Cover art: *The Feast of Saint George*, (oil on panel), Cleve, Marten van (1527–81) / Private Collection / Photo © Christie's Images / Bridgeman Images

About the Cover Image

The Feast of Saint George, (oil on panel), Marten van Cleve (1527–81)

Van Cleve was one of several Flemish painters from the time known for their depictions of peasant life, especially feast days, weddings and festivals. He established a major workshop in Antwerp, one of the major commercial centers of the time. He and his family were most likely in Antwerp during the religious conflicts of the 1560s and 1570s but he chose to depict mainly peaceful scenes.

SIXTH EDITION

The Making of the West

Peoples and Cultures

VOLUME I: TO 1750

Lynn Hunt
University of California, Los Angeles

Thomas R. Martin
College of the Holy Cross

Barbara H. Rosenwein
Loyola University Chicago

Bonnie G. Smith
Rutgers University

bedford/st.martin's
Macmillan Learning

Boston | New York

For Bedford/St. Martin's

Vice President, Editorial, Macmillan Learning Humanities: Edwin Hill

Senior Program Director for History: Michael Rosenberg

Senior Program Manager for History: William J. Lombardo

History Marketing Manager: Melissa Rodriguez

Director of Content Development, Humanities: Jane Knetzger

Senior Developmental Editor: Leah R. Strauss

Senior Content Project Manager: Kendra LeFleur

Senior Workflow Project Supervisor: Jennifer Wetzel

Production Coordinator: Brianna Lester

Editorial Assistant: Belinda Huang

Media Project Manager: Michelle Camisa

Project Management: Lumina Datamatics, Inc.

Editorial Services: Lumina Datamatics, Inc.

Composition: Lumina Datamatics, Inc.

Cartographer: Mapping Specialists, Ltd.

Photo Editor: Jennifer MacMillan

Photo Researcher: Bruce Carson

Permissions Editor: Kalina Ingham

Design Director, Content Management: Diana Blume

Text Design: Lisa Buckley

Cover Design: William Boardman

Cover Art: The Feast of Saint George, (oil on panel), Cleve, Marten van (1527–81)/Private Collection/Photo © Christie's
   Images/Bridgeman Images

Printing and Binding: LSC Communications

Manufactured in the United States of America.

1 2 3 4 5 6   23 22 21 20 19 18

For information, write: Bedford/St. Martin's, 75 Arlington Street, Boston, MA 02116

ISBN 978-1-319-10344-6 (Combined Edition)
ISBN 978-1-319-10365-1 (Vol. I)
ISBN 978-1-319-10363-7 (Vol. II)

Preface: Why This Book This Way

We are delighted to present the sixth edition of *The Making of the West: Peoples and Cultures*. With this edition, *The Making of the West* combines the best of the print and digital platforms while staying true to the fundamental approach that has made this book a popular choice for both instructors and students. New for this edition, the **primary source features** that have made this book so useful **are now available in both the print and digital editions**. We continue to **link the history of the West to wider developments in the world**. We continue to offer a **synthetic approach to history**—from military to gender—that integrates different approaches rather than privileging one or two. And we continue to believe that students benefit from a **solid chronological framework** when they are trying to understand events of the past. This new edition is priced affordably, to save students money and keep the overall course budget manageable. Bedford's learning platform, known as **LaunchPad**, is loaded with the full-color e-book plus **LearningCurve**, an adaptive learning tool; the popular *Sources of The Making of the West* documents collection; **additional primary sources**; a wealth of **assessment tools**; **chapter summative quizzes**; and more.

Helping Instructors Teach with Digital Resources

We are pleased to offer *The Making of the West* in **LaunchPad**, Macmillan's premier learning platform that offers an intuitive, interactive e-book and course space. Free when packaged with a bound text or available at a low price when used alone, LaunchPad is ready to use as is, or it can be edited and customized with your own material and assigned right away.

Developed with extensive feedback from history instructors and students, **LaunchPad for** *The Making of the West* includes the complete narrative of the print book, the companion reader *Sources of The Making of the West* by Katharine Lualdi, and **LearningCurve** adaptive quizzing that is designed to get students to read before they come to class. With new source-based questions in the test bank and in LearningCurve and the ability to sort test bank questions by chapter learning objectives, instructors now have more ways to test students on their understanding of sources and narrative in the book.

With LearningCurve, students move through questions based on the narrative text at their own pace and accumulate points as they go in a game-like fashion. Feedback for incorrect responses explains why the answer is incorrect and directs students back to the text to review. The end result is a better understanding of the key elements of the text. Quizzes in LaunchPad that have been designed for the features such as "Contrasting Views" (which compares two primary sources) and the "Mapping the West" maps will enable instructors to check their students' comprehension of assigned exercises.

NEW! Skill-Building Features in Both Print and Digital

Whether you find the print book, the LaunchPad digital platform, or some combination of the two most suitable for your course, your students will have access to features that are crucial to student learning. The following three **features appear in each chapter of the book, whether print or digital,** and provide a solid introduction to historical argument and critical thinking. In LaunchPad, there is an autograded multiple-choice quiz for the primary source features.

- **Primary Source Analysis** gives students a more direct experience of the past through original voices. Whether it is an excerpt from an anonymous Sophist's handbook of the late fifth century B.C.E. (Chapter 3), twelfth-century letters between two anonymous lovers (Chapter 11), or Marie de Sévigné's description of the French court (Chapter 16), primary documents offer windows into the thoughts and actions of the past. Each document is introduced by a headnote and followed by Questions to Consider.
- **Contrasting Views** compares two or more conflicting primary sources focused on a central event, person, or development—such as the Roman attitudes toward Cleopatra (Chapter 4), the Mongols (Chapter 12), and the consumer revolution of the eighteenth century (Chapter 17)—enabling students to understand history from a variety of contemporaneous perspectives. Each document pairing is introduced with a headnote and is followed by Questions to Consider.
- **NEW! Terms of History, now in every chapter,** looks not only at the origin of a term—such as *democracy* (Chapter 3), *barbarian* (Chapter 7), and *gothic* (Chapter 11)—but also at the changing meaning of the term over time, which further underscores historical skill building.

About *The Making of the West*

Even with all the exciting digital alternatives now available, our primary goal remains the same: to demonstrate that the history of the West is the story of an ongoing process, not a finished result with one fixed meaning. There is not one Western people or culture that has existed from the beginning until now. Instead, the history of the West includes many different peoples and cultures. To convey these ideas, we have written a sustained story of the West's development in a broad, global context that reveals the cross-cultural interactions fundamental to the shaping of Western politics, societies, cultures, and economies. To highlight the importance of this broad notion of the West, the first chapter opens with a section on the origins and contested meaning of the term *Western civilization*.

New Coverage and Current Scholarship

As always, we have also **incorporated the latest scholarly findings** throughout the book so that students and instructors have a text on which they can confidently rely, including **updated Suggested References** at the end of each chapter. In the sixth edition, we have included **new and updated discussions** of topics such as the agency of women in ancient Greece, the structures of Islamic societies in the Middle Ages, the growth of the European slave trade in the eighteenth and nineteenth centuries, and a host of new developments in the past few years. The final chapter now includes a discussion of the economic, technological, and cultural changes since the downturn of 2008 that have shaped the rise of populism, including rising immigration, the increasingly interventionist policies of Russia, and the unraveling of the "Arab Spring" with the catastrophe of the Syrian civil war and the continuing threat of ISIS.

Chronological Framework

We know from our own teaching that introductory students need a solid chronological framework, one with enough familiar benchmarks to make the material easy to grasp. Each chapter is organized around the main events, people, and themes of a period in which the West significantly changed; thus, students learn about political and military events and social and cultural developments as they unfolded. This **chronological integration** also makes it possible for students to see the **interconnections among varieties of historical experience**—between politics and cultures, between public events and private experiences, between wars and diplomacy and everyday life. For teachers, our chronological approach ensures a balanced account and provides the opportunity to present themes within their greater context. But perhaps best of all, this approach provides a text that reveals history as a process that is constantly alive, subject to pressures, and able to surprise us.

An Expanded Vision of the West

Cultural borrowing between the peoples of Europe and their neighbors has characterized Western civilization from the beginning. Thus, we have insisted on an **expanded vision of the West** that includes the United States and fully incorporates Scandinavia, eastern Europe, and the Ottoman Empire. Now this vision encompasses **an even wider global context** than before, as Latin America, Africa, China, Japan, and India also come into the story. We have been able to offer sustained treatment of crucial topics such as Islam and to provide a more thorough examination of globalization than any competing text. Study of Western history provides essential background to today's events, from debates over immigration to conflicts in the Middle East. Instructors have found this synthesis essential for helping students understand the West amid today's globalization.

Study Aids to Support Active Reading and Learning

We know from our own teaching that students need all the help they can get to absorb and make sense of information, to think analytically, and to understand that history itself is often debated and constantly revised. With these goals in mind, we retained the class-tested learning and teaching aids that worked well in the previous editions, but we have also done more to help students distill the central story of each age.

Focused Reading

Each chapter begins with a vivid **anecdote** that draws readers into the atmosphere of the period and introduces the chapter's main themes, accompanied by a full-page illustration. The **Chapter Focus** poses an overarching question at the start of the narrative to help guide students' reading. Strategically placed at the end of each major section, a **Review Question** helps students assimilate core points in digestible increments. **Key Terms** and names that appear in boldface in the text have been updated to concentrate on likely test items; these terms are defined in the **Glossary of Key Terms and People** at the end of the book. To make the reading as meaningful as possible to students, each chapter now includes a new pointed question, **What Would You Do?** It encourages the students to think about how they might have reacted to a crisis in the past and would have made choices with immense consequences. It is our hope that such questions will help bring history to life.

Reviewing the Chapter

At the end of each chapter, the **Conclusion** further reinforces the central developments covered in the chapter. The **Chapter Review** begins by asking students to revisit the key terms, identifying each and explaining its significance. **Review Questions** are also presented again so that students can revisit the chapter's core points. **Making Connections** questions then follow and prompt students to think across the sections of a given chapter. A chronology of **Important Events** enables students to see the sequence and overlap of important events in a given period and asks students a guiding question that links two or more events in the chapter. Finally, a list of author-selected and updated **Suggested References** directs students to print and online resources for further investigation.

Geographic Literacy

The map program of *The Making of the West* has been praised by reviewers for its comprehensiveness. In each chapter, we offer three types of maps, each with a distinct role in conveying information to students. Up to five **full-size maps** show major developments, up to four **"spot" maps**—small maps positioned within the discussion right where students need them—serve as immediate locators, and a *Mapping the West* **summary map** at the end of each chapter provides a snapshot of the West at the close of a transformative period and helps students visualize the West's changing contours over time. In this edition, we have carefully considered each of the existing maps, simplifying them where possible to better highlight essential information, and clarifying and updating borders and labels where needed.

Images and Illustrations

We have integrated art as fully as possible into the narrative. Over **240 images and illustrations** were carefully chosen to reflect this edition's broad topical coverage and geographic inclusion, reinforce the text, and show the varieties of visual sources from which historians build their narratives and interpretations. All artifacts, illustrations, paintings, and photographs are contemporaneous with the chapter; there are no anachronistic illustrations. The captions for the maps and art help students learn how to read visuals, and we have frequently included specific questions or suggestions for comparisons that might be developed.

Acknowledgments

In the vital process of revision, the authors have benefited from repeated critical readings by many talented scholars and teachers. Our sincere thanks go to the following instructors, whose comments often challenged us to rethink or justify our interpretations and who always provided a check on accuracy down to the smallest detail: David S. Bachrach, *University of New Hampshire*; Robert Bond, *Mira Costa College*; Curtis Bostick, *Southern Utah University*; Trevor Corless, *Cégep Heritage College*; Michael Frassetto, *University of Delaware*; William L. Grose, *Wytheville Community College*; Joanne Klein, *Boise State University*; Rosemary Moore, *University of Iowa*; Lisa Payne Ossian, *Des Moines Area Community College*; Svanur Petursson, *Rutgers University, Newark*; David Pizzo, *Murray State University*; Allison E. Stein, *Pellissippi State Community College*; Kathryn Steinhaus, *Seminole State College*; Erin W. Stone, *University of West Florida*; Sarah L. Sullivan, *McHenry County College*; Nancy Vavra, *University of Colorado at Boulder*; and Mirna Zakic, *Ohio University, Main Campus*.

Many colleagues, friends, and family members have made contributions to this work. They know how grateful we are. We also wish to acknowledge and thank the publishing team at Bedford/St. Martin's who did so much to bring this revised edition to completion: editorial director Edwin Hill; publisher for history Michael Rosenberg; program manager for history Bill Lombardo; developmental editor Leah Strauss; media editor Tess Fletcher; editorial assistant Belinda Huang; marketing manager Melissa Rodriguez; content production manager Kendra LeFleur; project manager, Andrea Stefanowicz; art researcher Bruce Carson; and cover designer Billy Boardman.

Our students' questions and concerns have shaped much of this work, and we welcome all our readers' suggestions, queries, and criticisms. Please contact us at our respective institutions or via **history@macmillanhighered.com**.

Lynn Hunt
Thomas Martin
Barbara Rosenwein
Bonnie Smith

Versions and Supplements

Adopters of *The Making of the West* and their students have access to abundant print and digital resources and tools, including documents, assessment and presentation materials, the acclaimed *Bedford Series in History and Culture* volumes, and much more. The LaunchPad course space for *The Making of the West* provides access to the narrative as well as a wealth of primary sources and other features, along with assignment and assessment opportunities at the ready. Achieve Read & Practice supplies adaptive quizzing and our mobile, accessible Value Edition e-book, in one easy-to-use, affordable product. See the following text for more information, visit the book's catalog site at macmillanlearning.com, or contact your local Bedford/St. Martin's sales representative.

Get the Right Version for Your Class

To accommodate different course lengths and course budgets, *The Making of the West* is available in several different formats to best suit your course needs. The comprehensive *The Making of the West* includes a full-color art program and a robust set of features. *The Making of the West* Value Edition offers a trade-sized two-color option with the unabridged narrative and selected art and maps at a steep discount. The Value Edition is also offered at the lowest price point in loose-leaf format, and these versions are available as e-books. To get the best value of all, package a new print book with LaunchPad or Achieve Read & Practice at no additional charge to get the best that each format offers. LaunchPad users get a print version for easy portability with an interactive e-book for the full-feature text and course space, along with LearningCurve and loads of additional assignment and assessment options; Achieve Read & Practice users get a print version with a mobile, interactive Value Edition e-book plus LearningCurve adaptive quizzing in one exceptionally affordable, easy-to-use product.

- **Combined Volume** (Chapters 1–29): available in paperback, Value, loose-leaf, and e-book formats and in LaunchPad and Achieve Read & Practice

- **Volume 1: To 1750** (Chapters 1–17): available in paperback, Value, loose-leaf, e-book formats and in LaunchPad and Achieve Read & Practice
- **Volume 2: Since 1500** (Chapters 14–29): available in paperback, Value, loose-leaf, and e-book formats and in LaunchPad and Achieve Read & Practice

As noted in the following text, any of these volumes can be packaged with additional titles for a discount. To get ISBNs for discount packages, visit macmillanlearning.com or contact your Bedford/St. Martin's representative.

LaunchPad macmillan learning Assign LaunchPad—An Assessment-Ready Interactive E-book and Course Space

Available for discount purchase on its own or for packaging with new books at no additional charge, LaunchPad is a breakthrough solution for history courses. Intuitive and easy to use for students and instructors alike, LaunchPad is ready to use as is and can be edited, customized with your own material, and assigned quickly. LaunchPad for *Making of the West* includes Bedford/ St. Martin's high-quality content all in one place, including the full interactive e-book and companion reader, *Sources of The Making of the West*, plus LearningCurve adaptive quizzing; guided reading activities designed to help students read actively for key concepts; autograded quizzes for primary sources, and chapter summative quizzes. Through a wealth of adaptive and summative assessment, including the adaptive learning program of LearningCurve (see the full description ahead), students gain confidence and get into their reading before class. These features, plus additional primary source documents, video tools for making video assignments, map activities, flashcards, and customizable test banks, make LaunchPad an invaluable asset for any instructor.

LaunchPad easily integrates with course management systems, and with fast ways to build assignments, rearrange chapters, and add new pages, sections, or links, it lets teachers build the courses they want to teach and to hold students accountable. For more information, visit launchpadworks .com or to arrange a demo, contact us at historymktg@macmillan.com.

☑ Assign LearningCurve So Your Students Come to Class Prepared

Students using LaunchPad receive access to LearningCurve for *The Making of the West*. Assigning LearningCurve in place of reading quizzes is easy for instructors, and the reporting features help instructors track overall class trends and spot topics that are giving students trouble so they can adjust their lectures and class activities. This online learning tool is popular with students because it was designed to help them rehearse content at their own pace in a nonthreatening, gamelike environment. The feedback for wrong answers provides instructional coaching and sends students back to the book for review. Students answer as many questions as necessary to reach a target score, with repeated chances to revisit material they haven't mastered. When LearningCurve is assigned, students come to class better prepared.

Assign Achieve Read & Practice So Your Students Can Read and Study Wherever They Go

Available for discount purchase on its own or for packaging with new books at no additional charge, Achieve Read & Practice is Bedford/St. Martin's most affordable digital solution for history courses. Intuitive and easy to use for both students and instructors, Achieve Read & Practice is ready to use as is, and can be assigned quickly. Achieve Read & Practice for *The Making of the West* includes the Value Edition interactive e-book, LearningCurve formative quizzing, assignment tools, and a gradebook. All this is built with an intuitive interface that can be read on mobile devices and is fully accessible and available at a discounted price so anyone can use it. Instructors can set due dates for reading assignments and LearningCurve quizzes in just a few clicks, making it a simple and affordable way to engage students with the narrative and hold students accountable for course reading so they will come to class better prepared. For more information, visit **macmillanlearning.com/ReadandPractice** or to arrange a demo, contact us at **historymktg@macmillan.com**.

iClicker, Active Learning Simplified

iClicker offers simple, flexible tools to help you give students a voice and facilitate active learning in the classroom. Students can participate with the devices they bring to class using our iClicker Reef mobile apps (which work with smartphones, tablets, or laptops) or iClicker remotes. We've now integrated iClicker with Macmillan's LaunchPad to make it easier than ever to synchronize grades and promote engagement—both in and out of class. iClicker Reef access cards can also be packaged with LaunchPad or your textbook at a significant savings for your students. To learn more, talk to your Macmillan Learning representative or visit us at **www.iclicker.com**.

Take Advantage of Instructor Resources

Bedford/St. Martin's has developed a rich array of teaching resources for this book and for this course. They range from lecture and presentation materials and assessment tools to course management options. Most can be found in LaunchPad or can be downloaded or ordered at macmillanlearning.com.

Bedford Coursepack for Blackboard, Canvas, Brightspace by D2L, or Moodle. We can help you integrate our rich content into your course management system. Registered instructors can download coursepacks that include our popular free resources and book-specific content for *The Making of the West.* Visit macmillanlearning.com to find your version or download your coursepack.

Instructor's Resource Manual. The instructor's manual offers both experienced and first-time instructors tools for presenting textbook material in engaging ways. It includes content learning objectives, annotated chapter outlines, and strategies for teaching with the textbook, plus suggestions on how to get the most out of LearningCurve and a survival guide for first-time teaching assistants.

Guide to Changing Editions. Designed to facilitate an instructor's transition from the previous edition of *The Making of the West* to this new edition, this guide presents an overview of major changes as well as of changes in each chapter.

Online Test Bank. The test bank includes a mix of fresh, carefully crafted multiple-choice, matching, short-answer, and essay questions for each chapter. Many of the multiple-choice questions feature a map, an image, or a primary source excerpt as the prompt. All questions appear in easy-to-use test bank software that allows instructors to add, edit, resequence, and print questions and answers. Instructors can also export questions into a variety of course management systems.

The Bedford Lecture Kit: Lecture Outlines, Maps, and Images. Observe carefully and save time with *The Bedford Lecture Kit.* These presentation materials are downloadable individually from the Instructor Resources tab on macmillanlearning.com. They include fully customizable multimedia presentations built around chapter outlines that are embedded with maps, figures, and images from the textbook and are supplemented by more detailed instructor notes on key points and concepts.

Print, Digital, and Custom Options for More Choice and Value

For information on free packages and discounts up to 50%, visit macmillanlearning.com, or contact your local Bedford/St. Martin's sales representative.

Sources of The Making of the West, Sixth Edition. Thoroughly revised, this companion reader provides written and visual sources to accompany each chapter of *The Making of the West.* A broad range of source types and themes illuminate historical experience from a diversity of perspectives. Now with a visual source as well as a comparative source pairing in every chapter, this reader offers instructors even more opportunities to promote classroom discussion of primary documents and to help students develop essential historical thinking skills. This companion reader is an exceptional value for students and offers plenty of assignment options for instructors. Available free when packaged with the bound text and included in the LaunchPad e-book with autograded quizzes for each source. In LaunchPad, each chapter of the reader includes special primary source online activities—self-graded exercises that challenge students to assess whether a specific piece of evidence drawn from the sources supports or challenges a conclusion related to a guiding question. *Sources of The Making of the West* is also available on its own as a downloadable e-book.

NEW *Bedford Select for History.* Create the ideal textbook for your course with only the chapters you need. Starting from one of our Value Edition history texts, you can rearrange chapters, delete unnecessary chapters, select primary sources from *Sources of The Making of the West*, Sixth Edition, and add document projects from the Bedford Document Collections, or choose to improve your students's historical thinking skills with the Bedford Tutorials for History. In addition, you can add your own original content to create just the book you're looking for. With Bedford Select, students pay only for material that will be assigned in the course, and nothing more. Order your textbook every semester, or modify from one term to the next. It is easy to build your customized textbook, without compromising the quality and affordability you've come to expect from Bedford/St. Martin's. For more information, visit **macmillanlearning.com/bedfordselect**.

NEW *The Bedford Document Collections for World History.* Available to customize the print text, this collection provides a flexible repository of discovery-oriented primary source projects ready to assign. Each curated project—written by a historian about a favorite topic—poses a historical question and guides students through analysis of the sources. Examples include "The Silk Road: Travel and Trade in Pre-Modern Inner Asia," "The Spread of Christianity in the Sixteenth and Early Seventeenth Centuries," "The Singapore Mutiny of 1915: Understanding World War I from a Global Perspective," and "Living through Perestroika: The Soviet Union in Upheaval, 1985–1991." For more information, visit **macmillanlearning.com**.

NEW *The Bedford Document Collections for World History Print Modules.* Choose one or two document projects from the collection (see above) and add them in print to a Bedford/St. Martin's title, or select several to be bound together in a custom reader created specifically for your course. Either way, the modules are affordably priced. For more information, contact your Bedford/St. Martin's representative.

NEW *Bedford Tutorials for History.* Designed to customize textbooks with resources relevant to individual courses, this collection of brief units, each 16 pages long and loaded with examples, guides students through basic skills such as using historical evidence effectively, working with primary sources, taking effective notes, avoiding plagiarism and citing sources, and more. Up to two tutorials can be added to a Bedford/St. Martin's history survey title at no additional charge, freeing you to spend your class time focusing on content and interpretation. For more information, visit **macmillanlearning.com/historytutorials**.

The Bedford Series in History and Culture. More than 100 titles in this highly praised series combine first-rate scholarship, historical narrative, and important primary documents for undergraduate courses. Each book is brief, inexpensive, and focused on a specific topic or period. Recent titles in the series include *The Prince by Niccolò Machiavelli with Related Documents, Second Edition*, edited by William J. Connell; *The Enlightenment: A Brief History with Documents, Second Edition*, by Margaret C. Jacob; *Candide by Voltaire with Related Documents, Second Edition*, edited by Daniel Gordon; and *The French Revolution and Human Rights: A Brief History with Documents, Second Edition*, by Lynn Hunt, and are now available. For a complete list of titles, visit **macmillanlearning.com**. Package discounts are available.

Rand McNally Atlas of Western Civilization. This collection of more than fifty full-color maps illustrates social, political, and cross-cultural change and interaction from classical Greece and Rome to the postindustrial Western world. Each map is thoroughly indexed for fast reference. Free when packaged.

Trade Books. Titles published by sister companies Hill and Wang; Farrar, Straus and Giroux; Henry Holt and Company; St. Martin's Press; Picador; and Palgrave Macmillan are available at a 50% discount when packaged with Bedford/St. Martin's textbooks. For more information, visit **macmillanlearning .com/tradeup**.

A Pocket Guide to Writing in History. Updated to reflect changes made in the 2017 *Chicago Manual of Style* revision, this portable and affordable reference tool by Mary Lynn Rampolla provides reading, writing, and research advice useful to students in all history courses. Concise yet comprehensive advice on approaching typical history assignments, developing critical reading skills, writing effective history papers, conducting research, using and documenting sources, and avoiding plagiarism—enhanced with practical tips and examples throughout—has made this slim reference a best-seller. Package discounts are available.

A Student's Guide to History. This complete guide to success in any history course provides the practical help students need to be successful. In addition to introducing students to the nature of the discipline, author Jules Benjamin teaches a wide range of skills from preparing for exams to approaching common writing assignments, and explains the research and documentation process with plentiful examples. Package discounts are available.

Brief Contents

Contents

CHAPTER 17

The Atlantic System and Its Consequences, 1700–1750 575

Maps, Figures, and Special Features

FIGURES

PRIMARY SOURCE ANALYSIS

CONTRASTING VIEWS

TERMS OF HISTORY

The B.C.E./C.E. Dating System

When were you born? What year is it? We customarily answer questions like these with a number, such as "1991" or "2008." Our replies are usually automatic, taking for granted the numerous assumptions Westerners make about how dates indicate chronology. But to what do numbers such as 1991 and 2008 actually refer? In this book the numbers used to specify dates follow a recent revision of the system most common in the Western secular world. This system reckons the dates of solar years by counting backward and forward from the traditional date of the birth of Jesus Christ, more than two thousand years ago.

Using this method, numbers followed by the abbreviation B.C.E., standing for "before the common era" (or, as some would say, "before the Christian era"), indicate the number of years counting backward from the assumed date of the birth of Jesus Christ. The abbreviation B.C.E. therefore indicates the same chronology marked by the traditional abbreviation B.C. ("before Christ"). The larger the number preceding B.C.E. (or B.C.), the earlier in history is the year to which it refers. The date 431 B.C.E., for example, refers to a year 431 years before the birth of Jesus and therefore comes earlier in time than the dates 430 B.C.E., 429 B.C.E., and so on. The same calculation applies to numbering other time intervals calculated on the decimal system: those of ten years (a decade), of one hundred years (a century), and of one thousand years (a millennium). For example, the decade of the 440s B.C.E. (449 B.C.E. to 440 B.C.E.) is earlier than the decade of the 430s B.C.E. (439 B.C.E. to 430 B.C.E.). "Fifth century B.C.E." refers to the fifth period of 100 years reckoning backward from the birth of Jesus and covers the years 500 B.C.E. to 401 B.C.E. It is earlier in history than the fourth century B.C.E. (400 B.C.E. to 301 B.C.E.), which followed the fifth century B.C.E. Because this system has no year "zero," the first century B.C.E. covers the years 100 B.C.E. to 1 B.C.E. Dating millennia works similarly: the second millennium B.C.E. refers to the years 2000 B.C.E. to 1001 B.C.E., the third millennium to the years 3000 B.C.E. to 2001 B.C.E., and so on.

To indicate years counted forward from the traditional date of Jesus's birth, numbers are followed by the abbreviation C.E., standing for "of the common era" (or "of the Christian era"). The abbreviation C.E. therefore indicates the same chronology marked by the traditional abbreviation A.D., which stands for the Latin phrase *anno Domini* ("in the year of the Lord"). The abbreviation A.D. properly comes before the date being marked. The date A.D. 1492, for example, translates as "in the year of the Lord 1492," meaning 1492 years after the birth of Jesus. Under the B.C.E./C.E. system, this date would be written as 1492 C.E. For dating centuries, the term "first century C.E." refers to the period from 1 C.E. to 100 C.E. (which is the same period as A.D. 1 to A.D. 100). For dates C.E, the smaller the number, the earlier the date in history. The fourth century C.E. (301 C.E. to 400 C.E.) comes before the fifth century C.E. (401 C.E. to 500 C.E.). The year 312 C.E. is a date in the early fourth century C.E., while 395 C.E. is a date late in the same century. When numbers are given without either B.C.E. or C.E., they are presumed to be dates C.E. For example, the term *eighteenth century* with no abbreviation accompanying it refers to the years 1701 C.E. to 1800 C.E.

No standard system of numbering years, such as B.C.E./C.E., existed in antiquity. Different people in different places identified years with varying names and numbers. Consequently, it was difficult to match up the years in any particular local system with those in a different system. Each city of ancient Greece, for example, had its own method for keeping track of the years. The ancient Greek historian Thucydides, therefore, faced a problem in presenting a chronology for the famous Peloponnesian War between Athens and Sparta, which began (by our reckoning) in 431 B.C.E. To try to explain to as many of his readers as possible the date the war had begun, he described its first year by three different local systems: "the year when Chrysis was in the forty-eighth year of her priesthood at Argos, and Aenesias was overseer at Sparta, and Pythodorus was magistrate at Athens."

A Catholic monk named Dionysius, who lived in Rome in the sixth century C.E., invented the system of reckoning dates forward from the birth of Jesus. Calling himself *Exiguus* (Latin for "the little" or "the small") as a mark of humility, he placed Jesus's birth 754 years after the foundation of ancient Rome. Others then and now believe his date for Jesus's birth was in fact several years too late. Many scholars today calculate that Jesus was born in what would be 4 B.C.E. according to Dionysius's system, although a date a year or so earlier also seems possible.

Counting backward from the supposed date of Jesus's birth to indicate dates earlier than that event represented a natural complement to reckoning forward for dates after it. The English historian and theologian Bede in the early eighth century was the first to use both forward and backward reckoning from the birth of Jesus in a historical work, and this system gradually gained wider acceptance because it provided a basis for standardizing the many local calendars used in the Western Christian world. Nevertheless, B.C. and A.D. were not used regularly until the end of the eighteenth century; B.C.E. and C.E. became common in the late twentieth century.

The system of numbering years from the birth of Jesus is far from the only one in use today. The Jewish calendar of years, for example, counts forward from the date given to the creation of the world, which would be calculated as 3761 B.C.E. under the B.C.E./C.E. system. Under this system, years are designated A.M., an abbreviation of the Latin *anno mundi*, "in the year of the world." The Islamic calendar counts forward from the date of the Prophet Muhammad's flight from Mecca, called the *Hijra*, in what is the year 622 C.E. The abbreviation A.H. (standing for the Latin phrase *anno Hegirae*, "in the year of the Hijra") indicates dates calculated by this system. Anthropology commonly reckons distant dates as "before the present" (abbreviated B.P.).

History is often defined as the study of change over time; hence the importance of dates for the historian. But just as historians argue over which dates are most significant, they disagree over which dating system to follow. Their debate reveals perhaps the most enduring fact about history—its vitality.

The Making of the West

Peoples and Cultures

Early Western Civilization

400,000–1000 B.C.E.

Kings in ancient Egypt believed the gods judged them after death. In *Instructions for Merikare*, written around 2100–2000 B.C.E., a king advises his son: "Secure your place in the cemetery by being upright, by doing justice, upon which people's hearts rely.... When a man is buried and mourned, his deeds are piled up next to him as treasure." Being judged pure of heart led to an eternal reward: "abiding [in the afterlife] like a god, roaming [free] like the lords of time."

Other Egyptians also believed they should live justly by worshipping the gods and obeying the king. A guidebook instructing mummies about the underworld, the *Book of the Dead*, explained the jackal-headed god Anubis would weigh the dead person's heart against the goddess Maat and her feather of Truth, with the bird-headed god Thoth recording the result. Pictures in the book show the Swallower of the Damned—with a crocodile's head, a lion's body, and a hippopotamus's hind end—crouching ready to eat the heart of anyone who failed. Egyptian mythology thus taught people that living a just life was their most important goal because it won them a blessed existence after they died.

This belief—that there are divine beings more powerful than humans—goes back to the time before civilization, when people in the Stone Age lived as hunter-gatherers. Ten to twelve thousand years ago, when global warming promoted the invention of agriculture and the domestication of animals, human life changed in revolutionary ways that powerfully affect our lives today. Civilization first emerged around 4000–3000 B.C.E. in cities in Mesopotamia (the region between the

CHAPTER PREVIEW

From the Stone Age to Mesopotamian Civilization, 400,000–1000 B.C.E.
How did life change for people in and nearby Mesopotamia, first after the Neolithic Revolution and then when they began to live in cities?

Egypt, the First Unified Nation, 3050–1000 B.C.E.
How did religion guide the lives of both rulers and ordinary people in ancient Egypt?

The Hittites, the Minoans, and the Mycenaeans, 2200–1000 B.C.E.
How did war determine the fate of early Western civilization in Anatolia, Crete, and Greece?

«**Remembering the Dead in Ancient Egypt** This illustration on papyrus from a copy of the *Book of the Dead*, which belonged to an Egyptian named Hunefer, portrays the jackal-headed god Anubis in the Underworld with the mummified Hunefer (in a case). A priest and others are presenting offerings in a funeral ceremony honoring the deceased at the entrance of the tomb and providing supplies for the journey to the world of the dead. Egyptians believed they had to observe justice in their lives so that they could be rewarded with a comfortable existence after death. (The British Museum, London, UK/Album/Art Resource, NY.)

Euphrates and Tigris Rivers, today Iraq). Historians define **civilization** as a way of life based on agriculture and trade, with cities containing large buildings for religion and government; technology to produce metals, textiles, pottery, and other manufactured objects; and knowledge of writing. Archaeological research indicates that those conditions first developed in Mesopotamia. (See Terms of History.)

Civilization always arose with religion at its core. In Mesopotamian civilization, rulers believed they were judged for maintaining order on earth and honoring the gods. Egyptian civilization, which began about 3100–3000 B.C.E., built enormous temples and pyramids. Civilizations emerged starting about 2500 B.C.E. in India, China, and the Americas. By 2000 B.C.E., civilizations appeared in Anatolia (today Turkey), on islands in the eastern Mediterranean Sea, and in Greece. The development of civilization produced intended and unintended consequences. The spread of metallurgy (using high heat to extract metals from ores), for example, created better tools and weapons but also increased preexisting social **hierarchy** (ranking people as superiors or inferiors).

The peoples of Mesopotamia, Egypt, the eastern Mediterranean, and Greece created Western civilization by exchanging ideas, technologies, and objects through trade, travel, and war. Building on concepts from the Near East, Greeks originated the idea of the West as a separate region, identifying Europe as the West (where the sun sets) and different from the East (where the sun rises). The making of the West depended on cultural, political, and economic interaction among diverse groups. The West remains an evolving concept, not a fixed region with unchanging borders and members.

CHAPTER FOCUS
What changes did Western civilization bring to human life?

From the Stone Age to Mesopotamian Civilization, 400,000–1000 B.C.E.

People in the Stone Age created patterns of life that still exist. The most significant of those early developments were (1) the evolution of hierarchy in society and (2) the invention of agriculture and the domestication of animals,

CHAPTER TIMELINE

50,000–45,000 B.C.E
Homo sapiens migrate from Africa into southwest Asia and Europe

4000–1000 B.C.E
Bronze Age in southwestern Asia, Egypt, and Europe

50,000   10,000   5000

10,000–8000 B.C.E
Neolithic Revolution in Fertile Crescent and Sahara

4000–3000 B.C.E
Mesopotamians invent writing and establish first cities

TERMS OF HISTORY   Civilization

The word *civilization* comes from the ancient Roman word *civilis*, which meant "suitable for a private citizen" and "behaving like an ordinary, down-to-earth person." Historians connect civilization especially with urbanization and the ways of life that characterize city existence. Also, the word *civilization* often expresses the judgment that being civilized means achieving a superior way of life. Consider, for example, these definitions from *The Random House Webster's College Dictionary* (1997), page 240:

> *civilization.* **1.** an advanced state of human society, in which a high level of culture, science, and government has been reached. **2.** those people or nations that have reached such a state. **3.** any type of culture, society, etc. of a specific place, time, or group: *Greek civilization.* **4.** the act or process of civilizing or being civilized. **5.** cultural and intellectual refinement. **6.** cities or populated areas in general, as opposed to unpopulated or wilderness areas. **7.** modern comforts and conveniences, as made possible by science and technology.

All these definitions imply that *civilization* means an "advanced" or "refined" way of life compared to a "savage" or "rude" way. Ancient peoples often drew this sort of comparison between themselves and those whom they saw as crude. Much later, this notion of superiority became prominent in European thought after voyagers to the Americas reported on what they saw as the barbarian life of the peoples they called Indians. Because these Europeans saw Native American life as lacking discipline, government, and above all Christianity, it seemed to them to be "uncivilized." Today, this sense of comparative superiority in the word *civilization* has become so accepted that it can even be used in nonhuman contexts, such as in the following startling comparison: "some communities of ants are more advanced in civilization than others."[1]

Sometimes *civilization* is used without much definitional content at all, as in the Random House dictionary's third definition. Can the word have any deep meaning if it can be used to mean "any type of culture, society, etc. of a specific place, time, or group"? This broad definition reveals that studying civilization and deciding what it does—and should—mean still presents difficult challenges to students of history today. Should it not be their task to make *civilization* a word with intellectual content and a reality with meaning for improving human life, as those who first used the word thought that it was?

[1]Sir John Lubbock, *On the Origin and Metamorphoses of Insects*, 2nd ed. (London, 1874), 13.

2687–2190 B.C.E	**2300–2200 B.C.E**	**2061–1665 B.C.E**	**1569–1081 B.C.E**	**1200–1000 B.C.E**
Old Kingdom in Egypt	Enheduanna, princess of Akkad, composes poetry	Middle Kingdom in Egypt	New Kingdom in Egypt	Period of violence ends many kingdoms

3000 · · · **2000** · · · **1000**

3050 B.C.E	**2350 B.C.E**	**2200 B.C.E**	**1792–1750 B.C.E**	**1400 B.C.E**
Narmer (Menes) unites Upper and Lower Egypt into one kingdom	King Sargon of Akkad establishes world's first empire	Minoans build their first palaces	Hammurabi rules Babylon and issues his law code	Mycenaeans build their first palaces in Greece and take over Minoan Crete

which allowed people to stay in one place and raise their own food instead of wandering around to find things to eat in the wild. This change in how human beings met their most basic need—nutrition—led them to settle down in permanent communities for the first time. Eventually, some of these communities grew large enough in population and area to be considered cities. The conditions of life in these populous settlements incubated civilization, beginning in the fertile plains of the two great rivers of the Near East, the Euphrates and the Tigris. There, the Mesopotamians learned to work metals, and their rulers' desire to acquire and control the sources of these increasingly precious resources generated the drive to create empires. That drive in turn set the world on a course that extends to the modern age.

Life and Change in the Stone Age

About four hundred thousand years ago, people whose brains and bodies resembled ours appeared first in Africa. Called *Homo sapiens* ("wise human beings"), they were the immediate ancestors of modern people. Spreading out from Africa, they gradually populated the rest of the earth. Anthropologists call this time the Stone Age because people made tools and weapons from stone as well as from bone and wood; they did not yet know how to work metals. The Stone Age is divided into an early part, the Paleolithic ("Old Stone"), and a later part, the Neolithic ("New Stone").

In the Paleolithic Age, people existed as **hunter-gatherers** who originally lived in mostly egalitarian bands (meaning all adults enjoyed a rough equality in making group decisions). They roamed in groups of twenty to fifty, hunting animals, catching fish and shellfish, and gathering plants, fruits, and nuts. Women with young children foraged for plants close to camp; they provided the group's most reliable supply of nourishment. Men did most of the hunting of wild animals far from camp, although archaeological evidence shows that women also participated, especially in hunting with nets. Objects from distant regions found in burial sites show that hunter-gatherer bands traded with one another. Trade spread knowledge—especially technology, such as techniques for improving tools, and art for creating beauty and expressing beliefs. The use of fire for cooking was a major innovation because it allowed people to obtain nourishment from wild grains that they could not digest if eaten raw.

Evidence from graves shows that hierarchy emerged in Paleolithic times. Some Paleolithic burial sites contain weapons, tools, animal figurines, ivory beads, seashells, and bracelets alongside the corpses; the objects indicate that certain dead persons had greater status and wealth than others. Hierarchy probably began when men acquired prestige from bringing back meat after long hunts and from fighting in wars. (The many traumatic wounds seen in male skeletons show warfare was frequent.) Older women and men also earned status from their experience and longevity, in an age when illness or accidents killed most people before age thirty. The decoration of corpses with red paint and valuable objects suggests that Paleolithic people thought about the mystery of death and perhaps believed in an afterlife. Paleolithic artists also sculpted statuettes of human figures, probably for religious purposes.

Climate and geography—the fundamental features of our natural environment—defined a new way of life for human beings beginning about 10,000 B.C.E. A slow process of transformation started when climate change in the late Paleolithic period brought warmer temperatures and more rainfall at higher elevations. This weather increased the amount of wild grains people could gather in the foothills of the Near East's Fertile Crescent, an arc of territory extending up from the Jordan valley in Israel, through eastern Turkey, and down into the foothills and plains of Iraq and Iran (Map 1.1).* Paleolithic hunter-gatherers came to settle where wild grains grew abundantly and game animals grazed. Recent archaeological excavation in Turkey suggests that around eleven thousand years ago, groups organized to erect stone

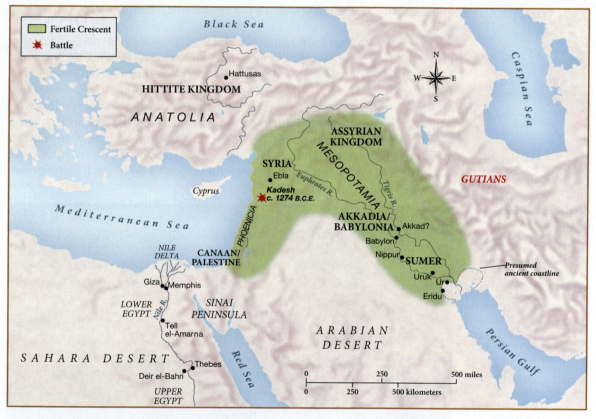

MAP 1.1 The Ancient Near East, 4000–3000 B.C.E.
The diverse region we call the ancient Near East included many different landscapes, climates, peoples, and languages. Kings ruled its independent city-states, the centers of the world's first civilizations, beginning around 4000–3000 B.C.E. Trade by land and sea for natural resources, especially metals, and wars of conquest kept the peoples of the region in constant contact and conflict with one another. How did geography facilitate—or hinder—the development of civilization in the Near East?

*In this book, we observe the common usage of the term *Near East* to mean the lands of southwestern Asia and Egypt.

monuments to worship gods who they believed helped them to survive, and they started growing food nearby. A more reliable food supply allowed people to raise more children, and increased social organization promoted larger settlements. More people being born, however, in turn, created a greater need for food.

After thousands of years of trial and error, people in the Fertile Crescent invented reliable agriculture by sowing seeds from wild grains to produce harvests year after year. This marked the start of the Neolithic Age. Since women had the most experience gathering plants, they probably played the major role in developing farming, while men continued to hunt. Archaeology shows that people learned to domesticate animals about the same time. By nine thousand years ago, keeping herds for food was widespread in the Near East, which was home to wild animals that could be domesticated, such as sheep, goats, pigs, and cattle.

Historians call agriculture and the domestication of animals the "farming package," which created the Neolithic Revolution. The farming package had revolutionary effects because it produced many permanent settlements and food surpluses. Some Neolithic people lived as pastoralists (herders moving around to find grazing land for their animals), while others were farmers who had to reside in a settled location to raise crops. Fixed settlements marked a turning point in the relationship between human beings and the environment, as farmers increasingly channeled streams for irrigation. DNA evidence from ancient bones and modern populations shows that by 4000 B.C.E., immigrants

Model of a House at Çatalhöyük
Archaeologists built this model of a house to show how Neolithic villagers lived in Çatalhöyük (today in central Turkey) from around 6500 to 5500 B.C.E. The wall paintings and bull-head sculpture had religious meaning, perhaps linked to the graves that the residents dug under the floor for their dead. The main entrance to the house was through the ceiling, as the houses were built right next to one another without streets in between, only some space for dumping refuse; the roofs served as walkways. Why do you think the villagers chose this arrangement for their settlement? (Çatalhöyük Research Project.)

and traders from the Fertile Crescent had helped spread knowledge of agriculture and domestication as far as the European shores of the Atlantic Ocean. When farmers began producing more food than they needed, the surpluses allowed other people in the community to specialize in architecture, arts, crafts, metalwork, textile production, and trade.

The Neolithic Revolution generated more hierarchy because positions of authority were needed to allow some people to supervise the complex irrigation systems that supported agricultural surpluses, and because greater economic activity created a stricter division of labor by gender. Men began to dominate agriculture after the invention of heavy wooden plows pulled by oxen, sometime after 4000 B.C.E. Not having to bear and nurse babies, men took over long-distance trade. Women and older children mastered new domestic tasks such as turning milk from domesticated animals into cheese and yogurt and making clothing for themselves and their families. This gendered division of labor arose as an efficient response to the conditions and technologies of the time, but it had the unintended consequence of increasing men's status.

The Emergence of Cities in Mesopotamia, 4000–2350 B.C.E.

Significant changes in human society took place when the first cities—and therefore the first civilization—emerged in Mesopotamia about 4000–3000 B.C.E. on the plains bordering the Tigris and Euphrates Rivers (see Map 1.1 on page 7). Cities developed there because the climate and the soil could support large populations. Mesopotamian farmers operated in a challenging environment; temperatures soared to 120 degrees Fahrenheit and little rain fell in the low-lying plains, yet the rivers flooded unpredictably. The farmers maximized agricultural production by devising the technology and administrative arrangements necessary to irrigate the arid flatlands with water diverted from the rivers. A vast system of canals controlled flooding and made the desert fertile with food crops. The need to construct and maintain a system of irrigation canals in turn led to the centralization of authority in Mesopotamian cities, whose rulers took control of the farmland and irrigation systems outside their fortified walls. This political arrangement—an urban center exercising control over the surrounding countryside—is called a **city-state**. Mesopotamian city-states were independent communities competing with each other for land and resources.

The people of Sumer (southern Mesopotamia) established the earliest city-states. Unlike other Mesopotamians, the Sumerians did not speak a Semitic language (the group of languages from which Hebrew and Arabic came); the origins of the Sumerians' language remain a mystery. By 3000 B.C.E., the Sumerians had created twelve independent city-states, including Uruk, Eridu, and Ur, which repeatedly battled each other for territory. By 2500 B.C.E., most of the cities had expanded to twenty thousand residents or more. The rooms in Sumerians' mud-brick houses surrounded open courts. Large homes had a dozen rooms or more.

The Sumerian city-states became prosperous from agricultural surpluses and trade in commodities and manufactured goods. Their residents bartered grain, vegetable oil, woolens, and leather with one another, and they acquired metal, timber, and precious stones from foreign trade. The invention of the wheel for use on transport wagons around 3000 B.C.E. strengthened the Mesopotamian economy. Traders traveled as far as India, where the cities of Indus civilization emerged about 2500 B.C.E. Two groups dominated the Sumerian economy: religious officials controlled the temples, and ruling families controlled large farms and gangs of laborers. Some private households also became rich.

Increasingly rigid forms of hierarchy evolved in Sumerian society. Slaves, owned by temple officials and by individuals, had the lowest status. People were enslaved by being captured in war, being born to slaves, voluntarily selling themselves or their children (usually to escape starvation), or being sold by their creditors when they could not repay loans (debt slavery). Children whose parents dedicated them as slaves to the gods could rise to prominent positions in temple administration. In general, however, slaves existed in near-total dependence on other people and were excluded from normal social relations. They usually worked without pay and lacked almost all legal rights. Considered as property, they could be bought, sold, beaten, or even killed by their masters.

Slaves worked in domestic service, craft production, and farming, but historians dispute whether slaves or free laborers were more important to the economy. Free persons performed most government labor, paying their taxes with work rather than with money, which was measured in amounts of food or precious metal (monetary currency was not invented until much later). Although some owners liberated slaves in their wills and a few allowed slaves to keep enough earnings to purchase their freedom, most slaves had little chance of becoming free.

Hierarchy became so strong in Mesopotamian society that it led to monarchy—the political system that became the most common form of government in the ancient world. In a monarchy, the king was at the top of the hierarchy, like the ruler of the gods. If he had male descendants, they inherited his position, sometimes competing violently to become the king. Royal families lived in elaborate palaces that served as administrative centers and treasure houses. Archaeologists excavating royal graves in Ur have revealed the rulers' dazzling riches—spectacular possessions crafted in gold, silver, and precious stones. These graves also have yielded grisly evidence of the top-ranking status of the king and queen: servants who were killed to care for their royal masters after death.

Patriarchy, the domination by men in political, social, and economic life, already existed in Mesopotamian city-states, probably as an inheritance from the development of hierarchy in Paleolithic times. A Sumerian queen was respected because she was the king's wife and the mother of the royal children, but her husband held supreme power. The king formed a council of older men as his advisers but acknowledged the gods as his rulers; this concept made the state a theocracy (government by gods) and gave priests and priestesses public influence. The king's greatest responsibility was to please the gods and to defeat attacks from rival cities. The king collected taxes from the working population to support his family, court, palace, army, and officials. The kings, along with the priests of the large temples, regulated most of the economy in their kingdoms by controlling the exchange of food and goods between farmers and craft producers in a system known as a **redistributive economy**.

In religion, Mesopotamians continued earlier traditions by practicing **polytheism**, worshipping many gods thought to control different aspects of life, including the weather, fertility, and war. People believed that their safety depended on the goodwill of the gods, and each city-state honored a deity as its special protector. To please the gods, city dwellers offered sacrifices and built ziggurats (temple towers) soaring as high as ten stories. Mesopotamians believed that if human beings angered the gods, divinities such as the sky god, Enlil, and the goddess of love and war, Inanna (also called Ishtar), would punish them by sending disease, floods, famine, and defeats in war.

Myths related in long poems such as the *Epic of Creation* and the *Epic of Gilgamesh* expressed Mesopotamian ideas about the challenges and violence that human beings faced in struggling with the natural environment and creating civilization. Gilgamesh was a legendary king of Uruk who forced the young men of Uruk to labor like slaves and the young women to sleep with him. When his subjects begged the mother of the gods to grant them a protector, she created Enkidu, "hairy all over … dressed as cattle are." A week of sex with a prostitute tamed this brute, preparing him for civilization: "Enkidu was weaker; he ran slower than before. But he had gained judgment, was wiser." After wrestling to a draw, Gilgamesh and Enkidu became friends; together they defeated Humbaba (the ugly giant of the Pine Forest) and the Bull of Heaven. The gods doomed Enkidu to die soon after these triumphs. Depressed about the human condition and longing to cheat death, Gilgamesh sought the secret of immortality, but a thieving snake ruined his quest. He decided that the only immortality for mortals was winning fame for deeds. Only memory and gods could live forever. (See Contrasting Views on pages 12–13.)

Mesopotamian myths recounted in poetry, song, and art greatly influenced other peoples. A version of the Gilgamesh story recounted how the gods sent a flood over the earth. They warned one man, instructing him to build a boat.

The Ziggurat at Ur in Sumer
Sumerian royalty built this massive temple (called a ziggurat) in the twenty-first century B.C.E. To construct its three huge terraces (connected with stairways), workers glued bricks together with tar around a central core. The walls had to be more than seven feet thick to hold the weight of the building, whose original height is uncertain. The first terrace reached forty-five feet above the ground. Still, the Great Pyramid in Egypt dwarfed even this large monument. (© World Religions Photo Library/ Bridgeman Images.)

CONTRASTING VIEWS

The Gains and the Losses of Life in Civilization versus Life in Nature

The ancient Mesopotamian poem referred to as the Epic of Gilgamesh *told a long and complicated story about the quest of the hero Gilgamesh to obtain fame and, most of all, immortality. Gilgamesh ultimately learns, to his sorrow, that human beings cannot escape their mortal nature and therefore their inevitable death.*

Gilgamesh is the king of the Sumerian city Uruk; he encounters Enkidu, a man living a completely different kind of life in the wilderness among wild animals. Their meeting comes from a hunter complaining to his father that Enkidu is making it impossible for him to be successful in catching wild animals.

His father ... spoke ... to the Hunter: "My son, in Uruk lives a man, Gilgamesh: no one has greater strength than his. In all the land he is the most powerful; power belongs to him.... Let him, the knowing one, hear of it ..."

The Hunter went to Gilgamesh.... Gilgamesh said to him, the Hunter, "Go, Hunter, and take with you a love-priestess, a temple courtesan [a status whose history and significance is disputed by modern scholars]. When he [that is, Enkidu] waters the animals at the watering place, have her take off her clothes, have her show him her strong beauty. When he sees her, he will come near her. His animals, who grew up in his wilderness, will turn from him...."

The woman saw him, the man-as-he-was-in-the-beginning, the man-and-killer from the wilderness.... The courtesan untied her wide belt and spread her legs, and he struck her wildness like a storm. She was not shy; she took his wind away. Her clothing she spread out, and he lay upon her. She made him know, the man-as-he-was, what a woman is. His body lay on her; six days and seven nights Enkidu attacked, having sex with the priestess. After Enkidu was glutted on her richness he set his face toward his animals. Seeing him, Enkidu, the gazelles scattered, wheeling: the beasts of the wilderness fled from his body. Enkidu tried to rise up, but his body pulled back. His knees froze. His animals had turned from him. Enkidu grew weak; he could not gallop as before. Yet he had knowledge, wider mind.... The

He loaded his vessel with his relatives, workers, and possessions; domesticated and wild animals; and "everything there was." After a week of torrential rains, they left the boat to repopulate the earth and regenerate civilization. This story recalled the frequent floods of the Mesopotamian environment and was echoed later in the biblical account of a global flood and Noah's ark.

The invention of writing in Mesopotamia transformed the way people exchanged stories and ideas. Sumerians originally invented this new technology to do accounting. Before writing, people drew small pictures on clay tablets to keep count of objects or animals. Writing developed when people created symbols to represent the sounds of speech instead of pictures to represent concrete things. Sumerian writing did not use an alphabet (a system in which each symbol represents the sound of a letter), but rather a system of wedge-shaped marks pressed into clay tablets to represent the sounds of syllables and entire words (Figure 1.1). Today this form of writing is called **cuneiform** (from *cuneus*, Latin for "wedge"). For a long time, writing was a professional skill for accounting mastered by only a few men and women known as scribes.

The possibilities for communication over time and space exploded when people began writing down nature lore, mathematics, foreign languages, and

woman said to him, to Enkidu: "You have become wise, like a god, Enkidu. Why did you range the wilderness with animals? Come, let me lead you to the heart of Uruk of the Sheepfold, to the stainless house, holy place of Anu and Ishtar, where Gilgamesh lives, completely powerful, and like a wild bull stands supreme, mounted above his people." She speaks to him, and they look at one another. With his heart's knowledge, he longs for a deeply loving friend....

[Following some adventures with Gilgamesh, Enkidu, conscious of his coming death, has come to regret his choice to leave the wilderness and becomes angry at the woman who introduced him to civilization.]

"His heart urged him to curse the temple courtesan, the woman.... [The god] Shamash heard, opened his mouth, and from afar, ... from the heavens called to him: "Why, Enkidu, do you curse the love-priestess, the woman who would feed you with the food of the gods, and would have you drink wine that is the drink of kings,

and would clothe you in a great garment, and would give you beautiful Gilgamesh as a companion? Listen: hasn't Gilgamesh, your beloved friend, made you lie down in a great bed? Hasn't he made you lie down in a bed of honor, and placed you on the peaceful seat at his left hand? The world's kings have kissed your feet ..." Enkidu listened to the words of Shamash the warrior [and] his angry heart grew still, ... grew quiet.

Source: Translation adapted from John Gardner and John Maier. *Gilgamesh* (1984), 73–74, 77–78, 172–173.

QUESTIONS TO CONSIDER

1. Why do you think sex provides the way to transform Enkidu from a man of the wild to a man of civilization?
2. What does this passage imply are the gains and the losses for human beings of living in civilization as opposed to living in wild nature?
3. Why do you think Enkidu "grew quiet" at the end of this story?

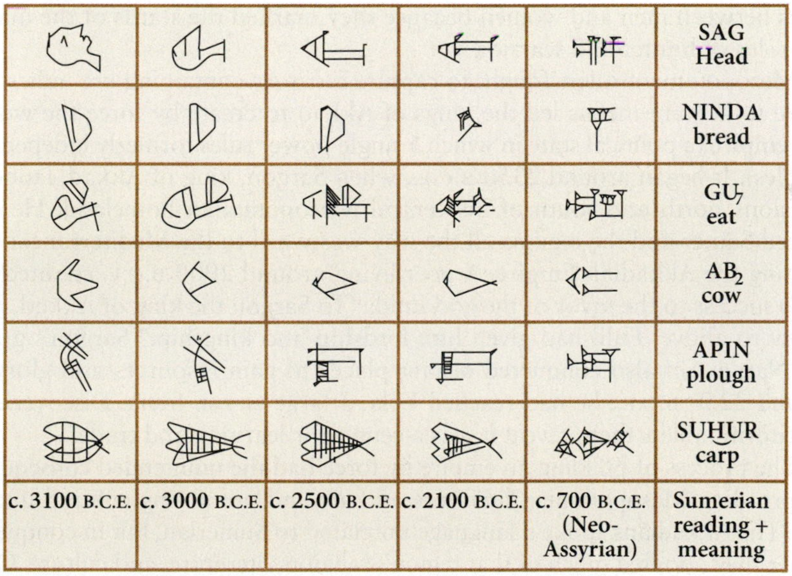

					SAG Head
					NINDA bread
					GU₇ eat
					AB₂ cow
					APIN plough
					SUHUR carp
c. 3100 B.C.E.	c. 3000 B.C.E.	c. 2500 B.C.E.	c. 2100 B.C.E.	c. 700 B.C.E. (Neo-Assyrian)	Sumerian reading + meaning

FIGURE 1.1 Cuneiform Writing
The earliest known form of writing developed in different locations in Mesopotamia in 4000–3000 B.C.E., when people began linking meaning and sound to signs such as those shown in the chart. Some scribes who mastered the system used sticks or reeds to press dense rows of small wedge-shaped marks into damp clay tablets; others used chisels to engrave them on stone. Cuneiform was used for at least fifteen Near Eastern languages and continued to be written for three thousand years.

literature. In the twenty-third century B.C.E., Enheduanna, the daughter of King Sargon of the city of Akkad, composed the oldest written poetry whose author is known. Written in Sumerian, her poetry praised the life-giving goddess of love, Inanna: "The great gods scattered from you like fluttering bats, unable to face your intimidating gaze, … knowing and wise queen of all the lands, who makes all creatures and people multiply." Later princesses who wrote love songs, lullabies, dirges, and prayers continued the Mesopotamian tradition of royal women becoming authors.

Metals and Empire Making: The Akkadians and the Ur III Dynasty, c. 2350–c. 2000 B.C.E.

The riches for which people now fought had a new component—metal. Early metallurgy demonstrates how technological innovation can generate social and political change. Pure copper, which people had long been using, lost its shape and edge quickly, so craftsmen were motivated to invent ways to smelt ore and to make metal alloys at high temperatures. The invention of bronze, a copper-tin alloy hard enough to hold a razor edge, enabled metalsmiths to produce durable and deadly swords, daggers, and spearheads. The period from about 4000 to 1000 B.C.E. is called the Bronze Age because at this time bronze was the most important metal for weapons and tools; iron was not yet commonly used. The ownership of metal objects strengthened status divisions in society between men and women and rich and poor. This technology allowed the Mesopotamian social elite to acquire new luxury goods in metal, improved tools for agriculture and construction, and bronze weapons. The desire to accumulate wealth and status symbols stimulated demand for decorated weapons and elaborate jewelry. Rich men ordered bronze swords and daggers with expensive inlays. Such weapons increased visible social differences between men and women because they marked the status of the masculine roles of hunter and warrior.

Mesopotamian rulers fought to capture territory containing ore mines. The desire to acquire metals led the kings of Akkad to create by force the world's first **empire** (a political state in which a single power rules formerly independent peoples). It began around 2350 B.C.E., when Sargon, king of Akkad, launched invasions north and south of his central Mesopotamian homeland. He conquered Sumer and the regions all the way westward to the Mediterranean Sea, creating the Akkadian Empire. A poet living around 2000 B.C.E. credited Sargon's success to the favor of the god Enlil: "To Sargon the king of Akkad, from below to above, Enlil had given him lordship and kingship." Sargon's grandson Naram-Sin also conquered distant places to gain resources and glory. By around 2250 B.C.E., he had reached Ebla, a large city in Syria. Discoveries of cuneiform tablets there reveal it was a center for learning and trade.

The process of building an empire by force had the unintended consequence of spreading Mesopotamian literature and art and promoting cultural interaction. The Akkadians spoke a language unrelated to Sumerian, but in conquering Sumer they adopted much of that region's religion, literature, and culture. Other peoples conquered by the Akkadians were then exposed to Sumerian beliefs and traditions, which they in turn adapted to suit their own purposes.

Civil war ended the Akkadian Empire. A newly resurgent Sumerian dynasty called Ur III (2112–2004 B.C.E.) seized power in Sumer. The Ur III rulers created a centralized economy, presided over a flourishing of Sumerian literature, published the earliest preserved law code, and justified their rule by proclaiming their king to be divine. The best-preserved ziggurat was built in their era. Royal hymns, a new literary form, glorified the king; one example reads: "Your commands, like the word of a god, cannot be reversed; your words, like rain pouring down from heaven, are without number."

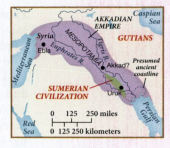

The Akkadian Empire, 2350–2200 B.C.E.

Mesopotamia remained politically unstable, however. When civil war weakened the Ur III kingdom, nearby Amorite marauders conducted damaging raids. The Ur III dynasty collapsed after only a century of rule.

The Achievements of the Assyrians, the Babylonians, and the Canaanites, 2000–1000 B.C.E.

New kingdoms emerged in Assyria and Babylonia in the second millennium B.C.E. At the time, Mesopotamia was experiencing extended economic troubles caused by climate change and agricultural pollution. By around 2000 B.C.E., intensive irrigation had unintentionally raised the soil's salt level so high that crop yields declined. When decreased rainfall made the situation worse, economic stress generated political instability lasting for centuries.

The Assyrians, who inhabited northern Mesopotamia, took advantage of their geography to create a kingdom whose rulers permitted long-distance trade conducted by private entrepreneurs. Assyrians became prosperous by acting as intermediaries in the trade for wood and metals between Anatolia and Mesopotamia. They exported woolen textiles to Anatolia in exchange for raw materials, which they sold to the rest of Mesopotamia.

Centralized state monopolies in which the government controlled international trade and redistributed goods dominated the Mesopotamian economy. This kind of redistributive economy persisted in Mesopotamia, but by 1900 B.C.E., Assyrian kings were allowing individuals to transact commerce. This market-based system let private entrepreneurs maximize profits in successful ventures. Private Assyrian investors, for example, financed traders to export cloth. The traders formed donkey caravans to travel hundreds of miles to Anatolia, where, if they survived the dangerous journey, they could make huge profits, split with their investors. Royal regulators settled any complaints of trader fraud or losses in transit.

To maintain social order, Mesopotamians established written laws made known to the people. Private commerce and property created a need to guarantee fairness in contracts. Mesopotamians believed that the king had a sacred duty to make divine justice known to his subjects by rendering judgments in all sorts of cases, from commercial disputes to crime. Once written down, the record of the king's decisions became what historians call a law code.

Hammurabi, king of Babylon (r. c. 1792–c. 1750 B.C.E.), became the most famous lawgiver in Mesopotamia. His laws for his kingdom straddling the Euphrates River drew on earlier Mesopotamian codes, such as that of the Ur III dynasty, and reveal details on city life in particular.

Hammurabi proclaimed that he was supporting "the principles of truth and equity" and protecting the weak. His law code was based on an ideal of justice. Its eye-for-an-eye principle matched the crime and punishment as literally as possible. The code punished fraudulent prosecutions by imposing the death penalty on anyone failing to prove a serious accusation. It also relied on "nature-decided justice" by allowing accused persons to leap into a river: if they sank, they were guilty; if they floated, they were innocent. King Hammurabi emphasized relieving the poor's burdens as crucial to royal justice. His laws divided society into free persons, commoners, and slaves. These categories reflected a social hierarchy in which some people were assigned a higher value than others. An attacker who caused a pregnant woman of the free class to miscarry, for example, paid twice the fine for the same offense against a commoner. Between social equals, the code specified an eye for an eye. A member of the free class who killed a commoner, however, was not executed, only fined.

Many of Hammurabi's laws concerned the king's interests as a property owner leasing land to tenants. His laws were harsh for offenses against property, including mutilation or a gruesome death for crimes ranging from theft to wrongful sales and careless construction. Women had limited legal rights, but they could make contracts and appear in court. Marriages were arranged between the bride's father and the groom and sealed with a legal contract. A wife could divorce her husband for cruelty; a husband could divorce his wife for any reason. The law protected the wife's interests by requiring a husband to restore his divorced wife's property.

Hammurabi's laws were not always strictly followed, and penalties were often less severe than specified. The people themselves assembled in courts to determine most cases by their own judgments. Why, then, did Hammurabi have his laws written down? He explained that it was to show Shamash, the Babylonian sun god and god of justice, that he had fulfilled his responsibility as a divinely installed king—to ensure justice and the moral and material welfare of his people: "So that the powerful may not oppress the powerless, to provide justice for the orphan and the widow … let the victim of injustice see the law which applies to him, let his heart be put at ease."

Hammurabi's laws for physicians reveal that there were doctors in the cities. (See Primary Source Analysis.) Because people believed that angry gods or evil spirits caused serious diseases, Mesopotamian medicine included magic: a doctor might prescribe an incantation along with potions and diet recommendations. Magicians or exorcists offered medical treatment that depended on spells and interpreting signs, such as the patient's dreams or hallucinations.

Babylonian cities had many taverns and wine shops, often run by women proprietors. Contaminated drinking water caused many illnesses because sewage disposal was rudimentary. Citizens found relief from a city's odors and

PRIMARY SOURCE ANALYSIS

Hammurabi's Laws for Physicians

In Hammurabi's collection of 282 laws, the following decisions set the fees for successful operations and the punishments for physicians' errors. The prescription of mutilation of a surgeon as the punishment for mutilation of a patient from the highest social class (law number 218) squares with the legal principle of equivalent punishment ("an eye for an eye") that occurs throughout Hammurabi's law code—a principle applied differently to patients of lower social classes.

215. If a physician performed a major operation on a freeman with a bronze scalpel and has saved the freeman's life, or he opened up the eye-socket of a freeman with a bronze scalpel and has saved the freeman's eye, he shall receive ten shekels[1] of silver.

216. If it was a commoner, he shall receive five shekels of silver.

217. If it was a freeman's slave, the owner of the slave shall give two shekels of silver to the physician.

218. If a physician performed a major operation on a freeman with a bronze scalpel and has caused the freeman's death, or he opened up the eye-socket of a freeman and has destroyed the freeman's eye, they shall cut off his hand.

219. If a physician performed a major operation on a commoner's slave with a bronze scalpel and has caused his death, he shall make good slave for the slave.

220. If he opened up [the slave's] eye-socket with a bronze scalpel and has destroyed his eye, he shall pay half his value in silver.

Source: Adapted from James B. Pritchard, *Ancient Near Eastern Texts Relating to the Old Testament*, 3rd ed. with supplement (Princeton, NJ: Princeton University Press, 1969), 175.

QUESTIONS TO CONSIDER

1. What does the nature of these punishments reveal about the different social worth of the physician and his patients?

2. Why do you think these laws were based on the principle of "an eye for an eye"?

---

[1] A shekel is a measurement of weight (about three-tenths of an ounce), not a coin. A hired laborer earned about one shekel per week. The average price of a slave was about twenty shekels.

---

crowding in its open spaces. The world's oldest known map, an inscribed clay tablet showing the outlines of the city of Nippur about 1500 B.C.E., indicates a large park.

Cities allowed large numbers of people from different places to interact, which stimulated intellectual developments. Mesopotamian achievements in mathematics and astronomy had an enduring effect. Mathematicians devised algebra, including the derivation of roots of numbers. They invented place-value notation, which makes a numeral's position in a number indicate ones, tens, hundreds, and so on. The system of reckoning based on sixty, still used in the division of hours and minutes and in the degrees of a circle, also comes from Mesopotamia. Mesopotamian expertise in recording the paths of the stars and planets probably arose from the desire to make predictions about the future, following the astrological belief that the movement of celestial bodies directly affects human life. The charts and tables compiled by Mesopotamian stargazers underlay later advances in astronomy.

REVIEW QUESTION
How did life change for people in and nearby Mesopotamia, first after the Neolithic Revolution and then when they began to live in cities?

In Canaan (ancient Palestine), west of Mesopotamia, the population grew by absorbing foreign merchants. The interaction of traders and travelers from many different cultures encouraged innovation in recording business transactions. This multilingual business environment produced the alphabet about 1600 B.C.E. In this new writing system, a simplified picture—a letter—stood for only one sound in the language, a large change from cuneiform. The Canaanite alphabet later became the basis for the Greek and Roman alphabets and therefore of modern Western alphabets.

Egypt, the First Unified Nation, 3050–1000 B.C.E.

The other earliest example of Western civilization arose in Egypt, in northeastern Africa. The Egyptians built a wealthy, profoundly religious, and strongly centralized society ruled by kings. Unlike the separate Mesopotamian city-states, Egypt became unified. Its prosperity and stability depended on the king maintaining strong central authority and defeating enemies. Egypt was located close enough to Mesopotamia to learn from peoples there but was geographically separate enough to develop its own distinct culture, which Egyptians believed was superior to any other. The Egyptians believed that a just society respected the gods, preserved hierarchy, and obeyed the king. The Egyptian rulers' belief in the soul's immortality and a happy afterlife motivated them to construct the largest tombs in history, the pyramids. Egyptian architecture, art, and religious ideas influenced later Mediterranean peoples, especially the Greeks.

From the Unification of Egypt to the Old Kingdom, 3050–2190 B.C.E.

When climate change dried up the grasslands of the Sahara region of Africa about 5000–4000 B.C.E., people slowly migrated from there to the northeast corner of the continent, settling along the Nile River. Recent radiocarbon dating of skeletons, hair, and plants has confirmed that Egypt became a united political state by about 3050 B.C.E., when King Narmer (also called Menes)* united the previously separate territories of Upper (southern) and Lower (northern) Egypt. (*Upper* and *Lower* refer to the direction of the Nile River, which begins south of Egypt and flows northward to the Mediterranean.) The Egyptian ruler therefore referred to himself as King of the Two Lands. By

---

*Since the Egyptians did not include vowel sounds in their writing, we are not sure how to spell their names. The spelling of names here is taken from *The Oxford Encyclopedia of Ancient Egypt*, edited by Donald B. Redford (2001), with alternate names given in cases where they seem more familiar. Dates are approximate and uncertain, and scholars bitterly disagree about them. (For an explanation of the problems, see Redford, "Chronology and Periodization," *The Oxford Encyclopedia*, vol. 1, 264–268.) The dates appearing in this book are compiled with as much consistency as possible from articles in *The Oxford Encyclopedia* and in the "Egyptian King List" given at the back of each of its volumes.

around 2687 B.C.E., Egypt's monarchs had created a large centralized state, called the Old Kingdom. It lasted until around 2190 B.C.E. (Map 1.2). Egyptian kings built only a few large cities. The first capital, Memphis (south of modern Cairo), grew into a metropolis packed with mammoth structures.

The most spectacular—and mysterious—of the Old Kingdom architectural marvels is the so-called Great Sphinx. The world's oldest monumental sculpture, this stone statue has a human head on the body of a lion lying on its four paws. It is nearly 250 feet long and almost 70 feet high. A temple was built in front of it, perhaps to worship the sun as a god. The Sphinx's purpose and date remain hotly debated. No records exist to explain its original meaning. Most scholars believe that it was erected sometime in the Old Kingdom. A few, however, citing its weathering and erosion patterns, argue that it is as old as 5000 B.C.E. If this date is ever confirmed, then the history of early Egypt will have to be rewritten. This is just one of the many controversies about ancient Egypt that archaeology may someday settle.

The Old Kingdom's costly architecture demonstrates the prosperity and power of Narmer's unified state. Its territory consisted of a narrow strip of fertile land running along both sides of the Nile River. This ribbon of green fields zigzagged for seven hundred miles southward from the Mediterranean Sea. The deserts flanking the fields on the west and the east protected Egypt; invasion was possible only through the northern Nile delta and from Nubia in the south. The deserts also were sources of wealth because they contained large deposits of metal ores.

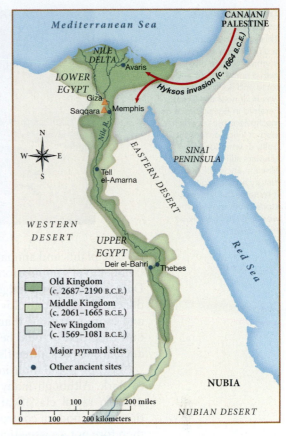

MAP 1.2 Ancient Egypt
Large deserts enclosed the Nile River on the west and the east. The Nile provided Egyptians with water to irrigate their fields and a highway for traveling north to the Mediterranean Sea and south to Nubia. The only easy land route into and out of Egypt lay through the northern Sinai peninsula into the coastal area of the eastern Mediterranean; Egyptian kings always fought to control this region to secure their land.

Egypt's geography also contributed to its prosperity by supporting seaborne commerce in the Mediterranean Sea and the Indian Ocean, as well as overland trade with central Africa.

Agriculture was Egypt's most important economic resource. Usually, the Nile River overflowed its channel for several weeks each year, when melting snow from central African mountains swelled its waters. This predictable annual flood enriched the soil with nutrients from the river's silt and diluted harmful mineral salts, thereby making farming more productive and supporting strong population growth. Unlike the unpredictable floods that harmed Mesopotamia, the regular flooding of the Nile benefited Egyptians. Trouble came in Egypt only if the usual flood did not take place, as happened when too little winter precipitation fell in the mountains.

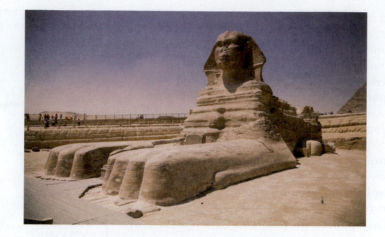

The Great Sphinx of Egypt
This enormous stone sculpture of a sphinx, a mythical female creature with a human head and torso and lion's body, was built near the Great Pyramid in Egypt. Since no inscriptions tell us which king or kings ordered it built, or when or why, scholars still debate its place in ancient Egyptian history and thought. It remains the largest stone monument in the world. (Emad Omar Farouk/Shutterstock.)

The plants and animals raised by Egypt's farmers fed a fast-growing population. Egypt's population totaled several million people by around 1500 B.C.E. Date palms, vegetables, grass for pasturing animals, and grain grew in abundance. The Egyptians loved beer, which people of all ages consumed. Thicker and more nutritious than modern brews, Egyptian beer was such an important food that it could be used to pay workmen's wages. Egyptians, like other ancient societies, often flavored their beer with fruits.

Egypt's population included people whose skin color ranged from light to dark. Although many ancient Egyptians would be regarded as black by modern racial classification, ancient peoples did not observe such distinctions. The modern controversy over whether Egyptians were people of color is therefore not an issue that ancient Egyptians would have considered. If asked, they would probably have identified themselves by geography, language, religion, or traditions rather than skin color. Like many other ancient groups, the Egyptians called themselves simply The People. Later peoples, especially the Greeks, recognized the ethnic and cultural differences between themselves and the Egyptians, but they deeply admired Egyptian civilization for its long history and strongly religious character.

Although Egyptians absorbed knowledge from both the Mesopotamians and the Nubians, their African neighbors to the south, they developed their own written scripts. For official documents they used a pictographic script known as **hieroglyphic** (Figure 1.2). They developed other, simpler scripts for everyday purposes.

Some scholars believe that Nubian society was the outside influence that most deeply affected early Egypt. A Nubian social elite lived in dwellings much grander than the small huts housing most of the population. Egyptians interacted with Nubians while trading for raw materials such as gold, ivory, and animal skins, and Nubia's hierarchical political and social organization possibly influenced the development of Egypt's politically centralized Old Kingdom. Eventually, however, Egypt's greater power led it to dominate its southern neighbor.

Keeping Egypt unified and stable was difficult. When the kings were strong, as during the Old Kingdom, the country was peaceful, with flourishing international trade. Regional governors rebelling against weak kings, however, could create political turmoil. Kings gained strength by fulfilling their public religious obligations. Egyptians worshipped a great variety of gods, often shown in paintings and sculptures as creatures with both human and animal features, such as the head of a jackal or a bird atop a human body. These images reflected the belief that the gods each had a particular animal through which they revealed themselves to human beings. Egyptian gods were associated with powerful natural objects, emotions, qualities, and technologies—examples are Re, the sun god; Isis, the goddess of love and fertility; and Thoth, the god of wisdom and the inventor of writing. People worshipped the gods with rituals, prayers, and festivals that expressed their respect and devotion to these divine powers.

Egyptians regarded their king as a helpful divinity in human form, identified with the hawk-headed god Horus. They saw the king's rule as divine because he helped generate *maat* ("what is right"), the supernatural force that brought order and harmony to human beings if they maintained a stable hierarchy. The goddess **Maat**—the embodiment of the divine force of justice—therefore oversaw a society that the Egyptians believed would fall apart violently if the king ruled unjustly. The king therefore had the duties of pleasing the gods, making law, and waging war on enemies.

Art expressed the king's legitimacy as ruler by representing him doing his religious and military duties. The requirement to show piety (proper religious belief and behavior) demanded strict regulation of the king's daily activities; he had specific times to take a bath, go for a walk, and make love to his wife. Most important, he had to ensure the country's fertility and prosperity. If the Nile flood failed to occur, this was seen as the king's fault and weakened his authority by leaving many people hungry and angry, thus encouraging rebellions by rivals.

FIGURE 1.2 Egyptian Hieroglyphs

Ancient Egyptians used pictures such as these to develop their own system of writing around 3000 B.C.E. Egyptian hieroglyphs include around seven hundred pictures in three categories: ideograms (signs indicating things or ideas), phonograms (signs indicating sounds), and determinatives (signs clarifying the meaning of the other signs). Because Egyptians employed this formal script mainly for religious inscriptions on buildings and sacred objects, Greeks referred to it as *ta hieroglyphica* ("the sacred carved letters"), from which comes the modern word *hieroglyphic*, used to designate this system of writing. Eventually, Egyptians also developed the handwritten cursive script called demotic (Greek for "of the people"), a much simpler and quicker form of writing. The hieroglyphic writing system continued until about 400 C.E., when it was replaced by the Coptic alphabet. Compare hieroglyphs with cuneiform shapes (see page 13).

Hieroglyph	Meaning	Sound value
	vulture	glottal stop
	flowering reed	consonantal I
	forearm and hand	ayin
	quail chick	W
	foot	B
	stool	P
	horned viper	F
	owl	M
	water	N
	mouth	R
	reed shelter	H
	twisted flax	slightly guttural
	placenta (?)	H as in "loch"
	animal's belly	slightly softer than h
	door bolt	S
	folded cloth	S
	pool	SH
	hill	Q
	basket with handle	K
	jar stand	G
	loaf	T

Successful Old Kingdom rulers used expensive building programs to demonstrate their piety and status. They erected their huge tombs—pyramids—in the desert outside Memphis. Temples and halls accompanied the tombs for religious ceremonies and royal funerals. Although the pyramids were not the first monuments built from enormous worked stones (the temples, admittedly much smaller in scale, on the Mediterranean island of Malta are earlier), they rank as the grandest, much larger even than the Great Sphinx.

Old Kingdom rulers spent vast resources on these giant complexes to proclaim their divine status and protect their mummified bodies for existence in the afterlife. King Khufu (r. 2609–2584 B.C.E.; also known as Cheops) commissioned the hugest monument of all—the Great Pyramid at Giza. Taller than a forty-story skyscraper at 480 feet high, it covered thirteen acres and stretched 760 feet long on each side. It required more than two million blocks of limestone, some weighing fifteen tons. Its exterior blocks were quarried along the Nile, floated down the river on barges, and pulled to the site on sleds over sand dampened to reduce friction. Free workers then dragged the blocks up ramps into position using rollers and wooden pads.

The Old Kingdom rulers' expensive preparations for death reflected their belief in the afterlife. One text says: "O [god] Atum, put your arms around King Neferkare Pepy II [r. c. 2300–2206 B.C.E.], around this construction work, around this pyramid.... May you guard lest anything happen to him evilly throughout the course of eternity." The royal family equipped their tombs with many comforts to use in the underworld. The kings had gilded furniture, sparkling jewelry, and precious objects placed alongside the coffins holding their mummies. Archaeologists have even uncovered two full-sized cedar ships buried next to the Great Pyramid, meant to carry King Khufu on his journey into eternity.

The Old Kingdom ranked Egyptians in a strict hierarchy to preserve their kings' authority and support what they regarded as the proper order of a just society. Egyptians, believing their ordered society was superior to any other, despised foreigners. The king and queen headed the hierarchy. Brothers and sisters in the royal family could

The Pyramids at Giza in Egypt

The kings of the Egyptian Old Kingdom built massive stone pyramids for their tombs. The largest pyramid shown here is the Great Pyramid of King Khufu (Cheops). Erected at Giza in the desert outside what is today Cairo in the twenty-sixth century B.C.E., it stands almost 480 feet high, not much shorter than the 550-foot-high Washington Monument in Washington, D.C. The pyramids formed the centerpieces of large complexes of temples and courtyards stretching down to the banks of the Nile River or along a canal leading there. The hidden burial chambers of the kings lay at the end of narrow tunnels snaking deep into the pyramids' interiors. (Guido Alberto Rossi/TIPS Images RM/age-fotostock.)

marry each other, perhaps because such matches were thought to preserve the purity of the royal line and imitate the gods' marriages. The priests, royal administrators, provincial governors, and army commanders ranked second. Then came the free common people, who mostly worked in agriculture. Free workers had heavy obligations to the state. In a system called corvée labor, the kings commanded commoners to work on the pyramids during slack times in farming. The state fed, housed, and clothed the workers while they performed this seasonal work; their labor was a way of paying taxes. Taxation reached 20 percent on the farmers' produce. Slaves captured in foreign wars served the royal family and the priests; privately owned slaves became numerous only after the Old Kingdom. The king hired mercenaries, many from Nubia, to form the majority of the army.

Egyptians preserved more of the gender equality of the early Stone Age than did their neighbors. Women generally enjoyed the same legal rights as free men. They could own land and slaves, inherit property, pursue lawsuits, transact business, and initiate divorces. Portrait statues show the equal status of wife and husband; each figure is the same size and sits on the same kind of chair. Men dominated public life, while women devoted themselves mainly to private life, managing their households and property. When their husbands went to war or were killed in battle, however, women often took on men's work. Women could serve as priestesses, farm managers, or healers in times of crisis.

The formal style of Egyptian art illustrates the high value placed on order and predictability. Statues represent the subject either standing stiffly with the left leg advanced or sitting on a chair or throne, stable and poised. The concern for decorum (suitable behavior) also appears in the Old Kingdom literature called **wisdom literature**—texts giving instructions for appropriate behavior. One text instructs a young man to seek advice from ignorant people as well as the wise and to avoid arrogant overconfidence. This kind of literature had a strong influence on later civilizations, especially the ancient Israelites.

The Middle and New Kingdoms in Egypt, 2061–1081 B.C.E.

The Old Kingdom began to disintegrate in the late third millennium B.C.E. Climate change perhaps caused the annual Nile flood to shrink, making people believe the kings had betrayed Maat. Rivalry for power erupted among leading families, and civil war between a northern dynasty and a southern dynasty ripped the country apart. This disunity allowed regional governors to increase their power, and some now seized independence for their regions. Famine and civil unrest during the so-called First Intermediate Period (2190–2061 B.C.E.) prevented the reestablishment of political unity.

The kings of the Middle Kingdom (2061–1665 B.C.E.) restored the strong central authority their Old Kingdom predecessors had lost. They waged war to extend Egypt's southern boundaries, and they expanded diplomatic and trade contacts in the eastern Mediterranean region and with the island of Crete. Middle Kingdom literature reveals that restored unity contributed to a deeply felt pride in the homeland. The Egyptian narrator of *The Story of Sinuhe*, for example, reports that he lived luxuriously during a forced stay in Syria but still longed to return: "Whichever god you are who ordered my exile, have mercy and bring me home! Please allow me to see the land where my heart dwells! Nothing is more important than that my body be buried in the country where I was born!" For this lonely man, love for Egypt outranked personal riches and comfort in a foreign land.

The Middle Kingdom lost its unity during the Second Intermediate Period (1664–1570 B.C.E.), when the kings proved too weak to control foreign migrants who had established independent communities in Egypt. By 1664 B.C.E., diverse bands of a Semitic people originally from the eastern Mediterranean coast seized power. The Egyptians called these foreigners Hyksos ("rulers of the foreign countries"). Hyksos settlers transplanted foreign cultural elements to Egypt; their capital, Avaris, boasted wall paintings done in the Minoan style of the island of Crete. The Hyksos promoted frequent contact between Egypt and other Near Eastern states and apparently introduced bronze-making technology, new musical instruments, humpbacked cattle, and olive trees. Hyksos rulers strengthened Egypt's military capacity by increasing the use of war chariots and more powerful bows.

The leaders of Thebes, in southern Egypt, reunited the kingdom after long struggles with the Hyksos. The series of dynasties they founded is called the New Kingdom (1569–1081 B.C.E.). Thebes drew strength from its connections with prosperous settlements that emerged far out in the western desert, such as at Kharga Oasis. Oases featured abundant water from underground aquifers in the middle of a scorching environment. Oasis settlements flourished by providing stopping points for the caravans of merchants who crossed harsh deserts to profit from commerce. Thebes's expansion of contact with the western desert settlements reveals that Egyptian society did not remain unchanged by completely shutting itself off behind its natural boundaries along the Nile. Similarly, contacts with peoples to the east across the Red Sea and along the Indian Ocean expanded in the New Kingdom.

The kings of the New Kingdom, known as pharaohs, rebuilt central authority by restricting the power of regional governors and promoting national identity. To prevent invasions, the pharaohs created a standing army, another significant change in Egyptian society. These kings still employed mercenaries, but they formed an Egyptian military elite as commanders. Recognizing that knowledge of the rest of the world was necessary for safety, the pharaohs promoted diplomacy with neighboring monarchs to increase their international contacts. The pharaohs exchanged official letters with their "brother kings," as they called them, in Mesopotamia, Anatolia, and the eastern Mediterranean region.

The New Kingdom pharaohs sent their army into foreign wars to gain territory and show their superiority. Their imperialism has earned them the title "warrior pharaohs." They waged many campaigns abroad and presented themselves in official propaganda and art as the incarnations of warrior gods.

They invaded lands to the south to win access to gold and other precious materials, and they fought up and down the eastern Mediterranean coast to control that crucial land route into Egypt.

Massive riches supported the power of these aggressive pharaohs. Egyptian traders exchanged local fine goods, such as ivory, for foreign luxury goods, such as wine and olive oil transported in painted pottery from Greece. Egyptian rulers displayed their wealth most conspicuously in the enormous sums spent to build stone temples. Queen Hatshepsut (r. 1502–1482 B.C.E.), for example, built her massive mortuary temple at Deir el-Bahri, near Thebes, including a temple dedicated to the god Amun (or Amen), to express her claim to divine birth and the right to rule. After her husband (who was also her half-brother) died, Hatshepsut proclaimed herself "female king" as co-ruler with her young stepson. In this way, she sidestepped the restrictions of Egyptian political tradition, which did not recognize the right of a queen to reign by herself. Hatshepsut also had herself represented in official art as a king, with a royal beard and male clothing. Hatshepsut succeeded in her unusual rule because she demonstrated that a woman could ensure safety and prosperity by maintaining the goodwill of the gods toward the country and its people.

Egyptians believed that the gods oversaw all aspects of life and death, and therefore they built large temples and held festivals to honor their deities. A calendar based on the moon governed the dates of religious ceremonies. (The Egyptians also developed a calendar for administrative and fiscal purposes that had 365 days, divided into 12 months of 30 days each, with the extra 5 days added before the start of the next year. Our modern calendar follows their invention.) The early New Kingdom pharaohs promoted their state god

Hatshepsut's Temple at Deir el Bahri
The massive mortuary temple of the famous Egyptian New Kingdom Queen Hatshepsut (r. 1502–1482 B.C.E.) was built as a series of terraces at the base of a looming rock cliff near Thebes in southern Egypt. Statues and gardens decorated the wide terraces, and a temple to the god Amun (or Amen) proclaimed the special relationship to the divine that Hatshepsut enjoyed as royalty. This visually impressive stone monument proclaimed her glory and perpetuated the memory of her having ruled essentially on her own. (James Morris/akg-images.)

Amun-Re (a combination of Thebes's patron god and the sun god) so energetically that he became far more important than the other gods. This Theban cult subordinated the other gods, without denying their existence or the continued importance of their priests. The pharaoh Akhenaten (r. 1372–1355 B.C.E.) went a step further, however; he proclaimed that official religion would concentrate on worshipping Aten, who represented the pure power of the sun. Akhenaten made the king and the queen the only people with direct access to the cult of Aten, excluding commoners. Some scholars identify Akhenaten's religious reform as a step toward monotheism, with Aten meant to be the state's sole god.

To showcase the royal family and the concentration of power that he desired, Akhenaten moved 40,000 Egyptians from their original locations to construct a new capital for Aten at Tell el-Amarna (Map 1.2 on page 19). Archaeology shows that the workers had very hard lives, suffering from poor nutrition and dangerous labor conditions. The pharaoh tried to force his revised religion on the priests of the old cults, who resisted fiercely. Historians have blamed Akhenaten's religious zeal for leading him to neglect his kingdom's defense, but international correspondence found at Tell el-Amarna has shown that the pharaoh tried to use diplomacy to turn foreign enemies against one another so that they would remain too weak to threaten Egypt. His policy failed, however, when the Hittites from Anatolia defeated the Mitanni, Egypt's allies in eastern Syria. Akhenaten's religious reform also died with him. During the reign of his successor, Tutankhamun (r. 1355–1346 B.C.E.)—famous today through the discovery in 1922 of his rich, unlooted tomb—the cult of Amun-Re reclaimed its leading role. The crisis created by Akhenaten's attempted reform emphasizes the overwhelming importance of religious conservatism in Egyptian life and the control of religion by the rulers and priests.

Most New Kingdom Egyptians' lives revolved around their labor and the annual flood of the Nile. During the months when the river stayed between its banks, they worked the fields, rising early in the morning to avoid the searing heat. When the flooding halted agricultural work, the king required laborers to work on his building projects. They lived in workers' quarters erected next to the construction sites. Although slaves became more common as household workers in the New Kingdom than they had been before, free workers—who were obliged to perform a certain amount of labor for the king—did most of the work on this period's mammoth royal construction projects. Workers lightened their burden by singing songs, telling adventure stories, and drinking a lot of beer. They accomplished a great deal; the majority of the ancient temples remaining in Egypt today were built during the New Kingdom.

Egyptians worshipped many different gods, especially those believed to protect them in their daily existence. They venerated Bes, for instance, a dwarf with the features of a lion, as a protector of the household. They carved his image on amulets, beds, headrests, and mirror handles. By this time, people believed that they could have a blessed afterlife and put great effort into preparing for it. Those who could afford it arranged to have their tombs outfitted with all the goods needed for the journey in the underworld. Most important, they paid burial experts to turn their corpses into mummies so that they could have a complete body for eternity. Making a mummy required removing the brain (through the nose with a long-handled spoon), cutting out the internal organs to store separately in stone jars, drying the body with mineral salts to the consistency of old leather, and wrapping the shrunken flesh in linen soaked with ointments.

Every mummy had to go to the afterlife with a copy of the *Book of the Dead*, which included magic spells for avoiding dangers along the way, as well as instructions on how to prepare for the judgment-day trial before the gods. To prove that they deserved a good fate, the dead had to convincingly recite claims such as the following: "I have not committed crimes against people; I have not mistreated cattle; I have not robbed the poor; I have not caused pain; I have not caused tears."

Magic played a significant role in Egyptians' beliefs. Professional magicians sold spells and charms, both written and oral, which the buyers used to promote eternal salvation, protect against demons, smooth the rocky course of love, exact revenge on enemies, and find relief from disease and injury. Egyptian doctors treated patients with medicinal herbs (knowledge passed on to later civilizations) and performed major surgeries, including opening the skull. Still, no doctor could cure severe infections, and the sick continued to ask supernatural beings for help through prayers and spells.

REVIEW QUESTION
How did religion guide the lives of both rulers and ordinary people in ancient Egypt?

The Hittites, the Minoans, and the Mycenaeans, 2200–1000 B.C.E.

The first societies of Western civilization in the central Mediterranean region were located in Anatolia, dominated by the warlike Hittite kingdom (Map 1.1 on page 7); on the large island of Crete and nearby islands, home to the Minoans; and on the Greek mainland, where the Mycenaeans grew rich from raiding and trade. As early as 6000 B.C.E., people from southwestern Asia, especially Anatolia, began migrating westward and southward across the sea to inhabit islands in the Mediterranean. From this migration, the rich civilization of the Minoans gradually emerged on Crete and other islands in the Aegean Sea by around 2200 B.C.E. In mainland Greece, civilization eventually arose among peoples who had moved into the area perhaps as early as 8000 B.C.E., again most likely from southwestern Asia.

The Hittites, the Minoans, and the Mycenaeans had advanced military technologies, elaborate architecture, striking art, a desire for luxury, and extensive trade contacts with Egypt and the Near East. The Hittites, like the Egyptians, created a unified state under a single central authority. The Minoans and the Mycenaeans, like the Mesopotamians, established separate city-states. All three peoples inhabited a dangerous world in which repeated raids and violent disruptions lasting from around 1200 to 1000 B.C.E. ultimately destroyed their prosperous cultures. Nevertheless, their accomplishments paved the way for the later civilization of Greece, which greatly influenced Western civilization.

The Hittites, 1750–1200 B.C.E.

By around 1750 B.C.E., the Hittites had made themselves the most powerful people of central Anatolia. Having migrated from the Caucasus area, between the Black and Caspian Seas, they defeated indigenous Anatolian peoples to found their centralized kingdom. It flourished because they inhabited a fertile upland plateau in the peninsula's center, excelled in war and diplomacy, and controlled trade in their region and southward. The Hittites' military campaigns eventually threatened Egypt's possessions on the eastern Mediterranean coast, creating conflict with the New Kingdom pharaohs.

Since the Hittites spoke an Indo-European language, they belonged to the linguistic family that over time populated most of Europe. The original Indo-European speakers, who were pastoralists and raiders from western Asia, migrated as separate groups into Anatolia and Europe, including Greece. Archaeological discoveries in that region have revealed graves of women buried with weapons. These burials suggest that women in these groups originally occupied positions of leadership in war and peace alongside men; the prominence of Hittite queens in documents, royal letters, and foreign treaties sprang from that tradition.

As in other early civilizations, rule in the Hittite kingdom based its legitimacy on religion. Hittite religion combined worship of Indo-European gods with worship of deities inherited from the original Anatolian population. The king served as high priest of the storm god, and Hittite belief demanded that he maintain a strict purity in his life as a demonstration of his justice and guardianship of social order. His drinking water, for example, always had to be strained. The king's water carrier was executed if so much as one hair was found in the liquid. Like Egyptian kings, Hittite rulers felt responsible for maintaining the gods' goodwill toward their subjects. King Mursili II (r. 1321–1295 B.C.E.), for example, issued a set of prayers begging the gods to end a plague: "What is this, o gods, that you have done? Our land is dying…. We have lost our wits, and we can do nothing right. O gods, whatever sin you behold, either let a prophet come forth to identify it … or let us see it in a dream!"

The kings conducted many religious ceremonies in their capital, Hattusas. Ringed by massive defensive walls and stone towers, it featured huge palaces aligned along straight, gravel-paved streets. Sculptures of animals, warriors, and, especially, the royal rulers decorated public spaces. Hittite kings maintained their rule by forging personal alliances—cemented by marriages and oaths of loyalty—with the noble families of the kingdom.

These rulers aggressively employed their troops to expand their power. In periods when ties between kings and nobles remained strong and the kingdom preserved its unity, they launched far-reaching military campaigns. In 1595 B.C.E., for example, the royal army raided as far southeast as Babylon in Mesopotamia, destroying that kingdom. Although Hittite craftsmen knew how to smelt iron, from which they made ceremonial implements, scholars no longer accept the idea that the kingdom owed its success in war to a special knowledge of making weapons from iron. Weapons made from iron did not become common in the Mediterranean world until well after 1200 B.C.E., at the end of the Hittite kingdom. The Hittite army excelled in the use of chariots, a tactic that gave it an edge on the battlefield.

The economic strength of the Hittite kingdom came from control over long-distance trade routes for raw materials, especially metals. The Hittites dominated the lucrative trade moving between the Mediterranean coast and inland northern Syria, despite the New Kingdom pharaohs' resistance against Hittite expansion to the south toward the Mediterranean coast and the benefits that access to the sea brought. In the bloody battle of Kadesh, around 1274 B.C.E., the Hittites fought the Egyptians to a standstill in Syria, leading to a political stalemate in the eastern Mediterranean. Fear of neighboring Assyria eventually led the Hittite king to negotiate with his Egyptian rival, and the two war-weary kingdoms became allies sixteen years after the battle of Kadesh by agreeing to a treaty that is a landmark in the history of international diplomacy. In it, the two monarchs pledged to be "at peace and brothers forever." The alliance lasted; thirteen years later the Hittite king gave his daughter in marriage to his Egyptian "brother."

The Minoans, 2200–1400 B.C.E.

Study of early Greek civilization traditionally begins with the people today known as Minoans, who inhabited Crete and other islands in the Aegean Sea by the late third millennium B.C.E. The word *Minoan* comes from the archaeologist Arthur Evans (1851–1941), who was searching the island for traces of King Minos, famous in Greek myth for building the first great navy and keeping the half-human/half-bull Minotaur in a labyrinth at his palace. Scholars today, however, are not sure whether to count the Minoans as the earliest Greeks because they are uncertain whether the Minoan language, written in a script called Linear A that is not fully deciphered, was related to Greek or belongs to another linguistic tradition. If research confirms that Minoan was a member of the Indo-European family of languages (the ancestor of many languages, including Greek, Latin, and, much later, English), then, based on the criterion of language, Minoans can be seen as the earliest Greeks. In any case, Minoans' interactions with the mainland deeply influenced later Greek civilization.

By around 2200 B.C.E., Minoans on Crete and nearby islands had created a **palace society**, a name pointing to its sprawling multichambered buildings housing not only the rulers, their families, and their servants, but also the political, economic, and religious administrative offices of the state. Minoan rulers combined the functions of ruler and priest, dominating both politics and religion. The palaces seem to have been independent, with no single Minoan community imposing unity on the others. The general population clustered around each palace in houses adjacent to one another; some of these settlements reached the size and density of small cities. The Cretan site Knossos is the most famous such palace complex. Other, smaller settlements dotted

Palace at Knossos
The Minoans on the island of Crete and neighboring islands in the Mediterranean Sea south of mainland Greece constructed large, multilevel buildings called palaces containing many rooms, corridors, worship spaces, and porches. They housed royal families, servants, administrators, and managers of enormous storage complexes. The walls were decorated with colorful paintings showing diverse scenes of nature, elaborately dressed people, and ceremonies. Urban settlements grew up around these palaces. The palace at Knossos is the largest known. It controlled a fertile agricultural area that provided the rulers with a luxurious lifestyle. (DEA/A. Vergani/age-fotostock.)

outlying areas of the island, especially on the coast. The Minoans' numerous ports supported extensive international trade, above all with the Egyptians and the Hittites.

The most surprising feature of Minoan communities is their lack of strong defensive walls. Palaces, towns, and even isolated country houses had no fortifications. The remains of the newer palaces—such as that at Knossos, with its hundreds of rooms in five stories, indoor plumbing, and colorful scenes painted on the walls—have led some historians to the controversial conclusion that Minoans avoided war among themselves, despite their having no single central authority over their independent settlements. Others reject this hypothesis of peaceful Minoans, arguing that the most powerful Minoans on Crete dominated neighboring islands. Recent discoveries of tombs on Crete have revealed weapons caches, and a find of bones cut by knives has even raised the possibility of human sacrifice. The prominence of women in palace frescoes and the numerous figurines of large-breasted goddesses found on Minoan sites have also prompted speculation that women dominated Minoan society, but no Linear A texts verify this. Minoan art certainly depicts women prominently and respectfully, but the same is true of other civilizations of the time controlled by men. More research is needed to resolve the controversies concerning gender roles in Minoan civilization.

Scholars do agree that the development of **Mediterranean polyculture**—the cultivation of olives, grapes, and grains in a single, interrelated agricultural system—greatly increased the health and wealth of Minoan society. This innovation made the most efficient use of a farmer's labor by combining crops that required intense work at different seasons. This system of farming, which still characterizes Mediterranean agriculture, had two major consequences. First, the combination of crops provided a healthy way of eating (the "Mediterranean diet"), which in turn stimulated population growth. Second, agriculture became both more diversified and more specialized, increasing production of the valuable products olive oil and wine.

Agricultural surpluses on Crete and nearby islands spurred the growth of specialized crafts. To store and transport surplus food, Minoan artisans manufactured huge storage jars (the size of a modern refrigerator) and in the process created another specialized industry. Craft workers, producing sophisticated goods using time-consuming techniques, no longer had time to grow their own food or make the things, such as clothes and lamps, they needed for everyday life. Instead, they exchanged the products they made for food and other goods. In this way, Minoan society experienced increasing economic interdependence.

The vast storage areas in their palaces suggest that the Minoan rulers, like some Mesopotamian kings before them, controlled their society's exchanges through a redistributive economic system. The Knossos palace, for example, held hundreds of gigantic jars capable of storing 240,000 gallons of olive oil and wine. Bowls, cups, and dippers crammed storerooms nearby. Palace officials decided how much each farmer or craft producer had to contribute to the palace storehouse and how much of those contributions would then be redistributed to each person in the community for basic subsistence or as an extra reward. In this way, people sent the products of their labor to the central authority, which redistributed them according to its own priorities.

The Mycenaeans, 1800–1000 B.C.E.

Ancestors of the Greeks had moved into the mainland region of Greece by perhaps 8000 B.C.E., yet the first civilization definitely identified as Greek because of its Indo-European language arose only in the early second millennium B.C.E. These first Greeks are called Mycenaeans, a name derived from the hilltop site of Mycenae, famous for its many-roomed palace, rich graves, and massive fortification walls. Located in the Peloponnese (the large peninsula forming southern Greece, Map 1.3), Mycenae dominated its local area, but no one settlement ever ruled all of Bronze Age Greece. Instead, the independent communities of Mycenaean civilization vied with one another in a fierce competition for natural resources and territory.

The nineteenth-century German millionaire Heinrich Schliemann (1822–1890) was the first to discover treasure-filled graves at Mycenae; he was on a self-financed personal quest to prove that the poems of Homer, Greece's first and most famous poet, were not just fiction. The burial objects he found revealed a warrior culture organized in independent settlements and ruled by aggressive kings. Constructed as stone-lined shafts, the graves contained entombed dead who had taken hordes of valuables with them: golden jewelry, including heavy necklaces loaded with pendants; gold and silver vessels; bronze weapons decorated with scenes of wild animals inlaid in precious metals; and delicately painted pottery.

In his excitement at finding treasure, Schliemann proudly announced that he had found the grave of Agamemnon, the legendary king who commanded the Greek army against Troy, a city in northwestern Anatolia, in the Trojan War. Homer had based his epic poem *The Iliad* on this war. Archaeologists

MAP 1.3 Greece and the Aegean Sea, 1500 B.C.E.
A varied landscape of mountains, islands, and seas defined the geography of Greece. The distances between settlements were mostly short, but rough terrain and seasonally stormy sailing made travel a chore. The distance from the mainland to the largest island in this region, Crete, where Minoan civilization arose, was long enough to keep Cretans isolated from the wars of most of later Greek history.

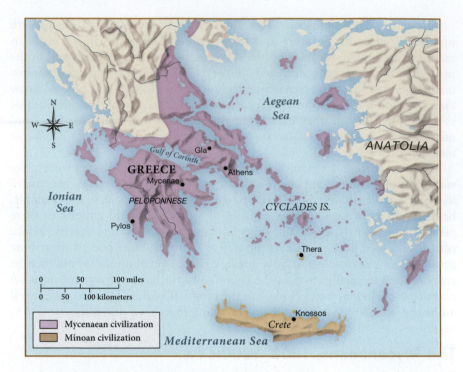

now know the shaft graves date to around 1700–1600 B.C.E., long before the Trojan War could have taken place. Still, Schliemann's discoveries at Mycenae, which had followed his excavations at Troy done to prove that the city had really existed, provided spectacular evidence for mainland Greece's earliest civilization.

Since the hilly terrain of Greece had little fertile land but many useful ports, settlements tended to spring up near the coast. Mycenaean rulers enriched themselves by dominating local farmers, conducting naval raids, and participating in seaborne trade. Palace records inscribed on clay tablets reveal that the Mycenaeans operated under a redistributive economy. On the tablets, scribes made detailed lists of goods received and goods paid out, recording everything from chariots to livestock, landholdings, personnel, and perfumes, even broken equipment taken out of service. Like the Minoans, the Mycenaeans did not use writing to record the oral literature that scholars believe they created.

Tholos tombs—massive underground burial chambers built in beehive shapes with closely fitted stones—reveal that by about 1500 B.C.E. some Mycenaeans had become very rich. The architecture of these tombs and the style of the burial goods in them testify to the far-flung expeditions for trade and war that Mycenaean rulers conducted throughout the eastern Mediterranean. Above all, their many decorative patterns clearly inspired by Minoan art indicate a close connection with that civilization on Crete.

Underwater archaeology has revealed the influence of international commerce during this period in promoting cultural interaction as a by-product of trade. Divers have discovered, for example, that a late-fourteenth-century B.C.E. shipwreck off Uluburun in Turkey carried a mixed cargo and varied personal possessions from many locations in the eastern Mediterranean, including Canaan, Cyprus, Greece, Egypt, and Babylon. The variety confirms that merchants and consumers involved in this sort of long-distance trade were exposed directly to the goods produced by others and indirectly to their ideas.

The sea brought the Mycenaean and Minoan civilizations into close contact, but they remained different in significant ways. The Mycenaeans spoke Greek and made burnt offerings to the gods; the Minoans did neither. The Minoans extended their religious worship outside their centers, establishing sacred places in caves, on mountaintops, and in country villas, while the mainlanders concentrated the worship of their gods inside their walled communities. When the Mycenaeans started building palaces in the fourteenth century B.C.E., they (unlike the palace-society Minoans) designed them around *megarons*—rooms with prominent ceremonial hearths and thrones for the rulers. Some Mycenaean palaces had more than one megaron, which could soar two stories high with columns to support a roof above the second-floor balconies.

Inscribed clay tablets found in the palace at Knossos reveal that by around 1400 B.C.E. the Mycenaeans had acquired dominance over Crete, possibly in a war over commerce in the Mediterranean. The documents were written in **Linear B**, a pictographic script based on Linear A. The architect Michael Ventris (1922–1956) proved that Linear B was used to write Greek, not Minoan. Because these tablets date from before the final destruction of Knossos in about 1370 B.C.E., they reveal that the palace administration had been keeping its records in this foreign language for some time and therefore that Mycenaeans were controlling Crete well before the end of Minoan civilization. By the middle of the fourteenth century B.C.E., then, the Mycenaeans had displaced the Minoans as the Aegean region's preeminent civilization.

By the time Mycenaeans took over Crete, war at home and abroad was the principal concern of well-off Mycenaean men, a tradition that they passed on to later Greek civilization. Contents of Bronze Age tombs in Greece reveal that no wealthy man went to his grave without his war equipment. Armor and weapons were so central to a Mycenaean man's identity that he could not do without them, even in death. Warriors rode into battle on revolutionary transport—lightweight two-wheeled chariots pulled by horses. These expensive vehicles, perhaps introduced by Indo-Europeans migrating from Central Asia, first appeared in various Mediterranean and Near Eastern societies not long after 2000 B.C.E.; the first picture of such a chariot in the Aegean region occurs on a Mycenaean grave marker from about 1500 B.C.E. Wealthy people evidently desired this new and costly equipment not only for war but also as proof of their social status.

The Mycenaeans apparently spent more on war than religion. They did not construct any giant religious buildings like Mesopotamia's ziggurats or Egypt's pyramids. Their most important deities were male gods concerned with war. The names of gods found in the Linear B tablets reveal that Mycenaeans passed down many divinities to later Greeks, for example Dionysus, the god of wine.

Decorated Dagger from Mycenae
The hilltop fortress and palace at Mycenae was the capital of Bronze Age Greece's most famous kingdom. The picture of a lion hunt inlaid in gold and silver on this sixteenth-century B.C.E. dagger expressed how wealthy Mycenaean men saw their roles in society: as courageous hunters and warriors overcoming the hostile forces of nature. The nine-inch blade was found in a circle of graves inside Mycenae's walls, where the highest-ranking people were buried with their treasures as evidence of their status. (National Archeological Museum, Athens, Greece/De Agostini Picture Library/Gianni Dagli Orti/Bridgeman Images.)

The Violent End to Early Western Civilization, 1200–1000 B.C.E.

A state of political equilibrium, in which kings corresponded with one another and traders traveled all over the area, characterized the Mediterranean and Near Eastern world around 1300 B.C.E. Within a century, however, violence and, perhaps, climate change had destroyed or weakened almost every major political state in the region, including Egypt, some kingdoms of Mesopotamia, and the Hittite and Mycenaean kingdoms. Neither the civilizations united under a single central authority nor the ones with independent states survived. Understanding this period of destruction from about 1200 to 1000 B.C.E. remains one of the most difficult puzzles in the history of Western civilization.

Research on fossilized pollen suggests that a prolonged period of severe drought at this time weakened the civilizations in the eastern Mediterranean by drastically reducing food production. Egyptian and Hittite records also reveal international military conflict. They document many invasions in this period, especially from the sea. According to one inscription, in about 1190 B.C.E. a warrior pharaoh defeated a powerful coalition of seaborne invaders from the north, who had fought their way to the edge of Egypt. These **Sea Peoples**, as historians call them, were made up of many different groups operating separately. No single, unified group of peoples originated the tidal wave of violence starting around 1200 B.C.E. Rather, many different bands devastated the region. A chain reaction of attacks causing their victims to flee seeking safety put even more bands on the move in a recurring and expanding cycle. Some attackers were mercenary soldiers who had deserted the rulers who had employed them; some were raiders by profession; some were displaced refugees. Many were probably Greeks. The story of the Trojan War recalls this period of violent, long-range attacks; it portrays an army from Greece crossing the Aegean Sea to attack and plunder Troy and the surrounding coastal region. The attacks also reached far inland. As a result, the Babylonian kingdom collapsed, the Assyrians were confined to their homeland, and much of western Asia and Syria was devastated.

It remains mysterious how so many attackers traveling great distances could be so destructive over such a long time, but the consequences for the eastern Mediterranean region are clear. The once mighty Hittite kingdom collapsed around 1200 B.C.E., when raiders cut off its trade routes for raw materials. Invaders razed its capital city, Hattusas, which never revived. Egypt's New Kingdom turned back the Sea Peoples after a strenuous military effort, but the raiders destroyed the Egyptian long-distance trade network. By the end of the New Kingdom, around 1081 B.C.E., Egypt had shrunk to its original territorial core along the Nile's banks. These problems ruined the Egyptian state's credit. For example, when an eleventh-century B.C.E. Theban temple official traveled to Phoenicia to buy cedar for a ceremonial boat, the city's ruler demanded cash in advance. Although the Egyptian monarchy hung on, power struggles between pharaohs and priests, made worse by frequent attacks from abroad, prevented the reestablishment of centralized authority. No Egyptian dynasty ever again became an expansionist international power.

In Greece, homegrown conflict apparently generated a tipping point for Mycenaean civilization at the time when the Sea Peoples became a threat. The Mycenaeans reached the zenith of their power around 1400–1250 B.C.E. The enormous domed tomb at Mycenae called the Treasury of Atreus testifies to the riches of this period. The tomb's elaborately decorated front and soaring roof reveal the pride and wealth of the Mycenaean warrior princes. The last phase of the extensive palace at Pylos on the west coast of the Peloponnese also dates from this time. It boasted vivid wall paintings, storerooms bursting with food, and a royal bathroom with a built-in tub and intricate plumbing. But these prosperous Mycenaeans did not escape the widespread violence that began around 1200 B.C.E. Linear B tablets record the disposition of troops to the coast to guard the palace at Pylos from raids from the sea. The palace inhabitants of eastern Greece constructed defensive walls so massive that the later Greeks said giants had built them. These fortifications protected coastal palaces against seafaring attackers, who could have been either outsiders or Greeks. The wall around the inland palace at Gla in central Greece, however, which foreign raiders could not easily reach, confirms that Mycenaean communities also had to defend themselves against other Mycenaean communities.

The internal conflict probably did more damage to Mycenaean civilization than the raids of the Sea Peoples. Major earthquakes also struck at this time, spreading further destruction among the Mycenaeans. Archaeology offers no evidence for the ancient tradition that Dorian Greeks invading from the north caused this damage. Rather, near-constant civil war by jealous local

WHAT WOULD YOU DO?

Imagine you and your family survived the crisis that ended Mycenaean civilization in most locations in mainland Greece. You, like your ancestors, had worked at a specialized job such as metalworking or accounting, making your living from the redistributive economic system of your society before disaster obliterated your way of life. What would you do now to try to keep yourself and your family alive, fed, safe, and with some hope for a future?

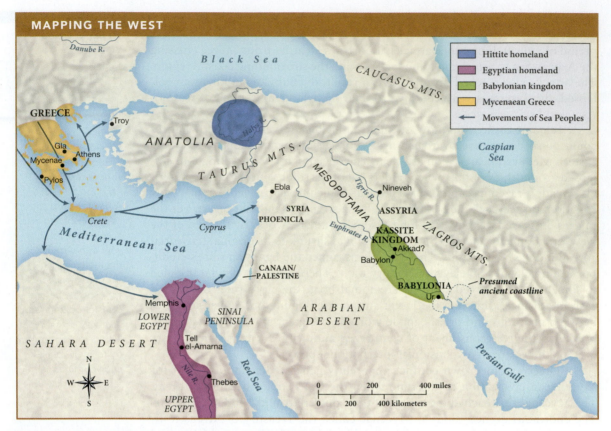

MAPPING THE WEST

The Violent End to Early Western Civilization, 1200–1000 B.C.E.

Bands of wandering warriors and raiders set the eastern Mediterranean aflame at the end of the Bronze Age. This violence displaced many people and ended the power of the Egyptian, Hittite, and Mycenaean kingdoms. Even some of the Near Eastern states well inland from the eastern Mediterranean coast felt the effects of this period of unrest, whose causes remain mysterious. The Mediterranean Sea was a two-edged sword for the early civilizations that grew up around and near it: as a highway for transporting goods and ideas, it was a benefit; as an easy access corridor for attackers, it was a danger. The raids of the Sea Peoples smashed the prosperity of the eastern Mediterranean region around 1200–1000 B.C.E. and set in motion the forces that led to the next step in our story, the reestablishment of civilization in Greece. Internal conflict among Mycenaean rulers turned the regional unrest of those centuries into a local catastrophe; fighting each other for dominance, they so weakened their monarchies that their societies could not recover from the effects of battles and earthquakes.

Analyze the Map: Which civilization depicted on this map does not lie on or very near a body of water? How would the geography of that civilization explain its attempts to expand its kingdom southward?

Make Connections: What other factors, besides geography, contributed to the violent end of early Western civilization?

Mycenaean rulers overburdened the intricate administrative balancing system of the palaces' redistributive economies and hindered recovery from earthquake damage. The violence killed many Mycenaeans, and the disappearance of the palace-based redistributive economy put many others on the road to starvation. The rulers' loss of power left most Mycenaean Greeks with no organized way to defend or feed themselves, forcing them to find new places to settle and to learn to farm on their own. Like people from the earliest times, they had to move to build a better life.

REVIEW QUESTION
How did war determine the fate of early Western civilization in Anatolia, Crete, and Greece?

Conclusion

The best way to create a meaningful definition of Western civilization is to study its history, which begins in Mesopotamia and Egypt; early societies there influenced the later civilization of Greece. Cities first arose in Mesopotamia around 4000–3000 B.C.E. Hierarchy had characterized society from the very beginning, and along with patriarchy it grew more prominent once civilization, larger populations, and political states with centralized authority became widespread.

Trade and war were constants, both aiming at profit and glory. Indirectly, they generated cultural interaction by putting civilizations into close contact. Technological innovation was also a prominent characteristic of this long period. The invention of metallurgy, monumental architecture, mathematics, and alphabetic writing changed people's ways of life. Religion was at the center of society; people believed that the gods demanded everyone, from king to worker, to display just and righteous conduct. But their faith did not protect the people of the early civilizations of the Mediterranean from the destruction inflicted by the Sea Peoples and from their own internal conflicts. Neither hierarchy nor central authority could preserve their prosperity, and so a Dark Age began around 1000 B.C.E.

Chapter 1 Review

Key Terms and People

Be sure that you can identify the term or person and explain its historical significance.

civilization (p. 4)

hierarchy (p. 4)

hunter-gatherers (p. 6)

city-state (p. 9)

patriarchy (p. 10)

redistributive economy (p. 11)

polytheism (p. 11)

cuneiform (p. 12)

empire (p. 14)

Hammurabi (p. 16)

hieroglyphic (p. 20)

Maat (p. 21)

wisdom literature (p. 23)

palace society (p. 29)

Mediterranean polyculture (p. 30)

Linear B (p. 33)

Sea Peoples (p. 34)

Review Questions

1. How did life change for people in and nearby Mesopotamia, first after the Neolithic Revolution and then when they began to live in cities?

2. How did religion guide the lives of both rulers and ordinary people in ancient Egypt?

3. How did war determine the fate of early Western civilization in Anatolia, Crete, and Greece?

Making Connections

1. Compare and contrast how the environmental factors in Mesopotamia and Egypt affected the emergence of the world's first civilizations.

2. What were the advantages and disadvantages of living in a unified country under a single central authority compared to living in a region with separate city-states?

3. Which was more important in influencing the development of early Western civilization: the intentional or the unintentional consequences of change?

Important Events

50,000–45,000 B.C.E.	*Homo sapiens* migrate from Africa into southwest Asia and Europe
10,000–8000 B.C.E.	Neolithic Revolution in Fertile Crescent and Sahara
4000–3000 B.C.E.	Mesopotamians invent writing and establish first cities
4000–1000 B.C.E.	Bronze Age in southwestern Asia, Egypt, and Europe
3050 B.C.E.	Narmer (Menes) unites Upper and Lower Egypt into one kingdom
2687–2190 B.C.E.	Old Kingdom in Egypt
2350 B.C.E.	King Sargon of Akkad establishes world's first empire
2300–2200 B.C.E.	Enheduanna, princess of Akkad, composes poetry
2200 B.C.E.	Minoans build their first palaces
2061–1665 B.C.E.	Middle Kingdom in Egypt
1792–1750 B.C.E.	Hammurabi rules Babylon and issues his law code
1569–1081 B.C.E.	New Kingdom in Egypt
1400 B.C.E.	Mycenaeans build their first palaces in Greece and take over Minoan Crete
1200–1000 B.C.E.	Period of violence ends many kingdoms

Consider three events

Mesopotamians invent writing and establish first cities (4000–3000 B.C.E.), King Sargon of Akkad establishes the world's first empire in Akkadia (2350 B.C.E.), and Enheduanna composes poetry (2300–2200 B.C.E.). How might the invention of writing have promoted the growth of stronger city-states and the first empire? How might the creation of the Akkadian Empire have fostered the development of literature?

Suggested References

The combination of archaeological and linguistic research informs scholarship on the history of the ancient Near East, Egypt, and Greece. New discoveries and new ideas both help historians achieve a clearer understanding of these earliest societies of Western civilization.

Bertman, Stephen. *Handbook to Life in Ancient Mesopotamia*. 2003.

Bryce, Trevor. *Life and Society in the Hittite World.* 2004.

_____. *The Routledge Handbook of the Peoples and Places of Ancient Western Asia.* 2009.

*Chavalas, Mark W., ed. *The Ancient Near East. Historical Sources in Translation.* 2006.

Cline, Eric H., ed. *The Oxford Handbook of the Bronze Age Aegean.* 2010.

Crouch, Carly L. *War and Ethics in the Ancient Near East.* 2009.

*Dalley, Stephanie, trans. *Myths from Mesopotamia: Creation, the Flood, Gilgamesh, and Others.* 1991.

Ikram, Salima. *Ancient Egypt: An Introduction.* 2010.

Mieroop, Marc Van De. *King Hammurabi of Babylon: A Biography.* 2005.

Partridge, Robert B. *Fighting Pharaohs: Weapons and Warfare in Ancient Egypt.* 2002.

Podany, Amanda H. *Brotherhood of Kings: How International Relations Shaped the Ancient Near East.* 2010.

Sanders, N. K. *The Sea Peoples: Warriors of the Ancient Mediterranean, 1250–1150 B.C.* Rev. ed. 1985.

Scarre, Chris. *The Human Past: World Prehistory and the Development of Human Societies.* 2009.

*Simpson, William Kelly, ed. *The Literature of Ancient Egypt. An Anthology of Stories, Instructions, and Poetry.* 3rd ed. 2003.

Suzman, James. *Affluence without Abundance: The Disappearing World of the Bushmen.* 2017.

Szapakowska, Kasia. *Daily Life in Ancient Egypt: Recreating Lahun.* 2008.

Tyldesley, Joyce. *Hatchepsut: The Female Pharaoh.* 1998.

_____

*Primary source.

Near East Empires and the Reemergence of Civilization in Greece

1000–500 B.C.E.

I n *The Iliad*, the eighth-century B.C.E. Greek poet Homer narrates bloody tales of the Trojan War. The story is rich with legends born from Greek and Near Eastern traditions, such as that of the Greek hero Bellerophon. Driven from his home by a false charge of sexual assault, Bellerophon has to serve as an enforcer for a foreign king, fighting his most dangerous enemies. In his most famous combat, Bellerophon is pitted against "the Chimera, an inhuman freak created by the gods, horrible with its lion's head, goat's body, and dragon's tail, breathing fire all the time." Bellerophon triumphs by mounting the winged horse Pegasus and swooping down on the Chimera for the attack. To reward such heroics, the king gives Bellerophon his daughter in marriage and half his kingdom.

Homer's story provides evidence for the intercultural contact between the Near East and Greece that helped Greek civilization reemerge after 1000 B.C.E. Greece's geography included many ports, which promoted contacts by sea through trade, travel, and war with the Near East. From 1000 to 500 B.C.E., these contacts—combined with the Greeks' value of competitive individual excellence, their sense of a communal identity, the contributions to the flourishing of families made by women (see, for example, the chapter opening illustration) and men alike, and their belief

CHAPTER PREVIEW

From Dark Age to Empire in the Near East, 1000–500 B.C.E.

In what ways was religion important in the Near East from c. 1000 B.C.E. to c. 500 B.C.E.?

The Reemergence of Greek Civilization, 1000–750 B.C.E.

What factors proved most important in the Greek recovery from the troubles of the Dark Age?

The Creation of the Greek City-State, 750–500 B.C.E.

How did the physical, social, and intellectual conditions of life in the Archaic Age promote the emergence of the Greek city-state?

New Directions for the Greek City-State, 750–500 B.C.E.

What were the main differences among the various forms of government in the Greek city-states?

‹‹ Black-Figure Vase Showing Women Weaving Cloth This vase, made in the 500s B.C.E., is decorated in the black-figure style, which was replaced by the red-figure style (see figure of A Greek Woman at an Altar, page 61) because the latter style allowed the artists to include more detail. The scene shows women weaving cloth. This activity emphasized women's foundational contribution to their families and therefore to human society overall, as clothing was the elemental form of protection—and expressive decoration—for the human body. During the Dark Age, Greeks had lost the knowledge of how to paint human and animal figures in their art, but they regained that skill by studying such representations in the art of the Near East. (Lekythos, c. 550–530 B.C.E. (terracotta)/Amasis Painter (fl. c. 560–515 B.C.E.)/The Metropolitan Museum of Art, New York, NY, USA/Bridgeman Images.)

that people in their communities were responsible for maintaining justice and the goodwill of the gods toward them—aided Greeks in reinventing their civilization.

Western peoples' desire for trade and cross-cultural contact increased as conditions improved after 1000 B.C.E. The Near East, which retained monarchy as its traditional form of government, recovered more quickly than Greece. Near Eastern kings extracted surpluses from subject populations to fund their palaces and armies. They also pursued new conquests to win glory, exploit the labor of conquered peoples, seize raw materials, and conduct long-distance trade.

During Greece's initial recovery from poverty and depopulation from 1000 to 750 B.C.E., new political and social traditions arose that rejected the rule of kings. In this period, Greeks maintained trade and cross-cultural contact with the Near East. Their mythology, as in Homer, and their art, which influenced Greek images of the Chimera, reveal that Greeks imported ideas and technology from their Near Eastern neighbors. By the eighth century B.C.E., however, Greeks had begun to create their own kind of city-state, the polis. The polis was a radical innovation because it made citizenship—not subjection to kings—the basis for society and politics, and included the poor as citizens. Women in the polis had legal, though not political, rights; slaves still had neither. With the exception of occasional tyrannies, Greek city-states governed themselves by having male citizens share political rights. In some places, small groups of upper-class men dominated, but many city-states were governed by all the free men, even the poor, eventually creating the world's first democracies. The Greeks' invention of a form of democratic political association, seriously incomplete though it was by incorporating gender inequality, represents a turning point in the history of Western civilization. (See Terms of History on page 44.)

CHAPTER FOCUS
How did the forms of political and social organization that Greece developed after 1000 B.C.E. differ from those of the Near East?

CHAPTER TIMELINE

1000–900 B.C.E. Greatest depopulation and economic loss	**1000–750 B.C.E.** Greece experiences Dark Age	**900–800 B.C.E.** Early revival of population and agriculture; beginning of the use of iron tools and weapons in Greece	**750 B.C.E.** Greeks begin to create the polis	**750 B.C.E.** Homeric poetry is recorded in writing after Greeks learn to write again; Hesiod composes his poetry

1000 ● ● ● **900** ● ● **800** ● ●

1000 B.C.E. Almost all important Mycenaean sites except Athens are destroyed by this time	**900 B.C.E.** Neo-Assyrian Empire emerges **800 B.C.E.** Greeks learn to write with an alphabet **800 B.C.E.** Greek trading contacts are initiated with Al Mina in Syria	**775 B.C.E.** Euboeans from Greece establish trading post on island in the Bay of Naples **776 B.C.E.** Olympic Games are founded in Greece **776 B.C.E.** First Olympic Games are held

New ways of belief and thought also developed in the Near East and Greece that deeply influenced Western civilization. In religion, the Persians developed beliefs that saw human life as a struggle between good and evil, and the Israelites evolved their monotheism. In philosophy, the Greeks began to use reason and logic to supplement mythological explanations of nature.

From Dark Age to Empire in the Near East, 1000–500 B.C.E.

The widespread violence in 1200–1000 B.C.E. had devastated many communities and populations in the eastern Mediterranean. Historians have traditionally used the term *Dark Age* to refer to the times following this period of violence, both because economic conditions were so gloomy for so many people and because the surviving evidence is so limited.

By 900 B.C.E., the Neo-Assyrian Empire had emerged in Mesopotamia. It inspired first the Babylonians and then the Persians to form empires after Assyrian power collapsed. By comparison, the Israelites had little military power, but they established a new path for civilization during this period by changing their religion. They developed monotheism and produced the Hebrew Bible (as it is known today), later called the Old Testament by Christians.

The New Empire of Assyria, 900–600 B.C.E.

By 900 B.C.E., Assyrian armies had punched westward all the way to the Mediterranean coast. The Neo-Assyrian kings conquered Babylon and then Egypt. Foot soldiers were the Assyrians' main strike force. They deployed siege towers

700 B.C.E.	657 B.C.E.		597 and 586 B.C.E.	546–510 B.C.E.	508–500 B.C.E.
Spartans conquer Messenia, enslave its inhabitants as helots	Cypselus becomes tyrant in Corinth		Israelites are exiled to Babylon	Peisistratus's family rules Athens as tyrants	Cleisthenes's reforms extend democracy in Athens

700 — **600** — **500**

700–500 B.C.E.	630 B.C.E.	594 B.C.E.	539 B.C.E.
Ionian philosophers develop rationalism	The lyric poet Sappho is born	Solon's reforms promote early democracy in Athens	Persian king Cyrus captures Babylon, permits Israelites to return to Canaan

TERMS OF HISTORY

The State

The modern term *state* comes from a Latin word meaning "having been firmly established," but social scientists disagree about what it means when applied to political associations forming large communities, especially to indicate what we commonly refer to as a nation or a country. Ideas about what the essential characteristic of a state are usually involve having authority over a clearly defined territory, sole control of the use of coercion in internal matters, the power to remain independent and free of external interference, and being recognized as legal, autonomous entities by other entities possessing the same characteristics. Some scholars refine the definition by focusing on ethnocultural identity, or developing as a functional unit, or possessing a monopoly of legitimate violence within a society, or being a set of autonomous bureaucracies, or even being a pluralist community.

Modern political scientists routinely deny that ancient political communities belong under the concept of state because, the argument goes, in the pre-modern world there was no distinction between government and ownership. In this context, "ownership" means not just slavery, but also political systems such as monarchies and empires in which the rulers operate as if they "own" the human and material resources of their communities. Some scholars, however, see the Greek city-states (see Chapter 3) and the Roman Republic (see Chapter 5) as exceptions to this generalization because they were not "kingly states" like those of medieval Europe and also satisfied the modern criteria for being recognized as a state, which is to say they possessed territoriality, sovereignty, and recognition as the legal equal of other states.

In most discussions, the term *state* remains in wide use to refer to other kinds of political association in the pre-modern world, if only for convenience, to avoid having to say, for example, "the Persian pre-modern form of political association that began with the Achaemenid Cyrus as ruler in the sixth century B.C.E.," instead of just saying "the Achaemenid Persian state." In thinking about the political history of Western civilization from antiquity to modern times, we should always keep in mind the debate over exactly what is meant by the concept of "the state."

and battering rams, while chariots carried archers. Foreign wars brought in revenues to supplement agriculture, herding, and long-distance trade.

Neo-Assyrian kings treated conquered peoples brutally. Those allowed to stay in their homelands had to make annual payments to the Assyrians. The kings also deported many defeated people to Assyria for work on huge building projects. One unexpected consequence of this policy was pressure on the kings' native language; so many Aramaeans, for example, were deported from Canaan to Assyria that Aramaic had largely replaced Assyrian as the land's everyday language by the eighth century B.C.E.

Neo-Assyrian men displayed their status and masculinity in waging war and hunting wild animals. The king hunted lions to demonstrate his vigor and power and thus his capacity to rule. Practical technology and knowledge also mattered to the kings. One boasted that he invented new irrigation equipment and a novel method of metal casting. Another one proclaimed, "I have read complicated texts, whose versions in Sumerian are obscure and in Akkadian hard to understand. I do research on the cuneiform texts on stone from before the Flood." Women of the social elite could become literate, but they were excluded from the male dominions of war and hunting.

Public religion reflected the prominence of war in Assyrian culture: the cult of Ishtar, the goddess of love and war, glorified warfare. The Neo-Assyrian rulers' desire to demonstrate their respect for the gods motivated them to build huge temples. These shrines' staffs of priests and slaves grew so large that the revenues from temple lands became insufficient; the kings had to supply extra funds from the spoils of conquest.

The Neo-Assyrian kings' harsh rule and demand for revenue made their own people resentful, especially the social elite whose riches were at risk. Rebellions therefore occurred, and a seventh-century B.C.E. revolt finally undid the kingdom. The Medes, an Iranian people, and the Chaldeans, a Semitic people who had driven the Assyrians from Babylonia, combined forces to defeat the Neo-Assyrian Empire.

The Neo-Babylonian Empire, 600–539 B.C.E.

The Chaldeans seized the lion's share of territory. Originating among semi-nomadic herders along the Persian Gulf, by 600 B.C.E. the Chaldeans had established the Neo-Babylonian Empire. They made Babylon a spectacular sight, rebuilding the great temple of Marduk, the chief god, and constructing an elaborate city gate dedicated to the goddess Ishtar. Blue-glazed bricks and lions molded in yellow, red, and white decorated the gate's walls, which soared thirty-six feet high.

The Neo-Babylonians preserved much Mesopotamian literature, such as the *Epic of Gilgamesh*. They also created many works of prose and poetry, which the educated minority would read aloud publicly to the illiterate. Particularly popular were fables, proverbs, essays, and prophecies teaching morality and proper behavior. This so-called wisdom literature, a tradition going back at least to the Egyptian Old Kingdom, was a Near Eastern tradition that also became prominent in the religious writings of the Israelites.

The Neo-Babylonians passed their knowledge to others outside their region. Their advances in astronomy became so influential that the Greeks later used the word *Chaldean* to mean "astronomer." The primary motivation for observing the stars was the belief that the gods communicated their will to humans through natural phenomena like the movements of celestial bodies and eclipses. (Other signs included abnormal births, patterns of smoke curling upward, and the trails of ants.)

The Persian Empire, 557–500 B.C.E.

Cyrus (r. c. 557–530 B.C.E.) founded the Persian Empire in what is today Iran through his skills as a general and a diplomat who saw respect for others' religious practices as advantageous imperial policy. He conquered Babylon in 539 B.C.E. Cyrus won support by proclaiming himself the restorer of traditional religion.

Cyrus's successors expanded Persian rule on the same principles of military strength and cultural tolerance. At its height, the Persian Empire extended on

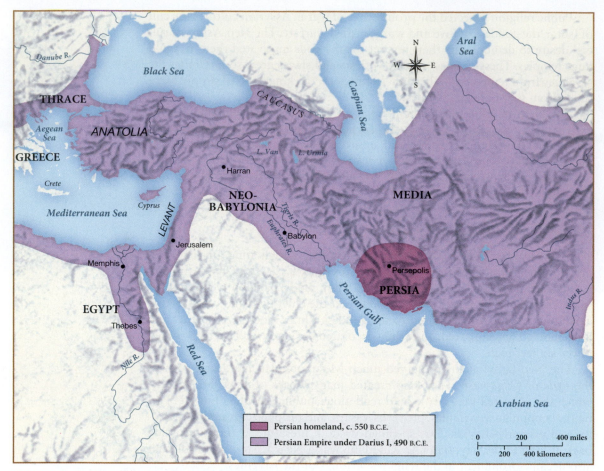

MAP 2.1 Expansion of the Persian Empire, c. 550–490 B.C.E.
Cyrus founded the Persian Empire, which his successors expanded to be even larger than the Neo-Assyrian Empire that it replaced. The Persian kings made war outward from their inland center to gain coastal possessions for access to seaborne trade and naval bases. By late in the reign of Darius I, the Persian Empire had expanded eastward as far as the western edge of India, while to the west it reached Thrace, the eastern edge of Europe. Unlike their imperial predecessors, the Persian kings won their subjects' loyalty with tolerance of local customs and religion, although they treated rebels harshly.

the west from Anatolia (today Turkey), the eastern Mediterranean coast, and Egypt, to present-day Pakistan on the east (Map 2.1). Believing they had a divine right to rule everyone in the world, Persian kings continually tried to expand their empire.

Everything about the Persian king emphasized his magnificence. His robes of purple outshone everyone else's; only he could step on the red carpets spread for him; his servants held their hands before their mouths so that he would not breathe the same air. As in other Near Eastern royal art, the Persian king was shown as larger than any other person in the sculpture adorning his immense palace at Persepolis. To display his concern for his loyal subjects and the gigantic scale of his resources, the king provided meals for fifteen thousand nobles and other guests every day—although he ate hidden from their view. The king punished criminals by mutilating their bodies and executing their families.

So long as his subjects—numbering in the millions and of many different ethnicities—remained peaceful, the king let them live and worship as they pleased. The empire's satraps (regional governors) ruled enormous territories with little interference from the king. In this decentralized system, the governors' duties included keeping order, enrolling troops when needed, and sending revenues to the royal treasury.

Darius I (r. 522–486 B.C.E.) extended Persian power eastward to westernmost India and westward to Thrace, northeast of Greece, creating the Near East's greatest empire. Darius assigned each region taxes payable in precious metals, grain, horses, and slaves. Royal roads and a courier system provided communication among the far-flung provincial centers. The Greek historian Herodotus reported that neither snow, nor rain, nor heat, nor darkness slowed the couriers from completing their routes as swiftly as possible.

Persian kings ruled as the agents of Ahura Mazda, the supreme god of Persia. Persian religion, Zoroastrianism, made Ahura Mazda the center of its devotion and took its doctrines from the teachings of the legendary prophet Zarathustra. Zarathustra taught that Ahura Mazda demanded purity from his worshippers and helped people who lived truthfully and justly. The most important doctrine of Zoroastrianism was **moral dualism**, which saw the world as a battlefield between the divine forces of good and evil. Ahura Mazda, the embodiment of good and light, struggled against the evil darkness represented by the Satan-like figure Ahriman. Human beings had to choose between the way of the truth and the way of the lie, between purity and impurity. Only those judged righteous after death made it across "the bridge of separation" to heaven and avoided falling from its narrow span into hell. Persian religion's emphasis on ethical behavior and on a supreme god had a lasting influence on others, especially the Israelites.

The Great King of Persia

Like their Assyrian predecessors, the Persian kings decorated their palaces with large relief sculptures emphasizing royal dignity and success. This one from Persepolis shows officials and petitioners giving the king proper respect when entering his presence. To symbolize their elevated status, the king and his son, who stands behind the throne, are shown larger than everyone else, as is done in other Near Eastern royal art. (National Museum of Iran, Tehran/Bridgeman Images.)

The Israelites, Origins to 539 B.C.E.

The Israelites never rivaled the political and military power of the great empires in the Near East. Their influence on Western civilization comes from their religion, Judaism. It originally reflected influences from the Israelites' polytheistic neighbors in Canaan (ancient Palestine), but the Israelites' development of monotheism became a turning point in the history of religions. The Israelites' scripture, the Hebrew Bible, was significant not only for Judaism but also later for Christianity and then for Islam.

No source provides definitive evidence for the historical background of the Israelites. According to the Bible's account, Abraham and his followers migrated from the Mesopotamian city of Ur to Canaan, perhaps around 1900 B.C.E. Traditionally believed to have been divided into twelve tribes, the Israelites never formed a political state in this period. The Canaanites remained the political and military power in the region.

Abraham's grandson Jacob, the story continues, moved to Egypt when his son Joseph brought his family there to escape famine. Joseph had previously used his intelligence and charisma to rise to an important position in the Egyptian administration. In fact, Israelites had probably drifted into Egypt during the seventeenth or sixteenth century B.C.E. as part of the movement of peoples there under Hyksos rule. By the thirteenth century B.C.E., the pharaohs had forced the Israelite men into slave-labor gangs.

According to the biblical Book of Exodus, the Israelite deity, Yahweh, instructed Moses to lead the Israelites out of bondage in Egypt against the will of the pharaoh, perhaps around the mid-thirteenth century B.C.E. Yahweh sent ten plagues to compel the Egyptian king to free the Israelites, but he still tried to recapture them during their flight. Yahweh therefore miraculously parted the sea to allow them to escape eastward; the water swirled back together and drowned the pharaoh's army as it tried to follow.

Next in the biblical narrative comes the crucial event in the history of the Israelites: the formalizing of a contractual agreement (a covenant) between them and their deity, who revealed himself to Moses on Mount Sinai in the desert northeast of Egypt. This contract between the Israelites and Yahweh specified that, in return for their worshipping him exclusively as their only god and living by his laws, Yahweh would make them his chosen people and lead them into a promised land of safety and prosperity. The form of the covenant with Yahweh followed the ancient Near Eastern tradition of treaties between a superior and subordinates, but its content differed from that of other ancient Near Eastern religions because it made Yahweh the exclusive deity of his people.

This binding agreement demanded human obedience to divine law and promised punishment for unrighteousness. Yahweh described himself to Moses as "compassionate and gracious, patient, ever constant and true . . . forgiving wickedness, rebellion, and sin," but he also declared that he was "one who punishes sons and grandsons to the third and fourth generation for their fathers' iniquity" (Exod. 34:6–7).

The Hebrew Bible sets forth the religious and moral code the Israelites had to follow. The **Torah** (the first five books of the Hebrew Bible, called the Pentateuch by Christians) recorded laws for righteous living. Most famous are the Ten Commandments, which required Israelites to worship Yahweh exclusively; make no idols; keep from misusing Yahweh's name; honor their parents; refrain from work on the seventh day of the week (the Sabbath); and abstain from murder, adultery, theft, lying, and covetousness. Many of the Israelites' laws shared the traditional form and content of earlier Mesopotamian laws, such as those of Hammurabi. Like his code, Israelite law protected the lower classes and people without power, including strangers, widows, and orphans.

Israelite law and thus Israelite justice differed significantly from their Mesopotamian precedents, however, in applying the same rules and punishments to everyone regardless of social rank. Israelite law also eliminated eye-for-an-eye punishment—the Mesopotamian legal tradition discussed in the previous chapter (see page 16). Crimes against property did not carry the death penalty in Israelite jurisprudence, as in other Near Eastern societies. Israelite laws also protected slaves against flagrant mistreatment. Slaves who lost an eye or a tooth from a beating were to be freed. Like free people, slaves enjoyed the right to rest on the Sabbath. Israelite women and children, however, had fewer legal rights than men did.

According to the Bible, the Israelites who fled from Egypt with Moses made their way back to Canaan, joining their relatives who had remained there and somehow carving out separate territories for themselves. The twelve Israelite tribes remained politically distinct under the direction of separate leaders, called judges, until the eleventh century B.C.E., when according to tradition their first monarchy emerged. Their monotheism gradually developed over the succeeding centuries.

Controversy rages about the historical accuracy of the biblical account, which reports that the Israelites created a monarchy in the late eleventh century B.C.E., when Saul became the Israelites' first king. His successors David (r. 1010–970 B.C.E.) and Solomon (r. c. 961–922 B.C.E.) brought the Israelite kingdom to the height of its prosperity. The kingdom's wealth, based on international commerce, supported the great temple that Solomon built in Jerusalem as the house of Yahweh. The temple, richly decorated with gold leaf, and the daily animal sacrifices to God that priests performed on the altar there became the center of the Israelites' religion.

After Solomon's death, the monarchy split into two kingdoms: Israel in the north and Judah in the south. The Assyrians destroyed Israel in 722 B.C.E. and deported its population to Assyria. In 597 B.C.E., the Babylonians conquered Judah and captured its capital, Jerusalem. In 586 B.C.E., they destroyed the temple to Yahweh and banished the Israelite leaders, along with much of the population, to Babylon. In exile, the Israelites learned about Persian religion. Zoroastrianism and Judaism came to share ideas, such as the existence of God and Satan, angels and demons, God's day of judgment, and the arrival of a messiah (an "anointed one," that is, a divinely chosen leader with special powers).

When the Persian king Cyrus overthrew the Babylonians in 539 B.C.E., he permitted the Israelites to return to their part of Canaan. The Bible proclaimed Cyrus a messiah of the Israelites chosen by Yahweh as his "shepherd . . . to accomplish all his purpose" in restoring his people to their previous home (Isa. 44:28–45:1). This region was called Yehud, from the name of the southern Israelite kingdom, Judah. From this geographical term came the word *Jew*, a designation for the Israelites after their Babylonian exile. Cyrus allowed them to rebuild their main temple in Jerusalem and to practice their religion.

Jewish prophets, both men and women, preached that their defeats were divine punishment for neglecting the Sinai covenant and mistreating their poor. Some prophets also predicted the end of the present world following a great crisis, a judgment by Yahweh, and salvation leading to a new and better world. This apocalypticism ("uncovering," or revelation), recalling Babylonian prophetic wisdom literature, would later inspire the worldview of Christianity.

Jewish leaders developed complex religious laws to maintain ritual and ethical purity. Marrying non-Jews and working on the Sabbath were forbidden. Fathers had legal power over the household, subject to intervention by the male elders of the community; women gained honor as mothers. Only men could initiate divorce proceedings. Jews had to pay taxes and offerings to support and honor the sanctuary of Yahweh, and they had to forgive debts every seventh year.

Gradually, Jews created their monotheism by accepting that Yahweh was the only god and that they had to obey his laws. Jews retained their identity by following this religion regardless of their personal fate or their geographical location. Therefore, Jews who did not return to their homeland could maintain their Jewish identity by following Jewish law while living among foreigners. In this way, the **Diaspora** ("dispersion of population") came to characterize the history of the Jewish people.

Goddess Figurines from Judah

These figurines perhaps represent Astarte, a goddess of Canaan, or related female deities. Archaeologists have found many small statues of this kind in private houses in Judah. They appear to date from about 800 to 600 B.C.E. Israelites probably kept them in their homes as religious objects promoting fertility and prosperity. The Israelites' prophets fiercely condemned the worship of images such as these as part of their support of the development of monotheism and the abandonment of polytheism, the long-established type of religion in the ancient world. (The Israel Museum, Jerusalem, Israel/Bridgeman Images.)

Israelite monotheism made the preservation and understanding of a sacred text, the Hebrew Bible, the center of religious life. Making scripture the focus of religion proved the most crucial development for the history not only of Judaism but also of Christianity and Islam, because these later religions made their own sacred texts—the Christian Bible and the Qur'an, respectively—the centers of their belief and practice. Through the continuing vitality of Judaism and its impact on the doctrines of Christianity and Islam, the early Jews passed on ideas—chiefly monotheism and the notion of a covenant bestowing a divinely ordained destiny on a people if they obey divine will—whose effects have endured.

REVIEW QUESTION
In what ways was religion important in the Near East from c. 1000 B.C.E. to c. 500 B.C.E.?

The Reemergence of Greek Civilization, 1000–750 B.C.E.

The period of violence in 1200–1000 B.C.E. destroyed the prosperous large settlements of the Greeks and erased their knowledge of how to write. They therefore had to remake their civilization in Greece's Dark Age (c. 1000–750 B.C.E.). Trade, cultural interaction, and technological innovation led to recovery; contact with the Near East promoted intellectual, artistic, and economic revival, while the introduction of metallurgy for making iron made farming more efficient. As conditions improved, an elite distinguished by wealth and the competitive pursuit of individual excellence revived a social hierarchy like that of Mycenaean times. However, communal values helped create a radically new form of political organization in which shared authority was based on citizenship beginning in the eighth century B.C.E.

The Greek Dark Age

Greeks apparently lost their knowledge of writing when Mycenaean civilization fell. The Linear B script they had used was probably known only by a few scribes, who used writing to track the redistribution of goods. When the Mycenaean palaces collapsed, scribes and writing disappeared. Only oral transmission kept Greek cultural traditions alive.

Compared with their forebears, Greeks in the early Dark Age cultivated much less land and had many fewer settlements. There was no redistributive economy. The number of ships carrying Greek adventurers, raiders, and traders dwindled. Most people scratched out an existence as herders, shepherds, and subsistence farmers bunched in tiny settlements as small as twenty people. As agriculture declined, more Greeks than ever before made their living by herding animals. In this transient lifestyle, people built only simple huts and kept few possessions. Unlike their Bronze Age ancestors, Greeks in the Dark Age had no monumental architecture. They also stopped painting people and animals on their ceramics (their principal art form), instead putting only abstract designs on their pots.

The Greek Dark Age, 1000–750 B.C.E.

1000 B.C.E.	Almost all important Mycenaean sites except Athens are destroyed by this time
1000–900 B.C.E.	Greatest depopulation and economic loss
900–800 B.C.E.	Early revival of population and agriculture; beginning of the use of iron tools and weapons in Greece
800 B.C.E.	Greek trading contacts are initiated with Al Mina in Syria
776 B.C.E.	First Olympic Games are held
775 B.C.E.	Euboeans from Greece establish trading post on island in the Bay of Naples
750 B.C.E.	Homeric poetry is recorded in writing after Greeks learn to write again; Hesiod composes his poetry

Dark Age Greece did, however, retain a small but wealthy social elite. On the island of Euboea, for example, archaeologists have discovered the tenth-century B.C.E. grave of a couple who took such enormous riches with them to the next world that the woman's body was covered in gold ornaments. While the couple had done well in the competition for prestige and wealth, most people of the time were, by comparison, desperately poor.

Geography allowed the Greeks to continue seaborne trade with the civilizations of the eastern Mediterranean even during their Dark Age. Trade promoted cultural interaction, and the Greeks learned to write again about 800 B.C.E., adopting and adapting an alphabet from the Phoenicians, seafaring traders from Canaan. Near Eastern art inspired Greeks to resume the production of ceramics with figural designs (as on the vase in the chapter-opening illustration). International commerce encouraged better-off Greeks to produce agricultural surpluses and goods they could trade for luxuries, such as gold jewelry and gems from Egypt and Syria.

Most importantly, trade brought the new technology of iron metallurgy. Greeks learned this skill through their eastern trade contacts and mined their own iron ore, which was common in Greece. Iron eventually replaced bronze in agricultural tools, swords, and spear points. The Greeks still used bronze for shields and armor, however, because it was easier to shape into thin, curved pieces, such as for helmets. The iron tools' lower cost allowed more people to acquire them. Because iron is harder than bronze, implements kept their sharp edges longer. Better and more plentiful farming implements of iron helped increase food production, which sustained population growth. In this way, technology imported from the Near East improved people's chances for survival and thus helped Greece recover from the Dark Age's depopulation.

With the Mycenaean rulers long gone, leadership became an open competition in Dark Age Greece. Individuals who proved themselves excellent in action, words, charisma, and religious knowledge joined the social elite, enjoying higher prestige and authority in society. Excellence—*aretê* (ah-re-TAY) in Greek—was earned in competition. Men competed with others for aretê as warriors and persuasive public speakers. Women won their highest aretê by managing a household of children, slaves, and storerooms. Members of the elite accumulated wealth by controlling agricultural land, and people of lower status worked for them as tenants or slaves.

The Iliad and *The Odyssey*, the eighth-century B.C.E. poems of **Homer**, reflect the social elite's ideals. Homer was the last in a long line of poets who, influenced by Near Eastern mythology, had been singing these stories for centuries, orally transmitting cultural values from one generation to the next. In telling the story of the Greek army in the Trojan War, *The Iliad* focuses on the greatest Greek warrior, Achilles, who proves his aretê by choosing to die in battle rather than accept the gods' offer to return home safely but without glory. *The Odyssey* recounts not only the hero Odysseus's ten-year adventure sailing home after the fall of Troy but also emphasizes the struggle of his wife, Penelope, to protect their household from the schemes of rivals.

Homer reveals that the white-hot emotions inflamed by the competition for excellence could provoke a disturbing level of inhumanity. Achilles, in preparing to duel Hector, the prince of Troy, brutally rejects the Trojan's proposal that the winner return the loser's corpse to his family and friends: "Do wolves and lambs agree to cooperate? No, they hate each other to the roots of their being." The victor, Achilles, mutilates Hector's body. When Hecuba, the queen of Troy and Hector's mother, sees this outrage, she bitterly shouts, "I wish I could sink my teeth into his liver to eat it raw." Homer's poems suggest that the gods could sometimes help people achieve reconciliation after violent conflict, but the human suffering described in his stories shows that the pursuit of excellence was painful.

The Values of the Olympic Games

Greece had recovered enough population and prosperity by the eighth century B.C.E. to begin creating new forms of social and political organization. The most vivid evidence is the founding of the Olympic Games, traditionally dated to 776 B.C.E. This international religious festival showcased the competitive value of aretê.

Every four years, the games took place in a huge sanctuary dedicated to Zeus, the king of the gods, at Olympia, in the northwestern Peloponnese. Male athletes from elite families vied in sports, imitating the aretê needed for war: running, wrestling, jumping, and throwing. Horse and chariot racing were added to the program later, but the main event remained a two-hundred-yard sprint, at the *stadion* (the origin of the word *stadium*). The athletes competed as individuals, not on national teams. Winners received only a garland made from wild olive leaves to symbolize the prestige of victory.

The Olympics illustrate Greek notions of proper behavior for each gender: crowds of men flocked to the games, but women were prohibited on pain of

Athletic Competition
Greek vase painters often showed male athletes in action or training, perhaps in part because athletes were customers who would buy pottery with such scenes. As in this painting of an Athenian foot race from around 530 B.C.E., the athletes were usually shown nude, which was how they competed, revealing their superb physical condition and strong musculature. Being in excellent shape was a man's ideal for several reasons: it was regarded as beautiful, it enabled him to compete for individual glory in athletic contests, and it allowed him to fulfill his community responsibility by fighting as a well-conditioned soldier in the city-state's citizen militia. Why do you think the figure at the far left does not have a full beard? (Panathenaic prize amphora, c. 530 B.C.E./The Metropolitan Museum of Art, New York, NY, USA./Rogers Fund, 1914 (14.130.12)/Image copyright © The Metropolitan Museum of Art. Image source: Art Resource, NY.)

death. Women had their own separate Olympic festival on a different date in honor of Hera, queen of the gods. Only unmarried women could compete. In later times, professional athletes dominated the Olympics, earning their living from appearance fees and prizes at games held throughout the Greek world.

Once every four years an international truce of several weeks was declared so that competitors and fans from all Greek communities could safely travel to and from Olympia. The games were open to any socially elite Greek male. These rules represented beginning steps toward a concept of collective Greek identity. The Olympics helped channel the competition for individual excellence into a new context of social cooperation and community values, essential preconditions for the creation of Greece's new political form, the city-state ruled by citizens.

Homer, Hesiod, and Divine Justice in Greek Myth

The Greeks' belief in divine justice inspired them to develop the cooperative values that remade their civilization. This idea came not from scripture—Greeks had none—but from poetry that told myths about the gods and goddesses and their relationships to humans. Different myths often provided different lessons, teaching that human beings could not expect to have a clear understanding of the gods and had to make their own choices about how to live—and take the consequences.

Homer's poems reveal that the gods had plans for human existence but did not guarantee success. Bellerophon, for example, the hero whose brave efforts won him a princess bride and a kingdom, ended up losing everything. He became, in Homer's words, "hated by the gods and wandering the land alone, eating his heart out, a refugee fleeing from the haunts of men." The poem gives no explanation for this tragedy.

Hesiod's poetry from the eighth century B.C.E., by contrast, reveals how other myths describing divine support for justice contributed to the Greek feeling of community. Hesiod's vivid stories, which originated in Near Eastern creation myths, show that deities experienced struggle, sorrow, and violence but that the divine order of the universe included a concern for justice.

Hesiod's epic poem *Theogony* (whose title means "genealogy of the gods") recounted the birth of the race of gods—including Sky and numerous others—from the intercourse of primeval Chaos and Earth. Hesiod explained that when Sky began to imprison his siblings, Earth persuaded her fiercest son, Kronos, to overthrow him violently because "Sky first schemed to do shameful things." When Kronos later began to swallow his own children to avoid sharing power with them, his wife, Rhea (who was also his sister), had their son Zeus violently force his father from power.

In *Works and Days*, Hesiod's poem on conditions in his own time, he identified Zeus as the source of justice in human affairs: "Zeus commanded that fishes and wild beasts and birds should eat each other, for they have no justice; but to human beings he has given justice, which is far the best." People were responsible for administering justice, and in the eighth century B.C.E. this meant the male social elite. They controlled their family members and household servants. Hesiod insisted that a leader should demonstrate aretê by employing persuasion instead of force: "When his people in their assembly get on the wrong track, he gently sets matters right, persuading them with soft words."

Hesiod complained that many elite leaders in his time failed to exercise their power "gently," instead creating conflict between themselves and the peasants—free proprietors of small farms owning a slave or two, oxen to work their fields, and a limited amount of goods acquired by trading the surplus of their crops. Peasants' outrage at unjust treatment helped push the gradual movement toward a new form of social and political organization in Greece.

REVIEW QUESTION
What factors proved most important in the Greek recovery from the troubles of the Dark Age?

The Creation of the Greek City-State, 750–500 B.C.E.

The Archaic Age (c. 750–500 B.C.E.) saw the creation of the Greek city-state—the **polis**—an independent community of citizens inhabiting a city and the countryside around it. Greece's geography, dominated by mountains and islands, promoted the creation of hundreds of independent city-states around the Aegean Sea. From there, Greeks dispersed around the Mediterranean to settle hundreds more trading communities that often grew into new city-states. Individuals' drive for profit from trade, especially in raw materials, and for farmland in foreign territories started this process of founding new settlements.

Though it took varying forms, the Greek polis differed from the Mesopotamian city-state, primarily in being a community of citizens making laws and administering justice among themselves instead of being the subjects of a king. Another difference was that poor citizens of Greek city-states enjoyed a rough legal and political equality with the rich. Not different, however, were the subordination of women and the subjugation of slaves. (See Primary Source Analysis on page 56.)

The Physical Environment of the Greek City-State

Culturally, Greeks identified with one another because they spoke the same language and worshipped the same gods. Still, the ancient Greeks never unified into a single political state. Mountains separated independent and often

PRIMARY SOURCE ANALYSIS

Zaleucus's Law Code for a Greek City-State in Seventh-Century B.C.E. Italy

Zaleucus from the Greek city-state of Locri, in southern Italy, became the most famous early Greek lawmaker for his creation of a new law code for his community around 650 B.C.E. He founded his law code on belief in the gods as benefactors of human life. Some of his laws imposed harsh penalties for crimes, literally incorporating the eye-for-an-eye principle of equivalent punishment known from much earlier Mesopotamian law codes. Other laws took a different approach, as shown below. The Locrians respected Zaleucus's lawgiving so highly that three hundred years later they still required anyone who wished to change a law to make the proposal with a noose around his neck. If his proposal failed, he was strangled on the spot.

Zaleucus's family came from Locri in Italy, and he was from the upper class. He was a student of the philosopher Pythagoras. Gaining a high reputation in his homeland, he was chosen as lawmaker. Creating a new law code from the foundation up, he began, first of all, with the gods of the heavens.

Immediately in the introduction to the entire code he said that the inhabitants of the city first of all must accept and believe that gods exist, and that, using their minds to inspect the heavens and their beautiful arrangement and order, they should judge that these things had been arranged not by chance or by human beings. Also, the inhabitants must worship the gods as being responsible for everything fine and good in life. They must keep their souls pure from every kind of wrongdoing, believing that the gods rejoice not at the sacrifices or expensive gifts of bad people, but at the just and fine ways of life of good men.

After urging the citizens in this introduction to pious worshipping and justice, he added the command that they should not regard a fellow citizen as an enemy with whom they could never be reconciled. Serious conflict should be conducted in such a way that they could come to a settlement and friendship. Anyone who behaves contrary to this should be considered by the citizens to be savage and wild in his soul. He instructed the officials not to be self-willed or arrogant, and not to give legal judgments based on hatred or friendship.

Among his various laws he came up with many on his own very wisely and extraordinarily. For, although everywhere else women who behaved badly were made to pay fines in money, Zaleucus corrected their out-of-control behavior with an ingenious penalty. He wrote the following: a freeborn woman may not be accompanied by more than one female slave, unless she is drunk; she may not leave the city during the night, unless she is committing adultery; she may not wear gold jewelry or clothing with a woven purple border, unless she is a hired "companion." A man may not wear a ring gleaming with gold or a cloak in the luxurious style of the city-state of Miletus unless he is partying with a "companion" or committing adultery.

In this way, with his (on the surface) shameful removal of penalties, he easily turned people away from harmful luxury and out-of-control habits. For no one wanted to be the object of ridicule among the citizens by seeming to approve of shameful out-of-control behavior.

He made other fine laws, such as those on contracts and other sources of disputes in life.

Source: Diodorus Siculus, *Library of History*, Book 12, chapter 20. Translation by Thomas R. Martin.

QUESTIONS TO CONSIDER

1. What do you think might have been the reasons for the regulations regarding the gods?

2. What are the implications about ideas of appropriate behavior for women and men that you can extract from Zaleucus's laws?

3. Do you think that fear of public shame or humiliation is a strong enough deterrent to prevent crime? If so, is it acceptable to use this kind of fear to change people's behavior?

mutually hostile Greek communities. Because few city-states had enough farmland to support many people, most of them had populations of only several hundred to several thousand. A few, prosperous from international trade, grew to have a hundred thousand or more inhabitants.

Long-distance transportation in Greece overwhelmingly occurred by sea. Land travel was slow and expensive because roads were mostly just dirt paths. The most plentiful resource was timber from the mountains for building houses and ships. Deposits of metal ore were scattered throughout Greek territory, as were clays suitable for pottery and sculpture. Various quarries of fine stone such as marble provided materials for special buildings and works of art.

Only 20 to 30 percent of Greece's mountainous terrain could be farmed, making it difficult to raise large herds of cattle and horses. Pigs, sheep, goats, and chickens were the common livestock. Because the amount of annual precipitation varied greatly, farming was a precarious business of boom and bust. People preferred to eat wheat, but since that grain was expensive to cultivate, the cereal staple of the Greek diet became barley. Wine grapes and olives were the other most important crops.

Trade and "Colonization," 800–580 B.C.E.

Greece's jagged coastline made sea travel feasible; almost every community lay within forty miles of the Mediterranean Sea. But seaborne commerce faced dangers from pirates and, especially, storms. As Hesiod commented, merchants took to the sea, "because an income means life to poor mortals, but it is a terrible fate to die among the waves."

The Odyssey describes the strategy of Greek long-distance trade in commodities, when the goddess Athena appears disguised as a metal trader: "I am here . . . with my ship and crew on our way across the wine-dark sea to foreign lands in search of copper; I am carrying iron now." By 800 B.C.E., the Mediterranean swarmed with entrepreneurs of many nationalities. The Phoenicians established settlements as far west as Spain's Atlantic coast to gain access to inland mines there. Their North African settlement at Carthage (modern Tunis) would become one of the Mediterranean's most powerful cities.

The scale of trade soared near the end of the Dark Age; archaeologists have found only two tenth-century B.C.E. Greek pots that were carried abroad, but eighth-century pottery has turned up at more than eighty foreign sites. By 750 B.C.E., Greeks were settling far from home, sometimes living in others' settlements, especially those of the Phoenicians, and sometimes establishing trading posts of their own, as the Euboeans did on an island in the Bay of Naples. Everywhere they traded with the local populations, such as the Etruscans in central Italy, who imported large amounts of Greek goods. Traders were not the only Greeks to emigrate. As the population expanded following the Dark Age, a shortage of farmland in Greece drove some poor farmers abroad to find fields they could work. Apparently, only males left home on trading and land-hunting expeditions, so they had to find wives wherever they settled, either through peaceful negotiation or by kidnapping.

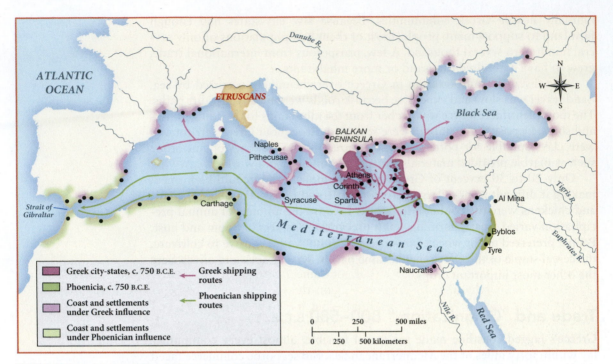

MAP 2.2 Phoenician and Greek Expansion, 750–500 B.C.E.
The Phoenicians were early explorers and settlers of the western Mediterranean. By 800 B.C.E., they had already founded the city of Carthage, which would become the main commercial power in the region. During the Archaic Age, groups of adventurous Greeks followed the Phoenicians' lead and settled all around the Mediterranean, hoping to improve their economic prospects by trade and farming. Sometimes they moved into previously established Phoenician settlements; sometimes they founded their own. Some Greek city-states established formal ties with new settlements or sent out their own expeditions to try to establish loyal colonies. Where did Phoenicians predominantly settle, and where did Greeks?

By about 580 B.C.E., Greek settlements had spread westward to Spain, present-day southern France, southern Italy, and Sicily, and southward to North Africa and eastward to the Black Sea coast (Map 2.2). The settlements in southern Italy and Sicily, such as Naples and Syracuse, eventually became so large and powerful that this region was called Magna Graecia ("Great Greece").

A Greek trading station had sprung up in Syria by 800 B.C.E., and in the seventh century B.C.E. the Egyptians permitted Greek merchants to settle in a coastal town. These close contacts with eastern Mediterranean peoples paid cultural as well as economic dividends. Near Eastern art inspired Greeks to reintroduce figures into their painting and provided models for statues that stood stiffly and stared straight ahead. When the improving economy of the later Archaic Age allowed Greeks again to afford monumental architecture in stone, their rectangular temples on platforms with columns reflected Egyptian architectural designs.

Historians have traditionally called the Greeks' settlement process in this era colonization, but recent research questions this term's accuracy because the word *colonization* implies the process by which modern European governments officially installed dependent settlements and regimes abroad. The evidence for these Greek settlements suggests rather that private entrepreneurship created most of them. Official state involvement was minimal, at least in the beginning.

Citizenship and Freedom in the Greek City-State

The creation of the polis filled the political vacuum left by Mycenaean civilization's fall. The Greek city-state was unique because it was based on the concept of citizenship for all its free inhabitants, rejected monarchy as its central authority, and made justice the responsibility of the citizens. Moreover, except in tyrannies, in which one man seized control of the city-state, at least some degree of shared governing was normal.

Power sharing reached its widest form in democratic Greek city-states. The philosopher Aristotle (384–322 B.C.E.), Greece's most famous analyst of politics and society, asserted "Humans are beings who by nature live in a city-state." Anyone who existed outside such a community, Aristotle remarked, must be either a simple fool or superhuman. The polis's innovation in making shared power the basis of government did not immediately change the course of history—monarchy later became once again the most common form of government in ancient Western civilization—but it was important as proof that power sharing was a workable system of political organization. (See Contrasting Views on page 60.)

Greek city-states were officially religious communities. As well as worshipping many deities, each city-state honored a particular god or goddess as its special protector, such as Athena at Athens. Different communities could choose the same deity; Sparta, Athens's chief rival in later times, also chose Athena as its defender. Greeks envisioned the twelve most important gods banqueting atop Mount Olympus, the highest peak in mainland Greece. Zeus headed this pantheon; the others were Hera, his wife; Aphrodite, goddess of love; Apollo, sun god; Ares, war god; Artemis, moon goddess; Athena, goddess of wisdom and war; Demeter, earth goddess; Dionysus, god of pleasure, wine, and disorder; Hephaestus, fire god; Hermes, messenger god; and Poseidon, sea god. The Greeks believed that their gods were immortal, occasionally experiencing temporary pain or sadness but immune to permanent suffering.

Most Greeks believed that humans must honor the gods to thank them for blessings received and to receive more blessings in return, and that the gods sent both good and bad into the world. Gods could punish offenders by sending disasters such as floods, famines, earthquakes, epidemic diseases, and defeats in battle. The relationship between gods and humans generated sorrow as well as joy, but with hope for favored treatment in this life and in the underworld after death for those who lived justly. An inscription on a seventh-century B.C.E. bronze statuette sums up the reciprocity that characterized these standard Greek religious ideas: "Mantiklos gave this from his share to [the god Apollo] the Far Darter of the Silver Bow; now you, Apollo, do something for me in return."

Mythology hinted at the gods' expectations of proper human behavior. For example, gods demanded hospitality for strangers, proper burial for family

alienated from regular society. Sometimes owners freed their slaves, and some promised freedom at a future date to encourage their slaves to work hard. Those slaves who gained their freedom did not become citizens in Greek city-states but instead mixed into the population of noncitizens officially allowed to live in the community.

Since they were usually of too many different origins and nationalities and too scattered to organize, Greek slaves rarely rebelled, except in Sparta, where they were local Greeks. The expansion of slavery in the Archaic Age reduced more and more people to a state of absolute dependence, and no Greeks ever called for the abolition of slavery.

Although only free men had the right to participate in city-state politics and to vote, free women counted as citizens legally, socially, and religiously. Citizenship gave women security and status because it guaranteed them access to the justice system and a respected role in a cult. Free women had legal protection against being kidnapped for sale into slavery and access to the courts in disputes over property, although they usually had to have a man speak for them. The traditional paternalism of Greek society required that all women have male guardians to regulate their lives and safeguard their interests (as defined by men). Before a woman's marriage, her father served as her legal guardian; after marriage, her husband took over that duty.

The expansion of slavery added new responsibilities for women. While their husbands farmed, participated in politics, and met with their male friends, well-off wives managed the household: raising the children, supervising the preservation and preparation of food, keeping the family's financial accounts, weaving fabric for clothing, directing the work of the slaves, and tending to household members, including slaves, when they were ill. Poor women worked outside the home, laboring in the fields or selling produce and small goods such as ribbons and trinkets in the market. Women's labor ensured the family's economic self-sufficiency and allowed male citizens the time to participate in public life.

Women's religious functions gave them prestige and freedom of movement. Women left the home to attend funerals, state festivals, and public rituals. They had access, for example, to the initiation rites of the popular cult of Demeter at Eleusis, near Athens. Women had control over cults reserved exclusively for them and also performed important duties in other official cults. In fifth-century B.C.E. Athens, for example, women officiated as priestesses for more than forty different deities, with benefits including salaries paid by the state.

Marriages were arranged by families and were not a concern of the state. Everyone was expected to marry. A woman's guardian would often engage her to another man's son while she was still a child, perhaps as young as five. The engagement was a public event conducted in the presence of witnesses. The guardian on this occasion repeated the statement that expressed the primary aim of the marriage: "I give you this woman for the plowing [procreation] of legitimate children." The actual marriage usually took place when the girl was in her early to mid-teens and the groom ten to fifteen years older.

A wedding consisted of the bride moving to her husband's dwelling; the procession to his house served as the ceremony. The bride's father bestowed on her

WHAT WOULD YOU DO?

If you could choose whether to live in the Persian Empire, in Israelite society, or in a Greek city-state, which would you choose? What factors would be most important in your decision and why? Your personal freedom? Your opportunities for economic prosperity? The chances of living a safe and secure family life? The political system? The majority religion?

A Bride's Preparation
This special piece of pottery was designed to fit over a woman's thigh to protect it while she sat down to spin wool. As a woman's tool, it appropriately carried a picture from a woman's life: a bride being helped to prepare for her wedding by her family, friends, and servants. The inscriptions indicate that this fifth-century B.C.E. piece shows the mythological bride Alcestis, famous for sacrificing herself to save her husband and then being rescued from Death by the hero Heracles. (Onos or epinetron, painted terracotta, by Diosphos, Greek, fifth century B.C.E./De Agostini Picture Library/Gianni Dagli Orti/ Bridgeman Images.)

a dowry (a certain amount of family property a daughter received at marriage); if she was wealthy, this could include land yielding an income as well as personal possessions that formed part of her new household's assets and could be inherited by her children. The husband was legally obliged to preserve the dowry, use it to support his wife and their children, and return it in case of a divorce.

Except in certain cases in Sparta, monogamy was the rule, as was a nuclear family (husband, wife, and children living together without other relatives in the same house). Citizen men, married or not, were free to have sexual relations with slaves, foreign concubines, female prostitutes, or willing pre-adult citizen males. Citizen women, single or married, lacked this freedom. Sex between a wife and anyone other than her husband carried harsh penalties for both parties.

Greek citizen men placed Greek citizen women under their guardianship, both to regulate marriage and procreation and to maintain family property. According to Greek mythology, women were a necessary evil. Zeus supposedly ordered the creation of the first woman, Pandora, as a punishment for men in retaliation against Prometheus, who had stolen fire from Zeus and given it to humans. To see what was in a container that had come as a gift from the gods, Pandora lifted its lid and accidentally released into a previously trouble-free world the evils that had been locked inside. When she finally slammed the lid back down, only hope still remained in the container. Hesiod described women as "big trouble" but thought any man who refused to marry to escape the "troublesome deeds of women" would come to "destructive old age" alone, with no heirs. In other words, a man needed a wife so that he could

REVIEW QUESTION
How did the physical, social, and intellectual conditions of life in the Archaic Age promote the emergence of the Greek city-state?

father children who would later care for him and preserve the family property after his death. This paternalistic attitude allowed Greek men to control human reproduction and consequently the distribution of property.

New Directions for the Greek City-State, 750–500 B.C.E.

Greek city-states developed three forms of social and political organization based on citizenship: oligarchy, tyranny, and democracy. Sparta provided Greece's most famous example of an oligarchy, in which a small number of men dominated policymaking in an assembly of male citizens. For a time Corinth had the best-known tyranny, in which one man seized control of the city-state, ruling it for the advantage of his family and loyal supporters, while acknowledging the citizenship of all—thereby distinguishing a tyrant from a king, who ruled over subjects. Athens developed Greece's best-known democracy.

Greeks in the Archaic Age also created new forms of artistic expression and new ways of thought. In this period they developed innovative ways of using reason to understand the physical world, their relations to it, and their relationships with one another. This intellectual innovation laid the foundation for the gradual emergence of scientific thought and logic in Western civilization.

Oligarchy in the City-State of Sparta, 700–500 B.C.E.

Sparta organized its society for military readiness. This oligarchic city-state developed the mightiest infantry force in Greece during the Archaic Age. Its citizens were famous for their militaristic self-discipline. Sparta's urban center was nestled in an easily defended valley on the Peloponnesian peninsula twenty-five miles from the Mediterranean coast. This separation from the sea kept the Spartans focused on being a land power.

The Spartan oligarchy included three components of rule. First came the two hereditary, prestigious military leaders called kings, who served as the state's religious heads and the generals of its army. Despite their title, they were not monarchs but just one part of the ruling oligarchy. The second part was a council of twenty-eight men over sixty years old (the elders), and the third part consisted of five annually elected officials called *ephors* ("overseers"), who made policy and enforced the laws.

In principle, legislation had to be approved by an assembly of all Sparta's free adult males, who were called the "Alike" to stress their common status and purpose. The assembly had only limited power to amend the proposals put before it, however, and the council would withdraw a proposal when the assembly's reaction proved negative. Spartan society demanded strict obedience to all laws. When the ephors took office, they

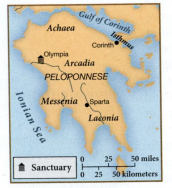

Sparta and Corinth, 750–500 B.C.E.

issued an official proclamation to Sparta's males: "Shave your mustache and obey the laws." Unlike other Greeks, the Spartans never wrote down their laws. Instead, they preserved their system with a unique, highly structured way of life. All Spartan citizens were expected to put service to their city-state before personal concerns because their state's survival was continually threatened by its own economic foundation: their great mass of Greek slaves, called helots, who did almost all the work for Spartan citizens.

A **helot** was a slave owned by the Spartan city-state. Helots were Greeks captured in neighboring parts of Greece that the Spartans defeated in war. Most helots lived in Messenia, to the west, which Sparta had conquered by around 700 B.C.E. The helots outnumbered Sparta's free citizens. Harshly treated by their Spartan masters, helots constantly looked for chances to revolt.

Helots had some family life because they were expected to produce children to maintain their population, and they could own some personal possessions and practice their religion. They labored as farmers and household slaves so that Spartan citizens would not have to do nonmilitary work. Spartan men wore their hair very long to show they were warriors rather than laborers.

Helots lived under the constant threat of officially approved violence by Spartan citizens. Every year the ephors formally declared war between Sparta and the helots, allowing any Spartan to kill a helot without legal penalty or fear of offending the gods. By beating the helots frequently, forcing them to get drunk in public as an object lesson to young Spartans, and humiliating them by making them wear dog-skin caps, the Spartans emphasized their slaves' "otherness." In this way Spartans created a justification for their harsh abuse of fellow Greeks. A later Athenian observed, "Sparta is the home of the freest of the Greeks, and of the most enslaved."

With helots to work the fields, male citizens devoted themselves full-time to preparation for war and training to protect their state from both hostile neighbors and its own slaves. Boys lived at home until their seventh year, when they were sent to live in barracks with other males until they were thirty. They spent most of their time exercising, hunting, practicing with weapons, competing to excel physically, and learning Spartan values by listening to tales of bravery and heroism at shared meals, where adult males in groups of about fifteen usually ate instead of at home. Discipline was strict, and the boys were purposely underfed so that they would learn stealth tactics by stealing food. If they were caught, punishment and disgrace followed immediately. One famous Spartan tale reported that a boy hid a stolen fox under his clothing and let the panicked animal rip out his insides rather than allow himself to be detected in the theft. A Spartan male who could not survive the tough training was publicly disgraced and denied the status of being an Alike.

Spending so much time in shared quarters schooled Sparta's young men in their society's values. The community took the place of a Spartan boy's family when he was growing up and remained his main social environment even after he reached adulthood. There he learned to call all older men "Father," to emphasize that his primary loyalty was to the group instead of his biological family. This way of life trained him for the one honorable occupation for

Spartan men: obedient soldier. A seventh-century B.C.E. poet expressed the Spartan male ideal: "Know that it is good for the city-state and the whole people when a man takes his place in the front row of warriors and stands his ground without flinching."

An adolescent boy's life often involved what in today's terminology would be called a homosexual relationship, although the ancient concepts of hetero-sexuality and homosexuality do not match modern notions. An older male would choose a teenager as a special favorite, in many cases engaging him in sexual relations. Their bond was meant to make each ready to die for the other in battle. Numerous Greek city-states included this form of sexuality among their customs, although some thought it disgraceful and made it illegal. The Athenian author Xenophon (c. 430–355 B.C.E.) wrote a work on the Spartan way of life denying that sex with boys existed there because he thought it a stain on the Spartans' reputation for virtue. However, other sources testify that such relationships did exist in Sparta and elsewhere.

In such relationships the elder partner (the "lover") was supposed to help educate the young man (the "beloved") in politics and community values, and not just exploit him for physical pleasure. Once they became adults, beloveds were expected to find a wife to start a family; they could also at that point become the "lover" of an adolescent "beloved." Sex between adult males was considered disgraceful, as was sex between females of all ages (at least according to men).

Spartan women were known throughout the Greek world for their personal freedom. Since their husbands were so rarely at home, women totally controlled the households, which included servants, daughters, and sons who had not yet left for their communal training. Consequently, Spartan women exercised even more power at home than did women elsewhere in Greece. They could own property, including land. Wives were expected to stay physically fit so that they could bear healthy children to keep up the population. They were also expected to drum Spartan values into their children. One mother became legendary for handing her son his shield on the eve of battle and sternly telling him, "Come back with it or [lying dead] on it."

Bronze Sculpture of a Spartan Youth
This sculpted handle of a bronze water jar from sixth-century B.C.E. Sparta shows a young male holding two lions by the tail on his shoulders. That spectacular pose portrayed the fearlessness and control over fierce nature that Sparta expected of its citizens. His hair is long in the self-conscious style of Spartan warriors, who prided themselves on not having the short hair that was common for laborers. (Greek, Archaic, about 540 B.C.E. Place of manufacture: Greece, Laconia, Sparta. Bronze. H. 12.8 cm [5 1/16 in.]. Museum of Fine Arts, Boston; Museum purchase with funds donated by contributions, 85.515. Photograph © 2018 Museum of Fine Arts, Boston.)

Demographics determined Sparta's long-term fate. The population of Sparta was never large. Adult males—who made up the army—numbered between eight and ten thousand in the Archaic period. Over time, the problem of producing enough children to keep the Spartan army from shrinking became desperate, probably because losses in war far outnumbered births and regulations on the timing of intercourse in marriage had the opposite of the intended effect, reducing instead of increasing fertility. Men became legally required to marry, with bachelors punished by fines and public ridicule. A woman could legitimately have children by a man other than her husband, if all three agreed.

Because the Spartans' survival depended on the exploitation of enslaved Greeks, they believed they had to avoid change in their way of life because it might make them vulnerable to internal revolts. Some Greeks criticized the Spartan way of life as repressive and monotonous, but the Spartans' discipline and respect for their laws also gained them widespread admiration.

Tyranny in the City-State of Corinth, 657–585 B.C.E.

In some city-states, competition among the social elite became so bitter that a single family would suppress all its rivals and establish itself in rule. The family's leader thus became a tyrant, a dictator who gained political dominance by force. Tyrants usually rallied support by promising support for poor citizens, such as public employment schemes. Since few tyrants successfully passed their dominance on to their heirs, tyrannies tended to be short-lived.

Tyrants usually preserved their city-states' existing laws and political institutions. If a city-state had a legislative assembly, for example, the tyrant would allow it to continue to meet, expecting it to follow his direction. Although today the word *tyrant* indicates a brutal or unwanted leader, tyrants in Archaic Greece did not always fit that description. Greeks evaluated tyrants according to their behavior, opposing the ruthless and violent ones but accepting the fair and generous ones.

The most famous early tyranny arose at Corinth in 657 B.C.E., when the family of Cypselus rebelled against the city's harsh oligarchic leadership. Corinth's location on the isthmus controlling land access to the Peloponnese and a huge amount of seaborne trade made it the most prosperous city-state of the Archaic Age. Cypselus "became one of the most admired of Corinth's citizens because he was courageous, prudent, and helpful to the people, unlike the oligarchs in power, who were insolent and violent," according to a later historian. Cypselus's son succeeded him at his death in 625 B.C.E. and aggressively continued Corinth's economic expansion by founding colonies to increase trade. He also pursued commercial contacts with Egypt. Unlike his father, the son lost popular support by ruling harshly. He held on to power until his death in 585 B.C.E., but the hostility he had provoked soon led to the overthrow of his own heir. The social elite, to prevent tyranny, then installed an oligarchic government based on a board of officials and a council.

Democracy in the City-State of Athens, c. 700–500 B.C.E.

Athens, located at the southeastern corner of central Greece, became the most famous of the democratic city-states because its government gave political rights to the greatest number of people, financed magnificent temples and public buildings, and, in the fifth century B.C.E., became militarily strong enough to induce numerous other city-states to follow Athenian leadership in a maritime empire. Athenian democracy did not reach its full development until the mid-fifth century B.C.E., but its first steps in the Archaic Age from around 700 B.C.E. allowed all male citizens to participate in making laws and administering justice.

Athens's early development of a large middle class was a crucial factor in opening this new path for Western civilization. The Athenian population apparently expanded at a phenomenal rate when economic conditions improved rapidly from about 800 to 700 B.C.E. The ready availability of good farmland in Athenian territory and opportunities for seaborne trade allowed many families to improve their standing. These hardworking entrepreneurs felt that their self-won economic success entitled them to a say in government.

By the seventh century B.C.E., all freeborn adult Athenian male citizens had the right to vote on public matters in the assembly. They also elected officials called archons, who ran the judicial system by rendering verdicts in disputes and criminal accusations. Members of the elite dominated these offices; because archons received no pay, poor men could not afford to serve. The democratic unity forged by the Athenian masses was demonstrated in 632 B.C.E., when the people rallied to block an elite Athenian's attempt to install a tyranny.

An extended economic crisis beginning in the late seventh century B.C.E. almost destroyed Athens's infant democracy. The first attempt to solve the crisis was the emergency appointment around 621 B.C.E. of a man named Draco to revise the laws. Draco's changes, which made death the penalty for even minor crimes, proved too harsh to work. Later Greeks said Draco (whose harshness inspired the word *draconian*) had written his laws in blood, not ink. By 600 B.C.E., economic conditions had become so terrible that poor farmers had to borrow constantly from richer neighbors and deeply mortgage their land. As the crisis grew worse, impoverished citizens were sold into slavery to pay off debts.

Desperate, Athenians appointed another emergency official in 594 B.C.E., a war hero named **Solon**. To head off violence, Solon gave both rich and poor something of what they wanted, a compromise called the "shaking off of obligations." He canceled private debts, which helped the poor but displeased the rich; he decided not to redistribute land, which pleased the wealthy but disappointed the poor. He banned selling citizens into slavery to settle debts and liberated citizens who had become slaves in this way. His elimination of debt slavery was a significant recognition of citizen rights.

Solon balanced political power between rich and poor by reordering Athens's traditional ranking of citizens into four groups based on annual income. This change eliminated inherited aristocracy at Athens. The groupings did not affect a man's treatment at law, only his eligibility for government office. The higher a man's ranking, the higher the post to which he could be elected, but higher also was the contribution he was expected to make to the community with his service and his money. Men at the poorest level, called laborers, were not eligible for any office. Solon did, however, confirm the laborers' right to vote in the legislative assembly. His classification scheme was consistent with democratic principles because it allowed for upward social mobility; a man who increased his income could move up the scale of eligibility for office.

The creation of a smaller council to prepare the agenda for the assembly that voted on laws and policy was a crucial development in making Athenian democracy efficient. Four hundred council members were chosen annually from the adult male citizenry by lottery—the most democratic method possible—which prevented the social elite from capturing too many seats.

Solon's two reforms in the judicial system promoted democratic principles of equality. First, he directed that any male citizen could start a prosecution on behalf of any crime victim. Second, he gave people the right to appeal an archon's judgment to the assembly. With these two measures, Solon empowered ordinary citizens in the administration of justice. Characteristically, he balanced these democratic reforms by granting broader powers to the Areopagus Council ("council that meets on the hill of the god of war Ares"). This select body, limited to ex-archons, held great power because its members judged the most important cases—accusations against archons themselves.

Solon's reforms extended power through the citizen body and created a system of law that applied more equally than before to all the community's free men. A critic once challenged Solon, "Do you actually believe your fellow citizens' injustice and greed can be kept in check this way? Written laws are more like spiders' webs than anything else: they tie up the weak and the small fry who get stuck in them, but the rich and the powerful tear them to shreds." Solon replied that communal values ensure the rule of law: "People abide by their agreements when neither side has anything to gain by breaking them. I am writing laws for the Athenians in such a way that they will clearly see it is to everyone's advantage to obey the laws rather than to break them."

Some elite Athenians wanted oligarchy and therefore bitterly disagreed with Solon. The unrest they caused opened the door to tyranny at Athens. Peisistratus, helped by his upper-class friends and the poor whose interests he championed, made himself tyrant in 546 B.C.E. Like the Corinthian tyrants, he promoted the economic, cultural, and architectural development of Athens and bought the masses' support. He helped poorer men, for example, by hiring them to build roads, a huge temple to Zeus, and fountains to increase the supply of drinking water. He boosted Athens's economy and its image by minting new coins stamped with Athena's owl (a symbol of the goddess of wisdom; see the illustration on page 118) and organizing a great annual festival honoring the god Dionysus that attracted people from near and far to see its musical and dramatic performances.

Peisistratus's eldest son, Hippias, ruled harshly and was denounced as unjust by a rival elite family. These rivals convinced the Spartans, the self-proclaimed champions of Greek freedom, to liberate Athens from tyranny by expelling Hippias and his family in 510 B.C.E.

Peisistratus's support of ordinary people evidently had the unintended consequence of making them think that they deserved political equality. Tyranny at Athens thus opened the way to the most important step in developing Athenian democracy, the reforms of Cleisthenes. A member of the social elite, Cleisthenes found himself losing against rivals for election to office in 508 B.C.E. He turned his electoral campaign around by offering more political participation to the masses; he called his program "equality through law." Most people so strongly favored his plan that they spontaneously rallied to repel a Spartan army that Cleisthenes' bitterest rival had convinced Sparta's leaders to send to block his reforms.

By about 500 B.C.E., Cleisthenes had engineered direct participation in Athens's democracy by as many adult male citizens as possible. First he created constituent units for the city-state's new political organization by grouping country villages and urban neighborhoods into units called **demes**. The demes chose council members annually by lottery in proportion to the size of their populations. To allow for greater participation, Solon's Council of Four Hundred was expanded to five hundred members. Finally, Cleisthenes required candidates for public office to be spread widely throughout the demes.

The creation of demes suggests that Greek democratic notions stemmed from traditions of small-community life, in which each man was entitled to his say in running local affairs and had to persuade—not force—others to agree. It took another fifty years of political struggle, however, before Athenian democracy reached its full development with the democratization of its judicial system.

New Ways of Thought and Expression in Greece, 630–500 B.C.E.

The idea that persuasion, rather than force or status, should drive political decisions matched the spirit of intellectual change rippling through Greece in the late Archaic Age. In city-states all over the Greek world, artists, poets, and philosophers pursued new ways of thought and new forms of expression. Through their contacts with the Near East, the Greeks encountered traditions to learn from and alter for their own purposes.

By the sixth century B.C.E., Greeks were introducing innovations of their own into art. In ceramics, painters experimented with different clays and colors to depict vivid scenes from mythology and daily life. Sculptors gave their statues balanced poses and calm, smiling faces. Women were sculpted as wearing brightly decorated clothing, while men were represented nude to display their physiques.

Building on the Near Eastern tradition of poetry expressing personal emotions, Greeks created a new poetic form. This poetry, which sprang from popular song, was performed to the accompaniment of a lyre (a kind of harp) and thus called lyric poetry. Greek lyric poems were short, rhythmic, and diverse

Archaic Female Statue

This Archaic Age marble statue depicting an unmarried girl was displayed in public, as was customary for art at the time. It was probably a gift to a divinity. The traces of paint surviving on the hair and elaborately draped clothing reveal the bright coloring applied to ancient Greek statues. The colors that originally existed on most statues in museums today have usually faded or disappeared over the centuries, leading to the mistaken modern assumption that the statues were left in the original white color of the marble. The statue's calm and smiling face is typical of art depicting human beings in this era. Why do you think this choice might have been the custom? (DEA/M. Carrieri/Getty Images.)

in subject. Lyric poets wrote songs both for choruses and for individual performers. Choral poems honored gods on public occasions, celebrated famous events in a city-state's history, praised victors in athletic contests, and enlivened weddings.

Some lyric poems generated controversy because the ideas expressed in them valued individual expression and opinion over conventional views. Solon wrote poems justifying his reforms. Other poets criticized traditional values, such as strength in war. **Sappho**, a lyric poet from Lesbos born about 630 B.C.E. and famous for her poems on love, wrote, "Some would say the most beautiful thing on our dark earth is an army of cavalry, others of infantry, others of ships, but I say it's whatever a person loves." In this poem Sappho was expressing her longing for a woman she loved, who was now far away. Archilochus of Paros, who probably lived in the early seventh century B.C.E., became famous for poems mocking militarism, lamenting friends lost at sea, and regretting love affairs gone wrong. He became infamous for his lines about throwing away his shield in battle so that he could run away to save his life: "Oh, the hell with it; I can get another one just as good." When he taunted a family in verse after the father had ended Archilochus's affair with one of his daughters, the power of his ridicule reportedly caused the father and his two daughters to commit suicide.

The study of philosophy ("love of wisdom") began in the seventh and sixth centuries B.C.E., when some Greek thinkers created prose writing to express their innovative ideas, above all their new explanations of the human world and its relation to the gods. Some also composed poetry to explain their theories. Most of these philosophers lived in Ionia, on Anatolia's western coast, where they came in contact with Near Eastern knowledge in astronomy, mathematics, and myth. Because there were no formal schools, philosophers communicated their ideas by teaching privately and giving public lectures. People who studied with these philosophers or heard their presentations helped spread the new ideas.

Working from Babylonian discoveries about the regular movements of the stars and planets, Ionian philosophers such as Thales (c. 625–545 B.C.E.)

Ionia and the Aegean, 750–500 B.C.E.

and Anaximander (c. 610–540 B.C.E.), both of Miletus, reached the revolutionary conclusion that unchanging laws of nature (rather than gods' wishes) governed the universe. Pythagoras, who emigrated from the island of Samos to the Greek city-state Croton in southern Italy about 530 B.C.E., taught that numerical relationships explained the world. He began the Greek study of high-level mathematics and the numerical aspects of musical harmony.

Ionian philosophers insisted that natural phenomena were neither random nor arbitrary. They applied the word *cosmos*—meaning "an orderly arrangement that is beautiful"—to the universe. The cosmos included not only the motions of heavenly bodies but also the weather, the growth of plants and animals, and human health. Because the universe was ordered, it was knowable; because it was knowable, thought and research could explain it.

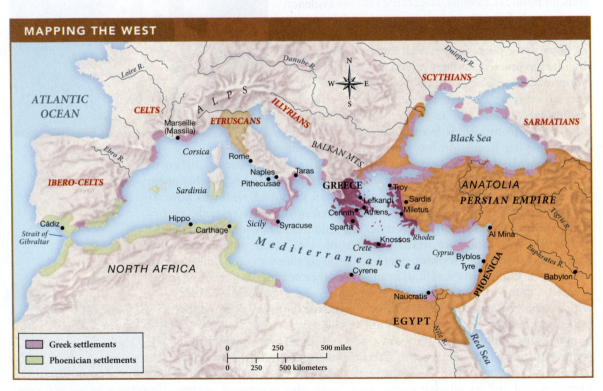

MAPPING THE WEST

Mediterranean Civilizations, c. 500 B.C.E.
At the end of the sixth century B.C.E., the Persian Empire was by far the most powerful civilization touching the Mediterranean. Its riches and its unity gave it resources that no Phoenician or Greek city could match. The Phoenicians dominated economically in the western Mediterranean, while the Greek city-states in Sicily and southern Italy rivaled the power of those in the heartland. In Italy, the Etruscans were the most powerful civilization; the Romans were still a small community struggling to replace monarchy with a republic.

Analyzing the Map: What can the locations of the Greek settlements tell us about their influence in the Mediterranean region in this period?

Making Connections: What geographic and other factors can account for the extent of Persian influence in this period?

Philosophers therefore looked for the first or universal cause of all things, a quest that scientists still pursue. These first philosophers believed they needed to give reasons for their conclusions and to persuade others by arguments based on evidence. That is, they believed in logic. This new way of thought, called **rationalism**, became the foundation for the study of science and philosophy. This rule-based view of the causes of events and physical phenomena contrasted sharply with the traditional mythological view. Many people had difficulty accepting such a startling change in their understanding of the world, and the older tradition of explaining events as the work of deities lived on alongside the new approach.

The early Greek philosophers deeply influenced later times by being the first to clearly separate scientific thinking from myth and religion. Their idea that people must give reasons to justify their beliefs, rather than simply make assertions that others must accept without evidence, was their most important achievement. This insistence on rationalism, coupled with the belief that the world could be understood as something other than the plaything of the gods, gave people hope that they could improve their lives through their own efforts. Xenophanes of Colophon (c. 570–c. 478 B.C.E.) concluded, "The gods have not revealed all things from the beginning to mortals, but, by seeking, human beings find out, in time, what is better." This saying expressed the value Archaic Age philosophers gave to intellectual freedom, corresponding to the value that citizens gave to political freedom in the city-state.

> **REVIEW QUESTION**
> What were the main differences among the various forms of government in the Greek city-states?

Conclusion

After its Dark Age, the Near East revived its traditional pattern of social and political organization: empire under a strong central authority. The Neo-Assyrians, the Neo-Babylonians, and the Persians succeeded one another as imperial powers. The moral dualism of Persian religion, Zoroastrianism, influenced later religions. The Israelites' development of monotheism based on scripture changed the course of religious history in Western civilization.

Greece's recovery from its Dark Age produced a new form of political and social organization: the polis, a city-state based on citizenship and shared governance. The growing population of the Archaic Age developed a communal sense of identity, personal freedom, and justice administered by citizens. The degree of power sharing varied in the Greek city-states. Some, like Sparta, were oligarchies; in others, like Corinth, rule was by tyranny. Over time, Athens developed the most extensive democracy, in which political power extended to all male citizens.

Greeks in the Archaic Age also developed new methods of artistic expression and new ways of thought. Building on Near Eastern traditions, Greek poets created lyric poetry to express personal emotion. Greek philosophers argued that laws of nature controlled the universe and that humans could discover these laws through reason and research, thereby establishing rationalism as the conceptual basis for science and philosophy.

Chapter 2 Review

Key Terms and People

Be sure that you can identify the term or person and explain its historical significance.

Cyrus (p. 45)

moral dualism (p. 47)

Torah (p. 49)

Diaspora (p. 50)

aretê (p. 53)

Homer (p. 53)

polis (p. 55)

cult (p. 61)

hoplite (p. 62)

helot (p. 67)

Solon (p. 70)

demes (p. 72)

Sappho (p. 73)

rationalism (p. 75)

Review Questions

1. In what ways was religion important in the Near East from c. 1000 B.C.E. to c. 500 B.C.E.?

2. What factors proved most important in the Greek recovery from the troubles of the Dark Age?

3. How did the physical, social, and intellectual conditions of life in the Archaic Age promote the emergence of the Greek city-state?

4. What were the main differences among the various forms of government in the Greek city-states?

Making Connections

1. What characteristics made the Greek city-state differ in political and social organization from the Near Eastern city-state?

2. How were the ideas of the Ionian philosophers different from mythic traditions?

3. To what extent were the most important changes in Western civilization in this period intentional or unintentional?

Important Events

1000–750 B.C.E.	Greece experiences Dark Age
900 B.C.E.	Neo-Assyrian Empire emerges
800 B.C.E.	Greeks learn to write with an alphabet
776 B.C.E.	Olympic Games are founded in Greece
750 B.C.E.	Greeks begin to create the polis
700 B.C.E.	Spartans conquer Messenia, enslave its inhabitants as helots
700–500 B.C.E.	Ionian philosophers develop rationalism
657 B.C.E.	Cypselus becomes tyrant in Corinth
630 B.C.E.	The lyric poet Sappho is born
597 and 586 B.C.E.	Israelites are exiled to Babylon
594 B.C.E.	Solon's reforms promote early democracy in Athens

546–510 B.C.E.	Peisistratus's family rules Athens as tyrants
539 B.C.E.	Persian king Cyrus captures Babylon, permits Israelites to return to Canaan
508–500 B.C.E.	Cleisthenes's reforms extend democracy in Athens

Consider three events

Ionian philosophers develop rationalism (700–500 B.C.E.), the lyric poet Sappho is born (630 B.C.E.), and Solon's reforms promote early democracy in Athens (594 B.C.E.). How did the development of the Greek city-state (polis) encourage new modes of thinking and expression in science, philosophy, and literature?

Suggested References

Scholars today emphasize the importance of contact and intercultural influence among different peoples around the Mediterranean in helping us understand the history of the region as it recovered from the economic troubles and depopulation of the Dark Age.

Ancient Olympic Games: http://www.perseus.tufts.edu/Olympics/

*Boyce, Mary, trans. *Textual Sources for the Study of Zoroastrianism.* 1990.

Bright, John. *A History of Israel.* 4th ed. 2000.

Bryce, Trevor. *Life and Society in the Hittite World.* 2004.

*Dalley, Stephanie, trans. *Myths from Mesopotamia: Creation, the Flood, Gilgamesh, and Others.* Rev. ed. 2009.

Finkelstein, Israel, and Amihai Mazar. *The Quest for the Historical Israel: Debating Archaeology and the History of Early Israel.* Ed. Brian B. Schmidt. 2007.

Hurwitt, Jeffrey M. *The Art and Culture of Early Greece, 1100–480 B.C.* 1985.

Kugel, James. *The God of Old: Inside the Lost World of the Bible.* 2003.

Larson, Jennifer. *Ancient Greek Cults: A Guide.* 2007.

Lewis, John. *Solon the Thinker: Political Thought in Archaic Athens.* 2008.

*Malandra, William W. *An Introduction to Ancient Iranian Religion: Readings from the Avesta and the Achaemenid Inscriptions.* 1983.

Martin, Thomas R. *Ancient Greece: From Prehistoric to Hellenistic Times.* 2nd ed. 2013.

Osborne, Robin. *Greece in the Making, 1200–479 B.C.* 2nd ed. 2009.

Shapiro, H. A. *The Cambridge Companion to Archaic Greece.* 2007.

*Waterfield, Robin. *The First Philosophers: The Presocratics and the Sophists.* 2000, 2009.

---

*Primary source.

The Greek Golden Age

c. 500–c. 400 B.C.E.

Fearing an attack to overthrow their democracy by the Spartans, the Athenians in 507 B.C.E. dispatched ambassadors to the Persian king Darius I (r. 522–486 B.C.E.) to request military assistance. Athens and Sparta so mistrusted each other that the Athenians chose to appeal to a foreign superpower for help against fellow Greeks. Darius's representative asked, "But who in the world are these people, and where do they live that they are begging for an alliance with the Persians?" Even so, the Persian king offered the Athenians help on his standard terms: that they acknowledge his superiority. Darius was eager to dominate more Greek city-states because their trade and growing wealth made them desirable prizes. The voters in the Athenian democratic assembly rejected the deal, unwilling to become Persian subjects.

This incident provides the background for the wars that dominated Greece's history throughout the fifth century B.C.E., first with Greeks fighting Persians and then with Greeks fighting Greeks. Conflicting interests and misunderstandings between Persia and Greece at the start of the century ignited a great conflict: the Persian Wars (499–479 B.C.E.), culminating in a massive Persian invasion of mainland Greece. Thirty-one Greek states united to defeat the Persians, surprising the world. After

«**Greek against Persian in Hand-to-Hand Combat (detail)** This red-figure painting appears on the interior of a Greek wine cup. Painted about 480 B.C.E. (during the Persian Wars), it shows a Greek hoplite (armored infantryman) striking a Persian warrior in hand-to-hand combat with swords. The Greek has lost his principal weapon, a spear, and the Persian can no longer shoot his, the bow and arrow. The Greek artist has designed the painting to express multiple messages: the Persian's colorful outfit with sleeves and pants stresses the "otherness" of the enemy in Greek eyes, and the soldiers' serene expressions at such a desperate moment dignify the horror of killing in war. Greek warriors often had heroic symbols painted on their shields, such as the winged horse Pegasus, an allusion to the brave exploits of Bellerophon. (The Triptolemos Painter (fl. 460 B.C.E.)/© National Museums of Scotland/Bridgeman Images.)

their victory, however, they once again began fighting one another. Despite nearly constant warfare, fifth-century B.C.E. Greeks, especially Athenians, created their most famous innovations in architecture, art, and theater. This Golden Age, as historians later named it, is the first part of the period called the Classical Age of Greece, which extends from around 500 B.C.E. to the death of Alexander the Great in 323 B.C.E.

New ideas in education and philosophy that became deeply controversial in the fifth century B.C.E. have had a lasting influence on Western civilization. The controversies arose because many people saw the changes as attacks on ancient traditions, especially religion; they feared the gods would punish their communities for abandoning ancestral beliefs. Political change also characterized the Athenian Golden Age. First, Athenian citizens made their city-state government more democratic than ever. Second, Athens grew internationally powerful by using its navy to establish dominance over other Greek city-states in a system criticized as "empire" by modern scholars. Athens's naval power also promoted seaborne trade, and the profits from its commerce and international power generated unprecedented revenue for the city-state. Athenians voted to use this money to finance new public buildings, art, and theater festivals, and to pay for poorer men to serve as officials and jurors in an expanded democratic government.

The Golden Age ended when Sparta defeated Athens in the Peloponnesian War (431–404 B.C.E.) and the Athenians subsequently fought a brief but bloody civil war (404–403 B.C.E.). The Peloponnesian War and its aftermath bankrupted and divided Athens.

CHAPTER FOCUS
Did war bring more benefit or more harm—politically, socially, and intellectually—to Golden Age Athens?

Wars between Persia and Greece, 499–479 B.C.E.

When the envoys from Athens met with the Persian king's representative in 507 B.C.E., they submitted to the monarch's demand: to present tokens of earth and water as symbolic acknowledgment of their city-state's submission to the Persian king. When the Athenian assembly subsequently repudiated

CHAPTER TIMELINE

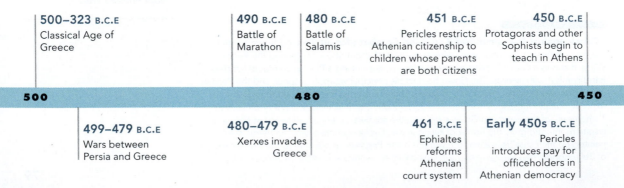

500–323 B.C.E
Classical Age of Greece

490 B.C.E
Battle of Marathon

480 B.C.E
Battle of Salamis

451 B.C.E
Pericles restricts Athenian citizenship to children whose parents are both citizens

450 B.C.E
Protagoras and other Sophists begin to teach in Athens

500   480   450

499–479 B.C.E
Wars between Persia and Greece

480–479 B.C.E
Xerxes invades Greece

461 B.C.E
Ephialtes reforms Athenian court system

Early 450s B.C.E
Pericles introduces pay for officeholders in Athenian democracy

their representatives' acceptance of these terms, it failed to inform King Darius. He therefore continued to believe that Athens had agreed to obey him in return for his support. This misunderstanding planted the seed for two Persian attacks on Greece. Since the Persian Empire dwarfed the Greek city-states in size and strength, the conflict pitted the equivalent of a huge bear against a pack of undersized dogs.

From the Ionian Revolt to the Battle of Marathon, 499–490 B.C.E.

In 499 B.C.E., the Greek city-states in Ionia rebelled against their Persian-installed tyrants. The Athenians sent troops because they saw the Ionians as close kin. By 494 B.C.E., a Persian counterattack had crushed the revolt (Map 3.1). Darius exploded in anger when he learned that the Athenians had helped the Ionian rebels. He ordered a slave to repeat three times at every meal, "Lord, remember the Athenians."

In 490 B.C.E., Darius sent a force to punish Athens and install a puppet ruler. The Athenians confronted the invaders near the town of Marathon on their eastern coast. The Athenian soldiers were stunned by the Persians' strange garb—colorful pants instead of the short tunics and bare legs that Greeks regarded as proper dress (see the chapter-opening photo)—but the Greek commanders had their infantry charge the enemy at a dead run. The soldiers in their heavy armor clanked across the plain through a hail of Persian arrows. In the hand-to-hand combat, the Greek hoplites used their long spears to over-whelm the Persian infantry.

The Athenian infantry then hurried the twenty-six miles to Athens to guard the city against the Persian navy. (Today's marathon races commemorate the legend of a runner speeding ahead to announce the victory, and then dropping dead.) The unexpected success of the Athenians strengthened their sense of community. When a rich strike was made in Athens's publicly owned silver mines in 483 B.C.E., **Themistocles** (c. 524–c. 460 B.C.E.) convinced the assembly to spend the windfall to double the size of the navy instead of dividing it among the citizens.

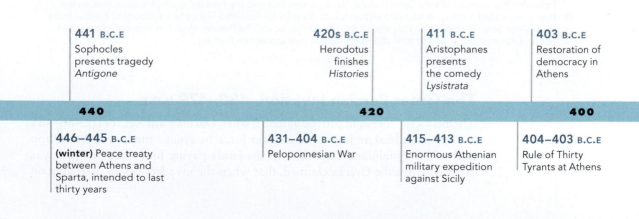

441 B.C.E	420s B.C.E	411 B.C.E	403 B.C.E
Sophocles presents tragedy *Antigone*	Herodotus finishes *Histories*	Aristophanes presents the comedy *Lysistrata*	Restoration of democracy in Athens

440 **420** **400**

446–445 B.C.E	431–404 B.C.E	415–413 B.C.E	404–403 B.C.E
(winter) Peace treaty between Athens and Sparta, intended to last thirty years	Peloponnesian War	Enormous Athenian military expedition against Sicily	Rule of Thirty Tyrants at Athens

MAP 3.1 The Persian Wars, 499–479 B.C.E.
Following the example of King Cyrus (r. 557–530 B.C.E.), who founded the Persian Empire, his successors on the throne expanded the empire eastward and westward. King Darius I invaded Thrace (in southeastern Europe) more than fifteen years before the conflict against the Greeks that we call the Persian Wars. The Persians' unexpected defeat in Greece put an end to their attempt to extend their power into Europe.

The Great Persian Invasion, 480–479 B.C.E.

Themistocles' foresight proved valuable when Darius's son Xerxes I (r. 486–465 B.C.E.) assembled an immense invasion force to avenge the loss at Marathon and add the mainland city-states to the lands paying him taxes. So vast was Xerxes' army, the Greeks claimed, that when the invaders began marching on

Greece in 480 B.C.E. it took them seven days and seven nights to cross the strip of sea between Asia and Europe.

The thirty-one states that allied to defend their freedom represented only a small portion of the Greek world. This coalition desperately wanted the rich Greek city-states in Italy and Sicily to join. Syracuse, for example, the most powerful Greek state at the time, controlled a regional empire built on agriculture in Sicily's plains and seaborne commerce on the Mediterranean's western trading routes. The tyrant ruling Syracuse rejected the allies' appeal for help because he was fighting his own war against Carthage, a Phoenician city in North Africa, over control of this lucrative trade. None of the western Greeks aided their mainland compatriots.

So, left on their own, the allies chose Sparta as leader because of its military excellence. The Spartans demonstrated their courage in 480 B.C.E. when three hundred of their infantry (and a few thousand fighters from other city-states) blocked Xerxes' army for several days at the pass called Thermopylae in central Greece. Told the Persian archers were so numerous that their arrows darkened the sun, one Spartan reportedly remarked, "That's good news; we'll get to fight in the shade." They did—to the death. Their tomb's memorial proclaimed, "Go tell the Spartans that we lie buried here obedient to their orders."

When the Persians marched south, the Athenians evacuated their homeland rather than surrender. The Persians burned Athens. Themistocles and his political rival Aristides (c. 530–c. 468 B.C.E.) cooperated to convince the other allies' generals to fight a naval battle. Themistocles tricked the Persian king into attacking the Greek fleet in the narrow channel between the island of Salamis and the west coast of Athens, where Xerxes could not send all his fleet (twice the size of the Greeks') into battle simultaneously. The heavier Greek warships won the battle by ramming the flimsier Persian craft. The battle of Salamis induced Xerxes to return home. In 479 B.C.E., the Spartans commanded victories over the Persian land forces.

A Signet of Persia's King Darius
Like other kings in the ancient Mediterranean region, the Persian king hunted lions to show his courage and his ability to overcome nature's threats. In this scene from a signet, used to impress the royal seal into wet clay to verify documents, Darius I shoots arrows from a chariot driven for him by a charioteer. He is depicted wearing his crown so that his status as ruler would be obvious. The symbol of Ahura Mazda, the chief god of Persian religion, hovers in the sky to indicate that the king enjoys divine favor. (akg-images.)

REVIEW QUESTION
How did the Greeks overcome the dangers of the Persian invasions?

The Greeks won these epochal battles against the Persians because their generals had better strategic foresight, their soldiers had stronger weapons, and their warships were more effective. Above all, the Greeks won the war because enough of them took the innovative step of uniting to fight for freedom. Because the Greek forces included both the social elites and the poorer men who rowed the warships, their success showed that rich and poor Greeks alike treasured political independence.

Athenian Confidence in the Golden Age, 478–431 B.C.E.

Victory fractured the Greek alliance because the allies resented the harshness of the Spartans as commanders, and the Athenians now competed with them for leadership. This competition created the so-called Athenian Empire. The growth of Athens's power inspired its citizens to broaden their democracy and spend vast amounts to fund officials and jurors, public buildings, art, and religious festivals.

The Establishment of the Athenian Empire

Sparta and Athens built up separate alliances to strengthen their own positions, believing that their security depended on winning a competition for power. Sparta led strong infantry forces from the Peloponnese region, and its ally Corinth had a sizable navy. The Spartan alliance had an assembly to decide policy, but Sparta dominated.

Athens allied with city-states in northern Greece, on the islands of the Aegean Sea, and along the Ionian coast—the places most threatened by Persia. This alliance, the **Delian League**, was built on naval power. It began as a democratic alliance, but Athens soon controlled it because the allies allowed the Athenians to command and to oversee the financing of the league's fleet. At its height, the league included some three hundred city-states. Each paid dues according to its size; Athens determined how the dues were spent. Larger city-states paid their dues by sending **triremes**—warships propelled by 170 rowers on three levels and equipped with a battering ram at the bow (Figure 3.1)—complete with trained crews and their pay. Smaller states could share in building one ship or contribute money instead of ships and crews.

Over time, more and more Delian League members voluntarily paid cash because it was easier. Athens used this money to construct triremes and pay men to row them; oarsmen who brought a slave to row alongside them earned double pay. Drawn primarily from the poorest citizens, rowers gained both income and also political influence in Athenian democracy because the navy became the city-state's main force. These benefits made poor citizens eager to expand Athens's power over other Greeks. The increase in Athenian naval power thus promoted the development of a wider democracy at home, but it undermined the democracy of the Delian League.

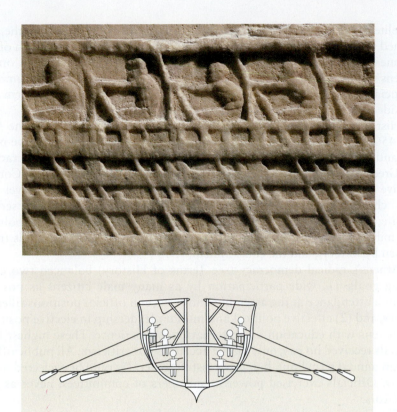

FIGURE 3.1 Triremes, the Foremost Classical Greek Warships Innovations in military technology and training propelled a naval arms race in the fifth century B.C.E. when Greek shipbuilders designed larger and faster ramming ships powered by 170 rowers seated in three rows, each above the other. (See the line illustration of the rowers from behind.) Called triremes, these ships were expensive to build and required extensive crew training. Only wealthy and populous city-states such as Athens could afford to build and man large fleets of triremes. The relief sculpture found on the Athenian acropolis and dating from about 400 B.C.E. gives a glimpse of what a trireme looked like from the side when being rowed into battle. (Sails were used for power only when the ship was not in combat.) (Gianni Dagli Orti/REX/Shutterstock.)

The Athenian assembly could use the league fleet to force disobedient allies to pay cash dues. Athens's dominance of the Delian League has led historians to label it *Athenian Empire*. By about 460 B.C.E., the Delian League's fleet had expelled all Persian garrisons from northern Greece and driven the enemy fleet from the Aegean Sea. This sweep eliminated the Persian threat for the next fifty years.

Military success made Athens prosperous by bringing in spoils and cash dues from the Delian League and making seaborne trade safe. The prosperity benefited rich and poor alike—the poor with good pay, the elite commanders by enhancing their chances for election to high office if they spent their war spoils on public festivals and buildings. In this way, the democracy of Golden Age Athens benefited from what modern scholars often call *imperialism*.

Radical Democracy and Pericles' Leadership, 461–431 B.C.E.

In the late 460s B.C.E., the trireme rowers decided that in their own interest they should make Athens's court system as democratic as its legislative assembly, in which all free adult male citizens participated. They wanted to prevent

WHAT WOULD YOU DO?

If you lived in a direct democracy like that of Athens in the Classical Age, would you advocate for any changes in the political or judicial systems? If so, what changes and why? Do you think citizens of the contemporary democracy of the United States should advocate for changes to align it more closely with institutions and principles of Athenian democracy—for example, wide participation in public office and selection of officials by holding lotteries? Why or why not?

the elite from rendering unfair verdicts in legal cases. Members of the elite pushed this judicial reform, to win popular support for election to high office; the measure passed in 461 B.C.E. **Pericles** (c. 495–429 B.C.E.), from one of Athens's most distinguished families, became Golden Age Athens's dominant politician by spearheading reforms to democratize its judicial system and provide pay for most public offices.

Historians have labeled the changes to Athenian democracy in the 460s and 450s B.C.E. *radical* ("from the roots") because the new system gave political and judicial power to all adult male citizens (the "roots" of democracy, in the Greek view). This direct democracy consisted of the assembly, the Council of Five Hundred chosen annually by lottery, nine archons (higher-level officials) chosen by lottery, the Council of the Areopagus of ex-archons serving for life, an executive board of ten "generals" elected annually with political and military responsibilities, hundreds of other annual minor officials (most chosen by lottery), and the court system.

Athens's **radical democracy** (see Terms of History) balanced two competing goals: (1) wide participation by as many male citizens as possible through attendance at the assembly and service in official positions filled by lottery, and (2) effective political and military leadership in elective positions by citizens with education and international experience. These highest-level officials received no pay, only public acclaim—or criticism. All public offices had an annual term limit, but a successful "general" could be reelected indefinitely. Officials exercised power as members of committees, never as sole operators.

The changes in the judicial system strongly supported radical democracy. Previously, archons and the Council of the Areopagus had decided most legal cases. Reform happened when, as with Cleisthenes before (see Chapter 2), an elite man proposed it in support of greater political influence for poorer citizens—to win their votes against his rivals. In 461 B.C.E., it was Ephialtes who convinced the assembly to establish a new system taking jurisdiction from the archons and giving it to courts manned by citizen jurors. To increase participation and prevent bribery, jurors were selected by lottery from male citizens over thirty years old. They received pay to serve on juries numbering from several hundred to several thousand members. No judges or lawyers existed, and jurors voted by secret ballot after hearing speeches from the persons involved, with every trial completed in a single day. As in the assembly, a majority vote decided; no appeals of verdicts were allowed.

In Athenian radical democracy, the majority could overrule legal protections for individuals. In **ostracism**, all male citizens could cast a ballot on which they scratched the name of one man they thought should be exiled for ten years. If at least six thousand ballots were cast, the man whose name appeared on the greatest number was expelled from Athens. He suffered no other penalty; his family and property remained undisturbed. Usually a man was ostracized because a majority feared he would overthrow the democracy to rule as a tyrant. There was, however, no guarantee of motives in an ostracism, as a story about Aristides illustrates. He was nicknamed "the Just"

TERMS OF HISTORY: Democracy

The term *democracy* comes from the ancient Greek word *dēmokratia*, formed from the words *dēmos* ("people, population of a land or region") and *kratos* ("power, strength"). So, *dēmokratia* originally meant something like "the power/strength of the inhabitants of a certain territory."

The first democratic states developed in ancient Greece; monarchy remained the most common form of government in the rest of the ancient Western world. The best known is Athens, whose government was a direct, not a representative, democracy. It is referred to as a "radical democracy" because it was direct rather than representative. Athenian democracy was direct because making law and policy and the power to punish belonged not to a voting body of elected representatives but to the *dēmos*, meeting either in the citizen assembly (*ecclesia*), the institution with ultimate power in political decision-making including the ability to declare war and peace, or convening as juries. Both these institutions made decisions by majority vote of a quorum of the adult male citizens who happened to be participating on that occasion. Since the attendance at an Assembly meeting represented by any standard a statistically significant sample of the population and the size of juries numbered from hundreds to thousands of men, their votes genuinely expressed the majority will of the *dēmos*—thought of as male citizens in the first instance. Decision-making had wider roots, however. Aristophanes' comic plays *Lysistrata* and *Women at the Assembly* provide evidence to be taken seriously, that Athenian women made their opinions on important civic matters known to their male relatives and were seen by men as having the capability to take action.

Finally, most public officials were chosen by lottery, and they as well as the limited number of top officials chosen by election had annual terms limits and were constantly liable for removal from office by prosecution by fellow citizens for malfeasance or incompetence. This meant Athenian democracy was much more in the hands of the *dēmos* than in a modern representative democracy such as in the United States.

---

because he had proved himself so fair-minded in setting the original level of dues for Delian League members. On the day of an ostracism, an illiterate citizen handed him a pottery fragment and asked him to scratch a name on it:

> "Certainly," said Aristides. "What name shall I write?" "Aristides," replied the man. "All right," said Aristides as he inscribed his own name, "but why do you want to ostracize Aristides? What has he done to you?" "Oh, nothing," the man muttered, "I don't even know him I just can't stand hearing everybody call him 'the Just.'"

True or not, this tale demonstrates that most Athenians believed the best way to support democracy was to trust majority vote.

Some socially elite citizens bitterly criticized Athens's democracy for giving political power to the poor. These critics insisted that oligarchy—the rule of the few—was morally superior to radical democracy because they believed that the poor lacked the education and moral values needed for leadership and would use majority rule to strip the rich of their wealth by making them provide benefits to poorer citizens.

Pericles convinced the assembly to pass reforms to strengthen citizens' equality, making him the most influential leader of his era. He introduced

The Nature of Women and Marriage

Greeks believed that women had different natures from men and that both genders were capable of excellence in their own ways. Marriage was supposed to bring these natures together in a partnership of complementary strengths and obligations to each other.

1. Melanippe's Rejection of Men's Criticism of Women

The heroine of Euripides' tragedy (only partially preserved) Melanippe the Captive was a mother who overcomes hardship and treachery to save her family.

Men's blame and criticism of women are empty, like the twanging sound a bowstring makes without an arrow. Women are superior to men, and I'll demonstrate it. They make contracts with no need of witnesses [to swear they are honest]. They manage their households and keep safe the valuable possessions, shipped from abroad, that they have inside their homes. Without a woman, no household is elegant or happy. And then in the matter of people's relationship with the gods—this I judge to be most important of all—there we have the greatest role. For women prophesy the will of Apollo in his oracles [at Delphi], and at the hallowed oracle of Dodona by the sacred oak tree a woman reveals the will of Zeus to all

Greeks who seek it. And then there are the sacred rites of initiation performed for the Fates and the Goddesses Without Names: these can't be done with holiness by men, but women make them flourish in every way. In this way women's role in religion is right and proper.

Therefore, should anyone put down women? Won't those men stop their empty fault-finding, the ones who strongly believe that all women should be blamed if a single one is found to be bad? I will make a distinction with the following argument: nothing is worse than a bad woman, but nothing is more surpassingly superior than a worthy one.

Source: Euripides, *Melanippe the Captive*, fragment 660 Mette. Translation by Thomas R. Martin.

2. A Husband Discusses Gender Roles in Marriage

Isomachus, an upper-class friend of Socrates, reports a discussion with his wife, who is represented as needing to be instructed by her husband concerning her full capability as a woman.

Ischomachus: I said to her: . . . I for my sake and your parents for your sake [arranged our marriage] by considering who would be the best partner for forming a household and having children. I chose

pay for all offices filled by lottery and for jury service, so that the poor could afford to serve. In 451 B.C.E., Pericles sponsored a law restricting citizenship to those whose mother and father were both Athenian by birth. Previously, wealthy men had often married foreign women from elite families. This change increased the status of Athenian women, rich or poor, as potential mothers of citizens, and it made Athenian citizenship more valuable by reducing the number of people eligible for its legal and financial benefits. (See Contrasting Views.)

Pericles convinced the assembly to launch naval campaigns when war with Sparta broke out in the 450s B.C.E. The assembly was so eager to compete for power and plunder against other Greeks and against Persians in the eastern Mediterranean that it voted for up to three major expeditions at once. These efforts slowed in the late 450s B.C.E., after a large naval force sent to aid an

you, and your parents chose me as the best they could find. If God should give us children, we will then plan how to raise them in the best possible way. For our partnership provides us this good: the best mutual support and the best maintenance in our old age. We have this sharing now in our household, because I've contributed all that I own to the common resources of the household, and so have you. We're not going to count up who brought more property, because the one who turns out to be the better partner in a marriage has made the greater contribution.

Ischomachus's wife: But how will I be able to partner you? What ability do I have? Everything rests on you. My mother told me my job was to behave with thoughtful moderation.

Ischomachus: Well, my father told me the same thing. Thoughtful moderation for a man, as for a woman, means behaving in such a way that their possessions will be in the best possible condition and will increase as much as possible by good and just means . . . So, you must do what the gods made you naturally capable of and what our law requires . . . Since the work both outside and inside required effort and

care, God, it seems to me, from the start fashioned women's nature for indoor work and men's for outdoor . . . But since both men and women have to manage things, [God] gave them equal shares in memory and attentiveness . . . God gave both an equal ability to practice self-control . . .

Precisely because they have different natures, they have greater need of each other and their yoking together is the most beneficial, with the one being capable where the other one is lacking.

Source: Xenophon, *Oeconomicus* 7.10–30. Translation by Thomas R. Martin.

QUESTIONS TO CONSIDER

1. What evidence and arguments for differing natures for men and women do these documents offer?

2. What do you see as the strengths and the weaknesses of Ischomachus' description of marriage as a partnership?

3. Do you think Athenian women of all social classes would have found these arguments convincing? Why or why not?

Egyptian rebellion against Persian rule suffered a horrendous defeat, losing tens of thousands of oarsmen. In 446–445 B.C.E., Pericles arranged a peace treaty with Sparta for thirty years, to preserve Athenian control of the Delian League.

The Urban Landscape in Athens

Golden Age Athens prospered from Delian League dues, war spoils, and profits and taxes from seaborne trade. Its artisans produced goods traded far and wide; the Etruscans in central Italy, for example, imported countless painted vases. All these activities boosted Athens to its greatest prosperity.

Athenians spent their public resources on pay for citizens participating in its democracy and on public buildings, art, and religious festivals. In private life, rich urban dwellers splurged on luxury goods influenced by Persian designs, but most houses remained modest and plain. Archaeology at the city of Olynthus in northeastern Greece has revealed typical homes grouping bedrooms, storerooms, and dining rooms around open-air courtyards. Poor city residents rented small apartments. Toilets consisted of pots indoors and a pit outside the front door. The city paid collectors to dump the waste in the countryside.

Generals won votes by spending their war spoils on public running tracks, shade trees, and buildings. The super-rich commander Cimon (c. 510–c. 450 B.C.E.), for example, paid for the Painted Stoa to be built on the edge of Athens's **agora**, the central market square. There, shoppers could admire the building's paintings commemorating the military achievements of the family of Cimon. This sort of financial contribution was voluntary, but the city-state also required wealthy citizens to pay for festivals and warship equipment. This obligation on the rich was essential because Athens, as usual in ancient Greece, had no regular property or income taxes.

On Athens's acropolis (the rocky hill at the city's center, Map 3.2), Pericles had the most famous buildings of Golden Age Athens erected during the 440s and 430s B.C.E.: a mammoth gateway and also an enormous marble temple of Athena called the **Parthenon** ("virgin goddess's house"). These two buildings cost well more than the equivalent of a billion dollars today, a phenomenal sum for even a large Greek city-state. Pericles' political rivals slammed him for spending too much public money on the project and diverting Delian League funds to beautify Athens. Research in surviving financial records reveals this accusation was false: Athens's own revenues financed the building program.

The Parthenon is the foremost symbol of Athens's Golden Age. It honored Athena, the city's chief deity. Inside the temple, a gold-and-ivory statue nearly forty feet high depicted the goddess in armor, holding a six-foot-tall statue of Nike, the goddess of victory. Like all other Greek temples, the Parthenon was a

MAP 3.2 Fifth-Century B.C.E. Athens The urban center of Athens, with the agora and acropolis at its heart, measured about one square mile; it was surrounded by a stone wall with a circuit of some four miles. Gates guarded by towers and various smaller entries allowed traffic in and out of the city. Much of the Athenian population lived in the many demes (villages) of the surrounding countryside. Most of the city's water supply came from wells and springs inside the walls, but, unlike some Greek cities, Athens also had water piped in from outside. The Long Walls provided a protected corridor connecting the city to its harbor at Piraeus, where the Athenian navy was anchored and grain was imported to feed the people.

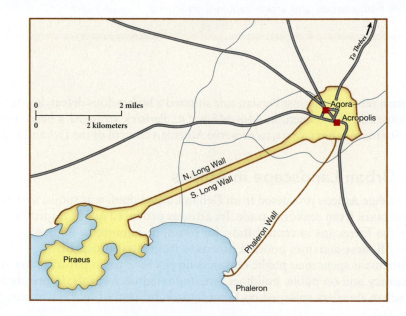

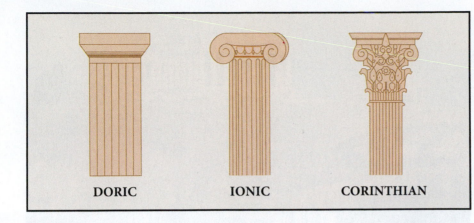

DORIC   IONIC   CORINTHIAN

FIGURE 3.2 Styles of Greek Capitals
The Greeks decorated the capitals, or tops, of columns in these three styles to fit the different architectural "canons" (their word for precise mathematical systems of proportions) that they devised for designing buildings. These styles were much imitated in later times, as on many U.S. state capitols and the U.S. Supreme Court Building in Washington, D.C.

divinity's residence, not a hall for worshippers. Its design was standard: a rectangular box on a raised platform lined with columns, a plan probably taken from Egypt. The Parthenon's soaring columns fenced in a porch surrounding the interior chamber. They were carved in the simple style called Doric, in contrast to the more elaborate Ionic and Corinthian styles (Figure 3.2).

The Parthenon's massive size and innovative style proclaimed the self-confidence of Golden Age Athens and its competitive drive to build a monument more spectacular than any other in Greece. Constructed from twenty thousand tons of local marble, the temple stretched 230 feet long and 100 feet wide. Its complex architecture demonstrated the Athenian ambition to use human skill to improve nature: because perfectly rectilinear architecture appears curved to the human eye, subtle curves and inclines were built into the Parthenon to produce an illusion of completely straight lines and emphasize its massiveness.

The Parthenon's many sculptures communicated confident messages: the gods ensure triumph over the forces of chaos, and Athenians enjoy the gods' goodwill more than anyone else. The sculptures in each pediment (the triangular space atop the columns at either end of the temple) portrayed Athena as the city-state's benefactor. The metopes (panels sculpted in relief above the outer columns around all four sides) portrayed victories over hostile centaurs (creatures with the body of a horse but torso and head of a man) and other enemies of civilization. Most strikingly of all, a frieze (a continuous band of figures carved in relief) ran around the top of the walls inside the porch and was painted in bright colors to make it more visible. The Parthenon's frieze was special because usually only Ionic-style buildings had one. The frieze showed Athenian men, women, and children parading before the gods, the procession shown in motion like the pictures in a graphic novel today.

No other Greeks had ever adorned a temple with representations of themselves. The Parthenon staked a claim of unique closeness between the city-state and the gods, reflecting the Athenians' confidence after helping turn back the Persians, achieving leadership of a powerful naval alliance, and accumulating great public wealth. Their city-state's success, the Athenians believed, proved that the gods were on their side, and their fabulous buildings displayed their gratitude.

REVIEW QUESTION

What factors produced political change in fifth-century B.C.E. Athens?

Like the unique Parthenon frieze, the innovations that Golden Age artists made in representing the human body shattered tradition. By the time of the Persian Wars, Greek sculptors had begun replacing the stiffly balanced style of Archaic Age statues with statues in motion in new poses. This style of movement in stone expressed an energetic balancing of competing forces, echoing radical democracy's principles. Sculptors began carving anatomically realistic but perfect-looking bodies, suggesting that humans could be confident about achieving beauty and perfection. Female statues now displayed the shape of the curves underneath clothing, while male ones showed athletic muscles. The faces showed a more relaxed and self-confident look in place of the rigid smiles of Archaic Age statues.

Freestanding Golden Age statues, whether paid for with private or government funds, were erected to be seen by the public. Privately commissioned statues of gods were placed in sanctuaries as symbols of devotion. Wealthy families paid for statues of their deceased relatives, especially if they had died young in war, to be placed above their graves as memorials of their excellence and signs of the family's social status.

Tradition and Innovation in Athens's Golden Age

Golden Age Athens's prosperity and international contacts created unprecedented innovations in architecture, art, drama, education, and philosophy, but the drive to innovate conflicted with traditional ways. In keeping with tradition, women were expected to limit their public role to participation in religious ceremonies. The controversial ideas of philosophers and teachers called Sophists and the Athenian philosopher Socrates' views on personal morality and responsibility upset many people, who feared the gods would become angry at the community for harboring these nontraditional thinkers. The tragic and comic plays presented in publicly funded drama festivals reflected the clash between innovation and tradition by examining problems in city-state life.

Religious Tradition in a Period of Change

Greeks maintained religious tradition as protection against life's dangers. They participated in the city-state's sacrifices and festivals and also worshipped privately. Different gods were worshipped with different rituals, from animal sacrifices to offerings of fruits, vegetables, and pastries. State-funded sacrifices of large animals gathered the community to reaffirm its ties to the divine world and to feast on roasted meat from the sacrificed beast. For poor people, the free food provided at religious festivals was often the only meat they ever tasted.

The biggest festivals featured parades and contests in music, dancing, poetry, and athletics. Laborers' contracts specified how many days off they received to attend such ceremonies. Some festivals were for women only, such as the three-day festival for married women in honor of Demeter, goddess of agriculture and fertility.

Families marked significant events such as birth, marriage, and death with prayers, rituals, and sacrifices. They honored their ancestors with offerings made at their tombs, consulted seers about the meanings of dreams and omens, and paid magicians for spells to improve their love lives or curses to harm their enemies. Hero cults included rituals performed at the tomb of an extraordinarily famous man or woman because their remains were thought to retain special power to provide oracles, heal sickness, and protect the army. The strongman Herakles (or Hercules, as the Romans spelled his name) had cults all over the Greek world because his superhuman reputation gave him international appeal. **Mystery cults** initiated members into "secret knowledge" about the divine and human worlds. Initiates believed that they gained divine protection both while alive and after death.

The Athenian mystery cult of Demeter and her daughter Persephone was internationally famous. The cult's central rite was the Mysteries, a series of initiation ceremonies. They were so popular that an international truce—as with the Olympic Games—allowed people to travel from distant places to participate. The Mysteries were open to any free Greek-speaking individuals—women and men, adults and children—if they were clear of ritual pollution (for example, if they had not committed sacrilege, been convicted of murder, or had recent contact with a corpse or blood from a birth). Some slaves who worked in the sanctuary were also eligible to participate. The main stage of initiation took more than a week. A sixth-century B.C.E. poem explained the initiation's benefits: "Richly blessed is the mortal who has seen these rites; but whoever is not an initiate and has no share in them, that one never has an equal portion after death, down in the gloomy darkness."

Women, Slaves, and Metics

Women, slaves, and **metics** (foreigners granted permanent residence status in return for taxes and military service) made up the majority of Athens's population, but they lacked political rights. Citizen women enjoyed legal privileges and social status, earning respect through their family roles and religious activities. Upper-class women managed their households, visited female friends, and participated in religious cults. Poor women worked as small-scale merchants, crafts producers, and agricultural laborers. Slaves and metics performed a variety of jobs in agriculture and commerce; some metics started their own successful businesses.

Bearing children in marriage earned women public and family status. Men were expected to respect and support their wives. Childbirth was dangerous under the medical conditions of the time. In *Medea*, a play of 431 B.C.E. by Euripides (c. 480–406 B.C.E.), the heroine shouts in anger at her husband, who has selfishly betrayed their marriage: "People say that we women lead a safe life at home, while men have to go to war. What fools they are! I would much rather fight in battle three times than give birth to a child even once."

Wives were partners with their husbands in owning and managing the household's property. Rich women acquired property, including land—the most valued possession in Greek society because it could be farmed or rented out for income—through inheritance and dowry. A husband often had to put up valuable land of his own as collateral to guarantee repayment to his wife of the amount of her dowry if he squandered it.

Like fathers, mothers were expected to hand down property to their children to keep it in the family through male heirs, since only sons could maintain their father's family line; married daughters became members of their husband's family. The goal of keeping property in the possession of male heirs shows up most clearly in Athenian law about heiresses (daughters whose fathers died without any sons, which happened in about one of every five families): the closest male relative of the heiress's father—her official guardian after her father's death—was required to marry her. The goal was to produce a son to inherit the father's property. This rule applied regardless of whether either party was already married (unless the heiress had sons); the heiress and the male relative were both supposed to divorce their present spouses and marry each other. In real life, however, people often used legal technicalities to get around this requirement so that they could remain with their chosen partners.

Tradition restricted women's freedom of movement to protect them, men said, from seducers and rapists. Men wanted to ensure that their family property went only to their biological children. Well-off city women were expected to avoid contact with male strangers. Research has discredited the idea that Greek homes had a defined "women's quarter" to which women were confined. Rather, women were granted privacy in certain rooms under their control. In their homes women would spin wool for clothing, converse with visiting friends, direct their children, supervise the slaves, and express opinions on everything, including politics, to their male relatives. Poor women had to leave the house, usually a crowded rental apartment, to sell vegetables, bread, cloth, or decorative objects they had made.

Vase Painting of Women Fetching Water (detail)
This vase painting shows women filling water jugs at a public fountain to take back to their homes. Both freeborn and slave women fetched water for their households, as few Greek homes had running water. Cities built attractive fountain houses such as this one, which dispensed fresh water from springs or piped it in through small aqueducts (compare the large Roman aqueduct on page 163). Women often gathered at fountains for conversation with people from outside their household. (Black-figure water jar (hydria) with women at the fountain, Attica, Athens, Archaic Period, c. 520 B.C.E. (ceramic)/Priam Painter (fl. c. 530–510 B.C.E.)/Museum of Fine Arts, Boston, Massachusetts, USA/William Francis Warden Fund/Bridgeman Images.)

An elite woman left home for religious festivals, funerals, childbirths at the houses of relatives and friends, and shopping. Often her husband escorted her, but sometimes she took only a slave, setting her own itinerary. Most upper-class women probably viewed their limited contact with men as a badge of superior social status. For example, a pale complexion, from staying inside much of the time, was much admired as a sign of an enviable life of leisure and wealth.

Women who bore legitimate children gained increased respect and freedom, as an Athenian man explained in his speech defending himself for having killed his wife's lover:

> After my marriage, I at first didn't interfere with my wife very much, but neither did I allow her too much independence. I kept an eye on her. . . . But after she had a baby, I started to trust her more and put her in charge of all my things, believing we now had the closest of relationships.

Bearing male children brought a woman special honor because sons meant security. Sons could appear in court to support their parents in lawsuits and protect them in the streets of Athens, which for most of its history had no regular police force. By law, sons were required to support elderly parents.

Some women escaped traditional restrictions by working as a **hetaira** ("companion"). Hetairas, usually foreigners, were unmarried, physically attractive, witty in speech, and skilled in music and poetry. Men hired them to entertain at a symposium (a drinking party to which wives were not invited). Their skill at clever teasing and joking with men gave hetairas a freedom of speech that "proper" women did not exercise in public. Hetairas nevertheless lacked the social status and respectability that married women possessed.

Sometimes hetairas sold sex for high prices; they could control their own sexuality by choosing their clients. Athenian men (but not women) could buy sex as they pleased without legal hindrance. Men (but not women) could also have sex freely with female or male slaves, who could not refuse their masters.

The most skilled hetairas earned enough to live in luxury on their own. The most famous hetaira in Athens was Aspasia from Miletus, who became Pericles' lover and bore him a son. She dazzled men with her brilliant talk and wide knowledge of society and politics. Pericles fell so deeply in love with her that he wanted to marry her, despite his own law of 451 B.C.E. restricting citizenship to the children of two Athenian parents.

Great riches freed a woman from traditional restrictions. The most outspoken rich Athenian woman was Elpinike. She once criticized Pericles to his face by sarcastically remarking in front of a group of women who were praising him for an attack on a rebellious Delian League ally, "This really is wonderful, Pericles. . . . You have caused the loss of many good citizens, not in battle against Phoenicians or Persians . . . but in suppressing an allied city of fellow Greeks."

Slaves and metics were considered outsiders. Both individuals and the city-state owned slaves, who could be purchased from traders or bred in the household. Some people picked up unwanted newborns abandoned by their parents (in an accepted practice called infant exposure) and raised them as slaves. Athens's commercial growth increased the demand for slaves, who in Pericles' time made up around 100,000 of the city-state's total of perhaps 250,000 inhabitants. Slaves worked in homes, on farms, and in crafts shops; rowed alongside their owners in the navy; and toiled in Athens's dangerous silver mines. Unlike those in Sparta, slaves in Athens almost never rebelled, probably because they originated from too many different places to be able to unite.

Golden Age Athens's wealth and cultural activities attracted metics from all around the Mediterranean. By the late fifth century B.C.E., they constituted perhaps 50,000 to 75,000 of the estimated 150,000 free men, women, and children in the city-state. Metics paid for the privilege of living and working in Athens through a special foreigners' tax and army service, but they could not usually become citizens.

Innovative Ideas in Education, Philosophy, History, and Medicine

Thinkers in the Greek Golden Age developed innovative ideas in education, philosophy, history, and medicine. These innovations angered some people, who worried that these departures from tradition would undermine society, especially in religion, thereby provoking punishment from angry gods. Eventually, these changes promoted the development of scientific study as an enduring characteristic of Western civilization.

Education and philosophy provided the hottest battles between tradition and innovation. Parents had traditionally controlled their children's education, which occurred in the home and included hired tutors (there were no public schools). Controversy erupted when men known as Sophists appeared in the mid-fifth century B.C.E. and offered, for pay, classes to young males on nontraditional philosophy and religious doctrines as well as new techniques for public speaking. Some philosophers' ideas challenged traditional religious views. The philosopher Socrates' views on personal morality provoked another fierce controversy. In writing history, innovators created novel models of interpretation to explore human experience; medical specialists developed scientific methods to investigate the human body.

Disagreement over whether these intellectual changes were dangerous for Athenian society added to the political tension that had arisen at Athens by the 430s B.C.E. concerning Athens's harsh treatment of its own allies and its economic sanctions against Sparta's allies. Athenians connected philosophic ideas about the nature of justice with their decisions about the city-state's domestic and foreign policy, while also experiencing anxiety concerning the gods' attitude toward the community.

Wealthy families sent their sons to private teachers to learn to read, write, play a musical instrument or sing, and to develop athletic skills. Physical training was considered vital because it made men's bodies handsome and prepared them to fight in the city-state's army and navy (all males from eighteen to sixty could be summoned to war anytime). Men exercised nude every day in gymnasia, public open-air facilities paid for by wealthy families. The daughters of wealthy families usually received instruction at home from educated slaves. Young girls learned reading, writing, and arithmetic to be able to help their future husbands by managing the household.

Poor girls and boys learned a trade and perhaps a little reading, writing, and arithmetic by assisting their parents in their daily work or by serving as apprentices to skilled craft workers. Most people probably were weak readers, but they could always find someone to read written texts aloud. Oral communication remained central to Greek life, in political speeches, songs, plays, and stories about the past.

Rich young men learned to participate in public life by observing their fathers, uncles, and other older men as they debated in the Council of Five Hundred and the assembly, served in public office, and spoke in court. Often an older man would choose an adolescent boy as his special favorite to educate. The teenager would learn about public life by spending time with the older man. During the day the boy would listen to his mentor talking politics in the agora, help him perform his duties in public office, and work out with him in a gymnasium. They would spend their evenings at a symposium, whose agenda could range from serious political and philosophical discussion to riotous partying.

This older mentor/younger favorite relationship could lead to sexual relations between the youth and the older (married) male. Sex between mentors and favorites was considered acceptable in elite circles in many city-states, including Athens, Sparta, and Thebes. Some city-states banned this behavior, believing it reflected an adult man's shameful inability to control his lustful desires.

By the time radical democracy emerged in Athens, young men could obtain higher education in a new way: paying expensive professional teachers called **Sophists** ("men of wisdom"). Sophists challenged tradition by teaching new skills of persuasion in speaking and new ways of thinking based on rational arguments. Sophists became notorious for using complex reasoning to make what many people considered deceptive arguments.

By 450 B.C.E., Athens was attracting Sophists from around the Greek world. These entrepreneurs competed with one another to attract students able to pay a high tuition. Sophists strove for excellence by offering specialized training in rhetoric—the skill of speaking persuasively. Every ambitious man

Vase Painting of a Symposium

Upper-class Greek men often spent their evenings at a symposium, a drinking party that always included much conversation and usually featured music and entertainers. Wives were not included. The discussions could range widely, from literature to politics to philosophy. The man on the right is about to fling the dregs of his wine, playing a messy game called *kottabos*. The nudity of the female musician indicates she is a hired prostitute. (Detail, Athenian red-figured cup, 500–450 B.C.E./Lewis Collection, courtesy of Corpus Christi College, Cambridge, UK/photo © Fitzwilliam Museum, Cambridge/Art Resource, NY.)

wanted rhetorical training because it promised power in Athens's assembly, councils, and courts. The Sophists alarmed those who feared their teachings would destroy the tradition that preserved democracy. Speakers trained by silver-tongued Sophists, they believed, might be able to mislead the assembly while promoting their personal interests.

The most notorious Sophist was Protagoras (c. 490–c. 420 B.C.E.), a contemporary of Pericles. Emigrating to Athens from Abdera, in northern Greece, around 450 B.C.E., Protagoras expressed views on the nature of truth and morality that outraged many Athenians. He argued that there could be no absolute standard of truth because every issue had two irreconcilable sides. For example, if one person feels a breeze is warm but another person finds it cool, neither judgment can be absolutely correct because the wind simply is warm to one and cool to the other. Protagoras summed up this subjectivism—the belief that there is no absolute reality behind and independent of appearances—in his work *Truth:* "The human being is the measure of all things, of the things that are that they are, and of the things that are not that they are not."

The subjectivism of Protagoras and other Sophists contained two main ideas: (1) human institutions and values are matters of *nomos* ("statute law, tradition, or convention") and not creations of *physis* ("nature"), and (2) since truth is subjective, speakers should be able to argue either side of a question with equal persuasiveness and rationality. The first view implied that traditional human institutions were arbitrary and changing rather than natural and permanent, while the second seemed to make questions of right and wrong irrelevant. (See Primary Source Analysis.)

The Sophists' critics accused them of teaching moral relativism that threatened the shared values of the democratic city-state. Aristophanes (c. 446–c. 386 B.C.E.), author of comic plays, satirized Sophists for harming Athens by instructing students in persuasive techniques "to make the weaker argument the stronger." Protagoras energetically responded that his doctrines were not hostile to democracy, arguing that every person had a natural capability for

PRIMARY SOURCE ANALYSIS   How to Argue Both Sides of a Case

The Sophist Protagoras taught his students to argue both sides of any case, but he insisted he did not teach this skill for immoral purposes. Some teachers following in his footsteps were less ethical. This excerpt comes from an anonymous handbook of the late fifth century B.C.E. entitled Double Arguments, *which provided examples of how Sophists could make arguments in the fashion of Protagoras.*

Greek philosophers put forward double arguments concerning the good and the bad. Some say that the good is one thing and the bad another, but others say that they are the same, and that a thing might be good for some persons but bad for others, or at one time good and at another time bad for the same person. I myself agree with those who hold the latter opinion, which I shall examine using as an example human life and its concern for food, drink, and sexual pleasures: these things are bad for someone if the person is sick but good if the person is healthy and needs them. And, further, overindulgence in these things is bad for the one who overindulges but good for those who make a profit by selling these things. And again, sickness is bad for the sick but good for the doctors. And death is bad for those who die but good for the undertakers and makers of grave monuments. . . . Shipwrecks are bad for the ship owners but good for the ship builders. When tools are blunted and worn away it is bad for others but good for the blacksmith. And if a pot gets smashed, this is bad for everyone else but good for the potter. When shoes wear out and fall apart it is bad for others but good for the shoemaker. . . . In the *stadion* race for runners, victory is good for the winner but bad for the losers.

Source: *Dissoi Logoi* 1.1–6. Translation adapted from Rosamund Kent Sprague, ed., *The Older Sophists* (Columbia: University of South Carolina Press, 1972), 279–280.

QUESTIONS TO CONSIDER

1. Do you think it is possible ever to reach a firm conclusion about whether something is good or bad? Why or why not?

2. Do think it could be harmful to teach people to make arguments of this kind in law or politics or business? Why or why not?

excellence and that human society depended on the rule of law based on a sense of justice. Members of a community, he explained, must be persuaded to obey the laws, not because laws were based on absolute truth, which did not exist, but because rationally it was advantageous for everyone to be law-abiding. A thief, for example, who might claim that stealing was a part of nature, would have to be persuaded by reason that a man-made law forbidding theft was to his advantage because it protected his own property and the community in which he, like all humans, had to live to survive.

Even more disturbing to Athenians than the Sophists' ideas about truth were their ideas about religion. Protagoras angered people with his agnosticism (the belief that supernatural phenomena are unknowable): "Whether the gods exist I cannot discover, nor what their form is like, for there are many impediments to knowledge, [such as] the obscurity of the subject and the brevity of human life." He upset those who thought he was saying that conventional religion had no meaning. They worried that his words would provoke divine anger against the community where he now resided.

Other fifth-century B.C.E. philosophers and thinkers also proposed controversial new scientific theories about the nature of the cosmos and the origin of religion. A philosopher friend of Pericles, for example, argued that the sun was a lump of flaming rock, not a god. Democritus, who visited Athens, invented an atomic theory of matter to explain how change was constant in the universe. Everything, he argued, consisted of tiny, invisible particles in eternal motion. Their random collisions caused them to combine and recombine in an infinite variety of forms, with no divine purpose guiding their collisions and combinations. These ideas seemed to invalidate traditional religion, which explained events as governed by the gods' will. Even more provocative was a play written by the wealthy Athenian aristocrat Critias that denounced religion as a clever but false system invented by powerful men to fool ordinary people into obeying moral standards through fear of divine punishment.

Many poorer citizens saw the Sophists and the philosophers as threats to Athenian democracy because only wealthy men could afford their classes or spend time conversing with them, thereby gaining yet more advantages by learning to speak persuasively in the assembly's debates or in court speeches. Moral relativism and the physical explanation of the universe struck many Athenians as especially dangerous to religion. These ideas so infuriated some Athenians that in the 430s B.C.E. they sponsored a law allowing citizens to bring charges of impiety against "those who fail to respect divine things or teach theories about the cosmos." Not even Pericles could prevent his philosopher friend from being convicted on this charge and expelled from Athens.

Socrates (469–399 B.C.E.), the most famous philosopher of the Golden Age, became well-known during this troubled time of the 430s, when people were anxious not just about new ways of thinking but also about war with Sparta. Socrates devoted his life to questioning people about their beliefs, but he insisted he was not a Sophist because he took no pay. Above all, he rejected the view that justice in fact amounted to power over others. Insisting that true justice was always better than injustice, he created an emphasis on ethics (the study of ideal human values and moral duties) in Greek philosophy.

Socrates lived an eccentric life attracting constant attention. Sporting a stomach that he called "a bit too big to be convenient," he wore the same cheap cloak summer and winter and always went barefoot no matter how cold the weather. His physical stamina—including both his tirelessness as a soldier and his ability to outdrink anyone—was legendary. He lived in poverty and disdained material possessions, though he supported a wife and several children by accepting gifts from wealthy admirers.

Socrates spent his time in conversations all over Athens: participating in a symposium with friends, strolling in the agora, or watching young men exercise in a gymnasium. He wrote nothing. Our knowledge of his ideas comes from others' writings, especially those of his famous follower Plato (c. 428–348 B.C.E.). Plato portrays Socrates as a relentless questioner of his fellow citizens, foreign friends, and leading Sophists. Socrates pushed his conversational partners to examine their basic assumptions about life. Giving few answers, Socrates never directly instructed anyone. Instead, he led people to draw conclusions in response to his probing questions and refutations of their unexamined beliefs. Today this procedure is called the **Socratic method**.

Socrates frequently outraged people because his method made them feel ignorant and baffled. His questions forced them to admit that they did not in fact know what they had assumed they knew very well. Even more painful to them was Socrates' fiercely argued view that the way they lived their lives—pursuing success in politics or business or art—was merely an excuse for avoiding the hard work of understanding and developing genuine *aretê* ("excellence"). Socrates insisted that he was ignorant of the definition of excellence and what was best for human beings, but that his wisdom consisted of knowing that he did not know. He vowed he wanted to improve, not undermine, people's ethical beliefs, even though, as a friend put it, a conversation with Socrates made a man feel numb—as if a jellyfish had stung him.

Socrates especially wanted to use reasoning to discover universal, objective standards for individual ethics. He attacked the Sophists for their relativistic claim that conventional standards of right and wrong were merely "the chains that handcuff nature." This view, he protested, equated human happiness with power and "getting more."

Socrates insisted that the only way to achieve true happiness was to behave according to a universal, transcendent standard of just behavior that people could understand rationally. He argued that just behavior and excellence were identical to knowledge, and that true knowledge of justice would inevitably lead people to choose good over evil. They would therefore have truly happy lives, regardless of how rich or poor they were. Since Socrates believed that ethical knowledge was all a person needed for the good life, he argued that no one knowingly behaved unjustly and that behaving justly was always in the individual's interest. It was simply ignorant to believe that the best life was the life of unlimited power to pursue whatever one desired. The most desirable human life was concerned with excellence and guided by reason, not by dreams of personal gain.

Though very different from the Sophists' doctrines, Socrates' ideas proved just as disturbing to the masses because they rejected the Athenians' traditional way of life. His ridicule of commonly accepted ideas about the importance of wealth and public success angered many people. Unhappiest of all were the fathers whose sons, after listening to Socrates' questions reduce someone to utter bewilderment, came home to try the same technique on their parents, employing the Socratic method to criticize their parents' values as old-fashioned and worthless. Men who experienced this reversal of the traditional educational hierarchy—the father was supposed to educate the son—felt that Socrates was undermining the stability of society by making young men question Athenian traditions. Socrates evidently did not teach women, but Plato portrays him as ready to learn from exceptional women, such as Pericles' companion Aspasia.

The worry that Socrates' ideas presented a danger to conventional society inspired Aristophanes to write his comedy *The Clouds* (423 B.C.E.). This play portrays Socrates as a cynical Sophist who, for a fee, offers instruction in Protagoras's technique of making the weaker argument the stronger. When Socrates' school transforms a youth into a public speaker arguing persuasively that a son has the right to beat his parents, his father burns the place down. None of these plot details was real, but people did have a genuine fear that Socrates' radical views on individual morality endangered the city-state's traditional practices.

Just as the Sophists and Socrates antagonized many people with their new ideas, the men who first wrote Greek history created controversy because they took a critical attitude in their descriptions of the past. Herodotus of Halicarnassus (c. 485–425 B.C.E.) and Thucydides of Athens (c. 455–399 B.C.E.) became Greece's most famous historians and established Western civilization's tradition of writing history. The fifth century B.C.E.'s unprecedented events—a coalition Greek victory over the world's greatest power and then the longest war ever between Greeks—inspired them to create history as a subject based on strenuous research. They explained that they wrote histories because they wanted people to remember the past and to understand why wars had taken place.

Herodotus's long, groundbreaking work *The Histories* ("Inquiries" in Greek) explained the Persian Wars as a clash between the cultures of the East and West. A typically competitive Greek intellectual, Herodotus—who by Roman times had become known as the Father of History—made the justifiable claim that he surpassed all those who had previously recorded the past by taking an in-depth and investigative approach to evidence, examining the culture of non-Greeks as well as Greeks, and expressing explicit and implicit judgments about people's actions. Because Herodotus recognized the necessity (and the delight) of studying other cultures with respect, he pushed his inquiries deep into the past, looking for long-standing cultural differences to help explain the Persian-Greek conflict. He showed that Greeks and non-Greeks were equally capable of good and evil. Unlike poets and playwrights, he focused on human psychology and interactions, not the gods, as the driving forces in history.

Thucydides innovated—and competed with Herodotus—by writing contemporary history and creating the kind of analysis of power that today underlies political science. His *History of the Peloponnesian War* made power politics, not divine intervention, history's primary force. Deeply affected by the war's brutality, Thucydides used his experiences as a politician and failed military commander (he was exiled for losing a key outpost) to make his narrative vivid and frank in describing human moral failings. His insistence that historians should energetically seek out the most reliable sources and evaluate their testimony with objectivity set a high standard for later writers. Like Herodotus, he challenged tradition by revealing that Greek history included not just glorious achievements but also some share of shameful acts (such as the Athenian punishment of the Melians in the Peloponnesian War—see page 109).

Hippocrates (c. 460–c. 370 B.C.E.) of Cos, a contemporary of Thucydides, challenged tradition by grounding medical diagnosis and treatment in clinical observation. His fame continues today in the oath bearing his name (the Hippocratic oath), which doctors swear at the beginning of their professional careers. Previously, medicine had depended on magic and ritual. People believed that evil spirits caused diseases, and various cults offered healing to patients through divine intervention. Competing to refute these earlier doctors' theories, Hippocrates insisted that only physical factors caused illnesses. He may have been the author of the view, dominant in later medicine, that four humors (fluids) made up the human body: blood, phlegm, black bile, and yellow bile. Health depended on keeping the proper balance among them; being healthy was to be "in good humor." This system for understanding the body corresponded to the division of the inanimate world into four elements: earth, air, fire, and water.

Hippocrates taught that the physician's most important duty was to base his knowledge on careful observation of patients and their responses to different treatments. Clinical experience, not abstract theory or religious belief, was the proper foundation for establishing effective cures. By putting his innovative ideas and practices to the test in competition with those of traditional medicine, Hippocrates established the truth of his principle, which later became a cornerstone of scientific medicine.

The Development of Greek Tragedy

Ideas about the problematic relationship between gods and humans inspired Golden Age Athens's most prominent cultural innovation: tragic drama. Plays called tragedies were presented in a contest for playwrights held before large audiences as part of multiday festivals for the god Dionysus. Most Greek plays have not survived: only thirty-three still exist of the hundreds of tragedies produced at Athens.

Public revenues and mandatory contributions by the rich paid for Athenian dramas. The competition in this public art began with an official choosing three authors from a pool of applicants. Each of the finalists presented four plays in one day: three tragedies in a row (a trilogy), followed by a semicomic play featuring satyrs (mythical half-man, half-animal beings) to end the day on a lighter note. Tragedies were written in verses of solemn language, and many were based on stories about the violent possibilities when gods and humans interacted. The plots often ended with a resolution to the trouble—but only after enormous suffering and loss.

At Athens, as in many other cities in Greece, plays were presented during the daytime in an outdoor theater. The one at Athens was built into the southern slope of the acropolis and held about fourteen thousand spectators overlooking an open, circular area in front of a slightly raised stage. A tragedy had eighteen cast members, all of whom were men: three actors to play the speaking roles (both male and female characters) and fifteen chorus members. Although the chorus leader sometimes engaged in dialogue with the actors, the chorus primarily performed songs and dances in the circular area in front of the stage, called the orchestra.

A successful tragedy offered a vivid spectacle. The chorus wore elaborate costumes and performed intricate dance routines. The actors, who wore masks, used broad gestures and booming voices to reach the upper tier of seats. A powerful voice was crucial to a tragic actor because words represented the heart of the plays, which featured extensive dialogue and long speeches. Special effects were popular. Actors playing the roles of gods swung from a crane to fly suddenly onto the stage. Actors playing lead roles, called the protagonists ("first competitors"), competed to win the "best actor" award. A skilled

Theater of Dionysus at Athens Around 14,000 spectators packed this theater in Athens on the southern side of the acropolis as the audience for plays (tragedies and comedies) presented as part of multiday festivals honoring the god Dionysus. Originally the theater had only a few permanent seats in the front rows for VIPs, but eventually stone seating was built on the slope of the hill, curving around the flat circular area down front where the chorus would dance and sing; the actors appeared on a temporary stage set up at the edge of this area. (Katie Singletary/age-fotostock.)

protagonist was so important to a play's success that actors were assigned by lottery to the competing playwrights so that all three had an equal chance to have a winning cast. Great actors became enormously popular.

Playwrights came from the social elite because only men with wealth could afford the amount of time and learning this work demanded. They served as authors, directors, producers, musical composers, choreographers, and occasionally actors for their own plays. As citizens, playwrights fulfilled the military and political obligations of Athenian men. The best-known Athenian tragedians—Aeschylus (525–456 B.C.E.), Sophocles (c. 496–406 B.C.E.), and Euripides (c. 485–406 B.C.E.)—all served in the army, and Sophocles was elected to Athens's board of "generals." Authors of plays competed from a love of honor, not money. The prizes, determined by a board of judges, awarded high prestige but little cash. The competition was regarded as so important that any judge who took a bribe in awarding prizes was put to death.

Tragedy's plots set out the difficulties of telling right from wrong when humans came into conflict and the gods became involved. Even though most tragedies were based on stories that referred to a legendary time before city-states existed, such as the period of the Trojan War, the plays' moral issues were relevant to the society and obligations of citizens in a city-state. The plays suggest that human beings learn only by suffering but that the gods could, if they wished, provide justice in the long run. For example, Aeschylus's trilogy *Oresteia* (458 B.C.E.) explains the divine origins of democratic Athens's court system through the story of the gods finally stopping the murderous violence in the family of Orestes, son of King Agamemnon, the Greek leader against Troy.

Sophocles' *Antigone* (441 B.C.E.) presents the story of the cursed family of Oedipus of Thebes as a drama of harsh conflict between a courageous woman, Antigone, and the city-state's stern male leader, her uncle Creon. After her brother dies in a failed rebellion, Antigone insists on her family's moral obligation to bury its dead in obedience to divine command. Creon, however, takes harsh action to preserve order and protect community values by prohibiting the burial of his traitorous nephew. In a horrifying story of raging anger and suicide that features one of the most famous heroines of Western literature, Sophocles exposes the right and wrong on each side of the conflict. His play offers no easy resolution of the competing interests of divinely sanctioned moral tradition and the state's political rules.

By basing their plots on difficult moral dilemmas, authors of tragedies stimulated spectators to consider the dangers to democracy from ignorance, arrogance, and violence. Audiences reacted strongly to the messages of these tragedies. For one thing, spectators realized that the plays' central characters were people who experienced disaster even though they held positions of power and prestige. The characters' reversals of fortune came about not because they were absolute villains but because, as humans, they were susceptible to a lethal mixture of error, ignorance, and **hubris** (violent arrogance that transformed one's competitive spirit into a self-destructive force). The Athenian Empire was at its height when audiences at Athens attended the tragedies written by competing playwrights. Thoughtful playgoers could reflect on the possibility that Athens's current power and prestige, managed as they were by humans, might fall victim to the same kinds of mistakes and conflicts that brought down the heroes and heroines of tragedy. Thus, these publicly funded plays both entertained through their spectacle and educated through their stories and words. In particular, they reminded male citizens—who governed the city-state in its assembly, council, and courts—that success created complex moral problems that self-righteous arrogance turned into community-wide catastrophes.

The Development of Greek Comedy

Golden Age Athens developed comedy as its second distinctive form of public theater. Like tragedies, comedies were written in verse, performed in festivals honoring the god Dionysus, and subsidized with public funds and contributions from the rich. Unlike tragedies, comedies commented *directly* on public policy and *bluntly* criticized current politicians and intellectuals. They also portrayed women as powerfully concerned with the fate of their city-state. The plots and casts of comedies presented outrageous fantasies of contemporary life. Comic choruses, which had twenty-four dancing singers, could be colorfully costumed as talking birds or dancing clouds, or an actor could fly on a giant dung beetle to visit the gods.

Authors competed to win the award for the festival's best comedy by creating beautiful poetry, raising laughs with constant jokes and puns, and mocking self-important citizens and political leaders. The humor, delivered in a stream of imaginative profanity full of "dirty words," frequently concerned sex and bodily functions. Well-known men of the day were targets for insults as cowards or weaklings. Women characters when portrayed as figures of fun and ridicule seem to have been fictional, to protect the dignity of actual female citizens.

Athenian comedies often made fun of political leaders. As the leading politician of radical democracy, Pericles was the subject of fierce criticism in comedy. Comic playwrights ridiculed his policies, his love life, even the shape of his skull ("Old Turnip Head" was a favorite insult). Aristophanes (c. 455–385 B.C.E.), Athens's most famous comic playwright, so fiercely satirized Cleon, the city's most prominent leader early in the Peloponnesian War, that Cleon sued him. A citizen jury ruled in Aristophanes' favor, upholding the Athenian tradition of free speech.

In several of Aristophanes' comedies, the main characters are powerful women who force the men of Athens to change their policy to preserve family life and the city-state. These plays even criticize the assembly's policy during wartime. Most famous is *Lysistrata* (411 B.C.E.), named after the female lead character of the play. In this fantasy, the women of Athens and Sparta unite to force their husbands to end the Peloponnesian War. To make the men agree to a peace treaty, they first seize the acropolis, where Athens's financial reserves are kept, to prevent the men from squandering them further on the war. They then use sarcasm and pitchers of cold water to beat back an attack on their position by the old men who have remained in Athens while the younger men are away at war with Sparta. Above all, the women steel themselves to refuse to sleep with their husbands returning from battle. The effects of their sex strike on the men, portrayed in a series of explicit episodes, finally drive the warriors to make peace.

Lysistrata presents women acting bravely and aggressively against men who seem bent on destroying traditional family life—the men are absent from home for long stretches while on military campaigns and ruin the city-state by prolonging a pointless war. Lysistrata insists that women have the intelligence and judgment to make political decisions: "I am a woman, and, yes, I have brains. And I'm pretty good in my judgment. My education hasn't been bad: it came from my listening often to the conversations of my father and the elders among the men." Lysistrata's old-fashioned training and good sense allow her to see what needs to be done to protect the community. Like the heroines of tragedy, Lysistrata is a conservative, even a reactionary. She wants to put things back the way they were before the war fractured family life. To do that, she has to act like an impatient revolutionary. That irony sums up the challenge that fifth-century B.C.E. Athens faced in trying to resolve the tension between the dynamic innovation of its Golden Age and the importance of tradition in Greek life. At the same time, the plot of this comic play, like that of others by Aristophanes such as *Women at the Assembly*, reveals that men in fact recognized the political capability of women. (Compare the speech by Melanippe from a tragedy by Euripides quoted in Contrasting Views on pages 88–89.)

The remarkable freedom of speech of Athenian comedy allowed frank, even brutal, commentary on current issues and personalities. It is significant that this energetic, critical drama emerged in Athens at the same time as radical democracy, in the mid-fifth century B.C.E. The feeling that all (male) citizens should have a stake in determining their government's policies evidently fueled a passion for using biting humor to keep the community's (male) leaders from becoming arrogant and aloof.

REVIEW QUESTION
How did new ways of thinking in the Golden Age change traditional ways of life?

The End of Athens's Golden Age, 431–403 B.C.E.

A war between Athens and Sparta (431–404 B.C.E.) ended the Golden Age. This long conflict is called the Peloponnesian War because it matched Sparta's Peloponnese-based alliance against Athens and the Delian League. The war started, according to Thucydides, because the growth of Athenian power alarmed the Spartans, who feared that their interests and allies would fall to the Athenians' restless energy. Pericles, who deeply distrusted the Spartans, persuaded Athens's assembly to take a hard line when Sparta demanded that Athens ease restrictions on city-states allied with Sparta. Corinth and Megara, crucial Spartan allies, complained bitterly to Sparta about Athens. Finally, Corinth told Sparta to attack Athens, or else Corinth and its navy would change sides to the Athenian alliance. Sparta's leaders therefore gave Athens an ultimatum—stop mistreating our allies. Pericles convinced the Athenian voters to reject the ultimatum on the grounds that Sparta had refused to settle the dispute through the third-party arbitration process called for by the 446–445 B.C.E. treaty. Pericles' critics claimed he was insisting on war against Sparta to revive his fading popularity. His supporters replied that he was defending Athenian honor and protecting foreign trade, a key to the economy. By 431 B.C.E., these disputes had shattered the peace treaty between Athens and Sparta that Pericles had negotiated fifteen years before.

The Peloponnesian War, 431–404 B.C.E.

Lasting longer than any previous war in Greek history, the Peloponnesian War (Map 3.3) took place above all because Spartan leaders believed they had to fight now to keep the Athenians from using their superior long-distance offensive power—the Delian League's naval forces—to destroy Sparta's control of their Peloponnesian League. Sparta made the first strike of the war, but the conflict dragged on so long because the Athenian assembly failed to negotiate peace with Sparta when it had the chance and because the Spartans were willing to make a deal with Persia to secure money to build a fleet to win the war.

Dramatic evidence for the anger that fueled the war comes from Thucydides' version of Pericles' stern oration to the Athenian assembly about not yielding to Spartan pressure:

> If we do go to war, have no thought that you went to war over a trivial affair. For you this trifling matter is the assurance and the proof of your determination. If you yield to their demands, they will immediately confront you with some larger demand, since they will think that you only gave way on the first point out of fear. But if you stand firm, you will show them that they have to deal with you as equals. . . . When our equals, without agreeing to arbitration of the matter under dispute, make claims on us as neighbors and state those claims as

commands, it would be no better than slavery to give in to them, no matter how large or how small the claim may be.

When Sparta invaded Athenian territory, Pericles advised a two-pronged strategy to win what he saw would be a long war: (1) use the navy to raid the lands of Sparta and its allies; and (2) avoid large infantry battles with the superior land forces of the Spartans, even when the enemy hoplites plunder the Athenian countryside outside the city. Athens's citizens could retreat to safety behind the city's impregnable walls, massive barriers of stone that encircled the city and the harbor, with the fortification known as the Long Walls protecting the land corridor between the urban center and the port (Map 3.2 on page 90). He insisted that Athenians should sacrifice their vast and valuable country property to save their population. In the end, he predicted, Athens, with its superior resources, would win a war of attrition, especially because the Spartans, lacking a base in Athenian territory, could not support long invasions.

Pericles' strategy and leadership might have made Athens the winner in the long run, but an epidemic struck Athens in 430 B.C.E., killing Pericles the next year and depriving Athens of his leadership. This plague ravaged Athens's population for four years, killing thousands among the people packed in behind the walls to avoid Spartan attacks. Despite their losses and their fears that the gods had sent the disease to punish them, the Athenians fought on. Over time, however, they abandoned the disciplined strategy that Pericles' prudent plan had required. The generals elected after his death, especially Cleon, pursued a much more aggressive strategy. At first this succeeded, especially when a group of Spartan hoplites laid down their arms after being blockaded by Cleon's forces at Pylos in 425 B.C.E. Their surrender shocked the Greek world and led Sparta to ask for a truce, but the Athenian assembly refused, believing their army could now crush their enemy. When the daring Spartan general Brasidas captured Athens's possessions in northern Greece in 424 and 423 B.C.E., however, he turned the tide of war in the other direction by crippling the Athenian supply of timber and precious metals from this crucial region. When Brasidas and Cleon were both killed in 422 B.C.E., mutual exhaustion made Sparta and Athens agree to a peace treaty in 421 B.C.E.

Athens's most innovative and confident new general, Alcibiades, soon persuaded the assembly to reject the peace and to attack Spartan allies in 418 B.C.E. In 416–415 B.C.E., the Athenians and their allies overpowered the tiny and strategically meaningless Aegean island of Melos because it refused to abandon its allegiance to Sparta. Thucydides, in his history of the Peloponnesian War, dramatically represents Athenian messengers telling the Melians they had to be conquered to show that Athens permitted no defiance to its dominance. Following their victory, the Athenians executed the Melian men, sold the women and children into slavery, and colonized the island.

The turning point in the war came soon thereafter, when, in 415 B.C.E., Alcibiades persuaded the Athenian assembly to launch the greatest and most expensive campaign in Greek history. The expedition of 415 B.C.E. was directed against Sparta's allies in Sicily, far to the west. Alcibiades had dazzled his fellow citizens with the dream of conquering that rich island and especially its greatest city, Syracuse. Alcibiades' political rivals had him removed from his

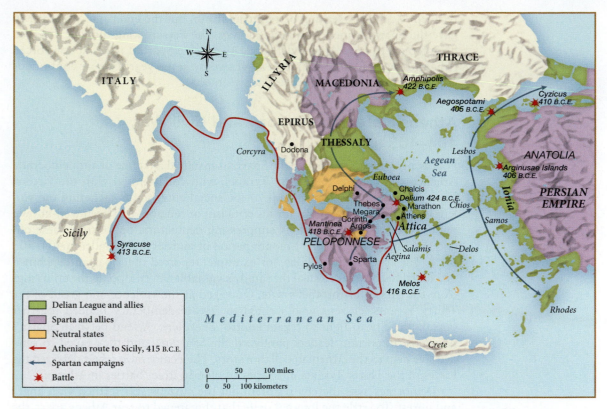

MAP 3.3 The Peloponnesian War, 431–404 B.C.E.
For the first ten years, the Peloponnesian War's battles took place largely in mainland Greece. Sparta, whose armies usually avoided distant campaigns, shocked Athens when its general Brasidas led successful attacks against Athenian forces in northeast Greece. Athens stunned the entire Greek world in the war's next phase by launching a huge naval expedition against Spartan allies in far-off Sicily. The last ten years of the war saw the action move to the east, on and along the western coast of Anatolia and its islands, on the boundary of the Persian Empire. Feeling threatened, the Persian king helped the Spartans build a navy there to defeat the famous Athenian fleet. Look at the route of Athens's expedition to Sicily; why do you think the Athenians took this longer voyage, rather than a more direct route?

command, however, and the other generals blundered into catastrophic defeat in Sicily in 413 B.C.E. (see Map 3.3). The victorious Syracusans destroyed the allied invasion fleet and packed the survivors like sardines into quarries under the blazing sun, with no toilets and only half a pint of drinking water and a handful of food a day.

On the advice of Alcibiades, who had deserted to their side in anger at having lost his command, the Spartans in 413 B.C.E. seized a permanent base of operations in the Athenian countryside for year-round raids, now that Athens was too weak to drive them out. Constant Spartan attacks devastated Athenian agriculture, and twenty thousand slave workers crippled production in Athens's silver mines by deserting to the enemy. The democratic assembly became so upset over these losses that in 411 B.C.E. it voted itself out of existence in favor of an emergency government run by the wealthier citizens. When an oligarchic group illegally took charge, however, the citizens restored the radical democracy and kept fighting for another seven years. They even recalled Alcibiades, seeking better generalship, but the end came when Persia gave the Spartans money to build a navy. The Persian king thought it served his interests to have Athens defeated. Aggressive Spartan naval action forced Athens to surrender in 404 B.C.E. After twenty-seven years of near-continuous war, the Athenians were at their enemy's mercy.

Athens Defeated: Tyranny and Civil War, 404–403 B.C.E.

Following Athens's surrender, the Spartans installed a regime of antidemocratic Athenians known as the Thirty Tyrants, who collaborated with the victors. The collaborators were members of the social elite; some, including the violent leader Critias, infamous for his criticism of religion, had been well-known pupils of the Sophists. Brutally suppressing democratic opposition, these oligarchs embarked on an eight-month period of murder and plunder in 404–403 B.C.E. The speechwriter Lysias, for example, reported that Spartan henchmen murdered his brother to steal the family's valuables, even ripping the gold rings from the ears of his brother's wife. Outraged at the violence and greed of the Thirty Tyrants, citizens who wanted to restore democracy banded together outside the city to fight to regain control of Athens. A feud between Sparta's two most important leaders paralyzed the Spartans, and they failed to send decisive help to the Athenian collaborators. The democratic rebels defeated the forces of the Thirty Tyrants in a series of bloody street battles in Athens.

Democracy was thereby restored, but the citizens still seethed with anger and unrest. To settle the internal strife that threatened to tear Athens apart, the newly restored democratic assembly voted the first known amnesty in Western history, a truce agreement forbidding any official charges or recriminations from crimes committed in 404–403 B.C.E. Agreeing not to pursue grievances in court was the price of peace. As would soon become clear, however, some Athenians harbored grudges that no amnesty could dispel. In addition, Athens's financial and military strength had been shattered. At the end of the Golden Age, Athenians worried about how to remake their lives and restore the reputation that their city-state's innovative accomplishments had produced.

REVIEW QUESTION
What factors determined the course of the Peloponnesian War?

Conclusion

The Greek city-states that united early in the fifth century B.C.E. to resist the Persian Empire surprised everyone by defeating the invaders and preserving their political independence. Following the unexpected Greek victory, Athens competed with Sparta for power. The Athenian Golden Age that followed was based on empire and trade, and the city's riches funded the widening of democracy and famous cultural accomplishments.

As the money poured in, Athens built glorious and expensive temples, legislated pay for service in many government offices to strengthen democracy, and assembled the Mediterranean's most powerful navy as leaders of the

MAPPING THE WEST

Classical Greece, c. 400 B.C.E.

Greece, Europe, and the Mediterranean, 400 B.C.E.
No single power controlled the Mediterranean region at the end of the fifth century B.C.E. In the west, the Phoenician city of Carthage and the Greek cities on Sicily and in southern Italy were rivals for the riches to be won by trade. In the east, the Spartans, confident after their recent victory over Athens in the Peloponnesian War, tried to become an international power outside the mainland for the first time in their history by sending campaigns into Anatolia. This aggressive action aroused stiff opposition from the Persians because it threatened their westernmost imperial provinces. There was to be no peace and quiet in the Mediterranean, even after the twenty-seven years of the Peloponnesian War.

Analyzing the Map: The city of Syracuse is located on which large Mediterranean island?

Making Connections: To judge from the territories indicated on the map, why would it have been unexpected for a coalition of Greek city-states to defeat the Persian Empire?

Delian League—called the Athenian Empire by its critics. The poor men who rowed the ships demanded greater democracy; such demands led to political and legal reforms that guaranteed fairer treatment for all. Pericles became the most famous politician of the Golden Age by leading the drive for radical democracy.

Religious practice and women's lives reflected the strong grip of tradition on everyday life, but innovations in education and philosophy created social tension. The Sophists' moral relativism disturbed tradition-minded people, as did Socrates' definition of excellence, which questioned ordinary people's love of wealth and success. Art and architecture broke out of old forms, promoting an impression of balanced motion rather than stability, while medicine gained a more scientific basis. Tragedy and comedy developed at Athens as competitive public theater commenting on contemporary social and political issues.

The Athenians' harsh treatment of allies and enemies combined with Spartan fears about Athenian power to bring on the disastrous Peloponnesian War. Nearly three decades of battle brought the stars of the Greek Golden Age crashing to earth: by 400 B.C.E., the Athenians found themselves in the same situation as in 500 B.C.E., fearful of Spartan power and worried whether the world's most direct democracy could survive.

Chapter 3 Review

Key Terms and People

Be sure that you can identify the term or person and explain its historical significance.

Themistocles (p. 81)	ostracism (p. 86)	hetaira (p. 95)
Delian League (p. 84)	agora (p. 90)	Sophists (p. 97)
triremes (p. 84)	Parthenon (p. 90)	Socratic method (p. 100)
Pericles (p. 86)	mystery cults (p. 93)	hubris (p. 105)
radical democracy (p. 86)	metic (p. 94)	

Review Questions

1. How did the Greeks overcome the dangers of the Persian invasions?

2. What factors produced political change in fifth-century B.C.E. Athens?

3. How did new ways of thinking in the Golden Age change traditional ways of life?

4. What factors determined the course of the Peloponnesian War?

Making Connections

1. What were the most significant differences between Archaic Age Greece and Golden Age Greece?

2. For what sorts of things did Greeks of the Golden Age spend public funds? Why did they believe these things were worth the expense?

3. What price, in all senses, did Athens and the rest of Greece pay for the Golden Age? Was it worth it?

Important Events

500–323 B.C.E.	Classical Age of Greece
499–479 B.C.E.	Wars between Persia and Greece
490 B.C.E.	Battle of Marathon
480 B.C.E.	Battle of Salamis
480–479 B.C.E.	Xerxes invades Greece

461 B.C.E.	Ephialtes reforms Athenian court system
Early 450s B.C.E.	Pericles introduces pay for officeholders in Athenian democracy
451 B.C.E.	Pericles restricts Athenian citizenship to children whose parents are both citizens
450 B.C.E.	Protagoras and other Sophists begin to teach in Athens
446–445 B.C.E. **(winter)**	Peace treaty between Athens and Sparta, intended to last thirty years
441 B.C.E.	Sophocles presents tragedy *Antigone*
431–404 B.C.E.	Peloponnesian War
420s B.C.E.	Herodotus finishes *Histories*
415–413 B.C.E.	Enormous Athenian military expedition against Sicily
411 B.C.E.	Aristophanes presents the comedy *Lysistrata*
404–403 B.C.E.	Rule of Thirty Tyrants at Athens
403 B.C.E.	Restoration of democracy in Athens

Consider three events

Ephialtes reforms Athenian court system (461 B.C.E.), Protagoras and other Sophists begin to teach in Athens (450 B.C.E.), and Aristophanes presents the comedy *Lysistrata* (411 B.C.E.). How did the principles of radical democracy during the Athenian Golden Age help to make possible these different events?

Suggested References

The Greek city-states, especially Athens, reached the height of their political, economic, and military power in the fifth century B.C.E., following the defeat of the Persian invasion of mainland Greece; scholars continue to investigate how the frequent wars of this period influenced not only the democracy of Athens but also the famous dramatists and philosophers of this so-called Golden Age.

Blundell, Sue. *Women in Ancient Greece*. 1995.

Camp, John M. *The Archaeology of Athens*. 2004.

*Dillon, John, and Tania Gergel. *The Greek Sophists*. 2003.

Foxhall, Lin. *Studying Gender in Classical Antiquity*. 2013.

*Grene, David, and Richmond Lattimore, eds. *The Complete Greek Tragedies*. 1992.

Herman, Gabriel. *Morality and Behavior in Democratic Athens*. 2006.

*Herodotus. *The Histories*. Trans. Aubrey de Sélincourt. Revised by John Marincola. Rev. ed. 2003.

Martin, Thomas R. *Pericles: A Biography in Context*. 2016.

Parker, Robert. *Athenian Religion: A History*. 1996.

Patterson, Cynthia B. *The Family in Greek History*. 1998.

*Strassler, Robert B., ed. *The Landmark Thucydides: A Comprehensive Guide to the Peloponnesian War*. 1996.

Strauss, Barry. *The Battle of Salamis: The Naval Encounter That Saved Greece — and Western Civilization*. 2005.

Thorley, John. *Athenian Democracy*. 2004.

Waters, Matt. *Ancient Persia: A Concise History of the Achaemenid Empire, 550–330 BCE*. 2014.

Wees, Han van, ed. *War and Violence in Ancient Greece*. 2000.

———————

*Primary source.

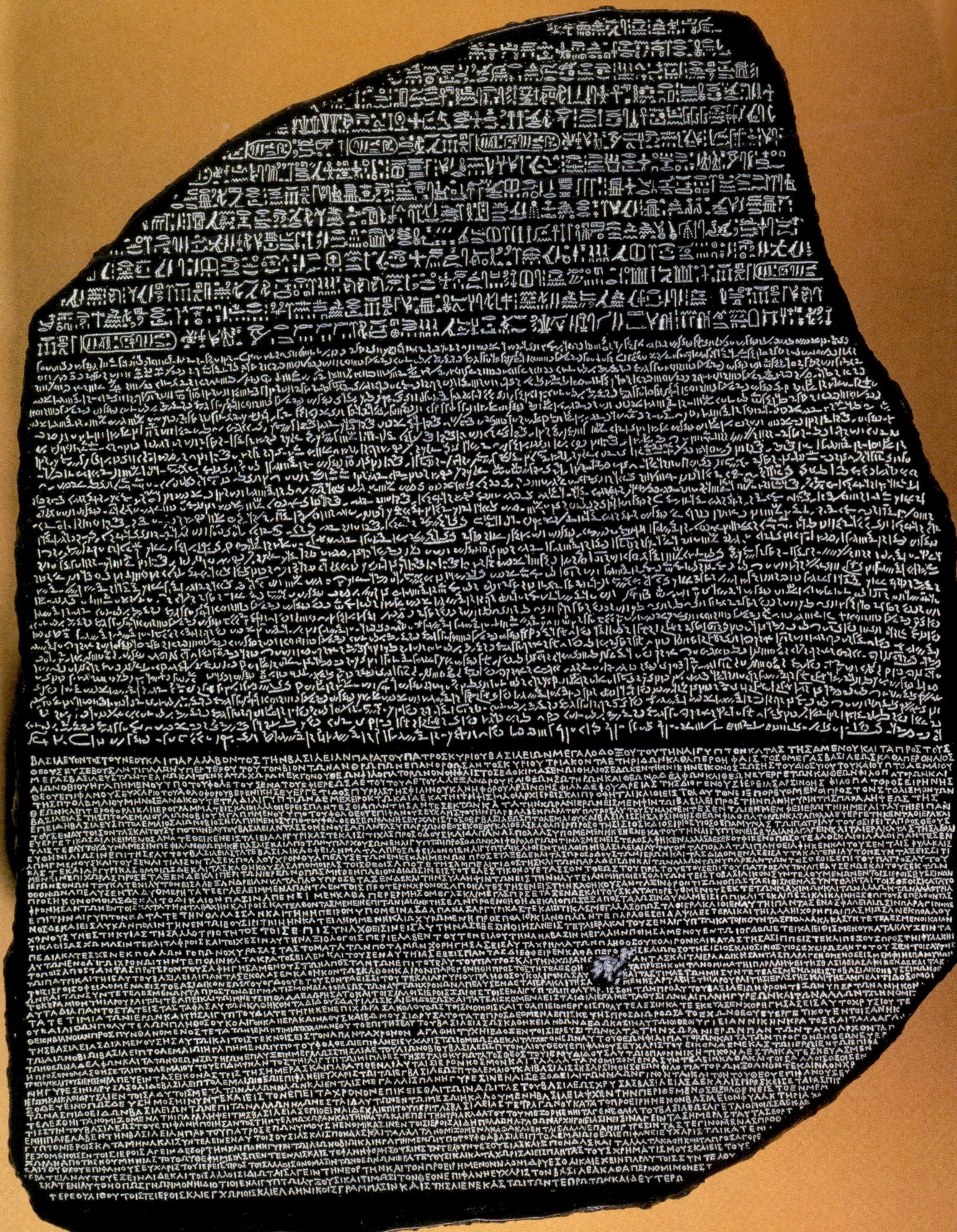

From the Classical to the Hellenistic World

400–30 B.C.E.

About 255 B.C.E., an Egyptian camel trader far from home sent a letter of complaint to his Greek employer back in Egypt:

> You know that when you left me in Syria with Krotos I followed all your instructions concerning the camels and behaved blamelessly towards you. But Krotos has ignored your orders to pay me my salary; I've received nothing despite asking him for my money over and over. He just tells me to go away. I waited a long time for you to come, but when I no longer had life's necessities and couldn't get help anywhere, I had to run away . . . to keep from starving to death. . . . I am desperate summer and winter. . . . They have treated me like dirt because I am not a Greek. I therefore beg you, please, order them to pay me so that I won't go hungry just because I don't know how to speak Greek.

The trader's plea for help from a foreigner living in his homeland reflects the changes in the eastern Mediterranean world during the Hellenistic Age (323–30 B.C.E.). The movement of Greeks into the Near East increased the cultural interaction between the Greek and the Near Eastern worlds and set a new course for Western civilization in politics, art, philosophy, science, and religion. Above all, Alexander the Great (356–323 B.C.E.) changed the course of history by conquering the Persian Empire, leading an army of Greeks and Macedonians to the border of

▬▬▬▬▬

«The Rosetta Stone Dug out of the wall of a fort in 1799 by a soldier in Napoleon's army near Rosetta, in the Nile River delta, this Hellenistic inscription in two different languages and three different forms of writing unlocked the lost secrets of how to read Egyptian hieroglyphs. The bands of text repeat the same message (priests praising King Ptolemy V in 196 B.C.E.) in hieroglyphs, demotic (a cursive form of Egyptian invented around 600 B.C.E.), and Greek. Bilingual texts were necessary to reach the mixed population of Hellenistic Egypt. Scholars deciphered the hieroglyphs by comparing them to the Greek version. They started with the hieroglyphs surrounded by an oval, which they correctly theorized were royal names. (Granger/Granger—All rights reserved.)

India, taking Near Easterners into his army and imperial administration, and planting colonies of Greeks as far east as Afghanistan. His amazing expedition shocked the world and spurred great change in Western civilization by combining Near Eastern and Greek traditions as never before.

Politics changed in the Greek world when Alexander's successors (who had been commanders in his army) created new kingdoms that became the dominant powers of the Hellenistic Age. The existing Greek city-states retained local rule but lost their independence in international affairs. The Hellenistic kings imported Greeks to fill royal offices, man their armies, and run businesses, generating tension with their non-Greek subjects. Egyptians, Syrians, or Mesopotamians who wanted to rise in Hellenistic society had to win the support of these Greeks and learn their language.

The Near East's local cultures interacted with the Greek overlords' culture to spawn a multicultural synthesis. Although Hellenistic royal society always remained hierarchical, its kings and queens financed innovations in art, philosophy, religion, and science that combined Near Eastern and Greek traditions. The Hellenistic kingdoms collapsed in the second and first centuries B.C.E., when the Romans overthrew them one by one. But the cultural interaction between diverse peoples and the emergence of new ideas—unintended consequences of Alexander's military campaigns—would strongly influence Roman civilization.

CHAPTER FOCUS
What were the major political and cultural changes in the Hellenistic Age?

Classical Greece after the Peloponnesian War, 400–350 B.C.E.

The Greek city-states regained political stability after the Peloponnesian War (431–404 B.C.E.), but daily life remained financially hard for many. The war's aftermath dramatically affected Greek philosophy. At Athens, citizens who blamed Socrates for inspiring the Thirty Tyrants' crimes prosecuted him in court; the jury condemned him to death. His execution helped persuade the philosophers Plato and Aristotle to detest democracy and develop new ways of thinking about right and wrong and how human beings should live.

CHAPTER TIMELINE

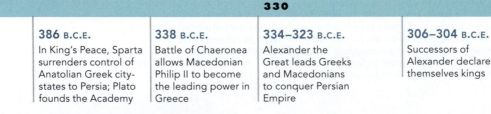

| **399 B.C.E.** Socrates is executed | **362 B.C.E.** Battle of Mantinea leaves power vacuum in a disunited Greece | | **335 B.C.E.** Aristotle founds the Lyceum | **307 B.C.E.** Epicurus founds his philosophical group in Athens | **c. 300 B.C.E.** Euclid teaches geometry at Alexandria | **300–260 B.C.E.** Theocritus writes poetry at Ptolemaic court |

400   **330**   **240**

| | **386 B.C.E.** In King's Peace, Sparta surrenders control of Anatolian Greek city-states to Persia; Plato founds the Academy | **338 B.C.E.** Battle of Chaeronea allows Macedonian Philip II to become the leading power in Greece | **334–323 B.C.E.** Alexander the Great leads Greeks and Macedonians to conquer Persian Empire | | **306–304 B.C.E.** Successors of Alexander declare themselves kings |

The Greek city-states' continuing competition for power in the fourth century B.C.E. drained their resources. Sparta's attempt to dominate central Greece and western Anatolia by collaborating with the Persians provoked violent resistance from Thebes and Athens. By the 350s B.C.E., the Greek city-states had so weakened themselves that they were unable to prevent the Macedonian kingdom from taking control of Greece.

Athens's Recovery after the Peloponnesian War

The devastation of Athens's economy in the Peloponnesian War and overcrowding of refugees from the country in the wartime city produced social conflict. Life became difficult for middle-class women whose male relatives had been killed. With no man to provide for them and their children, many war widows had to work outside the home. The only jobs open to them — such as wet-nursing, weaving, or laboring in vineyards — were low-paying.

Resourceful Athenians found ways to profit from women's skills. The family of one of Socrates' friends, for example, fell into poverty when several widowed sisters, nieces, and female cousins moved in. The friend complained to Socrates that he was too poor to support his new family of fourteen plus their slaves. Socrates replied that the women knew how to make clothing, so they should sell it. This plan succeeded financially, but the women then complained that Socrates' friend was the household's only member who ate without working. Socrates advised the man to reply that the women should think of him as sheep did a guard dog — he earned his share of the food by keeping the wolves away.

Athens's postwar economy recovered somewhat as international trade was revived once its Long Walls, which protected the transportation corridor from the city to the port, were rebuilt and mining for silver to produce the city's coinage resumed. Greek businesses producing manufactured goods were small and usually family-run; the largest known was a shield-making company with 120 slave workers. Some changes occurred in occupations formerly defined by gender. For example, men began working alongside women in cloth production when the first commercial weaving shops outside the home sprang up.

195 B.C.E.
Seleucid queen
Laodice endows
dowries for girls

30 B.C.E.
Cleopatra VII dies
and Rome takes over
Ptolemaic Empire

210   **120**   **30**

167 B.C.E.
Maccabee revolt after
Antiochus IV turns temple
in Jerusalem into a Greek
sanctuary

Silver Coins of Athens
The city-state of ancient Athens owned rich silver mines that financed its silver coinage, famous around the Greek world for purity and reliability. This coin from the fifth century B.C.E. was a decadrachm ("ten drachmas"), which was the amount that a worker or rower in the Athenian navy earned in ten days. The images show Athena, the city-state's main goddess, and an owl with an olive branch, also symbols of Athena. The style of the images was kept old-fashioned and mostly unchanging so as not to harm the trust that people in foreign lands had in accepting Athenian coins in trade and commerce as a form of international currency.

Some women made careers in the arts, especially painting and music, which men had traditionally dominated.

Making a living remained a struggle for working people. Most workers earned barely enough to feed and clothe their families. They ate two meals a day, with bread baked from barley as their main food; only rich people could afford wheat bread. A family bought bread from small bakery stands, often run by women, or made it at home, with the wife directing the slaves in grinding the grain, shaping the dough, and baking it in a clay oven heated by charcoal. People topped their bread with greens, beans, onions, garlic, olives, fruit, and cheese. The few households rich enough to afford meat boiled or grilled it over a fire. Everyone of all ages drank wine, diluted with water, with every meal.

The Execution of Socrates, 399 B.C.E.

Socrates, Athens's best known philosopher in the Golden Age of the fifth century, fell victim to the bitterness many Athenians felt about the rule of the Thirty Tyrants following the Peloponnesian War. Some prominent Athenians hated Socrates because his follower Critias had been one of the Thirty Tyrants' most violent leaders. These citizens charged Socrates with impiety, claiming he rejected the city-state's gods, introduced new divinities, and lured young men away from Athenian moral traditions. Speaking to a jury of 501 male citizens, Socrates refused to beg for sympathy, as defendants customarily did, and repeated his dedication to goading his fellow citizens into examining how to live justly. He vowed to remain their stinging gadfly.

When the jurors narrowly voted to convict Socrates, Athenian law required them to decide between the penalty proposed by the prosecutors and that proposed by the defendant. The prosecutors proposed death. Socrates dramatically rejected the tradition of proposing exile to escape execution, saying he deserved a reward for his conduct; horrified, his friends made him propose a fine as his penalty. The jury chose death, requiring him to drink a poison concocted from powdered hemlock. Socrates calmly accepted his sentence with the words, "No evil can come to a good man either in life or in death, and the gods do not fail to pay

Athens's Long Walls as Rebuilt after the Peloponnesian War

attention to what he does." Many Athenians soon regretted Socrates' execution as a tragic mistake and a severe blow to their reputation.

The Philosophy of Plato

Socrates' death helped make his follower **Plato** (429–348 B.C.E.) hate democracy. Plato, who became Greece's most famous philosopher of all time, started out as a political consultant supporting philosopher-tyrants as the best rulers, but their misdeeds performed against his advice convinced him that politicians could never avoid violence and greed. So, he turned to talking and writing about philosophy as the guide to life, establishing a school in Athens around 386 B.C.E. Called the Academy, it was an association of apparently only men studying philosophy, mathematics, and theoretical astronomy under the leader's guidance. It attracted intellectuals to Athens for the next nine hundred years, and Plato's ideas about the nature of reality, ethics, and politics have remained central to philosophy and political science to this day.

Plato's interests included astronomy, mathematics, political philosophy, ethics, and **metaphysics** (ideas about the ultimate nature of reality beyond the reach of the human senses). Plato wrote dialogues, to provoke readers into thoughtful reflection without prescribing definite beliefs. Nevertheless, he always maintained one essential idea based on his view of reality: ultimate moral qualities are universal, unchanging, and absolute. He emphatically rejected the relativism espoused by the Sophists.

Plato's dialogues explore his theory that justice, goodness, beauty, and equality exist on their own in a higher realm. He used the word *Forms* (or *Ideas*) to describe the abstract, invariable, and ultimate nature of these ethical qualities. Moreover, he argued that the Forms are the only genuine reality. All things that humans perceive with their senses are only dim and imperfect copies of these metaphysical absolutes.

Plato believed that humans possess immortal souls distinct from their bodies; this idea established the concept of **dualism**, a separation between soul (or mind) and body. Plato further explained that the human soul possesses preexisting knowledge put there by a god. Humans' present, impure existence is only a temporary stage in cosmic existence because, while the body does not last, the soul is immortal. Plato argued that people must seek perfect order and purity in their souls by using rational thought to control thoughtless and therefore harmful desires. People who yield to such desires fail to consider the future of their body and soul. The desire to drink too much alcohol, for example, is flawed because the binge drinker fails to consider the painful hangover that will follow.

Plato presented his most famous ideas on politics and justice in his dialogue *The Republic*. This work, whose Greek title *Politeia* (pol-ee-TAY-uh) means "system of government," discusses the nature of justice and the reasons people should never commit injustice. Democracy, Plato wrote, fails to produce justice because people cannot rise above their own self-interests to knowledge of the transcendent reality of universal truth. Justice can come only under the rule of an enlightened oligarchy or monarchy.

Plato's *Republic* describes an ideal society with a hierarchy of three classes distinguished by their ability to grasp the truth of Forms. Plato did not think humans could actually create the model society described in *The Republic*, but he did believe that imagining it was an important way to help people learn to live justly. The highest class in his envisioned hierarchy consists of the rulers, or "guardians," who must be educated in mathematics, astronomy, and metaphysics. Next are the "auxiliaries," who defend the community. "Producers" make up the bottom class; they grow food and make objects for the other classes. According to Plato's *Republic*, women can be guardians because they possess the same virtues and abilities as men, except that the average woman has less physical strength than the average man. To minimize distraction, guardians have neither private property nor nuclear families. Male and female guardians live in houses shared in common, eat in the same dining halls, and exercise in the same gymnasia. They have sex with various partners so that the best women can mate with the best men to produce the best children. The children are raised together by special caretakers, not their parents. Guardians who achieve the highest level of knowledge can rule as philosopher-kings.

Aristotle, Scientist and Philosopher

After studying with Plato, **Aristotle** (384–322 B.C.E.) founded his own school, the **Lyceum**, in Athens. He taught his own life-guiding philosophy, emphasizing practical reasoning. Like Plato, he thought Athenian democracy constituted bad government because it did not restrict decision making to the most educated and moderate citizens. His vast writings have made him one of the world's most influential thinkers to this day.

Aristotle's achievements included scientific investigation of the natural world, development of systems of logical argument, and practical ethics based on experience. He believed that the search for knowledge brought the good life and genuine happiness. His lectures covered biology, botany, zoology, medicine, anatomy, psychology, meteorology, physics, chemistry, mathematics, music, metaphysics, rhetoric, literary criticism, political science, and ethics. By creating a system of logic for precise argumentation, Aristotle also established grounds for determining whether an argument was logically valid. Aristotle's thought process stressed rationality and common sense, not metaphysics. He rejected Plato's theory of Forms and insisted that understanding depended on observation. He coupled detailed investigation with careful reasoning in biology, botany, and zoology. He collected information on more than five hundred different kinds of animals, including insects. His recognition that whales and dolphins are mammals was not rediscovered for another two thousand years.

Some of Aristotle's observations justified inequalities characteristic of his time. He argued that some people were slaves by nature because their souls lacked the rationality to be fully human. Mistaken biological information led Aristotle to evaluate females as inferior on the grounds they were incomplete males. However, he also believed that human communities could be successful and happy only if women and men both contributed.

In ethics, Aristotle emphasized the need to develop practical habits of just behavior in order to achieve happiness. Ethics, he taught, cannot work if it consists only of abstract reasons for just behavior. People should achieve self-control by training their minds to overcome instincts and passions. Self-control meant finding "the mean," or balance, between denying and indulging physical pleasures.

Greek Political Disunity

During the period that Plato and Aristotle developed their philosophies as guides to life, the Greek city-states engaged in constant wars. Sparta, Thebes, and Athens competed to dominate Greece, but none succeeded. Their endless fighting drained their finances and morale.

Thebes, Athens, Corinth, and Argos formed an anti-Spartan coalition, but the Spartans checkmated the alliance by negotiating with the Persian king. Betraying their long-standing claim to be fighters for Greek freedom, the Spartans acknowledged the Persian ruler's right to control the Greek city-states of Anatolia—in return for permission to wage war in Greece without Persian interference. This agreement of 386 B.C.E., called the King's Peace, sold out the Greeks of Anatolia, returning them to submission to the Persian Empire. Athens rebuilt its navy, again becoming the leader of a naval alliance. In the 370s B.C.E., Thebes attacked Sparta and freed many helots to weaken the enemy. The Theban success alarmed the Athenians, who allied with their hated enemies, the Spartans. The allied armies confronted the Thebans in the battle of Mantinea in the Peloponnese in 362 B.C.E. Thebes won the battle but lost the war when its best general was killed with no capable replacement available. This stalemate left the Greek city-states disunited and weak. By the 350s B.C.E., no Greek city-state controlled anything except its own territory. By failing to cooperate with one another, the Greeks opened the way for yet more war linked to the rise of a new power—the kingdom of Macedonia.

REVIEW QUESTION
How did daily life, philosophy, and the political situation change in Greece during the period 400–350 B.C.E.?

The Rise of Macedonia, 359–323 B.C.E.

The kingdom of Macedonia's rise to superpower status counts as one of the greatest surprises in ancient military and political history. Located north of central Greece, Macedonia rocketed from being a minor state to ruling the Greek and Near Eastern worlds. Two aggressive and charismatic Macedonian kings led this transformation: Philip II (r. 359–336 B.C.E.) and his son **Alexander the Great**. Their conquests ended the Greek Classical Age and set in motion the Hellenistic Age's cultural changes.

Macedonian Power and Philip II, 359–336 B.C.E.

Macedonian kings governed by maintaining the support of local leaders, who ranked as their social equals and controlled many followers. Men spent their time training for war, hunting, and drinking heavily. The king had to excel in these activities to show that he deserved to lead the state. Queens and royal mothers received respect because they came from powerful families or the ruling houses of neighboring regions.

Macedonian kings thought of themselves as ethnically Greek; they spoke Greek in addition to their native Macedonian. Macedonians as a whole looked down on Greeks as too soft to survive life in their northern region. The Greeks called Macedonians "barbarians," regarding them as less civilized but brave.

In 359 B.C.E., the Illyrians, neighbors to the west, slaughtered Macedonia's king and four thousand troops. Philip, the new king, restored the Macedonians' confidence by teaching them to use thrusting spears sixteen feet long. He trained them to maneuver in battle while maintaining formation. Deploying cavalry as a strike force, Philip routed the Illyrians. During the 340s B.C.E., Philip persuaded or forced most of northern and central Greece into alliance with him. Seeking glory for Greece and fearing the instability his strengthened army would create in his kingdom if the soldiers had nothing to do, he decided to lead a united Macedonian and Greek army to conquer the Persian Empire. He justified attacking Persia as revenge for its invasion of Greece 150 years earlier.

Athens and Thebes rallied a coalition of southern Greek city-states to combat Philip, but in 338 B.C.E. the Macedonian king and his Greek allies crushed this group's forces at the battle of Chaeronea in central Greece. The defeated city-states retained their internal freedom, but Philip forced most of them to join his alliance. The battle of Chaeronea marked a turning point in Greek history: never again would the city-states of Greece be independent agents in international affairs.

The Rule of Alexander the Great, 336–323 B.C.E.

Philip was murdered in 336 B.C.E. Some scholars think his son Alexander and his son's mother, Olympias, arranged the killing to seize power for the twenty-year-old Alexander, but the murderer, one of Philip's bodyguards, was probably motivated by personal anger at the king. Alexander secured his rule by eliminating rivals and defeating Macedonia's enemies to the west and north with swift attacks. He forced the southern Greeks, who had defected from the alliance at the news of Philip's death, to rejoin. To demonstrate the cost of disloyalty, in 335 B.C.E., Alexander destroyed Thebes for having rebelled.

In 334 B.C.E., Alexander launched the most astonishing military campaign in ancient history, leading a Macedonian and Greek army against the Persian Empire to fulfill Philip's dream of avenging Greece. Alexander's conquest of all the lands from Turkey to Egypt to the western edge of India while still in his twenties led later peoples to call him Alexander the Great. Alexander inspired his troops by leading charges against the enemy, riding his warhorse Bucephalas ("Oxhead"). Everyone saw him speeding ahead in his plumed helmet, polished armor, and vividly colored cloak. He was so intent on conquest that he rejected advice to delay the war until he had fathered an heir. He gave away nearly all of his land and property as gifts to strengthen ties with his

Mosaic Portrait of Alexander the Great

This detail from a large-scale mosaic (a picture created with many tiny pieces of colored tile or glass) shows a representation of the famous commander Alexander the Great. The mosaic as a whole showed Alexander on horseback fighting Darius, the Persian king, in a crowded battle scene. Archaeologists discovered the mosaic in a private residence in Italy from the time of the Roman Empire. In the actual battle, Alexander would have worn a metal helmet. Why do you think this representation shows him bare-headed and seems to emphasize his looking intently toward his opponent? (Universal History Archive/Getty Images.)

army officers. Alexander aimed at becoming more famous even than Achilles; he always kept a copy of Homer's *Iliad* under his pillow—along with a dagger.

Building on Near Eastern traditions of siege technology and Philip's innovations, Alexander developed even better military technology. When Tyre, a heavily fortified city on an island off the eastern Mediterranean coast, refused to surrender to him in 332 B.C.E., he built a massive stone pier as a platform for artillery towers, armored battering rams, and catapults flinging boulders to breach Tyre's walls. Knowing that Alexander could overcome their fortifications made enemies much readier to negotiate a deal.

In his conquest of Egypt and the Persian heartland, Alexander revealed his strategy for ruling a vast empire: keep an area's traditional administrative system and religious practices in place while founding cities of Greeks and Macedonians in the conquered territory. In Egypt, he established his first new city, naming it Alexandria after himself. In Persia, he proclaimed himself the king of Asia and relied on Persian administrators.

Alexander led his army past the Persian heartland farther east into territory hardly known to the Greeks (Map 4.1). He aimed to outdo the heroes of legend by marching to the end of the world. Shrinking his army to reduce the need for supplies, he marched northeast into what is today Afghanistan and Uzbekistan. Unable to subdue the local guerrilla forces, Alexander settled for an alliance sealed by his marriage to the Bactrian princess Roxane.

Alexander then headed east into India. Seventy days of marching through monsoon rains extinguished his soldiers' fire for conquest. In the spring of 326 B.C.E., they mutinied, forcing Alexander to turn back. The return journey through southeastern Iran's deserts cost many casualties from hunger and thirst; the survivors finally reached safety in the Persian heartland in 324 B.C.E. Alexander immediately began planning an invasion of the Arabian peninsula and North Africa. He also announced that he wanted to receive the honors due a god. Most Greek city-states obeyed by sending religious delegations to him. Personal motives best explain Alexander's announcement: he had come to believe he was truly the son of Zeus and that his superhuman accomplishments demonstrated that he must himself be a god in a human body present among other human beings.

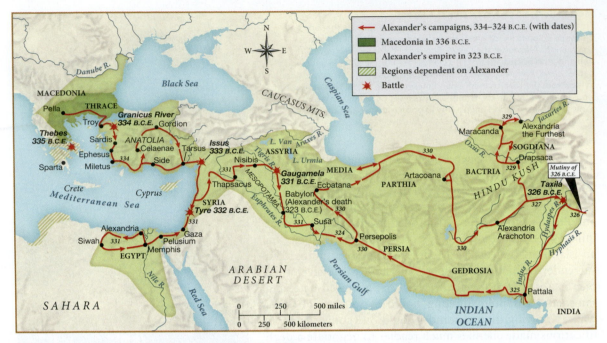

MAP 4.1 Conquests of Alexander the Great, r. 336–323 B.C.E.
From the time Alexander led his army against Persia in 334 B.C.E. until his death in 323 B.C.E., he was continually fighting military campaigns. His charismatic and fearless generalship, combined with effective intelligence gathering about his targets, generated an unbroken string of victories and made him a legend. His founding of garrison cities and preservation of local governments kept his conquests largely stable during his lifetime.

Alexander died from a fever in 323 B.C.E. Unfortunately for the stability of his immense conquests, he had no heir ready to take over his rule; Roxane gave birth to their son only after Alexander's death. The story goes that, when at Alexander's deathbed his commanders asked him to whom he left his kingdom, he replied, "To the most powerful."

Modern scholars express different evaluations of Alexander, ranging from condemning him as a bloodthirsty warmonger to praising him as a visionary creating a multiethnic world encompassing all cultures. The ancient sources suggest that Alexander had interlinked goals reflecting his restless and ruthless nature: to conquer and administer the known world with a new ruling class mixing competent people from all ethnic groups, to outdo the exploits and glory of legendary heroes, and to earn the status no living human had ever achieved—that of a god-man on earth.

It is certain that Alexander's explorations benefited scientific fields from geography to botany because he took along knowledgeable writers to collect and catalog new knowledge. He had vast quantities of scientific observations and money for research dispatched to his old tutor Aristotle. Alexander's new cities promoted trade between Greece and the Near East. Most of all, his career brought the two cultures into closer contact than ever before. This contact represented his career's most enduring impact.

REVIEW QUESTION
What were the accomplishments of Alexander the Great, and what were their effects both for the ancient world and for later Western civilization?

The Hellenistic Kingdoms, 323–30 B.C.E.

New kingdoms arose when Alexander's empire fragmented after his death. The time from Alexander's death in 323 B.C.E. to the death of Cleopatra VII, the last Macedonian queen of Egypt, in 30 B.C.E. is the Hellenistic Age. (See Terms of History on page 126.) This period reintroduced monarchy into Greek culture for the first time in a thousand years. Commanders from Alexander's army created the kingdoms by seizing portions of his empire and proclaiming themselves kings. This process of state formation took more than fifty years of war. The self-proclaimed kings—called Alexander's successors—had to transform their families into dynasties and accumulate enough power to force the Greek city-states to obey them. In the second and first centuries B.C.E., the Romans overthrew the Hellenistic kingdoms.

Creating New Kingdoms

Alexander's successors divided his conquests among themselves. Antigonus (c. 382–301 B.C.E.) took over Anatolia, the Near East, Macedonia, and Greece; Seleucus (c. 358–281 B.C.E.) seized Babylonia and the East as far as India; and Ptolemy (c. 367–282 B.C.E.) took over Egypt. These successors had to create their own form of monarchy based on military power and personal prestige because they were self-proclaimed rulers with no connection to Alexander's royal line.

The kingdoms' territories were never completely stable because the Hellenistic monarchs never stopped competing (Map 4.2). Conflicts repeatedly arose over border areas. The Ptolemies and the Seleucids, for example, fought to control the eastern Mediterranean coast, just like the Egyptians and Hittites. The wars between the major kingdoms created openings for smaller kingdoms to establish themselves. The most famous of these smaller kingdoms was that of the Attalids in western Anatolia, with the wealthy city of Pergamum as its capital. In Bactria in Central Asia, the Greeks—originally colonists settled by Alexander—broke off from the Seleucid kingdom in the mid-third century B.C.E. to found their own regional kingdom, which flourished for a time from the trade in luxury goods between India and China and the Mediterranean world.

The Hellenistic kingdoms imposed foreign rule by Macedonian kings and queens on indigenous populations, though the monarchies took over local traditions to build legitimacy. The Ptolemaic royal family, for example, observed the Egyptian royal tradition of brother-sister marriage and respected traditional Egyptian gods. Royal power was the ultimate source of control over the kingdoms' subjects, in keeping with the Near Eastern monarchical tradition that Hellenistic kings adopted. Seleucus justified his rule on what he claimed as a universal truth of monarchy: "It is not the customs of the Persians and other people that I impose upon you, but the law which is common to everyone, that what is decreed by the king is always just." The survival of these dynasties depended on their ability to create strong armies, effective administrations,

Hellenistic

The term *Hellenistic* involves a story of controversy about historians' judgments on cultures of the past. Invented by modern historians, the word means "Greek-like" or "Greek-ish." It is derived from the ancient Greek word for "Greek," which was *Hellēn*. (The term *Greek* comes from the Latin word *Graecus*, from the tribal name of the first Greeks whom the early Romans encountered.)

Hellen was the name of a Greek mythological figure; he was the grandson of Prometheus, the divine being who defied Zeus by teaching human beings to use fire for cooking and technology. Hellen survived a great flood that almost destroyed life on earth, much like Noah in the Hebrew Bible. This personal history made Hellen a worthy namesake for all Greeks.

"Hellenistic" was invented by early modern scholars to express the interpretation that the long-term consequences of Alexander the Great's expedition into Asia in the late fourth century B.C.E. constituted a turning point in world history because the interactions of Greeks and non-Greeks that the expedition produced indirectly prepared the way for the emergence of Christianity. It must have been God's plan, the argument proposed, that there would be a "Hellenistic Age" of cultural changes lasting from the time of Alexander to that of the apostles of Jesus and the early Roman Empire.

Later scholars proposed a nonreligious interpretation of the centuries after Alexander as having been a period during which Greek culture transformed the non-Greek cultures of southwest Asia into more "Greek-like" forms. This idea valued Greek, that is, "Western," culture more highly than "Eastern" culture. At the same time, Greek culture during the Hellenistic period was itself seen as inferior to that of Greece's earlier Classical or Golden Age (another modern concept).

Most recently, scholarly interpretation stresses that southwest Asia in the aftermath of Alexander's conquest remained a diverse region, from cultures to languages to religions. There were many more Greeks living there than ever before, and in many places these immigrants dominated politically, at least until the Roman conquest. Greek did become the "common language" for much interaction among the many different linguistic groups there, and aspects of Greek culture from architecture to sport did gain a presence as well, as archaeology especially has revealed. But Greeks were also deeply influenced by the new level of cultural interactions; change happened to most everyone, and its direction was never one-way.

In fact, "Hellenistic" today seems appropriate only as a chronological, not an interpretive, term, designating the period from the death of Alexander in 323 B.C.E. to the defeat and death of Cleopatra and Mark Antony in 31–30 B.C.E. But even that designation remains arbitrary: the cultural interactions between "West" and "East" that changed the world began before 323 B.C.E. and continued after 32–30 B.C.E.

---

and close ties to urban elites. A letter from a Greek city summed up the situation while praising the Seleucid king Antiochus I (c. 324–261 B.C.E.): "His rule depends above all on his own excellence [aretê], and on the goodwill of his friends, and on his forces."

Professional soldiers manned Hellenistic royal armies and navies. To develop their military might, the Seleucid and Ptolemaic kings encouraged immigration by Greeks and Macedonians, who received land grants in return for military service. When this source of manpower gave out, the kings had to employ local men as troops. Military competition put tremendous financial pressure on the kings to pay growing numbers of mercenaries and to purchase

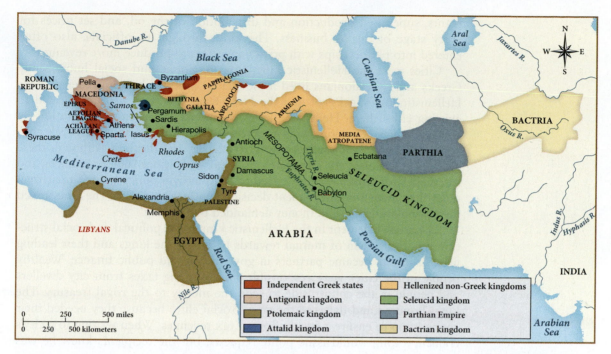

MAP 4.2 Hellenistic Kingdoms, 240 B.C.E. Monarchy became the dominant political system in the areas of Alexander's conquests. By about eighty years after his death, the three major kingdoms established by his successors had settled their boundaries, after the Seleucids gave up their easternmost territories to an Indian king and the Attalids carved out their kingdom in western Anatolia.

expensive new military technology. To compete effectively, a Hellenistic king had to provide giant artillery, such as catapults capable of flinging a 170-pound projectile up to two hundred yards. His navy cost a fortune because warships were now huge, requiring crews of several hundred men. War elephants became common after Alexander brought them back from India, but they were extremely costly to maintain.

Hellenistic kings needed effective administrations to collect revenues. Initially, they recruited mostly Greek and Macedonian immigrants to fill high-level posts. The Seleucids and the Ptolemies also employed non-Greeks for middle- and low-level positions, where officials had to be able to deal with the subject populations and speak their languages. Local men who wanted a government job bettered their chances if they could read and write Greek in addition to their native language. Bilingualism qualified them to fill positions communicating the orders of the Greek and Macedonian top officials to local farmers, builders, and crafts producers. Non-Greeks who had successful government careers were rarely admitted to royal society, because Greeks and Macedonians saw themselves as too superior to mix with locals. Greeks and non-Greeks therefore tended to live in separate communities.

Administrators' principal responsibilities were to maintain order and to direct the kingdoms' tax systems. The Ptolemaic administration used methods of central planning and control inherited from earlier Egyptian history. Its officials continued to administer royal monopolies to maximize the king's revenue. In the case of vegetable oil, widely used for cooking, cosmetics, and lubrication, they decided how much land farmers could sow in oil-bearing plants, supervised production and distribution of the oil, and set prices for every stage of the oil business. The king, through his officials, also often entered into partnerships with private investors to produce more revenue.

Cities were the Hellenistic kingdoms' economic and social hubs. Many Greeks and Macedonians lived in new cities founded by Alexander and the Hellenistic kings in Egypt and the Near East, and they also immigrated to existing cities there. Hellenistic kings promoted this urban immigration by adorning their new cities with architectural features of classical Greek city-states, especially colonnaded streets, gymnasia, and theaters. Although these cities often retained the city-state's political institutions such as councils and assemblies for citizen men, the need to follow royal policy limited their freedom; they made no independent decisions on foreign policy. The cities taxed their populations to send money demanded by the king.

The crucial element in the Hellenistic kingdoms' political and social structure was the system of mutual rewards by which the kings and their leading urban subjects became partners in government and public finance. Wealthy people in the cities were responsible for collecting taxes from city dwellers and people in the countryside to send the money to the royal treasury. The kings honored and flattered the cities' social elites because they needed their cooperation to ensure a steady flow of tax revenues. When writing to a city's council, a king would issue polite requests, but the recipients knew he was giving commands.

This system thus continued the Greek tradition of requiring the wealthy elite to contribute financially to the common good. Cooperative cities received gifts from the king to pay for expensive public works like theaters and temples or for reconstruction after natural disasters such as earthquakes. Wealthy men and women in turn helped keep the general population peaceful by subsidizing teachers and doctors, financing public works, and providing donations and loans to ensure a reliable supply of grain to feed the city's residents.

To keep their vast kingdoms peaceful and profitable, the kings established relationships with well-to-do non-Greeks living in the old cities of Anatolia and the Near East. In addition, non-Greeks and non-Macedonians from eastern regions began moving westward to the new Hellenistic Greek cities in increasing numbers. Jews in particular moved from their ancestral homeland to Anatolia, Greece, and Egypt. The Jewish community eventually became an influential minority in Egyptian Alexandria, the most important Hellenistic city. In Egypt, as the Rosetta stone shows, the king also had to build good relationships with the priests who controlled the temples of the traditional Egyptian gods because the temples owned large tracts of rich land worked by tenant farmers.

The Layers of Hellenistic Society

The royal family and the king's friends had the highest social rank. The Greek and Macedonian elites of the major cities came next. Then came indigenous urban elites, leaders of large minority urban populations, and local lords in rural regions. Merchants, artisans, and laborers made up the free population's bottom layer. Slaves still lacked any social status.

The kingdoms' growth increased the demand for slave labor throughout the eastern Mediterranean; a market on the island of Delos sold up to ten thousand slaves a day. The luckier ones were purchased as servants for the royal court or elite households and lived physically comfortable lives, so long as they pleased their owners. The luckless ones labored, and often died, in the mines. Enslaved children could be taken far from home to work. For example, a sales contract from 259 B.C.E. records that a Greek bought a seven-year-old girl named Gemstone to work in an Egyptian textile factory. Originally from an eastern Mediterranean town, she had previously labored as the slave of a Greek mercenary soldier employed by a Jewish cavalry commander in the Transjordan region.

Poor people—the majority of the population—mostly labored in agriculture, the foundation of the Hellenistic kingdoms' economies. There were large cities, above all Alexandria in Egypt, but most people lived in country villages. Many of the poor were employed on the royal family's huge estates, but free peasants still worked their own small fields in addition to laboring for wealthy landowners. Perhaps as many as 80 percent of all adult men and women had to work the land to produce enough food to sustain the population. In cities, poor women and men worked as small merchants, peddlers, and artisans, producing and selling goods such as tools, pottery, clothing, and furniture. Men could sign on as deckhands on the merchant ships that sailed the Mediterranean Sea and Indian Ocean.

Many country people in the Seleucid and Ptolemaic kingdoms existed in a state of dependency between free and slave. The "peoples," as they were called, were tenants who farmed the estates belonging to the king. Although they could not be sold like slaves, they were not allowed to move away or abandon their tenancies. They owed a large quota of produce to the king, a high compulsory rent that left these tenant farmers little chance to escape poverty.

Hellenistic queens had great social status and commanded enormous riches and honors. They exercised power as the representatives of distinguished families, as the mothers of a line of royal descendants, and as patrons of artists, thinkers, and even entire cities. Later Ptolemaic queens co-ruled with their husbands. Queens ruled on their own when no male heir existed. For example, Arsinoe II (c. 316–270 B.C.E.), the daughter of Ptolemy I, first married the Macedonian successor Lysimachus, who gave her four towns as her personal domain. After his death, she married her brother, Ptolemy II of Egypt, and was his partner in making policy. Public praise for a queen reflected traditional Greek values for women. A city decree from about 165 B.C.E. honored Queen Apollonis of Pergamum by praising her piety toward the gods, her reverence toward her parents, her distinguished conduct toward her husband, and her harmonious relations with her "beautiful children born in wedlock."

Some queens paid special attention to the condition of women. About 195 B.C.E., for example, the Seleucid queen Laodice gave a ten-year endowment to a city to provide dowries for needy girls. Laodice's gift shows that she recognized the importance to women of controlling property, which was the surest guarantee of respect.

Most women remained under the legal control of men. A common saying by men was, "Who can judge better than a father what is to his daughter's interest?" Most of the time, elite women continued to be separated from men outside their families, while poor women worked in public. Greeks continued to abandon infants they did not want to raise—girls more often than boys—but other populations, such as the Egyptians and the Jews, did not practice infant exposure. Exposure differed from infanticide in that the parents expected someone to find the child and rear it, usually as a slave. A third-century B.C.E. comic poet was exaggerating by writing, "A son, one always raises even if one is poor; a daughter, one exposes, even if one is rich," because daughters of wealthy parents were not usually abandoned; but probably up to 10 percent of other infant girls suffered that sorrowful fate.

A woman of exceptional wealth could enter public life by making donations or loans to her city and in return be rewarded with an official post in local government. In Egypt, women of all classes acquired greater say in married life as the marriage contract evolved from an agreement between the bride's parents and the groom, to one in which the bride made her own arrangements with the groom.

Rich people showed increasing concern for the welfare of poorer people during the Hellenistic period. They were following the lead of the royal families, who emphasized philanthropy to build a reputation for generosity that would support their legitimacy in ruling. Sometimes wealthy citizens funded a foundation to distribute free grain to eliminate food shortages, and they also funded schools for children in various Hellenistic cities, the first public schools in the Greek world. In some places, girls as well as boys could attend school. Many cities also began sponsoring doctors to improve medical care: patients still had to pay, but at least they could count on finding a doctor.

The donors funding these services were repaid by the respect and honor they earned from their fellow citizens. When an earthquake devastated Rhodes, many cities joined kings and queens in sending donations to help the residents recover. In return, the city-state's citizens showered honors on their benefactors by appointing them to prestigious municipal offices and erecting inscriptions expressing the city's gratitude. In this system, the masses' welfare depended more and more on the generosity of the rich. Lacking democracy, the poor had no political power to demand support.

The End of the Hellenistic Kingdoms

All the Hellenistic kingdoms eventually lost their riches and power, mostly through internal rivalries in their ruling families. Thus weakened, they could not prevent takeovers by the Romans, who over time intervened forcefully in conflicts among kingdoms and Greek city-states in the eastern Mediterranean.

The Roman interventions caused wars. Rome first established dominance over the Antigonid kingdom by the middle of the second century B.C.E.

REVIEW QUESTION
How did the political and social organization of the new Hellenistic kingdoms compare with that of the earlier Greek city-states?

Sculpture of Cleopatra
This fragment of a sculpture in relief (that is, not in the round) shows Cleopatra, the queen of Egypt in the late first century B.C.E. Descended from the royal line called the Ptolemies, who were originally Macedonians, Cleopatra was famous for her intelligence, wit, and political ambition. She formed alliances—and initiated love affairs—with the Roman commanders Julius Caesar and Mark Antony to try to protect her kingdom. She committed suicide in 30 B.C.E. after Octavian (soon to become Augustus) defeated her army and converted Egypt into a Roman province. Why do you think Cleopatra is shown here in Egyptian clothing and in the style of Egyptian art? (Musee du Louvre, Paris, France/De Agostini Picture Library/Gianni Dagli Orti/Bridgeman Images.)

Next, the Seleucid kingdom fell to the Romans in 64 B.C.E. The Ptolemaic kingdom in Egypt survived until the 50s B.C.E., when its royal family split into warring factions; the resulting weakness forced the rivals for the throne to seek Roman support. The end came when the famous Ptolemaic queen Cleopatra VII, the last Macedonian to rule Egypt, chose the losing side in the civil war between Mark Antony and the future emperor Augustus in the late first century B.C.E. An invading Roman army ended her rule in 30 B.C.E. (see Contrasting Views on pages 132–133). Rome then became the heir to all the Hellenistic kingdoms (see Mapping the West on page 142).

Hellenistic Culture

Hellenistic culture reflected three principal influences: (1) the overwhelming impact of royal wealth, (2) increased emphasis on private life and emotion, and (3) greater interaction of diverse peoples. The kings drove developments in literature, art, science, and philosophy by deciding which scholars and artists to put on the royal payroll. The obligation of authors and artists to the kings meant that they did not have freedom to criticize public policy; their works mostly concentrated on everyday life and personal feelings.

Cultural interaction between Near Eastern and Greek traditions occurred most prominently in language and religion. These developments deeply influenced the Romans as they took over the Hellenistic world. The Roman poet Horace (65–8 B.C.E.) described the effect of Hellenistic culture on his own Roman culture by saying that "captive Greece captured its fierce victor."

The Arts under Royal Support

Hellenistic kings became the supporters of scholarship and the arts on a vast scale, competing with one another to lure the best scholars and artists to their capitals with lavish salaries. They funded intellectuals and artists because they

Roman Attitudes toward Cleopatra VII, the Last Hellenistic Queen

Cleopatra VII was the ruler of Egypt, the last Hellenistic kingdom to fall to the Romans. She had relationships with, first, Julius Caesar and then, after his death in 44 B.C.E., with Mark Antony. In the 30s B.C.E., Antony fought a civil war for control of Rome with Octavian, the adopted son of Julius Caesar who would later become the first Roman emperor. In the aftermath of their defeat by Octavian in a naval battle at Actium in Greece in 31 B.C.E., Antony and then Cleopatra committed suicide in 30 B.C.E. to escape capture by Octavian. This excerpt from the biographer Plutarch (c. 50–c. 120 C.E.) describes Cleopatra's interactions with the Roman leaders fighting to control Egypt.

1. Cleopatra's Personal Qualities and Abilities

[To meet Julius Caesar] Cleopatra only took one other person with her, Apollodorus from Sicily. She approached the palace [at Alexandria] in a little rowboat, landing as it got dark outside. Since she was sure to have been found out otherwise [by her brother's hostile forces], she crawled into the kind of large sack used to hold bed sheets and pillows, stretching out fully. Apollodorus then cinched up the bag and toted it inside the royal quarters to Julius Caesar. This stratagem, people said, made Caesar intrigued by her, as she demonstrated that she was unconventionally inventive. Spending time with her won him over—her charisma won the victory, and so he arranged for a political reconciliation between her and her brother, making her the co-ruler of Egypt. [When Cleopatra's brother later treacherously betrays this alliance, Julius Caesar narrowly escapes with his life but manages to defeat the rebel.] Caesar then departed

for Syria, having made Cleopatra the ruler of Egypt. Not too much later she gave birth to their son, whom the Egyptians called "Little Caesar."

[Some years later, after Caesar's assassination, Cleopatra makes a political and personal alliance with the Roman general Mark Antony, now the opponent and rival of Octavian for power at Rome.] . . . As soon as Dellius, the messenger that Mark Antony had sent [to open negotiations with the Egyptian ruler], laid eyes on Cleopatra and realized her eloquent way of speaking and how sharp she was in making persuasive arguments, he concluded that Antony would never do her any harm and that in fact she was likely to become a central focus in his life. . . . [At her first meeting with Antony, Cleopatra entrances him.] Her physical beauty was not in itself without parallel [among other women]; it was not the kind that astonished people who saw her. But her personality inevitably fascinated those whom she met; her attractive presence combined with her charmingly persuasive style of conversation and the personal aura that she projected in company to enable her to inspire others. The quality of her voice was graceful, and she had a facility with languages . . . that allowed her to learn any foreign tongue that she wanted. Therefore, she needed a translator only on very exceptional occasions when she interacted with foreigners. Usually she could respond to them herself, regardless of whether they were Ethiopians, Troglodytes, Hebrews, Arabs, Scythians, Medes, or Parthians. Indeed, she was reported to have learned many other languages as well, although the kings of Egypt before her had not bothered even to learn Egyptian . . .

wanted to boost their reputations by having these famous people produce books, poems, sculptures, and other prestigious creations at their courts.

The Ptolemies turned Alexandria into the Mediterranean's leading arts and sciences center, establishing the world's first scholarly research institute with its own massive library. The librarians were instructed to collect all the books in the world. The library grew to hold half a million scrolls, an enormous number for the time. Linked to it was the building in which the hired research scholars dined together and produced encyclopedias of knowledge such as

[In the civil war between Mark Antony and Octavian, Cleopatra sides with Antony.] Antony definitely did not judge Cleopatra to be less intelligent than any of the foreign kings fighting as his allies [against Octavian]; she had ruled a great kingdom by herself for many years, and she had been his companion for a long time, competent to manage important matters.

[After Octavian defeats Antony and Cleopatra at the naval battle at Actium in Greece in 31 B.C.E. and then captures Cleopatra in her capital at Alexandria, he wants to take her back from Egypt to Rome to display as a prize in his victory parade, a plan that she subverts by committing suicide by allowing a venomous snake to bite her. Octavian then discovers her corpse.] He was angry that she was dead, but he was amazed at her nobility; he commanded that her body be buried next to Antony in the splendid style appropriate for royalty.

Source: Plutarch, *Life of Julius Caesar* 49; *Life of Antony* 25, 27, 56, and 86. Translation by Thomas R. Martin.

2. "Celebrating" Cleopatra's Defeat and Death

The contemporary Roman poet Horace wrote this poem in the aftermath of the suicide of Cleopatra. It starts out as a celebration of Rome's triumph in Egypt, but then the tone seems to shift when the focus shifts to Cleopatra's decision to take her own life.

Now it's time to drink, now it's time to dance, now, friends, it's time to drag out the couches with images of the gods for a banquet! Before now it would have been an abomination to pour out fine wine from the vintage casks, while in her insanity that queen was preparing to ruin and bury our Capitol and our empire, with her polluted gang of men sick in their filth. She was out of her mind in her expectations and drunk from her sweet luck. But she dropped her fury when scarcely a single ship from her fleet got away [from the battle of Actium] without being burned up, and Caesar [that is, Octavian] reduced her spirit, inflamed by Egyptian wine, to genuine terror. He chased her flying away from Italy, just like a hawk pursues gentle doves, or a hunter speeds after a rabbit over fields of snow, so that he could put chains on this deadly monster. She, however, sought to die in a nobler way, and she was not afraid of the sword like a woman and did not try to reach some hidden shores on her fast-sailing ships. She had the daring to look upon her fallen palace with a calm expression and bravely to handle the cruel snakes, so that she could drink in their dark poison throughout her body, so fierce in her decision to die. She scornfully refused to be transported by enemy warships, knocked down to an ordinary person's status to be shown off in a boastful victory parade [by Octavian in Rome]; she was not a woman without pride.

Source: Horace, *Odes* Book 1, no. 37. Translation by Thomas R. Martin.

QUESTIONS TO CONSIDER

1. What were Cleopatra's most important talents and qualities according to Plutarch and to Horace? Do these authors agree or disagree?

2. What insights into gender in the ancient world do these documents reveal?

3. What issues about gender do these documents raise that are relevant in today's world?

The Wonders of the World and *On the Rivers of Europe.* We still use the name of the research institute's building, the Museum ("place of the Muses," the Greek goddesses of learning and the arts), to designate institutions preserving knowledge.

The writers and artists paid by Hellenistic kings had to please their paymasters. The poet Theocritus (c. 300–260 B.C.E.) spelled out the deal underlying royal support in a poem flattering King Ptolemy II: "The spokesmen of the Muses [that is, poets] celebrate Ptolemy in return for his benefactions."

PRIMARY SOURCE ANALYSIS

Epigrams on Love and Sex by Women Poets

Anyte, Nossis, and Erinna were three of the most famous women poets of the Hellenistic period. They composed short poems about love, sex, and death that often centered on women. They also invented the tradition of writing poems about speaking animals. None of them was hired by a Hellenistic king to be a resident poet at court, so they had to create their poetic masterpieces on their own.

Anyte on Mourning a Young Woman

The virgin Antibia I mourn for; many
young men came to her father's house seeking to marry
    her,
drawn by the fame of her beauty and wisdom. But every-
    one's
hopes deadly Fate tossed away.

Anyte on a Dolphin Speaking after Death

No longer taking joy in surging seas
will I stretch out my neck as I leap from the depths,
no longer around the lovely bows of the ship
will I jump, delighting in the figurehead, my likeness.
No, the purple surge of the sea cast me onto the land;
here I lie on this narrow strip of beach.

Nossis on the Joy of Sex

Nothing is sweeter than sexual passion; every other
    blessing is second;
I spit out from my mouth even honey.
This is what Nossis says: anyone that Aphrodite has not
    kissed
doesn't know what kind of flowers her roses are.

Nossis on a Woman's Present to Aphrodite

The picture of herself Callo dedicated in the temple of
    blond Aphrodite,
having her portrait made to look exactly like herself.
How gracefully it stands; see how great is the grace that
    blooms on it.
Best wishes to her! For she has no blame in her life.

Erinna on the Death of the Bride Baukis

I am the grave marker of the bride Baukis. As you pass by
this most wept-for pillar, say this to Hades in the underworld:
"You are jealous of Baukis, Hades!" The lovely letters
    that you see
announce the brutal fate Chance brought to Baukis,
how with the pine-torches from the wedding that they
        were using to worship Hymenaeus [the god of mar-
        riage]
the groom's father set afire her funeral pyre.
And you, Hymenaeus, the tuneful song of the wedding
converted to the sad cries of lamentation.

Source: *Palatine Anthology,* 7.490, 7.215, 5.170, 9.605, 7.712. Translations by Thomas R. Martin.

QUESTIONS TO CONSIDER

1. What do these women's poems reveal about women's lives and concerns in the Hellenistic age?

2. Since these authors could have chosen any subjects they wanted, on any aspect of life, whether personal or public, female or male, why do you think they concentrated on the themes that they did?

Poets such as Theocritus avoided political topics and exploited the social gap that existed between the intellectual elite—to which the kings belonged—and the uneducated masses. They filled their new poetry with erudite references to make it difficult to understand and therefore exclusive. Only people with a deep literary education could appreciate the mythological allusions that studded these authors' elaborate poems.

No Hellenistic women poets seem to have enjoyed royal financial support; rather, they created their art independently. (See Primary Source Analysis.) They excelled in writing **epigrams,** short poems in the style of those originally used on tombstones to remember the dead. Highly literary poems by women from diverse regions of the Hellenistic world still survive. Many epigrams were about women, from courtesans to respectable matrons, expressing the writer's personal feelings. No other Hellenistic literature better conveys the depth of human emotion than the epigrams written by women poets.

Hellenistic comedies also emphasized stories about emotions and stayed away from politics. Comic playwrights presented plays concerning the troubles of fictional lovers. These comedies became enormously popular because, like modern situation comedies (sitcoms), they offered humorous views of daily life. Papyrus discoveries have restored previously lost comedies of Menander (c. 342–289 B.C.E.), the most famous Hellenistic comic poet, noted for his skill in depicting human personality. Hellenistic tragedy could take a multicultural approach. Ezechiel, a Jew living in Alexandria, wrote *Exodus*, a tragedy in Greek about Moses leading the Hebrews out of captivity in Egypt.

Hellenistic sculptors and painters featured emotions in their works as well. Classical artists had given their subjects' faces an idealized serenity, but now Hellenistic sculptures depicted intense personal feelings. Athletes, for example, could be shown realistically as exhausted and scarred by the exertion required to compete at a high level. The increasing diversity of subjects that emerged in Hellenistic art presumably represented a trend approved by kings, queens, and the elites. Sculpture best reveals this new preference for depicting people who had never before appeared in art: heartbreaking victims of war, drunkards, battered athletes, wrinkled old people. The female nude became common. A statue of Aphrodite by Praxiteles, which portrayed the goddess completely naked for the first time, became renowned as a religious object and also a tourist attraction in the city of Cnidos, which had commissioned it. The king of Bithynia offered to pay off the citizens' entire public debt if he could have the work of art. They refused.

Philosophy for a New Age

New philosophies arose in the Hellenistic period, all asking the same question: "What is the best way to live?" They recommended different paths to the same answer: individuals must achieve inner personal tranquility to achieve freedom from the disruptive effects of outside forces, especially chance. These philosophies became popular because outside forces—the Hellenistic kings—had robbed

Seated Boxer Statue
The bronze sculpture from the first century B.C.E. shows a boxer apparently resting after a hard bout. The metal and leather bands on his hands and forearms represent the "boxing gloves" used in this Greek sport. The sculptor revealed the damage done to the fighter in this brutal form of competition by depicting many scars on his body. His eyes would have been represented realistically by inserted, colored stones. Why do you think this figure was shown in this pose, instead of in an "action" posture he would use during a boxing match? (akg-images.)

the Greek city-states of their independence in foreign policy, with their citizens' fates ultimately dependent on unpredictable monarchs. More than ever, human life seemed out of individuals' control. It was therefore appealing to look to philosophy for personal solutions to the unsettling new conditions of Hellenistic life.

Hellenistic philosophers concentrated on **materialism**, the doctrine that only things made of matter truly exist. This idea corresponded to Aristotle's teaching that only things identified through logic or observation exist. Hellenistic philosophy was divided into three areas: (1) logic, the process for discovering truth; (2) physics, the fundamental truth about the nature of existence; and (3) ethics, how humans should achieve happiness and well-being through logic and physics.

One of the two most significant new Hellenistic philosophies was **Epicureanism**, named for its founder, Epicurus (341–271 B.C.E.). He settled his followers around 307 B.C.E. in an Athenian house surrounded by greenery — hence, his school came to be known as the Garden. Epicurus broke tradition by admitting women and slaves to study philosophy in his group.

Epicurus's key idea was that people should be free of worry about death. Because all matter consists of tiny, invisible, and irreducible pieces called atoms in random movement, as Democritus had argued (see page 100), death is nothing more than the painless separating of the body's atoms. Moreover, all human knowledge must be empirical, that is, derived from experience and perception. Phenomena that most people perceive as the work of the gods, such as thunder, do not result from divine intervention in the world. The gods live far away in perfect tranquility, ignoring human affairs. People therefore have nothing to fear from the gods.

Epicurus believed people should pursue true pleasure, meaning an "absence of disturbance." Thus, people should live free from the turmoil, passions, and desires of ordinary existence. A sober life spent with friends and separated from the cares of the common world provided Epicurean pleasure. Epicureanism thus challenged the Greek tradition of political participation by citizens.

The other most prominent Hellenistic philosophy, **Stoicism**, prohibited an isolationist life. Its name derives from the Painted Stoa in Athens, where Stoic philosophers discussed their ideas. Stoics believed that fate controls people's lives but that individuals should still make the pursuit of excellence their goal and participate in public life. Stoic excellence meant putting oneself in harmony with the divine, rational force of universal nature by cultivating good sense, justice, courage, and temperance. These doctrines applied to women as well as men. Some Stoics advocated equal citizenship for women, unisex clothing, and abolition of marriage and families.

The Stoic belief in fate raised the question of whether humans have free will. Stoic philosophers concluded that purposeful human actions do have significance even if fate rules. Nature, itself good, does not prevent evil from occurring, because excellence would otherwise have no meaning. What matters in life is striving for good. A person should therefore take action against evil by, for example, participating in politics. To be a Stoic also meant to shun

WHAT WOULD YOU DO?

If you were an aspiring philosopher in the Hellenistic period, which school of thought would you choose: Epicureanism, Stoicism, Skepticism, or Cynicism? What would your ideas say about how to live a good and meaningful life, and how to participate in society, if at all? How would your conclusions on these questions differ from the ideas of Socrates, Plato, and Aristotle?

desire and anger while calmly enduring pain and sorrow, an attitude that yields the modern meaning of the word *stoic*. Through endurance and self-control, Stoics gained inner tranquility. They did not fear death because they believed that people live the same life over and over again. This repetition occurred because the world is periodically destroyed by fire and then re-formed.

Several other Hellenistic philosophies competed with Epicureanism and Stoicism. Philosophers called Skeptics aimed for a state of personal calm, as did Epicureans, but from a completely different basis. They believed that secure knowledge about anything was impossible because the human senses perceive contradictory information about the world. All people can do, the Skeptics insisted, is depend on perceptions and appearances while suspending judgment about their ultimate reality. These ideas had been influenced by the Indian ascetics (who practiced self-denial as part of their spiritual discipline) encountered on Alexander the Great's expedition.

Cynics rejected every convention of ordinary life, especially wealth and material comfort. The name *Cynic*, which means "like a dog," came from the notion that dogs had no shame. Cynics believed that humans should aim for complete self-sufficiency and that whatever was natural was good and could be done without shame before anyone. Therefore, such things as bowel movements and sex acts in public were acceptable. Above all, Cynics rejected life's comforts. The most famous early Cynic, Diogenes (c. 412–c. 324 B.C.E.), wore borrowed clothing and slept in a storage jar. Also notorious was Hipparchia, a female Cynic of the late fourth century B.C.E. who once defeated a philosophical opponent named Theodorus the Atheist with the following remarks: "Anything that would not be considered wrong if done by Theodorus would also not be considered wrong if done by Hipparchia. Now if Theodorus punches himself, he does no wrong. Therefore, if Hipparchia punches Theodorus, she does no wrong."

Philosophy in the Hellenistic Age reached a wider audience than ever before. Although the working poor were too busy to attend philosophers' lectures, many well-off members of society studied philosophy. Greek settlers took their interest in philosophy with them to even the most remote Hellenistic cities. Archaeologists excavating a city in Afghanistan—thousands of miles from Greece—uncovered a Greek philosophical text and inscriptions of moral advice recording Apollo's oracle at Delphi as their source. This site, called Ai-Khanoum, was devastated in the twentieth century during the Soviet war in Afghanistan.

Scientific Innovation

Historians have called the Hellenistic period the golden age of ancient science. Scientific innovation flourished because Alexander's expedition had encouraged curiosity and increased knowledge about the world's extent and diversity, royal families supported scientists financially, and the concentration of scientists in Alexandria promoted the exchange of ideas.

The greatest advances in scientific knowledge came in geometry and mathematics. Euclid, who taught at Alexandria around 300 B.C.E., made

Tower of the Winds
This forty-foot octagonal tower, built in Athens about 150 B.C.E., used scientific knowledge developed in Hellenistic Alexandria to tell time and predict the weather. Eight sundials (now missing) carved on the walls displayed the time of day all year; a huge interior water clock showed hours, days, and phases of the moon. A vane on top showed wind direction. The carved figures represented the winds, which the Greeks saw as gods. Each figure's clothing predicted the typical weather from that direction, with the cold northern winds wearing boots and heavy cloaks, while the southern ones have bare feet and gauzy clothes. What were the goals, do you imagine, in erecting such a large clock in a public place? (De Agostini Picture Library/S. Vannini/Bridgeman Images.)

revolutionary discoveries in analyzing two- and three-dimensional space. Euclidean geometry is still useful. Archimedes of Syracuse (287–212 B.C.E.) calculated the approximate value of π (pi) and invented a way to manipulate very large numbers. He also invented hydrostatics (the science of the equilibrium of fluid systems) and mechanical devices, such as a screw for lifting water to a higher elevation and cranes to disable enemy warships. Archimedes' shout of delight when he solved a problem while soaking in his bathtub has been immortalized in the expression *Eureka!*, meaning "I have found it!"

Advances in Hellenistic mathematics energized other fields that required complex computation. Early in the third century B.C.E., Aristarchus was the first to propose the correct model of the solar system: the earth revolving around the sun. Later astronomers rejected Aristarchus's heliocentric model in favor of the traditional geocentric one (with the earth at the center), because conclusions drawn from his calculations of the earth's orbit failed to correspond to the observed positions of celestial objects. Aristarchus had assumed a circular orbit instead of an elliptical one, an assumption not corrected until much later. Eratosthenes (c. 275–194 B.C.E.) pioneered mathematical geography. He calculated the circumference of the earth with astonishing accuracy by measuring the length of the shadows cast by widely separated but identically tall structures. Together, these researchers gave Western scientific thought an important start toward its fundamental procedure of reconciling theory with observed data through measurement and experimentation.

Hellenistic science and medicine made gains even though no technology existed to measure very small amounts of time or matter. The science of the age was as quantitative as it could be, given these limitations. Ctesibius invented pneumatics by creating machines operated by air pressure. He also built a working water pump, an organ powered by water, and the first accurate water clock. Hero of Alexandria built a rotating sphere powered by steam. As in most of Hellenistic science, these inventions did not lead to usable applications in daily life. The scientists and their royal patrons were more interested in new theoretical discoveries than in practical results, and the technology did not exist to produce the pipes, fittings, and screws needed to build metal machines.

Hellenistic science produced impressive military technology, such as more powerful catapults and huge siege towers on wheels. The most famous large-scale application of technology for nonmilitary purposes was the construction of the Pharos, a lighthouse three hundred feet tall, for the harbor at Alexandria. Using polished metal mirrors to reflect the light from a large bonfire, the Pharos shone many miles out over the sea. Awestruck sailors called it one of the wonders of the world.

Medicine also benefited from the Hellenistic quest for new knowledge. Increased contact between Greeks and people of the Near East made Mesopotamian and Egyptian medical knowledge better known in the West and promoted research on what made people ill. Hellenistic medical researchers discovered the value of measuring the pulse in diagnosing illness and studied anatomy by dissecting human corpses. It was rumored that they also dissected condemned criminals while they were still alive; they had access to these subjects because the king authorized the research. Some of the diagnostic terms then invented are still used, such as the blood pressure measurement designations *diastolic* (Greek for "dilated") and *systolic* (Greek for "contracted"). Other Hellenistic advances in anatomy included the discovery of the nerves and nervous system.

Cultural and Religious Transformations

Cultural transformations also shaped Hellenistic society. Wealthy non-Greeks increasingly adopted a Greek lifestyle to join the Hellenistic world's social hierarchy. Greek became the common language for international commerce and communication. The widespread use of the simplified form of the Greek language called **Koine** ("common") reflected the emergence of an international culture employing a common language; this was the reason the Egyptian camel trader stranded in Syria mentioned at the beginning of this chapter was at a disadvantage because he did not speak Greek. The most striking evidence of this cultural development comes from Afghanistan. There, King Ashoka (r. c. 268–232 B.C.E.), who ruled most of the Indian subcontinent, used Greek as one of the languages in his public inscriptions meant to teach Buddhist self-control, such as abstinence from eating meat. Local languages did not disappear in the Hellenistic kingdoms, however. In one region of Anatolia, for example, people spoke twenty-two different languages.

Religious diversity also grew. Traditional Greek cults (as described in Chapters 2 and 3) remained popular, but new cults, especially those deifying kings, reflected changing political and social conditions. Preexisting cults that previously had only local significance gained adherents all over the Hellenistic world. In many cases, Greek cults and local cults from the eastern

Greek-Style Buddha
The style of this statue of the founder of Buddhism, who expounded his doctrines in India, shows the mingling of Eastern and Western art. The Buddha's appearance, gaze, and posture stem from Indian artistic traditions, while the flowing folds of his garment recall Greek traditions. This combination of styles is called Gandharan, after the region in northwestern India where it began. What do you think are the possible motives for combining different artistic traditions? (National Museum of India, New Delhi/Borromeo/Art Resource, NY.)

Mediterranean influenced each other. Sometimes, local cults and Greek cults existed side by side and even overlapped. Some Egyptian villagers, for example, continued worshipping their traditional crocodile god and mummifying their dead, but they also honored Greek deities. As polytheists (believers in multiple gods), people could worship in both old and new cults.

New cults incorporated a concern for the relationship between the individual and what seemed the arbitrary power of divinities such as *Tychê* (TWO-kay; "chance" or "luck"). Since advances in astronomy had furthered knowledge about the movement of the universe's celestial bodies, religion now had to address the disconnect between the idea of heavenly uniformity contrasted with that of a shapeless chaos in earthly life. One increasingly popular approach to bridging that gap was to rely on astrology, which was based on the movement of the stars and planets, thought of as divinities. Another common choice was to worship Tychê in the hope of securing good luck in life.

The most revolutionary approach in seeking protection from Tychê's unpredictable tricks was to pray for salvation from deified kings, who expressed their divine power in **ruler cults**. Various populations established these cults in recognition of great benefactions. The Athenians, for example, deified the Macedonian Antigonus and his son Demetrius as savior gods in 307 B.C.E., when they liberated the city from an oppressive tyranny and donated magnificent gifts. Like most ruler cults, this one expressed the population's spontaneous gratitude to the rulers for their physical salvation, in hopes of preserving the rulers' goodwill toward them by addressing the kings' own wishes to have their power respected. Many cities in the Ptolemaic and Seleucid kingdoms set up ruler cults for their kings and queens. An inscription put up by Egyptian priests in 238 B.C.E. concretely described the qualities appropriate for a divine king and queen who saved the people:

> King Ptolemy III and Queen Berenice, his sister and wife, the Benefactor Gods, . . . have provided good government . . . and [after a drought] sacrificed a large amount of their revenues for the salvation of the population, and by importing grain . . . they saved the inhabitants of Egypt.

The Hellenistic monarchs' tremendous power and wealth gave them the status of gods to the ordinary people who depended on their generosity and protection. The idea that a human being could be a god, present on earth to save people from evils, was now firmly established and would prove influential later in Roman imperial religion and Christianity.

Healing divinities offered another form of protection to anxious individuals. The cult of the god Asclepius, who offered cures for illness and injury at his many shrines, grew in popularity during the Hellenistic period. Suppliants seeking Asclepius's help would sleep in special locations at his shrines to await dreams in which he prescribed healing treatments. These prescriptions emphasized diet and exercise, but numerous inscriptions commissioned by grateful patients also testified to miraculous cures and surgery performed while the sufferer slept. The following example is typical:

> Ambrosia of Athens was blind in one eye. . . . She . . . ridiculed some of the cures [described in inscriptions in the sanctuary] as being incredible and impossible. . . . But when she went to sleep, she saw a vision; she thought the god was standing next to her. . . . He split open the diseased eye and poured in a medicine. When day came she left cured.

People's faith in divine healing gave them hope that they could overcome the constant danger of illness, which appeared to strike at random; there was no knowledge of germs as causing infections.

Underground Labyrinth for Healing
This underground stone labyrinth formed part of the enormous healing sanctuary of the god Asclepius at Epidaurus in Greece. Patients flocked to the site from all over the Mediterranean world. They descended into the labyrinth, which was covered and dark, as part of their treatment, which centered on reaching a trance state to receive dreams that would provide instructions on their healing and, sometimes, miraculous surgery. Do you think such treatment could be effective? (Gianni Dagli Orti/REX/Shutterstock.)

Mystery cults promised initiates secret knowledge for personal safety. The cults of the Greek god Dionysus and the Egyptian goddess Isis attracted many people. Isis became the most popular female divinity in the Mediterranean because her powers protected her worshippers in all aspects of their lives. Her cult involved rituals and festivals mixing Egyptian religion with Greek elements. Disciples of Isis strove to achieve personal purification and the goddess's aid in overcoming the demonic power of Tychê. This popularity of an Egyptian deity among Greeks (and, later, Romans) is clear evidence of the cultural interaction of the Hellenistic world.

Cultural interaction between Greeks and Jews influenced Judaism during the Hellenistic period. King Ptolemy II made the Hebrew Bible accessible to a wide audience by having his Alexandrian scholars produce a Greek translation—the Septuagint. Many Jews, especially those in the large Jewish communities that had

MAPPING THE WEST

Roman Takeover of the Hellenistic World, to 30 B.C.E.
By the death of Cleopatra VII of Egypt in 30 B.C.E., the Romans had taken over the Hellenistic kingdoms of the eastern Mediterranean. This territory became the eastern half of the Roman Empire.

Analyzing the Map: How did the geographical location of the Roman republic allow the Romans to expand their power throughout the Mediterranean area?

Making Connections: Compare the political divisions on this map with those on Mapping the West for Chapter 3. What accounts for the differences?

grown up in Hellenistic cities outside their homeland, began to speak Greek and adopt Greek culture. These Greek-style Jews mixed Jewish and Greek customs, while retaining Judaism's rituals and rules and not worshipping Greek gods.

Internal conflict among Jews erupted in second-century B.C.E. Palestine over how much Greek tradition was acceptable for traditional Jews. The Seleucid king Antiochus IV (r. 175–164 B.C.E.) intervened to support Greek-style Jews in Jerusalem, who had taken over the high priesthood that ruled the Jewish community. In 167 B.C.E., Antiochus converted the great Jewish temple in Jerusalem into a Greek temple and outlawed Jewish religious rites such as observing the Sabbath and performing circumcision. This action provoked a revolt led by Judah the Maccabee, which won Jewish independence from Seleucid control after twenty-five years of war. The most famous episode in this revolt was the retaking of the Jerusalem temple and its rededication to the worship of the Jewish god, Yahweh, commemorated by the Hanukkah holiday.

That Greek culture attracted some Jews in the first place provides a striking example of the transformations that affected many—though far from all—people of the Hellenistic world. By the time of the Roman Empire, one of those transformations would be Christianity, whose theology had roots in the cultural interaction of Hellenistic Jews and Greeks and their ideas on apocalypticism (religious ideas revealing the future) and divine human beings.

REVIEW QUESTION
How did the political changes of the Hellenistic period affect art, science, and religion?

Conclusion

The aftermath of the Peloponnesian War led ordinary people as well as philosophers like Plato and Aristotle to question the basis of morality. The disunity of Greek international politics allowed Macedonia's aggressive leaders Philip II and Alexander the Great to make themselves the masters of the competing city-states. Inspired by Greek heroic ideals, Alexander the Great conquered the Persian Empire and set in motion the Hellenistic period's enormous political, social, cultural, and religious changes.

When Alexander's commanders transformed themselves into Hellenistic kings after his death, they reintroduced monarchy into the Greek world, adding an administrative layer of Greek and Macedonian officials to the conquered lands' existing governments. Local elites cooperated with the new Hellenistic monarchs in governing and financing their hierarchical society, which was divided along ethnic lines, with the Greek and Macedonian elite ranking above local elites. To enhance their own reputations, Hellenistic kings and queens funded writers, artists, scholars, philosophers, and scientists, thereby energizing intellectual life. The traditional city-states continued to exist in Hellenistic Greece, but their freedom extended only to local governance; the Hellenistic kings controlled foreign policy.

Increased contacts between diverse peoples promoted greater cultural interaction in the Hellenistic world. Artists and writers expressed emotion in their works, philosophers discussed how to achieve true happiness, scientists conducted research with royal support, and royal rulers were often worshipped as a new kind of divinity. More anxious than ever about the role of chance in life, many people looked for new religious experiences, especially in cults promising secret knowledge to initiates. What changed most of all was the Romans' culture once they took over the Hellenistic kingdoms' territory and came into close contact with their diverse peoples' traditions. Rome's rise to power took centuries, however, because Rome originated as a tiny, insignificant place that no one except Romans ever expected to amount to anything in the wider world.

Chapter 4 Review

Key Terms and People

Be sure that you can identify the term or person and explain its historical significance.

Plato (p. 119)	Alexander the Great (p. 121)	Stoicism (p. 136)
metaphysics (p. 119)	Hellenistic (p. 126)	Koine (p. 139)
dualism (p. 119)	epigrams (p. 134)	ruler cults (p. 140)
Aristotle (p. 120)	materialism (p. 136)	
Lyceum (p. 120)	Epicureanism (p. 136)	

Review Questions

1. How did daily life, philosophy, and the political situation change in Greece during the period 400–350 B.C.E.?

2. What were the accomplishments of Alexander the Great, and what were their effects both for the ancient world and for later Western civilization?

3. How did the political and social organization of the new Hellenistic kingdoms compare with that of the earlier Greek city-states?

4. How did the political changes of the Hellenistic period affect art, science, and religion?

Making Connections

1. What made ancient people see Alexander as "great"? Would he be regarded as "great" in today's world?

2. What are the advantages and disadvantages of governmental support of the arts and sciences? Compare such support in the Hellenistic kingdoms to that in the United States today (e.g., through the National Endowment for the Humanities, the National Endowment for the Arts, and the National Science Foundation).

3. Is inner personal tranquility powerful enough to make a difficult or painful life bearable?

Important Events

399 B.C.E.	Socrates is executed
386 B.C.E.	In King's Peace, Sparta surrenders control of Anatolian Greek city-states to Persia; Plato founds the Academy
362 B.C.E.	Battle of Mantinea leaves power vacuum in a disunited Greece
338 B.C.E.	Battle of Chaeronea allows Macedonian Philip II to become the leading power in Greece

335 B.C.E.	Aristotle founds the Lyceum
334–323 B.C.E.	Alexander the Great leads Greeks and Macedonians to conquer Persian Empire
307 B.C.E.	Epicurus founds his philosophical group in Athens
306–304 B.C.E.	Successors of Alexander declare themselves kings
300–260 B.C.E.	Theocritus writes poetry at Ptolemaic court
c. 300 B.C.E.	Euclid teaches geometry at Alexandria
195 B.C.E.	Seleucid queen Laodice endows dowries for girls
167 B.C.E.	Maccabee revolt after Antiochus IV turns temple in Jerusalem into a Greek sanctuary
30 B.C.E.	Cleopatra VII dies and Rome takes over Ptolemaic Empire

Consider three events

Alexander the Great leads Greeks and Macedonians to conquer Persian Empire (334–323 B.C.E.), Epicurus founds his philosophical group in Athens (307 B.C.E.), and Euclid teaches geometry at Alexandria (c. 300 B.C.E.). How might Alexander's expeditions have influenced developments in politics, philosophy, and science?

Suggested References

After the Peloponnesian War, the structure of international relations changed radically in the Greek world as the city-states became secondary in political power to the kingdom of Macedonia, and then to the kingdoms of the Hellenistic period. Long-lasting cultural changes accompanied this political transformation.

Amitay, Ory. *From Alexander to Jesus*. 2010.

*Barnes, Jonathan, ed. *The Complete Works of Aristotle: The Revised Oxford Translation*. 1984.

Chaniotis, Angelos. *War in the Hellenistic World*. 2005.

Collins, John Joseph. *Between Athens and Jerusalem: Jewish Identity in the Hellenistic Diaspora*. 1999.

Erskine, Andrew, ed. *A Companion to the Hellenistic Age*. 2003.

Evans, J. A. S. *Daily Life in the Hellenistic Age: From Alexander to Cleopatra*. 2008.

*Hamilton, Edith, and Huntington Cairns, eds. *The Collected Dialogues of Plato, including the Letters*. 1961.

Holt, Frank L. *Lost World of the Golden King: In Search of Ancient Afghanistan*. 2012.

Martin, Thomas R., and Christopher W. Blackwell. *Alexander the Great: The Story of an Ancient Life*. 2012.

Mikalson, Jon D. *Religion in Hellenistic Athens*. 1998.

Pollitt, J. J. *Art in the Hellenistic Age*. 1986.

Ptolemaic Egypt: http://www.houseofptolemy.org/

*Scott-Kilvert, Ian, trans. *The Age of Alexander: Nine Greek Lives*. 1973.

Sharples, R. W. *Stoics, Epicureans, and Sceptics: An Introduction to Hellenistic Philosophy*. 1996.

Shipley, Graham. *The Greek World after Alexander 323–30 B.C.* 1999.

Snyder, Jane M. *The Woman and the Lyre: Women Writers in Classical Greece and Rome*. 1989.

_____

*Primary source.

The Rise of Rome and Its Republic

753–44 B.C.E.

The Romans treasured legends about their state's transformation from a tiny village to a world power. They especially loved stories about their city's legendary first king, Romulus. When early Rome needed more women to bear children to increase its population and build a strong army, Romulus begged Rome's neighbors for permission for its men to marry their women. Everyone turned him down, mocking Rome's poverty and weakness. Enraged, Romulus hatched a plan to use force where diplomacy had failed. Inviting the neighboring Sabines to a religious festival, he had his men kidnap the unmarried women who attended. The Roman kidnappers immediately married these Sabines, promising to cherish them as beloved wives and new citizens. When the Sabine men attacked Rome to rescue their kin, the women rushed into the midst of the bloody battle, begging their brothers, fathers, and new husbands either to stop slaughtering one another or to kill them—their devoted sisters, daughters, and wives—to end the war. The men on both sides made peace on the spot and agreed to merge their populations under Roman rule.

This legend emphasizes that Rome, unlike the city-states of Greece, expanded by absorbing outsiders into its citizen body—and recognized the valor of women. Rome's growth was the ancient world's greatest expansion of population and territory, as a people originally housed in a few huts gradually created a state that fought countless wars and relocated an unprecedented number of citizens to gain control of most

«The Wolf Suckling Romulus and Remus This bronze statue relates to the myth that a she-wolf nursed the twin brothers Romulus and Remus, the offspring of the war god Mars and the future founders of Rome. Romans treasured this story because it meant that Mars loved their city so dearly that he sent a wild animal to nurse its founders after a cruel tyrant had forced their mother to abandon the infants. The myth also taught Romans that their state had been born in violence: Romulus killed Remus in an argument over who would lead their new settlement. The wolf is an Etruscan sculpture from the fifth century B.C.E.; the babies were added in the Renaissance. (Musei Capitolini, Rome, Italy/Scala/Art Resource, NY.)

CHAPTER FOCUS
How did traditional
Roman values affect
the rise and then
the downfall of the
Roman republic?

of Europe, North Africa, Egypt, and the Mediterranean region. The social, cultural, political, legal, and economic traditions that Romans developed to rule this vast area created greater connections between diverse peoples than had ever existed before. Unlike the Greeks and Macedonians, the Romans maintained the unity of their state for centuries. The empire's long existence allowed many Roman values and traditions to become influential components of Western civilization.

Greek literature, art, and philosophy influenced Rome's culture greatly. Romans learned from their neighbors, adapting foreign traditions to their own purposes and forging their own cultural identity.

The legend about Romulus belongs to Rome's earliest history as a monarchy, when kings ruled (753–509 B.C.E.). Rome's later history is divided into the republic (see Terms of History on page 150) and the Empire, as it is called today. (See Terms of History in Chapter 6.) Under the republic (founded 509 B.C.E.), male citizens elected government officials and passed laws (although an oligarchy of the social elite dominated politics). The so-called empire, which by modern reckoning began in the late first century B.C.E., arose in the violent aftermath of the death of Julius Caesar. From then on, actual monarchs (whom we call emperors) once again ruled while denying they were kings by claiming to continue the Roman republic. Rome's greatest expansion came during the time of the original republic. Romans' belief in a divine destiny fueled this tremendous growth. They believed that the gods wanted them to rule the world and improve it by making everyone adhere to their social and moral values.

Roman values emphasized family loyalty, selfless political and military service to the community, individual honor and public status, the importance of the law, and shared decision making. By the first century B.C.E., power-hungry leaders such as Sulla and Julius Caesar had plunged Rome into civil war. By putting their personal ambition before the good of the state, they destroyed the republic.

CHAPTER TIMELINE

753 B.C.E.
Traditional
date of Rome's
founding as
monarchy

451–449 B.C.E.
Creation of Twelve
Tables, Rome's first
written law code

387 B.C.E.
Gauls sack Rome

760   **520**   **320**

509 B.C.E.
Roman republic
is established

509–287 B.C.E.
Struggle of the orders

396 B.C.E.
Defeat of Etruscan
city of Veii; first great
expansion of Roman
territory

Roman Social and Religious Traditions

Rome's citizens believed that eternal moral values connected them to one another and required them to honor the gods in return for divine support. Hierarchy affected everyone: people at all social levels were obligated to patrons or to clients; in families, fathers dominated legally but mothers held great status; in religion, people at all levels of society owed sacrifices, rituals, and prayers to the gods who protected the family and the state.

Roman Moral Values

Roman values defined relationships with other people and with the gods. Romans guided their lives by the **mos maiorum** ("the way of the elders"), values passed down from their ancestors. The Romans preserved these values because, for them, *old* equaled "tested by time," while *new* meant "dangerous." Roman morality emphasized virtue, faithfulness, and respect. A reputation for behaving morally was crucial to Romans because it earned them the respect of others.

Virtus ("manly virtue") meant strength, loyalty, and courage, especially in war. It also included wisdom and moral purity; in this broader sense, women, too, could possess virtus. In the second century B.C.E., the Roman poet Lucilius defined it this way:

> *Virtus* is to know the human relevance of each thing,
> To know what is humanly right and useful and honorable,
> And what things are good and what are bad, useless, shameful, and
> dishonorable. . . .
> And, in addition, *virtus* is putting the country's interests first,
> Then our parents', with our own interests third and last.

Fides (FEE-dehs, "faithfulness") meant keeping one's obligations no matter the cost. Failing to meet an obligation offended the community and the gods.

---

220 B.C.E.
Rome controls Italy south of Po River

218–201 B.C.E.
Rome and Carthage fight Second Punic War

168–149 B.C.E.
Cato writes *The Origins*, first history of Rome in Latin

133 B.C.E.
Tiberius Gracchus is elected tribune; assassinated in same year

60 B.C.E.
First Triumvirate of Caesar, Pompey, and Crassus

44 B.C.E.
Caesar is appointed dictator with no term limit; assassinated in same year

280   **160**   **40**

264–241 B.C.E.
Rome and Carthage fight First Punic War

149–146 B.C.E.
Rome and Carthage fight Third Punic War

146 B.C.E.
Carthage and Corinth are destroyed

91–87 B.C.E.
Social War between Rome and its Italian allies

49–45 B.C.E.
Civil war, with Caesar the victor

45–44 B.C.E.
Cicero writes his philosophical works on *humanitas*

TERMS OF HISTORY

Republic

The modern term *republic* comes from two Latin words, the noun *res* ("thing; matter") and the adjective *publicus, -a, -um* ("belonging to the people, public"). Originally, when Romans referred to **res publica**, they meant the "body politic," meaning the state giving at least some political rights to all (male) citizens that they created in 509 B.C.E. after the monarchy founded by Romulus had been overthrown in response to the rape and suicide of Lucretia, a woman from the social elite violently assaulted by a royal son (see page 158).

The "Roman republic" lasted, as modern historians see it, until the foundation of the "Roman Empire" by Augustus in the late first century B.C.E. The ancient Romans, however, persisted in using the term "republic" to refer to their government even following the time of Augustus, when what we called its emperors (called "first men" by Romans) ruled as if they were kings.

Why did Romans hold on to this name for their government even after they all realized that it had become a (disguised) monarchy? The answer probably lies in another meaning of *res publica*: "the public good, the well-being of the state, the resources belonging the people as a whole." That is, the Roman idea of "republic" was always intertwined with the notion of what was advantageous to the community, of what was foundational for its survival and flourishing. Even when the nature of their government changed, Romans could derive psychological comfort from the positive connotations of referring to it as a republic—unless, of course, this reference was purely propaganda put out by Roman emperors to try to mask the uncomfortable reality that they ruled as kings. Probably both these interpretations apply.

Ancient observers of government of the Roman republic praised it as a "mixed constitution," meaning that it combined positive aspects of monarchy, oligarchy, and democracy. In this context, it is important to remember that ancient Rome had no written constitution and that the notion of a republic does not require one.

What exactly the notion of a republic should be remains a debated issue. From the republics of the city-states in Renaissance Italy discussed by, among other contemporaries, Nicolò Machiavelli (see Chapter 14) , to the Dutch Republic and the "Republic of Virtue" in France (see Chapter 19), to the founding of the United States as a "federal republic," no single definition of the term emerged. James Madison, an "American founder," in 1787 in *Federalist Paper* no. 10 wrote that a republic was a state that was not a direct democracy, but rather one that elected representatives to whom the people delegated the power to govern; this structure, he argued, minimized the chances of conflict among factions that could destabilize the state. Article IV, Section 4, of the Constitution of the United States specifies that "The United States shall guarantee to every state in this union a republican form of government"—without defining what is meant by "a republican form of government" (i.e., a government in the form of a republic; the reference is not to the modern political party called "Republican"). The question of how to understand the term *republic* is still open.

Faithful women remained virgins before marriage and monogamous afterward. Faithful men kept their word, paid their debts, and treated everyone with justice—which did not mean treating everyone equally, but rather appropriately, according to whether the person was a social superior, an equal, or an inferior. Showing respect and devotion to the gods and to one's family was the supreme form of faithfulness. Romans believed they had to worship the gods faithfully to maintain the divine favor that protected their community.

Roman values required that each person maintain self-control and limit displays of emotion. So strict was this value that not even wives and husbands could kiss in public without seeming emotionally out of control. It also meant that a person should never give up, no matter how hard the situation.

The reward for living these values was respect from others. Women earned respect by bearing legitimate children and educating them morally. Men became respected through military service and helping others. They relied on their reputations to help them win election to the republic's government posts. A man of the highest reputation commanded so much respect that others would obey him regardless of whether he held an office with formal power over them. A man with this much prestige was said to possess authority. The concept of authority based on respect reflected the Roman belief that some people were by nature superior to others and that society had to be hierarchical to be just. Romans believed that aristocrats, people born into the "best" families, automatically deserved high respect. In return, aristocrats were supposed to live strictly by the highest values to serve the community.

In legends about the early days of Rome, a person could be poor and still remain a proud aristocrat. Over time, however, money became overwhelmingly important to the Roman elite, to purchase showy luxuries, large-scale entertainment, and costly gifts to the community. In this way, wealth became necessary to maintain high social status.

The Patron-Client System

The **patron-client system** was an interlocking network of personal relationships that obligated people to one another. A patron was a man of superior status able to provide benefits to lower-status people; these were his clients, who in return owed him duties and paid him special attention. In this hierarchical system, a patron was often himself the client of a higher-status man.

Benefits and duties created mutual exchanges of financial and political help. Patrons would help their clients get started in business by giving them a gift or a loan and connecting them with others who could help them. In politics, a patron would promote a client's candidacy for elective office and provide money for campaigning. Patrons also supported clients if they had legal trouble.

Clients had to support their patrons' campaigns for election to public office and lend them money to build public works and to fund their daughters' dowries. A patron expected his clients to gather at his house at dawn to accompany him to the forum, the city's public center, to show his great status. A Roman leader needed a large house to hold this throng and to entertain his social equals.

Patrons' and clients' mutual obligations endured for generations. Ex-slaves, who became the clients for life of the masters who freed them, often handed down this relationship to their children. Romans with contacts abroad could acquire clients among foreigners; Roman generals sometimes had entire foreign communities obligated to them. The patron-client system demonstrated the Roman idea that social stability and well-being were achieved by faithfully maintaining established ties.

The Roman Family

The family was Roman society's bedrock because it taught values and determined the ownership of property. Men and women shared the duty of teaching their children values, though by law the father possessed the *patria potestas* ("father's power") over his children—no matter how old—and his slaves. This power made him the sole owner of all his dependents' property. As long as he was alive, no son or daughter could officially own anything, accumulate money, or possess any independent legal standing. Unofficially, however, adult children did control personal property and money, and favored slaves could build up savings. Fathers also held legal power of life and death over these members of their households, but they rarely exercised this power except through exposure of newborns, an accepted practice to limit family size and dispose of physically imperfect infants.

Patria potestas did not allow a husband to control his wife; instead, under the common arrangement called a "free" marriage, the wife formally remained under her father's power as long as the father lived. But in the ancient world, few fathers lived long enough to oversee the lives of their married daughters or sons; four out of five parents died before their children reached age thirty. A Roman woman without a living father was relatively independent. Legally, she needed a male guardian to conduct her business, but guardianship was largely an empty formality by the first century B.C.E. As a commentator explained: "The common belief seems more false than true that, because of their instability of judgment, women are often deceived and that therefore it is only fair to have them controlled by the authority of guardians. In fact, women of full age manage their affairs themselves."

A Roman woman had to grow up fast. Tullia (c. 79–45 B.C.E.), daughter of Rome's most famous politician and orator, Cicero, was engaged at twelve, married at sixteen, and widowed by twenty-two. Like every other wealthy

Sculpture of a Woman Running a Store
This sculpture portrays a woman selling food from a small shop while customers make purchases or chat. Since Roman women could own property, it is possible that the woman is the store owner. The man standing behind her could be her husband or a servant. Much like malls of today, markets in Roman towns were packed with small stores. (Art Resource, NY.)

married Roman woman, she managed the household slaves, monitored the nurturing of the young children by wet nurses, kept account books to track the property she personally owned, and accompanied her husband to dinner parties—something a Greek wife was not allowed to do.

A mother's responsibility for shaping her children's values constituted the foundation of female virtue. Women like Cornelia, a famous aristocrat of the second century B.C.E., won enormous respect for loyalty to family. When her husband died, Cornelia refused an offer of marriage from King Ptolemy VIII of Egypt so that she could continue to oversee the family estate and educate her surviving daughter and two sons (her other nine children had died). The boys, Tiberius and Gaius Gracchus, grew up to be among the most influential political leaders in the late republic. The number of children Cornelia bore reveals the fertility and stamina required of a Roman wife to ensure the survival of her husband's family line. Cornelia also became famous for her stylishly worded letters, which were still being read a century later.

Roman women could not vote or hold political office, but wealthy women like Cornelia influenced politics by expressing their opinions to men at home and at dinner parties. Marcus Porcius Cato (234–149 B.C.E.), a famous politician and author, described this clout: "All mankind rule their wives, we [Roman men] rule all mankind, and our wives rule us."

Women could acquire property through inheritance and entrepreneurship. Archaeological discoveries reveal that by the end of the republic some women owned large businesses. Prenuptial agreements determining the property rights of husband and wife were common. In divorce fathers kept the children. Most poor women worked as field laborers or in shops. Women and men both worked in manufacturing, which mostly took place in the home. The men worked the raw materials—cutting, fitting, and polishing wood, leather, and metal—while the women sold the finished goods. The poorest women earned money through prostitution, which was legal but considered disgraceful.

Education for Public Life

Roman education aimed to make men and women effective speakers and exponents of traditional values. Most children received their education at home; there were no public schools, but the rich hired private teachers. Wealthy parents bought literate slaves called pedagogues to educate their children, especially to teach them Greek. In upper-class families, both daughters and sons learned to read. The girls were taught literature and music and how to make educated conversation at dinner parties. The aim of women's education was to prepare them to teach traditional social and moral values to their children.

Sons received physical training and learned to fight with weapons, but rhetorical training dominated an upper-class Roman boy's education because a successful political career depended on the ability to speak persuasively in public. A boy would learn winning techniques by listening to speeches in political meetings and arguments in court cases. The orator Cicero said, "[Young men must learn to] excel in public speaking. It is the tool for controlling men at Rome."

Public and Private Religion

Romans followed Greek models of religion. Their chief deity, Jupiter, corresponded to the Greek god Zeus and was seen as a powerful, stern father. Juno (the Greek Hera), queen of the gods, and Minerva (the Greek Athena), goddess of wisdom, joined Jupiter to form the state religion's central triad. These three deities shared Rome's most revered temple.

Protecting Rome's safety and prosperity was the gods' major function. They were supposed to help Rome defeat enemies in war and support agriculture. Prayers requested the gods' aid in winning battles, growing abundant crops, healing disease, and promoting reproduction for animals and people. In times of crisis, Romans sought foreign gods for help in bringing salvation to their community, such as when the government imported the cult of the healing god Asclepius from Greece in 293 B.C.E., praying he would stop an epidemic.

The republic supported many other cults, including that of Vesta, goddess of the hearth and protector of the family. Her shrine housed Rome's official eternal flame, which guaranteed the state's permanent existence. The Vestal Virgins, six unmarried women sworn to chastity and Rome's only female priests, tended Vesta's shrine. They earned high status and freedom from their fathers' control by performing their most important duty: keeping the flame from going out. If the flame went out, the Romans assumed that one of the Vestal Virgins had had sex and buried her alive.

Religion was important in Roman family life. Each household maintained small indoor shrines that housed statuettes of the spirits of the household and those of the ancestors, protectors of the family's health and morality. Upper-class families kept death masks of famous ancestors hanging in the main room and wore them at funerals to display their status.

Religious rituals accompanied everyday activities, such as breast-feeding babies or fertilizing crops. Many public religious gatherings promoted the community's health and stability. For example, during the Lupercalia festival (whose name recalled the wolf, *luper* in Latin, that had reared Romulus and his twin, Remus, according to legend), near-naked young men streaked around the Palatine hill, lashing any woman they met with strips of goatskin. Women who had not yet borne children would run out to be struck, believing this would help them become fertile.

The Romans did not regard the gods as guardians of human morality. As Cicero explained, "We call Jupiter the Best and Greatest not because he makes

Ahenobarbus Relief Sculpture

This relief sculpture from Rome about 100 B.C.E. shows young men being registered for service in the army (part of the Roman process called a "census"). Mars, the god of war dressed in armor, is depicted as presiding over this important ceremony involving both citizen identity and national defense. Large animals are being led in to be sacrificed (and then roasted and eaten) to sanctify and celebrate the occasion. The sculpture was probably paid for by a man named Ahenobarbus, who had risen to the elected office of consul, to demonstrate both his dedication to the community and his own success in a public career. (Musée du Louvre, Paris, France/ photo: Herve Lewandowski/ © RMN-Grand Palais/Art Resource, NY.)

us just or sober or wise but, rather, healthy, unharmed, rich, and prosperous." Roman officials preceded important actions with the ritual called taking the auspices, in which they sought Jupiter's approval by observing natural signs such as birds' flight direction or eating habits or the appearance of thunder and lightning.

Romans regarded values as divine forces. *Pietas* ("piety"), for example, meant devotion and duty to family, friends, the state, and the gods; a temple at Rome held a statue personifying pietas as a female divinity. The personification of abstract moral qualities provided a focus for cult rituals.

The duty of Roman religious officials was to maintain peace with the gods. Socially prominent men served as priests, conducting sacrifices, festivals, and prayers. Priests were citizens performing public service, not religious professionals. The chief priest, the *pontifex maximus* ("greatest bridge-builder"), served as the head of state religion, a position carrying political prominence. The most prominent religious ceremonies at which priests presided were sacrifices of large animals, whose meat would be shared among the worshippers.

Disrespect for religious tradition brought punishment. Admirals, for example, took the auspices by feeding sacred chickens on their warships: if the birds ate energetically, Jupiter favored the Romans and an attack could begin. In 249 B.C.E., the commander Publius Claudius Pulcher grew frustrated when his chickens, probably seasick, refused to eat. Determined to attack, he finally hurled the birds overboard in a rage, sputtering, "Well then, let them drink!" When he promptly suffered a huge defeat, he was fined heavily.

REVIEW QUESTION

What common themes underlay Roman values, and how did Romans' behavior reflect those values?

From Monarchy to Republic

Romans' values and their belief in a divine destiny fueled their astounding growth from a tiny settlement into the Mediterranean's greatest power. The Romans spilled much blood as they gradually expanded their territory through war. From the eighth to the sixth century B.C.E., they were ruled by kings, but the later kings' violence provoked members of the social elite to overthrow the monarchy and create the republic, which lasted until the first century B.C.E. The Roman republic gained land and population by winning aggressive wars and by absorbing other peoples. Its economic and cultural growth depended on contact with many other peoples around the Mediterranean.

Roman Society under the Kings, 753–509 B.C.E.

Seven kings ruled from 753 to 509 B.C.E. and created Rome's most famous and enduring government body: the Senate, a group of distinguished men chosen as the king's personal council. This council played the same role—advising government leaders—for a thousand years, as Rome changed from a monarchy to a republic and back to a monarchy (the Empire). It was always a Roman tradition that one should never make decisions by oneself but only after consulting advisers and friends.

Rome's expansion depended on taking in outsiders conquered in war and, uniquely in the ancient world, giving citizenship to freed slaves. Although these so-called freedmen and freedwomen owed special obligations to their former owners and could not hold elective office or serve in the army, they enjoyed all other citizens' rights, such as legal marriage. Their children possessed citizenship without any limits. By the late republic, many Roman citizens were descendants of freed slaves.

By 550 B.C.E., Rome had grown to some forty thousand people and, through war and diplomacy, had won control of three hundred square miles of surrounding territory. Archaeological excavation confirms that the Romans had already built substantial temples to their gods by this date. Rome's geography propelled its further expansion. The Romans originated in central Italy, a long peninsula with a mountain range down its middle like a spine and fertile plains on either side. Rome also controlled a river crossing on a major north–south route. Most important, Rome was ideally situated for international trade: the Italian peninsula stuck so far out into the Mediterranean that east–west seaborne traffic naturally encountered it (Map 5.1), and the city had a good port nearby.

The Italian ancestors of the Romans lived by herding animals, farming, and hunting. They became skilled metalworkers, especially in iron. The earliest Romans' neighbors in central Italy were poor villagers, too, and spoke the same language, Latin. Greeks lived to the south in Italy and Sicily, and contact with them deeply affected Roman cultural development. Romans developed a love-hate relationship with Greece, admiring its literature and art but despising its lack of military unity. Romans adopted many elements from Greek culture — from the deities for their national cults to the models for their poetry, prose, and architectural styles.

The Etruscans, a people to the north, also influenced Roman culture. Brightly colored wall paintings in tombs, portraying funeral banquets and festive games, reveal the splendor of Etruscan society. In addition to producing their own art, jewelry, and sculpture, the Etruscans imported luxurious objects from Greece and the Near East. Most of the intact Greek vases known today were found in Etruscan tombs, and Etruscan culture was deeply influenced by that of Greece.

MAP 5.1 Ancient Italy, 500 B.C.E.
When the Romans overthrew the monarchy to found a republic in 509 B.C.E., they controlled a relatively small territory in central Italy. Many different peoples lived in Italy at this time, with the most prosperous occupying fertile agricultural land and sheltered harbors on the peninsula's west side. The early republic's most urbanized neighbors were the Etruscans to the north and the Greeks in the city-states to the south, including on the island of Sicily. Immediately adjacent to Rome were the people of Latium, called Latins. How did geography aid early Roman expansion in the Italian peninsula?

Etruscan Tomb of the Leopards
This detail from a wall painting in an Etruscan tomb shows a banquet in honor of the dead person buried in the underground chamber. Like Greeks, the banqueters recline on couches, propped up on an elbow. The servant, shown nude, is carrying a wine jug to refill. Unlike Greeks, the Etruscans mixed women and men as guests at dinner and drinking parties, a tradition they passed on to the Romans. The men are depicted with darker skin tones, while the woman has lighter skin, reflecting the tradition that upper-class women stayed out of the sun to avoid getting a tan. (O. Louis Mazzatenta/ National Geographic Creative.)

Romans adopted ceremonial features of Etruscan culture, such as musical instruments, religious rituals, and lictors (attendants who walked before the highest officials carrying the fasces, a bundle of rods around an ax, symbolizing the officials' right to command and punish). The Romans also borrowed from the Etruscans the ritual of divination—determining the will of the gods by examining organs of slaughtered animals. Other prominent features of Roman culture were probably part of the ancient Mediterranean's shared practices, such as the organization of the Roman army (a citizen militia of heavily armed infantry troops fighting in formation) and the use of an alphabet.

The Early Roman Republic, 509–287 B.C.E.

A woman's response to a gender-related abuse of power initiated the epoch-making change in Roman history in which the monarchy was replaced by a republic. In 509 B.C.E., the son of the king raped Lucretia, a socially elite woman who first made her male relatives swear to take vengeance and then defied their wishes for her by committing suicide in front of them to preserve her honor. Inspired to action by her iron will, her relatives and friends then ousted the king to found the republic. Thereafter, the Romans prided themselves on having a political system based on sharing political power among (male) citizens, to avoid the abuse of power by a sole ruler and to try to tamp down violent competition among the socially elite for supreme prominence in the state. (See Primary Source Analysis on page 158.)

The Romans struggled for 250 years to shape a stable government for the republic. Roman social hierarchy split the population into two **orders:** the

PRIMARY SOURCE ANALYSIS

The Rape and Suicide of Lucretia

This story explaining why the Roman elite expelled the monarchy in 509 B.C.E., thus opening the way to the republic, centers on female virtue and courage, as do other famous stories about significant political changes in early Roman history. The historian Livy composed this narrative in the late first century B.C.E., at another crucial point in Roman history—the violent transition from republic to empire—when Romans were deeply concerned with the values of the past as a guide to the present.

Sextus Tarquinius, the son of Rome's king [Tarquin the Proud, r. 534–510 B.C.E.], came to Lucretia's home. She greeted him warmly and asked him to stay [as Roman hospitality demanded for such a high-status visitor]. Crazy with lust, he waited until he was sure the household was sleeping. Drawing his sword, he snuck into Lucretia's bedroom and placed the blade against her left breast, whispering, "Quiet, Lucretia; I am Sextus Tarquinius, and I am holding a sword. If you cry out, I'll kill you!" Rudely awakened, the desperate woman realized that no one could help her and that she was close to death. Sextus Tarquinius said he loved her, begging and threatening her in turn, trying everything to wear her down. When she wouldn't give in, even in the face of threats of murder, he added another intimidation. "After I've murdered you, I am going to put the naked corpse of a slave next to your body, and everybody will say that you were killed during a disgraceful adultery." This final threat defeated her, and after raping her he left, having stolen her honor.

Lucretia, overwhelmed by sadness and shame, sent messengers to her husband, Tarquinius Conlatinus, who was away, and her father at Rome, telling them, "Come immediately, with a good friend, because something horrible has happened." Her father arrived with a friend, and her husband came with Lucius Junius Brutus. . . . They found Lucretia in her room, overcome with grief. When she saw them, she started weeping. "How are you?" her husband asked. "Very bad," she replied. "How can any-

thing be fine for a woman who has lost her honor? Traces of another man are in our bed, my husband. My body is defiled, though my heart is still pure; my death will be the proof. But give me your right hand and promise that you will not let the guilty escape. It was Sextus Tarquinius who returned our hospitality with hostility last night. With his sword in his hand, he came to have his fun, to my despair, but it will also be his sorrow—if you are real men." They pledged that they would catch him, and they tried to ease her sadness, saying that the soul did wrong, not the body, and where there were no bad intentions there could be no blame. "It is your responsibility to ensure that he gets what he deserves," she said; "I am blameless, but I will not free myself from punishment. No dishonorable woman shall hold up Lucretia as an example." Then she grabbed a dagger hidden underneath her robe and stabbed herself in the heart. She fell dead, as her husband and father cried out.

Brutus, leaving them to their tears, pulled the blade from Lucretia's wound and held it up drenched in blood, shouting, "By this blood, which was completely pure before the crime of the king's son, I swear before you, O gods, to drive out the king himself, his criminal wife, and all their children, by sword, fire, and everything in my power, and never to allow a king to rule Rome ever again, whether from that family or any other."

Source: Livy, *From the Foundation of the City*, 1.57–59. Translation by Thomas R. Martin.

QUESTIONS TO CONSIDER

1. What notions of honor for men and for women are reflected in Livy's tale?

2. The values attributed here to Lucretia certainly reflect Roman men's wishes for women's behavior, but do you think women could have held similar opinions? Why or why not?

---

patricians (a small group of the most aristocratic families) and the **plebeians** (the rest of the citizens). These two groups' conflicts over power created the so-called struggle of the orders. The struggle finally ended in 287 B.C.E., when plebeians won the right to make laws in their own assembly.

Patricians constituted a tiny percentage of the population—numbering only about 130 families—but in the beginning of the republic their inherited status entitled them to control public religion and to monopolize political office. Many patricians were much wealthier than most plebeians. Some plebeians, however, were also rich, and they resented the patricians' dominance, especially their ban on intermarriage with plebeians. Poor plebeians demanded farmland and relief from crushing debts. Patricians inflamed tensions by wearing special red shoes to set themselves apart; later, they changed to black shoes adorned with a small metal crescent. To pressure the patricians, the plebeians periodically refused military service. This tactic worked because Rome's army depended on plebeian manpower for its citizen militia.

In response to plebeian unrest, the patricians agreed to the earliest Roman law code. This code, enacted between 451 and 449 B.C.E. and known as the **Twelve Tables**, guaranteed greater equality and social mobility. The Twelve Tables prevented patrician judges from giving judgments in legal cases only according to their own wishes. The Roman belief in fair laws as the best protection against social strife helped keep the republic united until the late second century B.C.E.

The voting to elect officials took place around the forum in the city center (Map 5.2). All officials worked as part of committees, to ensure power sharing. The highest officials, two elected each year, were called consuls. Their most important duty was to command the army.

To be elected consul, a man had to win elections all the way up a **ladder of offices** (*cursus honorum*). Before politics, however, came ten years of military service from about age twenty. The ladder's first step was getting elected quaestor (a financial administrator). Next was election as an aedile (supervisors of Rome's streets, sewers, aqueducts, temples, and markets). The third step was election as praetor (a powerful office with judicial and military duties). The most successful praetors competed to be one of the two consuls elected each year. Praetors and consuls held imperium (the power to command and punish) and served as army generals. Families with a consul among their ancestors were honored as nobles. By 367 B.C.E., the plebeians had forced passage of a law requiring that at least one of the two consuls be a plebeian. Ex-consuls competed to become one of the censors, elected every five years to conduct censuses of the citizen body and to

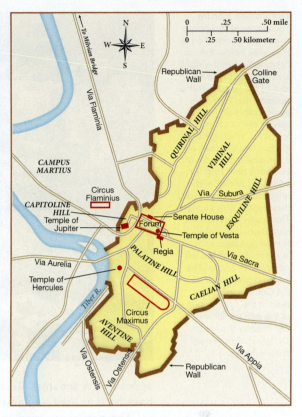

MAP 5.2 The City of Rome during the Republic
Roman tradition said that a king built Rome's first defensive wall in the sixth century B.C.E., but archaeology shows that the first wall encircling the city's center and seven hills on the east bank of the Tiber River belongs to the fourth century B.C.E.; this wall covered a circuit of about seven miles. By the second century B.C.E., the wall had been extended to soar fifty-two feet high and had been fitted with catapults to protect the large gates. Like the open agora surrounded by buildings at the heart of a Greek city, the forum remained Rome's political and social heart. Do you think that modern cities would benefit from having a large public space at their center?

The Roman Forum
The center of this photo shows the Roman Forum, the valley below the Palatine hill (on the right) and the Capitoline hill (out of the picture at the bottom) that from the earliest days of the city served as the central space for meetings of all kinds. Over the centuries, it became crowded with buildings designed for political, judicial, and religious purposes; today, they survive only as ruins. The later version of the meetinghouse of the Roman Senate stands at the middle of the left edge of the photo. The huge amphitheater of the Colosseum can be seen in the upper right of the picture, located just outside the forum. (De Agostini Picture Library/ Bridgeman Images.)

appoint new senators. To be eligible for selection to the Senate, a man had to have been at least a quaestor.

The patricians tried to monopolize the highest offices, but after violent struggle from about 500 to 450 B.C.E., the plebeians forced the patricians to create ten annually elected plebeian officials, called tribunes, who could stop actions that would harm plebeians or their property. The tribunate did not count as a regular ladder office. Tribunes based their special power on the plebeians' sworn oath to protect them, and on their authority to block officials' actions, prevent laws from being passed, suspend elections, and contradict the Senate's advice. The tribunes' extraordinary power to veto government action often made them agents of political conflict.

Men competed in elections to win respect and glory, not money. Only well-off men could serve in government because officials earned no salaries and were expected to spend their own money to pay for public works and for expensive shows featuring gladiators and wild animals. In the early republic, officials' only reward was respect, but as Romans conquered overseas territory, the desire for money from war spoils overcame many men's adherence to traditional Roman values of faithfulness, honesty, and the idea that respect should not be linked to wealth. By the second century B.C.E., military officers were also enriching themselves by extorting bribes as administrators of conquered territories.

The Senate directed government policy by giving advice to the consuls. If a consul rejected the Senate's advice, a political crisis ensued. The senators' social standing gave their opinions great weight. To make their status visible, the senators wore black high-top shoes and robes with a broad purple stripe. To maintain his rank as a senator by the late republic, a man had to be able to prove that he possessed a large amount of wealth.

Three different assemblies made legislation, conducted elections, and rendered judgment in certain trials. The Centuriate Assembly, which elected praetors and consuls, was dominated by patricians and rich plebeians. The Plebeian Assembly, which excluded patricians, elected the tribunes. In 287 B.C.E., its resolutions, called **plebiscites** (PLEB-uh-sites), became legally binding on all Romans. The Tribal Assembly mixed patricians with plebeians and became the republic's most important assembly. Each assembly was divided into groups, with each group comprising a different number of men based on status and wealth; each group had one vote.

Before assembly meetings, orators gave speeches about issues. Everyone, including women and noncitizens, could listen to these pre-vote speeches. The crowd expressed its opinions by either applauding or hissing. This process mixed a small measure of democracy with the republic's oligarchy.

Early on, the praetors decided most legal cases. A separate jury system arose in the second century B.C.E., and senators repeatedly clashed with other upper-class Romans over whether these juries should consist exclusively of senators. Accusers and accused had to speak for themselves in court, or have friends speak for them. Priests dominated in legal knowledge until the third century B.C.E., when senators with legal expertise, called jurists, began to offer advice about cases.

The Roman republic's complex political and judicial system evolved in response to conflicts over power. Laws could emerge from different assemblies, and legal cases could be decided by various institutions. Rome had no single highest court, such as the U.S. Supreme Court, to give final verdicts. The republic's stability therefore depended on maintaining the mos maiorum. Because they defined this tradition, the most socially prominent and richest Romans dominated politics and the courts.

> **REVIEW QUESTION**
> How and why did the Roman republic develop its complicated political and judicial systems?

Roman Imperialism and Its Consequences

From the fifth to the third century B.C.E., the Romans fought war after war in Italy until Rome became the most powerful state on the peninsula. In the third and second centuries B.C.E., Romans warred far from home in every direction, above all against Carthage across the Mediterranean Sea to the south. Their success in these campaigns made Rome the premier power in the Mediterranean by the first century B.C.E.

Fear of enemies and the desire for wealth propelled this Roman imperialism (the term modern scholars use to label the process of expansion of Rome's power internationally). The senators' worries about national security spurred them to recommend preemptive attacks against foreign powers. Poor soldiers hoped to pull their families out of poverty; the elite, who commanded the armies, wanted to strengthen their campaigns for office by acquiring glory and greater wealth.

The state of being at war transformed Roman life. Romans had no literature until around 240 B.C.E., when contact with conquered peoples stimulated their first written history and poetry. Repeated military service away from home created stresses on small farmers and undermined the stability of Roman society; so, too, did the relocation of numerous citizens and the importation of countless war captives to work as slaves on wealthy people's estates. Rome's great conquests turned out to be a double-edged sword: they brought expansion and wealth, but their unexpected social and political consequences disrupted the traditional values and stability of the community.

Expansion in Italy, 500–220 B.C.E.

After defeating their Latin neighbors in the 490s B.C.E., the Romans spent the next hundred years warring with the nearby Etruscan town of Veii. Their 396 B.C.E. victory doubled their territory. By the fourth century B.C.E., the Roman infantry legion of five thousand men had surpassed the Greek and Macedonian infantry phalanx as an effective fighting force because in the legion's more flexible battle line, the soldiers were trained to throw javelins from behind their long shields and then rush in to finish off the enemy with swords. A devastating sack of Rome in 387 B.C.E. by marauding Gauls (Celts) from beyond the Alps made Romans forever fearful of foreign invasion. By around 220 B.C.E., Rome controlled all of Italy south of the Po River, at the northern end of the peninsula.

The Romans combined brutality with diplomacy to control conquered peoples. Sometimes they enslaved the defeated or forced them to surrender large parcels of land. Other times they offered generous peace terms to former enemies but required them to join in fighting against other foes, for which they received a share of the spoils, mainly slaves and land.

To increase homeland security, the Romans planted numerous colonies of relocated citizens and constructed roads up and down the peninsula to allow troops to travel faster. By connecting Italy's diverse peoples, these settlements promoted a unified culture dominated by Rome. Latin became the common language, although some local tongues lived on.

The wealth of Rome's army attracted hordes of people to Rome, where new aqueducts provided fresh running water and a massive building program provided employment. By 300 B.C.E., about 150,000 people lived within Rome's walls (Map 5.2 on page 159). Outside the city, about 750,000 free Roman citizens inhabited various parts of Italy on land that had been taken from local peoples. Much conquered territory was declared public land, open to any Roman for grazing cattle.

Roman Roads, 110 B.C.E.

Rich plebeians and patricians cooperated to exploit the expanding Roman territories, deriving their wealth from agricultural land and war plunder. Since Rome had no regular income or inheritance taxes, families could freely pass down their wealth from generation to generation.

Aqueduct at Nîmes in France
The Romans excelled at building complex delivery systems of tunnels, channels, bridges, and fountains to transport fresh water from far away. One of the best-preserved sections of a major aqueduct is the so-called Pont-du-Gard near Nîmes (ancient Nemausus) in France, erected in the late first century B.C.E. to serve the flourishing town there. Built of stones fitted together without clamps or mortar, the span soars 160 feet high and 875 feet long, carrying water along its topmost level from 35 miles away in a channel constructed to fall only one foot in height for every 3,000 feet in length so that the flow would remain steady but gentle. What sort of social and political organization would be necessary to construct such a system? (Hubertus Kanus/Science Source.)

Wars with Carthage and in the East, 264–121 B.C.E.

The Roman republic fought its three most famous foreign wars against the wealthy city of Carthage in North Africa, which Phoenicians had founded around 800 B.C.E. Carthage, governed as a republic like Rome, controlled a powerful empire rich from farming in Africa and seaborne trade in the Mediterranean. Carthage seemed both a dangerous rival and a fine prize. Horror at the Carthaginians' reported tradition of incinerating infants to placate their gods in times of trouble also fed Romans' hostility against people they saw as barbarians.

Rome's wars with Carthage are called the Punic Wars (from the Latin word for "Phoenician"). The first one (264–241 B.C.E.) erupted over Sicily, where Carthage wanted to preserve its trading settlements, while Rome wanted to block Carthaginian power close to Italy. This long conflict revealed why the Romans won wars: the large Italian population provided deep manpower reserves, and the citizens were prepared to sacrifice as many troops, spend as much money, and fight as long as it took to defeat the enemy. Previously unskilled at naval warfare, the Romans expended vast sums to build warships to combat Carthage's experienced navy; they lost more than five hundred ships and 250,000 men while learning how to win at sea.

The Romans' victory in the First Punic War made them masters of Sicily, where they set up their first province (a foreign territory ruled and taxed by Roman officials). This innovation proved so profitable that they soon seized the islands of Sardinia and Corsica from the Carthaginians to create another

MAP 5.3 Roman Expansion, 500–44 B.C.E.
During its first two centuries, the Roman republic used war and diplomacy to extend its power north and south in the Italian peninsula. In the third and second centuries B.C.E., conflict with Carthage in the south and west and the Hellenistic kingdoms in the east extended Roman power outside Italy and led to the creation of provinces from Spain to Greece. The first century B.C.E. saw the conquest of Syria by Pompey and of Gaul by Julius Caesar.

province. These first successful foreign conquests increased the Romans' appetite for expansion outside Italy (Map 5.3). Fearing a renewal of Carthage's power, the Romans cemented alliances with local peoples in Spain, where the Carthaginians were expanding from their southern trading posts.

The Carthaginians decided to strike back. In the Second Punic War (218–201 B.C.E.), their general Hannibal terrified the Romans by marching troops and war elephants over the Alps into Italy. Slaughtering thirty thousand Romans at Cannae in 216 B.C.E., Hannibal tried to convince Rome's Italian allies to desert, but most refused to rebel. Hannibal's alliance in 215 B.C.E. with the king of Macedonia forced the Romans to fight on a second front in Greece. Still, they refused to crack despite Hannibal's ravaging of Italy from 218 to 203 B.C.E. Invading the Carthaginians' homeland, the Roman army won the battle of Zama in 202 B.C.E. The Senate forced Carthage to scuttle its navy, pay huge war indemnities, and hand over its Spanish territory, rich with silver mines.

The Third Punic War (149–146 B.C.E.) began when the Carthaginians retaliated against the aggression of the king of Numidia, a Roman ally. After winning the war, the Romans heeded the senator Cato's demand, "Carthage must be destroyed!" They obliterated the city and converted its territory into a province. This disaster did not destroy Carthaginian culture, however, and under the Roman Empire this part of North Africa flourished economically and intellectually, creating a synthesis of Roman and Carthaginian traditions.

The aftermath of the Punic Wars extended Roman power to Spain, North Africa, Macedonia, Greece, and western Asia Minor. Hannibal's alliance with the king of Macedonia had brought Roman troops east of Italy for the first time. After defeating the Macedonian king for revenge and to prevent any threat of his invading Italy, the Roman commander proclaimed the "freedom of the Greeks" in 196 B.C.E. to show respect for Greece's glorious past. The Greek cities and federal leagues understood the proclamation to mean that they, as "friends" of Rome, could behave as they liked. They were mistaken. The Romans expected them to behave as clients and follow their new patrons' advice.

The Romans repeatedly intervened to make the kingdom of Macedonia and the Greeks observe their obligations as clients. The Senate in 146 B.C.E. ordered Corinth destroyed for asserting its independence and converted Macedonia and Greece into a province. In 133 B.C.E., a Hellenistic king increased Roman power with a stupendous gift: in his will he bequeathed to Rome his kingdom in western Asia Minor. In 121 B.C.E., the Romans made the lower part of Gaul across the Alps (modern southern France) into a province. By the late first century B.C.E., Rome governed and profited from two-thirds of the Mediterranean region; only the easternmost Mediterranean lay outside its control (see Map 5.3).

Greek Influence on Roman Literature and the Arts

Roman expansion eastward generated extensive cross-cultural contact with Greece. Roman authors and artists found inspiration in Greek literature and art. The earliest Latin poetry was a translation of Homer's *Odyssey* by a Greek ex-slave, composed sometime after the First Punic War. About 200 B.C.E., the first Roman historian used Greek to write his narrative of Rome's founding and the wars with Carthage.

Many famous early Latin authors were not native Romans but came from different regions of Italy, Sicily, and even North Africa. All found inspiration in Greek literature. Roman comedies, for example, took their plots and stock characters from Hellenistic comedy such as that of Menander, which featured jokes about family life and stereotyped personalities, such as the braggart warrior and the obsessed lover.

In the mid-second century B.C.E., Cato established Latin prose writing with his history of Rome, *The Origins*, and his instructions on running a large farm, *On Agriculture*. He predicted that if the Romans adopted Greek values, they would lose their power. In fact, early Latin literature reflected traditional Roman values. For example, the path-breaking Latin epic *Annals*, a poetic version of Roman history by the poet Ennius, shows the influence of the

Greek epic but praises ancestral Roman traditions, as in this famous line: "The Roman state rests on the ways and the men of old." Later Roman writers also took inspiration from Greek literature. The first-century B.C.E. poet Lucretius wrote *On the Nature of Things* to persuade people not to fear death. His ideas reflected Democritus's "atomic theory," which said that matter was composed of tiny, invisible particles (see Chapter 3). Dying, the poem taught, simply meant the dissolving of the union of atoms, which had come together temporarily to make up a person's body. There could be no eternal punishment or pain after death because a person's soul perished along with the body.

Hellenistic Greek authors inspired Catullus in the first century B.C.E. to write witty poems ridiculing prominent politicians for their sexual behavior and lamenting his own disastrous love life. His most famous love poems revealed his obsession with a married woman named Lesbia. The orator and politician **Cicero** (106–43 B.C.E.) wrote speeches, letters, and treatises on political science, philosophy, ethics, and theology. He adapted Greek philosophy to Roman life and stressed the need to appreciate each person's uniqueness. His doctrine of *humanitas* ("humaneness," "the quality of humanity") expressed an ideal for human life based on generous and honest treatment of others and a commitment to morality based on natural law (the rights that belong to all people because they are human beings, independent of the differing laws and customs of different societies).

Greece also influenced Rome's art and architecture. Hellenistic sculptors had pioneered a realistic style showing the ravages of age and pain on the human body. They portrayed only stereotypes, however, such as the "old man" or the "drunken woman," not specific people. Their portrait sculpture presented actual individuals in the best possible light, much like a digitally enhanced photograph today. By contrast, Roman artists applied Greek realism to male portraiture, as contemporary Etruscan sculptors also did. They sculpted men without hiding their unflattering features: long noses, receding chins, deep wrinkles, bald heads, and worried looks. Portraits of women, by contrast, were more idealized, probably representing the traditional vision of the bliss of family life. Because the men depicted in the portraits (or their families) paid for the busts, they may have wanted their faces sculpted realistically—showing the damage of age and effort—to emphasize how hard they had worked to serve the republic.

Stresses on Society from Imperialism

The wars of the third and second centuries B.C.E. ruined many families living on small farms because the husband, absent during a protracted war, had to rely on a hired hand or slave to manage his crops and animals, or have his wife try to do the impossible by doing the farming in addition to her usual family responsibilities. This intolerable burden created grave social and economic difficulties for the republic. In the end, the long deployments of troops abroad disrupted Rome's agricultural system, the economy's foundation.

The story of the consul Regulus, who won a great victory in Africa in 256 B.C.E., revealed the problems that prolonged absence caused. When the man who managed Regulus's farm died while the consul was away fighting, a worker stole all the farm's tools and livestock. Regulus begged the Senate to send a replacement fighter so that he could return to save his wife and children from starving. The senators instead sent help to preserve Regulus's family and property because they wanted to keep him on the battle lines.

Ordinary soldiers received no special aid, and economic troubles hit them hard when, in the second century B.C.E., for unknown reasons, there was no longer enough farmland to support the population. The rich had deprived the poor of land, but recent research suggests that an increase in the number of young people created the crisis. Not all regions of Italy suffered as severely as others, and some impoverished farmers and their families survived by working as agricultural laborers for others. Many homeless people, however, relocated to Rome, where the men begged for work and women made cloth or, in desperation, became prostitutes.

This flood of landless poor created an explosive element in Roman politics by the late second century B.C.E. The government had to feed its poor citizens to avert riots, so Rome needed to import grain. The poor's demand for low-priced (and eventually free) food distributed at state expense became one of the most divisive issues in the late republic.

While the landless poor struggled, imperialism meant political and financial rewards for Rome's social elite. The need for commanders to lead military campaigns abroad created opportunities for successful generals to enrich their families. The elite enhanced their reputations by spending their gains to finance public works that benefited the general population. Building new temples, for example, won praise because the Romans believed it pleased their gods to have many shrines.

The troubles of small farmers enriched landowners who could buy bankrupt farms to create large estates. Some landowners also illegally occupied public land carved out of territory seized from defeated enemies. The rich

Bedroom in a Rich Roman House
This bedroom from about 40 B.C.E. was in the house of a rich Roman family near Naples; it was buried—and preserved—by the eruption of the volcano Vesuvius in 79 C.E. The bright paintings showed a dazzling variety of outdoor scenes and architecture. The stone floor helped create a sensation of coolness in the summer. (Cubiculum (bedroom) from the Villa of P. Fannius Synistor at Boscoreale, c. 50–40 B.C.E./The Metropolitan Museum of Art, New York, NY, USA/Rogers Fund, 1903 (03.14.13a-g). Image copyright © The Metropolitan Museum of Art. Image source: Art Resource, NY.)

worked their huge farms, called *latifundia*, with free laborers as well as slaves who had been taken captive in the same wars that displaced so many farmers. The size of the latifundia slave crews made their periodic revolts so dangerous that the army had to fight hard to suppress them.

The elite profited from Rome's expansion by filling the governing offices in the new provinces. Some governors ruled honestly, but others used their power to extort the locals. Since martial law ruled, no one in the provinces could curb a greedy governor's appetite for graft and extortion. Often, socially elite offenders escaped punishment because their fellow senators excused their crimes.

The new opportunities for rich living strained the traditional values of moderation and frugality. Previously, a man could become legendary for his life's simplicity: Manius Curius (d. 270 B.C.E.), for example, boiled turnips for his meals in a humble hut despite his glorious military victories. Now the elite acquired showy luxuries, such as large country villas for entertaining friends and clients. Money had become more valuable to them than the republic's ancestral values.

REVIEW QUESTION

What advantages and disadvantages did Rome's victories over foreign peoples create for both rich and poor Romans?

Civil War and the Destruction of the Republic

Conflict among members of the Roman upper class in the late second century B.C.E. turned politics into a violent competition. This conflict exploded into civil wars in the first century B.C.E. that destroyed the Roman republic. Senators introduced violence to politics by murdering the tribunes Tiberius and Gaius Gracchus when the brothers pushed for reforms to help the poor by giving them land. When a would-be member of the elite, Gaius Marius, opened military service to the poor to boost his personal status, his creation of "client armies" undermined faithfulness to the general good of the community. The people's unwillingness to share citizenship with Italian allies sparked a damaging war in Italy. Finally, the competition for power by the "great men" Sulla, Pompey, and Julius Caesar peaked in destructive civil wars.

The Gracchus Brothers and Violence in Politics, 133–121 B.C.E.

Tiberius and Gaius Gracchus based their political careers on pressuring the rich to make concessions to strengthen the state. Their policies supporting the poor angered many of their fellow members of the social elite. Tiberius explained the tragic circumstances motivating them:

> The wild beasts that roam over Italy have their dens. . . . But the men who fight and die for Italy enjoy nothing but the air and light. They wander about homeless with their wives and children. . . . They fight and die to protect the wealth and luxury of others. They are called masters of the world, but have not a lump of earth they call their own.

When Tiberius became tribune in 133 B.C.E., he took the radical step of blocking the Senate's will by having the Plebeian Assembly vote to redistribute public land to landless Romans and to spend the Attalid king's gift of his kingdom to equip new farms on the land. Tiberius next announced he would run for reelection as tribune for the following year, violating the prohibition against consecutive terms. His opponents therefore led a band of senators and their clients to murder him and many of his clients, shouting, "Save the republic."

Gaius, elected tribune for 123 B.C.E. and, contrary to tradition, again for the next year, also pushed measures that outraged his fellow elite: more farming reforms, subsidized prices for grain, public works projects to employ the poor, and colonies abroad with farms for the landless. His most revolutionary measures proposed Roman citizenship for many Italians, and new courts to try senators accused of corruption as provincial governors. The new juries would be manned by *equites* (EH-kwee-tehs, "equestrians" or "knights"). These were wealthy businessmen whose focus on commerce instead of government made their interests different from the senators' interests. To keep their rank, they were required to own a large amount of property, though not as much as those ranked as senators. Because they did not serve in the Senate, the equites could convict senators for crimes without having to face peer pressure.

When the senators blocked Gaius's plans in 121 B.C.E., he threatened violent resistance. The senators then advised the consuls "to take all measures necessary to defend the republic," meaning they should kill anyone identified as dangerous to public order. When his enemies came to murder him, Gaius committed suicide by having a slave cut his throat. The senators then killed hundreds of his supporters.

The conflict over reforms introduced factions (aggressive interest groups) into Roman politics. Members of the elite now identified themselves as either supporters of the people, the *populares* (pah-poo-LAH-rehs) faction, or supporters of "the best," the *optimates* (op-tih-MAH-tehs) faction. Some chose a faction from genuine allegiance to its policies; others supported whichever side better promoted their own political advancement. The elite's splintering into bitterly hostile factions remained a source of murderous political violence until the end of the republic.

Marius and the Origin of Client Armies, 107–100 B.C.E.

A new kind of leader arose to meet the need to combat slave revolts and foreign invasions in the late second and early first centuries B.C.E. The "new man" was an upper-class man without a consul among his ancestors, whose ability led him to fame, fortune, and—his ultimate goal—the consulship.

Gaius Marius (c. 157–86 B.C.E.), from the equites class, set the pattern for the influential "new man." Gaining fame for his brilliant military record, Marius won election as a consul for 107 B.C.E. Marius's success as a commander, first in North Africa and next against German tribes attacking southern France and Italy, led the people to elect him consul six times, breaking all tradition.

For his victories, the Senate voted Marius a triumph, Rome's ultimate military honor. In this ceremony, crowds cheered as he rode a chariot through Rome's streets. His soldiers shouted obscene jokes about him, to ward off the evil eye at his moment of supreme glory. Despite Marius's triumph, the optimates never accepted him as an equal. His support came from the common people, whom he had won over with his revolutionary reform of entrance requirements for the army. Previously, only men with property could usually enroll as soldiers. Marius opened the ranks to **proletarians**, men who had no property and could not afford weapons. For them, serving in the army meant an opportunity to better their life by acquiring plunder and a grant of land.

Marius's reform created armies that were more loyal to their commander than to the republic. Poor Roman soldiers behaved like clients following their commander as patron, who gave them financial gifts of war spoils. They in turn supported his political ambitions. Commanders after Marius used client armies to advance their careers more ruthlessly than he had, accelerating the republic's internal conflict.

Sulla and Civil War, 91–78 B.C.E.

One such commander, Lucius Cornelius Sulla (c. 138–78 B.C.E.), took advantage of uprisings by non-Romans in Italy and Asia Minor in the early first century B.C.E. to use his client army to seize Rome's highest offices and force the Senate to support him. His career revealed the dirty secret of politics in the late republic: traditional values no longer restrained commanders who prized their own advancement over peace and the good of the community.

The uprisings in Italy occurred because many of Rome's Italian allies lacked Roman citizenship and therefore had no vote in decisions that affected them. Their upper classes also wanted to share the prosperity that war brought to Rome's citizen elite. The Roman people rejected the allies' demand for citizenship, afraid that sharing such status would lessen their own privileges.

The Italians' discontent erupted in 91–87 B.C.E. in the Social War. They demonstrated their commitment by the number of their casualties — 300,000 dead. Although Rome's army prevailed, the rebels won the political war: the Romans granted citizenship and the vote to all freeborn people in Italy south of the Po River. The Social War's bloodshed therefore reestablished Rome's tradition of strengthening the state by granting citizenship to outsiders.

Sulla's generalship in the war won him election as consul for 88 B.C.E. When Mithridates VI (120–63 B.C.E.), king of Pontus on the Black Sea's southern coast, rebelled against Roman control and high taxation, Sulla seized his chance. Victory against Mithridates would mean capturing unimaginable riches from Asia Minor's cities as war spoils and allow him to restore his patrician but impoverished family's status. When the Senate gave Sulla the command, Marius had it transferred to himself by plebiscite. Outraged, Sulla marched his client army against Rome. All his officers except one deserted him in horror at this shameful attack, but his common soldiers followed him. After capturing Rome, Sulla killed or exiled his opponents. He let his men rampage through the city and then led them off to Asia Minor, ignoring a summons to stand trial and sacking Athens on the way. In Sulla's absence, Marius embarked on his own reign of terror in Rome to try to regain his former power. In 83 B.C.E., Sulla returned victorious, having allowed his soldiers to plunder Asia Minor. Civil war erupted for two years until Sulla crushed his enemies at home.

Sulla then exterminated his opponents. He used proscription—posting a list of people accused of being traitors so that anyone could hunt them down and execute them. Because proscribed men's property was confiscated, the victors fraudulently added to the list anyone whose wealth they coveted. The terrorized Senate appointed Sulla dictator—an emergency office supposed to be held only temporarily—and gave him permanent immunity from prosecution. Sulla reorganized the government to favor the optimates—his social class—by making senators the only ones allowed to judge cases against their colleagues and forbidding tribunes from sponsoring legislation or holding any other office after their term.

Sulla's career revealed the strengths and weaknesses of Roman values. First, the purpose of war had changed from defending the community to acquiring financial benefits for common soldiers as well as commanders. Second, the patron-client system led proletarian soldiers to feel stronger ties of loyalty to their generals than to the republic.

Finally, the traditional competition for status worked both for and against political stability. When that value motivated men to seek office to promote the community's welfare, it promoted social unity and prosperity. But pushed to its extreme, the contest for individual prestige and wealth destroyed the republic.

Julius Caesar and the Collapse of the Republic, 83–44 B.C.E.

Powerful generals after Sulla proclaimed their loyalty to the community while in reality ruthlessly pursuing their own advancement. The competition for power and money between two Roman aristocrats and famous generals, Gnaeus Pompey (106–48 B.C.E.) and Julius Caesar (100–44 B.C.E.; see Contrasting Views on pages 172–173), generated the civil war that ended the Roman republic and led to the return of monarchy.

Pompey already was a military star in his early twenties, winning battles to support Sulla. In 71 B.C.E., he led the final victories, suppressing a massive slave rebellion inspired by the gladiator Spartacus, who had terrorized southern Italy for two years and defeated consuls with his army of 100,000 escaped slaves. Pompey claimed the glory for this success instead of giving it to the senior Roman general, Marcus Licinius Crassus (115–53 B.C.E.), and then shattered tradition by demanding and receiving a consulship for 70 B.C.E. even though he was nowhere near the legal age of forty-two and had not been elected to any lower post on the ladder of offices. Three years later, he received a command to exterminate the pirates who were then infesting the Mediterranean, a task he accomplished in a matter of months. This success made him wildly popular with many groups: the urban poor, who depended on a

What Was Julius Caesar Like?

Julius Caesar provoked strong reactions among people: some loved him, some hated him, some ridiculed him (Document 2), and some changed their minds (Document 3)—but only fools failed to recognize his extraordinary energy and will (Document 1). These excerpts, including one in his own words (Document 4), offer sample assessments of what different sources said this most famous Roman was like.

1. Julius Caesar and the Pirates

About a century and a half after Caesar's death, the Greek scholar Plutarch wrote a biography to reveal the famous leader's character. He tells this story of Caesar as an eighteen-year-old (well before he became famous) refusing the dictator Sulla's politically motivated order to divorce his wife. When the teenage Caesar fled Rome to escape being murdered by Sulla's henchmen, he was captured by pirates while trying to get to safety in Asia Minor.

[To escape Sulla], Caesar sailed to King Nicomedes in Bithynia [in Asia Minor]. On his voyage home, pirates from Cilicia captured him and held him on an island. When they demanded twenty talents [a huge sum] for his ransom, he laughed at them for not knowing who he was, and spontaneously promised to give them fifty talents instead. Next, after he had dispatched friends to various cities to gather the money, he had only one friend and two attendants left while a captive of the most murderous men in the world. Nevertheless, he felt so superior to them that whenever he wanted to sleep, he would order them to be quiet.

For thirty-eight days, as if the pirates were not his kidnappers but rather his bodyguards, he participated in their games and exercises with a carefree spirit. He also composed poems and speeches that he read aloud to them, and anyone who failed to admire his work he would call an illiterate barbarian to his face, and often with a laugh threatened to crucify them. The pirates loved this, and attributed his free speech to simplemindedness and youthful spirit.

After Caesar had paid the ransom and was released, he immediately manned ships and put to sea against the pirates. He caught them still anchored, and captured most of them. He took their loot as his booty and threw the men into prison, telling the Roman provincial governor that it was his job to punish them. But since the governor had his eyes on the pirates' rich loot and kept saying that he would consider their case when he had time, Caesar took the pirates out of prison and crucified them all, just as he had often warned them on the island that he was going to do, when they thought he was joking.

Source: Plutarch, *Life of Julius Caesar,* 1–2 (excerpted). Translation by Thomas R. Martin.

2. A Poet Mocks Julius Caesar about Sex

In about 58 B.C.E., the twenty-something Catullus ridiculed Caesar (in his early forties) and his follower Mamurra in several acid-tongued poems filled with vulgar terms of insult. The biographer Suetonius (Life of Julius Caesar 73) reports that Caesar said the ridicule inflicted a permanent blot on his name, but that when Catullus apologized, Caesar invited the poet to dinner that very same day.

> They're a pretty good match, those fags,
> Mamurra and that queer, Caesar.
> And no wonder. They've both got the same stains,
> One of them a City guy and the other from Formiae,
> And they won't wash out.
> One's just as sick as the other, those twins,
> Two little brainiacs on the same little couch,
> This one's just as greedy an adulterer as the other,
> They're allies competing even for little girlies;
> So, they're a pretty good match, those fags.

Source: Catullus, Poem 57. Translation by Thomas R. Martin.

3. Cicero Writes to a Friend about Julius Caesar

Cicero, Rome's most famous orator, wrote many private letters that have survived. In this one, written to his friend Atticus a few days after Caesar began the civil war by crossing the Rubicon River in January 49 B.C.E., Cicero worriedly expresses his opinion of Caesar at the time.

What's going on? I'm in the dark. . . . That awful fool Caesar, who has never had even the slightest thought of "the good and the fair"! He claims he's doing all this for the sake of honor? But how can you have honor if you have no ethics? Is it ethical to lead an army without official confirmation of your command, to capture cities of Roman citizens to force your way more easily to our mother city, to plot abolition of debts and the recall of exiles, a thousand outrages, "all to obtain the greatest of divinities, sole rule"?

In this letter, written on March 1 of the same year, Cicero offers a different opinion.

Just look at the kind of man who has taken over the republic: clear thinking, sharp, on the ball. By god, if he doesn't murder anyone and doesn't take away people's property, the very people who lived in fear of him will worship him the most.

Source: Cicero, *Letters to Atticus*, 7.11, 8.13. Translation by Thomas R. Martin.

4. Julius Caesar Explains Why He Fought the Civil War

In his memoirs, Julius Caesar provided his own account of the civil war that made him Rome's most powerful man. Here he reports what he said to the Senate on April 1, 49 B.C.E., after Pompey left the capital and Caesar took it without a struggle. In his own writings, Caesar refers to himself in the third person (i.e., the "he" in this excerpt is Caesar).

A meeting of the Senate convened, and he spoke about the wrongs his enemies had done him. He explained that he had only wanted a usual office [i.e., consul] . . . and was content with what any citizen could obtain. . . . He emphasized his moderation in asking on his own initiative that both his army and Pompey's be disbanded [to prevent war], a concession that would have cost him both status and office. He talked about how bitter his enemies had been . . . and how they had not laid down their command and armies, even at the cost of anarchy. He stressed how unfair they had been to try to deprive him of his legions, and how savage and arrogant in putting restrictions on the tribunes [who favored him]. He spoke about the offers he had made, the meeting that he had suggested but they had rejected. Given all this, he encouraged, he asked the Senators to take responsibility for the state and govern it together with him. But, he added, if they ran away out of fear, he would not run away from the job and would govern the state by himself. His opinion was that the Senate should send delegates to Pompey to arrange a settlement; he was not intimidated by Pompey's recent remark in the Senate that to receive a delegation implied authority but sending it implied fear. That sort of thought revealed a weak and superficial spirit. He, by contrast, wished to win the competition to be just and fair in the same way in which he had striven to excel in his achievements.

Source: Julius Caesar, *The Civil War*, 1.32. Translation by Thomas R. Martin.

QUESTIONS TO CONSIDER

1. Based on these sources, what do you think were the keys to Julius Caesar's popularity with so many Romans?
2. What does the case of Julius Caesar reveal about how and why a leader's personal characteristics matter for political success or failure?
3. How should historians go about evaluating a leader when the evidence is inconsistent or conflicting?

steady flow of imported grain; merchants, who depended on safe sea lanes; and coastal communities, which were vulnerable to pirates' raids. In 66 B.C.E., he defeated Mithridates, who was still stirring up trouble in Asia Minor. By annexing Syria as a province in 64 B.C.E., Pompey ended the Seleucid kingdom and extended Rome's power to the Mediterranean's eastern coast.

People compared Pompey to Alexander the Great and added *Magnus* ("the Great") to his name. He ignored the tradition of consulting the Senate about conquering and administering foreign territories, behaving like an independent king. He summed up his attitude by replying to some foreigners who criticized his actions as unjust: "Stop quoting the laws to us," he told them. "We carry swords."

Pompey's enemies at Rome undermined his popularity by seeking the people's support, declaring sympathy for the problems of citizens in financial trouble. By the 60s B.C.E., Rome's urban population had soared to more than half a million. Hundreds of thousands of the poor lived crowded together in slum apartments, surviving on subsidized food distributions. Jobs were scarce. Danger haunted the streets because the city had no police force. Even many formerly wealthy property owners were in trouble: Sulla's confiscations had caused land values to plummet and produced a credit crunch by flooding the real estate market with properties for sale.

The senators, jealous of Pompey's glory, blocked his reorganization of the former Seleucid kingdom and his distribution of land to his army veterans. Pompey then negotiated with his fiercest political rivals, Caesar and Crassus. In 60 B.C.E., they formed an unofficial arrangement called the **First Triumvirate** (tree-UHM-vir-ate, "group of three"). Pompey forced through laws confirming his plans, reinforcing his status as a generous patron. Caesar got the consulship for 59 B.C.E. and a special command in Gaul, where he could build his own client army. Crassus received financial breaks for the Roman tax collectors in Asia Minor, who supported him politically and financially.

This coalition of political rivals revealed how private relationships had largely replaced communal values in politics. To cement their political bond, Caesar arranged to have his daughter, Julia, marry Pompey in 59 B.C.E., even though she had been engaged to another man. Pompey soothed Julia's jilted fiancé by offering the hand of his own daughter, who had been engaged to yet somebody else. Through these marital machinations, the two powerful antagonists now had a common interest: the fate of Julia, Caesar's only daughter and Pompey's new wife. (Pompey had earlier divorced his second wife after Caesar allegedly seduced her.) Pompey and Julia apparently fell deeply in love in their arranged marriage. As long as Julia lived, Pompey's affection for her kept him from breaking his alliance with her father.

During the 50s B.C.E., Caesar won his soldiers' loyalty with victories and war spoils in Gaul, which he added to the Roman provinces. His political enemies in Rome dreaded his return, and the bond allying him to Pompey shattered in 54 B.C.E., when Julia died in childbirth. The two leaders' rivalry exploded into violence: gangs of their supporters battled each other in Rome's streets. The violence became so bad in 53 B.C.E. that it prevented elections. The

First Triumvirate dissolved, and in 52 B.C.E., Caesar's enemies convinced the Senate to make Pompey consul alone, breaking the republic's long tradition of two consuls sharing power as the head of the state.

Civil war exploded when the Senate ordered Caesar to surrender his command. Like Sulla, Caesar led his army against Rome. In 49 B.C.E., when he crossed the Rubicon River, the official northern boundary of Italy, he uttered the famous words signaling there was now no turning back: "We have rolled the dice." His troops and the people in the countryside cheered him on. He had many backers in Rome, with the masses counting on his legendary generosity for handouts and impoverished members of the elite hoping to regain their fortunes.

The support for Caesar convinced Pompey and most senators to flee to Greece. Caesar entered Rome peacefully, left soon thereafter to defeat enemies in Spain, and then sailed to Greece. There he nearly lost the war when his supplies ran out, but his soldiers stayed loyal even when they were reduced to eating bread made from roots. When Pompey saw what Caesar's men were willing to live on, he exclaimed, "I am fighting wild beasts." Caesar defeated Pompey and the Senate at the battle of Pharsalus in central Greece in 48 B.C.E. Pompey fled to Egypt, where the pharaoh's ministers treacherously murdered him.

Caesar then invaded Egypt, winning a difficult campaign that ended when he restored Cleopatra VII (69–30 B.C.E.) to the Egyptian throne. As determined as she was intelligent, Cleopatra charmed Caesar into sharing her bed and supporting her rule. Their love affair shocked the general's friends and enemies alike: they thought Rome should seize power from foreigners, not share it with them.

By 45 B.C.E., Caesar had won the civil war. He apparently believed that only a sole ruler could end the chaotic violence of the factions, but the republic's oldest tradition prohibited monarchy. So Caesar decided to rule as a king without the title, taking instead the traditional Roman title of *dictator*, used for a temporary emergency ruler. In 44 B.C.E., he announced he would continue as dictator with no term limit. "I am not a king," he insisted. The distinction, however, was meaningless. As ongoing dictator, he controlled the government. Elections for offices continued, but Caesar manipulated the results by recommending candidates to the assemblies, which his supporters dominated.

As sole ruler, Caesar imposed a moderate cancellation of debts; a cap on the number of people eligible for subsidized grain; a large program of public works, including public libraries; colonies for his veterans in Italy and abroad; plans to rebuild Corinth and Carthage as commercial centers; and citizenship for more non-Romans. Caesar treated his opponents mildly, thereby obligating them to become his grateful clients. Caesar's decision not to seek revenge earned him unheard-of honors, such as a special golden seat in the Senate house and the renaming of the seventh month of the year after him (July). He also regularized the Roman calendar by having each year include 365 days, a calculation based on an ancient Egyptian calendar that forms the basis for our modern one.

WHAT WOULD YOU DO?

If you were a Roman citizen trying to decide which side you should back in the civil war that broke out in the mid-first century B.C.E., what factors would you consider and how would you weigh them? Would you worry about which side would give your family a better chance of being safe and prosperous? Would you think about traditional communal values and how they had affected the history of Rome from its origins? What other thoughts would you have in this time of crisis?

Coin of Julius Caesar
This silver coin shows a portrait of Julius Caesar as an older man, with his skin showing the marks of age, to demonstrate visually his claim to have worked in the service of Rome as a military commander and political leader. The garland on his head symbolizes his victories. The words on the coin announce his official but unprecedented status: dictator *in perpetuity*. His assuming the office of dictator, a recognized position in times of national emergency, but with no term limit, which was not traditional, helped motivate his assassination in 44 B.C.E. and led to the end of the Roman republic. (The Art Archive/REX/Shutterstock.)

Caesar's dictatorship satisfied the people but outraged the optimates. They resented being dominated by one of their own, labeling him a traitor who had deserted to the people's faction. Some senators, led by Caesar's former close friend Marcus Junius Brutus (85–42 B.C.E.), conspired to murder him. They stabbed Caesar repeatedly in the Senate house on March 15 (the Ides of March), 44 B.C.E. When Brutus struck him, Caesar gasped his last words—in Greek: "You, too, son?" He collapsed dead at the foot of a statue of Pompey.

The liberators, as they called themselves, had no new plans for government. They naively expected the republic to revive automatically after Caesar's murder, ignoring the political violence of the past century and the deadly imbalance in Roman values, with "great men" placing their competitive private interests above the community's well-being. The liberators were stunned when the people rioted at Caesar's funeral to vent their anger against the upper class that had robbed them of their generous patron. Instead of then forming a united front, the elite resumed their personal vendettas. The traditional values of the republic failed to save it.

REVIEW QUESTION
What factors generated the conflicts that caused the Roman republic's destruction?

Conclusion

The two most remarkable features of the Roman republic's history were its tremendous expansion and its violent disintegration. Rome expanded to control vast territories because it incorporated outsiders, its small farmers produced agricultural surpluses to support a growing population and army, and its most influential men and women respected traditional values stressing the common good. The Romans' willingness to endure great loss of life and property—the proof of faithfulness—made their army unstoppable: Rome

MAPPING THE WEST

The Roman World at the End of the Republic, 44 B.C.E.
By the time of Julius Caesar's assassination in 44 B.C.E., the territory that would be the Roman Empire was almost complete. Caesar's young relative Octavian (the future Augustus) would conquer and add Egypt in 30 B.C.E. Geography, distance, and formidable enemies were the primary factors inhibiting further expansion, which Romans never stopped wanting, even when lack of money and political discord rendered it purely theoretical. The deserts of Africa and the once again powerful Persian kingdom in the Near East worked against expansion southward or eastward, while trackless forests and fierce resistance from local inhabitants made expansion into central Europe and the British Isles impossible to maintain.

Analyzing the Map: By the end of the Roman republic, which major territories remained outside Roman control?

Making Connections: What effect does it appear that the natural features of central Europe and northern Africa had in the long term on the Romans' attempts to expand their international power?

---

might lose battles, but never wars. Because wars of conquest brought profits to leaders and the common people alike, peace seemed a wasted opportunity.

But the victories over Carthage and in Macedonia and Greece had unexpected consequences. Long military service ruined many farming families, and poor people flocked to Rome to live on subsidized food, becoming an unstable political force. Members of the upper class increased their competition with one another for the career opportunities presented by constant war. These rivalries became dangerous to the state when successful generals began acting as patrons to client armies of poor troops. Violence and murder became common in political disputes. Communal values were submerged in the blood of civil war. No one could have been optimistic about the chances for an enduring peace following Caesar's assassination in 44 B.C.E. It would have seemed an impossible dream to imagine that Caesar's grandnephew and adopted son, Octavian—a teenage student at the time of the murder—would eventually bring peace by creating a new political system—the Empire—disguised as the restoration of the old republic.

Chapter 5 Review

Key Terms and People

Be sure that you can identify the term or person and explain its historical significance.

mos maiorum (p. 149)

res publica (p. 150)

patron-client system (p. 151)

patria potestas (p. 152)

orders: patricians and plebeians (p. 158)

Twelve Tables (p. 159)

ladder of offices (p. 159)

plebiscites (p. 161)

Cicero (p. 166)

humanitas (p. 166)

equites (p. 169)

populares (p. 169)

optimates (p. 169)

proletarians (p. 170)

First Triumvirate (p. 174)

Review Questions

1. What common themes underlay Roman values, and how did Romans' behavior reflect those values?

2. How and why did the Roman republic develop its complicated political and judicial systems?

3. What advantages and disadvantages did Rome's victories over foreign peoples create for both rich and poor Romans?

4. What factors generated the conflicts that caused the Roman republic's destruction?

Making Connections

1. How did the political and social values of the Roman republic compare to those of the Greek city-state in the Classical Age?

2. What were the positive and the negative consequences of war for the Roman republic?

3. How can people decide what is the best balance between individual advancement and communal stability?

Important Events

753 B.C.E.	Traditional date of Rome's founding as monarchy
509 B.C.E.	Roman republic is established
509–287 B.C.E.	Struggle of the orders
451–449 B.C.E.	Creation of Twelve Tables, Rome's first written law code
396 B.C.E.	Defeat of Etruscan city of Veii; first great expansion of Roman territory
387 B.C.E.	Gauls sack Rome

264–241 B.C.E.	Rome and Carthage fight First Punic War
220 B.C.E.	Rome controls Italy south of Po River
218–201 B.C.E.	Rome and Carthage fight Second Punic War
168–149 B.C.E.	Cato writes *The Origins*, first history of Rome in Latin
149–146 B.C.E.	Rome and Carthage fight Third Punic War
146 B.C.E.	Carthage and Corinth are destroyed
133 B.C.E.	Tiberius Gracchus is elected tribune; assassinated in same year
91–87 B.C.E.	Social War between Rome and its Italian allies
60 B.C.E.	First Triumvirate of Caesar, Pompey, and Crassus
49–45 B.C.E.	Civil war, with Caesar the victor
45–44 B.C.E.	Cicero writes his philosophical works on *humanitas*
44 B.C.E.	Caesar is appointed dictator with no term limit; assassinated in same year

Consider two events

Cato writes *The Origins* (168–149 B.C.E.) and Carthage and Corinth are destroyed (146 B.C.E.). What attitudes prompted Cato's writings, and how were similar ideas reflected in the destruction of Carthage and Corinth?

Suggested References

Scholars continue to debate the causes and the effects of the rise and fall of the Roman republic, focusing in particular on the intended and unintended political, social, and cultural consequences of the many wars that the Romans fought in this period.

Beard, Mary, et al. *Religions of Rome*. 2 vols. 1998.

Billows, Richard. *Julius Caesar: The Colossus of Rome*. 2008.

*Caesar, Julius. *The Civil War*. Trans. John Carter. 1997.

*Cicero. *On the Good Life*. Trans. Michael Grant. 1971.

Cornell, Tim. *The Beginnings of Rome: Italy and Rome from the Bronze Age to the Punic Wars (c. 1000–264 B.C.)*. 1995.

Daily life (and more): http://www.vroma.org/~bmcmanus/romanpages.html

Flower, Harriet. *Roman Republics*. 2009.

Gardner, Jane. *Women in Roman Law and Society*. 1986.

Goldworthy, Adrian. *The Punic Wars*. 2000.

Haynes, Sybill. *Etruscan Civilization: A Cultural History*. 2005.

Hoyos, Dexter. *The Carthaginians*. 2010.

Martin, Thomas R. *Ancient Rome: From Romulus to Justinian*. 2012.

*Plutarch. *The Fall of the Roman Republic*. Trans. Rex Warner. Rev. ed. 2006.

Ramage, Nancy H., and Andrew Ramage. *Roman Art*. 2008.

Roller, Duane W. *Cleopatra: A Biography*. 2010.

Rosenstein, Nathan, and Robert Morstein-Marx, eds. *A Companion to the Roman Republic*. 2006.

Tan, James. *Power and Public Finance at Rome, 264–49 B.C.E.* 2017.

───────────────

*Primary source.

The Creation of the Roman Empire

44 B.C.E.–284 C.E.

I n 203 C.E., Vibia Perpetua, wealthy and twenty-two years old, sat locked in a Carthage jail, nursing her infant. She had been condemned to death for treason after refusing to sacrifice to the gods for the Roman emperor's health and safety. Perpetua reportedly had this conversation with the local governor when he tried to persuade her to save her life:

> My father came carrying my son, shouting "Perform the sacrifice; take pity on your baby!" Then the governor said, "Think of your old father; show pity for your little child! Offer the sacrifice for the imperial family's well being." "I refuse," I answered. "Are you a Christian?" asked the governor. "Yes." When my father would not stop trying to change my mind, the governor ordered him thrown to the earth and whipped with a rod. I felt sorry for my father; it seemed they were beating me. I pitied his pathetic old age.

Gored by a wild cow and stabbed by a gladiator, Perpetua died because she placed her faith above her duty of loyalty to her family and the state.

Rome's rulers during what we call the Roman Empire punished disloyalty because it threatened to reignite the civil wars that had destroyed the Roman republic. The refusal of some Christians such as Perpetua to perform traditional sacrifice was considered treason because Romans believed the gods would punish them for sheltering people who refused to worship the ancient deities and rejected traditional religious beliefs.

«**Cameo Celebrating Augustus** On this nine-inch-wide cameo, the woman and man seated together are Livia and Augustus, the first "Roman Emperor." A figure representing the Inhabited World crowns Augustus for saving Roman citizens by his leadership in war. Livia is shown as Juno, queen of the gods, or Minerva, goddess of wisdom. Their appearing together emphasizes Livia's partnership with her husband in protecting the Roman people. The man stepping from a chariot at the left is probably Tiberius, their son, Livia's biological son whom Augustus adopted. Below, Roman soldiers dominate captured foreigners and erect a victory monument. (Kunsthistorisches Museum, Vienna, Austria/Erich Lessing/Art Resource, NY.)

Internal conflict among Romans was a cause of anxiety for the empire's first rulers because the transformation from republic to empire opened with seventeen years of civil war following Julius Caesar's death in 44 B.C.E. With internal peace finally restored, in 27 B.C.E. Caesar's adopted son, Octavian (thereafter known as Augustus), declared that he had restored the republic; in reality, he created a disguised monarchy. Augustus's new system retained traditional institutions for sharing power—the Senate, the consuls, the courts—but in reality he and his successors governed like kings ruling an empire. (See Terms of History on page 184.)

The fear of civil discord gradually receded as Augustus's innovations brought peace for two hundred years, except for a struggle between generals for rule in 69 C.E. This **Pax Romana ("Roman Peace")** allowed agriculture and trade to flourish in the provinces, but paying for the military eventually weakened Rome. Previously, foreign wars had won Romans huge amounts of land and money, but now the distances were too great and the enemies too strong. The army was no longer an offensive weapon for expansion that brought in new taxes but instead was a defense force that had to be paid for out of existing revenues. The financial strain drained the treasury and destabilized the government. Christianity emerged as a new religion that would slowly transform the Roman world, but it also created tension because the growing presence of Christians made other Romans worry about punishment from the gods. In the third century C.E., the always-present fear that Romans would literally battle Romans for political prominence proved accurate when generals competing to rule reignited civil war that lasted fifty years and finally precipitated political change.

CHAPTER FOCUS
How did Augustus's "restored republic" successfully keep the peace for more than two centuries, and why did it fail in the third century?

From Republic to Empire, 44 B.C.E.–14 C.E.

It takes time to invent the future. Augustus created his political system gradually, following his favorite saying, he "made haste slowly." He succeeded because he reinvented government, guaranteed the army's support, unhesitatingly used

CHAPTER TIMELINE

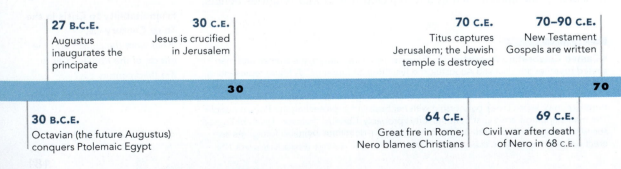

27 B.C.E.
Augustus inaugurates the principate

30 C.E.
Jesus is crucified in Jerusalem

70 C.E.
Titus captures Jerusalem; the Jewish temple is destroyed

70–90 C.E.
New Testament Gospels are written

30

70

30 B.C.E.
Octavian (the future Augustus) conquers Ptolemaic Egypt

64 C.E.
Great fire in Rome; Nero blames Christians

69 C.E.
Civil war after death of Nero in 68 C.E.

violence to win power, and built political legitimacy by communicating an image of himself as a dedicated leader and patron. By declaring his respect for tradition and establishing his disguised monarchy as Rome's political system, he saved the state from anarchy. Succeeding where Caesar had failed, Augustus preserved his power by making the new look old; old was what traditional Roman values enshrined as best.

Civil War, 44–27 B.C.E.

The main competitors in the civil war after Julius Caesar's death were Octavian (the future Augustus), Caesar's eighteen-year-old grandnephew and adopted son, and Mark Antony, a friend of Caesar. Octavian won over Caesar's soldiers by promising them money he had inherited from their general. Marching this army to Rome, the teenage Octavian forced the Senate to make him consul in 43 B.C.E., ignoring the ladder of offices.

Octavian and Mark Antony joined with a general named Lepidus to eliminate rivals. In 43 B.C.E., they formed the Second Triumvirate to reorganize the government. They murdered many of their enemies, including some of their own relatives, and seized their property.

Octavian and Antony then forced Lepidus out and fought each other. Antony controlled the eastern provinces by allying with Queen Cleopatra VII (69–30 B.C.E.), the ruler of Egypt who had earlier allied with Julius Caesar. Dazzled by her intelligence and magnetism, Antony, who was married to Octavian's sister, fell in love with Cleopatra. (See Contrasting Views in Chapter 4.) Octavian rallied support by claiming that Antony planned to make this foreign queen Rome's ruler. He made the residents of Italy and the western provinces swear an oath of allegiance to him. Octavian's victory in the naval battle of Actium in northwest Greece in 31 B.C.E. won the war. Cleopatra and Antony fled to Egypt, where they both committed suicide in 30 B.C.E. The general Mark Antony first stabbed himself, bleeding to death in his lover's embrace. Cleopatra then ended her life by allowing a poisonous snake to bite her. Octavian's revenues from the capture of Egypt made him Rome's richest citizen.

80s C.E.
Domitian leads campaigns against multiethnic invaders on northern frontiers

230s–280s C.E.
Third-century financial and political crisis

249–251 C.E.
Decius persecutes Christians

160   210   260

161–180 C.E.
Marcus Aurelius battles multiethnic bands attacking northern frontiers

212 C.E.
Caracalla extends Roman citizenship to almost all free inhabitants of the provinces

Empire

The term *empire* comes from the Latin word *imperium*, which referred to the supreme power to give orders to others; failure to comply would bring punishment, up to the death penalty. Originally the kings of Rome and then a small number of high-ranking magistrates under the republic held this power; later, the emperors possessed a "greater *imperium*."

This power had its roots in military discipline; commanders vested with it could execute disobedient soldiers in the field. Governors of provinces exercised this power within the boundaries of their assigned territory. In Rome itself, citizens could not be summarily put to death because they had a legal right of appeal.

In the mid-first century B.C.E., when the republic was being torn apart by factional conflict finally erupting into civil war, it became possible to vote "infinite imperium" for a leader, giving him power to command in any part of the world outside the city. It was in this same period that the word began to be used in the modern sense of "empire," to indicate domination of lands and peoples outside one's original territory.

In fact, the Roman republic had begun to amass an empire in this sense already in the third century B.C.E., following the First Punic War, and then continued to acquire domination over non-Roman territories. So, the Romans' acquisition of an empire preceded what we today call the Roman Empire.

The Roman Empire involved domination of a vast extent of non-Roman peoples and territories. Some of these regions were relatively peaceful under Roman control, while others could be more rebellious. Historians have not agreed about the Romans' primary motivation in fighting wars — and engaging in diplomacy — to construct their empire. Were they acting out of a perceived need to establish a defensive frontier abroad to protect their homeland, on the principle that "the best defense is a good offense"? Or were they intent on exploiting others by seizing war spoils and imposing taxes on areas converted into provinces?

Romans moved into many of these areas, bringing their own culture with them. Scholars often use the term "Romanization" to describe the interactions that transpired between the conquerors and the conquered. As with the debate over the meaning of the changes that took place during the earlier Hellenistic Age, scholars have disagreed over whether to see this process as beneficial or oppressive. The modern term *imperialism*, another coinage from imperium, refers to the oppression of other peoples dominated by another state. Recent research presents a more nuanced interpretation of the effects of empire without excusing conquest, for example by uncovering the negotiations over power that constantly took place between the powerful and the less powerful in the imperial system, and the need to build some level of cooperation by allowing local cultures and religions to continue while at the same time requiring demonstrations of loyalty by worship in the cult of the emperor in the provinces.

The Creation of the Principate, 27 B.C.E.–14 C.E.

In 27 B.C.E., Octavian proclaimed that he "gave back the state from [his] own power to the control of the Roman Senate and the people" and announced they should decide how to preserve it. Recognizing Octavian's power, the senators asked him to safeguard the state, granted him special civil and military powers, and bestowed on him the honorary title **Augustus**, meaning "divinely favored."

Augustus changed Rome's political system, but he retained the name *republic* and maintained the appearance of representative government in what is today called the Roman Empire. Citizens elected consuls, the Senate gave advice, and the assemblies met. Augustus occasionally served as consul, but mostly he let others hold that office so they could enjoy its prestige. He concealed his monarchy by referring to himself only with the honorary title *princeps*, meaning "first man" (among social equals), a term of status from the republic. The Romans used the Latin word *princeps* to describe the position that we call emperor, and so the Roman government in the early empire after 27 B.C.E. is most accurately labeled the **principate**. Each new princeps was supposed to be chosen only with the Senate's approval, but in practice each ruler chose his own successor, in the way a royal family decides who will be king. To preserve the tradition that no official should hold more than one post at a time, Augustus as princeps had the Senate grant him the powers, though not the office, of a tribune. In 23 B.C.E., the Senate agreed that Augustus should also have a consul's power to command (imperium): in fact, his power would be superior to that held by the actual consuls.

Holding the power of a tribune and a power even greater than a consul's meant that Augustus could rule the state without filling any formal executive political office. Augustus insisted that people obeyed him not out of fear but out of respect for his *auctoritas* ("authority"). Since Augustus realized that symbols affect people's perception of reality, he dressed and acted modestly, like a regular citizen, not an arrogant king. Livia, his wife, played a prominent role as his political adviser and partner in publicly upholding old-fashioned values. In fact, Augustus and the emperors who came after him were able to exercise supreme power because they controlled the army and the treasury. Later Roman emperors held the same power but continued to refer to the state as the republic; the senators and the consuls continued to exist, and the rulers continued to pretend to respect them.

Augustus made the military the foundation of the emperor's power by turning the republic's citizen militia into a professional, full-time army and navy. He established regular lengths of service and retirement benefits, making the emperor the troops' patron to solidify their loyalty to him. To pay the added costs, Augustus imposed Rome's first inheritance tax on citizens, angering the rich. He also stationed several thousand soldiers in Rome for the first time ever. These soldiers—the **praetorian guard**—would later play a crucial role in selecting the next emperor when the current one died. Augustus meant them to provide security for him and prevent rebellion in the capital by serving as a visible reminder that the superiority of the princeps was backed by the threat of armed force.

Augustus constantly promoted his image as patron and public benefactor. He used media as small as coins and as large as buildings. As a mass-produced medium for official messages, Roman coins functioned like modern political advertising. They proclaimed slogans such as "Father of His Country," to stress Augustus's superior authority, or "Roads have been built," to emphasize his care for the public.

Augustus used his personal fortune to erect spectacular public buildings in Rome. The huge Forum of Augustus, dedicated in 2 B.C.E., best illustrates his skill at communicating messages through architecture (Figure 6.1). This public gathering space centered on a temple to Mars, the god of war. Two-story

FIGURE 6.1 Cutaway Reconstruction of the Forum of Augustus
Augustus built this large forum (120 × 90 yards) to commemorate his victory over the assassins of Julius Caesar. The centerpiece was a marble temple to Mars Ultor ("Mars the Avenger"), and inside the temple were statues of Mars, Venus (the divine ancestor of Julius Caesar), and Julius Caesar (as a god), as well as works of art and Caesar's sword. The two spaces flanking the temple featured statues of Aeneas and Romulus, Rome's founders. The high stone wall behind the temple protected it from fire, a constant threat in the crowded neighborhood behind.

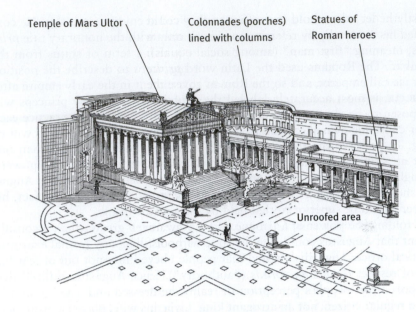

Temple of Mars Ultor

Colonnades (porches) lined with columns

Statues of Roman heroes

Unroofed area

colonnades held statues of famous Roman heroes to serve as inspirations to the young. Augustus's forum hosted religious rituals and the coming-of-age ceremonies of upper-class boys. As a symbol, it demonstrated his justifications for ruling: a new age of peace and security through military power, devotion to the gods protecting Rome, respect for tradition, and generosity in spending money on public works.

Augustus used the paternalism of the patron-client system to make the princeps everyone's most important patron, possessing the authority to guide their lives. When in 2 B.C.E. the Senate and the people proclaimed Augustus "Father of His Country," the title emphasized that the emperor governed like a father: stern but caring, expecting obedience and loyalty from his children, and taking care of them in return. The goal was stability and order, not freedom.

Augustus ruled until his death at age seventy-five in 14 C.E. As the historian Tacitus (c. 56–120 C.E.) remarked, by the time Augustus died after a reign of forty-one years, "almost no one was still alive who had seen the republic." His longevity, military innovations, support for the masses, and manipulation of political symbols had allowed Augustus to create the Roman Empire.

Daily Life in the Rome of Augustus

In Augustan Rome's population of nearly one million, many could not find regular jobs and often had too little to eat. The streets were packed: "One man jabs me with his elbow, another whacks me with a pole; my legs are smeared with mud, and big feet step on me from all sides," one poet wrote of walking in Rome. To ease congestion in the narrow streets, the city banned wagons in the daytime.

Most residents lived in small apartments in multistoried buildings called islands. The first floors housed shops, bars, and restaurants. The higher the floor, the cheaper the rent. The wealthy, who lived at ground level, had piped-in water. The less fortunate had to fill water jugs at public fountains, to which aqueducts delivered fresh water, and then lug the heavy jugs up the stairs. Most people had to use the public latrines or keep buckets for toilets at home and then carry the waste down to the streets for sewage collectors. Sanitation was a problem in this city that generated sixty tons of human waste daily.

However, low fees for public baths meant that almost everyone could bathe regularly. Baths were centers for exercising and socializing. Bathers progressed through a series of increasingly warm areas until they reached a sauna-like room. They swam naked in their choice of either hot or cold pools. Men and women bathed apart.

Augustus improved public safety and health. He instituted the first public fire department in Western history. He also established Rome's first permanent police force. He greatly enlarged the city's main sewer, but its contents still emptied untreated into the Tiber River. Also, poor people often left human and animal corpses in the streets, to be gnawed by birds and dogs. Flies and no refrigeration contributed to frequent gastrointestinal ailments. The wealthy splurged on luxuries such as snow rushed from the mountains to ice their drinks and slaves to clean their houses, which were built around courtyards and gardens. Roman architects built public structures with brick, stone, and concrete that lasted centuries; the cement used for underwater construction in harbors was better than anything available today. Still, also like the present, contractors sometimes cheated on materials for private building, causing apartment complexes to collapse. Augustus imposed a maximum height of seventy feet on multistory buildings to limit the danger.

A Roman Street
Like Pompeii, the town of Herculaneum on the Bay of Naples was frozen in time by the volcanic eruption of Mount Vesuvius in 79 C.E. Mud from the eruption buried the town and preserved its buildings. Herculaneum's straight roads paved with flat stones and sidewalks were typical for a Roman town. Balconies jutted from the houses, offering a shady viewing point for life in the streets. Roman houses often enclosed a garden courtyard instead of having yards in front or back. Why do you think urban homes had this arrangement? (Scala/Art Resource, NY.)

As the people's patron, Augustus paid for grain to feed the poor, upping the government's distribution of food to 250,000 heads of households. From this grain, people made bread or soup, adding beans, leeks, or cheeses if they could afford them; they washed down these meals with cheap wine. The rich ate more costly food, such as roast pork or seafood with honey and vinegar sauce.

Wealthy Romans increasingly spent money on luxuries and political careers instead of raising families. Fearing the falling birthrate would destroy the social upper level on which Rome relied for public service, Augustus granted privileges to the parents of three or more children. He criminalized adultery, even exiling his own daughter—his only child—and a granddaughter for sex scandals. His legislation failed, however, and the prestigious old families dwindled over time. With each generation, three-quarters of senatorial families lost their official status by either spending all their money and therefore not being able to show that they still possessed the amount of wealth required to maintain their senatorial rank or dying off without having children. The emperors filled the many places that came open in the Senate with equites and provincials.

Since imperial Rome still gave citizenship to freed slaves, all slaves hoped someday to become a free Roman citizen, regardless of how they had originally become enslaved (by being captured in war, stolen from their home region by slave traders, or born to slave women as the owner's property). Freed slaves' descendants, if they became wealthy, could become members of the social elite. This policy of giving citizenship to former slaves meant that over time most Romans descended from slave ancestors.

The harshness of slaves' lives varied widely. Slaves in agriculture and manufacturing had a grueling existence, while household slaves lived more comfortably. Modestly prosperous families owned one or two slaves, while rich houses and the imperial palace commanded huge staffs. Domestic slaves were often women, working as nurses, maids, kitchen helpers, and clothes makers. Some male slaves ran businesses for their masters and were often allowed to keep part of the profits, which they could save to purchase their freedom. Women had less opportunity to earn money, though masters sometimes granted tips for sexual favors to both female and male slaves. Many female prostitutes were slaves working for their owners in a brothel. Slaves with savings would sometimes buy other slaves, especially to have a mate; they were barred from legal marriage, because they and their children remained their master's property, but they could live as a shadow family. Some masters' tomb inscriptions express affection for a slave, but if slaves attacked their owner, the punishment was death.

Violence featured in much of Roman public entertainment. The emperors provided shows featuring hunters killing wild beasts, animals mangling condemned criminals, mock naval battles in flooded arenas, gladiatorial combats, and wreck-filled chariot races. Spectators were seated according to their social rank and gender. The emperor and senators sat up front, while women and the poor were in the upper tiers.

Gladiator after a Kill

This first-century C.E. mosaic covered a villa floor in North Africa. It shows a gladiator staring at the opponent he has just killed. What feelings do you think his expression conveys? Gladiatorial combats originated as part of wealthy people's funeral ceremonies, symbolizing the human struggle to avoid death. Training an expert gladiator took many years and great expense. Like boxers today, gladiators fought only a couple of times a year. Because it cost so much to replace a dead gladiator, most fights were not to the death intentionally; kills did happen, however, in the fury of combat. (Mosaic, Leptis Magna, Libya/photo (c) Gilles Mermet/Art Resource, NY.)

Criminals and slaves could be forced to fight as gladiators, but free people also voluntarily competed, hoping to become celebrities and win prizes. Most gladiators were men, though women could fight other women until such matches were banned around 200 C.E. Gladiators were often wounded or killed in the fights, but their contests rarely required a fight to the death, unless they were captives or criminals. To make the bouts unpredictable, pairs of gladiators often competed with different weapons. One favorite match pitted a lightly armored "net man" with a net and a trident against a heavily armored "fish man," so named from his helmet design. Betting was popular, and the crowds were rowdy.

Public entertainment supported communication between the ruler and the ruled. Emperors provided gladiatorial combats, chariot races, and theater productions for the masses, and ordinary citizens staged protests at them to express their wishes. Poor Romans regularly rioted to protest shortfalls in the free grain supply.

Changes in Education, Literature, and Art in Augustus's Rome

Elite culture changed in the Augustan period to serve the same goal as public entertainment: legitimizing the transformed political system. Orators skilled in persuasive public speaking lost their freedom of expression, as did artists. Under the republic, the ability to criticize political opponents in speeches had been such a powerful weapon that it could catapult a "new man" like Cicero to a leadership role. Now, the emperor's dominance limited frank political debate or subversive art. Criticism of the ruler became very dangerous.

With no public schools, only wealthy Romans received formal education. Most people learned only through working. As a character in a novel said, "I didn't study geometry and literary criticism and worthless junk like that. I just learned how to read the letters on signs and how to work out percentages, and I learned weights, measures, and the values of the different kinds of coins." Rich boys and girls attended private elementary schools to learn reading, writing, and arithmetic. Some went on to study literature, history, and grammar. Only a few male students then proceeded to study advanced literature and history, rhetoric, ethical philosophy, law, and dialectic (reasoned argument). (See Primary Source Analysis on page 190.) Mathematics and science were rarely studied as separate subjects, but engineers and architects became proficient at calculation. Highly educated Romans became fluently bilingual in Greek to supplement their native language, Latin.

Scholars call the Augustan period the Golden Age of Latin literature. The emperor was the patron for writers and artists. Augustus's favorite authors were Horace (65–8 B.C.E.) and Virgil (70–19 B.C.E.). Horace's poem celebrating Augustus's victory at Actium became famous for its opening line: "Now it's time to drink!" Virgil's epic poem *The Aeneid* became Rome's most famous work of literature. Inspired by Homer, Virgil told the drama-filled story of the Trojan Aeneas, whom the Romans regarded as their heroic ancestor, as he established a community in Italy after fleeing from the burning ruins of his

PRIMARY SOURCE ANALYSIS

A Roman Stoic Philosopher on the Capabilities of Women

Musonius Rufus was a Roman philosopher in the first century C.E. who lectured (in Greek) on Stoicism as "the science of living." His ideas were regarded as subversive enough to be threatening to those in power: two different emperors expelled him from Rome, hoping to eliminate his influence. These excerpts reveal his views on the natural capacities of women, education in philosophy, and marriage.

The gods have given women the same ability to use their minds as men. . . . Women as well as men have an eagerness and a natural tendency towards excellence (virtue). . . . Therefore, why is it proper for men to investigate and examine to live rightly, that is, to study philosophy and live by its guidance, but not for women? Is it appropriate for men to be good, but not women?

To begin with, a woman must manage her household and pick out what is helpful for her home and take charge of the household slaves. I claim that philosophy is especially helpful for these actions, since each of them is a part of life, and philosophy is nothing other than the science of living. . . . Next, a woman must be chaste, and capable of keeping herself free from illegal love affairs, and pure in other self-indulgent pleasures. She must not delight in quarreling, not be extravagant, or overly concerned with her appearance. . . . She must control her anger, and not be overcome by grief, and stronger than every kind of emotion. . . .

It is easy to recognize that there are not different types of excellences for men and women. First, men and women both need to have common sense. . . . Second, both need to live just lives. An unjust man can not be a good citizen, and a woman can not run her household well, if she does not run it justly. . . . Third, a wife ought to be chaste, and so should a husband, for the laws punish both sides in cases of adultery. . . .

You might argue that only men need courage, but that is false. The best sort of woman must have the courage of a man and purge herself of cowardice, so that she will not give in to suffering or fear. If she can't do that,

then how can she be chaste, if someone by threatening her or torturing her can force her to act disgracefully? . . . That women are able to use weapons, we know from the Amazons, who fought many peoples in battle. . . .

It is reasonable, then, for me to think that women should be educated like men concerning excellence, and they must be taught, beginning in their childhood, that this is good and that is bad, and that they are the same for both genders, and that this is beneficial and that harmful, and that an individual must do this, and not do that. Such lessons develop reasoning in both girls and boys, and there is no distinction between them. . . .

[In marriage], husband and wife join together to live their lives in common and to have children. . . . They should consider all their property to be shared, and nothing to belong only to themselves, not even their bodies. . . . There must be complete companionship and concern for each other by both husband and wife, in health and in sickness and at all times, because they entered upon the marriage for this reason, as well as to have children. When such caring for one another is perfect, and the married couple provide it for each another, and each works to outdo the other, then this is marriage as it ought to be. . . . But when one partner looks to their own interests alone and neglects the other's concerns . . . or is unwilling to pull together with their partner or to cooperate, then inevitably the marriage is destroyed, and although the two live together, their common interests do poorly, and finally they get a divorce, or they live on in an existence that is worse than loneliness.

Source: Musonius Rufus 3, 4, 13A, Lutz edition. Translation by Thomas R. Martin.

QUESTIONS TO CONSIDER

1. What arguments does the Stoic philosopher make about the benefits of women studying philosophy?

2. How do you think the philosopher's apparent assumptions about differences between women and men affected his arguments?

Marble Statue of Augustus from Prima Porta
At six feet eight inches high, this statue of Augustus stood a foot taller than he did. Found at his wife Livia's country villa at Prima Porta ("First Gate"), the portrait was probably done about 20 B.C.E., when Augustus was in his forties; however, it shows him as younger, using the idealizing techniques of classical Greek art. The statue's symbols communicate Augustus's image: his bare feet hint he is a near-divine hero, the Cupid refers to the Julian family's descent from the goddess Venus (the Roman equivalent of Aphrodite, Greek goddess of love), and the breastplate's design shows a Parthian surrendering to a Roman soldier under the gaze of personified cosmic forces admiring the peace Augustus's regime has created. (Vatican Museums and Galleries, Vatican State/Bridgeman Images.)

home city. Virgil balanced his praise for Roman civilization with the acknowledgment that peace existed at the cost of freedom.

Livy (54 B.C.E.–17 C.E.) wrote a history of Rome recording Augustus's ruthlessness in the civil war after Caesar's murder. The emperor scolded but did not punish him, because Livy's work proclaimed that stability and prosperity depended on traditional values of loyalty and self-sacrifice. The poet Ovid (43 B.C.E.–17 C.E.), however, wrote *Art of Love* and *Love Affairs* to mock the emperor's moral legislation with snarky advice on sexual affairs and adultery. Ovid's work *Metamorphoses* undermined the idea of natural hierarchy with stories of supernatural shape-changes, with people becoming animals and mixing the human and the divine. Augustus exiled the poet in 8 B.C.E. for his alleged involvement in the scandal involving the emperor's granddaughter.

Changes in public sculpture also reflected the emperor's supremacy. Augustus preferred sculpture that had an idealized style. In the Prima Porta statue, Augustus had himself portrayed as serene and dignified, not weary and sick, as he often was. As he did with architecture, Augustus used sculpture to project a calm and competent image of himself as the "Restorer of the Roman Republic" and founder of a new age for Rome.

REVIEW QUESTION
How did the peace gained through Augustus's "restoration of the Roman republic" affect Romans's lives in all social classes?

Politics and Society in the Early Roman Empire

Since Augustus claimed his system was not a monarchy, his successor could inherit his power only with the Senate's approval. Augustus therefore decided to identify an heir for the Senate to recognize as princeps after his death. This strategy succeeded and kept rule in his family, called the **Julio-Claudians**, until the death in 68 C.E. of Nero, Augustus's last descendant. It established the tradition that family dynasties ruled the principate.

The Julio-Claudian emperors worked to prevent unrest, maintain loyalty, finance the administration and army, and govern the provinces. Augustus set the pattern for effective imperial rule: take special care of the army, communicate the emperor's image as a just ruler and generous patron, and promote Roman law and culture as universal standards. The citizens, in return for their loyalty, expected the emperors to be supportive patrons—but the difficulties of long-range communication imposed practical limits on imperial support of or intervention in the lives of the residents of the provinces.

The Perpetuation of the Principate after Augustus, 14–180 C.E.

Augustus needed the Senate to bestow legitimacy on his successor to continue his disguised monarchy. Having no son, he adopted Livia's son by a previous marriage, Tiberius (42 B.C.E.–37 C.E.). Since Tiberius had a brilliant career as a general, the army supported Augustus's choice. Augustus had the Senate grant Tiberius the power of a tribune and the power of a consul equal to his own; his hope was that the senators would recognize Tiberius as emperor after his death. The senators did just that when Augustus died in 14 C.E.

Tiberius (r. 14–37 C.E.) was able to stay in power for twenty-three years because he retained the army's loyalty. He built a fortified camp for the praetorian guard in Rome to help its soldiers protect the emperor. The guards would influence all future successions—no emperor could come to power without their support.

Tiberius's long reign made permanent the compromise between the elite and the emperor that promoted political stability. The offices of consul, senator, and provincial governor continued, with elite Romans filling them and enjoying their prestige, but the emperors not only decided who received the offices but also controlled law and government policy. The social elite supported the regime by staying loyal and managing the collection of taxes while governing provinces. (The emperor used his own assistants to govern the provinces that housed strong military forces.) Everyone saved face by pretending that the republic's traditional offices retained their original power.

Tiberius paid a bitter price to rule. To strengthen their family tie, Augustus had forced Tiberius to divorce his beloved wife, Vipsania, to marry Augustus's daughter, Julia—a marriage that proved disastrously unhappy. When Tiberius's sadness led him to spend his reign's last decade in seclusion far from Rome, his neglect of the government permitted abuses in the capital and kept him from training a decent successor.

Tiberius designated Gaius, better known as Caligula (r. 37–41 C.E.), to be the next emperor, and the Senate approved him because the young man was Augustus's great-grandson. The third Julio-Claudian emperor might have been successful because he knew about soldiering: *Caligula* means "baby boots," the nickname the soldiers gave him as a child because he wore little leather shoes like theirs when he was growing up in the military garrisons his father commanded. Caligula, however, bankrupted the treasury to satisfy his desires. His biographer labeled him a monster for his murders and sexual crimes, which some said included incest with his sisters. He outraged the elite by fighting in mock gladiatorial combats and appearing in public in women's clothing or costumes imitating gods. He once said, "I'm allowed to do anything." The praetorian commanders murdered him in his fourth year of rule to avenge personal insults.

The senators then debated the idea of truly restoring the republic by refusing to approve a new emperor. They backed down, however, when Claudius (r. 41–54 C.E.), Augustus's grandnephew, bribed the praetorian guard to support him. The soldiers' insistence on having an emperor so that they would have a patron signaled that the original republic was never coming back.

Claudius was an active emperor, commanding a successful invasion of Britain in 43 C.E. that made much of the island into a Roman province. He promoted provincial elites' participation in government by enrolling men from Gaul in the Senate. In return for keeping their regions peaceful and ensuring tax payments, upper-class provincials received offices and prestige at Rome. Claudius also transformed imperial bureaucracy by employing freed slaves as powerful administrators who owed loyalty only to the emperor.

Claudius's successor, Nero (r. 54–68 C.E.), became emperor at sixteen. He loved performing music and acting, not governing. The poor loved him for his public entertainments and distributions of cash. His generals suppressed a revolt in Britain led by the woman commander Boudica in 60 C.E. and fought the Jewish rebels against Roman rule in Judaea beginning in 66 C.E., but he had no military career. A giant fire in 64 C.E. (the event behind the legend that Nero fiddled while Rome burned) aroused suspicions that he ordered the city torched to make space for a giant new residence. Nero emptied the treasury by building a huge palace. To raise money, he faked treason charges against senators and equites to seize their property. When his generals toppled his regime in 68 C.E., Nero had a servant help him cut his own throat.

Nero's death sparked a civil war in 69 C.E. during which four generals competed for power. Vespasian (r. 69–79 C.E.) won. To give his new dynasty (the Flavians) legitimacy, Vespasian had a law passed granting him the powers of previous good emperors, pointedly leaving Caligula and Nero off the list. He encouraged the imperial cult (worship of the emperor as a living god and sacrifices for his household's welfare) in the provinces beyond Italy but not in Italy itself, where it would have disturbed traditional Romans. The imperial cult communicated the image of the emperor as a superhuman who deserved Roman citizens' loyalty because he provided benefactions and salvation for them.

Vespasian's sons, Titus (r. 79–81 C.E.) and Domitian (r. 81–96 C.E.), conducted hardheaded fiscal policy and wars. Titus had suppressed the Jewish revolt, capturing Jerusalem in 70 C.E. In his role as "first man" protecting the people, Titus sent relief to Pompeii and Herculaneum when, in 79 C.E., Mount Vesuvius's volcanic eruption buried these towns. He built Rome's **Colosseum**, outfitting the fifty-thousand-seat amphitheater with awnings to shade the crowd. The Colosseum was constructed on the site of the private fishpond in Nero's palace to demonstrate the Flavian dynasty's commitment to the people.

When Titus died suddenly after only two years as emperor, his brother, Domitian, stepped in. Domitian balanced the budget and campaigned against the Germanic tribes threatening the empire's northern frontiers. Domitian's arrogance turned the senators against him; once he sent them a letter announcing, "Our lord god, myself, orders you to do this." Domitian executed numerous upper-class citizens as disloyal. Fearful that they, too, would become victims, his wife and members of his court murdered him in 96 C.E.

The next five emperors gained reputations for ruling well: Nerva (r. 96–98 C.E.), Trajan (r. 98–117 C.E.), Hadrian (r. 117–138 C.E.), Antoninus Pius (r. 138–161 C.E.), and Marcus Aurelius (r. 161–180 C.E.). Historians call this period the Roman political Golden Age because it had peaceful successions for nearly a century. Wars and rivalry among the elite continued, however. Trajan fought to expand Roman control across the Danube River into Dacia (today Romania) and eastward into Mesopotamia (Map 6.1); Hadrian executed several senators as alleged conspirators, punished a Jewish revolt by turning Jerusalem into a military colony, and withdrew Roman forces from Mesopotamia; and Marcus Aurelius fought off invaders from the Danube region as the dangers to imperial territory along the northern frontiers kept increasing.

Still, the five "good emperors" did preside over a political and economic Golden Age. They succeeded one another without murder or conspiracy—the first four, having no surviving sons, used adoption to find the best possible successor. The economy provided enough money to finance building projects such as the fortification wall Hadrian built across Britain. Most important, the army remained obedient. These reigns marked Rome's longest stretch without a civil war since the second century B.C.E.

Life in the Roman Golden Age, 96–180 C.E.

Peace and prosperity in Rome's Golden Age depended on defense by a loyal military, service by provincial elites in local administration and tax collection, common laws enforced throughout the empire, and a healthy population reproducing itself. The empire's vast size and the relatively small numbers of soldiers and imperial officials in the provinces meant that emperors had only limited control over these factors.

In theory, Rome's military goal was to expand perpetually because conquest brought land, money, and glory. In reality, the emperors lacked the resources to expand the empire much beyond the territory that Augustus had controlled, and they had to concentrate on defending imperial territory. The army of both Romans and noncitizens reflected the population's diversity. Serving under Roman officers, the non-Romans learned to speak Latin and follow Roman customs. Upon discharge, they received Roman citizenship. Thus, the army helped spread a common way of life.

Most provinces were peaceful, housing few troops. Most legions (units of five thousand troops) were stationed on frontiers to prevent invasions from

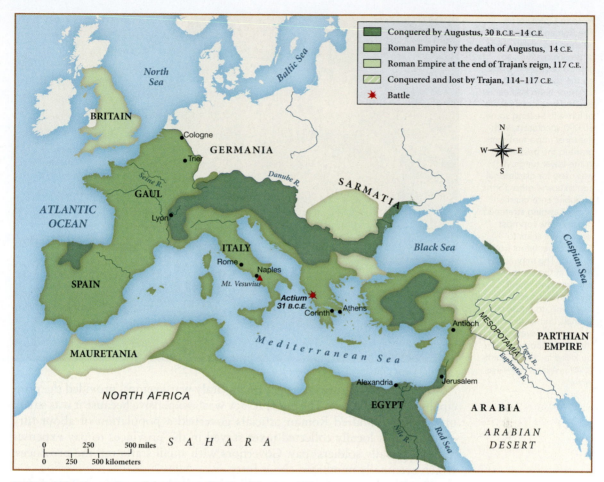

MAP 6.1 The Expansion of the Roman Empire, 30 B.C.E.–117 C.E.
When Octavian (the future Augustus) captured Egypt in 30 B.C.E., after the suicides of Mark Antony and Cleopatra, he greatly boosted Rome's economic strength. The land produced enormous amounts of grain and metals, and Roman power now almost encircled the Mediterranean Sea. When Emperor Trajan took over the southern part of Mesopotamia in 114–117 C.E., imperial conquest reached its height; Rome's control had never extended so far east. Egypt remained part of the empire until the Arab conquest in 642 C.E., but Mesopotamia was immediately abandoned by Hadrian, Trajan's successor, probably because it seemed too distant to defend. How did territorial expansion both strengthen and weaken the Roman Empire?

Germanic tribes to the north and Persians to the east. The peace allowed long-distance trade to import luxury goods, such as spices and silk, from as far away as India and China. Roman merchants regularly sailed from Egypt to India and back.

Paying for defense eventually became a problem too big to solve. Previously, foreign wars had brought in revenue from plunder and prisoners of war sold as slaves. Conquered territory also provided regular income from taxes. By the mid-second century C.E., the army was no longer making conquests, but the soldiers had to be paid well to maintain discipline. This made a soldier's career desirable but cost the emperors dearly.

Roman Colosseum
The Roman Emperor Titus finished the construction of the Colosseum, so named because it stood on the spot where the Emperor Nero had earlier erected a colossal statue of himself. Seating some 50,000 spectators, with the most important men granted the best seats in the lower rungs, it was used for gladiatorial combats and other forms of public entertainment. A giant awning stretched out from the topmost level of the seats to protect spectators from the sun. The ruins today reveal in the center the underground rooms and corridors used, for one thing, to house wild animals that were raised by manual elevators to the sandy floor above to be killed in bloody hunts. (© Alinari Archives/The Image Works.)

A tax on agriculture in the provinces (Italy was exempt) provided the principal source of revenue. The bureaucracy was inexpensive because it was small: only several hundred Roman officials governed a population of about fifty million. Most locally collected taxes stayed in the provinces to pay expenses there, especially soldiers' pay. Governors with small staffs ran the provinces, which eventually numbered about forty.

This lean bureaucracy was possible especially because elite civilians in the provinces were responsible for collecting the taxes that financed Roman government. Serving as **decurions** (members of municipal Senates), these wealthy men were required personally to guarantee that their area's financial responsibilities were met. If there was a shortfall in tax collection or local finances, the decurions had to pay the difference from their own pockets. Wise emperors kept taxes moderate. As Tiberius put it, when refusing a request for tax increases from provincial governors, "I want you to shear my sheep, not skin them alive." The financial liability in holding civic office made that honor expensive, but the accompanying prestige made the elite willing to take the risk. Rewards for decurions included priesthoods in the imperial cult, an honor open to both men and women.

The system worked because it observed tradition: the local elites were their communities' patrons and the emperor's clients. As long as there were enough rich, public-spirited provincials participating, the principate functioned by fostering the old ideal of community service by the upper class in return for respect and social status.

The provinces contained diverse peoples who spoke different languages, observed different customs, dressed in different styles, and worshipped different divinities (Map 6.2). In the countryside, Roman conquest only lightly affected local customs. In new towns that sprang up around Roman forts or settlements of army veterans, Roman influence predominated. Roman culture

MAP 6.2 Natural Features and Languages of the Roman World
The environment of the Roman world included a large variety of topography, climate, and languages. The inhabitants of the Roman Empire, estimated to have numbered as many as fifty million, spoke dozens of different tongues, many of which survived well into the late empire. The two predominant languages were Latin in the western part of the empire and Greek in the eastern. Latin remained the language of law even in the eastern empire. Vineyards and olive groves were important agricultural resources because wine was regarded as an essential beverage, and olive oil was the principal source of fat for most people as well as being used to make soap, perfume, and other products for daily life. Dates and figs were popular sweets in the Roman world, which had no refined sugar.

had the greatest effect on western Europe, spreading Latin (and the languages that would emerge from it) there, as well as Roman law and customs. Eventually, emperors came from citizen-families in the provinces; Trajan, from Spain, was the first princeps with an origin outside Italy.

Romanization, the spread of Roman law and culture in the provinces, raised the standard of living by providing roads and bridges, increasing trade, and establishing peaceful conditions for agriculture. The army's need for supplies created business for farmers and merchants. The increased prosperity that many provincials enjoyed under Roman rule made Romanization acceptable. In addition, Romanization was not a one-way street. In western regions as diverse as Gaul, Britain, and North Africa, interaction between the local people and Romans produced mixed cultural traditions, especially in religion and art. Therefore, Romanization merged Roman and local culture.

The eastern provinces, however, largely retained their Greek and Near Eastern characteristics. Huge Hellenistic cities such as Alexandria (in Egypt) and Antioch (in Syria) rivaled Rome in size and splendor. The eastern provincial elites readily accepted Roman governance because Hellenistic royal traditions had prepared them to see the emperor as their patron and themselves as his clients.

The continuing vitality of Greek language and culture contributed to new trends in literature. Lucian (c. 117–180 C.E.) composed satirical dialogues in Greek mocking stuffy and superstitious people. The essayist and philosopher Plutarch (c. 50–120 C.E.) also used Greek to write paired biographies of Greek and Roman men. His exciting stories made him favorite reading for centuries; William Shakespeare based several plays on Plutarch's biographies.

The late first century and early to mid-second century C.E. can be called the Silver Age of Latin literature. Tacitus wrote historical works that exposed the now-dead Julio-Claudian emperors' ruthlessness. Juvenal (c. 65–130 C.E.) wrote poems ridiculing pretentious Romans while complaining about living broke in the capital. Apuleius (c. 125–170 C.E.) excited readers with a sexually explicit novel called *The Golden Ass*, about a man turned into a donkey who regains his body and his soul through the kindness of the Egyptian goddess Isis.

To create an empire-wide legal system, the emperors issued laws based on the principle of equity, which meant doing what was "good and fair" even if that required ignoring the letter of the law. This principle taught that a contract's intent outweighed its words, and that accusers should prove the accused guilty because it was unfair to make defendants prove their innocence. In dealing with accusations against Christians, the emperor Trajan ruled that no one should be convicted on the grounds of suspicion alone because it was better for a guilty person to go unpunished than for an innocent person to be condemned.

The importance of hierarchy led Romans to continue formal distinctions in society based on wealth. The elites constituted a tiny portion of the population. Only about one in every fifty thousand had enough money to rank in the senatorial order, the highest-ranking class, while about one in a thousand belonged to the equestrian order, the second-ranking class. Different purple stripes on clothing identified these orders. The third-highest order consisted of decurions, the local Senate members in provincial towns.

The legal distinction between the elite and the rest of the population now became stricter. Under what was now an official distinction, the category "better people" included senators, equites, decurions, and retired army veterans. Everybody else—except slaves, who counted as property—made up the vastly larger group of "humbler people." The law imposed harsher penalties on them than on "better people" for the same crime. "Humbler people" convicted of serious crimes were regularly executed by being crucified or torn apart by wild animals before a crowd of spectators. "Better people" rarely received the death penalty, and those who did were allowed a quicker and more dignified execution by the sword. "Humbler people" could also be tortured in criminal investigations, even if they were citizens. Romans regarded these differences as fair on the grounds that an elite person's higher status required of him or her a higher level of responsibility for the common good. As one provincial governor expressed it, "Nothing is less equitable than mere equality itself."

Nothing mattered more to the empire's strength than steady population levels. Concerns about marriage and reproduction predominated in Roman society; remaining single and childless represented social failure for both women and men. The propertied classes usually arranged marriages. Girls often married in their early teens, to have as many years as possible to bear children. Because so many babies died young, families had to produce numerous offspring to keep from disappearing. The tombstone of Veturia, a soldier's wife, tells a typical story: "Here I lie, having lived for twenty-seven years. I was married to the same man for sixteen years and bore six children, five of whom died before I did."

Midwife's Sign
Childbirth carried the danger of death from infection or internal hemorrhage. This terracotta sign from Ostia, the ancient port city of Rome, probably hung outside a midwife's room to announce her expertise in helping women safely give birth. It shows a pregnant woman clutching the sides of her chair, with an assistant supporting her from behind and the midwife crouched in front to help deliver the baby. Why do you think the woman is seated for delivery instead of lying down? Such signs were especially effective for people who were illiterate; a person did not have to read to understand the services that the specialist inside could provide. (Museo Ostiense, Ostia, Italy/ Scala/Art Resource, NY.)

The social pressure to bear numerous children created many health hazards for women. Doctors possessed metal instruments for surgery and physical examinations, but many were poorly educated former slaves with only informal training. There was no official licensing of medical personnel. Complications in childbirth could easily kill the mother because doctors and midwives could not stop internal bleeding or cure infections. Romans controlled reproduction with contraception (by obstructing the vagina or by administering drugs to the female partner) or by abandoning unwanted infants.

The emperors regularly tried to support reproduction. They gave money to feed needy children, hoping they would grow up to have families. Wealthy people often adopted children in their communities. One North African man supported three hundred boys and three hundred girls each year until they grew up.

REVIEW QUESTION
In the early Roman Empire, what was life like in the cities and in the country for the elite and for ordinary people?

The Emergence of Christianity in the Early Roman Empire

Christianity began as what some scholars call "the Jesus movement," a Jewish splinter group in Judaea (today Israel and the Palestinian Territories). There, as elsewhere under Roman rule, Jews were allowed to worship in their ancestral religion. The emergence of the new religion was gradual: three centuries after the death of Jesus, Christians were still a minority in the Roman Empire. Moreover, Roman officials suspected that Christians' beliefs made them disloyal. Christianity grew because of the attraction of Jesus's charismatic career, its message of individual spiritual salvation, its early members' sense of mission, and the strong bonds of community it inspired. Ultimately, Christianity's emergence proved the most significant development in Roman history.

Jesus and His Teachings

Jesus (c. 4 B.C.E.–30 C.E.) grew up in a troubled region. Harsh Roman rule in Judaea had angered the Jews, and Rome's provincial governors worried about rebellion. Jesus's execution reflected the Roman policy of eliminating any threat to social order. In the two decades after his crucifixion, his followers, particularly Paul of Tarsus, elaborated on and spread his teachings beyond his region's Jewish community to the wider Roman world.

Christianity offered an answer to the question about divine justice raised by the Jews' long history of oppression under the kingdoms of the ancient and Hellenistic Near East: if God was just, as Hebrew monotheism taught, how could he allow the wicked to prosper and the righteous to suffer? Nearly two hundred years before Jesus's birth, persecution by the Seleucid king Antiochus IV (r. 175–164 B.C.E.) had provoked the Jews into revolt, a struggle that generated the concept of apocalypticism (see Chapter 2, page 50).

According to this doctrine, evil powers controlled the world, but God would end their rule by sending the Messiah ("anointed one," *Mashiach* in

Hebrew, **Christ** in Greek) to conquer them. A final judgment would follow, punishing the wicked and rewarding the righteous for eternity. Apocalypticism especially influenced the Jews living in Judaea under Roman rule and later, inspired Christians and Muslims.

During Jesus's life, Jews disagreed among themselves about what form Judaism should take in such troubled times. Some favored cooperation with Rome, while others preached rejection of the non-Jewish world. Unrest in Judaea led Augustus to install a Roman governor to suppress disorder.

The writings that would later become the New Testament Gospels, composed around 70 to 90 C.E., offer the earliest accounts of Jesus's life. Jesus wrote nothing down, and others' accounts of his words and deeds are often inconsistent. He began his career as a teacher and healer during the reign of Emperor Tiberius. Often, he expressed his teachings only indirectly, offering stories and parables to challenge his followers to reflect on what he meant.

Jesus's public ministry began with his baptism by John the Baptist, who preached a message of repentance before the approaching final judgment. After John was executed as a rebel, Jesus traveled around Judaea's countryside teaching that God's kingdom was coming and that people needed to prepare spiritually for it. Some saw Jesus as the Messiah, but his apocalypticism did not call for immediate revolt against the Romans. Instead, he taught that God's true kingdom was to be found not on earth but in heaven. He stressed that this kingdom was open to believers regardless of their social status or sinfulness, although his instructions on proper behavior could be direct and blunt. His emphasis on God's love for humanity and people's responsibility to love one another reflected Jewish religious teachings, such as the scriptural interpretations and moral teachings of the scholar Hillel, who lived in Jesus's time.

Realizing that he had to reach more than country people, Jesus took his message to the Jewish population of Jerusalem, the region's main city. The reports of his miraculous healings and exorcisms, combined with his powerful preaching, created a sensation. He became so popular that his followers created the Jesus movement; it was not yet Christianity but rather a Jewish sect, of which there were several, such as the Sadducees and Pharisees, competing for authority at the time. Jesus's popularity attracted the attention of Jewish leaders, who assumed that he wanted to replace them, a possibility they did not welcome. Fearing Jesus might lead a Jewish revolt, the Roman governor Pontius Pilate ordered his crucifixion in Jerusalem in 30 C.E.

Jesus's followers reported that they had seen him in person after his death, proclaiming that God had raised him from the dead. They convinced a few other Jews that he would soon return to judge the world and begin God's kingdom. At this time, his closest disciples, the twelve Apostles (Greek for "messengers"), still considered themselves faithful Jews and continued to follow the commandments of Jewish law. Their leader was Peter, who won acclaim as the greatest miracle worker of the Apostles, an ambassador to Jews interested in the Jesus movement, and the most important messenger proclaiming Jesus's teachings in the imperial capital. The later Christian church called him the first bishop of Rome.

Catacomb Painting of Christ as the Good Shepherd
Catacombs (tunnels with underground rooms) cut deep into soft rock outside major cities in the Roman Empire served as meeting places and burial chambers for Jews and Christians. Rome had 340 miles of catacombs. This painting from the catacomb at Rome named after Priscilla, who was probably a Christian from the first century C.E., shows Jesus as the Good Shepherd (John 10:10–11). He is carrying an animal back to the flock, symbolizing his role as savior; he is dressed in the traditional fashion for a Roman man on a special occasion. Catacomb paintings such as this one were the earliest form of Christian art. (From the Catacombs of Saint Priscilla, Rome, Italy/Erich Lessing/Art Resource, NY.)

A turning point came with the conversion of Paul of Tarsus (c. 10–65 C.E.), a pious Jew and a Roman citizen who had violently opposed Jews who accepted Jesus as the Messiah. A spiritual vision on the road to Damascus in Syria, which Paul interpreted as a divine revelation, inspired him to become a follower of Jesus as the Messiah, or Christ—a Christian, as members of the movement came to be known. Paul taught that accepting Jesus as divine and his crucifixion as the ultimate sacrifice for the sins of humanity was the only way of becoming righteous in the eyes of God. In this way alone could one prepare to attain salvation in the new world when it came; that it had not yet arrived created consternation among many of Jesus's earliest followers. Paul's mission opened the way for Christianity to endure and become a new religion separate from Judaism.

Seeking converts outside Judaea, Paul traveled to preach to Jews and Gentiles (non-Jews) who had adopted some Jewish practices in Asia Minor (today Turkey), Syria, and Greece. Although he stressed the necessity of ethical behavior as defined by Jewish tradition, especially the rejection of sexual immorality and polytheism, Paul also taught that converts did not have to live strictly according to Jewish law. To make conversion easier, he did not require male converts to undergo the Jewish initiation rite of circumcision. He also told his congregations that they did not have to observe Jewish dietary restrictions or festivals. These teachings generated tensions with Jewish authorities in Jerusalem as well as with followers of Jesus living there, who still believed that Christians had to follow Jewish law. Roman authorities arrested Paul as a troublemaker and executed him in 65 C.E.

Hatred of Roman rule provoked Jews to revolt in 66 C.E. After crushing the rebels in 70 C.E., the Roman emperor Titus destroyed the Jerusalem temple and sold most of the city's population into slavery. Following this catastrophe, which cost Jews their religious center, Christianity began to separate more and more clearly from Judaism. The destruction of the Jerusalem temple created a crisis for Judaism that eventually led to a reorientation of its teachings and interpretations through a long process of Jewish oral law and its interpretations being committed to writing.

Paul's importance in early Christianity shows in the number of letters—thirteen—attributed to him among the twenty-seven Christian writings that were eventually put together as the New Testament. Christians came to regard the New Testament as having equal authority with the Jewish Bible, which they then called the Old Testament. Since teachers like Paul preached mainly in the cities, congregations of Christians sprang up in urban areas. In early Christianity, women in some locations could be leaders—such as Lydia, a businesswoman who founded the congregation in Philippi in Greece—but many men, including Paul, opposed women's leadership.

Growth of a New Religion

Christianity faced serious obstacles as a new religion. Imperial officials, suspecting Christians of being traitors, could prosecute them for refusing to perform traditional sacrifices. Christian leaders had to build an organization from the ground up to administer their growing congregations. Finally, Christians had to decide whether women could continue as leaders in their congregations.

The Roman emperors found Christians baffling and troublesome. Unlike Jews, Christians professed a new faith rather than their ancestors' traditional "old" religion. Roman law therefore granted them no special treatment, as it did Jews out of respect for the great antiquity of Judaism. Most Romans feared that Christians' denial of the old gods and the imperial cult would bring divine punishment upon the empire. Secret rituals in which Christians symbolically ate the body and drank the blood of Jesus during communal dinners, called Love Feasts, led to accusations of cannibalism and sexual promiscuity.

Romans were quick to blame Christians for disasters. Nero declared that Christian arsonists set Rome's great fire, and he covered Christians in animal skins to be torn to pieces by dogs or fastened to crosses and set on fire at night. Nero's cruelty, however, earned Christians sympathy from Rome's population.

Persecutions like Nero's were infrequent. There was no law specifically prohibiting Christianity, but officials could punish Christians, as they could

CONTRASTING VIEWS	Christians in the Empire: Conspirators or Faithful Subjects?

Romans worried that new religions would disrupt the "peace with the gods" that guaranteed their national safety and prosperity. The early emperors tried to form a policy on religion that was fair both to Christian subjects and to those citizens who feared them (Excerpt 1). Christians insisted that they were loyal subjects who prayed for the safety of the emperors (Excerpt 2).

1. Pliny on Early Imperial Policy toward Christians, 112 C.E.

As governor of the province of Bithynia, Pliny wrote to the emperor Trajan to ask if he had acted correctly in deciding the fate of Christians accused of crimes by their neighbors. The emperor's reply set out official policy concerning Christians in the early empire.

[Pliny to the emperor Trajan]

I have never participated in trials of Christians. I therefore do not know what offenses it is the practice to punish or investigate, and to what extent. . . .

In the case of those who were denounced to me as Christians, I have observed the following procedure: I interrogated these as to whether they were Christians; those who confessed I interrogated a second and a third time, threatening them with punishment; those who persisted I ordered executed. For I had no doubt that, whatever the nature of their religion, stubbornness and inflexible obstinacy surely deserve to be punished. There were others possessed of the same madness; but because they were Roman citizens, I signed an order for them to be transferred to Rome.

Soon accusations spread, as usually happens, because of the proceedings going on, and several incidents occurred. An anonymous document was published containing the names of many persons. Those who denied that they were or had been Christians, when they called on the gods in words dictated by me, offered prayer with incense and wine to your image, which I had ordered to be brought for this purpose together with statues of the gods, and moreover cursed Christ—none of which those who are really Christians, it is said, can be forced to do—these I thought should be set free. Others named by the informer declared that they were Christians, but then denied it, asserting that they had been but had ceased to be, some three years before, others many years, some as much as twenty-five years. They all worshiped your image and the statues of the gods, and cursed Christ.

They asserted, however, that the sum and substance of their fault or error had been that they were accustomed to meet on a fixed day before dawn and sing responsively a hymn to Christ as to a god, and to bind themselves by oath, not to some crime, but not to commit fraud, theft, or adultery, not to break their word, nor to refuse to return a trust when called upon to do so. When this was over, it was their custom to depart and to assemble again to eat together—but ordinary and innocent food. Even this, they affirmed, they had stopped doing after my edict by which, in accordance with your instructions, I had forbidden political associations. Accordingly, I judged it all the more necessary to find out what the truth was by torturing two female slaves who were called attendants. But I discovered nothing else except depraved, excessive superstition.

I therefore postponed the investigation and hastened to consult you. For the matter seemed to me to require consulting you, especially because of the numbers involved. For the infection of this superstition has spread not only to the cities but also to the villages and farms. But it seems possible to check and cure it. It is certainly quite clear that the temples, which had been almost deserted, have begun to be frequented, that the established religious rites, long neglected, are being resumed, and that from everywhere sacrificial animals

anyone, to protect public order. Pliny's actions as a provincial governor in Asia Minor illustrated the situation. (See Contrasting Views.) In about 112 C.E., Pliny asked a group of people accused of following this new religion if they were really Christians. When some said yes, he asked them to reconsider.

are coming, for which until now very few purchasers could be found. Hence it is easy to imagine what a multitude of people can be reformed if an opportunity for repentance is given.

[Emperor Trajan to Pliny]

You followed proper procedure, my dear Pliny, in handling the cases of those who had been denounced to you as Christians. For it is not possible to lay down any general rule to serve as a kind of fixed standard. They are not to be searched for; if they are denounced and proved guilty, they are to be punished, with this reservation, that whoever denies that he is a Christian and really proves it—that is, by worshipping our gods—even though he was under suspicion in the past, shall obtain pardon through repentance. But anonymously posted accusations ought to have no place in any prosecution. For this is both a dangerous kind of precedent and out of keeping with [the spirit of] our age.

Source: Pliny, *Letters*, Book 10, nos. 96 and 97. Translation (here modified) by Betty Radice, 1969.

2. Tertullian's Defense of His Fellow Christians, 197 C.E.

A theologian from North Africa, Tertullian vehemently insisted that Christians supported the empire.

So that is why Christians are public enemies—because they will not give the emperors vain, false, and reckless honors; because, being men of a true religion, they celebrate the emperors' festivals more in heart than in a festival mood. . . .

On the contrary, the name faction may properly be given to those who join to hate the good and honest, who shout for the blood of the innocent, who use as a pretext to defend their hatred the absurdity that they take the Christians to be the cause of every disaster to the state, of every misfortune of the people. If the Tiber reaches the walls, if the Nile does not rise to water the fields, if the sky does not move [i.e., if there is no rain] or the earth does, if there is famine, if there is plague, the cry at once arises: "The Christians to the lions!"

For we do pray to the eternal God, the true God, the living God, for the safety of the emperors. . . . Looking up to heaven, the Christians—with hands outspread because innocent, with head bare because we do not blush, yes!, and without a prompter because we pray from the heart—are ever praying for all the emperors. We pray for a fortunate life for them, a secure rule, a safe house, brave armies, a faithful Senate, a virtuous people, a peaceful world. . . .

Should not our sect [i.e., Christianity] have been listed among the legal associations, when it commits no such actions as are commonly feared from unlawful associations? For unless I am mistaken, the reason for prohibiting associations clearly lay in care for public order—to save the state from being torn into factions, a thing very likely to disturb election assemblies, public gatherings, local Senates, meetings, even the public games, with the clashing and rivalry of partisans. . . . We, however, whom all the passion for glory and rank leave cold, have no need to combine; nothing is more foreign to us than the state. One state we recognize for all—the universe.

Source: Tertullian, *Apology*, 30.1, 30.4; 35.1; 38.1–3; 40.1–2. Translation (here modified) by T. R. Glover, 1931.

QUESTIONS TO CONSIDER

1. Do you think that Pliny's procedure in dealing with the accused Christians respected the Roman legal principle of equity? Why or why not?

2. How should a society treat a minority of its members whose presence severely disturbs the majority, especially if the source of the conflict is rooted in religious beliefs?

He freed those who denied Christianity, so long as they sacrificed to the gods, swore loyalty to the imperial cult, and cursed Christ. He executed those who refused these actions. Christians argued that Romans had nothing to fear from their faith. Christianity, they insisted, taught morality and respect for

WHAT WOULD YOU DO?

If you were a Roman provincial governor like Pliny how would you deal with religious conflict among the people in your region? How would you maintain order? And how would you try to prevent disruptions in the local economy, as had occurred in Pliny's province?

authority. It was the true philosophy, they explained, combining the best features of Judaism and Greek thought.

The occasional persecutions in the early empire did not stop Christianity. Christians like Vibia Perpetua regarded public executions as an opportunity to become a **martyr** (Greek for "witness"), someone who dies for his or her religious faith. Martyrs' belief that their deaths would send them directly to paradise allowed them to face torture. Some Christians actively sought to become martyrs. Tertullian (c. 160–240 C.E.) proclaimed that "martyrs' blood is the seed of the Church." Ignatius (c. 35–107 C.E.), bishop of Antioch, begged Rome's congregation, which was becoming the most prominent Christian group, not to ask the emperor to show him mercy after his arrest: "Let me be food for the wild animals [in the arena] through which I can reach God," he pleaded. "I am God's wheat, to be ground up by the teeth of beasts so that I may be found pure bread of Christ." Stories reporting the martyrs' courage showed that the new religion gave its believers spiritual power to endure suffering.

Christians continued to expect Jesus to return to pass judgment on the world during their lifetimes. When that did not happen, they began transforming their religion from an apocalyptic Jewish sect expecting the immediate end of the world into one that could survive indefinitely. This transformation was painful because early Christians fiercely disagreed about what they should believe, how they should live, and who had the authority to decide these questions. Some insisted Christians should withdraw from the everyday world to escape its evil, abandoning their families and shunning sex and reproduction. Others believed they could follow Christ's challenging teachings while living ordinary lives. Many Christians worried they could not serve as soldiers without betraying their faith because the army participated in the imperial cult. This dilemma raised the further issue of whether Christians could remain loyal subjects of the emperor. Disagreement over these doctrinal questions raged in the many congregations that arose in the early empire around the Mediterranean, from Gaul to Africa to the Near East (Map 6.3).

The need to deal with such tensions, to administer the congregations, and to promote spiritual communion among believers led Christians to create an official hierarchy of men, headed by bishops. They spearheaded the drive to build the connection between congregations and Christ that promised salvation to believers. Bishops possessed authority to define Christian doctrine and administer practical affairs for congregations. The emergence of bishops became the most important institutional development in early Christianity. Bishops received their positions according to the principle later called **apostolic succession**, which states that the Apostles appointed the first bishops as their successors, granting these new officials the authority Jesus had originally given to the Apostles. Those designated by the Apostles in turn appointed their own successors. Bishops had authority to ordain ministers with the holy power to administer the sacraments, above all baptism and communion, which believers regarded as necessary for achieving eternal life. Bishops also controlled their congregations' memberships and finances. The money financing the early church came from members' donations.

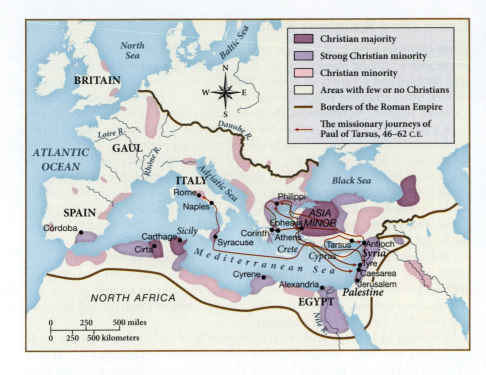

MAP 6.3
Christian Populations in the Late Third Century c.e.
Christians were still a minority in the Roman world three hundred years after Jesus's crucifixion. However, certain areas of the empire—especially Asia Minor, where Paul had preached—had a concentration of Christians. Most Christians lived in cities and towns, where the missionaries had gone to find crowds to hear their message. *Paganus*, a Latin word for "country person" or "rural villager," came to mean a believer in traditional polytheistic cults—hence the word *pagan* that modern historians sometimes use to indicate traditional polytheism. Paganism lived on in rural areas for centuries.

The bishops tried to suppress the disagreements that arose in the new religion. They used their authority to define **orthodoxy** (true doctrine) and **heresy** (false doctrine). The meetings of the bishops of different cities constituted the church's organization in this period. Today this loose organization is referred to as the early Catholic (Greek for "universal") church. Since the bishops often disagreed about doctrine and about which bishops should have greater authority than others, unity remained impossible to achieve.

When the male bishops came to power, they demoted women from positions of leadership. This change reflected their view that in Christianity women should be subordinate to men, as in Roman imperial society in general. Some congregations took a long time to accept this shift, however, and women still claimed authority in some groups in the second and third centuries c.e. In late-second-century c.e., Asia Minor, for example, Prisca and Maximilla declared themselves prophetesses with the power to baptize believers in anticipation of the coming end of the world. They spread the apocalyptic message that the heavenly Jerusalem would soon descend in their region.

Excluded from leadership posts, many women chose a life without sex to demonstrate their devotion to Christ. Their commitment to celibacy gave these women the power to control their own bodies. Other Christians regarded women who reached this special closeness to God as holy and socially superior. By rejecting the traditional roles of wife and mother in favor of spiritual excellence, celibate Christian women achieved independence and status otherwise denied them.

Competing Religious Beliefs

Three centuries after Jesus's death, traditional polytheism was still the religion of the overwhelming majority of the Roman Empire's population. Polytheists, who worshipped a variety of gods in different ways in diverse kinds of sanctuaries, often reflecting regional religious rituals and traditions, never created a unified religion. Nevertheless, the power and prosperity of the early empire gave traditional believers confidence that the old gods and the imperial cult protected them. Even those who preferred religious philosophy, such as Stoicism's idea of divine providence, respected the old cults because they embodied Roman tradition. By the third century C.E., the growth of Christianity, along with the persistence of Judaism and polytheistic cults, meant that people could choose from a number of competing beliefs. Especially appealing were beliefs that offered people hope that they could change their present lives for the better and also look forward to a blessed afterlife.

Polytheistic religion aimed at winning the goodwill of all the divinities who could affect human life. Its deities ranged from the state cults' major gods, such as Jupiter, Juno, and Minerva, to spirits thought to inhabit groves and springs. International cults such as the mystery cults of Demeter and Persephone outside Athens remained popular.

The cults of Isis and Mithras demonstrate how polytheism could provide a religious experience arousing strong emotions and demanding a moral way of life. The Egyptian goddess Isis had already attracted Romans by the time of Augustus, who tried to suppress her cult because it was Cleopatra's religion. But the fame of Isis as a kind, compassionate goddess who cared for her followers made her cult too popular to crush: the Egyptians said it was her tears for starving humans that caused the Nile to flood every year and bring them good harvests. Her image was that of a loving mother, and in art she was often depicted nursing her son. Her cult's central doctrine concerned the death and resurrection of her husband, Osiris. Isis also promised her believers a life after death.

Isis required her followers to behave righteously. Many inscriptions expressed her high moral standards by listing her own civilizing accomplishments: "I broke down the rule of tyrants; I put an end to murders; I caused what is right to be mightier than gold and silver." The hero of Apuleius's novel *The Golden Ass* shouts out his intense joy after his rescue and spiritual rebirth through Isis: "O holy and eternal guardian of the human race, who always cherishes mortals and blesses them, you care for the troubles of miserable humans with a sweet mother's love. Neither day nor night, nor any moment of time, ever passes by without your blessings." Other cults also required worshippers to lead upright lives. Inscriptions from Asia Minor, for example, record people's confessions to sins such as sexual transgressions for which their local god had imposed severe penance.

Archaeology reveals that the cult of Mithras had many shrines under the Roman Empire, but no texts survive to explain its mysterious rituals and symbols, which Romans believed had originated in Persia. Mithras's legend said

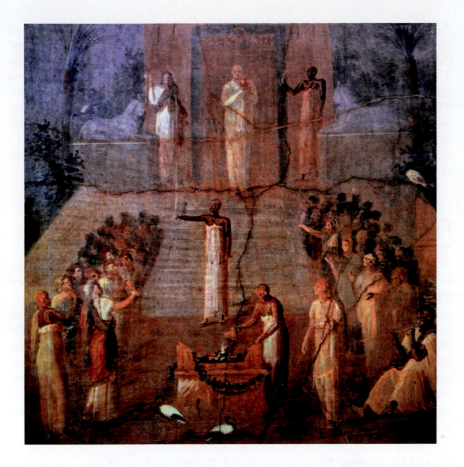

that he killed a bull in a cave, apparently as a sacrifice for the benefit of his worshippers. As pictures show, this was an unusual sacrifice because the animal was allowed to struggle as it was killed. Initiates in Mithras's cult proceeded through rankings named, from bottom to top, Raven, Male Bride, Soldier, Lion, Persian, Sun-runner, and Father—the latter a title of great honor.

Many upper-class Romans also guided their lives by Greek philosophy. Most popular was Stoicism, which presented philosophy as the "science of living" and required self-discipline and duty from men and women alike (see Chapter 4, page 136). Philosophic individuals put together their own set of beliefs, such as those on duty expressed by the emperor Marcus Aurelius in his memoirs expressing Stoic ideas, entitled *To Myself* (or *Meditations*). In this moving personal journal, the most powerful man in the Roman world told himself that "when it's hard to get out of bed in the morning, keep it in mind that you are getting up to do the work of a human being."

Christian and polytheist intellectuals debated Christianity's relationship to Greek philosophy. Origen (c. 185–255 C.E.) argued that Christianity was superior to Greek philosophical doctrines as a guide to correct living. At about

REVIEW QUESTION
Which aspects of social, cultural, and political life in the early Roman Empire supported the growth of Christianity, and which opposed it?

the same time, Plotinus (c. 205–270 C.E.) developed the philosophy that had the greatest influence on religion. His spiritual philosophy was influenced by Persian religious ideas and, above all, Plato's philosophy, for which reason it is called **Neoplatonism**. Plotinus's ideas deeply influenced many Christian thinkers as well as polytheists. He wrote that ultimate reality is a trinity of The One, of Mind, and of Soul. By rejecting the life of the body and relying on reason, individual souls could achieve a mystic union with The One, who in Christian thought would be God. To succeed in this spiritual quest required strenuous self-discipline in personal morality and spiritual purity as well as in philosophical contemplation.

From Stability to Crisis in the Third Century C.E.

In the third century C.E., military expenses provoked a financial crisis that fed a political crisis disrupting the empire from the 230s to the 280s C.E. Invasions on the northern and eastern frontiers had forced the Roman emperors to expand the army for defense, but no new revenues came in to meet the increased costs. The emperors' desperate schemes to pay for defense damaged the economy and infuriated the population. This anger at the regime encouraged generals to repeat the behavior that had destroyed the republic: commanding client armies to seize power in a prolonged civil war. Earthquakes and regional epidemics added to people's misery. By 284 C.E., this combination of troubles had destroyed the Pax Romana.

Threats to the Northern and Eastern Frontiers of the Early Roman Empire

Emperors since Domitian in the first century had combated invaders. The most aggressive attackers were the multiethnic bands from northern Europe that crossed the Danube and Rhine Rivers to raid Roman territory. These attacks perhaps resulted from pressure on the northerners caused by wars in central Asia that disrupted trade and the economy. These originally poorly organized northerners developed military discipline through their frequent fighting against the Roman army. They mounted especially damaging invasions during the reign of Marcus Aurelius (r. 161–180 C.E.).

A major threat also appeared at the eastern edge of the empire, when a new Persian dynasty, the Sasanids, defeated the Parthian Empire and fought to re-create the ancient Persian Empire. By the early third century C.E., Persia's renewed military power forced the Roman emperors to deploy a large part of the army to protect the rich eastern provinces, which took troops away from defense of the northern frontiers. The Atlantic Ocean on the west and the Sahara Desert to the south meant that threats to Roman territory were significantly less from those directions. (See Mapping the West: The Roman Empire in Crisis, 284 C.E. on page 214.)

Recognizing the northern warriors' bravery, the emperors had begun hiring them as auxiliary soldiers for the Roman army in the late first century C.E. and settling them on the frontiers as buffers against other invaders. By the early third century, the army had expanded to enroll perhaps as many as 450,000 troops (the size of the navy remains unknown). Training constantly, soldiers had to be able to carry forty-pound packs twenty miles in five hours, swimming rivers on the way. Since the early second century C.E., the emperors had built stone camps for permanent garrisons, but while on the march, an army constructed a fortified camp every night. Soldiers transported all the makings of a wooden walled city everywhere they went. As one ancient commentator noted, "Infantrymen were little different from loaded pack mules." At one temporary fort in a frontier area, archaeologists found a supply of a million iron nails—ten tons' worth. The same encampment required seventeen miles of timber for its barracks' walls. To outfit a single legion with tents required fifty-four thousand calves' hides.

The increased demand for pay and supplies strained imperial finances. The army had become a source of negative instead of positive cash flow to the treasury, and the economy had not expanded to make up the difference. To make matters worse, inflation had driven up prices. The principate's long period of peace promoted inflation by increasing demand for goods and services to a level that outstripped the supply.

In desperation, some emperors attempted to curb inflation by debasing imperial coinage. **Debasement of coinage** meant putting less precious metal in each coin and adding more metal of less worth without changing the coin's face value. In this way, the emperors created more cash from the same amount of precious metal. But merchants soon raised prices to make up for the debased coinage's reduced value; this in turn produced more inflation, causing prices to rise even more. Still, the soldiers demanded that their patrons, the emperors, pay them well. This pressure drove imperial finances into collapse by the 250s C.E.

Uncontrolled Spending, Natural Disasters, and Political Crisis, 193–284 C.E.

The emperor Septimius Severus (r. 193–211 C.E.) and his son and successor Caracalla (r. 211–217 C.E.) made financial crisis unavoidable when they drained the treasury to satisfy the army and their own dreams of glory. A soldier's soldier from North Africa, Severus became emperor when his predecessor's incompetence caused a government crisis and civil war. Seeking to restore imperial prestige and acquire money from foreign conquest, Severus campaigned beyond the frontiers of the provinces in Mesopotamia and Scotland.

Since extreme inflation had reduced their wages to almost nothing, soldiers expected the emperors to provide gifts of extra money. Severus spent large

Emperor Severus and His Family
This portrait of the emperor Septimius Severus; his wife, Julia Domna; and their sons, Caracalla (on the right) and Geta (with his face obliterated), was painted in Egypt about 200 C.E. The males hold scepters, symbolic of rule, but all four family members wear bejeweled golden crowns fit for royalty. Severus arranged to marry Julia without ever meeting her because her horoscope predicted she would become a queen, and she served as her husband's valued adviser. They hoped their sons would share rule, but when Severus died in 211 C.E., Caracalla murdered Geta so that he could rule alone. Why do you think the portrait's owner rubbed out Geta's face? (Staaliche Museen, Berlin, Germany/Bridgeman Images.)

sums on gifts and raised soldiers' pay by a third. The army's expanded size made this raise more expensive than the treasury could handle. The out-of-control spending did not trouble Severus. His deathbed advice to his sons, Caracalla and Geta, in 211 C.E. was to "stay on good terms with each other, be generous to the soldiers, and pay no attention to anyone else."

Ignoring the first part of his father's advice, Caracalla murdered his brother. He then went on to end the Roman Golden Age of peace and prosperity with his uncontrolled spending and cruelty. He increased the soldiers' pay by another 40 to 50 percent and spent gigantic sums on building projects, including the largest public baths Rome had ever seen, covering blocks and blocks of the city. These huge expenses put unbearable pressure on the local provincial elites responsible for collecting taxes, and they in turn squeezed ordinary citizens for even larger payments.

In 212 C.E., Caracalla tried to fix the budget by granting Roman citizenship to almost every man and woman in imperial territory except slaves. Since only citizens paid inheritance taxes and fees for freeing slaves, an increase in citizens meant an increase in revenues, most of which was earmarked for the army. But too much was never enough for Caracalla, whose cruelty to anyone who displeased him made his contemporaries whisper that he was insane. His attempted conquests of new territory failed to bring in enough funds, and he wrecked imperial finances. Once when his mother reprimanded him for his excesses he replied, as he drew his sword, "Never mind, we won't run out of money as long as I have this."

The financial crisis generated political instability that led to a half century of civil war. This period of violent struggle destroyed the principate. More than two dozen men, often several at once, held or claimed power in this period. Their only qualification was their ability to command a frontier army and to reward the troops for loyalty to their general instead of to the state.

The civil war devastated the population and the economy. Violence and hyperinflation made life miserable in many regions. Agriculture withered as farmers could not keep up normal production when armies searching for food ravaged their crops. City council members faced constantly escalating demands for tax revenues from the swiftly changing emperors. The endless financial pressure destroyed members' will to serve their communities.

Earthquakes and epidemics also struck the provinces in the mid-third century. In some regions, the population declined significantly as food supplies became less dependable, civil war killed soldiers and civilians alike, and infection raged. The loss of population meant fewer soldiers for the army, whose strength as a defense and police force had been gutted by political and financial chaos. This weakness made frontier areas more vulnerable to raids and allowed roving bands of robbers to range unchecked inside the borders.

The Fragmented Roman Empire of the Third Century

Foreign enemies to the north and east took advantage of the third-century crisis to attack. Roman fortunes hit bottom when Shapur I, king of the Sasanid Empire of Persia, invaded the province of Syria and captured the emperor Valerian (r. 253–260 C.E.). By this time, Roman imperial territory was in constant danger of being captured. Zenobia, the warrior queen of Palmyra in Syria, for example, seized Egypt and Asia Minor. Emperor Aurelian (r. 270–275 C.E.) won back these provinces only with great difficulty. He also had to encircle Rome with a larger wall to ward off attacks from northern raiders, who were smashing their way into Italy.

Polytheists explained the third-century crisis in the traditional way: the state gods were angry about something. But what? To them, the obvious answer was the presence of Christians, who denied the existence of the Roman gods and refused to worship them. Emperor Decius (r. 249–251 C.E.) therefore launched a systematic persecution to eliminate Christians and restore the goodwill of the gods. He ordered all the empire's inhabitants to prove their loyalty to the state by sacrificing to its gods. Christians who refused were killed. This persecution did not stop the civil war, economic failure, and natural disasters that threatened Rome's empire, and Emperor Gallienus (r. 253–268 C.E.) ordered Christians to be left alone and their property restored. The crisis in government continued, however, and by the 280s C.E., the principate had reached a political and financial dead end. Against long odds, the coming decades would bring a transformation under new, more autocratic emperors.

REVIEW QUESTION
What were the causes and the effects of the Roman crisis in the third century C.E.?

MAPPING THE WEST

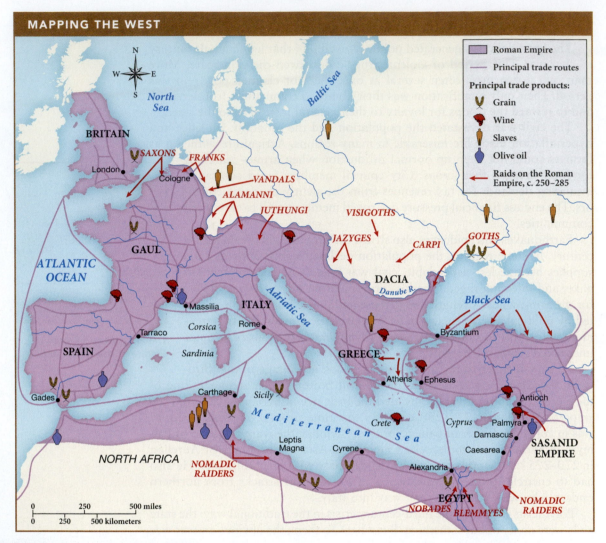

The Roman Empire in Crisis, 284 C.E.

By the 280s C.E., fifty years of civil war had torn the principate apart. Imperial territory retained the outlines inherited from the time of Augustus (compare Map 6.1 on page 195), except for the loss of Dacia to the Goths a few years before. Attacks from the north and east had repeatedly penetrated the frontiers, however. Long-distance trade had always been important to the empire's prosperity, but the decades of violence had made transport riskier and therefore more expensive, contributing to the crisis.

Analyzing the Map: From which direction—north and east or west and south—did the Roman Empire face the greater number of threats from raiders or another empire, and in what ways do you think this difference affected the fate of the Roman Empire?

Making Connections: What do you think would have been the greatest challenges in ruling such a vast empire in an age without swift communications or fast travel?

Conclusion

Augustus created the principate and the Pax Romana by constructing a disguised monarchy while insisting that he was restoring the republic. He succeeded by ensuring the loyalty of both the army and the people to him by becoming their patron. He bought off the upper class by letting them keep their traditional offices and status. The imperial cult provided a focus for building and displaying loyalty to the emperor.

The emperors provided food to the poor, built baths and arenas for public entertainment, paid their troops well, and gave privileges to the elite. By the second century, peace and prosperity created a Golden Age. Long-term financial difficulties set in, however, because the army, now concentrating on defense, no longer brought in money from conquests. Severe inflation made the situation desperate. Ruined by the demand for more tax revenues, provincial elites lost their public-spiritedness and avoided their communal responsibilities.

The emergence of Christianity generated tension because Romans doubted Christians' loyalty. The new religion had evolved from Jewish apocalypticism to a hierarchical organization. Its believers argued with one another and with the authorities. Martyrs such as Vibia Perpetua worried the government by placing their beliefs ahead of loyalty to the state.

When financial ruin, natural disasters, and civil war combined to create a political crisis in the mid-third century C.E., the emperors lacked the money and the popular support to solve it. Not even their persecution of Christians had convinced the gods to restore Rome's good fortunes. Threatened with the loss of peace, prosperity, and territory, the empire needed a political transformation to survive. That process would begin under the relentlessly tough emperor Diocletian (r. 284–305 C.E.). Under his equally determined successor, Constantine (r. 306–337 C.E.), the Roman Empire also began the slow process of becoming officially Christian.

Chapter 6 Review

Key Terms and People

Be sure that you can identify the term or person and explain its historical significance.

Pax Romana ("Roman Peace") (p. 182)
Augustus (p. 184)
principate (p. 185)
praetorian guard (p. 185)
Julio-Claudians (p. 191)
Colosseum (p. 193)
decurions (p. 196)
Romanization (p. 198)
Christ (p. 201)
martyr (p. 206)
apostolic succession (p. 206)
orthodoxy (p. 207)
heresy (p. 207)
Neoplatonism (p. 210)
debasement of coinage (p. 211)

Review Questions

1. How did the peace gained through Augustus's "restoration of the Roman republic" affect Romans's lives in all social classes?

2. In the early Roman Empire, what was life like in the cities and in the country for the elite and for ordinary people?

3. Which aspects of social, cultural, and political life in the early Roman Empire supported the growth of Christianity, and which opposed it?

4. What were the causes and the effects of the Roman crisis in the third century C.E.?

Making Connections

1. What were the similarities and differences between the crisis in the first century B.C.E. that undermined the Roman republic and the crisis in the third century C.E. that undermined the principate?

2. Do you think that the factors that caused the crisis in the Roman Empire could cause a similar crisis in the Western world of today?

Important Events

30 B.C.E.	Octavian (the future Augustus) conquers Ptolemaic Egypt
27 B.C.E.	Augustus inaugurates the principate
30 C.E.	Jesus is crucified in Jerusalem
64 C.E.	Great fire in Rome; Nero blames Christians
69 C.E.	Civil war after death of Nero in 68 C.E.
70 C.E.	Titus captures Jerusalem; the Jewish temple is destroyed
70–90 C.E.	New Testament Gospels are written
80s C.E.	Domitian leads campaigns against multiethnic invaders on northern frontiers
161–180 C.E.	Marcus Aurelius battles multiethnic bands attacking northern frontiers
212 C.E.	Caracalla extends Roman citizenship to almost all free inhabitants of the provinces
230s–280s C.E.	Third-century financial and political crisis
249–251 C.E.	Decius persecutes Christians

Consider three events

Great fire in Rome, Nero blames Christians (64 C.E.); New Testament Gospels are written (70–90 C.E.); and Decius persecutes Christians (249–251 C.E.). How were these events similar to and different from one another, and what attitudes did they illustrate? How might polytheist and Christian ideas have contributed to these events?

Suggested References

Scholars continue to debate the nature and the significance of the many social, cultural, and (especially) religious changes that occurred under the early Roman Empire. Perhaps the most difficult question to answer is to what extent life became better or worse for most people—and indeed how to define *better* and *worse* in this context—once the empire stopped expanding into new territories.

Challet, Claude-Emmanuelle C. *Like Man, Like Woman: Roman Women, Gender Qualities, and Conjugal Relationships at the Turn of the First Century.* 2013.

Crossan, Dominic, and Jonathan Reed. *In Search of Paul: How Jesus's Apostle Opposed Rome's Empire with God's Kingdom.* 2005.

Dennison, Matthew. *Livia: Empress of Rome.* 2010.

Denzey, Nicola. *The Bone Gatherers: The Lost Worlds of Early Christian Women.* 2007.

*Futrell, Allison. *The Roman Games: Historical Sources in Translation.* 2006.

Galinsky, Karl, ed. *The Cambridge Companion to the Age of Augustus.* 2005.

Goldsworthy, Adrian. *The Complete Roman Army.* 2003.

Green, Bernard. *Christianity in Ancient Rome: The First Three Centuries.* 2010.

Harris, W. V. *Rome's Imperial Economy.* 2010.

*Josephus. *The Jewish War.* Trans. Martin Hammond. 2017.

Knapp, Robert C. *The Dawn of Christianity: People and Gods in an Age of Miracles and Magic.* 2017.

*Kraemer, Ross Shephard. *Her Share of the Blessings: Women's Religion among Pagans, Jews, and Christians in the Greco-Roman World.* 1992.

*Marcus Aurelius. *Meditations.* Trans. Robin Hard. Intro. Christopher Gill. 2011.

Mattingly, David J. *Imperialism, Power, and Identity: Experiencing the Roman Empire.* 2010.

Matz, David. *Life of the Ancient Romans: Daily Life through History.* 2008.

Roman emperors: http://www.roman-emperors.org/startup.htm/

*Suetonius. *Lives of the Caesars.* Trans. Catharine Edwards. 2009.

*Tacitus. *The Complete Works.* Trans. Alfred John Church and William Jackson Brodribb. 1964.

---

*Primary source.

The Transformation of the Roman Empire

284–600 C.E.

Around 300,* Emperor Diocletian (r. 284–305) proclaimed the reason why the Roman Empire was endangered: "The immortal gods in their foresight have taken care to proclaim and prescribe what is good and true, which the sayings of many good and distinguished men have approved and confirmed, along with the reasoned judgments of the wisest. It is wrong to oppose and resist these traditions, and a new cult should not find fault with ancient religion. It is a serious crime to question matters that our ancestors established and fixed once and for all. . . . Therefore, we are eager to punish the obstinate and perverse thinking of these utterly worthless people."

With this proclamation, Diocletian was blaming people who did not worship the traditional gods—including Christians—for having brought on divine anger and therefore causing the disasters experienced by the Roman world in the third century. By appointing a co-emperor with himself and two assistant emperors, Diocletian had ended the political strife that threatened to break apart the Roman Empire earlier in the

«**Vandal General Stilicho and His Family** This diptych ("folding tablet") made of ivory around 400 shows Stilicho, the top general in the Roman army in Europe and close adviser to the western Roman emperor, with his wife, Serena, and their son, Eucherius. Stilicho's life reveals the mixing of cultures in the later Roman Empire: his father was from the Vandal tribe in Germany, and his mother was Roman; he himself rose to prominence in Roman imperial government and society. Serena was the adoptive daughter of the emperor, and Stilicho and Serena's daughter Maria married the emperor's son. Stilicho is shown dressed in the richly decorated clothing appropriate for a member of the Roman elite, and he wears a metal clasp to fasten his robe, a symbol of his father's ethnicity. The images on his shield of the two emperors then ruling the divided Roman Empire proclaim his loyalty even as they point to the political and geographic fragmentation of the time. (Basilica di San Giovanni Battista, Monza, Italy/Bridgeman Images.)

---

*From this point on, dates are C.E. unless otherwise indicated.

third century. Still, suspicions endured that the gods might punish all Romans for not taking action against people who did not believe in them. Diocletian therefore convinced his co-rulers first to persecute the pagan Manichaeans (followers of the Iranian prophet Mani and the objects of his proclamation) and then the Christians. His successor Constantine (r. 306–337) ended the persecution by converting to Christianity and supporting his new faith with imperial funds and a policy of religious freedom. Nevertheless, it took a century more for Christianity to become the state religion. The social and cultural transformations produced by the Christianization of the Roman Empire came slowly because many Romans clung to their ancestral beliefs.

Diocletian's reform of government only postponed the division of imperial territory. In 395, Emperor Theodosius I split the Empire in two to try to provide better defense against the warlike peoples pressing into Roman territory, especially from the north; the Romans called them "barbarians," meaning "brave but uncivilized." (See Terms of History on page 222.) He appointed one of his sons to rule the west and the other the east. The two emperors were supposed to cooperate, but in the long run, this system of divided rule could not cope with the different pressures affecting the two regions.

CHAPTER FOCUS

What were the most important sources of unity and of division in the Roman Empire from the reign of Diocletian to the reign of Justinian, and why?

In the western Roman Empire, military and political events provoked social and cultural transformation when barbarian immigrants began living side by side with Romans. Both groups underwent changes: the barbarians created kingdoms and laws based on Roman traditions yet adopted Christianity, and the wealthy Romans fled from cities to seek safety in country estates when the western government became ineffective. These changes in turn transformed the political landscape of western Europe in ways that foreshadowed the later development of nations there. In the east, however, the Empire lived on for another thousand years, passing on the memory of classical traditions to later Western civilization. The eastern half endured as the continuation of the Roman Empire until Turkish invaders conquered it in 1453.

CHAPTER TIMELINE

293	**303**	**313**	**324**	**361–363**	**391**
Diocletian creates the tetrarchy	Diocletian launches Great Persecution of Christians	Religious freedom is proclaimed in the Edict of Milan	Constantine wins civil war and refounds Byzantium as Constantinople, the "New Rome"	Julian the Apostate tries to reinstate polytheism as official state religion	Theodosius I makes Christianity the official state religion

300

301	**312**	**323**	**325**	**378**
Diocletian issues Edict on Maximum Prices and Wages	Constantine sees vision, wins battle of the Milvian Bridge in Rome, and converts to Christianity	Pachomius in Upper Egypt establishes the first monasteries	Council of Nicaea defends Christian orthodoxy against Arianism	Barbarian massacre of Roman army in battle of Adrianople

From Principate to Dominate in the Late Roman Empire, 284–395

Diocletian and Constantine pulled Roman government out of its extended crisis by increasing the emperors' authority, reorganizing the Empire's defense, restricting workers' freedom, and changing the tax system to try to increase revenues. The two emperors firmly believed they had to win back divine favor to ensure their people's safety.

Diocletian and Constantine tried to solve the Empire's problems by becoming more autocratic. They transformed their appearance as rulers to make their power seem awesome beyond compare, taking ideas from the self-presentation of their most powerful rivals, the rulers of the Persian Empire. Diocletian and Constantine hoped that their assertion of supremacy would keep their empire united; in the long run, however, it proved impossible to preserve Roman imperial territory on the scale once ruled by Augustus.

The Political Transformation and Division of the Roman Empire

No one could have predicted Diocletian's rise to power: he began life as an uneducated peasant in the Balkans, but his leadership, courage, and intelligence propelled him through the ranks until the army made him emperor in 284. He ended a half century of civil war by imposing the most autocratic system of rule in Roman history.

Historians refer to Roman rule from Diocletian onward as the *dominate*, because he took the title *dominus* ("lord" or "master")—what slaves called their owners. The emperors of the dominate continued to refer to their government as the Roman republic, but in truth they ruled autocratically. This new

410	426	475	476		507	527–565
Visigoths sack Rome	Augustine publishes *The City of God*	Visigoths publish law code	German commander Odoacer deposes the final western emperor, the boy Romulus Augustulus ("the fall of Rome")		Clovis establishes Frankish kingdom in Gaul	Reign of eastern Roman Emperor Justinian

400			**500**			**600**

395	451		493–526	529–534		540
Theodosius I divides Empire into western and eastern halves	Council of Chalcedon attempts to forge agreement on Christian orthodoxy		Ostrogothic kingdom in Italy	Justinian publishes law code and handbooks		Benedict devises his rule for monasteries

TERMS OF HISTORY

Barbarian

The term *barbarian* originated in ancient Greece. The Greek word *barbaros* originally indicated a person from somewhere else, whether in Greece or elsewhere. The meaning eventually came to be "someone whose native language is not Greek." Over time, it also indicated people who were different from Greeks in their customs, clothing, and, sometimes, general physical appearance. Nevertheless, before the Persian Wars in the early fifth century B.C.E. (see Chapter 3), Greeks' designation of others as barbarian did not automatically imply cultural or moral inferiority. In fact, Greeks could regard non-Greeks as intelligent, brave, honest, and admirable—though on their own, not Greek, terms.

The decades of bitter and bloody warfare with the Persians changed this situation. Now, barbarians were often (although not always) seen as morally treacherous, culturally degenerate, and cruelly dangerous. Their clothing, jewelry, weapons, and riches in precious metals could be impressive, but the main point of this later, conflict-generated interpretation of "the other" was that barbarians were different from Greeks in negative ways.

Romans took over the word "barbarian" from the Greeks (whom Romans excluded from this category),

recognizing the valor of non-Greek foreigners in war but denigrating them as culturally inferior. Since the later Roman Empire came under great stress from attacks by barbarians from northern Europe who lived as raiders, it makes sense to think that Romans held apprehensive and negative views of all barbarians, especially when large groups of them moved into Roman territory as refugees from strife in their original locations.

Scholars debate whether to call these movements of people into the Roman Empire "barbarian invasions" or "migrations," and whether to think of their effects on the Roman world as leading to a "fall," or to a political and cultural "transformation and synthesis." What does seem clear is that these groups of barbarians did not have clearly defined or unitary ethnic identities—they were not uniformly "Germanic"—before entering the Roman Empire, where they then had to figure out how to survive in a hostile environment. It is also clear that investigating this process and its consequences for Romans and barbarians alike is key to understanding how Western civilization moved, again to employ modern terms, from "ancient" to "medieval"—and therefore eventually to "modern."

system eliminated the principate's ideal of the princeps ("first man") as the social equal of the senators. The emperors of the dominate now recognized no equals. The offices of senator, consul, and other traditional positions continued, but only as posts of honor. These officials had the responsibility to pay for public services, especially chariot races and festivals, but no power to govern. Imperial administrators were increasingly chosen from lower ranks of society, according to their competence and their loyalty to the emperor.

The dominate's emperors took ideas for emphasizing their superiority from the Sasanids in Persia, whose empire (224–651) they recognized as equal to their own in power and whose king and queen they addressed as "our brother" and "our sister." The Roman Empire's masters broadcast their majesty by surrounding themselves with courtiers and ceremony, presiding from a raised platform, and sparkling in jeweled crowns, robes, and shoes. Constantine took from Persia the tradition that emperors set themselves apart by wearing a diadem, a purple gem-studded headband. In another echo of Persian monarchy, a series of veils separated the palace's waiting rooms from the interior room where the emperor listened to people's pleas for help or justice. Officials marked their rank by wearing special shoes and belts and claiming grandiose titles such as "Most Perfect."

The dominate's emperors also asserted their supreme power through laws and punishments. They alone made law. To impose order, they raised punishments to brutal levels. New punishments included Constantine's order that the "greedy hands" of officials who took bribes "shall be cut off by the sword." The guardians of a young girl who allowed a lover to seduce her were executed by having molten lead poured into their mouths. Penalties grew ever harsher for the majority of the population, legally designated as "humbler people," who were punished more severely than the "better people" for comparable offenses (see Chapter 6). In this way, the dominate strengthened the divisions between ordinary people and the rich.

Diocletian appointed three "partners" (a co-emperor, Maximian, and two assistant emperors, Constantius and Galerius, who were the designated successors) to join him in ruling the Empire in a **tetrarchy** ("rule by four"). Each ruler controlled one of four districts. Diocletian served as supreme ruler and was supposed to receive the loyalty of the others. He also created smaller administrative units, called dioceses, under separate governors, who reported to the four emperor's assistants, the praetorian prefects (Map 7.1). This system was Diocletian's attempt to put imperial government into closer contact with the Empire's frontier regions, where the dangers of invasion and rebellious troops loomed.

Diocletian's reforms ended Rome's thousand years as the Empire's most important city. Diocletian did not even visit Rome until 303, nearly twenty years after becoming emperor. Italy became just another section of the Empire, now subject to the same taxation as everywhere else.

Diocletian resigned in 305 for unclear reasons, after which rivals for power abandoned the tetrarchy and fought a civil war until 324, when Constantine finally won. At the end of his reign in 337, Constantine designated his three sons to rule as co-emperors. Failing to cooperate, they waged war against one another.

Constantine's warring sons unofficially split the Empire on a north–south line along the Balkan peninsula, a division that Theodosius made permanent in 395. In the long run, the Empire's halves would be governed largely as separate territories despite the emperors' insistence that the Empire remained one state.

Each half had its own capital city. Constantinople ("Constantine's City")—formerly the ancient city of Byzantium (today Istanbul, Turkey)—was the eastern capital. Constantine made it his capital, a "new Rome," because of its strategic military and commercial location: it lay at the mouth of the Black Sea guarding principal routes for trade and troop movements. To recall the glory of Rome, Constantine constructed a forum, an imperial palace, a hippodrome for chariot races, and monumental statues of the traditional gods in his refounded city. Constantinople grew to be the most important city in the Roman Empire.

The Empire's East/West Division, 395

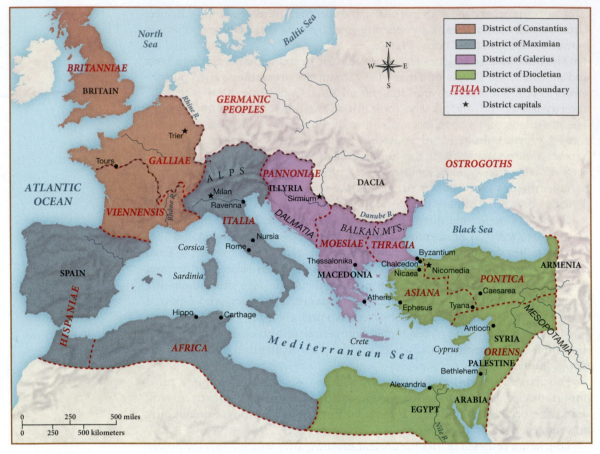

MAP 7.1 Diocletian's Reorganization of 293
Trying to prevent civil war, Emperor Diocletian reorganized Rome's imperial territory into a tetrarchy, to be ruled by himself, his co-emperor Maximian, and assistant emperors Constantius and Galerius, each the head of a large district. He subdivided the preexisting provinces into smaller units and grouped them into fourteen dioceses, each overseen by a regional administrator. The four districts as shown here reflect the arrangement recorded by the imperial official Sextus Aurelius Victor in about 360. What were the advantages and disadvantages of subdividing the Empire?

Honorius, Theodosius's son and successor in the west, wanted a headquarters that was easy to defend. In 404, he chose the port of Ravenna, a commercial center on Italy's northeastern coast housing a naval base. Marshes and walls protected Ravenna by land, while its harbor kept it from being starved out in a siege. Though the emperors enhanced Ravenna with churches covered in multicolored mosaics, it never rivaled Constantinople in size or splendor.

The Social Consequences of Financial Pressures

To try to control inflation and support his huge army, Diocletian imposed price and wage controls and a new taxation system. These measures failed because they imposed great financial pressures on both rich and poor. Diocletian also placed restrictions on many people's rights to choose their occupations.

Diocletian was desperate to reduce the hyperinflation resulting from the third-century crisis. As prices escalated, people hoarded whatever they could buy. "Hurry and spend all my money you have; buy me any kinds of goods at whatever prices they are available," wrote one official to his servant. Hoarding only worsened the inflation.

In 301, the inflation was so severe that Diocletian imposed harsh price and wage controls in the worst-hit areas. This mandate, which blamed high prices on merchants' "unlimited and frenzied greed," forbade hoarding of goods and set cost ceilings for about a thousand goods and services. The mandate failed to change people's behavior, despite penalties of exile or death. Diocletian's price and wage controls thus only increased financial pressure on everyone.

The emperors increased taxes mostly to support the army, which required enormous amounts of grain, meat, salt, wine, vegetable oil, military equipment, horses, camels, and mules. The major sources of revenue were a tax on land, assessed according to its productivity, and a head tax on individuals. To supplement taxes paid in coin, the emperors began collecting some payments in goods and services.

The Empire was too large to enforce the tax system uniformly. In some areas both men and women ages twelve to sixty-five paid the full tax, but in others women paid only half the tax assessment or none at all. The reasons for such differences are not recorded. Workers in cities periodically paid "in kind," that is, by laboring without pay on public works projects such as cleaning municipal drains or repairing buildings. People in commerce, from shopkeepers to prostitutes, still paid taxes in money, while members of the senatorial class were exempt from ordinary taxes but had to pay special levies.

The new tax system could work only if agricultural production remained stable and the government kept track of the people who were liable for the head tax. Diocletian therefore restricted the movement of tenant farmers, called *coloni* (cah-LOW-nee, "cultivators"), whose work provided the Empire's economic base. Now, male coloni, as well as their wives in areas where women were assessed for taxes, were increasingly tied to a particular plot of land. Their children, too, were bound to the family plot, making farming a hereditary obligation.

The government also regulated other occupations deemed essential. Bakers, who were required to produce free bread for Rome's poor, a tradition begun under the republic to prevent food riots, could not leave their jobs. Under Constantine, the sons of military veterans were obliged to serve in the army. However, conditions were not the same everywhere in the Empire. Free workers who earned wages apparently remained important in the economy of Egypt in the late Roman Empire, and archaeological evidence suggests that some regions may actually have become more prosperous.

The emperors also decreed oppressive regulations for the **curials** (CURE-ee-uhls), the social elite in the cities and towns. During this period, many men in the curial class were obliged to serve as decurions (unsalaried members of their city Senate) and to spend their own funds to support the community. Their financial responsibilities ranged from maintaining the water supply to feeding troops, but their most expensive duty was paying for shortfalls in tax collection. The emperors' demands for revenue made this a crushing obligation.

The Empire had always depended on property owners to fill local offices in return for honor and the emperor's favor. Now this tradition broke down as some wealthy people avoided public service to escape financial ruin. Service on a municipal council could even be imposed as punishment for a crime. Eventually, to prevent curials from escaping their obligations, imperial policy decreed that they could not move away from the town where they had been born. Members of the elite sought exemptions from public service by petitioning the emperor, bribing imperial officials, or taking up an occupation that freed them from curial obligations (the military, imperial administration, or church governance). The most desperate simply abandoned their homes and property.

These restrictions eroded the communal values motivating wealthy Romans. The drive to increase revenues also produced social discontent among poorer citizens: the tax rate on land eventually reached one-third of the land's gross yield, impoverishing small farmers. Financial troubles, especially severe in the west, kept the Empire from ever regaining the prosperity of its Golden Age.

From the Great Persecution to Religious Freedom

To eliminate what he saw as a threat to national security from the anger of the traditional gods about the existence of Christians, Diocletian in 303 launched the so-called **Great Persecution** to suppress Christianity. He expelled Christians from official posts, seized their property, tore down churches, and executed anyone who refused to participate in official rituals honoring the "old" gods of Roman religion.

His three partners in the tetrarchy differed in their commitment to Diocletian's policy of suppressing Christians. In the western Empire, official violence against Christians stopped after about a year; in the east, it continued for a decade. The public executions of Christians were so gruesome that they aroused the sympathy of some polytheists. The Great Persecution ultimately failed: it undermined social stability without destroying Christianity.

Constantine changed the world's religious history forever by converting to Christianity. During the civil war after Diocletian's resignation, right before the crucial battle of the Milvian Bridge in Rome in 312, Constantine reportedly experienced a dream promising him God's support and saw Jesus's cross in the sky surrounded by the words, "Under this sign you will win the victory." Constantine ordered his soldiers to paint "the sign of the cross of Christ" on their shields. When his soldiers won a great victory in that battle, Constantine attributed his success to the Christian God and declared himself a Christian.

However, Constantine did not make polytheism illegal and did not make Christianity the official state religion. Instead, he and his polytheist co-emperor Licinius enforced religious freedom, as shown by the **Edict of Milan** of 313. (See Primary Source Analysis on page 228.) The edict proclaimed free choice of religion for everyone and referred to protection of the Empire

Coin Portrait of Emperor Constantine
Constantine had these special, extra-large coins minted to depict him for the first time as an overtly Christian emperor. The jewels on his helmet and crown, the fancy bridle on the horse, and the scepter indicate his status as emperor, while his armor and shield signify his military accomplishments. He proclaims his Christian rule with his scepter's new design—a cross with a globe—and the round badge sticking up from his helmet that carries the monogram signifying "Christ" that he had his soldiers paint on their shields to win God's favor in battle. (The Art Archive/REX/Shutterstock.)

by "the highest divinity"—a general term meant to satisfy both polytheists and Christians.

Constantine promoted his newly chosen religion while trying to placate traditional polytheists, who still greatly outnumbered Christians. For example, he returned all property confiscated from Christians during the Great Persecution, but he had the treasury compensate those who had bought it. When in 321, he made the Lord's Day of each week a holy occasion on which no official business or manufacturing work could be performed, he called it Sunday to blend Christian and traditional notions in honoring two divinities, God and the sun. He decorated his new capital of Constantinople with statues of traditional gods. Above all, he respected tradition by continuing to hold the office of pontifex maximus ("chief priest"), which emperors had filled ever since Augustus.

REVIEW QUESTION
What were Diocletian's policies to end the third-century crisis, and how successful were they?

The Official Christianization of the Empire, 312–c. 540

The process of Christianization of the Roman Empire was gradual: Christianity was not officially made the state religion until the end of the fourth century, and even then many people continued to worship the traditional gods in private. Eventually, Christianity became the religion of most people by attracting converts among women and men of all classes, assuring believers of personal salvation, offering the social advantages and security of belonging to the emperors' religion, nourishing a strong sense of shared identity and community, developing a hierarchy to govern the church, and creating communities of devoted monks (male and female). The transformation from a polytheist into a Christian state was the Roman Empire's most important long-term influence on Western civilization.

PRIMARY SOURCE ANALYSIS

The Edict of Milan on Religious Freedom

In 313, Constantine, recently converted to Christianity, and his co-emperor, Licinius, a follower of traditional Roman religion, met to discuss official policy on religion. They agreed to abolish restrictions on Christianity and proclaim religious freedom in the eastern parts of the Empire; Constantine had done this as early as 306 in the west. The document contains the letter of instructions later sent to governors in the eastern provinces; it is the best surviving evidence for the new policies. Its long sentences (which are here divided into shorter sentences) and lofty language reflect the official imperial style.

When I, Constantine Augustus, and I, Licinius Augustus, had a successful meeting at Milan and discussed everything pertaining to the public benefit and security, among other things that we regarded as going to be of use to many people, we believed that first place should go to those matters having to do with reverence for divinity, so that we might give the Christians and everyone the free power of worshipping in the religion that they wish. In this way, whatever divinity exists in the heavenly seat may be appeased and be kind to us and to all those who are established under our power. And thus, believing that we should initiate this policy on a wholesome and most upright basis, we thought that to no one whatsoever should the opportunity be denied, whether he dedicates his mind to the worship of the Christians or to that religion, which he felt best suited him. Our purpose is so that the highest divinity, whose religion we follow with free minds, may provide his customary favor and kindness in all things. Wherefore it has pleased us for your Devotedness [the provincial governor] to know that all the restrictions on the Christian name set forth in letters given to your office previously are completely removed and that whatever seemed utterly sinister and foreign to our clemency should be repealed, and that now any person of those also wishing to observe the religion of the Christians may strive to do so freely and plainly without any worry or interference. We believed that these things should

be made completely clear to your Solicitude so that you would know that we have given a free and absolute permission to these Christians to practice their religion. When you see that we have granted this to them, your Devotedness will know that we have likewise conceded an open and free power to others to practice their religion for the sake of the tranquility of our age, so that each person may have free permission to worship in the manner he has chosen. We did this so that we shall not seem to have detracted from any observance or religion.

[The emperors next ordered regional officials to inform people who bought or received Christians' property confiscated in the Great Persecution to return it at no cost and then to apply to an imperial representative for reimbursement through the emperors' "clemency."]

On all these matters you will be obligated to provide your most effectual aid to the body of Christians mentioned above, so that our orders may be carried out more quickly, whereby public tranquility may be served also by our clemency. In this way it will happen, as was explained above, that divine favor toward us, which we have experienced in so many things, will endure for all time to give prosperity to our successes in company with the public happiness. Moreover, so that the content of this ordinance and of our kindness may come to everyone's attention, it should be put up everywhere above an announcement of your own and brought to the knowledge of everyone, so that this ordinance of our kindness shall not be concealed.

Source: Lactantius, *On the Deaths of the Persecutors*, 48, and Eusebius, *Ecclesiastical History*, 10.5.2–14. Translation by Thomas R. Martin.

QUESTIONS TO CONSIDER

1. What reasons do Constantine and Licinius give for instituting this new policy of religious freedom?

2. Why do you think that the references to divinity are more abstract ("the highest divinity") than specific?

Polytheism and Christianity in Competition

Polytheism and Christianity competed for people's faith. They shared some similar beliefs. Both, for example, regarded spirits and demons as powerful and ever-present forces in life. Some polytheists focused their beliefs on a supreme god who seemed almost monotheistic; some Christians took ideas from Neoplatonist philosophy, which was based on Plato's ideas about God and spirituality from hundreds of years before the lifetime of Jesus.

Unbridgeable differences remained, however, between the beliefs of traditional polytheists and Christians. People disagreed over whether there was one God or many, and what degree of interest the divinity (or divinities) paid to the human world. Polytheists could not accept a divine savior who promised eternal salvation for believers but had apparently lacked the will or the power to overthrow Roman rule and prevent his own execution. The traditional gods by contrast, they believed, had given their worshippers a world empire. Moreover, polytheists could say, cults such as that of the goddess Isis and philosophies such as Stoicism insisted that only the pure of heart and mind could be admitted to their fellowship. Christians, by contrast, embraced sinners. Why, wondered perplexed polytheists, would anyone want to associate with such people? In short, as the Greek philosopher Porphyry (c. 234–c. 305) argued, Christians had no right to claim they possessed the sole version of religious truth, for no one had ever discovered a doctrine that provided "the sole path to the liberation of the soul."

The slow pace of Christianization revealed how strong polytheism remained in this period, especially at the highest social levels. In fact, the emperor known as **Julian the Apostate** (r. 361–363) rebelled against his family's Christianity—the word *apostate* means "renegade from the faith"—by trying to reverse official support of the new religion in favor of his philosophical interpretation of polytheism. Like Christians, he believed in a supreme deity, but he based his religious beliefs on Greek philosophy when he said, "This divine and completely beautiful universe, from heaven's highest arch to earth's lowest limit, is tied together by the continuous providence of god, has existed ungenerated eternally, and is imperishable forever."

Emperors after Julian provided financial support for Christianity, dropped the title pontifex maximus, and stopped paying for sacrifices. Symmachus (c. 340–402), a polytheist senator who also served as prefect (mayor) of Rome, objected to the suppression of religious diversity: "We all have our own way of life and our own way of worship. . . . So vast a mystery cannot be approached by only one path."

Christianity officially replaced polytheism as the state religion in 391 when **Theodosius I** (r. 379–395) enforced a ban on privately funded polytheist sacrifices. In 395, he also announced that all polytheist temples had to close. Nevertheless, some famous shrines, such as the Parthenon in Athens, remained open for a long time. Pagan temples were gradually converted to churches during the fifth and sixth centuries. Non-Christian schools were not forced to close—the Academy, founded by Plato in Athens in the early fourth century B.C.E., endured for 140 years more.

Jews posed a special problem for the Christian emperors. They seemed entitled to special treatment because Jesus had been a Jew. Previous emperors had allowed Jews to practice their religion, but the rulers now imposed legal restrictions. They banned Jews from holding office but still required them to assume the financial burdens of curials without the status. By the late sixth century, the law barred Jews from marrying Christians, making wills, receiving inheritances, or testifying in court.

These restrictions began the long process that turned Jews into second-class citizens in later European history, but they did not destroy Judaism. Magnificent synagogues had been built in Palestine, though following the earlier rebellions against Roman rule in Judea (see Chapter 6) most Jews had been dispersed throughout the cities of the Empire and the lands to the east. Written Jewish teachings and interpretations proliferated in this period, culminating in the vast fifth-century texts known as the Palestinian and the Babylonian Talmuds (learned opinions on the Mishnah, a collection of Jewish law) and the Midrash (commentaries on parts of Hebrew Scripture).

As the official religion, Christianity attracted more believers, especially in the military. Soldiers could convert and still serve in the army. Previously, some Christians had felt a conflict between the military oath and their allegiance to Christ. Once the emperors were Christians, however, soldiers viewed military duty as serving Christ's regime.

Christianity's social values contributed to its appeal by offering believers a strong sense of shared identity and community. When Christians traveled, they could find a warm welcome in the local congregation (Map 7.2). The faith also won converts by promoting the tradition of charitable works characteristic of Judaism and some polytheist cults, which emphasized caring for poor people, widows, and orphans. By the mid-third century, Rome's Christian congregation was supporting fifteen hundred widows and poor people.

Women were deeply involved in the new faith. **Augustine** (354–430), bishop of Hippo in North Africa and perhaps the most influential theologian in Western civilization, recognized women's contribution to the strengthening of Christianity in a letter he wrote to the unbaptized husband of a baptized woman: "O you men, who fear all the burdens imposed by baptism! Your women easily best you. Chaste and devoted to the faith, it is their presence in large numbers that causes the church to grow." Women could earn respect by giving their property to their congregation or by renouncing marriage to dedicate themselves to Christ. Consecrated virgins rejecting marriage and widows refusing to remarry joined donors of large amounts of money as especially admired women. Their choices challenged the traditional social order, in which women were supposed to devote themselves to raising families. Even these sanctified women, however, were largely excluded from leadership positions as the church's hierarchy came more closely to resemble the male-dominated world of imperial rule. There were still some women leaders in the church, even in the fourth century, but they were a small minority.

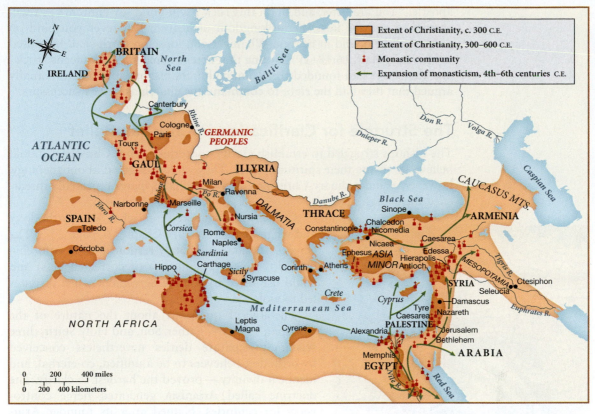

MAP 7.2 The Spread of Christianity, 300–600
Christians were a minority in the Roman Empire in 300, although congregations existed in many cities and towns, especially in the eastern provinces. The emperor Constantine's conversion to Christianity in the early fourth century gave a boost to the new religion. It gained further strength during that century as the Christian emperors supported it financially and eliminated subsidies for the polytheist cults that had previously made up the religion of the state. By 600, Christians were numerous in all parts of the Empire. (From Henry Chadwick and G. R. Evans, *Atlas of the Christian Church* [Oxford: Andromeda Oxford Ltd., 1987], 28. Reproduced by permission of Andromeda Oxford Limited.)

The hierarchy of male bishops replaced early Christianity's relatively loose communal organization, in which women held leadership posts. Over time, the bishops replaced the curials as the emperors' partners in local rule, taking control of the distribution of imperial subsidies to the people. Regional councils of bishops appointed new bishops and addressed doctrinal disputes. Bishops in the largest cities became the most powerful leaders in the church. The bishop of Rome eventually emerged as the church's supreme leader in the western Empire, claiming for himself a title previously applied to many bishops: pope (from *pappas*, a child's word for "father" in Greek), the designation still used for the head of the Roman Catholic church. Christians in the eastern Empire never conceded this title to the bishop of Rome.

The bishops of Rome claimed they had leadership over other bishops on the basis of the New Testament, where Jesus addresses Peter, his head apostle: "You are Peter, and upon this rock I will build my church. . . . I will entrust to you the keys of the kingdom of heaven. Whatever you bind on earth shall be bound in heaven. Whatever you loose on earth shall be loosed in heaven" (Matt. 16:18–19). Noting that Peter's name in Greek means "rock" and that Peter had founded the Roman church, bishops in Rome eventually argued that they had the right to command the church as Peter's successors.

The Struggle for Clarification in Christian Belief

The bishops struggled to establish clarity concerning what Christians should believe to ensure their spiritual purity. They often disagreed about theology, however, as did ordinary Christians, and doctrinal disputes repeatedly threatened the church's unity.

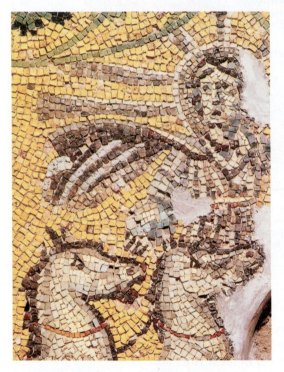

Jesus as Sun God
This heavily damaged mosaic, perhaps from the mid-third century, depicts Jesus like the Greek god of the sun, Apollo, riding in a chariot pulled by horses with rays of light shining forth around his head. This symbolism—God is light—reached back to ancient Egypt. Christian artists used it to portray Jesus because he had said, "I am the light of the world" (John 8:12). The mosaic artist arranged the sunbeams to suggest the shape of the Christian cross. The cloak flaring from Jesus's shoulder suggests the spread of his motion across the heavens. (Detail from a Roman mosaic, mid-3rd century CE/Crotte, St. Peter's Basilica, Vatican State/Scala/Art Resource, NY.)

Controversy centered on what was orthodoxy and what was heresy. (See Chapter 6, page 207.) The emperor became ultimately responsible for enforcing orthodox creed (a summary of correct beliefs) and could use force to compel agreement when disputes led to violence.

Theological questions about the nature of the Christian Trinity—Father, Son, and Holy Spirit, three seemingly separate deities nevertheless conceived by orthodox believers to be a unified, co-eternal, and identical divinity—proved the hardest to clarify. The doctrine called **Arianism** generated fierce controversy for centuries. Named after its founder, Arius (c. 260–336), a priest from Alexandria, it maintained that God the Father begot (created) his son Jesus from nothing and gave him his special status. Thus, Jesus was not identical with God the Father and was, in fact, dependent on him. Arianism found widespread support—the emperor Valens and his barbarian opponents were Arian Christians. Many people found Arianism appealing because it eliminated the difficulty of understanding how a son could be the equal of his father and because its subordination of son to father corresponded to the norms of family life. Arius used popular songs to make his views known, and people everywhere became engaged in the controversy. "When you ask for your change from a shopkeeper," one observer remarked in describing Constantinople, "he harangues you about the Begotten and the Unbegotten. If you inquire how much bread costs, the reply is that 'the Father is superior and the Son inferior.'"

Disputes such as this led Constantine to try to determine religious truth. In 325, he convened 220

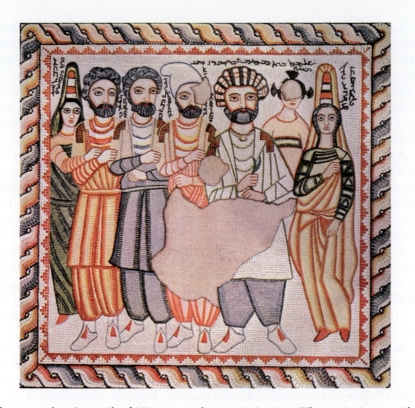

Mosaic of a Family from Edessa
This mosaic, found in a cave tomb from c. 218–238, depicts an elite family from Edessa in the late Roman Empire. Their names are given in Syriac, the dialect of Aramaic spoken in their region, and their colorful clothing reflects local Iranian traditions. The mosaic's border uses decorative patterns from Roman art, illustrating the combining of cultural traditions in the Roman Empire. Edessa was the capital of the small kingdom of Osrhoëne, annexed by Rome in 216. It became famous in Christian history because its king Abgar (r. 179–216) was the first monarch to convert to Christianity, well before Constantine. The eastern Roman emperors proclaimed themselves the heirs of King Abgar. (World History Archive/Alamy.)

bishops at the Council of Nicaea to discuss Arianism. The majority voted to banish Arius to the Balkans and declared in the **Nicene Creed** that the Father and the Son were *homoousion* ("of one substance") and co-eternal. So difficult were the issues, however, that Constantine later changed his mind twice, first recalling Arius from exile and then soon after reproaching him yet again.

Numerous other disputes divided believers. Orthodoxy taught that Jesus's divine and human natures commingled within his person but remained distinct. Monophysites (a Greek term for "believers in one nature") argued that the divine took precedence over the human in Jesus and that he therefore had essentially only a single nature. They split from the orthodox hierarchy in the sixth century to found independent churches in Egypt (the Coptic church), Ethiopia, Syria, and Armenia.

Nestorius, made bishop of Constantinople in 428, argued that Mary, in giving birth to Jesus, had produced the human being who became the temple for God dwelling within him. Nestorianism therefore offended Christians who accepted the designation of *theotokos* (Greek for "bearer of God") for Mary. The bishops of Alexandria and Rome had Nestorius deposed and his doctrines officially rejected at councils held in 430 and 431. Nestorian bishops then established a separate church centered in the Persian Empire, where for centuries Nestorian Christians flourished under the tolerance of non-Christian rulers. They later became important agents of cultural diffusion by establishing communities that still endure in Arabia, India, and China.

The heresy of Donatism best illustrates the ferocity that Christian disputes could generate. A conflict erupted in North Africa over whether to readmit to their old congregations Christians who had cooperated with imperial authorities during the Great Persecution initiated by Diocletian. The Donatists (followers of the North African priest Donatus) insisted that the church should not be polluted with such "traitors." So bitter was the clash that it even broke apart Christian families. One son threatened his mother, "I will join Donatus's followers, and I will drink your blood."

A council organized in Chalcedon (a suburb of Constantinople) in 451 to settle the still-raging disagreement over Nestorius's views was the most important attempt to clarify orthodoxy. The conclusions of the Council of Chalcedon form the basis of the doctrine of most Christians in the West today. At the time, however, it failed to create unanimity, especially in the eastern Empire, where Monophysites flourished.

By around 500, Augustine and other influential theologians such as Ambrose (c. 339–397) and Jerome (c. 345–420) earned the informal title *church fathers* because their views were cited as authoritative in disputes over orthodoxy. Augustine became the most famous of this group of patristic (from *pater*, Greek for "father") authors, and for the next thousand years his many works would be the most influential texts in western Christianity aside from the Bible.

In *The City of God*, Augustine expressed his views on the need for order in human life and asserted that the basic human dilemma lay in the conflict between desiring earthly pleasures and desiring spiritual purity. Emotion, especially love, was natural and commendable, but only when directed toward God. Humans were misguided to look for any value in life on earth. Only life in God's eternal city at the end of time had meaning.

Nevertheless, Augustine wrote, law and government are required on earth because humans are imperfect. God's original creation was perfect, but after Adam and Eve disobeyed God, humans lost their initial perfection and inherited a permanently flawed nature. According to this doctrine of original sin—a subject of theological debate since at least the second century—Adam and Eve's disobedience passed down to human beings a hereditary moral disease that made the human will a divisive force. This corruption made governments necessary, to suppress evil. The state therefore had a duty to compel people to remain loyal to the church, by force if that was the only way.

Christians, Augustine argued, had a duty to obey the emperor and participate in political life. Soldiers, too, had to follow their orders. Order was so essential, Augustine argued, that it even justified what he admitted was the unjust institution of slavery. Although he detested slavery, he believed it was a lesser evil than the social disorder that he thought its abolition would create.

In *The City of God*, Augustine argued that history has a divine purpose, even if people could not see it. History progressed toward an ultimate goal, but only God knew the meaning of his creation:

> To be truthful, I myself fail to understand why God created mice and frogs, flies and worms. Nevertheless, I recognize that each of these creatures is beautiful in its own way. For when I contemplate the body

and limbs of any living creature, where do I not find proportion, number, and order exhibiting the unity of concord? Where one discovers proportion, number, and order, one should look for the craftsman.

The question of how to understand and regulate sexual desire perplexed Christians in the search for religious truth. Augustine wrote that sex trapped human beings in evil and that they should therefore strive for **asceticism** (a-SET-uh-sism), the practice of self-denial and spiritual discipline. Augustine knew from personal experience how difficult it was to accept this doctrine. In his autobiographical work *Confessions*, written about 397, he described the deep conflict he felt between his sexual desires—which he enthusiastically followed in his earlier years—and his religious beliefs. Only after a long period of reflection and doubt, he wrote, did he find the inner strength to commit to chastity as part of his conversion to Christianity.

He advocated sexual abstinence as the highest course for Christians because he believed that Adam and Eve's disobedience had forever ruined the perfect harmony God created between the human will and human passions. According to Augustine, God punished his disobedient children by making sexual desire a disruptive force that human will would always struggle to control. He reaffirmed the value of marriage in God's plan, but he insisted that sexual intercourse even between loving spouses carried the unhappy reminder of humanity's fall from grace. Reproduction, not pleasure, was the only acceptable reason for sex.

This doctrine ennobled virginity and sexual renunciation as the highest virtues. By the end of the fourth century, Christians valued virginity so highly that congregations began to request virgin ministers and bishops.

The Emergence of Christian Monks

Christian asceticism peaked with the emergence of monks: men and women who withdrew from everyday society to live a life of extreme self-denial, imitating Jesus's suffering, while praying for divine mercy on the world. In monasticism, monks originally lived alone, but soon they formed communities for mutual support in the pursuit of holiness.

Polytheists and Jews had strong ascetic traditions, but Christian monasticism was distinctive for the huge numbers of people drawn to it and the high status that they earned in the Christian population. The fame of monks came from their rejection of ordinary pleasures and comforts. They left their families and congregations, renounced sex, worshipped almost constantly, wore rough clothes, and ate so little they were always nearly starving. To achieve inner peace, monks fought a constant spiritual battle against fantasies of earthly delights—plentiful, tasty food and the joys of sex.

The earliest monks emerged in Egypt in the second half of the third century. Antony (c. 251–356), the son of a well-to-do family, was among the first to renounce regular existence. After hearing a sermon stressing Jesus's command to a rich young man to sell his possessions and give the proceeds to the poor (Matt. 19:21), he left his property in about 285 and withdrew into the desert to devote the rest of his life to worshipping God through extreme self-denial.

Monastery of St. Catherine at Mount Sinai
The sixth-century eastern Roman Emperor Justinian built a wall to protect this monastery in the desert at the foot of Mount Sinai (on the peninsula between Egypt and Arabia). Justinian fortified the monastery to promote orthodoxy in a region dominated by Monophysite Christians. The monastery gained its name in the ninth century, when the story was circulated that angels had recently brought the body of Catherine of Alexandria there. Catherine was said to have been martyred in the fourth century for refusing to marry the emperor because, in her words, she was the bride of Christ. (Erich Lessing/Art Resource, NY.)

The opportunity to gain fame as a monk seemed especially valuable after the end of the Great Persecution. Becoming a monk—a living martyrdom—not only served as the substitute for dying a martyr's death but also emulated the sacrifice of Christ. In Syria, so-called holy women and holy men sought fame through feats of pious endurance; Symeon (390–459), for example, lived atop a tall pillar for thirty years, preaching to the people gathered at the foot of his perch. Egyptian Christians came to believe that their monks' supreme piety made them living heroes who ensured the annual flooding of the Nile (which enriched the soil, aiding agriculture), an event once associated with the pharaohs' religious power.

In a Christian tradition originating with martyrs, the relics of dead holy men and women—body parts or clothing—became treasured sources of protection and healing, as in ancient Greek hero cults (see Chapter 3). The power associated with the relics of saints (people venerated after their deaths for their holiness) gave believers faith in divine favor.

In about 323, an Egyptian Christian named Pachomius organized the first monastic community, establishing the tradition of single-sex settlements of male or female monks. This communal monasticism dominated Christian asceticism ever after. Communities of men and women were often built close together to share labor, with women making clothing, for example, while men farmed.

Some monasteries imposed military-style discipline, but there were large differences in the degree of control of the monks and the extent of contact allowed with the outside world. Some groups strove for complete self-sufficiency and strict rules to avoid transactions with outsiders. Basil of Caesarea (c. 330–379), in Asia Minor, started an alternative tradition of monasteries in service to society. Basil (later dubbed "the Great") required monks to perform charitable deeds, especially ministering to the sick, a development that led to the foundation of the first hospitals, which were attached to monasteries.

A milder code of monastic conduct became the standard in the west beginning about 540. Called the Benedictine rule after its creator, Benedict of Nursia (c. 480–553), it mandated the monastery's daily routine of prayer, scriptural readings, and manual labor. This was the first time in Greek and Roman history that physical work was seen as noble, even godly. The rule divided the day into seven parts, each with a compulsory service of prayers and lessons, called the office. Unlike the harsh regulations of other monastic communities, Benedict's code did not isolate the monks from the outside world or deprive them of sleep, adequate food, or warm clothing. Although it gave the abbot (the head monk) full authority, it instructed him to listen to other members of the community before deciding important matters. He was forbidden to beat disobedient monks. Communities of women, such as those founded by Basil's sister Macrina and Benedict's sister Scholastica, had rules like those of the male monasteries, emphasizing the particular decorum thought fitting for women.

Monastic piety held special appeal for women and the rich because women could achieve greater status and respect for their holiness than ordinary life allowed them, and the rich could win fame on earth and hope for favor in heaven by endowing monasteries with large gifts of money. Jerome wrote, "[As monks,] we evaluate people's virtue not by their gender but by their character, and judge those to be worthy of the greatest glory who have renounced both status and riches." Some monks did not choose their life; monasteries took in children from parents who could not raise them or who, in a practice called oblation, gave them up to fulfill pious vows. Jerome once advised a mother regarding her young daughter:

> Let her be brought up in a monastery, let her live among virgins, let
> her learn to avoid swearing, let her regard lying as an offense against
> God, let her be ignorant of the world, let her live the angelic life,
> while in the flesh let her be without the flesh, and let her suppose that
> all human beings are like herself.

When the girl reached adulthood as a virgin, he added, she should avoid the baths so that she would not be seen naked or give her body pleasure by dipping in the warm pools. Jerome emphasized traditional values favoring males when he promised that God would reward the mother with the birth of sons in compensation for the dedication of her daughter.

Monasteries could come into conflict with the church leadership. Bishops resented members of their congregations who withdrew into monasteries, especially because they then gave money and property to their new community instead of to their local churches. Monks represented a threat to bishops' authority because holy men and women earned their special status not by having it bestowed from the church hierarchy but through their own actions.

REVIEW QUESTION
How did Christianity both unite and divide the Roman Empire?

Non-Roman Kingdoms in the Western Roman Empire, c. 370–550s

The western Roman Empire came under great pressure from the incursions of non-Roman peoples—barbarians to the Romans—that took place in the fourth and fifth centuries. The emperors had traditionally admitted some multiethnic groups from east of the Rhine River and north of the Danube River into the Empire to fight in the Roman army, but eventually other barbarians fought their way in from the northeast. The barbarians wanted to flee attacks by the Huns (nomadic warriors from central Asia) and share in Roman prosperity. By the 370s, this human tide provoked violence and a loss of order in the western Empire.

The immigrants slowly transformed themselves from loosely organized tribes into kingdoms with newly defined identities. By the 470s, one of their commanders ruled Italy—the political change that has been said to mark the fall of the Roman Empire. However, the interactions of these non-Roman peoples with the Empire's residents in western Europe and North Africa seem closer to a political, social, and cultural transformation—based on force more than cooperation—that made the immigrants the heirs of the western Roman Empire and led to the formation of medieval Europe based on continuity of traditions and cultural synthesis

Non-Roman Migrations into the Western Roman Empire

The non-Roman peoples who flooded into the Empire had diverse origins; labeling them "Germanic peoples," as is sometimes done, underplays the diversity of their multiethnic languages and customs. These different barbarian peoples had no previously established sense of monolithic ethnic identity, and many of them had had long-term contact with Romans through trade across the frontiers and service in the Roman army. By encouraging this contact, the emperors unwittingly set in motion forces that they could not in the end control. By late in the fourth century, attacks by the Huns had destabilized life for these bands across the Roman frontiers, and the families of the warriors followed them into the Empire seeking safety. Hordes of men, women, and children crossed into the Empire as refugees, fleeing the Huns, who were themselves not just a single ethnicity. (See Contrasting Views on pages 240–241.) The refugees came into Roman territory with no political or military unity and no clear plan. They shared only their terror of the Huns and their custom of conducting raids for a living, in addition to farming small plots.

The inability to prevent immigrants from crossing the border or to integrate them into Roman society once they had crossed put great stress on the western central government. Persistent economic weakness rooted in the third-century crisis worsened this pressure. Tenant farmers and landlords fleeing crushing taxes had left as much as 20 percent of farmland unworked in the most seriously affected areas. The loss of revenue made the government unable to afford enough soldiers to control the frontiers. Over time, the immigrating non-Roman peoples forced the Roman government to grant them territory in the Empire. Remarkably, they then began to develop separate ethnic identities and create new societies for themselves and the Romans living under their control.

In their homelands, the barbarians had lived in chiefdom societies, whose members could only be persuaded, not ordered, to follow the chief. Chiefs maintained their status by giving gifts to their followers and leading raids to capture cattle and slaves. They led clans—groups of households organized by kinship lines, following maternal as well as paternal descent. Violence against a fellow clan member was the worst possible offense. Clans in turn grouped themselves into tribes—fluctuating coalitions that anyone could join. Tribes differentiated themselves by their clothing, hairstyles, jewelry, weapons, religious cults, and oral stories.

Family life was patriarchal: men headed households and held authority over women, children, and slaves. Warfare preoccupied men, as their ritual sacrifices of weapons preserved in northern European bogs reveal. Women were valued for their ability to bear children, and rich men could have more than one wife and perhaps concubines as well. A division of labor made women responsible for growing crops, making pottery, and producing textiles, while men worked iron and herded cattle. Women enjoyed certain rights of inheritance and could control property, and married women received a dowry of one-third of their husband's property.

Assemblies of free male warriors made major decisions in the tribes. Their leaders' authority was restricted mostly to religious and military matters. Tribes could be unstable and prone to internal conflict—clans frequently feuded, with bloody consequences. Tribal law tried to determine what forms of violence were and were not acceptable in seeking revenge, but laws were oral, not written, and thus open to wide dispute. Tribes frequently attacked other tribes.

The migrations became a flood of people when the Huns invaded eastern Europe in the fourth century. The Huns arrived on the Russian steppes shortly before 370 as the vanguard of ancient-Turkish-speaking nomads moving west. Their warriors' appearance terrified their victims, who reported their attackers had skulls elongated from having been bound between boards in infancy, faces grooved with decorative scars, and arms covered with fearsome tattoos. Huns excelled as raiders, launching cavalry attacks without warning. Skilled as horsemen, they could shoot their powerful bows accurately while riding full tilt and stay mounted for days, sleeping atop their horses and carrying snacks of raw meat between their thighs and the animal's back.

By later in the fourth century, the Huns had moved as far west as the Hungarian plain north of the Danube, terrifying the peoples there and launching raids southward into the Balkans. The emperors in Constantinople began paying the Huns to spare their territory, so the most ambitious Hunnic leader, Attila (r. c. 440–453), pushed his domain westward toward the Alps. He led his

| CONTRASTING VIEWS | Debate: Did Romans or Huns Better Protect Life, Law, and Freedom? |

In 448, a Roman named Priscus went as a diplomat to the court of Attila the Hun at a location north of the Danube River. His firsthand report of what he learned about life among the Huns during this visit includes this conversation with a stranger he met there. They exchanged contrasting views concerning whether life, law, and freedom were better protected among the Romans or the Huns (called Scythians here).

A man who I assumed was a barbarian from his Scythian-style clothes came up to me and said "Hello!" in Greek. I was surprised by a Scythian speaking Greek. … I asked him who he was and where he had come from into a barbarian land and chosen the Scythian lifestyle. When he asked me why I was eager to know, I told him that his speaking Greek had made me curious. Then he laughed and said that he was a Greek by birth and had gone as a merchant to trade in Viminacium, in the region of Moesia on the Danube River. He had lived there a long time and married a very rich wife. But barbarians captured the city, and his property was taken away. On account of his riches he was allotted as a captive to [the Hun] Onegesius in the division of the spoils, since it was customary that, after Attila, the chiefs of the Scythians, because they commanded many men, would keep the rich prisoners for themselves. He later fought bravely [in attacks by the Huns] against the Romans and the Acatiri tribe. Following the Scythian custom, he gave the spoils that he won to his master, and so got his freedom. He then married a barbarian wife and had children.

Since he had the privilege of eating at the table of Onegesius, he considered his new life among the Scythians better than his old life among the Romans. For he explained that once a war is over, the Scythians live at ease, each enjoying what he has got, with no, or only a little, bothering of others or being bothered themselves. The Romans, on the other hand, are very likely to be destroyed by war, as they have to pin their hopes of safety on other people: their tyrants do not permit everyone to use weapons. And Romans who do use them are harmed by the cowardly actions of their generals, who cannot stand up to the stresses of war. But the condition of Roman subjects in peacetime is far more burdensome than the evils of war, on account of the harshness of tax collection and the harm done by wrongdoers, since the laws do not apply to everyone. A member of the upper class who breaks the law does not face punishment. If a man is poor, however, and doesn't understand how to handle things, he suffers the penalty imposed by the law, if he doesn't leave this life before he gets to the trial, given how long lawsuits are dragged out and how much money has to be spent. The most painful thing of all is to have to pay in order to try to get justice. For no one will give his day in court to the man who has been treated unjustly unless he pays money to the judge and the judge's clerks.

As he was saying many other things like this, I calmly asked him to hear what I had to say. I insisted that the founders of the Roman Republic were wise and good

forces as far west as central France and into northern Italy. At Attila's death in 453, the Huns lost their fragile unity and faded from history. By this time, however, the terror that they had inspired in the peoples living in eastern Europe had provoked the migrations that eventually transformed the western Empire.

The first non-Roman group that created a new identity and society inside the Empire were barbarians from the north. Abused by the officers of the emperor Valens, these barbarians defeated and killed him at the battle of Adrianople in 378 (Map 7.3). Their history illustrates the pattern of the migrations: desperate people in barely organized groups with no uniform ethnic identity, who sought protection in the Roman Empire in return for military service but were brutalized, and then rebelled to form their own, new kingdom.

men. To prevent things from being done randomly, they arranged for some people to be guardians of the laws, while others were tasked with skill in weapons and to train for war, focused on nothing else but being ready for battle and having the spirit to go to war as if going to their usual exercises, having gotten rid of their fear ahead of time through their training. The founders arranged for others to do farming and care for the land, to feed both themselves and those who fought for them by contributing the tax that consists of the grain supply for the army. They arranged for others to pay attention to people who have been treated unjustly and to conduct rightful prosecutions for people who are too weak to advance their own case. Others they set up as judges to guard what the law wishes. Since the founders were concerned for those involved in the judicial process, they also arranged for others whose job it is to make sure that a person who wins a judgment in court will in fact receive the damages that have been awarded, as well as that the person who was found guilty does not pay more than the legal judgment specified....

You ought to thank chance for the freedom you enjoy, not the master who led you into war, where as a result of your inexperience you could have been killed by the enemy or punished by the one who possessed you if you ran away from the battlefield. The Romans usually treat even their household slaves better than this. They act like fathers or teachers to them, to restrain them from behaving stupidly and to get them to do what is considered right, and they teach them self-control when they make mistakes, just as with the children in their families. It is not legal for them to punish them with death, as the Scythians do.

There are many ways to freedom among the Romans. Not just the living but even those who have died gladly give it, arranging their estates however they wish. The law is that whatever each person wishes to happen to his possessions when he dies is valid.

In tears, he said that the laws were excellent and the Roman Republic [as the Romans still called the Empire] was good, but the officials were corrupting it by not living up to the same moral standards that the officials of the past did.

Source: Priscus, fr. 11.2 Müller *Fragmenta Historicorum Graecorum* (*Exc. de Leg. Rom.* 3). Translation by Thomas R. Martin.

QUESTIONS TO CONSIDER

1. Do you think that this is a fabricated account written by Priscus to demonstrate a point, a documentation of an actual exchange, or a combination of both? What evidence from the document supports your argument?

2. Do you think Priscus, in his reply, adequately answers the points raised by the stranger? Why or why not?

3. What do you think is the intended effect of Priscus's giving the stranger the last word in this exchange?

An imperial policy aimed at integrating the immigrant northerners into Roman society and economic life might well have prevented, or at least moderated, this development that marked a turning point in the long-term fragmenting of the western Roman Empire.

When the emperor Theodosius died in 395, the barbarians whom he had allowed to settle in the Empire rebelled. United by the Gothic chief Alaric into a tribe known as the **Visigoths**, they fought their way into the western Empire. In 410, they stunned the world by sacking Rome itself. For the first time since the Gauls eight hundred years before, a foreign force occupied the ancient capital. They terrorized the population: "What will be left to us?" the Romans asked when Alaric demanded all the citizens' goods. "Your lives," he replied.

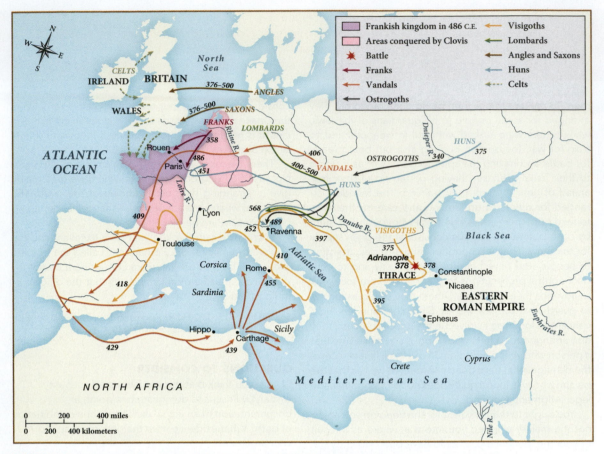

MAP 7.3 Migrations and Invasions of the Fourth and Fifth Centuries
The movements of non-Roman peoples into imperial territory transformed the Roman Empire. These migrations had begun as early as the reign of Domitian (r. 81–96), but in the fourth century they increased greatly when the Huns' attacks pushed numerous barbarian bands into the Empire's northern provinces. Print maps offer only a static representation of dynamic processes such as movements of populations, but this map helps illustrate the variety of peoples involved, the wide extent of imperial territory that they affected, and their prominence in the western Empire.

Too weak to fend off the invaders, the western emperor Honorius in 418 reluctantly agreed to settle the newcomers in southwestern Gaul (present-day France), where they completed their unprecedented transition from tribe to kingdom, organizing a political state and creating their identity as Visigoths. They had no precedents to follow from their previous existence, so they adapted the only model available: Roman tradition, including a code of written law. The Visigoths established mutually beneficial relations with local Roman elites, who used time-tested ways of flattering their new superiors to gain advantages. Sidonius Apollinaris (c. 430–479), for example, a well-connected noble from Lyon, once purposely lost a backgammon game to the Visigothic king as a way of winning a favor.

How the new non-Roman kingdoms raised revenues is uncertain. Did the newcomers become landlords by forcing Roman property owners to redistribute a portion of their lands, slaves, and movable property as "ransom" to them? Or did Romans directly pay the expenses of the kingdom's soldiers, who lived mostly in urban garrisons? Whatever the new arrangements were, the Visigoths found them profitable enough to expand into Spain within a century of establishing themselves in southwestern Gaul.

The western government's concessions to the Visigoths led other groups to seize territory and create new kingdoms and identities. In 406, the Vandals cut a swath through Gaul all the way to the Spanish coast. (The modern word *vandal*, meaning "destroyer of property," perpetuates their reputation for destruction.)

In 429, eighty thousand Vandals ferried to North Africa, where they broke their agreement to become federate allies with the western Empire and captured the region. They crippled the western Empire by seizing North Africa's tax payments of grain and vegetable oil and disrupting the importation of food to Rome. They threatened the eastern Empire with their navy, and in 455, sailed to Rome, plundering the city. Back in the Roman province of Africa, the Vandals caused tremendous hardship for local people by confiscating property rather than allowing owners to make regular payments on the land. As Arian Christians, they persecuted North African Christians whose doctrines they considered heresy.

Small non-Roman groups took advantage of the disruption caused by bigger bands to break off distant pieces of the Empire. The Anglo-Saxons, for example, were composed of Angles from what is now Denmark and Saxons from northwestern Germany. This mixed group invaded Britain in the 440s after the Roman army had been recalled from the province to defend Italy against the Visigoths. The Anglo-Saxons captured territory from the local Celtic peoples and the remaining Roman inhabitants. Gradually, their culture replaced the local traditions of the island's eastern regions. The Celts there lost most of their language, and Christianity gave way to Anglo-Saxon beliefs except in Wales and Ireland. Another barbarian group, the Ostrogoths, carved out a kingdom in Italy in the fifth century. By the time their king Theodoric (r. 493–526) came to power, there had not been a western Roman emperor for nearly twenty years, and there never would be again.

The details of the change in the later fifth century that has traditionally, but simplistically, been called the fall of the Roman Empire reveal the complexity of the political transformation of the western Empire under the new kingdoms. The weakness of the western emperors' army had obliged them to hire foreign officers to lead the defense of Italy. By the middle of the fifth century, one non-Roman general after another had come to decide who would serve as a puppet emperor under his control.

The last such unfortunate puppet was only a child. His father, a former aide to Attila, tried to establish a royal house by proclaiming his young son as western emperor in 475. He gave the boy ruler the name Romulus Augustulus ("Romulus the Little Augustus") to match his young age and to recall both Rome's founder and its first emperor. In 476, following a dispute over pay, the boy emperor's non-Roman soldiers murdered his father and deposed him. Little Augustus was given refuge and a pension. The rebels' leader, Odoacer, had the Roman Senate petition Zeno, the eastern emperor, to recognize his leadership in return for his acknowledging Zeno as sole emperor over west and east. Odoacer thereafter oversaw Italy nominally as the eastern emperor's subordinate, but he ruled on his own.

Theodoric established the Ostrogothic kingdom in Italy by eliminating Odoacer. He and his nobles wanted to enjoy the luxurious life of the Empire's elite and to preserve the Empire's prestige; they therefore left the Senate and consulships intact. An Arian Christian, Theodoric announced a policy of religious freedom. Like the other non-Romans, the Ostrogoths adopted and adapted Roman traditions that supported the stability of their own rule, thereby promoting cultural synthesis.

The Franks were especially significant in the reshaping of the western Roman Empire because they transformed Roman Gaul into Francia (from which comes the name *France*). In 507, their king Clovis (r. 485–511), with support from the eastern Roman emperor, overthrew the Visigothic king in Gaul. When the emperor named Clovis an honorary consul, Clovis celebrated this honor by having himself crowned with a diadem in the style of the emperors. He established western Europe's largest new kingdom in what is today mostly France, overshadowing the neighboring and rival kingdoms of the Burgundians and Alemanni in eastern Gaul. Probably persuaded by his wife, Clotilda, a Christian, to believe that God had helped him defeat the Alemanni, Clovis proclaimed himself an orthodox Christian and renounced Arianism. To build stability, he carefully fostered good relations with the bishops as the regime's intermediaries with the population.

Clovis's dynasty, called Merovingian after the legendary Frankish ancestor Merovech, endured for another two hundred years, foreshadowing the kingdom that would emerge much later as the forerunner of modern France. The Merovingians survived so long because they successfully combined their own traditions of military bravery with Roman social and legal traditions. In addition, their location in far western Europe kept them out of the reach of the destructive invasions sent against Italy by the eastern emperor Justinian in the sixth century to reunite the Roman world.

Social and Cultural Transformation in the Western Roman Empire

The gradual replacement of government in the western Roman Empire by barbarian kingdoms set in motion social and cultural transformations. The newcomers and their Roman subjects created novel ways of life by combining old traditions, as Athaulf, king of the Visigoths (r. 410–415), explained after marrying a Roman noblewoman:

> At the start I wanted to erase the Romans' name and turn their land into a Gothic empire, doing myself what Augustus had done. But

I have learned that the Goths' freewheeling wildness will never accept the rule of law, and that a state with no law is no state. Thus, I have more wisely chosen another path to glory: reviving the Roman name with Gothic vigor. I pray that future generations will remember me as the founder of a Roman restoration.

This process of social and cultural transformation through mixing diverse traditions promoted stability by producing new law codes but undermined long-term security by weakening the economic situation.

Roman law was the most influential precedent for the new kings in constructing states. Their tribes had never possessed written laws, but their new states required legal codes to create a sense of justice and keep order. The Visigothic kings issued the first "barbarian law code." Published in Latin in about 475, it made fines and compensation the primary method for resolving disputes. Clovis also emphasized written law for the Merovingian kingdom. His code, also published in Latin between about 507 and 511, promoted social order through clear penalties for specific crimes, formalizing a system of fines intended to defuse feuds and vendettas between individuals and clans. The most prominent component of this system was **wergild**, the payment a murderer had to make as compensation for his crime, to prevent endless cycles of revenge. The king received about one-third of the fine, with the rest paid to the victim's family.

Since laws indicate social values, the differing amounts of wergild in Clovis's code suggest the relative values of different categories of people in his kingdom. Murdering a woman of childbearing age, a boy under twelve, or a man in the king's retinue brought a massive fine of six hundred gold coins, enough to buy six hundred cattle. A woman past childbearing age (specified as sixty years), a young girl, or a freeborn man was valued at two hundred gold coins. Ordinary slaves rated thirty-five gold coins.

The migrations of new groups into Roman territory had the unintended consequence of harming the Empire's already weakened economy. The Vandals' violence battered many towns in Gaul, hastening a decline in urban population. In the countryside, now beyond the control of any central government, wealthy Romans built sprawling villas on extensive estates, staffed by tenants bound to the land like slaves. These establishments aimed to operate as self-sufficient units by producing all they needed, defending themselves against barbarian raids, and keeping their distance from any authorities. The owners shunned municipal offices and tax collection, the public services that had supplied the lifeblood of Roman administration. Provincial government slowly withered away.

In some areas now outside reach of the central government, the infrastructure of trade—roads and bridges—fell into disrepair with no public-spirited elite to maintain them. The elite holed up in their fortress-like households. They could afford to protect themselves: the annual income of the richest of them rivaled the revenue of an entire province in the old western Empire.

In some cases, these fortunate few helped pass down Roman learning to later ages. Cassiodorus (c. 490–585) founded a monastery on his ancestral estate in

REVIEW QUESTION
How did their migrations and invasions change the barbarians themselves and the Roman Empire?

Mosaic of Women Exercising
This picture covered a floor in a fourth-century country villa in Sicily that had more than forty rooms decorated with thirty-five hundred square meters of mosaics. The women shown in this mosaic were perhaps dancers getting in shape for public appearances or athletes performing as part of a festival show. Members of the Roman elite built such enormous and expensive houses as the centerpieces of estates meant to insulate them from increasingly dismal conditions in cities and protect them from barbarian attack. In this case, the strategy apparently failed: the villa was likely seriously damaged by Vandal invaders. (Detail from mosaic, Villa del Casale, Piazza Armerina, Sicily, Italy/Erich Lessing/Art Resource, NY.)

Italy in the 550s, after a career in imperial administration. He gave the monks the task of copying manuscripts to keep their contents from disappearing as old ones disintegrated. His own book, *Institutions*, summed up what he saw as the foundation of ancient Greek and Roman culture by listing the books an educated person should read; it included ancient classical literature as well as Christian texts.

The Roman Empire in the East, c. 500–565

The eastern Roman Empire (later called the Byzantine Empire — see Chapter 8) avoided the massive transformations that reshaped the western Roman Empire. Trade and agriculture kept the eastern Empire from poverty, while its emperors used force, diplomacy, and bribery to prevent invasions from the north and repel attacks by the powerful Sasanid Empire in Persia.

The eastern emperors believed it was their duty to rule a united Roman Empire and prevent barbarians from degrading its culture. The most famous eastern Roman emperor, **Justinian** (r. 527–565), and his wife and partner in rule, **Theodora** (500–548), waged war against the barbarian kingdoms in the west, aiming to reunite the Empire and restore the imperial glory of the Augustan period. Justinian increased imperial authority and tried to purify religion to satisfy what he saw as his duty to provide strong leadership and God's favor. He and his successors in the eastern Empire contributed to the preservation of the memory of classical Greek and Roman culture by preserving a great deal of earlier literature, both non-Christian and Christian.

Imperial Society in the Eastern Roman Empire

The sixth-century eastern Empire enjoyed a vitality that had vanished in the west. Its social elite spent freely on luxuries such as silk, precious stones, and pepper and other spices imported from India and China. Markets in its large cities teemed with merchants from abroad. Its churches' soaring domes testified to its confidence in the Christian God as its divine protector.

The eastern emperors sponsored religious festivals and entertainments on a massive scale to rally public support. Rich and poor alike crowded city squares, theaters, and hippodromes on these lively occasions. Chariot racing aroused the hottest passions. Constantinople's residents divided themselves into competitive factions called Blues and Greens after the racing colors of their favorite charioteers. Emperors sometimes backed one gang or the other to intimidate potential rivals.

The eastern emperors worked to maintain Roman tradition and identity, believing that "Romanness" was the best defense against what they saw as the barbarization of the western Empire. They hired foreign mercenaries but also tried to keep their subjects from adopting foreign ways. The emperors ordered Constantinople's residents not to wear barbarian-style clothing (especially heavy boots and furs, which the chariot racing fans favored) instead of traditional Roman attire (sandals or light shoes and cloth robes).

The emperors' push for compulsory cultural unity was doomed to failure because everyday society in the eastern Empire was widely multilingual and multiethnic. The inhabitants referred to themselves as Romans, but most of them spoke Greek in their daily lives and used Latin only for government and military communication. Many people also retained their traditional languages, such as Phrygian and Cappadocian in western Asia Minor, Armenian farther east, and Syriac and other Aramaic dialects along the eastern Mediterranean coast. The streets of Constantinople reportedly rang with seventy-two languages.

Romanness definitely included Christianity, but the eastern Empire's theological diversity rivaled its ethnic and linguistic complexity. Bitter controversies over doctrine divided eastern Christians; emperors used violence against Christians with different beliefs—heretics they called them—when persuasion failed. They had to employ force, they believed, to save lost souls and preserve the Empire's religious purity and divine goodwill.

Most women in eastern Roman society lived according to ancient Mediterranean tradition, concentrating on their households and minimizing contact with men outside that circle. Law barred them from performing many public functions, such as witnessing wills. Subject to the authority of their fathers and husbands, women veiled their heads (though usually not their faces) to show modesty. The strict views of Christian theologians on sexuality and reproduction made divorce more difficult and discouraged remarriage even for widows. Sexual offenses carried harsher legal penalties. Female prostitution remained legal and common, but emperors raised the penalties for those who forced girls or female slaves under their control into prostitution.

Women in the imperial family could achieve prominence unattainable for ordinary women. Empress Theodora demonstrated the influence high-ranking women could have in the eastern Empire. Uninhibited by her humble origins (she was the daughter of a bear trainer and had been an actress with a scandalous reputation), she came to rival anyone in influence and wealth. She

Theodora and Her Court in Ravenna
This mosaic shows the empress Theodora and members of her court presenting a gift to the church at San Vitale in Ravenna. It faced the matching scene of her husband Justinian and his attendants. Theodora wears the jewels, pearls, and rich robes characteristic of eastern Roman monarchs. She extends in her hands a gem-encrusted wine cup as her present. Her gesture imitates the gift-giving of the Magi to the baby Jesus, the scene illustrated on the hem of her garment. The circle around her head, called a nimbus (Latin for "cloud"), indicates special holiness. (Basilica/San Vitale, Ravenna, Italy/Bridgeman Images.)

participated in every aspect of Justinian's rule, advising him on personnel for his administration, advocating for her doctrinal views in Christian disputes, and rallying Justinian's courage at times of crisis. A contemporary called her "superior in intelligence to any man."

Government in the eastern Empire increased social divisions because it provided services according to people's wealth. Officials received fees for activities from commercial permits to legal grievances. People with money and status relied on their social connections and wealth to get what they wanted. The poor had trouble affording the payments that government officials expected.

This fee-based system allowed the emperors to pay their civil servants tiny salaries and spend imperial funds for other purposes. One top official reported that he earned thirty times his annual salary in payments from people seeking services. To keep the system from destroying itself through extortion, the emperors published an official list of the maximum fees that their employees could charge.

The Reign of Emperor Justinian, 527–565

Justinian became the most famous eastern emperor by waging war to reunite the Empire as it had been in the days of Augustus, making imperial rule more autocratic, constructing costly buildings in Constantinople, and instituting legal and religious reforms. Justinian had the same aims as all his predecessors:

Justinian and His Court in Ravenna
This mosaic scene dominated by the eastern Roman Emperor Justinian stands opposite Theodora's mosaic in San Vitale's Church in Ravenna. The emperor is shown presenting a gift to the church. Justinian and Theodora finished building the church, which the Ostrogothic king Theodoric had started, to commemorate their successful campaign to restore Italy to the Roman Empire and reassert control of the western capital, Ravenna. The inclusion of the portrait of Maximianus, bishop of Ravenna, standing on Justinian's left and identified by name, stresses the theme of cooperation between bishops and emperors in ruling the world. What do you think the inclusion of the soldiers at the left is meant to indicate? (Basilica/San Vitale, Ravenna, Italy/Bridgeman Images.)

to preserve social order based on hierarchy and maintain divine goodwill. The cost of his plans, however, forced him to raise taxes, generating civil strife.

Justinian's unpopular taxes provoked the Nika Riot in 532, when the Blue and Green factions, gathering to watch chariot races, united against the emperor, shouting "Nika! Nika!" ("Win! Win!"). After nine days of violence had left much of Constantinople in ashes, Justinian prepared to flee in panic. But Theodora sternly rebuked him: "Once born, no one can escape dying, but for one who has held imperial power it would be unbearable to be a fugitive. May I never take off my imperial robes of purple, nor live to see the day when those who meet me will not greet me as their ruler." Her reproach convinced her husband to send in troops, who ended the rioting by slaughtering thirty thousand rioters trapped in the racetrack.

Justinian's most ambitious goal was to restore the Empire to a unified territory, religion, and culture. Invading the former western provinces, his generals defeated the Vandals and Ostrogoths after campaigns that in some cases took decades to complete. At an enormous cost in lives and money, Justinian's armies restored the boundaries of the Roman Empire almost as in the time of Augustus, with its territory stretching from the Atlantic to the western edge of Mesopotamia. His successors, however, would not be able to retain these reconquests.

Justinian's success in reuniting much of the western and eastern Empires had unintended consequences: severe damage to the west's infrastructure and the east's finances. Italy endured the most physical destruction, while the eastern

Empire suffered because Justinian demanded even more taxes to finance his wars and pay the Persian kingdom not to attack. The tax burden crippled the economy, leading to constant banditry in the countryside. Crowds poured into the capital from rural areas, seeking relief from poverty and robbers.

Natural disaster compounded Justinian's problems. In the 540s, a horrific epidemic killed a third of his empire's inhabitants; a quarter of a million, half the capital's population, died in Constantinople alone. This was the first of many pandemics that erased millions of people in the eastern Empire over the next two centuries. Serious earthquakes increased the death toll. The loss of so many people created a shortage of army recruits, requiring the emperor to hire expensive mercenaries, and left countless farms vacant, reducing tax revenues.

He communicated his supremacy and piety through his building program in Constantinople, especially in Hagia Sophia ("Church of the Holy Wisdom"). Creating a new design for churches, Justinian's architects erected a huge building on a square plan capped by a dome 107 feet across and 160 feet high. Its interior walls glowed like the sun from the light reflecting off their four acres of gold mosaics. Imported marble of every color added to the sparkling effect. When he first entered his masterpiece, dedicated in 538, Justinian exclaimed, "I have defeated you, Solomon," claiming to have outdone the glory of the temple that the ancient king built for the Hebrews.

Justinian's autocratic rule reduced the autonomy of cities: imperial officials governed instead of their councils. Provincial elites still had to ensure full payment of their area's taxes, but they no longer controlled local matters or social status. Men of property from the provinces who aspired to power and prestige could satisfy their ambitions only by joining the imperial administration in the capital.

Justinian sought stability by emphasizing his closeness to God and increasing the autocratic power of his rule. Moreover, he proclaimed the emperor the "living law," recalling the Hellenistic royal doctrine that the ruler's decisions defined law. To streamline the mass of decisions that earlier emperors had made, Justinian codified the laws. His Codex (The Code of Justinian) appeared in 529, with a revised version completed in 534. A team of scholars also condensed millions of words of regulations to produce the *Digest* in 533, intended to expedite legal cases and provide a syllabus for law schools. This collection, like the *Codex* written in Latin and therefore readable in the western Empire, influenced legal scholars for centuries. Justinian's legal experts also compiled a textbook for students, the *Institutes*, which appeared in 533 and remained on law-school reading lists until modern times.

To fulfill the emperor's sacred duty to the welfare of his people, Justinian acted to enforce religious purity. He believed his world could not flourish if its god became angered by the presence of religious offenders. As emperor, Justinian decided who the offenders were. Zealously enforcing laws against polytheists, he compelled them to be baptized or forfeit their lands and official positions. He also purged heretical Christians opposing his version of orthodoxy.

Justinian's laws made male homosexual relations illegal for the first time in Roman history. Male same-sex unions had apparently been allowed, or at least officially ignored, until they were prohibited in 342 after Christianity became the emperors' religion. There had never before been any civil penalties imposed on men engaging in homosexual activity, perhaps because previous rulers considered it impractical to regulate men's sexuality, given that adult men lived their private lives free of direct oversight. All the previous emperors had, for example, simply taxed male prostitutes. The legal status of homosexual activity between women is uncertain, but homosexual activity between married women probably counted as adultery and thus as a crime.

Justinian tried to reconcile orthodox and Monophysite Christians by revising the creed of the Council of Chalcedon. But the church leaders in Rome and Constantinople could not agree. The eastern and western churches were therefore launched on diverging courses that would result in formal schism five hundred years later. Justinian's own ecumenical council in Constantinople ended in conflict in 553 when it jailed Rome's defiant pope Vigilius, while also managing to alienate Monophysite bishops. Justinian's efforts to impose religious unity only drove Christians further apart and undermined his vision of a restored Roman world.

The Preservation of Classical Traditions in the Late Roman Empire

Christianization of the late Roman Empire endangered the memory of classical traditions. The plays, histories, philosophical works, poems, speeches, and novels of classical Greece and Rome were polytheist and therefore potentially subversive of Christian belief, but the threat to their survival stemmed more from neglect than suppression. As many Christians became authors, their works displaced ancient Greek and Roman texts as the most important literature of the age.

Some classical texts survived, however, because Christian education and literature depended on non-Christian models, both Greek and Latin. Latin scholarship in the east received a boost when Justinian's Italian wars caused Latin-speaking scholars to flee to Constantinople. There they helped conserve many ancient Roman texts. Scholars preserved classical literature because they regarded it as a crucial part of an elite education. Some knowledge of pre-Christian classics was required for a successful career in government service, the goal of every ambitious student. An imperial decree from 360 stated, "No person shall obtain a post of the first rank unless it shall be shown that he excels in long practice of liberal studies, and that he is so polished in literary matters that words flow from his pen faultlessly."

Another factor promoting the preservation of classical literature was the use of classical rhetoric and its techniques for making persuasive arguments to present Christian theology. When Ambrose, bishop of Milan from 374 to 397, composed the first systematic description of Christian ethics for young ministers, he imitated the great Roman orator Cicero. Theologians refuted heresies among Christians by employing the dialogue form pioneered by Plato. Authors of the biographies of saints found inspiration in ancient literature that praised the heroes of traditional polytheist religion. Choricius, a Christian who held the official position of professor of rhetoric in Gaza, wrote works based on subjects from pre-Christian Greek mythology and history, such as the Trojan War or the Athenian general Miltiades. Similarly, Christian artists incorporated polytheist traditions in communicating their beliefs and emotions in paintings, mosaics, and carved reliefs. A favorite artistic motif of Christ with a sunburst surrounding his head, for example, took its inspiration from polytheist depictions of the radiant Sun as a god. (See the illustration on page 232.)

The growth of Christian literature generated a technological innovation that helped preserve classical literature. Polytheist scribes had written books on sheets of parchment (made from animal skin) or paper (made from papyrus). They then glued the sheets together and attached rods at both ends

Code of Justinian
This illustration from a medieval copy of the collection of laws called the *Codex Justinianus*, the legal code instituted by the Emperor Justinian (r. 527–565), shows the emperor at the center, while a prisoner is imprisoned in a cell on the right. The very first law listed in Justinian's long book prohibited any public disputation of or deviation from the doctrines of Christianity as believed and enforced by the emperor. He insisted that this law protected the truth of religion and therefore was for the good of all. Heretics—those who held different views—could expect harsh punishment, such as imprisonment, or worse—if they were convicted of breaking this law. (Leemage/Getty Images.)

to form a scroll. Readers faced an awkward task in unrolling scrolls to read. For ease of use, Christians produced their literature in the form of the codex—a book with bound pages. Eventually the codex became the standard form of book production.

Despite its continuing importance in education and rhetoric, classical Greek and Latin literature barely survived the war-torn world dominated by Christians. Knowledge of Greek in the west faded so drastically that by the sixth century almost no one there could read the original versions of Homer's *Iliad* and *Odyssey*, the foundations of a classical literary education. Latin fared better, and scholars such as Augustine and Jerome knew Rome's ancient literature extremely well. But they also saw its classics as potentially too seductive for a pious Christian because the pleasure that came from reading them could be a distraction from the worship of God. In fact, Jerome once had a nightmare of being condemned on Judgment Day for having been more dedicated to Cicero than to Christ.

The closing around 530 of the Academy, founded in Athens by Plato more than nine hundred years earlier, demonstrated the dangers for classical learning in the later Roman Empire. This most famous of classical schools finally went out of business when many of its scholars emigrated to Persia to escape Justinian's tightened restrictions on polytheist teachers and its revenues dwindled because the Athenian elite, its traditional supporters, were increasingly Christianized. The Neoplatonist school at Alexandria, by contrast, continued. Its leader John Philoponus (c. 490–570) was a Christian. In addition to Christian theology, Philoponus wrote commentaries on the works of Aristotle. Some of his ideas anticipated those of Galileo a thousand years later. He achieved the kind of synthesis of old and new that was one of the innovative outcomes of the cultural transformation of the late Roman world—he was a Christian subject of the eastern Roman Empire in sixth-century Egypt, heading a school founded long before by polytheists, studying the works of an ancient Greek philosopher as the inspiration for his forward-looking scholarship. The strong possibility that present generations could learn from the past would continue as Western civilization once again remade itself in medieval times.

> **REVIEW QUESTION**
> What policies did Justinian undertake to try to restore and strengthen the Roman Empire?

Conclusion

Diocletian ended the third-century crisis of the Roman Empire, but his reforms only delayed its fragmentation. In the late fourth century, migrations of barbarians fleeing the Huns weakened the Roman imperial government. Emperor Theodosius I divided the Empire into western and eastern halves in 395 to try to improve its administration and defense. When Roman authorities bungled the task of integrating barbarian tribes into Roman society, the newcomers created kingdoms that eventually replaced Roman rule in the west.

Large-scale and violent immigration transformed the western Empire's politics, society, and economy. The political changes and economic deterioration accompanying this transformation destroyed the public-spiritedness

MAPPING THE WEST

The eastern Roman Empire at the accession of Justinian, 527 C.E.

The eastern Roman Empire at the death of Justinian, 565 C.E.

Western Europe and the Eastern Roman (or Byzantine) Empire, c. 600

The eastern Roman Emperor Justinian employed brilliant generals and expended huge sums of money to reconquer Italy, North Africa, and part of Spain to reunite the western and eastern halves of the former Roman Empire. His wars to regain Italy and North Africa eliminated the Ostrogothic and Vandal kingdoms, respectively, but at a huge cost in effort, time—the war in Italy took twenty years—and expense. The resources of the eastern Empire were so depleted that his successors could not maintain the reunification. By the early seventh century, the Visigoths had taken back all of Spain. Africa, despite serious revolts by indigenous Berber tribes, remained under imperial control until the Arab conquest of the seventh century. Within five years of Justinian's death, however, the Lombards had set up a new kingdom controlling a large section of Italy. Never again would anyone in the ancient world attempt to reestablish a universal Roman Empire.

Analyzing the Map: In which direction did Justinian expand the Byzantine Empire?

Making Connections: What factors do you think might help explain why Justinian was not able to reconquer the territories occupied by the Frankish and the Visigothic kingdoms?

---

of the elite, as wealthy nobles retreated to self-sufficient country estates and shunned municipal office.

The eastern Empire fared better economically than the western and avoided the worst violence of the migrations. Eastern emperors attempted to preserve "Romanness" by maintaining Roman culture and political traditions. The financial pressure of wars to reunite the Empire drove tax rates to unbearable levels, while the concentration of authority in the capital weakened local communities.

Constantine's conversion to Christianity in 312 marked a turning point in Western history. Christianization of the Empire occurred gradually, and Christians disagreed among themselves over doctrines of faith, even to the point of deadly violence. Monastic life redefined the meaning of holiness by creating communities of "God's heroes" who withdrew from this world to devote their service to glorifying the next. In the end, the quest for unity fell short through the powerful effects of political and social transformation. Nevertheless, the memory of Roman power and culture remained potent, providing an influential inheritance to the peoples and states that would become Rome's heirs in the next stage of Western civilization.

Chapter 7 Review

Key Terms and People

Be sure that you can identify the term or person and explain its historical significance.

dominate (p. 221)

tetrarchy (p. 223)

coloni (p. 225)

curials (p. 225)

Great Persecution (p. 226)

Edict of Milan (p. 226)

Julian the Apostate (p. 229)

Theodosius I (p. 229)

Augustine (p. 230)

Arianism (p. 232)

Nicene Creed (p. 233)

asceticism (p. 235)

Visigoths (p. 241)

wergild (p. 245)

Justinian and Theodora (p. 246)

Review Questions

1. What were Diocletian's policies to end the third-century crisis, and how successful were they?

2. How did Christianity both unite and divide the Roman Empire?

3. How did their migrations and invasions change the barbarians themselves and the Roman Empire?

4. What policies did Justinian undertake to try to restore and strengthen the Roman Empire?

Making Connections

1. How did the principate and the dominate differ with regard to political appearance versus political reality?

2. What were the main similarities and differences between polytheism and Christianity as official state religions in the late Roman Empire?

3. What developments in the late Roman Empire would support the idea that it is possible for a state to be too large to be well governed and to remain united indefinitely?

Important Events

293	Diocletian creates the tetrarchy
301	Diocletian issues Edict on Maximum Prices and Wages
303	Diocletian launches Great Persecution of Christians
312	Constantine sees vision, wins battle of the Milvian Bridge in Rome, and converts to Christianity
313	Religious freedom is proclaimed in the Edict of Milan
323	Pachomius in Upper Egypt establishes the first monasteries
324	Constantine wins civil war and re-founds Byzantium as Constantinople, the "New Rome"
325	Council of Nicaea defends Christian orthodoxy against Arianism
361–363	Julian the Apostate tries to reinstate polytheism as official state religion
378	Barbarian massacre of Roman army in battle of Adrianople
391	Theodosius I makes Christianity the official state religion
395	Theodosius I divides Empire into western and eastern halves
410	Visigoths sack Rome
426	Augustine publishes *The City of God*
451	Council of Chalcedon attempts to forge agreement on Christian orthodoxy
475	Visigoths publish law code
476	German commander Odoacer deposes the final western emperor, the boy Romulus Augustulus ("the fall of Rome")
493–526	Ostrogothic kingdom in Italy
507	Clovis establishes Frankish kingdom in Gaul
527–565	Reign of eastern Roman Emperor Justinian
529–534	Justinian publishes law code and handbooks
540	Benedict devises his rule for monasteries

Consider three events

Augustine publishes *The City of God* (426), Council of Chalcedon attempts to forge agreement on Christian orthodoxy (451), and Justinian publishes law code and handbooks (529–534). What connections can be drawn between these events in terms of the attitudes that informed them, their goals, and their effects on society?

Suggested References

Some scholars regard the political, social, and cultural changes in the late Roman Empire as evidence of a sad "decline and fall"; others judge them to have had mixed positive and negative consequences. The rise of Christianity to the status of an official religion also changed Roman life in complex ways that are still being investigated.

Brown, Peter. *The Body and Society: Men, Women, and Sexual Renunciation in Early Christianity.* 1988.

Cameron, Averil. *The Mediterranean World in Late Antiquity AD 395–700.* 2nd ed. 2012.

Daryaee, Touraj. *Sasanian Iran (224–651 C.E.): Portrait of a Late Antique Empire.* 2008.

Dresken-Weiland, Jutta. *Mosaics of Ravenna: Image and Meaning.* 2017.

*Drew, Katherine Fischer, ed. *The Laws of the Salian Franks.* 1991.

Elsner, Jas. *Imperial Rome and Christian Triumph: The Art of the Roman Empire, A.D. 100–450.* 1998.

*Grubbs, Judith Evans. *Women and Law in the Roman Empire: A Sourcebook on Marriage, Divorce, and Widowhood.* 2002.

Heather, Peter. *Empires and Barbarians: The Fall of Rome and the Birth of Europe.* 2010.

Hebblewhite, Mark. *The Emperor and the Army in the Later Roman Empire, AD 235–395.* 2017.

Jacobsen, Torsten Cumberland. *A History of the Vandals.* 2012.

*Lee, A. D. *Pagans and Christians in Late Antiquity: A Sourcebook.* 2000.

MacMullen, Ramsay. *Christianity and Paganism in the Fourth to Eighth Centuries.* 1997.

Odahl, Charles. *Constantine and the Christian Empire.* 2nd ed. 2010.

*Procopius. *The Secret History.* Trans. G. A. Williamson and Peter Sarris. 2007.

*Procopius. *The Wars.* Vols. I–V. Trans. H. B. Dewing. 1914–1928.

Rosen, William. *Justinian's Flea: The First Great Plague and the End of the Roman Empire.* 2008.

Southern, Pat, and Karen R. Dixon. *The Late Roman Army.* 1996.

Wickham, Chris. *Framing the Early Middle Ages: Europe and the Mediterranean.* 2007.

---

*Primary source.

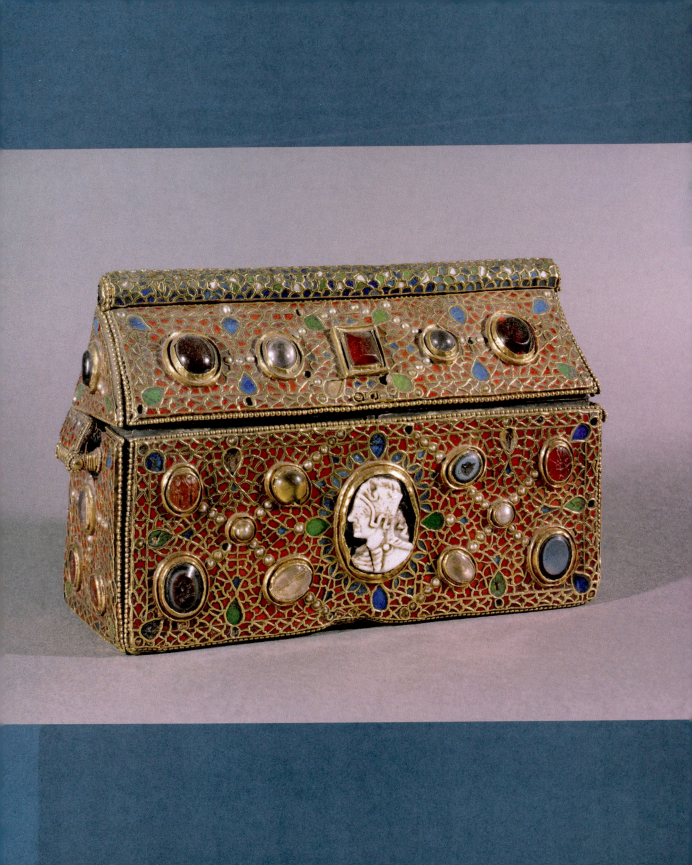

The Heirs of Rome: Islam, Byzantium, and Europe

600–750

At the end of the sixth century, Gregory, bishop of Tours, wrote about Clovis, an early king of the Franks. Under Clovis, the Franks took over Gaul. Yet, about a century later, Gregory described Clovis as if he were a legitimate Roman ruler. He wrote about the day in which Clovis was crowned in the church of Saint Martin at Tours:

> [He was] clad in a purple tunic and the military mantle, and he crowned himself with a diadem. He then rode out on his horse and with his own hand showered gold and silver coins among the people present all the way from the doorway of Saint Martin's church to Tours cathedral. From that day on he was called Consul or Augustus.

Consul or Augustus! Gregory thought that the Roman Empire lived on in the person of the barbarian Clovis. His words reveal that at the time people did not recognize the enormous transformations that were taking place in the sixth and seventh centuries. In fact, as the western and eastern parts of the Roman Empire went their separate ways, a third power—the Islamic world—was taking shape as well. These three powers have continued in various forms to the present day: the western Roman Empire became western Europe, the eastern Roman Empire became eastern Europe and Turkey and helped create Russia, and the Islamic world endures across North Africa and the Middle East and elsewhere as well.

«Reliquary The precious remains of a saint—or relics—were housed in this equally precious box—a seventh-century reliquary. Most of the decorative elements of the box—cloisonné enamel (bits of enamel framed by metal), garnets, and glass gems laid out in an abstract pattern—were drawn from barbarian artistic motifs. The pearls, however, form crosses that make clear the Christian purpose of the box. In the center, the maker put a cameo (or perhaps an imitation cameo) that was meant to recall Roman silhouettes, as if there were no contradiction between barbarian abstract styles and Roman forms. Like Gregory of Tours calling Clovis "Augustus," the maker of this box considered a Roman-type cameo to be a perfect complement to his otherwise geometrical design. (Treasury, Abbey, St. Maurice, Switzerland/Erich Lessing/Art Resource, NY.)

Diverse as these cultures are today, they share many of the same roots. Gregory had a good point: the successor states were heirs of Rome. This was most obvious in the instance of religion. All three adhered to monotheism. The western and eastern halves of the Roman Empire had Christianity in common, although they differed at times in interpreting it. Adherents of Islam believed in the same one God as the Jews and Christians.

The seventh and eighth centuries illustrate the Roman Empire's persistence and transformation. Changes in the eastern half of the empire were so important that historians have given it a new name—Byzantine Empire. The term *Byzantine Empire*, or *Byzantium*, which comes from the old Greek name for Constantinople, rightly implies that the center of power and culture in the eastern Roman Empire was now concentrated in this one city. Over the centuries, the Byzantine Empire expanded, shrank, and even nearly disappeared—but it hung on in one form or another until 1453.

During the period 600–750, which historians consider the beginning of the Middle Ages, all three heirs of the Roman Empire combined elements of their heritage with new values, interests, and conditions. Their differences should nevertheless not obscure the fact that the Byzantine, Muslim, and western European cultures were partly based on a common tradition.

CHAPTER FOCUS

What three cultures took the place of the Roman Empire, and how did each of them both draw on and reject Roman traditions?

Islam: A New Religion and a New Empire

In the early seventh century, a religion that called on all to believe in one God began in Arabia (today Saudi Arabia). Islam ("submission to God") took shape under **Muhammad** (c. 570–632). While many of the people living in Arabia were polytheists, Muhammad recognized the one God of the Jews and Christians. He saw himself as God's final prophet and thus became known as the Prophet. Invited by the people of Medina, in western Arabia, to come and act as a mediator in their disputes, Muhammad exercised the powers of

CHAPTER TIMELINE

| | | 572 Lombards conquer northern Italy |

c. 486–751 Merovingian dynasty

450   500

c. 570–632 Life of Muhammad, prophet of Islam

r. 573–594 Bishop Gregory of Tours

both a religious and a secular leader. This dual role became the model for his successors, known as caliphs. Through a combination of persuasion and force, Muhammad and his co-religionists, the Muslims ("those who submit to Islam"), converted most of the Arabian peninsula. By the time Muhammad died in 632, Muslims had begun to conquer Byzantine and Persian territories. In the next generation, they expanded both eastward and westward. Yet, within the territories they conquered, daily life went on much as before.

Nomads and City Dwellers

In the seventh century, the vast deserts of the Arabian peninsula were populated by both sedentary (settled) and nomadic peoples. The sedentary peoples, some farmers, others merchants and artisans, lived in oases. They far outnumbered the nomads, known as Bedouins, who herded livestock and raided one another for plunder, slaves, and wives (men practiced polygyny—having more than one wife at a time). They had a flourishing literary as well as oral culture, with poetry prized above all. These poems expressed their esteem for honor, friendship, bravery, and love.

Islam began as a religion of the sedentary, but it soon found support and military strength among the nomads. It started in Mecca, an important commercial and religious center south of Medina. Mecca was the home of the Ka'ba, a shrine that contained the images of many gods. It was a sacred place within which war and violence were prohibited. The tribe that dominated Mecca, the Quraysh, controlled access to the shrine, taxing the pilgrims who flocked there. Visitors, assured of their safety, bartered on the sacred grounds, transforming the plunder from raids into trade.

The Prophet Muhammad and the Faith of Islam

Muhammad was born in Mecca. Orphaned at the age of six, he went to live with his uncle, a leader of the Quraysh tribe. Eventually, Muhammad became a trader and married Khadija, a rich widow. They lived (to all appearances)

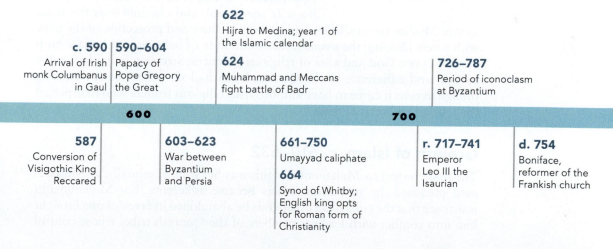

622
Hijra to Medina; year 1 of the Islamic calendar

c. 590
Arrival of Irish monk Columbanus in Gaul

590–604
Papacy of Pope Gregory the Great

624
Muhammad and Meccans fight battle of Badr

726–787
Period of iconoclasm at Byzantium

600   **700**

587
Conversion of Visigothic King Reccared

603–623
War between Byzantium and Persia

661–750
Umayyad caliphate

664
Synod of Whitby; English king opts for Roman form of Christianity

r. 717–741
Emperor Leo III the Isaurian

d. 754
Boniface, reformer of the Frankish church

Qur'an (568–645)
More than a holy book, the Qur'an represents for Muslims the very words of God that were dictated to Muhammad by the archangel Gabriel. The recent discovery of this fragment of a Qur'an, radiocarbon dated to 568–645, suggests that the text was compiled during Muhammad's lifetime or only shortly thereafter. The decoration in red ink marks the end of one sura and the beginning of the next. (Dan Kitwood/Getty Images.)

happily and comfortably. Yet Muhammad sometimes left home to pray in a nearby cave, practicing a type of piety similar to that of the early Christians.

Around 610, on one of these retreats, Muhammad heard a voice and had a vision that summoned him to worship the God of the Jews and Christians, Allah ("the God" in Arabic). Over the next years, he received messages that he understood to be divine revelations. Later, when these messages had been written down and compiled—a process completed perhaps as early as in the Prophet's lifetime—they became the **Qur'an**, the holy book of Islam. *Qur'an* means "recitation"; each of the book's parts, called suras, is understood to be God's revelation as told to Muhammad by the archangel Gabriel—the very Gabriel of the Hebrew and Christian Bibles—and then recited by Muhammad to others. Written entirely in verse and focused on the divine, the Qur'an stood apart from traditional Bedouin poetry, which emphasized the here and now.

Beginning with the Fatihah, which praises God as the "lord sustainer of the worlds," the Qur'an continues with suras of gradually decreasing length. They cover the gamut of human experience and the life to come after death. For Muslims, the Qur'an contains the legal and moral code by which men and women should live: "Do not set up another god with God. . . . Do not worship anyone but Him, and be good to your parents." It emphasizes the family—a man, his wife (or wives), and children—as the basic unit of Muslim society. Islam replaced the identity and protection of the tribe with a new identity: the *ummah*, the community of believers, who share both a belief in one God and a set of religious practices. Stressing individual belief in God and adherence to the Qur'an, Islam had no priests or sacraments, though in time it came to have authoritative religious leaders who interpreted the Qur'an and related texts.

Growth of Islam, c. 610–632

The first convert to Muhammad's faith was his wife. Eventually, as Muhammad preached the new faith, others became adherents. But Muhammad's insistence that the cults of all other gods be abandoned in favor of one brought him into conflict with leading members of the Quraysh tribe, whose control over the Ka'ba had given them prestige and wealth. Perceiving Muhammad as a threat, they insulted him and harassed his followers.

Disillusioned with the people of Mecca, Muhammad looked elsewhere for converts. In particular, he expected support from Jews because he thought their monotheism prepared them for his own faith. He eagerly accepted an invitation to go to Medina, in part because of its significant Jewish population. Muhammad's journey to Medina—called the **Hijra**—proved to be a crucial event for the new faith, and the year in which it occurred, 622, became the first year of the Islamic calendar.*

Although he was disappointed not to find much support among the Jews at Medina, Muhammad did find others there ready to listen to his religious message and to accept him as the leader of their community. Muhammad's political position in the community set the pattern by which Islamic society would be governed afterward; rather than simply adding a church to political and cultural life, Muslims made their political and religious institutions inseparable.

Muhammad felt threatened by the Quraysh tribe at Mecca, and he led raids against their caravans. At the battle of Badr in 624, the Muslims killed forty-nine of the Meccan enemy, took numerous prisoners, and confiscated considerable treasure. From the time of this conflict, the Bedouin tradition of plundering was grafted onto the Muslim duty of **jihad** ("striving in the way of God").

The battle of Badr was a great triumph for Muhammad, who now secured his position at Medina, gaining new adherents and silencing all doubters, including Jews. Turning against those who refused to convert, he expelled two Jewish tribes from Medina and executed the male members of another. Although Muslims had originally prayed in the direction of Jerusalem, the center of Jewish worship, Muhammad now had them turn in the direction of Mecca.

Around the same time, Muhammad instituted new religious obligations. Among these were the *zakat*, a tax on possessions to be used for alms; the fast of Ramadan, which took place during the ninth month of the Islamic year, the month in which the battle of Badr had been fought; the *hajj*, the pilgrimage to Mecca during the last month of the year, which each Muslim was to make at least once in his or her lifetime; and the *salat*, formal worship at least three times a day (later increased to five). The salat included the *shahadah*, or profession of faith: "There is no divinity but God, and Muhammad is the messenger of God." Detailed regulations for these practices, sometimes called the **Five Pillars of Islam**, were worked out in the eighth and early ninth centuries.

Meanwhile, Muhammad sent troops to subdue Arabs north and south. In 630, he entered Mecca with an army and took over the city. As the prestige of Islam grew, clans elsewhere converted. Through a combination of force, conversion, and negotiation, Muhammad was able to unite many, though not all, Arabic-speaking tribes under his leadership by the time of his death in 632.

Muhammad was responsible for social as well as religious change. The ummah included both men and women; Islam thus enhanced women's status.

---

*Thus, 1 anno Hegirae (1 A.H.) on the Muslim calendar is equivalent to 622 C.E.

At first, Muslim women joined men during the prayer periods that punctuated the day, but, beginning in the eighth century, women began to pray apart from men. Men were allowed to have up to four wives at one time but were obliged to treat them equally; wives received dowries and had certain inheritance rights. Islam prohibited all infanticide, a practice that Arabs had long used largely against female infants. Like Judaism and Christianity, however, Islam retained the practices of a patriarchal society in which women's participation in community life was limited.

The ummah functioned in many ways as a "supertribe," obligated to fight common enemies, share plunder, and peacefully resolve any internal disputes. Bedouin converts to Islam turned their traditional warrior culture to its cause. Unlike intertribal fighting, warfare was now the jihad of people who were carrying out God's command against unbelievers as recorded in the Qur'an: "Strive, O Prophet, against the unbelievers and the hypocrites, and deal with them firmly. Their final abode is Hell: And what a wretched destination!"

The Caliphs, Muhammad's Successors, 632–750

In the new political community he founded in Arabia, Muhammad reorganized traditional Arab society by cutting across clan allegiances and welcoming converts from every tribe. He forged the Muslims into a formidable military force, and his successors, the caliphs, took the Byzantine and Persian worlds by storm. They quickly conquered Byzantine territory in Syria and Egypt and invaded the Sasanid Empire, conquering the whole of Persia by 651 (Map 8.1). During the last half of the seventh century and the beginning of the eighth, Islamic warriors extended their sway westward to Spain and eastward to India.

How were such widespread conquests possible, especially in so short a time? First, the Islamic forces faced weakened empires. The Byzantine and Sasanid states were exhausted from fighting each other. Second, discontented Christians and Jews welcomed Muslims into both Byzantine and Persian territories. The Monophysite Christians in Syria and Egypt, for example, had suffered persecution under the Byzantines and were glad to have new, Islamic overlords. There were also internal reasons for Islam's success. Inspired by jihad, Arab fighters were well prepared: fully armed and mounted on horseback, using camel convoys to carry supplies and provide protection, they conquered with amazing ease. To secure their victories, they built garrison cities from which their soldiers requisitioned taxes and goods.

Yet the solidarity of the Muslim community was threatened by disputes over the successors to Muhammad, the caliphs. While the first two caliphs came to power without serious opposition, the third, Uthman (r. 644–656), a member of the Umayyad clan and son-in-law of Muhammad, was resented by some members of the inner circle and soldiers unhappy with his distribution of high offices and revenues. Accusing Uthman of favoritism, they supported his rival, Ali, a member of the Hashim clan (to which Muhammad had belonged) and the husband of Muhammad's only surviving child, Fatimah. After a group of discontented soldiers murdered Uthman, civil war broke out

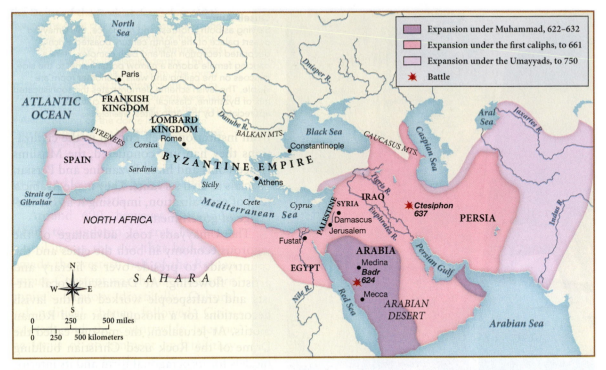

MAP 8.1 Expansion of Islam to 750
In little more than a century, Islamic armies conquered a vast region that included numerous different people, cultures, climates, and living conditions. Yet under the Umayyads, these disparate territories were administered by one ruler from the capital city at Damascus.

between the Umayyads and Ali's faction. It ended when Ali was killed by one of his own former supporters, and the caliphate remained in Umayyad hands from 661 to 750.

Despite defeat, the Shi'at Ali ("Ali's faction") did not fade away. Ali's memory lived on among **Shi'ite** Muslims, who saw in him a symbol of justice and righteousness. For them, Ali's death was the martyrdom of the true successor to Muhammad. They remained faithful to his dynasty, shunning the mainstream caliphs of Sunni Muslims (whose name derived from the word *sunna*, the practices of Muhammad). They awaited the arrival of the true leader—the imam—who in their view could come only from the house of Ali.

Peace and Prosperity in Islamic Lands

Ironically, the definitive victories of the Muslim warriors in the seventh and early eighth centuries ushered in a time of peace. While the conquerors stayed within their fortified cities or built magnificent castles in the deserts, the conquered, including Christians and Jews, went back to work, to study, to play, and to worship. Under the **Umayyad caliphate**, which lasted from 661 to 750, the Muslim world became a state, its capital at Damascus, in Syria. Borrowing

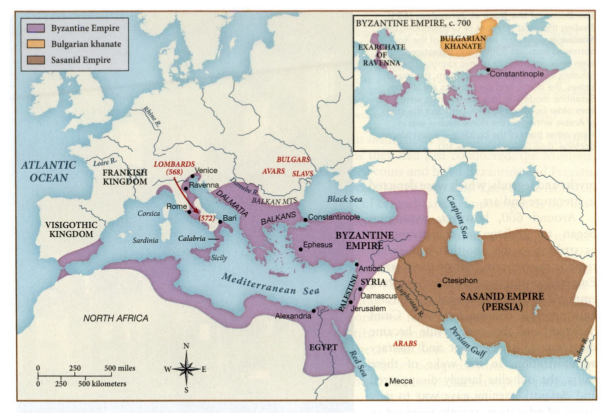

MAP 8.2 Byzantine and Sasanid Empires, c. 600

Emperor Justinian (r. 527–565) hoped to re-create the old Roman Empire, but just a century after his death, most of Italy was conquered by the Lombards. Meanwhile, the Byzantine Empire had to contend with the Sasanid Empire to its east. In 600, these two major powers faced each other uneasily. Three years later, the Sasanid king attacked Byzantine territory. The resulting wars, which lasted until 627, exhausted both empires and left them open to invasion by the Arabs. By 700, the Byzantine Empire was quite small. Compare the inset map here with Map 8.1 on page 265. Where had the Muslims made significant conquests of Byzantine territory?

and gave the men at their court titles such as priest of priests and scribe of scribes. With dreams of military glory, they invaded major areas of the Roman Empire, using the revenues from new taxes to strengthen the army. King Chosroes II (r. 590–628) took Syria and Jerusalem between 611 and 614, and he conquered Egypt in 620.

Responding to these attacks, the Byzantine emperor **Heraclius** (r. 610–641) inspired his troops to avenge the sack of Jerusalem. By 627, the Byzantines had regained all their lost territory. But the wars had changed much: Syrian, Egyptian, and Palestinian cities had grown used to being under Persian rule, and Christians who did not adhere to the orthodoxy at Byzantium preferred their Persian overlords, who did not persecute them. Even more important, the constant wars and plundering sapped the wealth of the region and the energy of the people who lived under Byzantine rule.

Preoccupied by war with Persia, Byzantium was ill equipped to deal with other groups who were pushing into parts of the empire at about the same time. The **Lombards**, a Germanic people, entered northern Italy in 568; by 572, they were masters of the Po valley and parts of Italy's south. In addition to Rome, the Byzantines retained only Italy's "foot," the island of Sicily, and a narrow swath of land through the middle of the peninsula called the Exarchate of Ravenna. The Byzantine army also contended with the Slavs and Bulgars just beyond the Danube River. Joined by the Avars, the Slavs attacked both rural and urban areas of Byzantium. Meanwhile, the Bulgars entered what is now Bulgaria in the 670s, defeating the Byzantine army, and in 681, forcing the emperor to recognize their new state. When the Arabs arrived under the banner of Islam, the Byzantine Empire was further diminished.

Even as it was facing military attacks on all fronts, Byzantium's power was being whittled away by more peaceful means. As Slavs and Avars, who were not subject to Byzantine rulers, settled in the Balkans, they often intermingled with the native peoples there, absorbing local agricultural techniques and burial practices while imposing their language and religious cults.

Byzantium's loss of control over the Balkans meant the shrinking of its empire (see inset on Map 8.2). It also exacerbated the growing separation between the eastern and western parts of the former Roman Empire. Avar and Slavic control of the Balkans effectively cut off trade and travel between Constantinople and the cities of the Dalmatian coast, while the new Bulgarian state served as a political barrier across the Danube. The two halves of the former Roman Empire communicated very little in the seventh century, a fact partly due to their different languages: Greek in the East, Latin in the West.

From an Urban to a Rural Way of Life

As Byzantium shrank, the conquered regions had to adjust to new rulers. Byzantine subjects in Syria and Egypt who came under Arab rule adapted to the new conditions, paying a special tax to their conquerors but practicing their Christian and Jewish religions in peace. Cities remained centers of government, scholarship, and business, while peasants were permitted to keep and farm their lands. In the Balkans, as Slavs and Bulgars came to dominate the peninsula, some cities disappeared when people fled to hilltop settlements. Nevertheless, the Balkan newcomers recognized the Byzantine emperor's authority and soon began to flirt with Christianity.

Some of the most radical transformations for seventh- and eighth-century Byzantines occurred not in the territories lost but in the shrunken empire itself. Under the ceaseless barrage of invaders, many towns, formerly bustling centers of trade and the imperial bureaucracy, vanished or became unrecognizable. The public activity of open marketplaces, theaters, and town squares largely ended. City baths, once places where people gossiped, made deals, and talked politics and philosophy, disappeared in most Byzantine towns—with the significant exception of Constantinople. Warfare reduced some cities to rubble, and the limited resources available for rebuilding went to construct thick city walls and solid churches instead of spacious marketplaces and baths.

Despite the general urban decay, Constantinople and a few other urban centers retained some of their old vitality. The manufacture and trade of fine silk textiles continued. Even though Byzantium's economic life became increasingly rural and barter-based in the seventh and eighth centuries, the skills, knowledge, and institutions of urban workers remained.

As urban life declined, agriculture, always the basis of the Byzantine economy, became the center of its social life as well. Unlike Europe, where peasants often depended on aristocratic landlords, the Byzantine Empire had many free peasants who grew food, herded cattle, and tended vineyards on their own small plots of land. As Byzantine cities declined, the curials (town councilors), the elite who for centuries had mediated between the emperor and the people, disappeared. Now on those occasions when farmers came into contact with the state—to pay taxes, for example—they felt the impact of the emperor or his representatives directly.

Byzantine emperors, drawing on the still-vigorous Roman legal tradition, promoted domestic life with new imperial legislation, strengthening the nuclear family by narrowing the grounds for divorce and setting new punishments for marital infidelity. Abortion was prohibited, and new protections were set in place against incest. Mothers were given equal power with fathers over their offspring; if widowed, they became the legal guardians of their minor children and controlled the household property.

New Military and Cultural Forms

The shift from an urban- to a rural-centered society meant changes not only in daily life and the economy, but also in the empire's military and cultural institutions. The Byzantine navy fought successfully at sea with its powerful weapon of "Greek fire," a mixture of crude oil and resin that was heated and shot via a tube over the water, engulfing enemy ships in flames. Determined to win wars on land as well, the imperial army, which previously had served to guard the frontiers, was now brought inside the empire. Posted in fortresses within large districts called *strategiai*, the soldiers served under district commanders known as *strategoi* (sing., *strategos*, general). Officials supplied the army with weapons and food purchased or requisitioned as taxes from local peasants. When attacks came, the troops went out to meet the enemy and afterward retreated to the safety of their fortresses.

The disappearance of the old cultural elite meant a shift in the focus of education. Whereas the curial class had promoted the study of the pagan classics, eighth-century parents showed far more interest in giving their children a religious education. Even with the decay of urban centers, cities and villages often retained an elementary school. There, teachers used the Book of Psalms (the Psalter) as their primer. Secular, classical learning remained decidedly out of favor throughout the seventh and eighth centuries; dogmatic writings, biographies of saints, and devotional works took center stage.

Religion, Politics, and Iconoclasm

The new stress on religious learning in the seventh century complemented both the autocratic imperial ideal and the powers of the bishops. While in theory imperial and church powers were separate, in practice they were interdependent. The emperor exercised considerable power over the church: he influenced the appointment of the chief religious official, the patriarch of Constantinople; he called church councils to determine dogma; and he regularly used bishops as local governors.

Bishops and their clergy, whose seats were in the cities, formed a rich and powerful upper class. They distributed food to the needy, sat as judges, functioned as tax collectors, and built military fortifications. They owed their appointment to metropolitans (bishops who headed an entire province), who in turn were appointed by the patriarchs (bishops with authority over whole regions). Monasteries were theoretically under the limited control of the local bishop, but in practice they were enormously powerful institutions that often defied the authority of bishops and even emperors.

Laypeople, clergy, and monks alike looked to relics and holy images to help them worship. Relics were the material remains of the saints: their bodies and body parts, even clothes and dust from their tombs. Holy images—of Christ, Mary (his mother), and the saints—gave people a visual focus for their piety.

As a series of setbacks rocked the Byzantine Empire—plagues, earthquakes, and wars against invading Slavs and Bulgars—images, known as **icons**, became more important than relics in focusing religious devotion. By the late seventh century, some groups within the empire understood icons to manifest in physical form not only the sacred person depicted but also his or her holiness. Monks, above all, centered their worship on icons and encouraged others to do so.

Soon there was a backlash against such intense devotion to icons. Emperor Leo III the Isaurian (r. 717–741) made that backlash

Icon of the Virgin and Child

Surrounded by two angels in the back and two soldier-saints at either side, the Virgin Mary and the Christ Child are depicted with still, otherworldly dignity. The sixth-century artist gave the angels transparent halos to emphasize their spiritual natures, while depicting the saints as earthly men, with hair and beards, and feet planted firmly on the ground. Icons like this were used for worship both in private homes and in Byzantine monasteries. (St. Catherine Monastery, Mount Sinai, Egypt/Erich Lessing/Art Resource, NY.)

WHAT WOULD YOU DO?

Given that icons had only recently become the focus of worship and that, at the very same time, Islamic forces were scoring unprecedented victories, if you were Emperor Leo, what would you do to strengthen your position in the eyes of God? Why or why not would you institute iconoclasm?

REVIEW QUESTION

What stresses did the Byzantine Empire endure in the seventh and eighth centuries, and how was iconoclasm a response to those stresses?

official. In 726, as Islamic armies swallowed up Byzantine territory and after a volcano erupted in the middle of the Aegean Sea, Leo denounced icons. The year 726 marks the beginning of **iconoclasm** ("icon breaking") in Byzantine history. It lasted until 787, and a modified ban was imposed between 815 and 843.

Legend has it that in 726, Leo tore down the great image of Christ that used to be at the gateway to the imperial palace. This is probably not true. But Leo did erect a cross nearby, and in 730, he demanded that both the pope at Rome and the patriarch of Constantinople remove sacred images. He and his successors had good political reasons to oppose icons. Icons diluted loyalties because they created intermediaries between worshippers and God that undermined the emperor's exclusive place in the divine and temporal order. In addition, the emphasis on icons in monastic communities made the monks potential threats to imperial power; the emperors hoped to use this issue to weaken the monasteries. Finally, the emperors opposed icons because the army did so. Byzantine soldiers, unnerved by Arab triumphs, attributed their misfortunes to icons, which disregarded the biblical command against graven (carved) images. They compared their defeats to Muslim successes and noted that Islam prohibited all visual images of the divine. The Byzantine emperors, who needed to keep the loyalty of their troops, adopted their soldiers' position on icons. They saw it as a renewal of pagan idolatry.

Iconoclasm had an enormous impact on Byzantium (see Contrasting Views on pages 274–275). The devout had to destroy their personal icons or worship them in secret. Iconoclasts (who were especially numerous at Constantinople) whitewashed the walls of churches, erasing all the images. They smashed portable icons. Artists largely ceased depicting the human form, and artistic production in general dwindled during this time. The power and prestige of the monasteries, which were associated with icons, diminished. As the tide of battle turned in favor of the Byzantines, imperial supporters and soldiers credited iconoclasm for their victories.

Western Europe: A Medley of Kingdoms

In contrast to Byzantium—where an emperor still ruled as the successor to Augustus and Constantine—western Europe saw a dispersal of political power. With the end of Roman imperial government there, independent monarchs ruled in Spain, Italy, England, and Gaul. These kings relied on kinship networks, the support of powerful men who attended them at court, the prestige that came from church patronage, and wealth derived from land and plunder.

In some places churchmen and rich magnates were even more powerful than royalty. So were saintly relics, which represented and were believed to wield the divine forces of God. Icons existed but were not very important in the West.

Frankish Kingdoms with Roman Roots

The most important kingdoms in post-Roman Europe were Frankish. The Franks dominated Gaul during the sixth century, and by the seventh century, their kingdoms roughly approximated the eastern borders of present-day

Merovingian kingdoms
Tributary regions

0   100   200 miles
0   100   200 kilometers

North Sea

ENGLAND

Rhine R.

SAXONS

Douai

Laon

Cologne

NEUSTRIA   Paris   Mosel R.   Mainz

Trier

AUSTRASIA

Nantes

Loire R.

Tours

Dijon

ALAMANNIA   BAVARIA

Salzburg

Limoges

BURGUNDY

AQUITAINE   Lyon

Bordeaux

Clermont

Rhône R.

BASQUES

Arles

KINGDOM OF
THE LOMBARDS   Adriatic Sea

Marseille   PROVENCE

KINGDOM OF
THE VISIGOTHS   Mediterranean Sea

MAP 8.3 The Merovingian Kingdoms in the Seventh Century By the seventh century, there were three powerful Merovingian kingdoms: Neustria, Austrasia, and Burgundy. The important cities of Aquitaine were assigned to these major kingdoms, while Aquitaine as a whole was assigned to a duke or other governor. Kings did not establish capital cities; they did not even stay in one place. Rather, they continually traveled throughout their kingdoms, making their power felt in person.

France, Belgium, the Netherlands, and Luxembourg (Map 8.3). Moreover, the Frankish kings who constituted the **Merovingian dynasty** (c. 486–751) subjugated many of the peoples beyond the Rhine River, foreshadowing the contours of the western half of modern Germany.

Where there were cities, there were reminders of Rome. Elsewhere, the Roman heritage was less obvious. Imagine, then, travelers going from Rome to Trier (near what is now Bonn, Germany) in the early eighth century, perhaps to visit its bishop and check up on his piety. They would have relied on river travel. Water routes were preferable to roads because land travel was slow, even though some Roman roads were still in fair repair, and because even large groups of travelers on the roads were vulnerable to attacks by robbers. Traveling northward on the Rhône River, our voyagers would have passed Roman walled cities and farmlands neatly and squarely laid out by Roman land surveyors. The great stone palaces of villas would still have dotted the countryside. Once at Trier, the travelers would have felt at home seeing the city's great gate (now called the Porta Nigra), its monumental baths (some still standing today), and its cathedral, built on the site of a Roman palace. Being in Trier was almost like being in Rome.

Nevertheless, these travelers would have noticed that the cities that they passed through were not what they had been in the heyday of the Roman Empire. True, cities still served as the centers of church administration. Bishops lived in them, and so did clergymen, servants, and others who helped the

Icons: Idols or Aids to Worship

After icons were condemned in 726 by Byzantine emperor Leo III the Isaurian (r. 717–741), a church synod (an assembly of the clergy) met in Constantinople in 754 to condemn icons formally (Excerpt 1). Throughout this time, no one living under Byzantine rule dared to publicly oppose iconoclasm. But Christians in the Islamic world had more freedom. Excerpt 2 was written on behalf of icons by John of Damascus (c. 675–749), a Christian living in Islamic-ruled Syria.

1. Icons Are Idols

The church council that met in 754 declared that veneration of icons was a "new idolatry." Idols were representations of God. The council, fearful of idols, declared that Christ—and by extension his saints and, indeed, all living creatures—could not be represented through material images.

The holy and Ecumenical synod . . . has decreed as follows.

Satan misguided men, so that they worshiped the creature instead of the Creator. The Mosaic law and the prophets co-operated to undo this ruin; but in order to save mankind thoroughly, God sent his own Son, who turned us away from error and the worshiping of idols and taught us the worshiping of God in spirit and in truth. As messengers of his saving doctrine, he left us his Apostles and disciples, and these adorned the Church, his Bride, with his glorious doctrines. This ornament of the Church the holy Fathers and the six Ecumenical Councils have preserved inviolate. . . . But [Satan] . . . could not endure the sight of this adornment and gradually brought back idolatry under the appearance of Christianity. As then Christ armed his Apostles against the ancient idolatry with the power of the Holy Spirit and sent them out into all the world, so has he awakened against the new idolatry his servants our faithful Emperors and endowed them with the same wisdom of the Holy Spirit. Impelled by the Holy Spirit they could no longer be witnesses of the Church being laid waste by the deception of demons

and summoned the sanctified assembly of the God-beloved bishops, that they might institute at a synod a scriptural examination into the deceitful coloring of the pictures which draws down the spirit of man from the lofty adoration of God to the low and material adoration of the creature, and that they, under divine guidance, might express their view on the subject.

Our holy synod therefore assembled, and we, its 338 members, follow the older synodal decrees and accept and proclaim joyfully the dogmas handed down, principally those of the six holy Ecumenical Synods. . . .

After we had carefully examined their decrees under the guidance of the Holy Spirit, we found that the unlawful art of painting living creatures blasphemed the fundamental doctrine of our salvation—namely, the Incarnation of Christ—and contradicted the six holy synods. . . .

Wherefore we thought it right to make clear with all accuracy in our present definition the error of such as make and venerate these, for it is the unanimous doctrine of all the holy Fathers and of the six Ecumenical Synods that no one may imagine any kind of separation or mingling in opposition to the unsearchable, unspeakable, and incomprehensible union of the two natures in the one hypostasis [underlying substance] or person. What avails, then, the folly of the painter, who from sinful love of gain depicts that which should not be depicted—that is, with his polluted hands he tries to fashion that which should only be believed in the heart and confessed with the mouth? He makes an image and calls it Christ. The name *Christ* signifies *God and man*. Consequently it is an image of God and man, and consequently he has in his foolish mind, in his representation of the created flesh, depicted the Godhead which cannot be represented and thus mingled what should not be mingled. Thus he is guilty of a double blasphemy—the one in making an image of the Godhead and the other in mingling the Godhead and manhood. Those fall into the same blasphemy who venerate the image, and the same woe rests upon both. . . . They fall into the abyss of impiety since they separate the flesh from the Godhead, ascribe to it a subsistence of its own, a personality of its own, which they depict, and thus introduce a fourth person into the Trinity. Moreover, they represent as not being divine that which has been made divine by being assumed by the Godhead. . . .

The only admissible figure of the humanity of Christ, however, is bread and wine in the holy Supper. This and no other form, this and no other type, has he chosen to represent his incarnation. Bread he ordered to be brought, but not a representation of the human form, so that idolatry might not arise. And as the body of Christ is made divine, so also this figure of the body of Christ, the bread, is made divine by the descent of the Holy Spirit; it becomes the divine body of Christ by the mediation of the priest who, separating the oblation [offering] from that which is common, sanctifies it. . . .

Supported by the Holy Scriptures and the Fathers, we declare unanimously, in the name of the Holy Trinity, that there shall be rejected and removed and cursed out of the Christian Church every likeness which is made out of any material and color whatever by the evil art of painters.

Whoever in future dares to make such a thing, or to venerate it, or set it up in a church, or in a private house, or possesses it in secret, shall, if bishop, presbyter, or deacon, be deposed; if monk or layman, be anathematized [i.e., excommunicated from the Church] and become liable to be tried by the secular laws as an adversary of God and an enemy of the doctrines handed down by the Fathers.

Source: *A Select Library of Nicene and Post-Nicene Fathers of the Christian Church,* 2nd ser., eds. Philip Schaff and Henry Wace, vol. 14: *The Seven Ecumenical Councils* (Grand Rapids, MI: Wm. B. Eerdmans, 1971), 543–45.

2. Icons as Aids to Proper Worship

John of Damascus was born in Syria after it came under Islamic rule. His father, though Christian, worked for the governor there, and John soon did so as well. John wrote a ringing defense of icons in the 730s or early 750s, shortly before he joined a monastery near Jerusalem. To be sure, the iconoclasts condemned his work, but he was vindicated in 787, when the ban was lifted (for a time).

I believe in one God, the source of all things, without beginning, uncreated, immortal, everlasting, incomprehensible, bodiless, invisible, uncircumscribed [i.e., in no one place], without form. I believe in one supersubstantial being [i.e., beyond all substance], one divine Godhead in three entities, the Father, the Son, and the Holy Ghost, and I adore Him alone with the worship [due God alone]. I adore one God, one Godhead but three Persons, God the Father, God the Son made flesh, and God the Holy Ghost, one God. I do not adore creation more than the Creator, but I adore the creature created as I am, adopting creation freely and spontaneously that He might elevate our nature and make us partakers of His divine nature. Together with my Lord and King I worship Him clothed in the flesh, not as if it were a garment or He constituted a fourth person of the Trinity—God forbid. That flesh is divine, and endures after its assumption. Human nature was not lost in the Godhead, but just as the Word made flesh remained the Word, so flesh became the Word remaining flesh, becoming, rather, one with the Word through union. Therefore I venture to draw an image of the invisible God, not as invisible, but as having become visible for our sakes through flesh and blood. I do not draw an image of the immortal Godhead. I paint the visible flesh of God, for if it is impossible to represent a spirit, how much more God who gives breath to the spirit.

Source: *St. John Damascene on Holy Images,* trans. Mary H. Allies (London: Thomas Baker, 1898), 1 (slightly modified).

QUESTIONS TO CONSIDER

1. According to the Synod of 754, what brought about the veneration of icons?

2. How does John's view of the nature of the Son (Jesus Christ) support his argument in favor of icons?

3. How do John and the Synod differ in their interpretations of what an icon represents?

The Porta Nigra at Trier
Although in Germania, Trier became one of Rome's capitals in the fourth century. The Porta Nigra was originally the northern gate of the city. During the course of the fifth century, the Porta Nigra came to be considered at best useless and at worst pagan, so bits and pieces of it were pillaged to be used in other building projects. However, this practice stopped in 1030, when a hermit named Simeon moved into its eastern tower. After Simeon's death in 1035, the Porta Nigra was turned into a two-story church, which it remained until the early nineteenth century, when Napoleon, who conquered Trier, ordered the church to be dismantled and the site returned (more or less) to its original shape. (De Agostini Picture Library/ Bridgeman Images.)

bishops. Cathedrals (the churches presided over by bishops) remained within city walls, and people were drawn to them for important rituals such as baptism. Nevertheless, many urban centers had lost their commercial and cultural vitality. Largely depopulated, they survived as skeletons of their former selves.

Whereas the chief feature of the Roman landscape had been cities, the Frankish landscape was characterized by dense forests, acres of marshes and bogs, patches of cleared farmland, and pastures for animals. These areas were not much influenced by Rome; they more closely represented the farming and village settlement patterns of the Franks.

On the vast plains between Paris and Trier, most peasants were only semi-free. They were settled in family groups on small holdings called manses, which included a house, a garden, and cultivable land. The peasants paid dues and sometimes owed labor services to a lord (an aristocrat who owned the land). Some of the peasants were descendants of the coloni (tenant farmers) of the late Roman Empire; others were the sons and daughters of slaves, now provided with a small plot of land; and a few were people of free Frankish origin who for various reasons had come down in the world. At the lower end of the social scale, the status of Franks and Romans had become identical.

Romans (or, more precisely, Gallo-Romans) and Franks had also merged at the elite level. Although people south of the Loire River continued to be called Romans and people to the north Franks, their cultures—their languages, their settlement patterns, their newly military way of life—were strikingly similar.

The language that aristocrats spoke and (often) read depended on location, not ethnicity. Among the many dialects in the Frankish kingdoms, some were Germanic, especially to the east and north, but most were derived from Latin, yet no longer the Latin of Cicero. At the end of the sixth century, Bishop **Gregory of Tours** (r. 573–594)—the man who described Clovis's coronation at the start of this chapter—wrote, "Though my speech is rude, ... to my surprise, it has often been said by men of our day, that few understand the learned words of the rhetorician but many the rude language of the common people." This beginning to Gregory's *Histories*, a valuable source for the Merovingian period, testifies to Latin's transformation; Gregory expected that his "rude" Latin—the plain Latin of everyday speech—would be understood and welcomed by the general public.

The Frankish elites, like Frankish peasants, tended to live in the countryside rather than in cities. In fact, peasants and aristocrats tended to live together in villages. In many cases, a village consisted of a large central building (probably for the aristocratic household to use), sometimes with stone foundations. Surrounding the central building were smaller structures, some of which were houses for peasant families, who lived with their livestock. Such villages might boast populations a bit over one hundred.

The elites of the Merovingian period cultivated military—rather than civilian—skills. They went on hunts and wore military-style clothing: the men wore trousers, a heavy belt, and a long cloak; both men and women bedecked themselves with jewelry. As hardened warriors, or wanting to appear so, aristocrats no longer lived in grand villas, choosing instead modest wooden structures without baths or heating systems. That explains why the village great house and the smaller ones nearby looked very much alike.

Sometimes villages formed around old villas. In other instances, they clustered around sacred sites. Tours—where Gregory was bishop—exemplified this new-style settlement. In Roman times, Tours was a thriving city; around 400, its population diminished, and it constructed walls around its shrunken perimeter. By Gregory's day, however, it had gained a new center *outside* the city walls. There a church had been built to house the remains of the most important and venerated person in the locale: St. Martin. This fourth-century soldier-turned-monk was long dead, but his relics remained at Tours, where he had served as bishop. The population of the surrounding countryside was pulled to his church as if to a magnet. Seen as a miracle worker, Martin acted as the representative of God's power: a protector, healer, and avenger. In Gregory's view, Martin's relics (or rather God *through* Martin's relics) not only cured the lame and sick but even prevented armies from plundering local peasants.

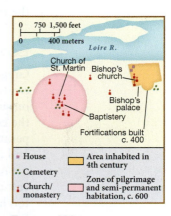

Tours, c. 600

The veneration of saints and their relics marked a major departure from practices of the classical age, in which the dead had been banished from the presence of the living. In the medieval world (see Terms of History on page 278), the holy dead held the place of highest esteem. The church had no formal procedures for proclaiming saints in the early Middle Ages, but holiness was "recognized" by influential local people and the local bishop. Everyone at

TERMS OF HISTORY Medieval

How did the word *medieval* come into being, and why is it a derogatory term today? No one who lived in the Middle Ages thought of himself or herself as "medieval." People did not say they lived in the Middle Ages. The whole idea of the Middle Ages began in the sixteenth century. At that time, writers decided to call their own age the Renaissance (French for "rebirth") because, in their view, it revived the civilizations of ancient Greek and Rome. They dubbed the period in between—from about 600 to about 1400—with a Latin term: the *medium aevum*, or the "middle age." It was not a flattering term. Renaissance writers considered the *medium aevum* a single unfortunate, barbaric, and ignorant period.

Only with the Romantic movement of the nineteenth century and the advent of history as an academic discipline did writers begin to divide that middle age into several ages. Often they divided it into three periods: Early (c. 600–1100), High (c. 1100–1300), and Late (c. 1300–1400). Today there is no hard-and-fast rule about this terminology: Chapter 11 of this book, for example, covers the period 1150–1215 as the High Middle Ages.

The period before the High Middle Ages was sometimes called the Dark Ages, a term that immediately brings to mind doom and gloom. However, recent research disputes this view of the period, stressing instead its creativity, multiethnicity, and localism.

Newspaper reporters and others still sometimes use *medieval* as a negative term: for example, by calling a primitive prison system "medieval." Little do they know that when they do that, they are stuck in the sixteenth century.

Tours (and beyond) recognized Martin as a saint, and to tap into the power of his relics, the local bishop built a church directly over his tomb. For a man like Gregory of Tours and his flock, the church building was, above all, a home for the relics of the saints.

Economic Activity in a Peasant Society

Gregory wrote about some sophisticated forms of economic activity that existed in early medieval Europe, such as long-distance trade, which depended on surpluses. But he also wrote about famines. Most people in his day lived on the edge of survival. From the fifth to the mid-eighth century, the mean temperature in Europe dropped. This climatic change spelled shortages in crops and the likelihood of famine and disease.

An underlying reason for these calamities was the weakness of the agricultural economy. Even the meager population of the Merovingian world was too large for the land's productive capacities. The heavy, wet soils of northern Europe were difficult to turn and aerate. Technological limitations meant a minimal food supply, and agricultural work was not equitably or efficiently allocated and managed. A leisure class of landowning warriors and churchmen lived off the work of peasant men, who tilled the fields, and peasant women, who wove cloth, gardened, brewed, and baked.

Occasionally surpluses developed, either from good harvests in peacetime or plunder in warfare, and these changed hands, although rarely in an impersonal, commercial manner. Most economic transactions of the seventh and eighth centuries were part of a gift economy, a system of give-and-take: the rich took plunder, demanded tribute, hoarded harvests, and minted coins—all to be redistributed to friends, followers, and dependents. Powerful men and women amassed gold, silver, ornaments, and jewelry in their treasuries and grain in their storehouses to mark their power, add to their prestige, and demonstrate their generosity. Those benefiting from the gifts of the rich included monasteries and churches. The gift economy was the dynamic behind most of the exchanges of goods and money in the Merovingian period.

However, some economic activity in this period was purely commercial and impersonal. Long-distance traders transported slaves and raw materials such as furs and honey from areas of northern Europe such as the British Isles and Sweden. These they sold to traders in Byzantium and the Islamic world, returning home with luxuries and manufactured goods such as silks and papyrus. Byzantine, Islamic, and western European descendants of the Roman Empire kept in tenuous contact with one another by making voyages for trade, diplomatic ventures, and pilgrimages. Seventh- and eighth-century sources speak of Byzantines, Syrians, and Jews as the chief intermediaries of such long-distance trade. Many of these merchants lived in the still-thriving port cities of the Mediterranean. Gregory of Tours associated Jews with commerce, complaining that they sold things "at a higher price than they were worth."

Although the population of the Merovingian world was overwhelmingly Christian, Jews were integrated into every aspect of secular life. They used Hebrew in worship, but otherwise they spoke the same languages as Christians and used Latin in their legal documents. Jews dressed as everyone else did, and they engaged in the same occupations. Many Jews planted and tended vineyards, partly because of the importance of wine in synagogue services and partly because they could easily sell the surplus. Some Jews were rich landowners, with slaves and dependent peasants working for them; others were independent peasants of modest means. Some Jews lived in towns with a small Jewish quarter that included both homes and synagogues, but most Jews, like their Christian neighbors, lived on the land.

The Powerful in Merovingian Society

The Merovingian elite—who included monks and bishops as well as kings and lay aristocrats—obtained their power through hereditary wealth, status, and personal influence. Many of them were extremely wealthy. The will drawn up by a bishop and aristocrat named Bertram of Le Mans, for example, shows that he owned estates—some from his family, others given him as gifts—scattered all over Gaul.

Along with administering their estates, male aristocrats spent their time honing their proficiency as warriors. To be a great warrior in Merovingian society meant perfecting the virtues necessary for leading armed men. Merovingian warriors affirmed their skills and comradeship in the hunt: they proved their worth in the regular taking of plunder, and they rewarded their followers afterward at generous banquets.

Merovingian aristocrats also spent time with their families. The focus of marriage was procreation. Important both to the survival of aristocratic families and to the transmission of their property and power, marriage was an expensive institution. It had two forms: in the most formal, the man gave a generous dowry of clothes, livestock, and land to his bride; after the marriage was consummated, he gave her a "morning gift" of furniture. Very wealthy men also might support one or more concubines, who enjoyed a less formal type of marriage, receiving a morning gift but no dowry. Churchmen in this period had many ideas about the value of marriages, but in practice they had little to do with the matter. Marriage was a family decision and a family matter: the couple exchanged rings before witnesses, and later the bride moved to the house of the groom.

In the sixth century, some aristocrats still patterned their lives on the old Roman model, teaching their children classical Latin poetry and writing to one another in phrases borrowed from Virgil. But this changed in the seventh century. The spoken language had become very different from classical Latin, and written Latin was learned mainly to read the Book of Psalms. Just as in Byzantium, a religious culture that emphasized Christian piety over the classics was developing in Europe.

The arrival on the continent around 590 of the Irish monk St. Columbanus (543–615) heightened this emphasis on religion. Columbanus's brand of monasticism—which stressed exile, devotion, and discipline—found much favor among the Merovingian elite. The monasteries St. Columbanus established in both Gaul and Italy attracted local recruits from the aristocracy. Some were grown men and women; others were young children, given to the monastery by their parents in the ritual called **oblation**. This practice was not only accepted but also often considered essential for the spiritual well-being of both the children and their families.

Alongside monks, bishops ranked among the most powerful men in Merovingian society. Gregory of Tours, for example, considered himself the protector of "his citizens." When representatives of the king came to collect taxes in Tours, Gregory stopped them in their tracks, warning them that St. Martin would punish anyone who tried to tax his people. "That very day," Gregory reported, "the man who had produced the tax rolls caught a fever and died." Little wonder that Frankish kings stopped collecting the old Roman land tax.

Like other aristocrats, many bishops were married, even though church councils demanded celibacy. As the overseers of priests and guardians of morality, bishops were expected to refrain from sexual relations with their wives. Since bishops were ordinarily appointed late in life, long after they had raised a family, this restriction did not threaten the ideal of a procreative marriage.

Noble parents generally decided whom their daughters would marry, for such unions bound together not only husbands and wives but entire extended families as well. Aristocratic brides received a dowry from their families in addition to their husband's gift. This was often land, over which they had some control; if they were widowed without children, they were allowed to sell, give away, exchange, or rent out their dowry estates as they wished. Moreover, people could give property to their women kinfolk outright in written testaments. Many aristocratic women were very rich, and like rich men, they frequently gave generous gifts to the church from their vast possessions.

Though legally under the authority of her husband, a Merovingian married woman often found ways to exercise some power and control over her life. Tetradia, wife of Count Eulalius, left her husband, taking all his gold and silver, because, as Gregory of Tours tells us,

> he was in the habit of sleeping with the women-servants in his household. As a result he neglected his wife. . . . As a result of his excesses, he ran into serious debt, and to meet this he stole his wife's jewelry and money.

A court of law ordered Tetradia to repay Eulalius four times the amount she had taken from him, but she was allowed to keep and live on her own property.

Other women were able to exercise behind-the-scenes control through their sons. A woman named Artemia, for example, used the prophecy that her son Nicetius would become a bishop to prevent her husband from becoming a bishop himself. After Nicetius fulfilled the prophecy, he nevertheless remained at home with his mother well into his thirties, working alongside the servants and teaching the younger children to read the Psalms.

Some women exercised direct power. Rich widows with fortunes to bestow wielded enormous influence. Some Merovingian women were abbesses, rulers in their own right over female monasteries and sometimes over "double monasteries," with separate facilities for men and women. Monasteries under the control of abbesses could be substantial centers of population: the convent at Laon, for example, had three hundred nuns in the seventh century. Because women lived in populous convents or were monopolized by rich men able to support several wives or mistresses at one time, unattached aristocratic women were scarce.

Atop the aristocracy were the Merovingian kings, rulers of the Frankish kingdoms. The Merovingian dynasty (c. 486–751) owed its longevity to good political sense: from the start it allied itself with local lay aristocrats and ecclesiastical (church) authorities. Bishops and abbots bolstered the power that kings also gained from their leadership in war, their access to the lion's share of plunder, and their takeover of the public lands and legal framework of Roman administration. Religious leaders often worked in tandem with Merovingian queens; the piety of a woman like Balthild (d. 680), wife of King Clovis II, benefited the church while adding luster to the royal court (see Primary Source Analysis on page 282). Such courts also functioned as schools for the sons of the elite. When kings sent officials—counts and dukes—to rule in their name in various regions of their kingdoms, these regional governors worked with and married into the aristocratic families who had long controlled local affairs.

Praising a Merovingian Queen

Queen Balthild (d. 680) was the wife of Merovingian King Clovis II. Her anonymous biographer, quite likely a nun writing shortly after Balthild's death, praised her for her piety. The excerpts below explore her life as wife of a king and later regent, ruling on behalf of her young sons. Further on in this 19-chapter biography, she "retired"—or perhaps was forced by political enemies—to enter a monastery.

CHAPTER 4

As she had the grace of prudence conferred upon her by God, with watchful eagerness she obeyed the king as her lord, and to the princes she showed herself a mother, to the priests as a daughter, and to the young and the adolescents as the best possible nurse. And she was friendly to all, loving the priests as fathers, the monks as brothers, the poor as a faithful nurse does, and giving to each generous alms. She preserved the honor of the princes and kept their fitting counsel, always exhorting the young to religious studies and humbly and steadfastly petitioning the king for the churches and the poor. While still in secular dress, she desired to serve Christ; she prayed daily, tearfully commending herself to Christ, the heavenly king. And the pious king [Clovis], taking care of her faith and devotion, gave his faithful servant, Abbot Genesius, to her as support, and through his hands she served the priests and the poor, fed the hungry, clothed the naked with garments, and conscientiously arranged the burial of the dead. Through him she sent most generous alms of gold and silver to the monasteries of men and women. And this servant of Christ, Lord Genesius, was later ordained bishop of Lyon at Christ's command. He was at that time regularly in the court of the Neustrians [the region around Paris. Clovis II was the king of Neustria and Burgundy.]. And through him, as we said, the lady Balthild, along with the authority of King Clovis and at the petition of this servant of God [Genesius], provided the generous alms of the king to all the poor throughout many places.

CHAPTER 5

What more is there to say? At God's command, her husband, King Clovis, went forth from his body, leaving a lineage of sons with their mother. In his place after him, his son, the late King Clothar [III], took the throne of the Franks and then also with the excellent princes, Chrodbert, bishop of Paris, Lord Audoin, and Ebroin, mayor of the palace, along with the other great magnates and very many of the rest [of the aristocracy]. And, indeed, the kingdom of the Franks was maintained in peace. Then indeed, a little while ago, the Austrasians [the region around Metz; this was the center of the third Merovingian kingdom] peacefully received her son Childeric [II] as king in Austrasia by the arrangement of Lady Balthild and, indeed, through the advice of the great magnates. But the Burgundians and the Neustrians were united. And we believe that, with God guiding, and in accordance with the great faith of Lady Balthild, these three kingdoms kept the harmony of peace among themselves.

CHAPTER 6

At that time it happened that the heresy of simony [buying church offices] stained the Church of God with its depraved practice in which they received the rank of bishop by paying a price for it. By the will of God [acting] through her, and at the urging of the good priests, the above-mentioned Lady Balthild stopped this impious evil so that no one would set a price on the taking of holy orders. Through her, the Lord also arranged for another very evil and impious practice to cease, one in which many men were more eager to kill their offspring than to provide for them in order to avoid the royal exactions which were inflicted upon them by custom, and from which they incurred a very heavy loss of property. This the lady prohibited for her own salvation so that no one presumed to do it. Because of this deed, truly a great reward awaits her.

Source: *Late Merovingian France: History and Hagiography (640–720),* eds. and trans. Paul Fouracre and Richard A. Gerberding (Manchester: Manchester University Press, 1996), pp. 121–25.

QUESTIONS TO CONSIDER

1. What sorts of virtues did the author stress and why?
2. How and why did a queen's reputation for piety enhance the power of Merovingian kings?

Both kings and aristocrats benefited from a powerful royal authority. The king acted as arbitrator and intermediary for the competing interests of the aristocrats. Gregory of Tours's history of the sixth century is filled with stories of bitter battles between Merovingian kings, as royal brothers fought continuously. Yet what seemed to the bishop like royal weakness and violent chaos was in fact one way the kings contained local aristocratic tensions, organizing them on one side or another, and preventing them from spinning out of royal control. By the beginning of the seventh century, three relatively stable Frankish kingdoms had emerged: Austrasia to the northeast; Neustria to the west, with its capital city at Paris; and Burgundy, incorporating the southeast (see Map 8.3 on page 273).

As the power of the kings in the seventh century increased, however, so did the might of their chief court official, the mayor of the palace. As we shall see, one mayoral family allied with the Austrasian aristocracy would in the following century displace the Merovingian dynasty and establish a new royal line, the Carolingians.

Christianity and Classical Culture in the British Isles

The Merovingian kingdoms exemplify some of the ways in which Roman and non-Roman traditions combined; the British Isles show others. Ireland had never been part of the Roman Empire, but the Irish people were early converts to Christianity, as were people in Roman Britain and parts of Scotland. Invasions by various Celtic and Germanic groups—particularly the Anglo-Saxons, who gave their name to England ("land of the Angles")—redrew the religious boundaries. Ireland, largely free of invaders, remained Christian. Scotland, also relatively untouched by invaders, had been slowly Christianized by the Irish from the west and in early years by the British from the south. England, which emerged from the invasions as a mosaic of about a dozen kingdoms ruled by separate Anglo-Saxon kings, became largely pagan until it was actively converted in the seventh century.

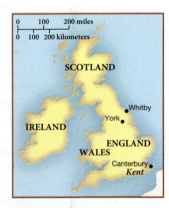

The British Isles

Christianity was introduced to Anglo-Saxon England from two directions. To the north, Irish monks brought their own brand of Christianity. Converted in the fifth century by St. Patrick and other missionaries, the Irish had evolved a church organization that corresponded to its rural clan organization. There, abbots and abbesses were more powerful than bishops. The Irish missionaries to England were monks, and they set up monasteries modeled on those at home—out in the countryside.

In the south, Christianity came to England in 597 via missionaries sent by the pope known as **Gregory the Great** (r. 590–604). These men, led by Augustine (not the same Augustine as the bishop of Hippo discussed on page 230), intended to convert the king and people of Kent, the southernmost kingdom, and then work their way northward. Augustine and his party brought with them Roman practices at odds with those of Irish Christianity, stressing ties to the pope and the authority of bishops. Using the Roman model, they divided England into territorial units, called dioceses, headed by an archbishop and bishops. Augustine became archbishop of Canterbury. Because he was a monk, he set up a monastery right next to his cathedral, and having a community of monks attached to the bishop's church became a characteristic of the English church. Later a second archbishopric was added in the north of England, at York.

A major bone of contention between the Roman and Irish churches involved the calculation of the date of Easter, celebrated by Christians as the day on which Christ rose from the dead. Because everyone agreed that believers could not be saved unless they observed Christ's resurrection properly and on the right date, the conflict was bitter. It was resolved by Oswy, king of Northumbria, who organized a meeting of churchmen, the **Synod of Whitby**, in 664. Convinced that Rome spoke with the voice of St. Peter, who was said in the New Testament to hold the keys of the kingdom of heaven, Oswy chose the Roman date. His decision paved the way for the triumph of the Roman brand of Christianity in England.

The authority of St. Peter was only one of the attractions of Roman Christianity. Rome had great prestige as a treasure trove of knowledge, piety, and holy objects. Benedict Biscop (c. 628–690), the founder of two important English monasteries, made many difficult trips to Rome, bringing back relics, liturgical vestments, and even a cantor to teach his monks the proper melodies in a time before written musical notation. Above all, he went to Rome to get books. At his monasteries in the north of England, he built up a grand library. In Anglo-Saxon England, as in Scotland and Ireland, all of which lacked a strong classical tradition from Roman times, a book was considered a precious object, to be decorated as finely as a jewel-studded reliquary (see the chapter-opening image on page 258).

The Anglo-Saxons and Irish Celts had a thriving oral culture but extremely limited uses for writing. Books became valuable only when these societies converted to Christianity. Just as Islamic reliance on the Qur'an made possible a literary culture under the Umayyads, so Christian dependence on the Bible, liturgy, and the writings of the church fathers helped make England and Ireland centers of literature and learning in the seventh and eighth centuries. Men like Benedict Biscop soon sponsored other centers of learning, using texts from the classical past. Although women did not establish famous schools, many abbesses ruled over monasteries that stressed Christian learning. Latin writings, even pagan texts, were studied diligently, in part because Latin was so foreign a language on the British Isles that mastering it required systematic and formal study. One of Benedict Biscop's pupils was Bede ("the Venerable," 673–735), an Anglo-Saxon monk and a historian of extraordinary breadth. Bede in turn taught a new generation of monks who became advisers to eighth-century rulers.

Much of the vigorous pagan Anglo-Saxon oral tradition was adapted to Christian culture. Bede encouraged and supported the use of the Anglo-Saxon language, urging priests, for example, to use it when they instructed their flocks. In contrast to other European regions, where Latin was the primary written language in the seventh and eighth centuries, England made use of the vernacular—the language normally spoken by the people. Written Anglo-Saxon (or Old English) was used in every aspect of English life, from government to entertainment.

Page from the Lindisfarne Gospels
The lavishly illuminated manuscript known as the Lindisfarne Gospels, of which this is one page, was probably produced in the first third of the eighth century. For the monks at Lindisfarne (a tidal island off the northeast coast of England) and elsewhere in the British Isles, books were precious objects. The page shown here depicts the Evangelist St. Mark, writing while also holding a book. Above his halo is his symbol, a winged lion; it is blowing a trumpet while its front paws rest on a book. What book might St. Mark and the lion be holding? (The British Library/The Image Works.)

The decision at the Synod of Whitby to favor Roman Christianity tied the English church to Rome by doctrine, friendship, and conviction. The Anglo-Saxon monk and bishop Wynfrith took the Latin name Boniface to symbolize his loyalty to the Roman church. Preaching on the continent, Boniface (d. 754) set up churches in Germany and Gaul that, like those in England, looked to Rome for leadership and guidance. Boniface was one of those travelers from Rome who went to Trier to check on the bishop's piety. He found it badly wanting! Boniface's efforts to reform the Frankish church gave the papacy new importance in Europe.

Unity in Spain, Division in Italy

Southern Gaul, Spain, and Italy, unlike the British Isles, had long been part of the Roman Empire and preserved many of its traditions. Nevertheless, as these areas were settled and fought over by new peoples, their histories diverged dramatically. When the Merovingian king Clovis (r. 481/482–511) defeated the Visigoths in 507, the Visigothic kingdom, which had sprawled across southern Gaul into Spain, was dismembered. By midcentury, the Franks had come into possession of most of its remnants in southern Gaul.

In Spain, the Visigothic king Leovigild (r. 569–586) established territorial control by military might. But no ruler could hope to maintain his position in Visigothic Spain without the support of the Hispano-Roman population, which included both the great landowners and leading bishops—and their backing was unattainable while the Visigoths remained Arian Christians, who maintained that Christ was not identical with God (see page 232). Leovigild's son Reccared (r. 586–601) took the necessary step in 587, converting to Roman Catholic Christianity. Two years later, at the Third Council of Toledo, most of the Arian bishops followed their king by announcing their conversion to Catholicism.

Thereafter, the bishops and kings of Spain cooperated to a degree unprecedented in other regions. While the king gave the churchmen free rein to set up their own hierarchy (with the bishop of Toledo at the top) and to meet regularly at synods to regulate and reform the church, the bishops in turn supported their Visigothic king, who ruled as a minister of

Visigothic Spain, c. 624

Votive Crown of King Recceswinth
The Church and the king of Spain were closely allied. After Reccared's conversion, the Spanish bishops recognized the Visigothic kings as successors of Constantine, and they anointed them, daubing them with holy oil like the Old Testament kings. The kings, in turn, supported the Church. This gorgeous crown made of gold and inlaid with rock crystal, pearls, and gems, was a gift of Visigothic King Recceswinth (r. 649–672) to a church. Its letters spell out "King Recceswinth offers this." This crown, like others like it, was not meant to be worn but rather hung over the altar during the liturgy. (Museo Arqueológico Nacional, Madrid, Spain/Photo (c) Tarker/Bridgeman Images.)

the Christian people. Rebellion against him was tantamount to rebellion against Christ. The Spanish bishops reinforced this idea by anointing the king, daubing him with holy oil in a ritual that paralleled the ordination of priests and demonstrated divine favor. Toledo, the city where the highest bishop presided, was also where the kings were "created" through anointment. While the bishops in this way made the king's cause their own, their lay counterparts, the great landowners, helped supply the king with troops, allowing him to maintain internal order and repel his external enemies.

Ironically, it was precisely the centralization and unification of the Visigothic kingdom that proved its undoing. When the Arabs arrived in 711, they needed only to kill the king, defeat his army, and capture Toledo to take the kingdom.

By contrast, in Italy the Lombard king faced a hostile papacy in the center of the peninsula and insubordinate dukes in the south. Theoretically the dukes of Benevento and Spoleto were royal officers, but in fact they ruled independently. Although many Lombards were Catholics, others were Arian. The "official" religion of the Lombards in Italy varied with the ruler in power. Their conversion to Catholic Christianity occurred gradually, ending only around the mid-seventh century. Partly as a result of this slow development, Lombard kings never gained the full support of the church.

Nevertheless, Lombard kings had strengths. Chief among these were the traditions of leadership associated with the royal dynasty, the kings' military ability, their control over large estates in northern Italy, and their hold on surviving Roman institutions. Lombard kings took advantage of the still-urban organization of Italian society and economy, assigning dukes to city bases and setting up a royal capital at Pavia. Recalling emperors like Constantine and Justinian, the kings built churches, monasteries, and other places of worship in the royal capital; they also maintained the city walls, issued laws, and minted coins. Revenues from tolls, sales taxes, port duties, and court fines filled their treasuries, although their inability to revive the Roman land tax was a major weakness. The greatest challenge for the Lombard kings came from sharing the peninsula with Rome. As soon as the kings began to make serious headway into southern Italy against the duchies of Spoleto

Lombard Italy, Early Eighth Century

and Benevento, the pope—located between north and south—began to fear for his own position and called on the Franks for help.

Political Tensions and the Power of the Pope

Around 600, the pope's position was ambiguous: he was both a ruler—successor of St. Peter and head of the church—and a subordinate, subject to the Byzantine emperor. Pope Gregory the Great in many ways laid the foundations for the papacy's spiritual and temporal ascendancy. During Gregory's reign, the papacy became the greatest landowner in Italy. Gregory organized the defenses of Rome and paid for its army; he heard court cases, made treaties, and provided welfare services. The missionary expedition Gregory sent to England was only a small part of his involvement in the rest of Europe.

A prolific author of spiritual works and biblical commentaries, Gregory digested and simplified the ideas of church fathers like St. Augustine of Hippo, making them accessible to a wider audience. His book *Pastoral Rule* was used as a guide for bishops throughout Europe.

Yet even Gregory was not independent, for he was subordinate to the emperor. For a long time the Byzantine views on dogma, discipline, and church administration prevailed at Rome. This authority began to unravel in the seventh century. Sheer distance, as well as diminishing imperial power in Italy, meant that the popes became, in effect, the leaders of the parts of Italy not controlled by the Lombards.

The gap between Byzantium and Rome widened in the early eighth century as Emperor Leo III tried to increase the taxes on papal property to pay for his war against the Arab invaders. The pope responded by leading a general tax revolt. Meanwhile, Leo's fierce policy of iconoclasm collided with the pope's tolerance of images. In Italy, as in other European regions, Christian piety focused more on relics than on icons. Nevertheless, the papacy would not allow sacred images and icons to be destroyed. The pope argued that holy images should be respected, though not worshipped.

These disputes with the emperor were matched by increasing friction between the pope and the Lombards. The Lombard kings had gradually managed to bring under their control the duchies of Spoleto and Benevento as well as part of the Exarchate of Ravenna. By the mid-eighth century, the popes feared that Rome would fall to the Lombards, and Pope Zachary (r. 741–752) looked northward for friends. He created an ally by giving his approval to the removal of the last Merovingian king and his replacement by the first Carolingian king, Pippin III (r. 751–768). In 753, Pope Stephen II (r. 752–757) called on Pippin to march to Italy with an army to fight the Lombards.

REVIEW QUESTION
What were the similarities and differences among the kingdoms that emerged in western Europe?

Conclusion

The Islamic world, Byzantium, and western Europe were heirs to the Roman Empire, but they built on its legacies in different ways. Muslims were the newcomers to the Roman world, but their religion, Islam, was influenced by

MAPPING THE WEST

Rome's Heirs, c. 750

The major political fact of the period 600–750 was the emergence of Islam and the creation of an Islamic state that reached from Spain to the Indus River. The Byzantine Empire, once a great power, was dwarfed—and half swallowed up—by its Islamic neighbor. To the west were fledgling European kingdoms, mere trifles on the world stage. The next centuries, however, would prove their resourcefulness and durability.

Analyzing the Map: How does the map's use of one color for Europe distort its real political situation c. 750?

Making Connections: What areas of the Byzantine Empire were incorporated into the Islamic world by 750, and what explains this change? (See Mapping the West in Chapter 7.)

---

both Jewish and Christian monotheism, each with roots in Roman culture. Under the guidance of Muhammad the Prophet, Islam became both a coherent theology and a way of life. Once the Muslim Arabs embarked on military conquests, they became the heirs of Rome in other ways: preserving Byzantine cities, hiring Syrian civil servants, and adopting Mediterranean artistic styles. Drawing on Roman and Persian traditions, the Umayyad dynasty created a powerful Islamic state, with a capital city in Syria and a culture that generally tolerated a wide variety of economic, religious, and social institutions as long as the conquered paid taxes to their Muslim overlords.

Byzantium directly inherited the central political institutions of Rome: its people called themselves Romans; its emperor was the Roman emperor; and its capital, Constantinople, was considered to be the new Rome. Byzantium also inherited the taxes, cities, laws, and Christian religion of Rome. The changes of the seventh and eighth centuries—contraction of territory, urban decline, disappearance of the old elite, and a ban on icons—whittled away at this Roman character. By 750, Byzantium was less Roman than it was a new, resilient political and cultural entity, a Christian state.

Western Europe also inherited—and transformed—Roman institutions. The Frankish kings built on Roman traditions that had earlier been modified by provincial and Germanic custom. In the seventh century, Anglo-Saxon England reimported the Roman legacy through Latin learning and the Christian religion. Visigothic kings in Spain converted from Arian to Roman Christianity and allied themselves with the Hispano-Roman elite. In Italy and at Rome itself, the traditions of the classical past endured. The roads remained, the cities of Italy survived (although depopulated), and both the popes and the Lombard kings ruled according to the traditions of Roman government.

Muslim, Byzantine, and western European societies all suffered the ravages of war. Social hierarchies became simpler, with the loss of "middle" groups like the curials at Byzantium and the near suppression of tribal affiliations among Muslims. Politics were tightly tied to religion: the Byzantine emperor was a religious force, the caliph was a religious and political leader, and western European kings allied with churchmen. Despite their many differences, all these leaders had a common understanding of their place in a divine scheme: they were God's agents on earth, ruling over God's people. In the next century they would consolidate their power. Little did they know that, soon thereafter, local elites would be able to assert greater authority than ever before.

Chapter 8 Review

Key Terms and People

Be sure that you can identify the term or person and explain its historical significance.

Muhammad (p. 260)	Umayyad caliphate (p. 265)	Gregory of Tours (p. 277)
Qur'an (p. 262)	Heraclius (p. 268)	oblation (p. 280)
Hijra (p. 263)	Lombards (p. 269)	Gregory the Great (p. 283)
jihad (p. 263)	icon (p. 271)	Synod of Whitby (p. 284)
Five Pillars of Islam (p. 263)	iconoclasm (p. 272)	
Shi'ite (p. 265)	Merovingian dynasty (p. 273)	

Review Questions

1. How and why did the Muslims conquer so many lands in the period 632–750?

2. What stresses did the Byzantine Empire endure in the seventh and eighth centuries, and how was iconoclasm a response to those stresses?

3. What were the similarities and differences among the kingdoms that emerged in western Europe, and how did their histories combine and diverge?

Making Connections

1. What were the similarities and the differences in political organizations of the Islamic, Byzantine, and western European societies in the period 600–750?

2. Compare and contrast the roles of religion in the Islamic, Byzantine, and western European worlds in the period 600–750.

3. Compare the material resources of the Islamic, Byzantine, and western European governments in the period 600–750.

Important Events

c. 486–751	Merovingian dynasty
c. 570–632	Life of Muhammad, prophet of Islam
572	Lombards conquer northern Italy
r. 573–594	Bishop Gregory of Tours
587	Conversion of Visigothic King Reccared
c. 590	Arrival of Irish monk Columbanus in Gaul
590–604	Papacy of Pope Gregory the Great
603–623	War between Byzantium and Persia
622	Hijra to Medina; year 1 of the Islamic calendar
624	Muhammad and Meccans fight battle of Badr
661–750	Umayyad caliphate
664	Synod of Whitby; English king opts for Roman form of Christianity
r. 717–741	Emperor Leo III the Isaurian
726–787	Period of iconoclasm at Byzantium
d. 754	Boniface, reformer of the Frankish church

Consider three events

Papacy of Pope Gregory the Great (r. 590–604); Hijra to Medina, year 1 of the Islamic calendar (622); and Emperor Leo III the Isaurian (r. 717–741). How did these events reshape religious faith? What were the broader implications of those changes for social and political life?

Suggested References

Hoyland offers insight into Islam's conquests. Haldon surveys the early Byzantine Empire. Fleming gives a brilliant account of the British Isles, while Alexander Callander Murray's collection of sources illuminates the Frankish world.

*Bede. *A History of the English Church and People.* Trans. Leo Sherley-Price. 1991.

*Byzantine Sourcebook: http://www.fordham.edu/halsall/sbook1c.html

Cameron, Averil. *The Byzantines.* 2006.

Fleming, Robin. *Britain after Rome: The Fall and Rise, 400 to 1070.* 2010.

*Gregory of Tours. *The History of the Franks.* Trans. Lewis Thorpe. 1976.

Haldon, John. *The Empire that Would Not Die: The Paradox of Eastern Roman Survival, 640–740.* 2016.

Hoyland, Robert G. *In God's Path: The Arab Conquests and the Creation of an Islamic Empire.* 2015.

*Islamic Sourcebook: http://www.fordham.edu/halsall/islam/islamsbook.html

*Murray, Alexander Callander. *From Roman to Merovingian Gaul: A Reader.* 2000.

Smith, Julia M. H. *Europe after Rome: A New Cultural History 500–1000.* 2005.

Stathakopoulos, Dionysios. *A Short History of the Byzantine Empire.* 2014.

Wickham, Chris. *Framing the Early Middle Ages: Europe and the Mediterranean, 400–800.* 2005.

*Primary source.

From Centralization to Fragmentation

750–1050

In 841, a fifteen-year-old boy named William went to serve at the court of Charles the Bald, king of the Franks. William's father, Bernard, was an extremely powerful noble. His mother, Dhuoda, was a well-educated, pious, and able woman; she administered the family's estates in the south of France while her husband was occupied with politics at court. In 841, however, politics had become a dangerous business. King Charles was fighting with his brothers over his portion of the Frankish Empire, and he doubted Bernard's loyalty. In fact, William was sent to Charles's court as a kind of hostage, to ensure Bernard's fidelity. Anxious about her son, Dhuoda wrote a handbook of advice for William, outlining his moral obligations. She emphasized duty to his father over loyalty to the king:

> Royal and imperial . . . power seem preeminent in the world, and the custom of men is to [put] their names ahead of all others. . . . But despite all this, I caution you to render first to him whose son you are special, faithful, steadfast loyalty as long as you shall live. . . . So I urge you . . . that first of all you love God. . . . Then love, fear, and cherish your father.

William heeded his mother's words, with tragic results: when Bernard ran afoul of Charles and was executed, William died in a failed attempt to avenge his father.

« King Charles Receives a Bible The importance of loyalty is clear in this ninth-century depiction of King Charles the Bald receiving a book. The painting appears at the very end of the manuscript (a large and splendid bible) accompanied by two poems. In the painting, the king sits on a throne. Two courtiers flank him on either side, and beside each of them is a warrior. Two canons from the monastery of St. Martin at Tours, where the bible was made, hold it aloft, while all the others make gestures of praise and prayer. Above, the hand of God reaches down to bless the king, whose throne touches the very scarf of heaven. The first poem begins "Kind King Charles, flourish with the power of the Almighty. . . . [You are] the patron of the church, a solace to the clergy and people." (From the *First Bible of Charles the Bald*, c. 843–851/Bibliothèque Nationale, Paris, France/Bridgeman Images.)

CHAPTER PREVIEW

The Byzantine Emperor and Local Elites
In what ways did the Byzantine emperor expand his power, and in what ways was that power checked?

The Rise and Fall of the Abbasid Caliphate
What forces contributed to the fragmentation of the Islamic world in the tenth and eleventh centuries, and what forces held it together?

The Carolingian Empire
What were the strengths and weaknesses of Carolingian institutions of government, warfare, and defense?

After the Carolingians: The Emergence of Local Rule
After the dissolution of the Carolingian Empire, what political systems developed in western, northern, eastern, and central Europe, and how did these systems differ from one another?

Dhuoda's handbook reveals the volatile political atmosphere of the mid-ninth century, and her advice to her son points to one of its causes: a crisis of loyalty. Devotion to emperors, caliphs, and kings competed with allegiances to local authorities, which, in turn, vied with family loyalties. The period from 600 to 750 had seen the startling rise of Islam, the whittling away of Byzantium, and the beginnings of stable political and economic institutions in an impoverished Europe. The period from 750 to 1050 would see all three societies contend with internal issues of diversity, even as they became increasingly conscious of their unity and uniqueness. At the beginning of this period, rulers built up and dominated strong, united political communities. By the end, these realms had fragmented into smaller, more local units.

In Byzantium, military triumphs brought emperors enormous prestige. A renaissance (French for "rebirth")—that is, an important revival—of culture and art took place at Constantinople. Yet at the same time, new elites began to dominate the Byzantine countryside. In the Islamic world, a dynastic revolution in 750 ousted the Umayyads from the caliphate and replaced them with a new family, the Abbasids. The Abbasid caliphs moved their capital to the east, from Damascus to Baghdad. Even though the Abbasids' power began to ebb as regional Islamic rulers came to the fore, the Islamic world, too, saw a renaissance. In western Europe, **Charlemagne**—a Frankish king from a new dynasty, the Carolingians—forged a huge empire and presided over yet another cultural renaissance. Yet this newly unified kingdom was fragile, disintegrating within a generation of Charlemagne's death. In western Europe, even more than in the Byzantine and Islamic worlds, power fell into the hands of local lords.

Along the borders of these realms, new political entities began to develop, shaped by the religion and culture of their more dominant neighbors. Rus, the ancestor of Russia, grew up in the shadow of Byzantium, as did Bulgaria and Serbia. Western Europe cast its influence over central European states. Meanwhile, the borders of the Islamic world remained stable or were pushed back. By the year 1050, the contours of what were to become modern Europe and the Middle East were dimly visible.

CHAPTER FOCUS
What forces led to the dissolution—or weakening—of centralized governments in the period from 750 to 1050, and what institutions took their place?

CHAPTER TIMELINE

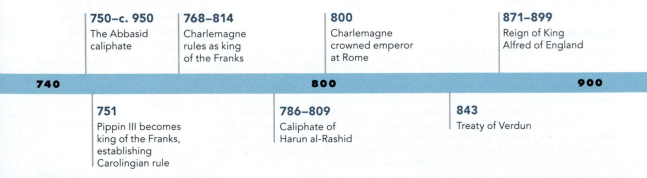

750–c. 950
The Abbasid caliphate

768–814
Charlemagne rules as king of the Franks

800
Charlemagne crowned emperor at Rome

871–899
Reign of King Alfred of England

740   800   900

751
Pippin III becomes king of the Franks, establishing Carolingian rule

786–809
Caliphate of Harun al-Rashid

843
Treaty of Verdun

The Byzantine Emperor and Local Elites

Between 750 and 850, Byzantium staved off Muslim attacks and began to rebuild. After 850, it expanded. Military victories brought new wealth and power to the imperial court, and the emperors supported a vast program of literary and artistic revival at Constantinople. But while the emperor dominated at the capital, a new landowning elite began to control the countryside. On its northern frontier, Byzantium helped create new Slavic realms.

Imperial Power

Byzantine rulers strengthened their army by dividing the *strategiai* into smaller districts called **themes**. Soldiers were recruited locally, and the inhabitants of each district were required to help pay for weapons and other supplies. While the *themes* handled attacks on Byzantine territory, *tagmata*—new mobile armies made up of the best troops—moved aggressively outward, beginning around 850. By 1025, the Byzantine Empire extended from the Danube in the north to the Euphrates in the south (Map 9.1).

Military victories gave new prestige and wealth to the army and to the imperial court. The Byzantine emperors drew revenues from vast and growing imperial estates. They could demand services and money from the general population at will, and they used their wealth to create a lavish court culture, surrounding themselves with servants, slaves, family members, and civil servants. From their powerful position, the emperors negotiated with other rulers, exchanging ambassadors and receiving and entertaining diplomats with elaborate ceremonies to express the serious, sacred, concentrated power of imperial majesty.

Some of the emperors' wealth derived from a prosperous agricultural economy organized for trade. Byzantine commerce depended on a careful balance of state regulation and individual enterprise. The emperor controlled craft and commercial guilds, while entrepreneurs organized most of the markets held throughout the empire. Foreign merchants were welcomed, but because

	955	**987–996**	**1001–1018**
	Battle of Lechfeld	Reign of King Hugh Capet of France	Byzantine conquest of Bulgaria

920	980		1060

929–1031	**962**	**c. 990**	**1000 or 1001**
Caliphate of Córdoba	King Otto I (r. 936–973) of Germany crowned emperor	Peace of God movement begins	Stephen I (r. 997–1038) crowned king of Hungary

MAP 9.1 The Byzantine Empire, 1025
Under Emperor Basil II, the Byzantine Empire once again embraced the entire area of the Balkans, while its eastern arm extended around the Black Sea and its southern fringe reached nearly to Tripoli. The year 1025 marked the Byzantine Empire's greatest size after the rise of Islam.

international trade intertwined with foreign policy, the Byzantine government insisted on controlling it, issuing privileges to certain "nations" (as the Venetians, Genoese, and Jews, among others, were called), regulating the fees they were obliged to pay and the services they had to render.

The emperors also negotiated privileges for their own traders in foreign lands. Byzantine merchants were guaranteed protection in Syria, for example, while the two governments split the income on sales taxes. Thus, Byzantine trade flourished in the Middle East and, thanks to Venetian intermediaries, with western Europe. Equally significant was trade to the north; from the conquerors of the area of Kiev, peoples known as the Kievan Rus, the Byzantines imported furs, slaves, wax, and honey.

The Macedonian Renaissance, c. 870–c. 1025

Flush with victory and recalling Byzantium's past glory, the emperors of the late ninth century revived classical intellectual pursuits. Basil I (r. 867–886) from Macedonia founded the imperial dynasty that presided over the so-called Macedonian renaissance. Basil's dynasty drew on an intellectual elite who—even in the anxious years of the eighth century—had persisted in studying the

The Macedonian Renaissance: The Veroli Casket (10th cent.) This plaque from a small casket made at Constantinople exemplifies the ways artists there inventively reused classical motifs and even improved on ancient carving techniques to produce an object for an unknown but clearly wealthy and cosmopolitan patron. Many of the themes depicted on the casket's seven plaques are comic, as if mocking ancient myths and persons, but the theme of this one is very serious: the sacrifice of Iphigenia by her father, Agamemnon. (Album/Oronoz/Newscom.)

classics. Now, with the empire slowly regaining its military eminence and with icons permanently restored in 843, this scholarly elite thrived again.

Under the patronage of the emperor and other members of the imperial court, scholars wrote summaries of classical literature, encyclopedias of ancient knowledge, and commentaries on classical authors. Some copied religious manuscripts and theological commentaries such as Bibles, Psalters, homilies, and liturgical texts. Liberated from the taboos of the iconoclastic period, some artists—such as those who carved the beautiful ivory casket on this page—exuberantly depicted classical myths and stories in a style that mimicked the ancients. Others merged classical and Christian traditions, as when an artist depicting King David, the supposed poet of the Psalms, borrowed from a picture of Orpheus, the beguiling musician of ancient Greek mythology. At the same time, still other artists picked up once again the frontal, hierarchical style of icons such as the one on page 271.

The *Dynatoi*: A New Landowning Elite

At Constantinople the emperor reigned supreme. But outside the capital, extremely powerful military families began to compete with imperial power. The *dynatoi* ("powerful men"), as this new hereditary elite was called, got rich on plunder and new lands taken in the aggressive wars of the tenth century. They took over or bought up whole villages, turning the peasants' labor to their benefit. For the most part they exercised their power locally, but they also sometimes occupied the imperial throne.

The Phocas family exemplifies the strengths as well as the weaknesses of the dynatoi. Probably originally from Armenia, they possessed military skills and exhibited loyalty to the emperor that together brought them high positions in both the army and imperial court in the last decades of the ninth century. In the tenth century, with new successes in the east, the Phocas family gained independent power. After some particularly brilliant victories, Nicephorus Phocas was declared emperor by his armies and ruled (as Nicephorus II Phocas) at Constantinople from 963 to 969. But opposing factions of the dynatoi brought him down. The mainstay of Phocas family power, as of that of all the dynatoi, was outside the capital, on the family's great estates.

As the dynatoi gained power, the social hierarchy of Byzantium began to resemble that of western Europe, where land owned by aristocratic lords was farmed by peasants bound by tax and service obligations to the fields they cultivated.

The Formation of Eastern Europe and Kievan Rus

The contours of modern eastern Europe took shape during the period from 850 to 950. By 800, Slavic settlements dotted the area from the Danube River down to Greece and from the Black Sea to Croatia. The ruler of the Bulgarians, called a *khagan*, presided over the largest realm. In the ninth century, Bulgarian rule stretched west to the Tisza River in modern Hungary. At about the same time, however, the Byzantine Empire began its own campaigns to conquer, convert, and control these Slavic regions, today known as the Balkans.

The Byzantine offensive began under Emperor Nicephorus I (r. 802–811), who waged war against the Slavs of Greece in the Peloponnese, set up a new Christian diocese there, organized it as a new military *theme*, and forcibly resettled Christians in the area to counteract Slavic paganism. The Byzantines followed this pattern of conquest as they pushed northward. By 900, Byzantium ruled all of Greece.

Still under Nicephorus I, the Byzantines launched a massive attack against the Bulgarians, took the chief city of Pliska, plundered it, burned it to the ground, and then marched against the khagan's encampment in the Balkan Mountains. But the Bulgarians successfully parried this attack. In 816, the two sides agreed to a temporary peace—though it was punctuated by hostilities—that lasted for most of the tenth century. Then Emperor **Basil II** (r. 976–1025) led the Byzantines in a slow, methodical conquest. Later dubbed the Bulgar-Slayer, Basil brought the entire region under Byzantine control and forced its ruler to accept the Byzantine form of Christianity. Around the same time, the Serbs, encouraged by Byzantium to oppose the Bulgarians, began to form the political community that would become Serbia.

Religion played an important role in the Byzantine conquest of the Balkans. In 863, the brothers Cyril and Methodius were sent as Christian missionaries from the Byzantines to the Slavs. Well educated in both classical and religious texts, they devised an alphabet for Slavic (until then an oral language) based on Greek forms. It was the ancestor of the modern Cyrillic alphabet used in Bulgaria, Serbia, and Russia today.

The region that would eventually become Russia lay outside the sphere of direct Byzantine rule in the ninth and tenth centuries. Like Serbia and Bulgaria, however, it came under increasingly strong Byzantine influence. In the ninth century, the Vikings—Scandinavian adventurers who ranged over vast stretches of ninth-century Europe seeking trade, riches, and land—penetrated the region below the Gulf of Finland, where they imposed their rule. By the end of the century, they had moved southward and had conquered the region around Kiev, a key commercial emporium. From there, the Rus, as the Viking conquerors were called, sailed the Dnieper River and crossed the Black Sea in search of markets for their slaves and furs.

The relationship between the Rus and Byzantium began with trade, continued with war, and ended with a common religion. By the beginning of the tenth century, the Rus had special trade privileges at Constantinople. But relations deteriorated, and the Rus unsuccessfully attacked Constantinople in 941. Soon they resumed trading with Byzantium.

Few Rus were Christian (most were polytheists, others Muslims or Jews), but that changed at the end of the tenth century, when good relations between the Rus and the Byzantines were sealed by the conversion of the Rus ruler Vladimir (r. 980–1015). In 988, Emperor Basil II sent his sister Anna to marry Vladimir in exchange for an army of Rus. To seal the alliance, Vladimir was baptized and took his brother-in-law's name. The general population seems to have quickly adopted the new religion.

Vladimir's conversion represented a wider pattern: the Christianization of Europe. In the southeast, orthodox Byzantine Christianity dominated, while in the west and northwest, Roman Catholicism tended to be most important. Slavic realms such as Moravia, Serbia, and Bulgaria adopted the Byzantine form of Christianity, while the rulers and peoples of Poland, Hungary, Denmark, and Norway were converted under the auspices of the Roman church. The conversion of the Rus was especially significant because they were geographically as close to the Islamic world as to the Christian and could conceivably have become Muslims. By converting to Byzantine Christianity, the Rus made themselves heirs to Byzantium and its church, customs, art, and political ideology. However, choosing the Byzantine form of Christianity, rather than the Roman Catholic, later served to isolate the region from western Europe.

For more than fifty years, Rus remained united under one ruler. But after 1054, civil wars broke out. Invasions by outsiders, particularly from the east, further weakened the Kievan rulers, who were eventually displaced by princes from the north. At the crossroads of East and West, Rus could meet and absorb a great variety of traditions, but its geographical position also opened it to unremitting military pressures.

The Rise and Fall of the Abbasid Caliphate

A new dynasty of caliphs—the Abbasids—first brought unity and then, in their decline, fragmentation to the Islamic world as regional rulers took over. Local traditions based on religious and political differences played an increasingly important role in people's lives. Yet, even in the eleventh century, the Islamic

WHAT WOULD YOU DO?

Imagine that you were a Rus living under the rule of Vladimir. To further good relations with Byzantium, Vladimir has just married the Byzantine emperor's sister, taken on the name of the emperor himself, and had himself baptized a Christian. Would you also convert to Christianity? Would it be a difficult decision? What sort of Christianity would it be?

REVIEW QUESTION

In what ways did the Byzantine emperor expand his power, and in what ways was that power checked?

world had a clear sense of its own unity, based on language, commerce, and artistic and intellectual achievements that transcended regional boundaries.

The Abbasid Caliphate, 750–936

In 750, a civil war ousted the Umayyads and raised the **Abbasids** to the caliphate. The Abbasids found support in an uneasy coalition of Shi'ites (the faction of Islam loyal to Ali's memory; see page 265) and non-Arabs who had been excluded from the Umayyad government. Under the Abbasids, the center of Islamic rule shifted from Damascus, with its roots in the Roman tradition, to the newly founded city of Baghdad in Iraq. Here the Abbasid caliphs adhered even more firmly than the Umayyads to Persian courtly models, with a centralized administration, a large staff, and control over the appointment of regional governors.

The Abbasid caliph Harun al-Rashid (r. 786–809) presided over a flourishing empire. His contemporary Frankish ruler, Charlemagne, was impressed with the elephant that Harun sent him as a gift, along with monkeys, spices, and medicines. Such items were mainstays of everyday commerce in Harun's Iraq. A mid-ninth-century catalog of imports listed "tigers, panthers, elephants, panther skins, rubies, white sandal [wood], ebony, and coconuts" from India as well as "silk, chinaware, paper, ink, peacocks, racing horses, saddles, felts [and] cinnamon" from China.

The Abbasid dynasty began to decline after Harun's death. While his sons waged war against each other, the caliphs lost control over many regions, including Syria and Egypt. They needed to recruit an army that would be loyal to them alone. This they found in "outsiders," many of them Turks from east of the Caspian Sea (today Kazakhstan). Many of the Turks, later called Mamluks, were bought as slaves. Once purchased, the Turks were freed and paid a salary. They were expert fighters, but the Abbasids needed a good tax base to be able to pay them, which they did not have. Serious uprisings just south of Baghdad kept huge swaths of territory outside the control of the caliphs. Other regions of the Islamic world easily went their own way when the caliphs lacked the money to keep them in line. In the tenth century, the caliphs became figureheads only, while independent regional rulers collected taxes and hired their own armies.

Thus, in the Islamic world, as in the Byzantine, new regional lords challenged the power of the central ruler. But the process advanced more quickly in Islamic territories than in Byzantine territories. Map 9.1 (page 296) correctly omits any indication of regional dynatoi because the key center of power in the Byzantine Empire continued to be Constantinople. Map 9.2, in contrast, shows how the Abbasid caliphate fragmented as local dynasties established themselves.

Regional Diversity in Islamic Lands

The splintering of the Islamic world was to be expected since central power there was based on the conquest of many diverse regions, each with its own deeply rooted traditions and culture. The Islamic religion, with its Sunni/Shi'ite

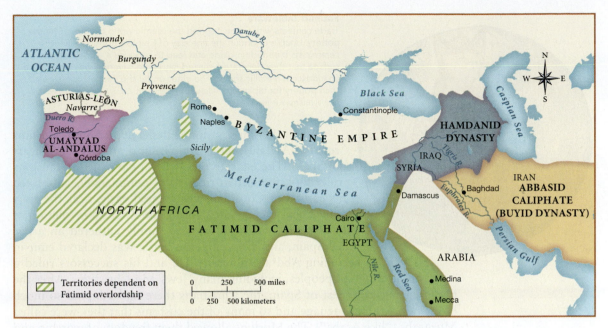

MAP 9.2 Islamic States, c. 1000
Comparing this map with Map 8.1 (page 265) will quickly demonstrate the fragmentation of the once united Islamic caliphate. In 750, one caliph ruled territory stretching from Spain to India. In 1000, there was more than one caliphate as well as several other ruling dynasties. The most important of those dynasties were the Fatimids, who began as organizers of a movement to overthrow the Abbasids. By 1000, the Fatimids had conquered Egypt and claimed hegemony over all of North Africa.

split, also became a source of polarization.* Western Europeans knew almost nothing about Muslims, calling all of them Saracens (from the Latin word for "Arabs") without distinction. But, as is still true today, Muslims were of different ethnicities, practiced different customs, and identified with different regions. With the fragmentation of political and religious unity, each of the tenth- and early-eleventh-century Islamic states built on local traditions under local rulers.

A good example of this trend was the Shi'ite group known as the **Fatimids**. Taking their name from Fatimah, daughter of Muhammad and wife of Ali, they established themselves in 909 as rulers in the region of North Africa now called Tunisia. The Fatimid ruler claimed to be not only the true imam—the descendant of Ali—but also the *mahdi*, the "divinely guided" messiah, come to bring justice on earth. In 969, the Fatimids declared themselves rulers of Egypt. Their dynasty lasted for about two hundred years. Fatimid leaders also controlled North Africa, Arabia, and even Syria for a time. They established a lavish court culture that rivaled the one at Baghdad, and they supported industries such as lusterware that had once been a monopoly of the Abbasids.

---

*The Shi'ites, originally followers of Ali, had by this time come to practice Islam differently from the Sunni. Each faction adhered to its own interpretation of the prophet Muhammad's life and message.

Fatimid Tableware
Trade contacts with China inspired the Islamic world to mimic Chinese pottery. Unable to obtain the fine clay of Chinese potters, Islamic ceramicists blended tin-oxide and lead to produce a white opaque surface that they decorated, glazed, and fired several times to produce an iridescent metallic sheen. The elites under the Fatimid rulers used such pottery for tableware. (Museum of Islamic Art, Cairo, Egypt/Werner Forman Archive/Bridgeman Images.)

While the Shiʿites dominated Egypt, Sunni Muslims ruled al-Andalus, the Islamic central and southern heart of Spain. The emirate of Córdoba (so called because its ruler took the secular title *emir*, "commander," and fixed his capital at Córdoba) was created early, near the start of the Abbasid caliphate. During the Abbasid revolution of 750, a member of the Umayyad family gathered an army, invaded Spain, and after only one battle was declared emir in 756, becoming Abd al-Rahman I. He and his successors ruled a broad range of peoples, including many Jews and Christians. After the initial Islamic conquest of Spain, the Christians there had adopted so much of the new Arabic language and so many of the customs that they were called Mozarabs ("like Arabs"). The Muslims allowed them freedom of worship and let them live according to their own laws. Some Mozarabs were content with their status, others converted to Islam, and still others intermarried.

Abd al-Rahman III (r. 912–961) was powerful enough to take the title of caliph, and the caliphate of Córdoba, which he created, lasted from 929 to 1031. His military triumphs were celebrated in poetry by Ibn ʿAbd Rabbihi, one of his courtiers (see Primary Source Analysis on pages 304–305). Under Abd al-Rahman, Spain flourished. Abd al-Rahman had diplomatic relations with European and Byzantine rulers, and during his reign, members of all religious groups enjoyed not only freedom of worship but also equal opportunity to rise in the civil service. Yet under later caliphs, al-Andalus experienced the same political fragmentation that was occurring everywhere else. The caliphate of Córdoba broke up in 1031, and rulers of small, independent regions, called *taifas*, took power.

Unity of Commerce and Language

Although the regions of the Islamic world were culturally and politically diverse, they maintained a measure of unity through trade networks and language. Their principal bond was Arabic, the language of the Qurʾan. At once poetic and sacred, Arabic was also the language of commerce and government from Baghdad to Córdoba. Moreover, despite political differences, borders were open. The primary reason for these open borders was Islam itself, but the openness extended to non-Muslims as well.

The commercial activities of the Tustari brothers, Jewish merchants from southern Iran, are a good example. By 1026, they had established a flourishing business in Egypt. Informal contacts with friends and family allowed them to import fine textiles from Iran to sell in Egypt and to export Egyptian fabrics to

A Princely Pyxis

A pyxis is a small container, and this one, about six inches high and carved out of ivory, was made for the younger son of Abd al-Rahman III, the caliph of Córdoba. The prince is depicted in a decorative lozenge, sitting on a rug and holding a bottle and a flower. One servant sits beside him to cool him with a fan; another stands and plays the lute. Underneath the rug are lions, symbols of power. Outside the princely enclosure, falconers stand by, ready to accompany the prince to the hunt. The whole scene suggests order, skill, and elegance, all important features of the Islamic renaissance. (Musée du Louvre, Paris, France/Peter Willi/Bridgeman Images.)

sell in Iran. The Tustari brothers held the highest rank in Jewish society and had contacts with Muslim rulers. At the same time, commercial networks even more vast than those of the Tustari family were common. Muslim merchants brought tin from England; salt and gold from Timbuktu in west-central Africa; amber, gold, and copper from Rus; and slaves from every region.

The Islamic Renaissance, c. 790–c. 1050

Unlike the Macedonian renaissance, which was concentrated in Constantinople, the Islamic renaissance occurred throughout the Islamic world. In fact, the dissolution of the caliphate into separate political entities multiplied the centers of learning and intellectual productivity. The Islamic renaissance was particularly dazzling in capital cities such as Córdoba (a city in southern Spain today), where tenth-century rulers presided over a brilliant court culture, patronizing scholars, poets, and artists.

Islamic scholarship was diverse. Some scholars read, translated, and commented on the works of ancient philosophers. Others studied astronomy or wrote on mathematical matters. Ibn Sina (980–1037), known in Christian Europe as Avicenna, wrote books on logic, the natural sciences, and physics. His *Canon of Medicine* systematized earlier treatises and reconciled them with his own experience as a physician.

Long before there were universities in Europe, there were institutions of higher learning in the Islamic world. A rich Muslim might demonstrate his piety and charity by establishing a madrasa, a school located within or attached to a mosque. Professors at madrasas held classes throughout the day on the interpretation of the Qur'an and literary or legal texts. Students, all male, attended the classes that suited their achievement level and interest. Most students paid a fee for learning, but there were also scholarship students. One tenth-century court official was so solicitous of the welfare of the scholars he supported that each day he set out iced refreshments, candles, and paper for them in his own kitchen.

The use of paper, made from flax and hemp or rags and vegetable fiber, points to a major difference among the Islamic, Byzantine, and (as we shall see) Carolingian renaissances. Byzantine scholars generally worked for the ruling classes. Their books, written on expensive parchment (made from animal skins), kept manuscripts out of the hands of all but the very rich. This was true

REVIEW QUESTION
What forces contributed to the fragmentation of the Islamic world in the tenth and eleventh centuries, and what forces held it together?

Ibn 'Abd Rabbihi Celebrates a Military Campaign in Verse

The tenth and eleventh centuries marked the golden age of Arabic poetry in al-Andalus. In the first of these centuries, the poets' patron was the emir or caliph at Córdoba. In the eleventh century, as al-Andalus broke up into taifas, each taifa ruler supported his own artists. One court poet for Abd al-Rahman III (r. 912–961) was Ibn 'Abd Rabbihi. In his long epic poem The Unique Necklace, he described the events of his day, including a military campaign undertaken by Abd al-Rahman in 306–307 (in the Islamic Calendar; 918–920 in the Christian calendar) against the rulers of León and Navarre to retaliate for their incursions into al-Andalus. The "hero" and "Imam" in the passages below are Abd al-Rahman himself.

The Year 306 (918 c.e.)

117. Then God retaliated against His enemies and decreed victory to His friends:

118. At the beginning of the year newly commencing, truth filled the soul of the hero,

119. For the purpose of the glorious Imām; the best of those begotten and the best begetter was

120. To take up the defense of the One, the Victorious, and to vent some of his anger upon the infidels.

121. So he mustered soldiers and troops and called together with his trumpet, both lord and vassal;

122. He enrolled [the men] of the borders and frontiers and shunned pleasures and good cheer,

123. Until, when the troops were complete and recruiters and recruits had been mustered,

124. He appointed Badr to command the group, for he was held in great awe.

125. So he set forth accompanied by troops like the torrent and an army like the blackness of night.

126. Until, when he descended upon Motunia [south of Toledo] in which the worst of creatures was [lurking],

127. He waged against them an open war that gave off sparks such that fire could be kindled from it,

128. And fighting was intense among them while the footsoldiers surrounded them on all sides.

129. So they waged war all day long, then spent the night with the archers banishing their sleep,

130. So that during the long passage of the night, they were like those fatigued whose wounds fester on their limbs.

131. Then they continued warring against them for a few days until death revealed itself to them suddenly and violently.

132. When they saw the clouds of Fate raining the thunderbolts of misfortune down upon them,

133. The non-Arabs hurriedly made a break for their foreign land and re-assembled under every star;

134. So the non-Arab came to their rescue on Thursday in the greatest haste:

135. In front of him went the footsoldiers and knights, and around him the crosses and bells,

136. For he was hoping to dislodge the army from the side of the fortress that had been destroyed,

137. So Badr impeded him with his own men, observing him attentively on his march towards him.

138. Until the right wing of one army met up with the left wing of the other and breaths got stuck in the windpipe.

of scholarship in Europe as well. By contrast, Islamic scholars wrote on paper, which was cheap, and they spoke to a broad audience.

The Carolingian Empire

Just as in the Byzantine and Islamic worlds, in Europe the period from 750 to 1050 saw first the formation of a strong empire, ruled by one man, and then its fragmentation as local rulers took power into their own hands. A new dynasty, the Carolingian, came to rule in the Frankish kingdom in 751, just one year after

139. Therefore God's partisans were victorious over the two infidels and the familiars of Satan were put to flight.

140. Thus they were massacred swiftly and dispersed, while the infidel retreated with blame and disgrace,

141. Whereas [our] people set out for Alcolea [a Muslim fortress] and met the enemy on Friday morning.

142. Then the two infidels met together on the road: the Pamplonan and the Galician,

143. And agreed to plunder the [Muslim] army, [or else] to die before that assembly.

144. They swore by enchantment and the devil that they would not be put to flight before death's encounter.

145. So they advanced with the greatest body of unbelievers who had covered the hills in general with horsemen,

146. Until [our] people drew near on Saturday, and O, what a moment it was!

147. For spears were aimed among them and cries of "God is very great!" and shouts rose high,

148. Swords forsook their sheaths and deaths opened wide their mouths;

149. Footsoldiers met with footsoldiers and plunged into the thick of the fray

150. In a place such that glances swerved away from it and in its length lives became too short,

151. And those gifted with patient forbearance and far-seeing prudence acted with brisk energy, for they rushed upon the non-believing enemy,

152. Until there took place the routing of the Basques [the Christians from the North] as though it were a stain of *wars*, [a dye]

153. For the eagles and hounds arose and they cried out, calling upon the captain of the Galicians [the Northeraers]:

154. The eagles of a death that snatches away souls and satiates swords and spears.

155. Thus was the pig put to flight at that time while his shame was revealed in that place;

156. Moreover, they were massacred in every river bottom and [their] heads were carried [aloft] on poles,

157. And the commander sent forward a thousand heads of the Galicians schooled in hardship.

158. In this way God's favor towards Islām was accomplished while the joy of that year embraced us all,

159. Though the greatest joy that occurred in its course was the death in it of Ibn Ḥafṣūn [a rebellious Muslim leader], the pig!

160. Thus one conquest was added to a second and one victory to another granted by the aid of God,

161. Hence this campaign is called "The Decisive" because after it this great calamity was to befall [the enemy].

QUESTIONS TO CONSIDER

1. What epithets does the poet use to characterize the enemies of Abd al-Rahman?

2. What sorts of arms and armies were involved in these battles?

3. What was Badr's role?

the Abbasids gained the caliphate. Charlemagne, the most powerful Carolingian monarch, conquered new territory, took the title of emperor, and presided over a revival of Christian classical culture known as the Carolingian renaissance. He ruled at the local level through counts and other military men. Nevertheless, the unity of the Carolingian Empire—based largely on conquest, a measure of prosperity, and personal allegiance to Charlemagne—was shaky. Its weaknesses were exacerbated by attacks from Viking, Muslim, and Magyar invaders. Charlemagne's successors divided his empire among themselves and saw it divided further as local leaders took defense—and rule—into their own hands.

The Rise of the Carolingians

The Carolingians were among many aristocratic families on the rise during the Merovingian period (see pages 272–283), but they gained exceptional power by monopolizing the position of palace mayor — a sort of prime minister — under the Merovingian kings. Charles Martel (Charles the Hammer), mayor 714–741, gave the name **Carolingian** (from *Carolus*, Latin for "Charles") to the dynasty. Renowned for defeating an invading army of Muslims from al-Andalus near Poitiers in 732, he also contended vigorously against other aristocrats who were carving out independent lordships for themselves. Charles Martel and his family turned aristocratic factions against one another, rewarded supporters, crushed enemies, and dominated whole regions by supporting monasteries that served as focal points for both religious piety and land donations.

The Carolingians also allied themselves with the Roman papacy. They supported Anglo-Saxon missionaries like Boniface (see page 285) who went to areas on the fringes of the Carolingian realm as the pope's ambassador. Reforming the Christianity that these regions had adopted, Boniface set up a hierarchical church organization and founded new monasteries. His newly appointed bishops were loyal to Rome and the Carolingians.

Pippin III (d. 768), Charles Martel's son, turned to the pope directly. When he deposed the Merovingian king in 751, taking over the kingship himself, Pippin petitioned Pope Zachary to legitimize the act; the pope agreed. The Carolingians returned the favor a few years later when the pope asked for their help against hostile Lombards. That papal request signaled a major shift. Before 754, the papacy had been part of the Byzantine Empire; after that, it turned to Europe for protection.

Pippin launched a successful campaign against the Lombard king that ended in 756 with the so-called Donation of Pippin, a peace accord between the Lombards and the pope. The treaty gave back to the pope cities that had been taken by the Lombard king. The new arrangement recognized what the papacy had long before created: a territorial "republic of St. Peter" ruled by the pope, not by the Byzantine emperor. Henceforth, the fate of Italy would be tied largely to the policies of the pope and the Frankish kings to the north, not to the eastern emperors.

Partnership with the Roman church gave the Carolingian dynasty a Christian aura, expressed in symbolic form by anointment. Bishops rubbed holy oil on the foreheads and shoulders of Carolingian kings during the coronation ceremony, imitating the Old Testament kings who had been anointed by God.

Charlemagne and His Kingdom, 768–814

The most famous Carolingian king was Charles, whom his contemporaries called "the Great" (*le Magne* in Old French) — thus, Charlemagne (r. 768–814). Charlemagne was complex, contradictory, and sometimes brutal. He loved listening to St. Augustine's *City of God* as it was read aloud, and he supported major scholarly enterprises, yet he never learned to write. He was devout, yet he flouted the advice of churchmen when they told him to convert pagans rather than force baptism on them. He admired the pope, yet he was furious when a pope placed the imperial crown on his head. He waged many successful wars, yet he thereby destroyed the buffer states surrounding the Frankish kingdoms, unleashing a new round of invasions.

Behind these contradictions, however, lay a unifying vision. Charlemagne dreamed of an empire that would unite the martial and learned traditions of the Roman and Germanic worlds with the legacy of Christianity. This vision lay at the core of his political activity, his building programs, and his support of scholarship and education.

During the early years of his reign, Charlemagne conquered lands in all directions (Map 9.3). He invaded Italy, seizing the crown of the Lombard kings and annexing northern Italy in 774. He then moved northward and

MAP 9.3 Expansion of the Carolingian Empire under Charlemagne
The conquests of Charlemagne temporarily united almost all of western Europe under one ruler. Although the great Carolingian Empire broke apart (see the inset showing how the empire was divided by the Treaty of Verdun), the legacy of that unity remained, even serving as one of the inspirations behind today's European Union.

| **CONTRASTING VIEWS** | # Charlemagne: Roman Emperor, Father of Europe, or the Chief Bishop? |

Charlemagne was crowned emperor, but was he really one of the successors of Augustus? Einhard (Excerpt 1) thought so. An anonymous poet at Charlemagne's court claimed still more (Excerpt 2): the king was the "father of Europe." Even while these secular views of Charlemagne were being expressed, other people—both in and outside the court—were stressing the king's religious functions and duties. Later on, these views became even more grandiose, as Notker the Stammerer's statement (Excerpt 3) reveals.

1. Charles as Emperor

Probably at some point in the mid-820s, Einhard, who had spent time at the Carolingian court and knew Charlemagne well, wrote a biography of the emperor that took as its model the Lives of the Caesars by Suetonius (c. 70–130). Although he did not emphasize Charlemagne's imperial title per se, Einhard stressed the classical moral values of his hero, including his "greatness of spirit" and steadfast determination.

It is widely recognized that, in these ways [i.e., through conquests, diplomacy, and patronage of the arts, Charlemagne] protected, increased the size of, and beautified his kingdom. Now I should begin at this point to speak of the character of his mind, his supreme steadfastness in good times and bad, and those other things that belong to his spiritual and domestic life.

After the death of his father [in 768], when he was sharing the kingdom with his brother [Carloman], he endured the pettiness and jealousy of his brother with such great patience, that it seemed remarkable to all that he could not be provoked to anger by him. Then [in 770], at the urging of his mother [Bertrada], he married a daughter of Desiderius, the king of the Lombards, but for some unknown reason he sent her away after a year and took Hildegard [758–783], a Swabian woman of distinct nobility. . . .

[Charlemagne] believed that his children, both his daughters and his sons, should be educated, first in the liberal arts, which he himself had studied. Then, he saw to it that when the boys had reached the right age they were trained to ride in the Frankish fashion, to fight, and to hunt. But he ordered his daughters to learn how to work with wool, how to spin and weave it, so that they might not grow dull from inactivity and [instead might] learn to value work and virtuous activity. . . .

Source: *Charlemagne's Courtier: The Complete Einhard,* ed. and trans. Paul Edward Dutton (Peterborough, Ont.: Broadview Press, 1998), 27–28.

2. The "Father of Europe"

Shortly after Pope Leo III fled northward to seek Charlemagne's help (799), an anonymous poet at the royal court composed an extremely flattering poem about the king. Here Charlemagne's virtues became larger than life.

The priests and the joyful people await the pope's advent.

Now father Charles [i.e., Charlemagne] sees his troops arrayed on the wide field;

He knows that Pepin [his son] and the highest pastor [the pope] are fast approaching;

He orders his people to wait for them.

He divides his troops into a ring-like shape,

In the center of which, he himself, that blessed one, stands,

Awaiting the advent of the pope, but higher up than his comrades

On the summit of the ring; he rises above the assembled [Franks].

Now Pope Leo approaches and crosses the front line of the ring.

He marvels at the many peoples from many lands whom he sees,

also prepared an improved edition of the Vulgate, the Latin Bible used by the clergy in all church services.

Art, like scholarship, served Carolingian political and religious goals. Carolingian artists turned to models from Italy and Byzantium (perhaps some refugees from Byzantine iconoclasm joined them) to illustrate Bibles, Psalters,

At their differences, their strange tongues, dress, and weapons.

At once Charles hastens to pay his reverent respects,
Embraces the great pontiff, and kisses him.

The two men join hands and walk together, speaking as they go.

The entire army prostrates itself three times before the pope,

And the suppliant throng three times pays its respects.

The pope prays from his heart for the people three times.

The king, the father of Europe, and Leo, the world's highest pastor,

Walk together and exchange views,

Charles inquiring as to the pope's case and his troubles.

He is shocked to learn of the wicked deeds of the [Roman] people.

He is amazed by the pope's eyes which had been blinded,

But to which sight had now returned,

And he marveled that a tongue mutilated with tongs now spoke.

Source: Paul Edward Dutton, ed., *Carolingian Civilization: A Reader*, 2nd ed. (Peterborough, Ont.: Broadview Press, 2004), 64–65.

3. The Chief Bishop

A monk at the Swiss monastery of St. Gall, Notker the Stammerer, wrote a biography of Charlemagne in 884 at the request of Charlemagne's great-grandson Charles the Fat. Here the emphasis is on Charlemagne's religious authority.

The Devil, who is skillful in laying ambushes and is in the habit of setting snares for us in the road which we are to follow, is not slow to trip us up one after another by means of some vice or other. The crime of fornication was imputed to a certain princely bishop—in such a case the name must be omitted. This matter came to the notice of his congregation, and then through tale-tellers it eventually reached the ears of the most pious Charles, the chief bishop of them all. . . . Charlemagne, that most rigorous searcher after justice, sent two of his court officials who were to turn aside that evening to a place near to the city in question and then come unexpectedly to the bishop at first light and ask him to celebrate Mass for them. If he should refuse, then they were to compel him in the name of the Emperor to celebrate the Holy Mysteries in person. The bishop did not know what to do, for that very night he had sinned before the eyes of the Heavenly Observer [God], and yet he did not dare to offend his visitors. Fearing men more than he feared God, he bathed his sweaty limbs in ice-cold spring-water and then went forward to offer the awe-inspiring sacraments. Behold, either his conscience gripped his heart tight, or the water penetrated his veins, for he was seized with such frosty chill that no attention from his doctors was of use to him. He was brought to his death by a frightful attack of fever and compelled to submit his soul to the decree of the strict and eternal Judge.

Source: *Einhard and Notker the Stammerer: Two Lives of Charlemagne*, trans. Lewis Thorpe (Harmondsworth, Eng.: Penguin, 1969), 121–22.

QUESTIONS TO CONSIDER

1. How does the anonymous poet describe the relationship between Charlemagne and the pope?

2. According to Notker, how important is the Mass?

3. What did Einhard consider to be the chief imperial virtues?

scientific treatises, and literary manuscripts. A great variety of artistic styles flourished, some of them (like the Saint Mark illustrated on page 309) drawing on classical traditions.

Many of the achievements of the Carolingian renaissance endured even after the dynasty itself had faded to a memory. The work of locating, understanding, and transmitting models of the past continued in a number of monastic schools. In the twelfth century, scholars would build on the foundations laid by the Carolingian renaissance. The very print of this textbook depends on one achievement of the period: modern typefaces are based on the clear and beautiful letter forms, called Caroline minuscule, invented in the ninth century to standardize manuscript handwriting.

Charlemagne's Successors, 814–911

Charlemagne's successor, Louis the Pious (r. 814–840), took his role as leader of the Christian empire even more seriously than his father did. In 817, he imposed on all the monasteries of the empire a uniform way of life, based on the Benedictine rule. Although some monasteries opposed this legislation, and in the years to come the king was unable to impose his will directly, this moment marked the effective adoption of the Benedictine rule as the monastic standard in Europe.

In a new development of the coronation ritual, Louis's first wife, Ermengard, was crowned empress by the pope in 816. In 817, their firstborn son, Lothar, was named emperor and made co-ruler with Louis. Their other sons, Pippin and Louis (later called Louis the German), were made subkings under imperial rule. Louis the Pious hoped in this way to ensure the unity of the empire while satisfying the claims of all his sons. Should any son die, only his firstborn could succeed him, a measure intended to prevent further splintering. But Louis's hopes were thwarted by events. Ermengard died, and Louis married Judith, reputed to be the most beautiful woman in the kingdom. In 823, she and Louis had a son, Charles (later known as Charles the Bald, to whose court Dhuoda's son William was sent). The sons of Ermengard, bitter over the birth of another royal heir, rebelled against their father and fought one another for more than a decade.

Finally, after Louis the Pious died in 840, the **Treaty of Verdun** (843) divided the empire among his three remaining sons (Pippin had died in 838). The arrangement roughly defined the future political contours of western Europe (see the inset in Map 9.3 on page 307). The western third, bequeathed to Charles the Bald (r. 843–877), would eventually become France, and the eastern third, handed to Louis the German (r. 843–876), became Germany. The "Middle Kingdom," which was given to Lothar (r. 843–855), had a different fate: parts of it were absorbed by France and Germany, and the rest eventually formed what became the modern states of the Netherlands, Belgium, Luxembourg, Switzerland, and Italy.

Thus, by 843, the European-wide empire of Charlemagne had dissolved. Forged by conquest, it had been supported by a small group of privileged aristocrats with lands and offices stretching across its entire expanse. Their loyalty—based on shared values, friendship, expectations of gain, and sometimes formal ties of vassalage and oaths of fealty (faithfulness)—was crucial to the success of the Carolingians. The empire had also been supported by an ideal, shared by educated laymen and churchmen alike, of conquest and Christian belief working together to bring good order to the earthly state.

But powerful forces operated against unity. Once the Carolingian Empire's borders were fixed and conquests ceased, the aristocrats could not hope for new lands and offices. They put down roots in particular regions and began to gather their own followings. Powerful local traditions such as different languages also undermined solidarity.

Finally, as Dhuoda revealed in the handbook she wrote for her son, some people disagreed with the imperial ideal. By asking her son to put his father before the emperor, Dhuoda demonstrated her belief in the primacy of the family and the personal ties that bound it together. Her values represented a new sensibility that saw real benefit in the breaking apart of Charlemagne's empire into smaller, more intimate local units.

Land and Power

The Carolingian economy, based on war profits, trade, and agriculture, contributed first to the rise and then to the dissolution of the Carolingian Empire. After the spoils of war ceased to pour in, the Carolingians still had access to money and goods. To the north, the Carolingian economy intermingled with that of the Abbasid caliphate. Silver from the Islamic world probably came north up the Volga River through Kievan Rus to the Baltic Sea. There the coins were melted down and the silver was traded to the Carolingians in return for wine, jugs, glasses, and other manufactured goods. The Carolingians turned the silver into coins of their own, to be used throughout the empire for small-scale local trade. The weakening of the Abbasid caliphate in the mid-ninth century, however, disrupted this far-flung trade network and contributed to the weakening of the Carolingians at about the same time.

Land provided the most important source of Carolingian wealth and power. Carolingian aristocrats held many estates, called manors, scattered throughout the Frankish kingdoms and organized for production. The names of the peasants who tilled the soil and the dues and services they owed were even sometimes carefully noted down in registers.

A typical manor was Villeneuve Saint-Georges, which belonged to the monastery of Saint-Germain-des-Prés (today in Paris) in the ninth century. Villeneuve consisted of arable fields, vineyards, meadows where animals could roam, and woodlands, all scattered about the countryside rather than connected in a compact unit. Peasant families did the farming. Each family had its own manse, which consisted of a house, a garden, and small sections of the arable land. Besides farming the land that belonged to them, the families also worked the demesne, the very large manse of the lord, in this case the abbey of Saint-Germain. Grown children would found their own families, and their parents' land would be subdivided to give them a share. In many ways, the peasant household of the Carolingian period was the precursor of the modern nuclear family.

Peasants at Villeneuve practiced the most progressive sort of plowing, known as the three-field system, in which they farmed two-thirds of the arable land at one time (see Figure 9.1). They planted one-third of the arable land in the fall with winter wheat, one-third in the spring with summer crops, and left the

FIGURE 9.1 Diagram of a Manor and Its Three-Field System

This schematic diagram of a manor shows that peasants lived clustered together in a village that consisted of houses and gardens. One of the buildings was a church. Nearby were vineyards. A bit beyond were the fields, pastureland, and meadows, well connected by dirt roads. The field sown with spring crops (such as oats) this year would have been sown with winter wheat the next year, while the fallow field would get a spring crop.

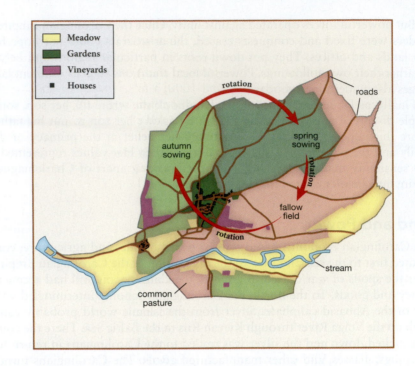

remaining third fallow to restore its fertility. The crops sown and the fallow field then rotated so that land use was repeated only every three years. This method of organizing the land produced larger yields (because two-thirds of the land was cultivated each year) than the still-prevalent two-field system, in which only half of the arable land was cultivated one year while the other half lay fallow.

All the peasants at Villeneuve were dependents of the monastery and owed dues and services to Saint-Germain. Their status and obligations varied enormously. One family, for example, owed four silver coins, wine, wood, three hens, and fifteen eggs every year, and the men had to plow the fields of the demesne. Another family owed the intensive labor of working the vineyards. Peasant women spent much time at the lord's house in the *gynaeceum*—the workshop where women made and dyed cloth and sewed garments—or in the kitchens, as cooks. Peasant men spent most of their time in the fields.

Manors organized on the model of Villeneuve were profitable. Like other lords, the Carolingians benefited from their extensive landholdings. Nevertheless, farming was still too primitive to return great surpluses, and as the lands belonging to the king were divided up in the wake of the partitioning of the empire and new invasions, the Carolingians' dependence on manors scattered throughout their kingdom proved to be a source of weakness.

Viking, Muslim, and Magyar Invasions, c. 790–955

Beginning around the time of Charlemagne's imperial coronation and extending to the mid-tenth century, new groups—Vikings, Muslims, and Magyars—confronted the Carolingian Empire and many of the other kingdoms of

Europe. The Vikings were the first invaders. About the same time as some Vikings made their eastward forays into what would become Rus, others moved westward. Traveling in small bands led by a chief, the Vikings were merchants, sailors, and pirates. Some crossed the Atlantic in their longships to settle Iceland and Greenland. Around 1000, a few landed on the coast of North America. Others navigated the rivers of continental Europe.

As pagans, Vikings considered monasteries and churches—with their reliquaries, chalices, and crosses—no more than convenient storehouses of plunder. They hit the British Isles particularly hard. By the middle of the ninth century, the Vikings were spending winters there, and in 876, they settled in the northeast quadrant as farmers. This region was later called the Danelaw.

In Wessex, the southernmost kingdom of England, King Alfred the Great bought time and peace from the Vikings by giving them hostages and tribute. The tribute, later called Danegeld, eventually became the basis of a relatively lucrative taxation system in England. After Alfred led his army against the Vikings, set up strongholds, and deployed new warships, the threat of invasions eased.

On the continent, too, the Vikings set up trading stations and settled where originally they had raided. Beginning about 850, their attacks became well-organized expeditions for regional control. At the end of the ninth century, one contingent settled in the region of France that soon took the name Normandy ("land of the Northmen"). In 911, the Frankish king Charles the Simple ceded the region to Rollo, the Viking leader there. In turn, Rollo converted to Christianity.

Normandy was not the only new Christian polity created in the north during the tenth and eleventh centuries. Scandinavia itself was transformed with the creation of the powerful kingdom of Denmark. There had been kings in Scandinavia before the tenth century, but they had been weak, their power challenged by nearby chieftains. Some of these chieftains led the Viking raids, competing with one another for foreign plunder in order to win prestige, land, and power back home. During the course of their raids, they and their followers came into contact with new cultures and learned from them.

Meanwhile, the Carolingians and the English supported missionaries in Scandinavia. By the middle of the tenth century, the Danes had become Christian. Following the model of the Christian kings to their south, the Danish kings built up an effective monarchy, with a royal mint and local agents who depended on them. By about 1000, the Danish monarchy had extended its control to parts of Sweden, Norway, and even England under King Cnut (also spelled Canute) (r. 1016–1035).

Southern Europe largely escaped the Vikings, but parts of it were attacked by Muslim adventurers from North Africa, Sicily, and northeastern al-Andalus who set up bases in the Mediterranean. Meanwhile, the Magyars (or Hungarians) settled in Europe's very center. A nomadic people from the Ural Mountains (today northeastern Russia), they arrived around 899 in the Danube basin, driving a wedge between the Slavs near the Frankish kingdom and those bordering on Byzantium. The Bulgarians, Serbs, and Rus were forced into the Byzantine orbit, while the Slavs nearer the Frankish kingdom came under the influence of Germany.

From their bases in present-day Hungary, the Magyars raided far to the west, attacking Germany, Italy, and even southern Gaul frequently between 899 and 955. Then in 955, the German king Otto I (r. 936–973) defeated a marauding party of Magyars at the battle of Lechfeld. Otto's victory, his subsequent military reorganization of his eastern frontiers, and the cessation of Magyar raids around this time made Otto a great hero to his contemporaries. However, historians today think the containment of the Magyars had more to do with their internal transformation from nomads to farmers than with their military defeat. Soon they converted to the Roman form of Christianity. Hungary's position between East and West made it a frontier region, vulnerable to invasion and immigration but also open to new experiments in assimilation and integration.

The Viking, Muslim, and Magyar invasions were the final onslaught western Europe experienced from outsiders. In some ways they were a continuation of the invasions that had rocked the Roman Empire in the fourth and fifth centuries. Loosely organized in war bands, the new groups entered western Europe looking for wealth but stayed on to become absorbed in the region's post-invasion society.

REVIEW QUESTION
What were the strengths and weaknesses of Carolingian institutions of government, warfare, and defense?

After the Carolingians: The Emergence of Local Rule

As royal power diminished, counts and other powerful men stopped looking to the king for new lands and offices; instead, they began to develop and exploit what they already had. Commanding the allegiance of vassals, controlling the local peasantry, building castles to dominate the countryside, setting up markets, collecting revenues, and keeping the peace, they regarded themselves as independent regional rulers. In this way, a new warrior class of lords and vassals came to dominate post-Carolingian society.

There were, to be sure, variations on this theme. In northern and central Italy, where urban life had never lost its importance, elites ruled from the cities rather than from rural castles. Everywhere kings retained a certain amount of power; in some places, such as Germany and England, they were extremely effective. Central European monarchies formed under the influence of Germany.* Still, throughout this period, local allegiances—between lord and vassal, castellan and peasant, bishop and layman—mattered most to the societies of Europe.

Public Power and Private Relationships

Both kings and less powerful men commanded others through institutions designed to ensure personal loyalty. This was true already under Charlemagne, and in the wake of the Viking, Magyar, and Muslim invasions, more and more warriors were drawn into networks of dependency, but not with the king: they became the faithful men—the vassals—of local lords, who often gave them

---

*Names such as *Germany, France,* and *Italy* are used here for the sake of convenience. They refer to regions, not to the nation-states that would eventually become associated with those names.

Feudalism

Feudalism is a modern word, like *capitalism* and *communism*. No one in the Middle Ages used it, or any of its related terms, such as *feudal system* or *feudal society*. Many historians today think that it is a misleading word and should be discarded. The term poses two serious problems. First, historians have used it to mean different things. Second, it implies that one way of life dominated the Middle Ages, when in fact social, political, and economic arrangements varied widely.

Consider the many different meanings that *feudalism* has had. Historians influenced by Karl Marx's powerful communist theory used (and still use) the word *feudalism* to refer to an economic system in which a class of landowners dominated subservient peasant cultivators. When they speak of feudalism, they are speaking of manors, lords, and serfs. Other historians, however, call that system *manorialism*. They reserve the word *feudalism* for a system consisting of vassals (who did no agricultural labor but only military service), lords, and fiefs. For example, in *Feudalism*, an influential book written in the mid-1940s, F. L. Ganshof considered the tenth to the thirteenth centuries to be the "classical age of feudalism," because during this period lords regularly granted fiefs to their vassals, who fought on their lord's behalf in return.

But, writing around the same time as Ganshof, Marc Bloch included in his definition of feudalism every aspect of the political and social life of the Middle Ages, including peasants, fiefs, knights, vassals, the fragmentation of royal authority, and even the survival of the state.

Today some historians argue that talking about feudalism distorts the realities of medieval life. The fief—whose Latin form, *feodum*, gave rise to the word *feudalism*—was by no means important everywhere. And even where it was important, it did not necessarily have anything to do with lords, vassals, or military obligations. For such historians, feudalism is a myth. Other historians, however, think that the term is extremely useful as long as its multiple forms are recognized. These historians are now starting to speak of "feudalisms"—in the plural.

fiefs (grants of land) in return for their military service. As sons often took the place of their fathers, this arrangement tended to be permanent. From the Latin *feodum* ("fief") comes the word *feudal*, and some historians use the term **feudalism** to describe the social and economic system created by the relationship among vassals, lords, and fiefs (see Terms of History).

Medieval people divided their society into three groups: those who prayed, those who fought, and those who worked. All these groups were involved in hierarchies of dependency and linked by personal bonds, but the upper classes—those who prayed (monks) and those who fought (knights)—were free. Their brand of dependency was prestigious, whether they were vassals, lords, or both. In fact, a typical warrior was lord of several vassals even while serving as the vassal of another lord. Monasteries (including women's monasteries) normally had vassals to fight for them, and their abbots (and abbesses) in turn were often vassals of a king or other powerful lord.

Vassalage served both as an alternative to public power and as a way to strengthen what little public power remained. Given the impoverished economic conditions of western Europe, its primitive methods of communication, and its lack of unifying traditions, lords of every sort needed faithful men to protect them and carry out their orders. And vassals needed lords. At the low end of the social scale, poor vassals depended on their lords to feed, clothe, house, and arm them. At the upper end of the social scale, landowning vassals looked to lords to give them still more land.

Many upper-class laywomen participated in the society of "those who fought" as wives and mothers of vassals and lords. A few women were themselves vassals, and some were lords (or, rather, ladies). Other women entered convents and joined the group of those who prayed. Through its abbess or a man standing in for her, a convent often had vassals as well. Many elite women engaged in property transactions, whether alone, with other family members, or as part of a group such as a convent.

Becoming a vassal involved both ritual gestures and verbal promises. In a ceremony witnessed by others, the vassal-to-be knelt and, placing his hands between the hands of his lord, said, "I promise to be your man." This act, known as homage, was followed by the promise of fealty—fidelity, trust, and service—which the vassal swore with his hand on relics or a Bible. Then the vassal and the lord kissed. In an age when many people could not read, a public ceremony such as this represented a visual and verbal contract. Vassalage bound the lord and vassal to one another with reciprocal obligations, usually military. Knights, as the premier fighters of the day, were the most desirable vassals.

At the bottom of the social scale were those who worked—the peasants. In the Carolingian period, many peasants were free; they did not live on a manor or, if they did, they owed very little to its lord. (Manors like Villeneuve were the exceptions.) But as power fell into the hands of local rulers, fewer and fewer peasants remained free. Rather, they were made dependent on lords, not as vassals but as serfs. A serf's dependency was completely unlike that of a vassal. Serfdom was not voluntary. No serf did homage or fealty to his lord; no serf kissed his lord as an equal. Whereas vassals served their lords as warriors, serfs worked as laborers on their lord's land and paid taxes and dues to that lord. Peasants constituted the majority of the population, but unlike knights, who were celebrated in song, they were barely noticed by the upper classes—except as a source of revenue. While there were still free peasants who could lease land or till their own soil without paying dues to a lord, serfs, who could not be kicked off their land but who were also not free to leave it, became the norm.

New methods of cultivation and a slightly warmer climate helped transform the rural landscape, making it more productive and thus able to support a larger population. But population increase meant more mouths to feed and the threat of food shortages. Landlords began reorganizing their estates to run more efficiently. In the tenth century, the three-field system became more prevalent; heavy plows that could turn wet, clayish northern soils came into wider use, and horses (more effective than oxen) were harnessed to pull the plows. The results were surplus food and a better standard of living for nearly everyone.

In search of greater profits, some lords lightened the dues and services of peasants, or turned them into fixed money payments that the lords could then use to pay laborers to open up new lands by draining marshes and cutting down forests. Money payments allowed lords to buy what they wanted, while peasants benefited because their dues were fixed despite inflation.

By the tenth century, many peasants had begun living in populous rural settlements, true villages. Surrounded by arable lands, meadows, woods, and wastelands, villages developed a sense of community. Boundaries—sometimes real fortifications, sometimes simple markers—told nonresidents to stay away or to find shelter in huts located outside the village limits.

The church often formed the focal point of village activity. There people met, received the sacraments, drew up contracts, and buried their dead. Religious feasts and festivals joined the rituals of farming to mark the seasons. The church dominated the village in another way: men and women owed it a tax called a tithe (one-tenth of their crops or income, paid in money or in kind), which was first instituted on a regular basis by the Carolingians.

Village peasants developed a sense of common purpose based on their interdependence, as they shared oxen or horses for the teams that pulled the plow or turned to village craftsmen to fix their wheels or shoe their horses. Village solidarity could be compromised, however, by conflicting loyalties and obligations. A peasant in one village might very well have one piece of land connected with a certain manor and another piece on a different estate; and he or she might owe several lords different kinds of dues. Even peasants of one village working for one lord might owe him varied services and taxes.

Obligations differed even more strikingly across the regions of Europe than within particular villages. The principal distinction was between free peasants—such as small landowners in Saxony and other parts of Germany, who had no lords—and serfs, who were especially common in France and England. In Italy, peasants ranged from small independent landowners to leaseholders.

As landlords consolidated their power over their manors, they collected not only dues and services but also fees for the use of their flour mills, bake houses, and breweries. Some built castles, fortified strongholds, collected taxes, heard court cases, levied fines, and mustered men for defense. In France, for example, as the king's power waned, political control fell into the hands of counts and other princes. By 1000, castles had become the key to their power. In the south of France, power was so fragmented that each man who controlled a castle—a **castellan**—was a virtual ruler, although often with a very limited reach. In northwestern France, territorial princes, basing their rule on the control of many castles, dominated much broader regions.

The development of virtually independent local political units, dominated by a castle and controlled by a military elite, marks an important turning point in western Europe. Although this development did not occur everywhere simultaneously (and in some places, it hardly occurred at all), the social, political, and cultural life of Europe was now dominated by landowners who were both military men and regional rulers.

Warriors and Warfare

Not all medieval warriors were alike. At the top of this elite group were the kings, counts, and dukes. Below them, but on the rise, were the castellans; and still further down the social scale were ordinary knights. Yet all shared in a common lifestyle.

Late Ninth-Century Warfare
This manuscript page illustrates the first lines of Psalm 60 (Douay 59): "when he set fire to Mesopotamia of Syria and Sobal; and Joab returned and slew of Edom, in the vale of the saltpits, twelve thousand men." The artist has depicted the scene as it would have looked in his own day: Joab's soldiers—led by a military standard in the shape of a dragon—are mounted on horseback. Some, the richest, are clad in chain mail; all are armed with lances, and one bears a round shield strapped to his back. (The Art Archive/REX/Shutterstock.)

Knights and their lords fought on horseback. High astride his steed, wearing a shirt of chain mail and a helmet of flat metal plates riveted together, the knight marked a military revolution. The war season started in May, when the grasses were high enough for horses to forage. Horseshoes allowed armies to move faster than ever before and to negotiate rough terrain previously unsuitable for battle. Stirrups, probably invented by nomadic Asiatic tribes, allowed the mounted warrior to hold his seat while thrusting at the enemy with a heavy lance. The light javelin of ancient Roman warfare was abandoned.

Lords and their vassals often lived together. In the lord's great hall they ate, listened to entertainment, and bedded down for the night. They went out hunting together, competed with one another in military games, and went off to the battlefield as a group. Some powerful vassals—counts, for example—lived on their own fiefs. These vassals hardly ever saw their lord (probably the king), except when doing homage and fealty—once in their lifetimes—or serving him in battles, for perhaps forty days a year (as was the custom in eleventh-century France). These powerful vassals were themselves lords of other men—typically unmarried knightly vassals who lived, ate, and hunted together with their lord.

No matter how old they might be, unmarried knights who lived with their lords were called youths by their contemporaries. Such perpetual bachelors were something new, the result of a profound transformation in the organization of families and inheritance. Before about 1000, noble families had recognized all their children as heirs and had divided their estates accordingly. Thereafter, adapting to diminished opportunities for land and office and wary of fragmenting the estates they had, French nobles (in particular) changed both their conception of their family and the way property passed to the next generation. Recognizing the overriding claims of one son, often the eldest, they handed down their entire inheritance to him. (The system of inheritance in which the heir is the eldest son is called **primogeniture**.) The heir, in turn, traced his lineage only through the male line, backward through his father and forward through his own eldest son. Such **patrilineal** families left many younger sons without an inheritance and therefore without the prospect of marrying and founding a family; instead, the younger sons lived at the courts of the great as youths, or they joined the church as clerics or monks. The development of territorial rule and patrilineal families went hand in hand, as fathers passed down to one son not only manors but also titles, castles, and authority over the peasantry.

Patrilineal inheritance tended to bypass daughters and so worked against aristocratic women, who lost the power that came with inherited wealth. In families without sons, however, widows and daughters did inherit property. And wives often acted as lords of estates when their husbands were at war. Moreover, all aristocratic women played an important role in this warrior society, whether in the monastery (where they prayed for the souls of their families) or through their marriages (where they produced children and helped forge alliances between their own natal families and the families of their husbands).

Efforts to Contain Violence

The rise of the castellans meant an increase in violence. Supported by their knights, castellans were keen to maintain their new authority over the peasants in their vicinity in the face of older regional powers, like counts and dukes. Threatened from below, those higher-ranking authorities looked to the bishops for help. The bishops, themselves resentful of local castellan claims and, moreover, generally members of the same elite families as counts and dukes, were glad to oblige. To do so, they enlisted the lower classes—peasants who were tired of wars that destroyed their crops or forced them to join regional infantries. The result was the **Peace of God**, which united bishops, counts, and peasants in an attempt to contain local violence. The movement began in the south of France around 990 and spread over a wide region by 1050. At impassioned meetings of bishops, lords, and crowds of enthusiastic men and women, the clergy set forth the provisions of this peace. "No man in the counties or bishoprics shall seize a horse, colt, ox, cow, ass, or the burdens which it carries. . . . No one shall seize a peasant, man or woman," ran the decree of one early council. Anyone who violated this peace was to be excommunicated: cut off from the community of the faithful, denied the services of the church and the hope of salvation.

The Peace of God proclaimed at local councils like this limited violence but did not address the problem of conflict between armed men. A second set of agreements, the Truce of God, soon supplemented the peace. The truce prohibited fighting between warriors at certain times. Enforcement fell to the local knights and nobles, who swore over saints' relics to uphold it and to fight anyone who broke it.

The Peace of God and the Truce of God were only two of the mechanisms that attempted to contain or defuse violent confrontations in the tenth and eleventh centuries. At times, lords and their vassals mediated wars and feuds at grand judicial assemblies. In other instances, monks or laymen tried to find solutions to disputes that would leave the honor of both parties intact. Rather than establishing guilt or innocence, winners or losers, these methods of adjudication often resulted in compromises on both sides.

Political Communities in Italy, England, and France

The political systems that emerged following the breakup of the Carolingian Empire were as varied as the regions of Europe. In northern and central Italy, cities were the centers of power, still reflecting, if feebly, the political organization of ancient Rome. Italian lords tended to construct their family castles within the walls of cities. From there they controlled the land and people in the surrounding countryside.

Italian cities also served as marketplaces where peasants sold their surplus goods, artisans and merchants lived and worked, and foreign traders offered their wares. These members of the lower classes were supported by the wealthy elite, who depended, here more than elsewhere, on cash to satisfy their desires. In the course of the ninth and tenth centuries, the peasants in the countryside became renters who paid in currency, helping to meet their landlords' need for cash.

Families in Italy organized themselves quite differently from the patrilineal families of France. To prevent dividing its properties among heirs, the Italian family became a kind of economic corporation in which all male members shared the profits of the family's inheritance and all women were excluded. In the coming centuries, this successful model would also serve as the foundation of most early Italian businesses and banks.

In contrast to Italy, most of England was rural. Having successfully repelled the Viking invaders, **Alfred the Great**, king of Wessex (r. 871–899), developed new mechanisms of royal government, instituting reforms that his successors continued. He fortified settlements throughout Wessex and divided the army into two parts, one with the duty of defending these fortifications, the other operating as a mobile unit. Alfred also started a navy. The money to pay for these military innovations came from assessments on peasants' holdings.

England in the Age of King Alfred, 871–899

[Map legend:]
Kingdom of Alfred
Dependent on Wessex
To Alfred in 878

North Sea
Northumbria
DANELAW
Mercia
East Anglia
Wales
Wessex
0   50   100 miles
0 50 100 kilometers

Along with its regional fortifications, Alfred sought to strengthen his kingdom's religious integrity. He began his program of religious reform by bringing scholars to his court to translate works by church fathers such as Gregory the Great and St. Augustine into Anglo-Saxon (Old English) so that everyone would understand them. Alfred himself did some of these translations. He even had the Psalms, until now sung only in Hebrew, Greek, and Latin, put into the vernacular—the common spoken language. In most of ninth- and tenth-century Europe, only the Latin language was used in writing. In England, however, the spoken language became a written language as well.

Alfred's reforms strengthened not only defense, education, and religion but also royal power. He consolidated his control over Wessex and fought the Danish kings, who by the mid-870s had taken Northumbria, northeastern Mercia, and East Anglia. Eventually, as he successfully fought the Danes who were pushing south and westward, he was recognized as king of all the English not under Danish rule. He issued a law code for all of the English kingdoms, becoming, in effect, the first king of all the English.

Alfred's successors rolled back the Danish rule in England even though many Vikings remained. Converted to Christianity, their great men joined Anglo-Saxons in attending the English king at court. As peace returned, new administrative subdivisions for judicial and tax purposes were established throughout England: shires (the English equivalent of counties) and hundreds (smaller units). The powerful men of the kingdom swore fealty to the king, promising to be enemies of his enemies, friends of his friends. England was united and organized to support a strong ruler.

Alfred's grandson Edgar (r. 959–975) commanded all the possibilities early medieval kingship offered. He was the sworn lord of all the great men of the kingdom. He controlled appointments to the English church and sponsored monastic reform. In 973, he was anointed king. The fortifications of the kingdom were in his hands, as was the army, and he took responsibility for keeping the peace by proclaiming certain crimes—arson and theft—to be under his special jurisdiction, and he mobilized the machinery of the shire and the hundred to find and punish thieves.

Despite its apparent centralization, England was not a unified state in the modern sense, and the king's control was often tenuous. Many royal officials were great landowners who (as on the European continent) worked for the king because it was in their best interest. When it was not, they allied with different claimants to the throne. This political fragility may have helped the Danish king Cnut conquer England. As king there from 1016 to 1035, Cnut reinforced the already strong connections between England and Scandinavia while keeping intact much of the administrative, ecclesiastical, and military apparatus already established in England by the Anglo-Saxons. By Cnut's time, Scandinavian traditions had largely merged with those of the rest of Europe and the Vikings were no longer an alien culture.

Across the English Channel, French kings had a harder time than the English in coping with invasions because their realm was much larger. They had no chance to build their defenses slowly from one powerful base. During most of the tenth century, Carolingian kings alternated on the throne with kings from a family that would later be called the Capetian. As the Carolingian dynasty waned, the most powerful men of the kingdom—dukes, counts, and important bishops—came together to elect as king Hugh Capet (r. 987–996), a lord of great prestige yet relatively little power. This choice marked the end of Carolingian rule and the beginning of the **Capetian dynasty**, which would hand down the royal title from father to son until the fourteenth century.

The Kingdom of the Franks under Hugh Capet, 987–996

In the eleventh century, nearby territorial lordships limited the reach of the Capetian kings. The king's scattered but substantial estates lay in the north of France, in the region around Paris—the Île-de-France ("island of France"). His castles and his vassals were there. Independent castellans, however, controlled areas nearby. In the sense that he was a neighbor of castellans and not much more powerful militarily than they, the king of the Franks—who would only later take the territorial title of king of France—was just another local leader. Yet the Capetian kings had considerable prestige. They were anointed with holy oil, and they represented the idea of unity inherited from Charlemagne. Most of the counts, at least in the north of France, became their vassals. But because they were powerful, these vassals' obligations to the king were minimal.

Emperors and Kings in Central and Eastern Europe

In contrast to the development of territorial lordships in France, Germany's fragmentation had hardly begun before it was reversed. In the late Carolingian period, five large duchies (regions dominated by dukes) emerged in Germany. When the last Carolingian king in Germany died, in 911, the dukes elected one of themselves as king. Then, as the Magyar invasions increased, the dukes gave the royal title to the duke of Saxony, Henry I (r. 919–936), who proceeded to set up fortifications and reorganize his army, crowning his efforts with a major defeat of a Magyar army in 933.

Otto I (r. 936–973), the son of Henry I, was an even greater military hero. In 951, he marched into Italy and took the Lombard crown. His defeat of the Magyar forces in 955 at Lechfeld gave him prestige and helped solidify his dynasty. Against the Slavs, with whom the Germans shared a border, Otto created marches (border regions specifically set up for defense) from which he could make expeditions and stave off counterattacks. After the pope crowned him emperor in 962, Otto claimed the Middle Kingdom carved out by the Treaty of Verdun and cast himself as the agent of Roman imperial renewal. His kingdom was called the Empire, as if it were the old Roman Empire revived. Some historians call it the Holy Roman Empire to distinguish it from the Roman Empire, but Otto and his successors made no such distinction; they considered it a continuation. In this book, it will be called the Empire.

Otto's victories brought tribute and plunder, ensuring him a following but also raising the German nobles' expectations for enrichment. The **Ottonian kings**—including Otto I and his successors Otto II (r. 961–983) and Otto III (r. 983–1002)—were not always able or willing to provide the gifts and inheritances their family members and followers expected. They did not divide their kingdom among their sons; instead, like castellans in France, they created a patrilineal pattern of inheritance. As a consequence, younger sons and other potential heirs felt cheated, and disgruntled royal kin led revolt after revolt against the Ottonian kings.

Relations between the Ottonians and the German clergy were more harmonious. Otto I appointed bishops, gave them extensive lands, and subjected the local peasantry to their overlordship. Like Charlemagne, Otto believed that the well-being of the church in his kingdom depended on him. The Ottonians gave bishops the right to collect revenues and call men to arms. Answering to the king and furnishing him with troops, the bishops became royal officials, while also carrying out their religious duties. German kings claimed the right to select bishops, even the pope at Rome, and to "invest" them (install them in their office) by participating in the ceremony that made them bishops.

Like all strong rulers of the day, the Ottonians presided over a renaissance of learning. They brought learned churchmen to court to write and teach. To an extent unprecedented elsewhere, noblewomen in Germany also acquired an education and participated in the intellectual revival. Living at home with their kinfolk and servants or in convents that provided them with comfortable private apartments, noblewomen wrote books and supported other artists and scholars.

Despite their military and political strength, the kings of Germany faced resistance from dukes and other powerful princes, who hoped to become

Otto III Receiving Gifts
These triumphal images are in a book of Gospels made for Otto III (r. 983–1002). The crowned women on the left are personifications of the four parts of Otto's empire: Sclavinia (the Slavic lands), Germania (Germany), Gallia (Gaul), and Roma (Rome). Each offers a gift in tribute and homage to the emperor, who sits on a throne holding the symbols of his power (orb and scepter) and flanked by representatives of the church (on his right) and of the army (on his left). Why do you suppose the artist separated the image of the emperor from that of the women? What does the body language of the women indicate about the relations Otto wanted to portray between himself and the parts of his empire? Can you relate this manuscript, which was made in 997–1000, to Otto's conquest over the Slavs in 997? (bpk Bildagentur/Bayerische Staatsbibliothek, Munich, Germany/Photo: Lutz Braun/Art Resource, NY.)

regional rulers themselves. The Salians, the dynasty that succeeded the Ottonians, tried to balance the power among the German dukes, but could not meld them into a corps of vassals the way the Capetian kings tamed their counts. In Germany, vassalage was considered beneath the dignity of free men. Instead of relying on vassals, the Salian kings and their bishops used ministerials (specially designated men who were legally serfs) to collect taxes, administer justice, and fight on horseback. Ministerials retained their servile status even though they often rose to wealth and high position. Under the Salian kings, ministerials became the mainstay of the royal army and administration.

Hand in hand with the popes, German kings created new, Catholic polities along their eastern frontier. The Czechs, who lived in the region of Bohemia, converted under the rule of Václav (r. 921–929), who thereby gained recognition in Germany as the duke of Bohemia. He and his successors did not become kings, remaining politically within the German sphere. Václav's murder by his younger brother made him a martyr and the patron saint of Bohemia, a symbol around which later movements for independence rallied.

The Poles gained a greater measure of independence than the Czechs. In 966, Mieszko I (r. c. 960–992), the leader of the Slavic tribe known as the Polanians, accepted baptism to forestall the attack that the Germans were

MAPPING THE WEST

Europe and the Mediterranean, c. 1050

The clear borders and distinct colors of the "states" on this map distort an essential truth: none of the areas shown had centralized governments that controlled whole territories, as in modern states. Instead, there were numerous regional rulers within each, and there were often competing claims of jurisdiction and conflicting allegiances. Consider Sicily: it was conquered by Muslims in the tenth century, but by 1060, it had been taken over by the Normans—adventurers from Normandy (in France). Its predominantly Greek-speaking population, however, was Greek Orthodox in religion, a legacy of its Byzantine past.

Analyzing the Map: What does this map tell you about the way Spain was ruled c. 1050?

Making Connections: Together the German kingdom and the north of Italy on this map formed an empire under what dynasty of rulers?

already mounting against pagan Slavic peoples along the Baltic coast and east of the Elbe River. Busily engaged in bringing the other Slavic tribes of Poland under his control, Mieszko adroitly shifted his alliances with various German princes to suit his needs. In 991, he placed his realm under the protection of the pope, establishing a tradition of Polish loyalty to the Roman church. Mieszko's son Boleslaw the Brave (r. 992–1025) greatly extended Poland's boundaries, at one time or another holding sway from the Bohemian border to Kiev. In 1000, he gained a royal crown with papal blessing.

Hungary's case was similar to that of Poland. As we have seen, the Magyars settled in the region known today as Hungary. Under Stephen I (r. 997–1038), they accepted Roman Christianity. According to legend, the crown placed on Stephen's head at his coronation (in late 1000 or early 1001) was sent to him by the pope. Stephen was canonized in 1083, and to this day the crown of St. Stephen remains the most hallowed symbol of Hungarian nationhood.

Symbols of rulership such as crowns, consecrated by Christian priests and accorded a prestige almost akin to saints' relics, were among the most vital sources of royal power in central Europe. The economic basis for the power of central European rulers was largely agricultural. As happened elsewhere, here, too, centralized rule gradually gave way to regional rulers.

REVIEW QUESTION
After the dissolution of the Carolingian Empire, what political systems developed in western, northern, eastern, and central Europe, and how did these systems differ from one another?

Conclusion

In 800, the three heirs of the Roman Empire all appeared to be organized like their parent: centralized, monarchical, imperial. Byzantine emperors commissioning learned books, Abbasid caliphs holding court in their new resplendent palace at Baghdad, and Carolingian emperors issuing their directives for reform all mimicked the Roman emperors. Yet leaders in the three realms confronted tensions and regional pressures that tended to put political power into the hands of local lords. Byzantium felt this fragmentation least, yet even there the emergence of a new elite, the dynatoi, weakened the emperor's control over the countryside. In the Islamic world, quarrels between Abbasid heirs, army disloyalty, economic weakness, and the ambitions of powerful local rulers decisively weakened the caliphate and opened the way to separate successor states. In Europe, powerful independent landowners strove with greater or lesser success (depending on the region) to establish themselves as effective rulers.

Local conditions determined political and economic organizations. Between 900 and 1000, for example, French society was transformed by the rise of castellans, the formation of patrilineal families, and the spread of ties of vassalage. These factors figured less prominently in Germany, where a central monarchy remained, buttressed by churchmen, ministerials, and conquests to the east. And in Italy, the cities remained crucial institutions.

After 1050, however, the German king would lose his supreme position as a storm of church reform whirled around him. The Italian cities gained effective independence. The economy changed, becoming more commercial and urban, and the papacy asserted itself with new force in the life of Europe.

Chapter 9 Review

Key Terms and People

Be sure that you can identify the term or person and explain its historical significance.

Charlemagne (p. 294)

themes (p. 295)

dynatoi (p. 297)

Basil II (p. 298)

Abbasid (p. 300)

Fatimids (p. 301)

Carolingian (p. 306)

Treaty of Verdun (p. 312)

fiefs (p. 317)

feudalism (p. 317)

castellan (p. 319)

primogeniture (p. 320)

patrilineal (p. 320)

Peace of God (p. 321)

Alfred the Great (p. 322)

Capetian dynasty (p. 323)

Ottonian kings (p. 324)

Review Questions

1. In what ways did the Byzantine emperor expand his power, and in what ways was that power checked?

2. What forces contributed to the fragmentation of the Islamic world in the tenth and eleventh centuries, and what forces held it together?

3. What were the strengths and weaknesses of Carolingian institutions of government, warfare, and defense?

4. After the dissolution of the Carolingian Empire, what political systems developed in western, northern, eastern, and central Europe, and how did these systems differ from one another?

Making Connections

1. How were the Byzantine, Islamic, and European economies similar? How did they differ? How did these economies interact?

2. How did the powers and ambitions of castellans compare with those of the dynatoi of Byzantium and of Muslim provincial rulers?

3. Compare the effects of the barbarian invasions into the Roman Empire with the effects of the Viking, Muslim, and Magyar invasions into Carolingian Europe.

Important Events

750–c. 950	The Abbasid caliphate
751	Pippin III becomes king of the Franks, establishing Carolingian rule
768–814	Charlemagne rules as king of the Franks
786–809	Caliphate of Harun al-Rashid
800	Charlemagne crowned emperor at Rome
843	Treaty of Verdun
871–899	Reign of King Alfred of England
929–1031	Caliphate of Córdoba

955	Battle of Lechfeld
962	King Otto I (r. 936–973) of Germany crowned emperor
987–996	Reign of King Hugh Capet of France
c. 990	Peace of God movement begins
1000 or 1001	Stephen I (r. 997–1038) crowned king of Hungary
1001–1018	Byzantine conquest of Bulgaria

Consider two events

Peace of God movement begins (c. 990) and Stephen I (r. 997–1038) crowned king of Hungary (1000 or 1001). How do these events illustrate Christianity's ability to unify and mobilize people in this era?

Suggested References

A few books, like the one edited by Brubaker and Smith, try to bridge the divides between the Byzantine, Islamic, and western European worlds. Nevertheless, for the most part these regions are treated separately. For Byzantium, see Neville. For insight into the Islamic world, see Benson and Brett. For the Carolingian world, De Jong provides a new approach.

Becher, Matthias. *Charlemagne*. 2003.

Benson, Bobrick. *The Caliph's Splendor: Islam and the West in the Golden Age of Baghdad*. 2012.

Berend, Nora, Przemysław Urbańczyk, and Przemysław Wiszewski. *Central Europe in the High Middle Ages: Bohemia, Hungary and Poland, c. 900–c.1300*. 2013.

Bolton, Timothy. *Cnut the Great*. 2017.

Brett, Michael. *The Fatimid Empire*. 2017.

Brubaker, Leslie, and Julia M. H. Smith. *Gender in the Early Medieval World: East and West, 300–900*. 2004.

Cooperson, Michael. *Al Ma'mun*. 2005.

De Jong, Mayke. *The Penitential State: Authority and Atonement in the Age of Louis the Pious, 814–840*. 2009.

*Dutton, Paul Edward, ed. *Carolingian Civilization: A Reader*. 2004.

*_____, ed. and trans. *Charlemagne's Courtier: The Complete Einhard*. 1998.

Garver, Valerie L. *Women and Aristocratic Culture in the Carolingian World*. 2009.

Herrin, Judith. *Women in Purple: Rulers of Medieval Byzantium*. 2002.

Jones, Anna Trumbore. *Noble Lord, Good Shepherd: Episcopal Power and Piety in Aquitaine, 877–1050*. 2009.

Kennedy, Hugh. *The Armies of the Caliphs: Military and Society in the Early Islamic State*. 2001.

Neville, Leonora. *Authority in Byzantine Provincial Society, 950–1100*. 2004.

*Psellus, Michael. *Fourteen Byzantine Rulers: The Chronographia*. Trans. E. R. A. Sewter. 1966.

Raffensperger, Christian. *Reimagining Europe: Kievan Rus' in the Medieval World*. 2012.

Whittow, Mark. *The Making of Byzantium, 600–1025*. 1996.

_____

*Primary source.

Commercial Quickening and Religious Reform

1050–1150

A bit after the year 1100, sculptors were hired to decorate the inner walls of the cloister porch at Moissac, a monastery in southern France. On one wall they carved in stone the New Testament story of the poor man Lazarus and the rich man Dives. Their fates could not have been more different. While the soul of Lazarus was carried to heaven by an angel, the rich man was shown plunging down to hell.

The sculptor's work reflected a widespread change in attitudes toward money. In the Carolingian and post-Carolingian period (up to, say, 1050), people generally considered wealth to be unproblematic. Rich kings were praised for their generosity; expensively produced manuscripts, illuminated with gold leaf and precious colors, were highly prized; and splendid churches like Charlemagne's chapel at Aachen were widely admired. Such views changed over the course of the eleventh century. Wealth came to be both highly prized—and vehemently rejected.

The most striking feature of the period from 1050 to 1150 was the rise of a money economy in western Europe. Agricultural production swelled, fueling the growth of trade and the expansion of cities. A new class of well-heeled merchants, bankers, and entrepreneurs emerged. These developments were met with a wide variety of responses. Some people fled the cities and their new wealth altogether, seeking isolation and poverty. Others, even the participants in the new economy, condemned it and emphasized its corrupting influence. Many people, however, embraced the new money economy.

«**Dives and Lazarus** At the time this sculpted depiction of Dives and Lazarus was made, the nearby city of Toulouse was expanding commercially. The parable of the rich man and the poor man (Luke 16:19-31) spoke to the concerns of a money economy. At the top right, Dives, the rich man, feasts. To his left, the poor man, Lazarus, lies dying. Above Lazarus is an angel who carries his soul to heaven. Further to the left, Lazarus's soul lies in the lap of Abraham. This is an image of heavenly bliss. By contrast, under the left-hand arch below Abraham, devils are welcoming the soul of Dives into Hell. The monks of Moissac, like the townspeople of Toulouse, by 1100 were attuned to moneymaking and well aware of both its pleasures and dangers. (St. Pierre, Moissac, France/Bridgeman Images.)

CHAPTER FOCUS
How did the commercial revolution affect religion and politics?

The development of a profit-based economy quickly transformed the landscape and lifestyles of western Europe. Many villages and fortifications became cities where traders, merchants, and artisans conducted business. In some places, town dwellers began to determine their own laws and administer their own justice. Although most people still lived in sparsely populated rural areas, the new cash economy touched their lives in many ways. Economic concerns helped drive changes within the church, where a movement for reform gathered steam and exploded in three directions: the Investiture Conflict, new monastic orders emphasizing poverty, and the crusades. Money allowed popes, kings, and princes to redefine the nature of their power.

The Commercial Revolution

A growing population, cities, long-distance trade networks, local markets, and new business arrangements meshed to create a profit-based economy. With improvements in agriculture and more land in cultivation, the great estates of the eleventh century produced surpluses that helped feed—and therefore make possible—a new urban population.

Commerce was not new to the history of western Europe, but the **commercial revolution** of the Middle Ages spawned the institutions that would be the direct ancestors of modern businesses: widespread use of money, corporations, banks, accounting systems, and, above all, urban centers that thrived on economic vitality (see Terms of History). Whereas ancient cities had primarily religious, social, and political functions, medieval cities were centers of production and economic activity. Wealth meant power: it allowed city dwellers to become self-governing.

Fairs, Towns, and Cities

The commercial revolution took place in three venues: markets, fairs, and permanent centers. In some places, markets met weekly to sell local surplus goods. In others, fairs—which lasted anywhere from several days to a few months—took place once a year and drew traders from longer distances.

CHAPTER TIMELINE

910
Founding
of Cluny

1054
Schism between eastern and
western churches begins

1020   **1040**   **1060**

1049–1054
Papacy of
Leo IX

1066
Battle of Hastings:
Norman conquest of
England under William I

The Commercial Revolution

The term *commercial revolution* was first coined by the Belgian (later American) economic historian Raymond de Roover in a series of publications starting in the 1940s. Reacting to the prevailing view that the economy of the Middle Ages had been dominated by petty shopkeepers and itinerant merchants and that the great economic transformations awaited the modern era, De Roover forcefully asserted that a decisive shift took place in the thirteenth century. Before then, it was true, medieval entrepreneurs had traveled to fairs, bringing their wares, selling them, and buying other items for sale back home. But in the thirteenth century there was a "drastic change"—as complete and as momentous as the much later industrial revolution. That change, initiated by Italian merchants, involved the establishment of permanent agencies that allowed businessmen to buy products right at the centers of production. Making this development possible were new, permanent partnerships, bills of exchange (ensuring payments without shipping coins), and the invention of double-entry bookkeeping. These thirteenth-century institutions were the ancestors of modern business methods.

De Roover's term was accepted but his dating challenged by Robert Lopez, a Jew who fled to the United States from fascist Italy. Lopez did not think that the crucial factor in the revolution was the change from itinerant petty traders to settled companies. Rather, he saw the entire period 950–1350 as witnessing a shift "for the first time in history" from an undeveloped to a developed economy. Indeed, he wanted to go even further back than 950—to ninth-century agricultural innovations like the three-field system. Such advances in the rural sector made the commercial revolution possible by helping to create the food surpluses that permitted some people to devote themselves to making money through long-distance trading-related pursuits. Global commerce, not stability, was the key to the commercial revolution. Its effects are still with us today.

Some fairs specialized in particular goods: at Saint-Denis, a monastery near Paris that had had a fair since at least the seventh century, the star attraction was wine. Most fairs offered a wide variety of products: at the Champagne fairs in France, there were woolen fabrics from Flanders; silks from Lucca, Italy; leather goods from Spain; and furs from Germany. Bankers attended as well, exchanging coins from one currency into another—and charging for their services. Local inhabitants did not have to pay taxes or tolls, but traders from the outside—protected by guarantees of safe conduct—were charged

1071
Battle between Byzantines and Seljuk Turks at Manzikert

1077
Henry IV does penance before Gregory VII at Canossa; war breaks out

1096–1099
First Crusade
1097
Establishment of commune at Milan

1122
Concordat of Worms ends Investiture Conflict

1080   **1100**   **1120**

1073–1085
Papacy of Gregory VII

1086
Domesday survey

1095
Council of Clermont; Pope Urban II calls First Crusade
1109
Establishment of the crusader states

1108–1137
Reign of Louis VI

c. 1140
Gratian's *Decretum* published

1147–1149
Second Crusade

stall fees as well as entry and exit fees. Local landlords reaped great profits, and as the fairs came under royal control, kings did so as well.

Permanent commercial centers (cities and towns) developed around castles and monasteries and within the walls of ancient Roman towns. Great lords in the countryside—and this included monasteries—were eager to take advantage of the profits that their estates generated. In the late tenth century, they reorganized their lands for greater productivity, encouraged their peasants to cultivate new land, and converted services and dues to money payments. With ready cash, they not only fostered the development of local markets and yearly fairs, where they could sell their surpluses and buy luxury goods, but also encouraged traders and craftspeople to settle down near them.

Some markets formed just outside the walls of older cities; these gradually merged into new and enlarged urban communities as towns built new walls to protect their inhabitants. Along the Rhine River and in other river valleys, cities sprang up to service the merchants who traversed the route between Italy and the north. Many long-distance traders were Italians and Jews. They supplied the fine wines, spices, and fabrics beloved by lords and ladies, their families, and their vassals. Italians took up long-distance trade because of Italy's proximity to Byzantine and Islamic ports, their opportunities for plunder and trade on the high seas, and their never entirely extinguished urban traditions.

The Jews of Mediterranean regions—especially Italy and Spain—had been involved in commerce since Roman times. That trade had centered on the Mediterranean; now it extended to the north as well. For Jews living in the port cities of the old Roman Empire, little had changed. But for many Jews in northern Europe, the story was different. They had settled on the land alongside other peasants, and during the Carolingian period their properties

Jewish Cemetery at Worms
Known as the Holy Sand graveyard, this is one of the oldest surviving Jewish cemeteries in Europe, built around the same time as the city's synagogue. It was used by the Jews in the city of Worms from the eleventh to the twentieth century, the oldest legible gravestone dating from 1058/1059. (Chris Howes/Wild Places Photography/Alamy.)

bordered those of their Christian neighbors. As political power fragmented over the course of the tenth century and the countryside was reorganized under local lords, many Jews were driven off the land. They found refuge in the new towns and cities. Some became scholars, doctors, and judges within their communities; many became small-time pawnbrokers; and still others became moneylenders and financiers.

By the eleventh century, most Jews lived in cities but were not citizens. They were generally serfs of the king or, in the Rhineland, under the safeguard of the local bishop. This status was ambiguous: the Jews were "protected" but also exploited since their protectors constantly demanded steep taxes. Regular town trade groups, craft organizations, and town governments often rested on a conception of the common good sealed by an oath among Christians—and thus, by definition, excluded Jews.

Nevertheless, Jews had their own institutions, centered on the synagogue, their place of worship. Although they often lived in a "Jewish quarter," they were not forcibly segregated from other townspeople. In many cities, they lived near Christians, purchased products from Christian craftspeople, and hired Christians as servants. In turn, Christians purchased luxury goods from Jewish long-distance traders and often borrowed money from Jewish lenders.

The fact that Jews and Christians could live side by side had less to do with tolerance than with lack of planning. Most towns in medieval Europe grew haphazardly. Typically, towns had a center, where the church and town government had their headquarters, and around this were the shops of tradespeople and craftspeople, generally grouped by specialty: butchers, for example, lived and worked on the Street of the Butchers.

The look and feel of such developing cities varied enormously, but nearly all included a marketplace, a castle, and several churches. The streets—made of packed clay or gravel—were often narrow, dirty, dark, and winding. Most people had to adapt to increasingly crowded conditions. Even so, most city dwellers tended a garden and perhaps livestock as well, living largely off the food they raised themselves.

Cities were part of a building boom. Towns put up specialized buildings for trade and for city government, charitable houses for the sick and indigent, city halls, and warehouses. They

The Tannery District at Metz
This photograph, taken in 1880, nevertheless reflects the location of many medieval tanneries, whose manufacturing techniques required great quantities of water. Tanners prepared the leather for boots, shoes, gloves, animal harnesses, sacks for liquids, scabbards, and many other items. Since their work involved treating the skins of dead animals obtained from butchers, and since the skins often needed to rot (to loosen the hairs) and then had to be treated with acids or alkalis for cleaning, tanneries were full of foul fumes and were normally sited at the outer edge of towns. (LL/Getty Images.)

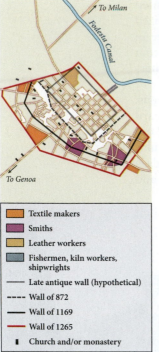

Textile makers

Smiths

Leather workers

Fishermen, kiln workers, shipwrights

Late antique wall (hypothetical)

Wall of 872

Wall of 1169

Wall of 1265

Church and/or monastery

The Walls of Piacenza

also expanded their walls. Workers at Piacenza, for example, first pulled down the late antique wall and replaced it with a more extensive one in 872. Then, in 1169, Piacentines took down the ninth-century wall and replaced it with one that was still more expansive.

Before the eleventh century, Europeans had depended on boats and waterways for bulky long-distance transport. In the twelfth century, carts could haul items overland because new roads through the countryside linked the urban markets and strengthened governments could protect overland travelers. Still, although commercial centers developed throughout western Europe, they grew fastest and most densely in regions along key waterways: the Mediterranean coasts of Italy, France, and Spain; northern Italy along the Po River; the Rhône-Saône-Meuse river system; the Rhineland; the English Channel; and the shores of the Baltic Sea. During the eleventh century, these waterways became part of a single interdependent economy.

What did townspeople look like? We can get an idea from a twelfth-century baptismal font cast in Liège. It shows Jesus speaking to the soldiers and publicans (tax collectors): the soldier is dressed as a medieval knight, while the publicans wear the caps and clothes of well-to-do city dwellers.

Organizing Crafts and Commerce

In the Middle Ages, most manufactured goods were produced by hand or with primitive machines and tools. Though not mechanized, most medieval industries, crafts, and trades were highly organized. The fundamental unit of organization was the **guild**. Originally, guilds were religious and charitable associations of people in the same line of business. In Ferrara, Italy, for example, the shoemakers' guild started as a prayer confraternity, an association whose members gathered and prayed for one another. But soon guilds became professional corporations defined by statutes and rules. They charged dues, negotiated with lords and town governments, set the standards of their trade, and controlled their membership.

The manufacture of finished products often required the cooperation of several guilds. The production of wool cloth, for example, involved numerous guilds—shearers, weavers, fullers (who thickened the cloth), dyers—generally working under the supervision of the merchant guild that imported the raw wool. Within each guild was a hierarchy, starting at the bottom with the **apprentices**, who were learning the trade, moving up to the **journeymen** and **journeywomen** (that is, male or female day laborers—the word comes from the Middle English for "a day's work"), ending with the **masters** at the top.

It was hard to become a master. Young people might spend many years as an apprentice and then as a day laborer hired by masters who needed extra help. Journeymen and journeywomen aspired to be masters because then they would be able to draw up regulations for the guild and serve as its chief overseers, inspectors, and treasurers. Most masters eventually had a chance to serve as guild officers. Occasionally they were elected, but more often they were appointed by town governments or local rulers.

In addition to guilds, medieval entrepreneurs created new kinds of business arrangements through partnerships, contracts, and large-scale productive enterprises—the ancestors of modern **capitalism**. Although they took many forms, all of these business agreements had the common purpose of bringing people together to pool their resources and finance larger initiatives. Short-lived partnerships were set up for the term of one sea voyage; longer-term partnerships were created for land trade. In northern and central Italy, for example, long-term ventures took the form of a family corporation formed by extended families. Everyone who contributed to this corporation bore joint and unlimited liability for all losses and debts. This provision enhanced family solidarity because each member was responsible for the debts of all the others, but it also risked bankrupting everyone in the family.

Pooling resources meant that money had to be available. Small silver coins were excellent for small-scale transactions; larger ones were also minted. The widespread use of coins meant that entrepreneurs got rich from mines and minters from stamping the coins. Where rulers were strong, they insisted on controlling or at least authorizing both mines and mints. Only in the thirteenth century did gold coinage become important in the West.

But commerce needed credit as well as coins. In the Middle Ages, as now, entrepreneurs had to take out loans to finance their projects. Creditors were induced to give out loans in return for interest. But the church banned usury—lending money at interest. This led to various ingenious ways to get around the prohibition. For example, often contracts specified a "penalty for late payment" rather than an interest charge. The new willingness to finance business enterprises with loans signaled a more positive attitude toward credit, risk, and profit.

Contracts and partnerships made large-scale productive enterprises possible. In fact, light industry began in the eleventh century. One of the earliest products to benefit from new industrial technologies was cloth. Water mills powered machines such as presses to extract oil from fibers, and flails to clean and thicken cloth. Machines also exploited raw materials more efficiently: new deep-mining technology provided Europeans with hitherto untapped sources of metals. Simultaneously, forging techniques improved, and for the first time since antiquity, iron was regularly used for agricultural tools and plows. Iron tools—which were more durable than wood tools—made farming more productive, which in turn fed the commercial revolution.

Baptismal Font at Liège, 1107–1118
This detail from a large bronze baptismal font cast at Liège (a city today in Belgium) illustrated the words of Luke 3:12–14: "Tax collectors also came to be baptized, and said to [Jesus], 'Teacher, what shall we do?' And he said to them, 'Collect no more than is appointed you.' Soldiers also asked him, 'And we, what shall we do?' And he said to them, 'Rob no one . . . and be content with your wages.'" In this representation, the tax collectors are dressed like twelfth-century city dwellers, while a soldier is dressed like a knight of the period. (Bildarchiv Monheim/akg-images.)

Communes: Self-Government for the Towns

In the eleventh and twelfth centuries, townspeople did not fit into the old categories of medieval types: those who prayed, those who fought, or those who labored on the land. Just knowing they were different from those groups gave townspeople a sense of solidarity. But practical reasons also contributed to their feeling of common purpose: they lived in close quarters, and they shared a mutual interest in laws to facilitate commerce, freedom from servile dues and duties, reliable coinage, and independence to buy and sell as the market dictated. To gain this freedom, townspeople petitioned the political powers that ruled them—bishops, kings, counts, castellans—for the right to govern themselves. Already in the early twelfth century, the king of England granted to the citizens of Newcastle-upon-Tyne the privilege that any unfree peasant who lived there unclaimed by his lord for a year and a day would thereafter be a free person. This became a common custom. But to gain their own laws and officials the townspeople often had to fight for their freedom and, if successful, paid a hefty sum for it. A type of town institution of self-government arose called a **commune**; citizens swore allegiance to the commune, forming a legal corporate body.

Communes were especially common in northern and central Italy, France, and Flanders. Even before the commercial revolution, Italian cities had become centers of regional political power; the commercial revolution swelled them with tradespeople, whose interest in self-government was often fueled by religious as well as economic concerns. At Milan in the second half of the eleventh century, popular discontent with the archbishop, who effectively ruled the city, led to numerous armed clashes. In 1097, the Milanese succeeded in transferring political power from the archbishop and his clergy to a government of leading men of the city, who called themselves consuls, recalling the ancient Roman republic. The consuls' rule extended beyond the town walls into the *contado*, the outlying countryside.

Outside Italy, movements for city independence took place within the framework of larger kingdoms or principalities. Such movements were sometimes violent, as at Milan, but at other times peaceful. For example, William Clito, who claimed the county of Flanders (today in Belgium), willingly granted the citizens of St. Omer the privileges they asked for in 1127; he recognized them as legally free, gave them the right to mint coins, allowed them their own laws and courts, and lifted certain tolls and taxes. In return, the citizens supported his claims to rule Flanders. Whether violently or peacefully, the men and women of many towns and cities gained a measure of self-rule.

The Commercial Revolution in the Countryside

The countryside, too, was caught in the web of trade. By 1150, rural life in many regions was organized for the marketplace. Great lords hired trained, literate agents to administer their estates, calculate profits and losses, and make marketing decisions. Aristocrats needed money not only because they relished luxuries but also because their honor and authority continued to depend on their personal generosity, patronage, and displays of wealth. In the twelfth century, when some townsmen could boast fortunes that rivaled the riches of the landed aristocracy, the economic pressures on the nobles increased as their extravagance exceeded their income. Many went into debt.

Peasants, too, participated in the new commercial economy. The increase in population and the resultant greater demand for food required bringing more land under cultivation. Sometimes lords sponsored land clearance. At other times peasants acted on their own to clear land and relieve the pressure of overpopulation, as when the small freeholders in England's Fenland region cooperated to build banks and dikes to reclaim the land that led out to the North Sea. Villages were founded on the drained land, and villagers shared responsibility for repairing and maintaining the dikes, even as each peasant family farmed its new holding individually.

On old estates the rise in population strained to the breaking point the Carolingian period's manse organization, in which each household had been settled on the land that supported it. Now, in the twelfth century, twenty peasant families might live on what had been, in the tenth century, the manse of one family. With the manse supporting so many more people, labor services and dues had to be recalculated, and peasants and their lords often turned services and dues into money rents, payable once a year.

The commercial revolution and the resulting money economy brought both benefits and burdens to peasants. They gained from rising prices, which made their fixed rents less onerous. They had access to markets where they could sell their surplus and buy what they lacked. Increases in land under cultivation and the use of iron tools meant greater productivity. Peasants also gained increased personal freedom as they shook off direct control by lords. Nevertheless, these advantages were partially canceled out by their cash obligations. Peasants touched by the commercial revolution ate better than their forebears had eaten, but they also had to spend more money.

REVIEW QUESTION
What new institutions resulted from the commercial revolution?

Church Reform

The commercial revolution affected the church no less than it affected other institutions of the time. Typically, kings or powerful local lords appointed bishops, who then ruled over the city. This transaction involved gifts: churchmen gave gifts and money to secular leaders in return for their offices. Soon the same sorts of people who appreciated the fates of Dives and Lazarus were condemning such transactions. The impulse to free the church from "the world"—from rulers, wealth, sex, money, and power—was as old as the origins of monasticism; but, beginning in the tenth century and increasing to fever pitch in the eleventh, reformers demanded that the church as a whole remodel itself and become free of secular entanglements.

This freedom was, from the start, as much a matter of power as of religion. Most people had long believed that their ruler—whether king, duke, count, or castellan—reigned by the grace of God and had the right to control the churches in his territory. But by the second half of the eleventh century, more and more people saw a great deal wrong with secular power over the church. They looked to the papacy to lead the movement of church reform. The matter came to a head during the so-called Investiture Conflict, when Pope Gregory VII clashed with Emperor Henry IV (whose empire embraced both Germany and Italy). The Investiture Conflict ushered in a major civil war in Germany and a great upheaval in the distribution of power across western Europe. By the early 1100s, a reformed church—with the pope at its head—was penetrating into areas of life never before touched by churchmen. Church reform began as a way to free the church from the world, but in the end the church was thoroughly involved in the new world it had helped create.

Beginnings of Reform

The project of freeing the church from the world began in the tenth century with no particular plan and only a vague idea of what it might mean. The Benedictine monastery of Cluny (today in France) may serve to represent the early phases of the reform. The duke and duchess of Aquitaine founded Cluny in 910 and endowed it with property. Then they did something new: instead of retaining control over the monastery, like most other monastic founders, they gave it and its worldly possessions to saints Peter and Paul. In this way, they put control of the monastery into the hands of heaven's two most powerful saints. They designated the pope, as the successor of St. Peter, to be the monastery's worldly protector if anyone should bother or threaten it.

The whole notion of "freedom" at this point was vague. But Cluny's prestige was great because of its status as St. Peter's property and the elaborate round of prayers that the monks carried out there with scrupulous devotion. The Cluniac monks fulfilled the role of "those who pray" in a way that dazzled their contemporaries. Through their prayers, they seemed to guarantee the salvation of all Christians. Rulers, bishops, rich landowners, and even serfs (if they could) donated land to Cluny, joining their lands to the land of St. Peter and the fate of their souls to Cluny's efficacious prayers. Powerful men and women called on the Cluniac monks to reform other monasteries along the Cluniac model. Cluny was rebuilt several times, and by 1100, it boasted the largest church in Christendom.

The abbots of Cluny came to see themselves as reformers of the world. They advocated

Investiture of a Bishop
This plaque, made of champlevé enamel around 1180, shows a seated ruler on the viewer's right. He holds an orb of the world in one hand, while with the other he gives the monk at the left a cross-standard. The inscription at the top says "E-P FIT," meaning "He becomes bishop." What is depicted here, then, is the investiture of a bishop by a king. In the eleventh century, this practice came under heavy criticism by church reformers. By the time this plaque was made, the reformers had made their point. The artist put the focus on the monk who was about to become bishop: he wears a halo and looms in size over the king. In addition, the inscription makes him—rather than the king—the subject of the story. (Museum for the Arts and Industry, Hamburg, Germany/Interfoto/akg-images.)

clerical celibacy and argued against the prevailing norm, in which parish priests and even some bishops were married. They thought that the laity (all Christians who were not part of the clergy) must become more virtuous. In particular, they sought to curb the oppression of the poor by the rich and powerful. In the eleventh century, the Cluniacs began to link their program of internal monastic and external worldly reform to the papacy. When bishops and laypeople encroached on their lands, they appealed to the pope for help. The causes that the Cluniacs championed were soon taken up by a small group of clerics and monks in the Empire, the political entity created by the Ottonians. They buttressed their arguments with new interpretations of canon law—the laws decreed over the centuries at church councils and by bishops and popes. They concentrated on two breaches of those laws: clerical marriage and **simony** (buying church offices).* Later they added the condemnation of **lay investiture**—the installation of clerics into their offices by lay rulers. In the investiture ritual, the emperor or his representative symbolically gave the church and the land that went with it to the priest or bishop or archbishop chosen for the job.

Other advocates of reform lived in the highly commercialized regions of the empire—Italy and the regions along the northern half of the Rhine River. Familiar with the impersonal practices of a profit economy, they regarded the gifts that churchmen usually gave in return for their offices as no more than crass purchases. At first the emperors supported them. Taking seriously his position as the anointed of God, Emperor Henry III (r. 1039–1056) felt responsible for the well-being of the church in his empire. He denounced simony and refused to accept money or gifts when he appointed bishops to their posts. When in 1046, three men, each representing a different faction of the Roman aristocracy, claimed to be pope, Henry, as ruler of Rome, traveled to Italy to settle the matter. There the emperor presided over the Synod of Sutri (1046), which deposed all three popes and elected another. In 1049, Henry appointed a bishop from the Rhineland to the papacy as Leo IX (r. 1049–1054). But this appointment did not work out as Henry had expected.

Leo set out to reform the church under his own, not the emperor's, control. He traveled to France and Germany, holding councils to condemn bishops guilty of simony. He brought to the papal court the most zealous reformers of his day, including Humbert of Silva Candida and Hildebrand (later Pope Gregory VII). In 1054, his last year as pope, Leo sent Humbert to Constantinople on a diplomatic mission to argue against the patriarch of Constantinople on behalf of the new, lofty claims of the pope. When the patriarch treated him with contempt, Humbert became furious and excommunicated him. In retaliation, the patriarch excommunicated Humbert and his party, threatening them with eternal damnation. Clashes between the two churches had occurred before and had been patched up, but this one, the

---

* The word *simony* comes from the name Simon Magus, the magician in the New Testament who wanted to buy the gifts of the Holy Spirit from St. Peter.

The World of the Investiture Conflict, c. 1070–1122

schism between the eastern and western churches (1054), proved insurmountable.* Thereafter, the Roman Catholic and the Greek Orthodox churches largely went their separate ways.

Leo also confronted a new power to his south. Under Count Roger I (c. 1031–1101), the Normans created a county that would eventually stretch from Capua to Sicily. Leo, threatened by this great power, tried to curtail it: in 1053, he sent a military force to Apulia, but it was soundly defeated. Leo's successors were obliged to change their policy. In 1058, the reigning pope "invested"—in effect, gave—Apulia, nearby Calabria, and even the still-unconquered Sicily to Roger's brother, even though none of this was the pope's to give. The papacy was particularly keen to see the Normans gain Sicily. Once part of the Byzantine Empire, the island had been taken by Muslims in the tenth century; now the pope hoped to bring it under Catholic control. Thus, the pope's desires to convert Sicily meshed nicely with the territorial ambitions of Roger and his brother. The agreement of 1058 included a promise that all of the churches of southern Italy and Sicily would be placed under papal jurisdiction. No wonder that when the Investiture Conflict broke out, the Normans played an important role as a military arm of the papacy.

The popes were in fact becoming more and more involved in military enterprises. They participated in wars of expansion in Spain, for example. There, political fragmentation into small and weak *taifas* (see page 302) made al-Andalus fair game for the Christians to the north. Slowly, the idea of the *reconquista*, the Christian "reconquest" of Spain from the Muslims, took shape, fed by religious fervor as well as by greed for land and power. In 1063, just before a major battle, the pope issued an incentive to all who would fight—an indulgence that lifted the knights' obligation to do penance, although it did not go so far as to forgive all sins.

The Gregorian Reform and the Investiture Conflict, 1075–1122

Historians associate the papal reform movement above all with Gregory VII (r. 1073–1085) and therefore often call it the **Gregorian reform**. Beginning as a lowly Roman cleric named Hildebrand, with the job of administering the papal estates, Gregory rose slowly through the hierarchy. A passionate advocate of papal primacy (the theory that the pope was the head of the church), Gregory was not afraid to clash with **Henry IV** (r. 1056–1106), ruler of Germany and much of Italy, over leadership of the church (see Contrasting Views on pages 344–346). As his views crystallized, Gregory came to see an anointed ruler as

---

*The mutual excommunications led to a breach between the churches until 1965, when Pope Paul VI and Patriarch Athenagoras I made a joint declaration regretting "the offensive words" and sentences of excommunication the two sides had exchanged more than nine hundred years before, deploring "the effective rupture of ecclesiastical communion," and expressing the hope that in time the "differences between the Roman Catholic Church and the Orthodox Church" would be overcome.

just another layman who had no right to meddle in church affairs. At the time, this was an astonishing position, given the traditional religious and spiritual roles associated with kings and emperors.

Gregory was, and remains, an extraordinarily controversial figure. As pope, he thought that he was acting as the vicar, or representative, of St. Peter on earth. In his view, the reforms he advocated and the upheavals he precipitated were necessary to free the church from the evil rulers of the world. But his great nemesis, Henry IV, had a very different view of Gregory. He considered him an ambitious and evil man who "seduced the world far and wide and stained the Church with the blood of her sons." Modern historians are only a bit less divided in their assessment of Gregory. Few deny his sincerity and deep religious devotion, but many speak of his pride, ambition, and single-mindedness.

Henry IV was less complex. He was raised in the traditions of his father, Henry III. He believed that he and his bishops—who were, at the same time, his most valuable supporters and administrators—were the rightful leaders of the church. He had no intention of allowing the pope to become head of the church; he didn't see that new religious ideals were sweeping away the old traditions. The great confrontation between Gregory and Henry that historians call the **Investiture Conflict*** began in 1075 over the appointment of the archbishop of Milan and a few other Italian prelates. When Henry insisted on appointing these clergymen, Gregory admonished the king. Henry responded by calling on Gregory to step down as pope. In turn, Gregory called a synod that both excommunicated and suspended Henry from office:

> I deprive King Henry [IV], son of the emperor Henry [III], who has rebelled against [God's] Church with unheard-of audacity, of the government over the whole kingdom of Germany and Italy, and I release all Christian men from the allegiance which they have sworn or may swear to him, and I forbid anyone to serve him as king.

It was this last part of the decree that made it politically explosive; it authorized everyone in Henry's kingdom to rebel against him. Henry's enemies, mostly German princes (as German aristocrats were called), now threatened to elect another king. They were motivated partly by religious sentiments and partly by political opportunism. Some bishops joined forces with Gregory's supporters, a great blow to royal power because Henry desperately needed the troops supplied by his churchmen.

Attacked from all sides, Henry traveled to intercept Gregory, who was journeying northward to visit the rebellious princes. In early 1077, king and pope met at a castle belonging to Matilda, countess of Tuscany, at Canossa, high in central Italy's snowy Apennine Mountains. Gregory remained inside the fortress there; Henry stood outside as a penitent, begging forgiveness.

---

*This movement is also called the Investiture Controversy, Investiture Contest, or Investiture Struggle. The epithets all refer to the same thing: the disagreement and eventually war between the pope and the emperor over the right to invest churchmen in particular and power over the church hierarchy in general.

Henry IV

Henry III was a church reformer in the old mold: he ensured the well-being of the church by appointing excellent prelates. When he died in 1056, he left his six-year-old son, Henry IV, as his heir. Excerpt 1 is a sympathetic account of the young king, whose minority gave many powerful groups in Germany a chance to exploit him. When he turned fifteen and was therefore no longer legally a minor, Henry freed himself from their grasp and began to restore royal power. This meant, in part, asserting his right to appoint bishops and archbishops, as he did in 1075 to the sees of Milan, Fermo, and Spoleto. In Excerpt 2, Gregory VII scolds Henry for these appointments and demands that he heed the pope, or rather St. Peter, in whose place the pope stands. In Gregory's view, Henry was disobeying God. Henry's response to Gregory's scolding letter is in Excerpt 3: there he portrays himself as the ordained of God and calls on Gregory to resign the papacy. Gregory reacted to this letter by excommunicating Henry, declaring him no longer king, and releasing all his subjects from their obedience to him. Suddenly Henry found himself nearly abandoned. To regain his position, he needed Gregory to lift the excommunication. In January 1077, Henry stood barefoot in the snow at Canossa, acting as a penitent. Excerpt 4 describes that moment.

1. Anonymous Account of Henry's Minority

A biographer of Henry IV wrote this account shortly after the emperor's death in 1106. By then, the Investiture Conflict had raged for decades, and most people had taken sides. This biographer was on Henry's side.

But since immature age inspires too little fear, and while awe languishes, audacity increases, the boyish years of the king excited in many the spirit of crime. Therefore everyone strove to become equal to the one greater than him, or even greater, and the might of many increased through crime; nor was there any fear of the law, which had little authority under the young boy-king.

And so that they could do everything with more license, they first robbed of her child the mother [Empress Agnes, wife of Henry III] whose mature wisdom and grave habits

they feared, pleading that it was dishonorable for the kingdom to be administered by a woman (although one may read of many queens who administered kingdoms with manly wisdom). But after the boy-king, once drawn away from the bosom of his mother, came into the hands of the princes to be raised, whatever they prescribed for him to do, he did like the boy he was. Whomever they wished, he exalted; whomever they wished, he set down; so that they may rightly be said not to have ministered to their king so much as to have given orders to him. When they dealt with the affairs of the kingdom, they took counsel not so much for the affairs of the kingdom as for their own; and in everything they did, it was their primary concern to put their own advantage above everything else....

But when [at the age of fifteen] he passed into that measure of age and mind in which he could discern what was honorable, what shameful, what useful, and what was not, he reconsidered what he had done while led by the suggestion of the princes and condemned many things which he had done. And, having become his own judge, he changed those of his acts which were to be changed. He also prohibited wars, violence, and rapine; he strove to recall peace and justice, which had been expelled to restore neglected laws, and to check the license of crime.

Source: "The Life of the Emperor Henry IV" in *Imperial Lives and Letters of the Eleventh Century*, trans. Theodor E. Mommsen and Karl F. Morrison (New York: Columbia University Press, 2000), 106.

2. Gregory VII Admonishes Henry (1075)

Gregory had written letters to Henry before 1075, but this was the first one that scolded him. The issue was Henry's attempt to appoint prelates to three Italian sees (the seat, jurisdiction, or office of a bishop). Gregory complained that Henry's candidates were unknown and inappropriate. He did not yet object to royal investiture.

We marvel exceedingly that you have sent us so many devoted letters and displayed such humility by the spoken words of your legates . . . and yet in action showing yourself most bitterly hostile to the canons and apostolic decrees in those duties especially required by loyalty to the Church. Not to mention other cases, the way you have observed your promises in the Milan affair, made through your mother and through bishops, our colleagues, whom we sent to you, and what your intentions were in making them is evident to all. And now, heaping wounds upon wounds, you have handed over the sees of Fermo and Spoleto—if indeed a church may be given over by any human power—to persons entirely unknown to us, whereas it is not lawful to consecrate anyone except after probation and with due knowledge.

It would have been becoming to you, since you confess yourself to be a son of the Church, to give more respectful attention to the master of the Church, that is, to Peter, prince of the Apostles. To him, if you are of the Lord's flock, you have been committed for your pasture, since Christ said to him: "Peter, feed my sheep" (John 21:17), and again: "To thee are given the keys of Heaven, and whatsoever thou shalt bind on earth shall be bound in Heaven and whatsoever thou shalt loose on earth shall be loosed in Heaven" (Matt. 16:19). Now, while we, unworthy sinner that we are, stand in his place of power, still whatever you send to us, whether in writing or by word of mouth, he [Peter] himself receives, and while we read what is written or hear the voice of those who speak, he discerns with subtle insight from what spirit the message comes.

Source: *The Correspondence of Pope Gregory VII*, trans. Ephraim Emerton (New York: W. W. Norton, 1969), 87.

3. Henry's Response to Gregory's Admonition (early 1076)

A meeting called by Henry and attended by nobles and bishops in Germany produced two documents in response to Gregory's scolding letter: a harsh retort meant to be circulated in Germany as propaganda for Henry, and a gentler version to be sent to Gregory himself. Both called on Gregory to step down as pope. The harsh letter, part of which is printed here, makes clear Henry's exalted view of his own role in the church.

Henry, King not by usurpation, but by the pious ordination of God, to Hildebrand, now not Pope, but false monk:

You have deserved such a salutation as this because of the confusion you have wrought; for you left untouched

no order of the Church which you could make a sharer of confusion instead of honor, of malediction instead of benediction.

For to discuss a few outstanding points among many: Not only have you dared to touch the rectors of the holy Church—the archbishops, the bishops, and the priests, anointed of the Lord as they are—but you have trodden them under foot like slaves who know not what their lord may do. . . .

And we, indeed, bore with all these abuses, since we were eager to preserve the honor of the Apostolic See. But you construed our humility as fear, and so you were emboldened to rise up even against the royal power itself, granted to us by God. You dared to threaten to take the kingship away from us—as though we had received the kingship from you, as though kingship and empire were in your hand and not in the hand of God.

Our Lord, Jesus Christ, has called us to kingship, but has not called you to the priesthood.

Source: *Imperial Lives and Letters of the Eleventh Century*, trans. Theodor E. Mommsen and Karl F. Morrison (New York: Columbia University Press, 2000), 150.

4. Lampert of Hersfeld Describes Henry at Canossa (c. 1077)

Lampert of Hersfeld was a German monk whose monastery, Hersfeld, supported Henry. However, in his Annales, *from which this excerpt is taken, Lampert emphasizes how weak the king had become as he awaited the pope's absolution at Canossa.*

Leaving Speyer a few days before Christmas with his wife and infant son, the journey [to Canossa] was begun. That noble man [Henry IV] left the realm accompanied by not a soul from Germany save one notable neither for his lineage nor his wealth. Since he needed resources for so long a journey, Henry sought aid from many men he had often benefited when his kingdom was intact. There were very few, however, who relieved his necessity to any extent, moved either by memory of past favors or by the present spectacle of human events. And thus the king descended suddenly from the

(Continued)

height of glory and greatest wealth to such distress and calamity! . . .

Henry came [to the walls of Canossa], as he was ordered to, and since that castle had been enclosed by a triple wall, having been received within the space of the second wall, his band of retainers having been left outside, his regalia laid aside, displaying nothing pertaining to the kingship, showing no ceremony, with bare feet and fasting from morning until vespers, he waited for the decision of the Roman Pontiff. He did this a second day, and then a third. On the fourth day, finally having been admitted into the pope's presence, after many opinions were voiced on each side, he was finally absolved from the excommunication under these conditions: that on the day and at the place designated by the pope, he promptly call a general council of the German princes . . .

[and there] it would be decided according to ecclesiastical law whether Henry should retain the realm.

Source: Maureen C. Miller, ed., *Power and the Holy in the Age of the Investiture Conflict: A Brief History with Documents* (Boston: Bedford/St. Martin's, 2005), 91–97.

QUESTIONS TO CONSIDER

1. How important was Henry's minority in weakening royal authority?

2. Why did Gregory consider Henry impious when he appointed churchmen?

3. Why did Henry consider Gregory a false pope?

4. If the events at Canossa led to the king's absolution, why did Lampert and others consider it a sign of royal weakness?

WHAT WOULD YOU DO?

If you were Henry IV, highly mindful of your status as emperor, angry about the claims of Gregory, but aware of the erosion of your supporters within Germany, would you have done penance at Canossa? Why or why not?

Henry's move was astute, for no priest could refuse absolution to a penitent; Gregory had to lift the excommunication and receive Henry back into the church. But, as Henry stood in the snow, Gregory had the advantage of enjoying the king's humiliation before the majesty of the pope.

Although Henry was technically back in the church's fold, nothing of substance had been resolved. The princes elected an antiking (a king chosen illegally), and Henry and his supporters elected an antipope. From 1077 until 1122, papal and imperial armies and supporters waged intermittent war in both Germany and Italy.

The Investiture Conflict was finally resolved long after Henry IV and Gregory VII had died. The **Concordat of Worms** of 1122 ended the fighting with a compromise. Henry V, the heir of Henry IV, gave up the right in the investiture ceremony to confer the ring and the pastoral staff—symbols of spiritual power. But he retained, in Germany, the right to be present when bishops were elected. In effect, he would continue to have influence over those elections. In both Germany and Italy, he also had the right to give the scepter to the churchman in a gesture meant to indicate the transfer of the temporal, or worldly, powers and possessions of the church (the lands by which it was supported).

Superficially, nothing much had changed; the Concordat of Worms ensured that secular rulers would continue to have a part in choosing and investing churchmen. In fact, however, few people would now claim that a king could act as head of the church. Just as the concordat broke the investiture ritual into two parts—one

Matilda of Tuscany
How often is a laywoman the dominant figure in medieval art? In this illustration, made around 1115, Matilda, countess of Tuscany, towers above the king (Henry IV) and upstages the abbot of Cluny (Hugh). Matilda was a key supporter of Pope Gregory VII. It was at her castle at Canossa that Henry IV did penance. The words underneath the picture emphasize Henry's abjection. They read: "The king begs the abbot and supplicates Matilda as well." (Biblioteca Apostolica Vaticana, Vatican State/Bridgeman Images.)

spiritual, with ring and staff, the other secular, with the scepter—so, too, it implied a new notion of kingship that separated it from priesthood. The Investiture Conflict did not produce the modern distinction between church and state—that would develop slowly—but it set the wheels in motion.

The most important changes brought about by the Investiture Conflict, however, were on the ground: the political landscape in both Italy and Germany was irrevocably transformed. In Germany, the princes consolidated their lands and their positions at the expense of royal power. In Italy, the emperor lost power to the cities. The northern and central Italian communes were formed in the crucible of the war between the pope and the emperor. In fierce communal struggles, city factions, often created by local grievances but claiming to fight on behalf of the papal or the imperial cause, created their own governing bodies. In the course of the twelfth century, these Italian cities became accustomed to self-government.

The Sweep of Reform

Church reform involved much more than the clash of popes, emperors, and their supporters. It penetrated into the daily lives of ordinary Christians. It inspired new ways to think about church personnel such as the priests and about church institutions such as the sacraments. It brought about a new systemization of church law, changed the way the papacy operated, inspired new monastic orders dedicated to poverty, and led to the crusades.

The **sacraments** were, in the Catholic church's terminology, the regular means by which God's heavenly grace infused mundane existence. They included rites such as baptism, the Eucharist (holy communion), and marriage. But this did not mean that Christians were clear about how many sacraments there were, how they worked, or even what their significance was. Eleventh-century church reformers began the process—which would continue into the thirteenth century—of emphasizing the importance of the sacraments and the special nature of the priest, whose chief role was to administer them.

Marriage, for example, became a sacrament only after the Gregorian reform. Before the twelfth century, priests had little to do with weddings, which were family affairs. After the twelfth century, however, priests were expected to consecrate marriages. Churchmen also began to assume jurisdiction over marital disputes, not simply in cases involving royalty (as they had always done) but also in those involving lesser aristocrats. The clergy's prohibition of marriage partners as distant as seventh cousins (since marriage between cousins was considered incest) had the potential to control dynastic alliances.

At the same time, churchmen began to stress the sanctity of marriage. Hugh of St. Victor, a twelfth-century scholar, dwelled on the sacramental meaning of marriage:

> Can you find anything else in marriage except conjugal society which makes it sacred and by which you can assert that it is holy? . . . Each shall be to the other as a same self in all sincere love, all careful solicitude, every kindness of affection, in constant compassion, unflagging consolation, and faithful devotedness.

In other words, Hugh saw marriage as a matter of Christian love.

The reformers also proclaimed the special importance of the sacrament of the Eucharist, received by eating the wafer (the body of Christ) and drinking wine (the blood of Christ) during the Mass. Gregory VII called the Mass "the greatest thing in the Christian religion." No layman, regardless of how powerful, and no woman of any class or status at all could perform anything equal to it, for the Mass was the key to salvation.

The new emphasis on the sacraments, along with a desire to distinguish the clergy more clearly from the laity, led to vigorous enforcement of an old element of church discipline: the celibacy of priests. The demand for a celibate clergy had far-reaching significance for the history of the church. It distanced western clerics even further from their eastern Orthodox counterparts (who did not practice celibacy), exacerbating the east–west church schism of 1054. It also broke with local practices in places where clerical marriage was customary. Undaunted, the reformers persisted, and in 1123, the pope proclaimed all clerical marriages invalid.

Clerics found other ways to distinguish themselves from the laity. Even before the Investiture Conflict, bishops made their power, prestige, and holiness visible by wearing gorgeous clothing when they carried out their ceremonial roles. Their donning of beautiful garb did not end once the conflict was over. In fact, in the twelfth and thirteenth centuries, the practice was extended to members of even the lower clerical orders, such as deacons and subdeacons.

What were the foundations of this new power? Some of it came from the consolidation and imposition of canon, or church, law. These laws had begun as rules determined at church councils. Later they were supplemented with papal declarations. Churchmen had made several attempts to gather together and organize these laws before the Gregorian reform. But that movement made systematization imperative. During the period 1085 to 1140, the anonymous *Collection in 74 Canons*, which brought canon laws together in such a way as to enhance the position of the pope, was enormously popular. It was superseded in 1140 by the *Decretum*, a massive work by Gratian, a teacher

of canon law at Bologna. Collecting nearly two thousand passages from the decrees of popes and councils as well as the writings of the church fathers, Gratian intended to demonstrate their essential agreement. In fact, his book's original title was *Harmony of Discordant Canons*. If he found any discord in his sources, Gratian usually imposed the harmony himself by arguing that the passages dealt with different situations. A bit later, another legal scholar revised and expanded the *Decretum*, adding ancient Roman law to the mix.

Even while Gratian was writing, the papal curia (government), centered in Rome, was beginning to resemble a court of law, complete with its own collection agency. In the course of the eleventh and twelfth centuries, the papacy developed a bureaucracy to hear cases, such as disputed elections of bishops. Churchmen went to the papal curia for other purposes as well: to petition for privileges for their monasteries or to be consecrated by the pope. All these services were expensive, requiring lawyers, judges, hearing officers, notaries, and collectors. The lands owned by the papacy were not sufficient to support the growing cost of its administrative apparatus, so the petitioners and litigants themselves had to pay. The pope, with his law courts, bureaucracy, and financial apparatus, had become a monarch.

New Monastic Orders of Poverty

Like the popes, the monks of Cluny and other Benedictine monasteries were reformers. Unlike the popes, they spent nearly their entire day in large and magnificently outfitted churches singing a long and complex liturgy consisting of Masses, prayers, and psalms. These "black monks"—so called because they dyed their robes black—reached the height of their popularity in the eleventh century. Their monasteries often housed hundreds of monks, though convents for Benedictine nuns were usually less populated. Cluny was one of the largest monasteries, with some four hundred brothers in the mid-eleventh century.

In the twelfth century, the black monks' lifestyle came under attack by groups seeking a religious life of poverty. They considered the opulence of a huge and gorgeous monastery like Cluny to be a sign of greed rather than honor. The Carthusian order founded by Bruno of Cologne in the 1080s was one such group. Each monk took a vow of silence and lived as a hermit in his own small hut. Monks occasionally joined others for prayer in a common prayer room, or oratory. When not engaged in prayer or meditation, the Carthusians copied manuscripts. They considered this task part of their religious vocation, a way to preach God's word with their hands rather than their mouths. The Carthusian order grew slowly. Each monastery was limited to only twelve monks, the number of the Apostles.

The Cistercians, by contrast, expanded rapidly. Their guiding spirit was **St. Bernard** (c. 1090–1153), who arrived at the Burgundian monastery of Cîteaux (in Latin, Cistercium, hence the name of the monks) in 1112 along

The Monastery of Cluny

Today, very little of Cluny's great monastery church is still standing, but this computer-enhanced image shows it as it likely looked in the twelfth century. The sound of the monks' chants would have reverberated in its enormous space, amplified still more by its stone construction. At the top of the apse (the easternmost part of the church), an image of Christ painted in bright colors floated in a mandorla—a large almond-shaped aureole. Around him were the symbols of the Evangelists (the authors of the four Gospels). Stained glass adorned its windows, and alternating light and dark stone enlivened the massive piers that reached from floor to vault. (Major Écclesia © on-situ/Arts et Métiers ParisTech/Centre des Monuments Nationaux – 2010.)

with about thirty friends and relatives. St. Bernard soon became abbot of Clairvaux, one of a cluster of Cistercian monasteries in Burgundy. By the mid-twelfth century, more than three hundred monasteries spread throughout Europe were following what they took to be the customs of Cîteaux. Nuns, too—as eager as monks to live the life of simplicity and poverty that they believed the Apostles had enjoyed and endured—adopted Cistercian customs. By the end of the twelfth century, the Cistercians were an order: all of their houses followed rules determined at the General Chapter, a meeting at which the abbots met to hammer out legislation.

Although they held up the rule of St. Benedict as the foundation of their monastic life, the Cistercians created a lifestyle all their own, largely governed by the goal of simplicity. Rejecting even the conceit of blackening their robes, they left them undyed (hence their nickname, the "white monks"). As shown in Figure 10.1, a diagram of Fountains Abbey in England, their monasteries were divided into two parts: the eastern half was for the monks, and the western half was for the lay brothers. The lay brothers did the hard manual labor necessary to keep the other monks—the "choir" monks—free to worship.

Cistercian churches reflected the order's emphasis on poverty. The churches were small, made of smoothly hewn, undecorated stone. Wall paintings and sculpture were prohibited. Their buildings cultivated a quiet beauty. Cistercian churches were bright, cool, and serene.

The white monks dedicated themselves to monastic administration as well as to private prayer and contemplation. Each house had large and highly organized farms and grazing lands called granges. Cistercian monks spent much of their time managing their estates and flocks, both of which were yielding

FIGURE 10.1 Plan of Fountains Abbey
Fountains Abbey's floor plan shows the key features of a Cistercian monastery. The eastern half of the monastery was reserved for the monks, who were dedicated to contemplation and prayer. The western half was for the lay brothers, who worked in the fields. The lay brothers slept above their storeroom and refectory, the monks above their common room. No one had a private bedroom, just as the rule of St. Benedict prescribed.

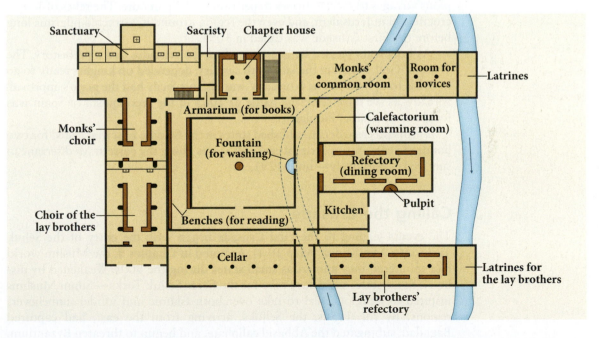

handsome profits by the end of the twelfth century. Although they had reacted against the wealth of the commercial revolution, the Cistercians became part of it, and managerial expertise was an integral part of their monastic life.

At the same time, the Cistercians emphasized a spirituality of intense emotion. They cultivated a theology that stressed the humanity of Christ and Mary. They regularly used maternal metaphors to describe the nurturing care that Jesus provided to humans. The Cistercian Jesus was approachable, human, protective, even mothering.

Many who were not members of the Cistercian order held similar views of God; their spirituality signaled wider changes. For example, around 1099, St. Anselm wrote a theological treatise entitled *Why God Became Man*, arguing that since man had sinned, only a sinless man could redeem him. St. Anselm's work represented a new theological emphasis on the redemptive power of human charity, including that of Jesus as a human being. As Anselm was writing, the crusaders were heading for the very place of Christ's crucifixion, making his humanity more real and powerful to people who walked in the holy "place of God's humiliation and our redemption," as one chronicler put it. Yet this new stress on the loving bonds that tied Christians together also led to the persecution of non-Christians, especially Jews and Muslims.

REVIEW QUESTION
What were the causes and consequences of the Gregorian reform?

The Crusades

The crusades were the culmination of two separate historical movements: pilgrimages and holy wars. Like pilgrimages to the Holy Land, the place where Jesus had lived and died, the crusades drew on a long tradition of making pious voyages to sacred shrines to petition for help or cure. The relics of Jesus's crucifixion in Jerusalem, and even the region around it, attracted pilgrims long before the First Crusade was called in 1095.

As holy wars blessed by church leaders, the crusades had a prehistory. The Truce of God, begun in the late tenth century, depended on knights ready to go to battle to uphold it. The Normans' war against Sicily had the pope's approval. Already, as we have seen, the battle of 1063 in the reconquista of Spain was fought with a papal indulgence.

European crusaders established states in the Middle East that lasted for two hundred years. A tiny strip of crusader states along the eastern Mediterranean survived—perilously—until 1291.

Calling the Crusade

The events leading to the First Crusade began with the entry of the Seljuk Turks into Asia Minor (Map 10.1). As noted in Chapter 9, the Muslim world had splintered into numerous small states during the 900s. Weakened by disunity, those states were easy prey for the fierce Seljuk Turks—Sunni Muslims inspired by religious zeal to take over both Islamic and infidel (unbeliever) regions. By the 1050s, the Seljuks, arriving from the east, had captured Baghdad, subjugated the Abbasid caliphate, and begun to threaten Byzantium.

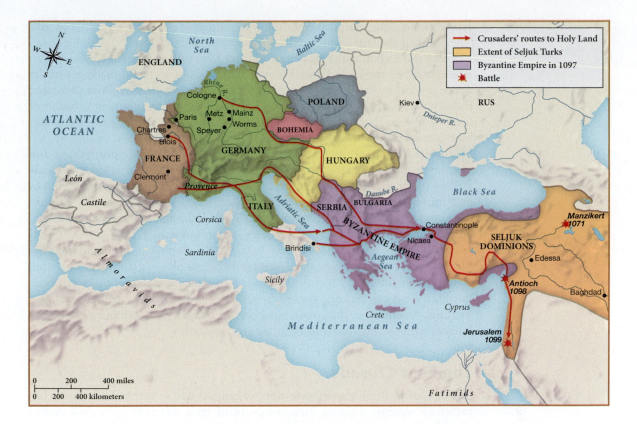

MAP 10.1 The First Crusade, 1096–1099
The First Crusade was a major military undertaking that required organization, movement over both land and sea, and enormous resources. Four main groups were responsible for the conquest of Jerusalem. One began at Cologne, in northern Germany; a second group started out from Blois, in France; the third originated just to the west of Provence; and the fourth launched ships from Brindisi, at the heel of Italy. All joined up at Constantinople, where their leaders negotiated with Alexius Comnenus for help and supplies in return for a pledge of vassalage to the emperor.

The difficulties that Byzantine ruler Romanus IV had in pulling together an army to attack the Turks reveal how weak the emperor's position had become. Unable to muster Byzantine troops—which either were busy defending their own districts or were under the control of dynatoi (see page 297) wary of sending support to the emperor—Romanus had to rely on a mercenary army made up of Normans, Franks, Slavs, and even Turks. This motley force met the Seljuks at Manzikert in what is today eastern Turkey. The battle was a disaster for Romanus: the Seljuks routed the Byzantine army and captured the emperor. The battle of Manzikert (1071) marked the end of Byzantine domination in the region.

Gradually settling in Asia Minor, the Turks extended their control across the empire and beyond, all the way to Jerusalem, which had been under Muslim control since the seventh century and most recently had been under the rule of the Shi'ite Fatimids. In 1095, the Byzantine emperor **Alexius I (Alexius Comnenus)** (r. 1081–1118) appealed for help to Pope Urban II, hoping to get new mercenary troops for a fresh offensive.

Urban II (r. 1088–1099) chose to interpret the request in his own way. At a church council in Clermont (France) in 1095, he addressed an already excited throng, telling them to "wrest that land"—he meant the Holy Land—"from the wicked race, and subject it to yourselves." The crowd responded with one voice: "God wills it." Urban offered all who made the difficult trek to

Jerusalem to fight against the Muslims an indulgence—the forgiveness of sins. The pains of the trip would substitute for ordinary penance.

Why did Urban make this call to arms? Certainly he hoped to win Christian control of the Holy Land. He was also anxious to fulfill the goals of the Truce of God by turning the crowd at Clermont into a peace militia dedicated to holy purposes. Finally, Urban's call placed the papacy in a new position of leadership, one that complemented in a military arena the position the popes had gained in the church hierarchy.

Inspired by local preachers, men and women, rich and poor, young and old, laypeople and clerics heeded Urban's call to go on the **First Crusade** (1096–1099). Between 60,000 and 100,000 people abandoned their homes and braved the rough journey to Jerusalem. They went to fight for God, to gain land and plunder, or to follow their lord. Although women were discouraged from going, some crusaders were accompanied by their wives. Other women went as servants; a few may have been fighters. Children and old people, not able to fight, made the cords for siege engines—giant machines used to hurl stones at enemy fortifications. As Christians undertook more crusades during the twelfth century, the transport and supply of these armies became a lucrative business for the commercial classes of maritime Italian cities such as Venice, strategically located on the route eastward.

The First Crusade

The armies of the First Crusade were organized not as one military force but rather as separate militias, each commanded by a different individual authorized by the pope. There were also irregular armies. Some of these, not heeding the pope's official departure date in August, left early. Historians call these loosely affiliated groups the People's (or Peasants') Crusade. Some of the participants were peasants, others knights. Inspired by the charismatic orator Peter the Hermit and others like him, they took off for the Holy Land via the Rhineland. This unlikely route was no mistake: the crusaders wanted to kill Jews, who, like the Muslims, did not accept Christ's divinity. By 1095, three cities of the Rhineland—Speyer, Worms, and Mainz—had especially large and flourishing Jewish populations with long-established relationships with the local bishops.

The People's Crusade—joined by local nobles, knights, and townspeople—vented its fury against the Jews of the Rhineland. As one commentator put it, the crusaders considered it ridiculous to attack Muslims when other infidels lived in their own backyards: "That's doing our work backward." The Rhineland Jews had to choose between conversion or death. Many Jews in Speyer found refuge in the bishop's castle, but at Worms and Mainz hundreds were massacred. Similar pogroms—systematic persecutions of Jews—took place a half century later, when the preaching of the Second Crusade led to new attacks on the Jews.

After they had vented their fury in the Rhineland, some members of the People's Crusade dropped out. The rest continued through Hungary to Constantinople, where Alexius I promptly shipped them to Asia Minor, where most of them died. In the autumn, the main armies of the crusaders began to arrive, their leaders squabbling with Alexius from the start.

Considering them too weak to bother with, the Turks spared the arriving crusaders, who made their way south to the Seljuk capital at Nicaea. At first, their armies were uncoordinated and their food supplies uncertain, but soon the crusaders organized themselves. They managed to defeat a Turkish army that attacked from nearby; then, surrounding Nicaea and besieging it with catapults and other war machines, they took the city on June 18, 1097.

Most of the crusaders then went toward Antioch, which stood in the way of their conquest of Jerusalem, but one led his followers to Edessa, where they took over the city and its outlying area, creating the first of the crusader states. Meanwhile, the main body of crusaders took Antioch after a long stalemate (see Primary Source Analysis on pages 356–357). From there, it was only a short march to Jerusalem. Quarrels among Muslim rulers eased the way. In early June 1099, a large force of crusaders amassed before the walls of Jerusalem; in mid-July, they attacked, breaching the walls and entering the city. "Now that our men had possession of the walls and towers, wonderful sights were to be seen," wrote Raymond d'Aguiliers, a priest serving one of the crusade leaders. "Some of our men (and this was the more merciful) cut off the heads of their enemies; others shot them with arrows, so that they fell from the towers; others tortured them longer by casting them into the flames."

The Crusader States in 1109

The Crusader States

The main objective of the First Crusade—to wrest the Holy Land from the Muslims and subject it to Christian rule—had now been accomplished. The leaders of the expedition did not give the conquered territories to Alexius but held on to them instead. By 1109, they had carved out several tiny states in the Holy Land.

Crusade Warfare
This battle scene, painted on paper (already common in the Islamic world) in the twelfth century, depicts an Islamic garrison defending against Western knights. At the center is a Muslim warrior wearing a large turban. Fully clad in chain mail, he sits atop a horse and wields a sword and shield. Behind him to the left are archers, also in mail armor and turbans. Above him and to the right are Muslim foot soldiers protected only by large shields. Their enemy, the knight on the black horse, has been defeated and is falling to the ground. (The Art Archive/ REX/Shutterstock.)

The First Crusade from the Muslim Point of View

Ibn al-Qalanisi (1073–1160) was a well-educated scholar who served in several public offices—including the position equivalent to mayor—in Damascus. Not only did he live through the First Crusade as a young man, but he also had access to eyewitness reports about it from the Muslim point of view.

(19th December, 1096, to 8th December, 1097)
In this year there began to arrive a succession of reports that the armies of the Franks had appeared from the direction of the sea of Constantinople with forces not to be reckoned for multitude. As these reports followed one upon the other and spread from mouth to mouth far and wide, the people grew anxious and disturbed in mind. The king, Da'ud b. Sulaiman b. Qutulmish [the Seljuk sultan of Anatolia], whose dominions lay nearest to them, having received confirmation of these statements, set about collecting forces, raising levies, and carrying out the obligation of Holy War. He also summoned as many of the Turkmens [mainly Seljuks] as he could to give him assistance and support against them, and a large number of them joined him along with the 'askar [the standing army of archers] of his brother. His confidence having been strengthened thereby, and his offensive power rendered formidable, he marched out to the fords, tracks, and roads by which the Franks must pass, and showed no mercy to all of them who fell into his hands. When he had thus killed a great number, they turned their forces against him, defeated him, and scattered his army, killing many and taking many captive,

and plundered and enslaved. The Turkmens, having lost most of their horses, took to flight. The King of the Greeks [Byzantine Emperor Alexius] bought a great many of those whom they had enslaved and had them transported to Constantinople. When the news was received of this shameful calamity to the cause of Islam, the anxiety of the people became acute and their fear and alarm increased. The date of this battle was the 20th of Rajab (4th July, 1097).

In the middle of Sha'ban (end of July) the emir Yaghi Siyan, lord [emir] of Antioch, accompanied by the emir Sukman b. Ortuq and the emir Karbuqa [lord of Mosul], set out with his 'askar towards Antioch, on receipt of news that the Franks were approaching it and had occupied al-Balana [a village in northern Syria]. Yaghi Siyan therefore hastened to Antioch and dispatched his son to al-Malik Duqaq at Damascus, to Janah al-Dawla at Hims, and to all the other cities and districts, appealing for aid and support, and inciting them to hasten to the Holy War, while he set about fortifying Antioch and expelling its Christian population. On the 2nd of Shawwal (12th September) the Frankish armies descended on Baghras and developed their attack upon the territories of Antioch, whereupon those who were in the castles and forts adjacent to Antioch revolted and killed their garrisons except for a few who were able to escape from them. The [Christian] people of Artah did likewise and called for reinforcements from the Franks. During Sha'ban a comet appeared in the West; it continued to rise for a space of about twenty days, and then disappeared.

Because the crusader states were created by conquest, they were treated as lordships. The rulers granted fiefs to their vassals, and some of these in turn gave portions of their holdings as fiefs to their own vassals. Since most Europeans went home after the First Crusade, the rulers who remained learned to coexist with the indigenous population, which included Muslims, Jews, and Greek Orthodox Christians. They encouraged a lively trade at their ports.

The main concerns of these rulers were military. They set up castles and recruited knights from Europe. So organized for war was this society that it produced a new and militant kind of monasticism: the Knights Templar. The Templars vowed themselves to poverty and chastity. But unlike monks, the Templars, whose name came from their living quarters in the area of the former Jewish

Meanwhile, a large detachment of the Frankish army, numbering about thirty thousand men, had left the main body and set about ravaging the other districts, in the course of which they came to al-Bara and slaughtered about fifty men there. Now the 'askar of Damascus had reached the neighborhood of Shaizar, on their way to support Yaghi Siyan, and when this detachment made its descent on al-Bara, they moved out against it. After a succession of charges by each side, in which a number of their men were killed, the Franks returned to al-Ruj, and thence proceeded towards Antioch. Oil, salt, and other necessaries became dear and unprocurable in Antioch, but so much was smuggled into the city that they became cheap again. The Franks dug a trench between their position and the city, owing to the frequent sallies made against them by the army of Antioch.

Now the Franks, on their first appearance, had made a covenant with the king of the Greeks, and had promised him that they would deliver over to him the first city which they should capture. They then captured Nicæa, and it was the first place they captured, but they did not carry out their word to him on that occasion, and refused to deliver it up to him according to the stipulation. Subsequently they captured on their way several frontier fortresses and passes.

A.H. 491

(9th December, 1097, to 27th November, 1098)
At the end of First Jumada (beginning of June, 1098) the report arrived that certain of the men of Antioch among the armorers in the train of the emir Yaghi Siyan had entered into a conspiracy against Antioch and had come to an agreement with the Franks to deliver the city up to them, because of some ill-usage and confiscations which they had formerly suffered at his hands. They found an opportunity of seizing one of the city bastions adjoining the Jabal [low-lying hills near Antioch], which they sold to the Franks, and thence admitted them into the city during the night. At daybreak they raised the battle cry, whereupon Yaghi Siyan took to flight and went out with a large body, but not one person amongst them escaped to safety. When he reached the neighbourhood of Armanaz, an estate near Ma'arrat Masrin, he fell from his horse to the ground. One of his companions raised him up and remounted him, but he could not maintain his balance on the back of the horse, and after falling repeatedly he died. As for Antioch, the number of men, women, and children killed, taken prisoner, and enslaved from its population is beyond computation. About three thousand men fled to the citadel and fortified themselves in it, and some few escaped for whom God had decreed escape.

QUESTION TO CONSIDER

What evidence does al-Qalanisi offer to suggest that the Muslims themselves were not united against the Crusaders?

Temple at Jerusalem, devoted themselves to warfare. Their first mission—to protect the pilgrimage routes from Palestine to Jerusalem—soon diversified. They manned the town garrisons of the crusader states, and they transported money from Europe to the Holy Land. In this way, the Order of the Templars became enormously wealthy (even though individual monks owned nothing), with branch "banks" in major cities across Europe.

The Disastrous Second Crusade

The presence of the Knights Templar did not prevent the Seljuks from taking the county of Edessa in 1144. This was the beginning of the slow but steady shrinking of the crusader states. It sparked the Second Crusade (1147–1149), which attracted, for the first time, ruling monarchs to the cause: Louis VII of France and Emperor Conrad III in Germany. (The First Crusade had been led by counts and dukes.) St. Bernard, the charismatic and influential Cistercian abbot, was its tireless preacher.

Little organization or planning went into the Second Crusade. The emperor at Byzantium was hardly involved. Louis VII and Conrad III had no coordinated strategy. A chronicler of the crusade wryly remarked, "Those whose common will had undertaken a common task should also use a common plan of action." All the armies were badly hurt by Turkish attacks. Furthermore, they largely acted at cross-purposes with the Christian rulers still in the Holy Land.

At last the leaders met at Acre (today in Israel) and agreed to storm Damascus, which was under Muslim control and a thorn in the side of the Christian king of Jerusalem. On July 24, 1148, they were on the city's outskirts, but, encountering a stiff defense, they abandoned the attack after five days, suffering many losses as they retreated. The crusade was over.

The Second Crusade had one decisive outcome: it led Louis VII to divorce his wife, Eleanor, the heiress of Aquitaine. He was disappointed that she had provided him with a daughter but no son, and he suspected her of infidelity. After the pope "dissolved" their marriage—that is, found it to have been uncanonical in the first place—Eleanor promptly married Henry, count of Anjou and duke of Normandy. This marriage had far-reaching consequences, as we shall see, when Henry became King Henry II of England in 1154.

The Long-Term Impact of the Crusades

The success of the First Crusade was a mirage. The European toehold in the Middle East could not last. Numerous new crusades were called, and eight major ones took place between the first in 1096 and the last at the end of the thirteenth century. But most Europeans were not willing to commit the vast resources and personnel that would have been necessary to maintain the crusader states, which fell to the Muslims permanently in 1291. In Europe, the crusades to the Holy Land became a sort of myth—an elusive goal that receded before more pressing ventures nearer to home. Yet they inspired far-flung expeditions like Columbus's in 1492. Although the crusades stimulated trade a bit, especially enhancing the prosperity of Italian cities like Venice, the commercial revolution would have happened without them. On the other hand, modern taxation systems may well have been stimulated by the machinery of revenue collection used to finance the crusades.

In the Middle East, the crusades worsened—but did not cause—Islamic disunity. Before the crusades, Muslims had a complex relationship with the Christians in their midst—taxing but not persecuting them, allowing their churches to stand and be used, permitting pilgrims into Jerusalem to visit the holy sites of Christ's life and death. In many ways, the split between Shi'ite and Sunni Muslims was more serious than the rift between Muslims and Christians. The crusades, and especially the conquest of Jerusalem, shocked and dismayed Muslims: "We have mingled blood with flowing tears," wrote one of their poets, "and there is no room left in us for pity."

REVIEW QUESTION
How and why was the First Crusade a success, and how and why was it a failure?

The Revival of Monarchies

Even as the papacy was exercising its authority by adjudicating clerical disputes, annulling marriages, and calling crusades, most kings and other rulers were enhancing and consolidating their own power. They created new ideologies and dusted off old theories to justify their hegemony (dominating influence), they hired officials to work for them, and they found vassals and churchmen to support them. Money gave them greater effectiveness, and the new commercial economy supplied them with increased revenues. The exception was the emperor in Germany, who was weakened by the Investiture Conflict.

Reconstructing the Empire at Byzantium

Ten years after the disastrous battle at Manzikert, Alexius Comnenus became the Byzantine emperor, Alexius I. He was an upstart—from a family of dynatoi—who saw the opportunity to seize the throne in a time of crisis. The people of Constantinople were suffering under a combination of high taxes and rising living costs. In addition, the empire was under attack on every side—from Normans in southern Italy, Seljuk Turks in Asia Minor, and new groups in the Balkans. However, the emperor managed to avert the worst dangers.

To wage all the wars he had to fight, Alexius relied on mercenaries and allied dynatoi, armed and mounted like European knights and accompanied by their own troops. In return for their services, he gave these nobles lifetime possession of large imperial estates and their dependent peasants. Meanwhile, Alexius satisfied the urban elite by granting them new offices. He normally got on well with the patriarch and Byzantine clergy, for emperor and church depended on each other to suppress heresy and foster orthodoxy. The emperors of the Comnenian dynasty (1081–1185) thus gained in prestige and military might, but at the price of significant concessions to the Byzantine nobility.

England under Norman Rule

In the twelfth century, the kings of England were the most powerful monarchs of Europe, in large part because they ruled their whole kingdom by right of conquest. When the Anglo-Saxon king Edward the Confessor (r. 1042–1066) died childless in 1066, three main contenders vied for the English throne: Harold, earl of Wessex, an Englishman close to the king but not of royal blood; Harald Hardrada, the king of Norway, who had unsuccessfully attempted to conquer the Danes and now turned hopefully to England; and William, duke of Normandy, who claimed that Edward had promised him the throne fifteen years earlier. On his deathbed, Edward had named Harold of Wessex to succeed him, and a royal advisory committee that had the right to choose the king confirmed the nomination. When he learned that Harold had been anointed and crowned, William (1027–1087) prepared for battle. Appealing to the pope, he received the banner of St. Peter and with this symbol of God's approval launched

Norman Conquest of England, 1066

the invasion of England, filling his ships with warriors recruited from many parts of France. Just before William's invasion force landed, Harold defeated Harald Hardrada at Stamford Bridge, near York, in the north of England. When he heard of William's arrival, Harold turned his forces south, marching them 250 miles and picking up new soldiers along the way to meet the Normans.

The two armies clashed at the **battle of Hastings** on October 14, 1066, in one of history's rare decisive battles. Most of Harold's men were on foot, armed with battle-axes and stones tied to sticks, which could be thrown with great force. William's army consisted of perhaps three thousand mounted knights, a thousand archers, and the rest infantry. At first William's knights broke rank, frightened by the deadly battle-axes thrown by the English; but then some of the English also broke rank as they pursued the knights. Gradually Harold's troops were worn down, particularly by William's archers, whose arrows flew a hundred yards, much farther than an Englishman could throw his battle-ax. (Some of the archers are depicted on the lower margin of the Bayeux "Tapestry.") By dusk, King Harold was dead and his army defeated.

Some Anglo-Saxons in England supported William. But William—known to posterity as William the Conqueror—wanted to replace, not assimilate, the Anglo-Saxons. During William's reign, families from the European continent almost totally supplanted the English aristocracy. Although the English peasantry remained—now with new Norman lords—many of them "perished . . . by famine or the sword," as William confessed on his deathbed. Modern historians estimate that one out of five people in England died as a result of the Norman conquest and its immediate aftermath. Yet, although the Normans destroyed a generation of English men and women, they preserved and extended many Anglo-Saxon institutions. For example, the new kings retained the old administrative divisions and legal system of the shires. At the same time, they drew from continental institutions. They set up a political hierarchy, culminating in the king, whose strength was reinforced by his castles. Because all of England was the king's by conquest, he could treat it as his booty. William kept about 20 percent of the land for himself and divided the rest, distributing it in large but

Bayeux "Tapestry" (detail)
This famous "tapestry" is misnamed; it is really an embroidery, 230 feet long and 20 inches wide, created to tell the story of the Norman conquest of England from William's point of view. In this detail, the Norman archers are lined up along the lower band. In the large central zone, the English warriors are on foot, while the Norman knights are on horseback. (The top border is decorated with animals and birds.) Who seems to be winning? (Musée de la Tapisserie, Bayeux, France/Bridgeman Images.)

scattered fiefs to a relatively small number of his barons and family members, lay and ecclesiastical, as well as to some lesser men. In turn, these fief-holders maintained their own vassals; they owed the king military service—and the service of a fixed number of their vassals—along with certain dues, such as reliefs (money paid upon inheriting a fief) and aids (payments made on important occasions).

In addition to these revenues from the nobles, the king of England made sure that he would get his share from the peasantry. In 1086, William ordered a survey and census of England, popularly called Domesday because, like the reckoning Christians expected at doomsday, it provided facts that could not be appealed. It was the most extensive inventory of land, livestock, taxes, and population that had ever been compiled in Europe. The king's men consulted Anglo-Saxon tax lists and took testimony from local men. From these inquests, scribes drew up reports, which were then summarized in Domesday itself.

William was not just the ruler of England; he was also duke of Normandy. The Norman conquest tied England to the languages, politics, institutions, and culture of the European continent. English commerce was linked to the wool industry in Flanders. St. Anselm, the archbishop of Canterbury and author of *Why God Became Man*, was born in Italy and served as the abbot of a monastery in Normandy before crossing the channel to England. Modern English is an amalgam of Anglo-Saxon and Norman French.

The barons of England retained their estates in Normandy and elsewhere, and the kings of England often spent more time on the continent than they did on the island. When William's son Henry I (r. 1100–1135) died without male heirs, civil war soon erupted: the throne of England was fought over by two French counts, one married to Henry's daughter, the other to his sister. The story of England after 1066 was, in miniature, the story of Europe.

Praising the King of France

The twelfth-century kings of France were much less obviously powerful than their English and Byzantine counterparts. Yet they, too, took part in the monarchical revival. Louis VI, called Louis the Fat (r. 1108–1137), was a tireless defender of royal power. We know a good deal about him and his reputation because a contemporary and close associate, Suger (1081–1152), abbot of Saint-Denis, wrote Louis's biography.

Although a churchman, Suger was a propagandist for his king. When Louis set about consolidating his rule in the Île-de-France, Suger portrayed him as a righteous hero. He thought that the king had rights over the French nobles because they were his vassals. He believed that the king had a religious role as the protector of the church and the poor. To be sure, the Gregorian reform had made its mark: Suger did not claim that Louis was the head of the church. But he nevertheless emphasized the royal dignity and its importance to the papacy. He stressed Louis's piety and active defense of the faith.

When Louis VI died in 1137, Suger's notion of the might and right of the king of France reflected reality in an extremely small area. Nevertheless, Louis laid the groundwork for the gradual extension of royal power in France. As the lord of vassals, the king could call on his men to aid him in times of war, though the most powerful among them sometimes disregarded the summons. As a king and landlord, he could obtain many dues and taxes. He drew revenues from Paris, a thriving city not only of commerce but also of scholarship. Officials called provosts enforced his royal laws and collected taxes. With money and land, Louis dispensed the favors and gave the gifts that added to his prestige and his power. Louis VI and Suger together created the territorial core and royal ideal of the future French monarchy.

Surviving as Emperor

Henry IV lost much of the power over the church and over Italy that his father had wielded. The Investiture Conflict meant that he could no longer control the church hierarchy in Germany and northern Italy, nor could he depend on bishops to work as government officials. The German princes rebelled against him, and the cities of northern Italy found ways to declare their independence of him.

The Concordat of Worms (1122) conceded considerable power within the church to the king, but said nothing about the ruler's relations with the German princes or the Italian cities. When Henry V (r. 1106–1125) died childless, the position of the emperor was extremely uncertain.

REVIEW QUESTION
Which ruler—Alexius I Comnenus, William the Conqueror, or Louis VI—was the strongest, which the feeblest, and why?

At such times, the great bishops and princes would meet together to elect the next emperor. In 1125, numerous candidates were put forward; the winner, Lothar II (r. 1125–1137), was chosen largely because he was *not* the person designated by Henry V. Lothar had little time to reestablish royal control before he, too, died childless, leaving the princes to elect Conrad III. It was Conrad's nephew, Frederick Barbarossa, who would find new sources of imperial power in the post-Gregorian age.

Conclusion

The commercial revolution and the building boom it spurred profoundly changed Europe. New trade, wealth, and business institutions became common in its thriving cities. Merchants and artisans became important. Mutual and fraternal organizations like the guilds and communes expressed and reinforced the solidarity and economic interests of city dwellers. The countryside became reorganized for the market.

Sensitized by the commercial revolution to the corrupting effects of money and inspired by the model of Cluny, which seemed to "free the church from the world," reformers began to demand a new and purified church. Under Pope Gregory VII, the reform movement asserted a new vision of the church with the pope at the top. But many people—especially rulers—depended on the old system. Henry IV was particularly affected; for him the Gregorian reform meant war. The Investiture Conflict, though officially ended by a compromise, in fact greatly enhanced the power of the papacy and weakened that of the emperor.

The First Crusade was both cause and effect of the pope's new power. But the crusades were not just papal projects. They were fueled by enormous

MAPPING THE WEST

Europe and the Mediterranean, c. 1150

A comparison with Mapping the West in Chapter 9 (page 326) reveals the major changes wrought during the century 1050–1150. England was politically tied to the continent with the Norman invasion of 1066. The Seljuk Turks settled most of Anatolia, pushing into territory previously held by Byzantium. At the end of the eleventh century, a narrow ribbon of crusader states was set up in the Holy Land. Meanwhile, Sicily and southern Italy came under Norman rule.

Analyzing the Map: What happened to the Byzantine Empire in the period 1050–1150?

Making Connections: What explains the growth of the northern kingdoms in Spain?

popular piety as well as by the ambitions of European rulers. They resulted in a ribbon of crusader states along the eastern Mediterranean.

Apart from the emperor, rulers in the period after the Investiture Conflict gained new prestige and, with the wealth of the commercial revolution, the ability to hire civil servants and impose their will as never before. The Norman ruler of England is a good example of the new-style king; William the Conqueror was interested not only in waging war but also in setting up the most efficient possible taxation system in times of peace. The successes of these rulers signaled a new era: the flowering of the Middle Ages.

Chapter 10 Review

Key Terms and People

Be sure that you can identify the term or person and explain its historical significance.

commercial revolution (p. 332)

guild (p. 336)

apprentices (p. 336)

journeymen/journeywomen (p. 336)

masters (p. 336)

capitalism (p. 337)

commune (p. 338)

simony (p. 341)

lay investiture (p. 341)

reconquista (p. 342)

Gregorian reform (p. 342)

Henry IV (p. 342)

Investiture Conflict (p. 343)

Concordat of Worms (p. 346)

sacraments (p. 347)

St. Bernard (p. 350)

Alexius I (Alexius Comnenus) (p. 353)

Urban II (p. 353)

First Crusade (p. 354)

battle of Hastings (p. 360)

Review Questions

1. What new institutions resulted from the commercial revolution?

2. What were the causes and consequences of the Gregorian reform?

3. How and why was the First Crusade a success, and how and why was it a failure?

4. Which ruler—Alexius I Comnenus, William the Conqueror, or Louis VI—was the strongest, which the feeblest, and why?

Making Connections

1. What were the similarities—and what were the differences—between the powers wielded by the Carolingian kings and those wielded by twelfth-century rulers?

2. In what ways was the movement for church reform a consequence of the commercial revolution?

3. How may the First Crusade be understood as a consequence of the Gregorian reform?

Important Events

910	Founding of Cluny
1049–1054	Papacy of Leo IX
1054	Schism between eastern and western churches begins
1066	Battle of Hastings: Norman conquest of England under William I
1071	Battle between Byzantines and Seljuk Turks at Manzikert
1073–1085	Papacy of Gregory VII
1077	Henry IV does penance before Gregory VII at Canossa; war breaks out
1086	Domesday survey
1095	Council of Clermont; Pope Urban II calls First Crusade
1096–1099	First Crusade

1097	Establishment of commune at Milan
1108–1137	Reign of Louis VI
1109	Establishment of the crusader states
1122	Concordat of Worms ends Investiture Conflict
c. 1140	Gratian's *Decretum* published
1147–1149	Second Crusade

Consider three events

Papacy of Gregory VII (1073–1085), Concordat of Worms ends Investiture Conflict (1122), and Gratian's *Decretum* published (c. 1140). How did these events serve to enhance the power of the papacy? How might the papacy have been different had any of these events not occurred?

Suggested References

Little makes crucial connections between the commercial revolution and religious reform. Miller's running narrative and primary sources provide the best introduction to the Investiture Conflict and its aftermath, and her book on clerical clothing shows that "fashion" is not a modern invention. Rubenstein's book offers a good mix of primary sources on the First Crusade. Yildiz introduces the Seljuks. Fuhrmann, Hallam, and Huscroft cover the new western monarchies, while Waley takes up the Italian republics.

*Bayeux Tapestry: http://www.bayeuxtapestry.org.uk/Index.htm

Clanchy, Michael. *From Memory to Written Record: England, 1066–1307*. 3rd ed. 2013.

Fuhrmann, Horst. *Germany in the High Middle Ages, c. 1050–1200*. 2002.

Hallam, Elizabeth M., and Judith Everard. *Capetian France, 987–1328*. 2nd ed. 2001.

Huscroft, Richard. *The Norman Conquest: A New Introduction*. 2009.

Little, Lester K. *Religious Poverty and the Profit Economy in Medieval Europe*. 1978.

Lopez, Robert S. *The Commercial Revolution of the Middle Ages, 950–1350*. 1976.

*_____, and Irving W. Raymond. *Medieval Trade in the Mediterranean World*. 1955.

Miller, Maureen C. *Clothing the Clergy: Virtue and Power in Medieval Europe, c. 800–1200*. 2014.

*_____. *Power and the Holy in the Age of the Investiture Conflict*. 2005.

Moore, Robert I. *The First European Revolution, c. 970–1215*. 2000.

Morris, Colin. *The Papal Monarchy: The Western Church from 1050 to 1250*. 1989.

*Peters, Edward, ed. *The First Crusade: The Chronicle of Fulcher of Chartres and Other Source Materials*. 1971.

*Rubenstein, Jay. *The First Crusade: A Brief History with Documents*. 2015

*Suger. *The Deeds of Louis the Fat*. Trans. Richard C. Cusimano and John Moorhead. 1992.

Tyerman, Christopher. *God's War: A New History of the Crusades*. 2006.

Waley, Daniel. *The Italian City-Republics*. 1969.

Yildiz, Sara Nur. *The Seljuk Empire of Anatolia*. 2016.

_____

*Primary source.

The Flowering of the Middle Ages

1150–1215

I n 1194, a raging fire burned most of the town of Chartres, in France, including its cathedral. Worried citizens feared that their most prized relic, the sacred tunic worn by the Virgin Mary when Christ was born, had gone up in flames as well. Had the Virgin abandoned the town? Suddenly the bishop and his clerics emerged from the cathedral crypt carrying the sacred tunic, which had remained unharmed. They took it as a sign that the Virgin had not only *not* abandoned her city but also wanted a new and more magnificent cathedral to house her relic. The town dedicated itself to the task; the bishop, his clerics, and the town guilds all gave generously to pay for stonecutters, carvers, glaziers, countless other workmen, and a master builder. Donations poured in from the counts, dukes, and even the king of France. The new cathedral was finished in twenty-six years—a very short time in an age when such churches usually took a century or more to build. Its vault soared 116 feet high; its length stretched more than 100 yards. Its western portals, which had been spared the flames, retained the sculptural decoration—carved around 1150—of the old church: three doorways surrounded and surmounted by figures that demonstrated the close relationship between the truths of divine wisdom, the French royal house, and the seven liberal arts—grammar, rhetoric, logic, arithmetic, geometry, music, and astronomy. The rest of the church was built in a new style: Gothic.

The rebuilt cathedral at Chartres sums up in stone the key features that characterized the period from 1150 to 1215 and would mark the rest of the Middle Ages. Its Gothic style—with its high vault, flying buttresses, and enormous stained-glass windows—became the quintessential style of medieval architecture. The celebration of the liberal arts on one of its doorways mirrored the new schools that flourished in the twelfth

«**Chartres Cathedral** Rebuilt after a fire in 1194, the cathedral of Chartres reconciled old and new. The three doorways of its west end (shown here) were remnants of the former church. But they were crowned by a rose window, a form newly in vogue. (Ingram Publishing/ Newscom.)

century and culminated in the universities of the thirteenth. The twenty-four statues of Old Testament figures flanking its western portals were meant to prefigure the kings of France; they demonstrate the extraordinary importance of powerful princes in this period, when monarchies and principalities ceased to be the personal creation of each ruler and became permanent institutions, with professional bureaucratic staffs. The outpouring of popular support that culminated in the building of the cathedral is evidence of a vibrant vernacular (non-Latin-speaking) culture, which expressed itself not only in stone but in literature as well. Finally, the emphasis at Chartres on the divine wisdom echoes the age's fervor about Christian truths, a zeal that led to the creation of new religious movements even as it stoked the fires of intolerance.

New Schools and Churches

Key to the flowering of the Middle Ages was a new emphasis on learning and a new form of church architecture termed Gothic. In many ways, these developments laid the foundation for other trends of the period. The schools trained men to staff new bureaucracies and at the same time fed religious fervor. The Gothic style gave luster to its rich patrons, the increasingly powerful rulers of the time, who offered needed support both to the schools and to the architects who produced the style.

The New Learning and the Rise of the University

CHAPTER FOCUS
What were the cultural and political achievements of the late twelfth century, and what downsides did they have?

Since the Carolingian period schools had been connected to monasteries and cathedrals, where they trained men to become either monks or priests. Some schools were better endowed with books and masters (or teachers) than others; a few developed a reputation for a certain kind of theological approach or specialized in a particular branch of learning, such as theology, medicine, or law. By the end of the eleventh century, the best schools were generally in the cathedrals of the larger cities: Reims, Paris, and Montpellier in France, and Bologna in Italy.

Finding these schools both exciting and practical, eager students flocked to them. Teachers were forced to search out larger halls to accommodate the

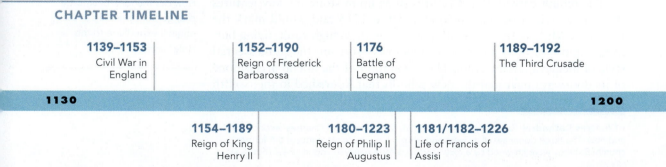

CHAPTER TIMELINE

1139–1153	1152–1190	1176	1189–1192
Civil War in England	Reign of Frederick Barbarossa	Battle of Legnano	The Third Crusade

1130 ── **1200**

1154–1189	1180–1223	1181/1182–1226
Reign of King Henry II	Reign of Philip II Augustus	Life of Francis of Assisi

crush. Some set up shop by renting a room. If a teacher could prove his mettle in the classroom, he had no trouble finding paying students.

Because schools hitherto had been the training grounds for clergymen, all of their students were considered clerics, whether or not they had been ordained. Using Latin, Europe's common language, students could drift from, say, Italy and Spain to France and England, wherever a noted master had settled. Students joined crusaders, pilgrims, and merchants to make the roads of Europe very crowded as the consolidation of castellanies, counties, and kingdoms made violence against travelers less frequent. Markets, taverns, and lodgings sprang up in urban centers to serve the needs of transients.

What the students sought, above all, was knowledge of the seven liberal arts. Grammar, rhetoric, and logic (or dialectic) belonged to the beginning arts, the so-called trivium. Logic, involving the technical analysis of texts as well as the application and manipulation of mental constructs, was a transitional subject leading to the second part of the liberal arts, the quadrivium. This comprised four areas of study that we might call theoretical math and science: arithmetic, geometry, music (theory), and astronomy. Of all these arts, logic appealed the most to twelfth-century students. Medieval students and masters were convinced that logic could order and clarify every issue, even questions about the nature of God.

After studying the trivium, students went on to schools of medicine, theology, or law. Paris was renowned for theology, Montpellier for medicine, and Bologna for law. All of these schools trained men for jobs. The law schools, for example, taught men who would later serve popes, bishops, kings, princes, and communes. Scholars interested in the quadrivium tended to pursue those studies outside the normal school curriculum, and few gained their living through such pursuits. With books expensive and hard to find, lectures were the chief method of communication. Students committed the lectures to memory.

The remarkable renewal of scholarship in the twelfth century had an unexpected benefit: we know a great deal about the men involved in it—and a few of the women—because they wrote so much, often about themselves. Three important figures may serve to typify the scholars of the period: Abelard and Heloise, who were early examples of the new learning; and Peter the Chanter, the product of a slightly later period.

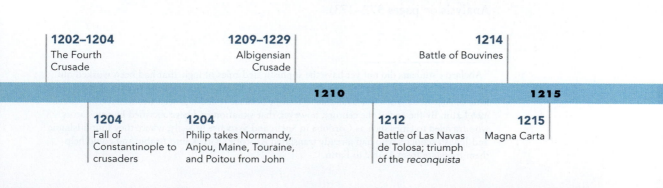

1202–1204
The Fourth
Crusade

1209–1229
Albigensian
Crusade

1214
Battle of Bouvines

1210

1215

1204
Fall of
Constantinople to
crusaders

1204
Philip takes Normandy,
Anjou, Maine, Touraine,
and Poitou from John

1212
Battle of Las Navas
de Tolosa; triumph
of the *reconquista*

1215
Magna Carta

Although Peter Abelard (1079–1142) was expected to become a lord and warrior, he gave up his inheritance to become one of the twelfth century's greatest thinkers. In his autobiographical account, *The Story of My Misfortunes*, Abelard described how he first studied with one of the best-known teachers of his day in Paris. Soon he began to lecture and to gather students of his own. Around 1122–1123, he composed a textbook for his students, *Sic et Non* (*Yes and No*). It consisted of opposing positions on 156 subjects, among them "That God is one and the contrary" and "That all are permitted to marry and the contrary." Abelard arrayed passages from the Bible, the church fathers, and other authorities on both sides of each question. The juxtaposition of such sources was nothing new; what was new was calling attention to their contradictions. Abelard's students loved the challenge: they were eager to find the origins of the quotes, consider the context of each one carefully, and seek to reconcile the opposing sides by using the tools of logic.*

Abelard's fame as a teacher was such that a Parisian cleric named Fulbert gave Abelard room and board and engaged him as tutor for his niece, Heloise (c. 1100–c. 1163/1164). Brought up under Fulbert's guardianship, Heloise had been sent as a young girl to a convent school, where she received a thorough literary education. Her uncle hoped to continue her education at home by hiring Abelard. Abelard, however, became Heloise's lover as well as her tutor. "Our desires left no stage of love-making untried," wrote Abelard in his *Misfortunes*.

At first their love affair was secret. But Heloise became pregnant, and Abelard insisted they marry. They did so clandestinely to prevent damaging Abelard's career, for the new emphasis on clerical celibacy meant that Abelard's professional success and prestige would have been compromised if news of his marriage were made public. After they were married, Heloise and Abelard rarely saw one another; Abelard's sister took in their child. Fulbert, suspecting that Abelard had abandoned his niece, plotted a cruel revenge against him: he paid a servant to castrate Abelard. Soon after, Abelard and Heloise entered separate monasteries.

For Heloise, separation from Abelard was a lasting blow. Although she became a successful abbess, carefully tending to the physical and spiritual needs of her nuns, she continued to call on Abelard for "renewal of strength." In a series of letters addressed to him, she poured out her feelings as "his handmaid, or rather his daughter, wife, or rather sister" (see Primary Source Analysis on pages 372–373).

---

* Abelard's students did not yet have the sophisticated rules of logic that had been worked out by the ancient philosopher Aristotle (see page 120). Until the middle of the twelfth century, very little of Aristotle's work was available in Europe because it had not been translated from Greek into Latin. By the end of the century, however, that situation had been rectified by translators who traveled to cities such as Córdoba in Spain and Syracuse in Sicily, where they found Islamic and Jewish scholars who had already translated Aristotle's Greek into Arabic and could help them translate from Arabic to Latin.

For Abelard, however, the loss of Heloise and even his castration were not the worst disasters of his life. The heaviest blow came later, and it was directed at his intellect. He wrote a book that applied "human and logical reasons" (as he put it) to the Trinity; the book was condemned at the Council of Soissons in 1121, and he was forced to throw it, page by page, into the flames. Bitterly weeping at the injustice, Abelard lamented, "This open violence had come upon me only because of the purity of my intentions and love of our Faith, which had compelled me to write."

By the second half of the twelfth century, masters like Abelard had become far more common. Many of them taught in Paris. Peter the Chanter (d. 1197) was one of the most influential and prolific. He studied at the cathedral school at Reims and was given the honorary title of chanter of Notre Dame in Paris in 1183. The chant consisted of the music and words of the church liturgy. But Peter was not very dedicated to that job. He had his underlings work with the choir singers; he himself was far more interested in lecturing, disputing, and preaching.

Peter's lectures followed the pattern established by other masters. The lecture began with the recitation of a passage from an important text. The master then explained the text, giving his comments. He then "disputed"—mentioning other explanations and refuting them, often drawing on the logic of Aristotle, which by Peter's time was fully available. Sometimes masters held public debates on their interpretations.

Peter chose to comment on biblical texts. There were many ways to interpret the Bible. Some commentators preferred to talk about it as an allegory; others favored stressing its literal meaning. Peter was interested in the morals it taught. While most theology masters commented on just the Psalms and the New Testament, Peter taught all the books of the Bible. His works were particularly devoted to exploring social issues and the sacrament of penance. He brought the fruits of his thinking to the public in sermons and he inspired a whole group of men to preach in and around Paris. One of his protégés, for example, was renowned for turning prostitutes, usurers, and immoral clerics from their sinful ways.

Around 1200, the pope wrote to the masters of theology, church law, and the liberal arts at Paris. He called their group a *universitas*—the Latin word for a corporation or guild. The pope was right. Like guilds, universities had apprentices (students) and masters (schoolmasters). They issued rules to cover their trade (the acquisition and dissemination of knowledge). They had

Peter the Chanter
Peter the Chanter, on the right, is here paired with another university master, Alain of Lille (d. 1203), in a thirteenth-century manuscript. The two were colleagues at the University of Paris, and the artist of this illumination depicts them in lively discussion. Certainly, Peter's thoughts about doctrine were influenced by Alain's teachings. But Peter's main interest was in practical morality, while Alain concentrated on speculative theology. (Portraits of Magister Alanus de Insulis and Pierre de Poitiers/ The British Library, London, UK/© British Library Board. All Rights Reserved./Bridgeman Images.)

PRIMARY SOURCE ANALYSIS Two Letters from Two Lovers

These twelfth-century letters between two anonymous lovers may in fact have been written by Abelard and Heloise. Whether or not that is the case, it is clear that the Woman is the Man's student, that they became lovers in the course of their relationship, and that both are very well educated and eager to show off their learning in their letters to one another. In the two printed here (a small sample from over 100 letters), the lovers refer to scientific lore, ancient poets such as Ovid (who wrote The Art of Love *in the first century), biblical texts, the historian Gregory of Tours (see page 277) and Pope Gregory the Great (see page 283). The ellipses [. . .] indicate where the scribe (probably out of squeamishness) made some abridgments.*

22. (Man)

To his gem, more gracious and luminous than the present light, from him who without you is wrapped in thick darkness. What else should I wish than for you to exult without end in your natural brilliance?

Scientists often say the moon cannot shine without the sun. So when it is deprived of that light, losing all benefit of the sun's warmth and splendor, it shows mortals a dim and pallid sphere. This is plainly a metaphor for you and me. For you are my sun, always inflaming and illumining me with the joyous splendor of your countenance. I have no light except yours; without you I am dull, obscure, weakened, and dead. And to speak truly, what you do for me is greater than what the sun does for the lunar orb, for the moon grows darker as it approaches the sun. As for me, the closer I come to you and the nearer I am, the more I burn. I am so inflamed that (as you have often noticed), when I am with you I become altogether fire. I burn down to the marrow of my bones.

What then shall I repay to match your countless acts of kindness? Nothing, to be sure, for you transcend your sweetest words in the abundance of your deeds. You surpass them in the very performance of love, so that you seem to me poorer in words than in deeds. Among the other countless gifts you possess beyond others, you have this outstanding quality too: you do more for your friend than you say, being poor in words but rich in deeds. This is all the more to your glory because it is harder to act than to speak.

[. . .]

You are immortally buried in my heart; from this tomb you shall never emerge while I live. There you lie down, there you rest. Until sleep comes you are with me; in sleep you do not forsake me; after sleep I see you as soon as I open my eyes, before the light of heaven itself. To others I direct my words, to you my intention. Often I stumble in speech because my thoughts are elsewhere. Who then could deny that you are truly buried within me?

[. . .]

Envious time threatens our love, yet you delay as if we had leisure.

Farewell.

23. (Woman)

To the sweetest support of her soul, deeply rooted in her charity, from the one in whose love you are firmly grounded, in whose honeyed passion you are truly founded: I send what is far from anger and hate.

Although I wished to reply to you, the greatness of the task—unequal to my strength—threw me back. I had

provisions for disciplining, testing, and housing students and regulated the masters in similar detail. For example, masters at the University of Paris were required to wear long black gowns, follow a particular order in their lectures, and set the standards by which students could become masters themselves. The University of Bologna was unique in having two guilds, one of students and one of masters. At Bologna, the students participated in the appointment of masters and paid their salaries.

the will but not the power; I began and faltered, I struggled and fell, my shoulders crushed by the burden. The fervent affection of my mind desired, but the defection of my arid talent refused. I endured the debates and quarrelsome urgings of these two and, having weighed the arguments of each, could not decide to which I should yield. For my mind's affection said:

Affect: "What are you doing, you ingrate? How long will you keep me waiting in this long and surely undeserved silence? Are you not stirred by the generous kindness, the kind generosity of your beloved? Compose a letter full of gratitude, offer the thanks you owe to his abundant goodness! For a favor does not seem welcome or pleasing unless it is repaid with ample thanks."

I thought I should heed these arguments and indeed wished to heed them. But my dry, meager talent resisted, chastising what I had rashly begun with the sharp scourge of reproach, saying:

Defect: "Where are you rushing, you weak, foolish woman? Where is the rash intention of your hasty mind driving you? Will you begin to speak of great things with rude, uncircumcised lips? For you are inadequate to such a magnificent theme. Indeed, whoever takes it upon himself to praise something ought to divide the subject into parts, weigh the qualities of each with the utmost care, and celebrate each according to its worth with suitable praise. Otherwise he insults what he meant to praise, diminishing its beauty with his overwrought account. But where should you obtain enough literary skill to speak of the sublime as it deserves? Attend to yourself and to what you wish to do. Manifold and great are the favors for which you intend to give thanks in your letter. Why do you burn with a swarm of tempestuous thoughts? Look at your icy, brutish heart; it lacks the salt of knowledge and swells only with the thick vapor of idleness. Draw in the sails of your boldness, the little boat in which you mean to cross the imperious sea—to be swiftly drowned unless you take heed!"

Oscillating thus between persuasion and dissuasion, I have until now deferred the thanksgiving I owe, obeying the advice of my talent which blushes at its own frailty. Let the excellence of that divine gentleness which abounds in you impute no fault to me, I pray. But since you are the son of true sweetness, let the virtue of your accustomed mildness abound the more toward me. I know indeed, and I confess, that from the riches of your philosophy, the most copious joy has flowed and still flows to me. But—if I may speak without offense—it is still less than enough to make me perfectly blessed in this respect. For I often come with parched throat, desiring to be refreshed with the sweet nectar of your mouth and to drink thirstily of the riches poured out in your heart. What need is there for more words? I swear, with God as my witness, there is no one who lives or breathes in this world whom I would rather love than you.

[. . .]

May this farewell, my beloved, sweetly pierce the very marrow of your bones.

QUESTION TO CONSIDER
What do these letters tell us about the education of women in the twelfth century?

University curricula differed in content and duration. At the University of Paris in the early thirteenth century, for example, a student had to spend at least six years studying the liberal arts before he could become a master and begin to teach. If he wanted to become a master in theology, he had to attend lectures on the subject for at least another five years.

Because masters and students were considered clerics, and clerics were male, women could be neither students nor masters—though, like Heloise, they might be educated in a monastery or at home. And because clerics were subject to church courts only, no secular jurisdiction, whether town courts or lords, could touch those who attended the university. For example, in 1200, the king of France promised that "neither our provost nor our judges shall lay hands on a student [at the University of Paris] for any offense whatever." The emperor in Germany declared that in his territories—Germany and northern Italy—"no one shall be so rash as to venture to inflict any injury on scholars."

The combination of clerical status and special privileges made universities virtually self-governing corporations within the towns. This sometimes led to friction. For example, when a student at Oxford was suspected of killing his mistress and the townspeople tried to punish him, the masters protested by refusing to teach and leaving town. Incidents such as this explain why historians speak of the hostility between "town" and "gown." Yet, as in our own time, university towns depended on scholars to patronize local restaurants, shops, and hostels. Town and gown normally learned to negotiate with each other to their mutual advantage.

Architectural Style: From Romanesque to Gothic

While Peter the Chanter lectured at Notre Dame, the cathedral itself was going up around him—in Gothic style. This was a new architectural style, associated at first with the Île-de-France and the Capetian kings of France. Elsewhere the reigning style was Romanesque. But in the course of the thirteenth century, Gothic style took much of Europe by storm, and by the fourteenth it was the quintessential cathedral style.

Romanesque is the term art historians use to describe the massive church buildings of eleventh-century monasteries like Cluny. Heavy, serious, and solid, Romanesque churches were decorated with brightly colored wall paintings and sculpture. The various parts of the church—the chapels in the *chevet*, or apse (the east end), for example—were handled as discrete units, with the forms of cubes, cones, and cylinders (Figure 11.1). Romanesque churches boasted "tunnel vaults" that emphasized their

Vézelay

In this view down the nave of a French monastic church built in the early twelfth century, almost all the elements of Romanesque architecture are visible: a "tunnel" vault, here enlivened with red and white stone ribbing; round arches between the piers (here made up of several columns); and relatively small windows. Romanesque churches impress by their sober solidity, which is, however, often relieved, as here, by carved capitals above the columns. Many Romanesque churches also boasted wall paintings. (Andrea Jemolo/akg-images.)

length. Inventive sculptural reliefs, both inside and outside the church, enlivened the geometrical forms. Emotional and sometimes frenzied, Romanesque sculpture depicted themes ranging from the beauty of Eve to the horrors of the Last Judgment. (See the frieze depicting Dives and Lazarus on page 330 for an example.)

Romanesque churches were above all houses for prayer, which was neither silent nor private. The musical style for prayer was called plainchant, or Gregorian chant. Monks sang plainchant melodies in unison and without instrumental accompaniment. Rhythmically free and lacking a regular beat, plainchant's melodies ranged from extremely simple to highly ornate and embellished. By the twelfth century, a large repertoire of melodies had grown up, at first composed and transmitted orally and then, starting in the ninth century, using written notation. Echoing within the stone walls and the cavernous choirs, plainchant worked well in a Romanesque church.

Gothic architecture, to the contrary, was a style of the cities, reflecting the self-confidence and wealth of merchants, guildspeople, bishops, and kings.* (See Terms of History on page 377.) Usually a cathedral—the bishop's principal church—rather than a monastic church, the Gothic church was the religious, social, and commercial focal point of a city. The style, popular from the twelfth to the fifteenth centuries, was characterized by pointed arches, ribbed vaults, and stained-glass windows. The arches began as architectural motifs but were soon adopted in every art form. Flying buttresses permitted much of the wall to be cut away and the open spaces to be filled with glass. Soaring above the west, north, south, and often east ends of many Gothic churches is a rose window: a large round window shaped like a flower. Gothic churches appealed to the senses the way that Peter the Chanter's lectures and disputations appealed to human logic and reason: both were designed to lead people to knowledge that touched the divine. The atmosphere of a Gothic church was a foretaste of heaven.

The style had its beginnings around 1135, with the project of Abbot Suger, the close associate of King Louis the Fat of France (see page 361), to remodel portions of his monastery's church at Saint-Denis. Suger's rebuilding was part

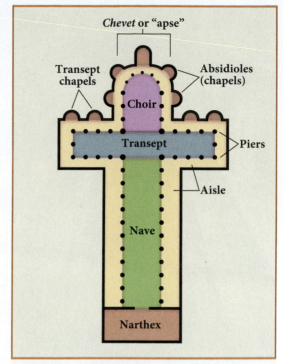

FIGURE 11.1 Floor Plan of a Romanesque Church
As churchgoers entered a Romanesque church, they passed through the narthex, an anteroom decorated with sculptures depicting scenes from the Bible. Walking through the portal of the narthex, they entered the church's nave, at the east end of which—just after the crossing of the transept and in front of the choir—was the altar. Walking down the nave, they passed tall, massive piers leading up to the vault (the ceiling) of the nave. Each of these piers was decorated with sculpture, and the walls were brightly painted. Romanesque churches were both lively and colorful (because of their decoration) and solemn and somber (because of their heavy stones and massive scale).

Gothic is a modern term, originally meant to denigrate the style's "barbarity" but now used admiringly.

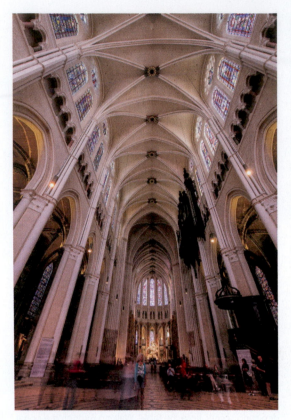

Chartres (interior)
The three doorways of Chartres' west end open onto this view of the nave. Chartres illustrates all the elements of a Gothic church: a multistory elevation made to seem even higher by pointed arches; a ribbed, pointed-arch vault; and (taking the place of walls) large lancet windows filled with stained glass that glowed with color as the sunlight poured in. Rose windows top the west and transept entryways (not shown here). The vault was supported not by walls but by flying buttresses on the church's exterior. (FORGET Patrick/age-fotostock.)

of the fruitful melding of royal and ecclesiastical interests and ideals in the north of France. At the west end of his church, the place where the faithful entered, Suger decorated the portals with figures of Old Testament kings, queens, and patriarchs, signaling the links between the present king and his illustrious predecessors. At the eastern end, behind the altar, Suger used pointed arches and stained glass to let in light, which Suger believed would transport the worshipper from the "slime of earth" to the "purity of Heaven." Suger said that the father of lights, God himself, "illuminated" the minds of the beholders through the light that filtered through the stained-glass windows.

By the mid-thirteenth century, Gothic architecture had spread from France to other European countries. The style varied by region, most dramatically in Italy. At Sant'Andrea in Vercelli, for example, there are only two stories, and light filters in from small windows. Yet because it has pointed arches and ribbed vaulting, Sant'Andrea is considered a Gothic church.

REVIEW QUESTION
What were the innovations in education and church architecture in the twelfth and early thirteenth centuries?

Governments as Institutions

Around the same time that architects, workers, patrons, theologians, and city dwellers were coming together to produce Gothic cathedrals, rulership was becoming institutionalized. By the end of the twelfth century, western Europeans for the first time spoke of their rulers not as kings of a people (for example, the king of the Franks) but as kings of a territory (for example, the king of France). This new designation reflected an important change in medieval rulership. However strong earlier rulers had been, their political power had been personal (depending on ties of kinship, friendship, and vassalage) rather than territorial (touching all who lived within the borders of their state). Renewed interest in Roman law, a product of the schools, served as a foundation for strong, centralized rule. Money allowed kings to hire salaried professionals—talented, literate officials, many of whom had been schooled in the new universities cropping up across Europe—to carry out the will of the ruler. The process of state building had begun.

Gothic

The noun *Goth* and the adjective *Gothic* have a long and varied history. Originally, Goth was a term for the Germanic tribespeople that split into the Visigoths and the Ostrogoths and, under those various identities, founded kingdoms within the boundaries of the former Roman empire. The Visigothic kingdom was centered in Spain; the Ostrogothic in Italy. To the sixth-century Bishop Gregory of Tours, the Goths were heretics (they were Arian Christians) and the destroyers of Rome.

The association of Goths with barbarians continued, so that in the seventeenth through nineteenth centuries, writers used the term Goth to describe robbers, enemies of learning, brutal killers, and anyone without culture. The adjective *Gothic* meant the Middle Ages, which was often denigrated, as when Henry Fielding (d. 1754) had a character in one of his novels speak of "Gothic Ignorance."

But during that same period, the very same term, in its adjectival form, was often used admiringly to refer to medieval church architecture. In a diary entry of 1641,

John Evelyn wrote, "Harlem [a city in Holland] . . . hath one of the fairest Churches of the Gotique designe, I had ever seene." He was thinking of the late medieval church of St. Bavo in Haarlem. Gothic churches were characterized then, as today, by their arched vaults, their lofty columns, and their great stained-glass windows. In the mid-nineteenth century, there was even a "Gothic Revival," during which architects sought to reintroduce the style. Some American universities were built when this movement was ascendant. At the same time, Gothic literature was invented, featuring a dark vision shot through with a shiver of excitement: the stories had supernatural or macabre plots, often in a medieval setting.

Today, the term *Gothic* is mainly used by art historians. But Gothic literature spawned a genre of cinema. The protagonists in such films inspired some rock groups in the 1980s to adopt dark makeup, black clothing, and heavy metal jewelry. A "goth" today is not exactly a member of a Germanic tribe, but as an adherent of punk rock culture, she presents herself as a rebel and even a modern-day barbarian.

In England, the governmental system was institutionalized early, with royal officials administering both law and revenues. In other regions, such as France and Germany, bureaucratic administration did not develop that far. In eastern Europe, it hardly existed at all. At Byzantium, the bureaucracy that had long been in place frayed badly, leaving the state open to conquest by western crusaders.

England: Unity through Common Law

In the mid-twelfth century, the government of England was by far the most institutionalized in Europe. The king hardly needed to be present: royal government functioned smoothly without him, since officials handled all the administrative matters and record keeping. The very circumstances of the English king favored the growth of an administrative staff—the king's frequent travels to and from the European continent meant that officials needed to work in his absence, and his enormous wealth meant that he could afford them.

Henry II (r. 1154–1189) was the driving force in extending and strengthening the institutions of English government. He took the throne in the wake of a terrible civil war (1139–1153) between two royal claimants. The chaos had benefited the English barons and high churchmen, who gained new privileges and powers as the monarch's authority waned. Newly built private castles, already familiar on the continent, now appeared in England as symbols of the rising power of the English barons. But when Henry was crowned king of England, ushering in the Angevin (from Anjou) dynasty there, he had the barons' castles either torn down or surrendered to him.* Then he proceeded to extend monarchical power, above all by imposing royal justice. His judicial reforms built on an already well-developed legal system. The Anglo-Saxon kings had royal district courts: the king appointed sheriffs to police the shires, muster military levies, and haul criminals into court. The Norman kings retained these courts and had the right to summon large landowners in the shire to attend them. To these established institutions, Henry II added a system of judicial visitations called eyres (from the Latin *iter*, "journey"). Under this system, royal justices made regular trips to every locality in England to judge those accused of murder, arson, or rape—all defined as crimes against the "king's peace." The justices summoned representatives of the knightly class to meet and either give the sheriff the names of those suspected of committing crimes in the vicinity or arrest the suspects themselves and hand them over to the royal justices.

During the eyres, the justices also heard cases between individuals, today called civil cases. Free men and women (that is, people of the knightly class or above) could bring their disputes over such matters as inheritance, dowries, and property claims to the king's justices. Earlier courts had generally relied on duels between litigants to determine verdicts. Henry's new system offered a different option, an inquest under royal supervision.

The new system of **common law**—law that applied to all of England—was praised for its efficiency, speed, and conclusiveness in a twelfth-century legal treatise known as *Glanvill* (after its presumed author). *Glanvill* might have added that the king also speedily gained a large treasury. The exchequer, as the financial bureau of England was called, recorded all the fines paid for judgments and the sums collected for writs. The amounts, entered on parchment sewn together and stored as rolls, became the Receipt Rolls and Pipe Rolls, the first of many such records of the English monarchy and an indication that writing had become a mechanism for institutionalizing royal power in England.

The stiffest opposition to Henry's extension of the royal courts came from the church, where a separate system of trial and punishment had long been available to the clergy and to others who enjoyed church protection. The punishments for crimes meted out by church courts were generally quite mild. Protective of their special status, churchmen refused to submit to the jurisdiction of Henry's courts. Henry insisted, and the ensuing contest between Henry II and his archbishop, Thomas Becket (1118–1170), became the greatest battle

---

*Henry's father, Geoffrey of Anjou, was nicknamed "Plantagenet," from the *genet*, a shrub he liked. Historians sometimes use the name to refer to the entire dynasty, so Henry II was the first Plantagenet as well as the first Angevin king of England.

Hanging Thieves

The development of common law in England meant mobilizing royal agents to bring charges and arrest people throughout the land. In 1124, the royal justice Ralph Basset hanged forty-four thieves. It could not have been very shocking in that context to see, in this miniature from around 1130, eight thieves hanged for breaking into the shrine of St. Edmund. Under Henry II, all cases of murder, arson, and rape were considered crimes against the king himself. The result was not just the enhancement of the king's power but also new definitions of crime, more thorough policing, and more systematic punishments. Even so, hanging was probably no more frequent than it had been before. (The Thieves Are Hanged. From *The Life, Passion, and Miracles of St. Edmund, King and Martyr*, in Latin. Bury St. Edmund's, c. 1130. Ms. M.736, f. 19v. The Pierpont Morgan Library, New York, NY, USA/The Morgan Library & Museum/Art Resource, NY.)

between the church and the state in the twelfth century. The conflict simmered for six years, with Becket refusing to allow "criminous clerics"—clergy suspected of committing a crime—to come before royal courts. Then Henry's henchmen murdered Becket, right in his own cathedral. The desecration unintentionally turned Becket into a martyr. Henry was forced by a general public outcry to do penance for the deed. In the end, both church and royal courts expanded to address the concerns of an increasingly litigious society.

In England, Henry II made the king's presence felt everywhere through his system of traveling royal courts. Even beyond England, Henry had enormous power. His marriage to Eleanor of Aquitaine in 1152, after her marriage to Louis VII of France was annulled, brought the enormous inheritance of the duchy of Aquitaine to the English crown. Although Henry was technically the vassal of the king of France for his continental lands, he effectively ruled a territory that stretched from England to southern France (Map 11.1).

Eleanor gave Henry not only an enormous inheritance but also the sons he needed to maintain his dynasty. He gave her much less. As queen of France, Eleanor had enjoyed an important position: she disputed with St. Bernard, the Cistercian abbot who was the most renowned churchman of the day, and when she accompanied Louis on the Second Crusade, she brought more troops than he did. Of independent mind, she determined to separate from Louis even before he considered leaving her. But with Henry, she lost much of her power, for he dominated her just as he came to dominate his barons. Turning to her offspring in 1173, Eleanor, disguised as a man, tried to join her eldest son, Henry the Younger, in a plot against his father. But the rebellion was put down, and she spent most of her years thereafter, until her husband's death in 1189, confined under guard at Winchester Castle. (In death, however, she gained dignity, with her tomb next to Henry's.)

Henry bequeathed to his sons Richard I (r. 1189–1199) and John (r. 1199–1216) an omnipresent and wealthy monarchy. Its omnipresence derived largely from its eyre system of justice and its administrative apparatus. Its wealth

MAP 11.1 Europe in the Age of Henry II and Frederick Barbarossa, 1150–1190

The second half of the twelfth century was dominated by two men, King Henry II and Emperor Frederick Barbarossa. Of the two, Frederick seemed to control more land, but this was deceptive. Although he was emperor, he had great difficulty ruling the territory that was theoretically part of his empire. Frederick's base was in central Germany, and even there he had to contend with powerful vassals. Henry II's territory was more compact but also more surely under his control.

came from court fees, income from numerous royal estates both in England and on the continent, taxes from cities, and customary feudal dues (reliefs and aids) collected from barons and knights. Enriched by the commercial economy of the late twelfth century, the English kings encouraged their knights and barons not to serve them personally in battle but, in lieu of service, to pay a tax called scutage. The monarchs preferred to hire mercenaries both as troops to fight external enemies and as police to enforce the king's will at home.

Richard I, known as the Lion-Hearted, went on the Third Crusade the very year he was crowned. On his way home, he was captured and held for ransom by political enemies for a long time; he died soon thereafter while defending his possessions on the continent. His successor, John, lived longer but gained no admiring epithet. In fact, he presided over the whittling away of the English empire. In 1204, the king of France confiscated the northern French territories held by John. Between 1204 and 1214, John did everything he could to add to

Eleanor and Henry
Nothing about their side-by-side tombs suggests the stormy relationship of Eleanor of Aquitaine and King Henry II of England. Their effigies, carved of limestone and walnut, suggest peace and piety. How does Eleanor's book help to project this image? What do you suppose she is reading? The placement of the couple's tombs also attests to their religious fervor: they were buried in the powerful monastery of Fontevraud, a "double monastery" that housed (in separate quarters) both monks and nuns. An abbess presided over all. (BRIAN HARRIS/Alamy.)

the crown revenues so that he could pay for an army to win back the territories. He forced his vassals to pay ever-increasing scutages, and he extorted money in the form of new feudal dues. He compelled the widows of his vassals either to marry men of his choosing or to pay him a hefty fee. Despite John's heavy investment in the war, his army was defeated in 1214 at the battle of Bouvines. The defeat caused discontented English barons to rebel openly against the king. At Runnymede in June 1215, John was forced to agree to the charter of baronial liberties that has come to be called **Magna Carta** ("Great Charter").

The English barons intended Magna Carta to be a conservative document defining the "customary" obligations and rights of the nobility and forbidding the king to break from these customs without consulting his barons. It maintained that all free men in the land had certain rights that the king was obligated to uphold. In this way, Magna Carta implied that the king was not above the law. In time, as the definition of *free men* expanded to include all the king's subjects, Magna Carta came to be seen as a guarantee of the rights of Englishmen (and eventually Englishwomen) in general (see Contrasting Views on pages 382–383).

France: Consolidation and Conquest

John's territorial loss was the gain of the French king **Philip II (Philip Augustus)** (r. 1180–1223). When Philip came to the throne, the royal domain, the Île-de-France, was sandwiched between territory controlled by the counts of Flanders, Champagne, and Anjou. King Henry II and the counts of Flanders and Champagne vied to control the young king. Philip, however, quickly learned to play the three rulers against one another. Contemporaries were astounded when Philip successfully gained territory: he wrested land from Flanders in

Magna Carta

Magna Carta ("Great Charter"), today often considered a landmark of constitutional government, began as a demand by English barons and churchmen for specific rights and privileges. Reacting to King John's "abuses," the barons and churchmen forced him in 1215 to affix his seal to a "charter of liberties" (Excerpt 1). It set forth the customs that the king was expected to observe and, in its sixty-first clause, in effect allowed the king's subjects to declare war against him if he failed to carry out the charter's provisions. In 1225, Henry III, John's son, issued a definitive version of the charter. By then, it had become more important as a symbol of liberty than for its specific provisions. It was, for example, invoked by the barons in 1242 when they were summoned to one of the first Parliaments (Excerpt 2).

1. Magna Carta, 1215

In these excerpts, the provisions that were dropped by Henry III in the definitive version of 1225 are starred. Explanatory notes are in brackets. The original charter had sixty-three clauses. In every clause, John refers to himself by the royal "we."

1. First of all we [i.e., John] have granted to God, and by this our present charter confirmed for us and our heirs for ever that the English church shall be free, and shall have its rights undiminished and its liberties unimpaired. . . .

8. No widow shall be forced to marry so long as she wishes to live without a husband, provided that she gives security [pledges] not to marry without our consent if she holds [her land] from us, or without the consent of her lord of whom she holds, if she holds of another.

9. Neither we nor our bailiffs will seize for any debt any land or rent, so long as the chattels [property] of the debtor are sufficient to repay the debt. . . .

*10. If anyone who has borrowed from the Jews any sum, great or small, dies before it is repaid, the debt shall not bear interest as long as the heir is under age, of whomsoever [lord] he holds [his land]; and if the debt falls into our hands [which might happen, as Jews were serfs of the crown], we will not take anything except the principal mentioned in the bond.

*12. No scutage or aid [money payments owed by a vassal to his lord] shall be imposed in our kingdom unless by common counsel of our kingdom, except for ransoming our person, for making our eldest son a knight, and for once marrying our eldest daughter; and for these only a reasonable aid shall be levied. . . .

30. No sheriff, or bailiff of ours, or anyone else shall take the horses or carts of any free man [for the most part, a member of the elite] for transport work save with the agreement of that freeman.

31. Neither we nor our bailiffs will take, for castles or other works of ours, timber which is not ours, except with the agreement of him whose timber it is. . . .

39. No free man shall be arrested or imprisoned or disseised [deprived of his land] or outlawed or exiled or in any way victimized, neither will we attack him or send anyone to attack him, except by the lawful judgment of his peers or by the law of the land. . . .

*61. Since . . . we have granted all these things aforesaid . . . we give and grant [the barons] the under-written security, namely, that the barons shall choose any twenty-five barons of the kingdom they wish, who must with all their might observe, hold, and cause to be observed, the peace and liberties which we have granted and confirmed to them by this present charter of ours, so that if we, or our justiciar [the king's chief minister], or our bailiffs or any one of

the 1190s and then, as we have seen, he took Normandy, Anjou, Maine, the Touraine, and Poitou from King John of England in 1204. No wonder he was given the epithet *Augustus*, after the first Roman emperor.

After Philip's army confirmed its triumph over most of John's continental territories in 1214, the French monarch could boast that he was the richest

our servants offend in any way against anyone or transgress any of the articles of the peace or the security . . . , [the barons] shall come to us . . . and laying the transgression before us, shall petition us to have that transgression corrected without delay. And if we do not correct the transgression . . . within forty days . . . those twenty-five barons together with the community of the whole land shall distrain and distress us in every way they can, namely, by seizing castles, lands, possessions, and in such other ways as they can, saving [not harming] our person.

Source: Harry Rothwell, ed., *English Historical Documents*, vol. 3 (London: Eyre & Spottiswoode, 1975), 317–23.

2. The Barons at Parliament Refuse to Give the King an Aid, 1242

Henry III convoked the barons to a meeting (parliament), expecting them to ratify his request for money to wage war for his French possessions. According to the writer of this document, Matthew Paris (a monk, artist, and chronicler of his time), the barons considered his request an excessive imposition. Magna Carta was a justification for their flat rejection of the king's request.

Since he had been their ruler they had many times, at his request, given him aid, namely, a thirteenth of their movable property, and afterwards a fifteenth and a sixteenth and a fortieth. . . . Scarcely, however, had four years or so elapsed from that time, when he again asked them for aid, and, at length, by dint of great entreaties, he obtained a thirtieth, which they granted him on the condition that neither that exaction nor the others before it should in the future be made a precedent of. And regarding that he gave them his charter. Furthermore,

he then [at that earlier time] granted them that all the liberties contained in Magna Carta should thenceforward be fully observed throughout the whole of his kingdom. . . .

Furthermore, from the time of their giving the said thirtieth, itinerant justices have been continually going on eyre [moving from place to place] through all parts of England, alike for pleas of the forest [to enforce the king's monopoly on forests] and all other pleas, so that all the counties, hundreds, cities, boroughs, and nearly all the vills of England are heavily amerced [fined]; wherefore, from that eyre alone the king has, or ought to have, a very large sum of money, if it were paid, and properly collected. They therefore say with truth that all in the kingdom are so oppressed and impoverished by these amercements and by the other aids given before that they have little or no goods left. And because the king had never, after the granting of the thirtieth, abided by his charter of liberties [namely, Magna Carta], nay had since then oppressed them more than usual . . . they told the king flatly that for the present they would not give him an aid.

Source: Harry Rothwell, ed., *English Historical Documents*, vol. 3 (London: Eyre & Spottiswoode, 1975), 355–56.

QUESTIONS TO CONSIDER

1. What do the clauses of Magna Carta that say what will henceforth *not* be done suggest about what the king *had been* doing?

2. How did the barons of 1242 use Magna Carta as a symbol of liberty?

3. What did it mean for John to affix his seal to Magna Carta?

and most powerful ruler in France. Philip was particularly successful in imposing royal control in Normandy. He received homage and fealty from most of the Norman aristocracy, and his officers carried out their work there in accordance with Norman customs. Later French kings gave most of the other territories conquered by Philip to various members of the royal family.

French royal domain (Île-de-France), c. 1180

Acquired by Philip Augustus, 1180–1223

French royal fiefs

★ **Battle**

The Consolidation of France under Philip Augustus, 1180–1223

Wherever he ruled, Philip instituted new administrative practices. Before Philip's day, most French royal arrangements were committed to memory rather than to writing. If decrees were recorded at all, they were saved by the recipient, not by the government. The king did keep some documents, which he generally carried with him in his travels like personal possessions. But during a battle in 1194, Philip lost his meager cache of documents along with much treasure when he had to abandon his baggage train. After 1194, the king had all his decrees written down, and he established a permanent repository in which to keep them.

Like the English king, Philip relied largely on members of the lesser nobility—knights and clerics, many of whom were masters educated in the city schools of France. They served as officers of his court, tax collectors, and overseers of the royal estates, making the king's power felt locally as never before.

Germany: The Revived Monarchy of Frederick Barbarossa

Theoretically, Henry V and his successors were kings of Germany and Italy, and at Rome they received the crown and title of emperor from the popes as well. But the Investiture Conflict (see pages 342–347) reduced their power and authority. Meanwhile, the German princes strengthened their position, enjoying near independence as they built castles on their properties and established control over whole territories. When they elected a new king, the princes made sure that he would give them new lands and powers. The German kings were in a difficult position: they had to balance the many conflicting interests of their royal and imperial offices, their families, and the German princes, and they had to contend with the increasing power of the papacy and the Italian communes. All this prevented the consolidation of power under a strong German monarch during the first half of the twelfth century.

During the Investiture Conflict, the two sides (imperial and papal) were represented by two noble families. Leading the imperial party was the Staufer, or Hohenstaufen, clan; opposing them were the Welfs. (Two later Italian factions, the Ghibellines and the Guelphs, corresponded, respectively, to the Hohenstaufens and the Welfs.) The enmity between these families was legendary, and warfare between the groups raged long after the Concordat of Worms in 1122. Decades of constant battles exhausted all parties, who began to long for peace. In an act of rare unanimity, they elected **Frederick I (Barbarossa)**. In Frederick (r. 1152–1190) they seemed to have a candidate who could end the strife: his mother was a Welf, his father a Staufer. Contemporary accounts of the king's career represented Frederick as the cornerstone that joined two houses and reconciled enemies.

Frederick's very appearance impressed his contemporaries—the name *Barbarossa* referred to his red-blond hair and beard. But beyond appearances, Frederick impressed those around him by what they called his firmness. He affirmed royal rights, even when he handed out duchies and allowed others to name bishops, because in return for these political powers Frederick required the princes to concede formally and publicly that they held their rights and territories from him as their lord. By making them his vassals, although with nearly royal rights within their principalities, Frederick defined the princes' subordinate relationship to the German king.

As the king of Germany, Frederick had the traditional right to claim the imperial crown. When, in 1155, he marched to Rome to be crowned emperor, the fledgling commune there protested that it alone had the right to give him the crown. Frederick interrupted them, asserting that the glory of Rome, together with its crown, came to him by right of conquest. He was equally insistent with the pope, who wrote to tell him that Rome belonged to St. Peter. Frederick replied that his imperial title gave him rights over the city. In part, Frederick was influenced by the revival of Roman law—the laws of Theodosius and Justinian—that was taking place in the schools of Italy. In part, too, he was convinced of the sacred—not just secular—origins of the imperial office. Frederick called his empire *sacer* ("sacred"), asserting that it was in its own way as precious, worthwhile, and God-given as the church.

Frederick buttressed this high view of his imperial right with worldly power. He married Beatrice of Burgundy, whose vast estates in Burgundy and Provence enabled him to establish a powerful political and territorial base centered in Swabia (today southwestern Germany). From Swabia, Frederick looked south to Italy, with its wealthy cities. Swabia and northern Italy together could give Frederick a compact and centrally located territory.

Nevertheless, Frederick's ambitions in Italy were problematic. Since the Investiture Conflict, the emperor had ruled Italy in name only. The communes of the northern cities guarded their liberties jealously, while the pope considered Italy his own sphere of influence. Frederick's territorial base just north of Italy threatened those interests (see Map 11.1 on page 380).

Despite the opposition of the cities and the pope, Frederick was determined to conquer northern Italy, which he managed to do by 1158. Adopting an Italian solution for governing the communes—appointing outsiders as magistrates—Frederick appointed his own men to these powerful positions. But that was where Frederick made a mistake. He chose German officials who lacked a sense of Italian communal traditions. Their heavy hand created enormous resentment. By 1167, most of the cities of northern Italy had joined with the pope to form the Lombard League against Frederick. Defeated by the

Frederick Barbarossa
In this image of Frederick, made during his lifetime, the emperor is dressed as a crusader, and the inscription tells him to fight the Muslims. The small figure on the right is the abbot of the Monastery of Schäftlarn, who gives Frederick a book that contains an account of the First Crusade. (Photo © Tarker/Bridgeman Images.)

league at the battle of Legnano in 1176, Frederick made peace and withdrew most of his forces from Italy. The battle marked the triumph of the cities over the crown in Italy, which would not have a centralized government until the nineteenth century; its political history would instead be that of its various regions and their dominant cities.

Frederick was the victim of traditions that were rapidly becoming outmoded. He based much of his rule in Germany on the bond of lord and vassal at the very moment when rulers elsewhere were relying less on such personal ties and more on salaried officials. He lived up to the meaning of *emperor*, with all its obligations to rule Rome and northern Italy, when other leaders were consolidating their territorial rule bit by bit. In addition, as "universal" emperor, he did not recognize the importance of local pride, language, customs, and traditions; he tried to rule Italian communes with his own men from Germany, and he failed.

Frederick also had problems in Germany, where he had to contend with princes of near-royal status who acted as independent rulers of their principalities, though acknowledging Frederick as their feudal lord. One of the most powerful was Henry the Lion (c. 1130–1195); as duke of both Saxony and Bavaria he had important bases in both the north and the south of Germany. A confident and aggressive ruler, Henry dominated his territories by investing bishops (usurping the role of the emperor as outlined in the Concordat of Worms), collecting dues from his estates, and exercising judicial rights. Henry also actively extended his rule, especially in Slavic regions, pushing northeast past the Elbe River to reestablish dioceses and to build the commercial city of Lübeck (today in northern Germany). He was lord of many vassals and ministerials (people of unfree status but high prestige). He organized a staff of clerics and ministerials to collect taxes and tolls and to write up his legal acts.

Yet like kings, princes could fall. Henry's growing power so threatened other princes as well as Frederick that in 1179, Frederick called Henry to the king's court for violating the peace. When Henry chose not to appear, Frederick exercised his authority as Henry's lord and charged him with violating his duty as a vassal. Because Henry refused the summons to court and avoided serving his lord in Italy, Frederick condemned him and confiscated his holdings. However, unlike Philip Augustus with Normandy, Frederick immediately granted Henry's duchies to some of his other vassals.

Eastern Europe and Byzantium: Fragmenting Realms

The importance of governmental and bureaucratic institutions such as those developed in England and France is made especially clear by comparing the experience of regions where they were not established. In eastern Europe, the characteristic pattern was for states to form under the leadership of one great ruler and then to fragment under his successor. For example, King Béla III of Hungary (r. 1172–1196) built up a state that looked superficially like a western European kingdom. He married a French princess, sent his officials to Paris to be educated, and built his palace in the French Romanesque style. The annual income from his estates, tolls, dues, and taxes equaled that of the richest western monarchs. But Béla did not set up enduring governmental institutions, and in the decades that followed his death, wars between his sons splintered his monarchical holdings, and aristocratic supporters divided the wealth.

Rus underwent a similar process. Although twelfth-century Kiev was politically fragmented, autocratic princes to the north constructed Vladimir (also known as Suzdalia), the nucleus of the later Muscovite state. Within the clearly defined borders of this principality, well-to-do towns prospered and monasteries and churches flourished; one chronicler wrote that "all lands trembled at the name [of its ruler]." Yet early in the thirteenth century this nascent state began to crumble as princely claimants fought one another for power, much as Béla's sons had done in Hungary. Soon Rus would be conquered by the Mongols (see pages 424–425).

Although the Byzantine Empire was already a consolidated bureaucratic state, after the mid-twelfth century it gradually began to show weaknesses. Traders from the west—the Venetians especially—dominated its commerce. The Byzantine emperors who ruled during the last half of the twelfth century downgraded the old civil servants, elevated imperial relatives to high offices, and favored the military elite, who nevertheless rarely came to the aid of the emperor. As Byzantine rule grew more personal and European rule became more bureaucratic, the two gradually became more alike.

The Byzantine Empire might well have continued like this for a long time. Instead, its heart was knocked out by the warriors of the Fourth Crusade (1202–1204). At the instigation of Venice, the crusaders made a detour to Constantinople on their way to the Holy Land, capturing the city in 1204. Although one of the crusade leaders was named "emperor" and ruled in Constantinople and its surrounding territory, the Byzantine Empire itself continued to exist, though disunited and weak. It retook Constantinople in 1261, but it never regained the power that it had in the eleventh century.

REVIEW QUESTION
What new sources and institutions of power became available to rulers in the second half of the twelfth century?

The Growth of a Vernacular High Culture

With their consolidation of territory, wealth, and power in the last half of the twelfth century, kings, barons, princes, and their wives and daughters supported new kinds of literature and music. For the first time on the continent, though long true in England, poems and songs were written in the vernacular, the spoken language, rather than in Latin. Meant to be read or sung aloud, sometimes with accompanying musical instruments, they celebrated nobles' lives and provided a common experience for aristocrats at court. Patrons and patronesses in the cities of Italy and in the more isolated courts of northern Europe spent some of the profits from their estates and commerce on the arts. Their support helped develop and enrich the spoken language while it heightened their prestige as aristocrats.

The Troubadours: Poets of Love and Play

Already at the beginning of the twelfth century, Duke William IX of Aquitaine (1071–1126), the grandfather of Eleanor of Aquitaine, had written lyric poems in Occitan, the vernacular of southern France. Perhaps influenced by

Arabic and Hebrew love poetry from al-Andalus, he was the first of the **troubadours**, lyric poets who wrote in Occitan. (Women poets using this language were known as **trobairitz**.) Their poems were clever and inventive. The final four-line stanza of one such poem demonstrates the poet's skill:

Per aquesta fri e tremble,	For this one I shiver and tremble,
quar de tan bon' amor l'am;	I love her with such a good love;
qu'anc no cug qu'en nasques semble	I do not think the like of her was ever born
en semblan de gran linh n'Adam.	in the long line of Lord Adam.

The rhyme scheme of this poem appears to be simple—*tremble* goes with *semble*, *l'am* with *n'Adam*—but the entire poem has five earlier verses, all six lines long and all containing the *am, am* rhyme in the fourth and sixth lines, while every other line within each verse rhymes as well.

Troubadours and trobairitz traveled from one aristocratic court to another in the south of France as well as northern Spain and Italy. They sang their own songs, perhaps accompanied by other musicians (*jongleurs*) or accompanying themselves on an instrument. Varying their rhymes and meters endlessly, they strove to dazzle their audiences with brilliant originality. Their most common topic, love, echoed the twelfth-century church's emphasis on the emotional relationship between God and humans. But the troubadours concentrated on the various forms of human love and its joys and sorrows. Thus the trobairitz comtessa de Dia (flourished c. 1160) sang about her unrequited love for a man (Figure 11.2):

I am so aggrieved by the one to whom I am the friend,
for I love him more than anything than can be.
Pity does not help me toward him, nor cortesia [fine manners],
nor my beauty, nor my good name, nor my wit.

The key to these lines, as to troubadour verse in general, is the idea of *cortesia*. The word refers to courtesy (the refinement of people living at court) and to the struggle to achieve an ideal of virtue.

Historians and literary critics used to use the term *courtly love* to emphasize one of the themes of this literature: the poet's overwhelming love for a beautiful married noblewoman who was far above him in status and utterly unattainable. But this motif was only one of many aspects of love that the troubadours sang about: some of the songs boasted of sexual conquests, others played with the notion of equality between lovers, and still others preached that love was the source of virtue. The underlying theme of this literature was not courtly love; it was the power of women. And no wonder: there were many powerful ladies (the female counterparts of lords) in southern France. They owned property, had vassals, led battles, decided disputes, and entered into and broke political alliances as their advantage dictated. Both men and women appreciated troubadour poetry, which recognized and praised women's power even as it eroticized it.

WHAT WOULD YOU DO?

If you were the comtessa de Dia, a woman with a literary and musical bent, where and how would you find opportunities to exercise your talents?

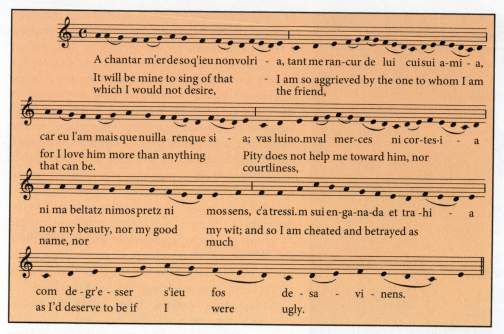

FIGURE 11.2 The Song "A chantar m'er de so"
This music is the first part of a song written by trobairitz comtessa de Dia in the mid-twelfth century. It has been adapted here for the treble clef. There is no time signature, but the music may easily be played by calculating one beat for each note, except for the two-note slurs, which fit into one beat together. Many recordings of this song are available on YouTube. ("A chantar," from *Lyrics of the Troubadours and Trouvères: An Anthology and a History*, translated by Frederick Goldin. Copyright © 1973 by Frederick Goldin. Used by permission of Doubleday, an imprint of the Knopf Doubleday Publishing Group, a division of Penguin Random House LLC. All rights reserved. Any third-party use of this material, outside of this publication, is prohibited. Interested parties must apply directly to Penguin Random House LLC for permission.)

The troubadours' songs were in the language of southern France. Similar poetry appeared in other vernacular languages: the *minnesingers* ("love singers") sang in German; the *trouvères* sang in the Old French of northern France. One trouvère was the English king Richard the Lion-Hearted. Taken prisoner on his return from the Third Crusade, Richard wrote a poem expressing his longing not for a lady but for the good companions of war, the knightly "youths" he had joined in battle:

> They know well, the men of Anjou and Touraine,
> . . . that I am arrested, far from them, in another's hands.
> There's no lordly fighting now on the barren plains,
> because I am a prisoner.

Clearly some troubadour poetry was about war rather than love.

The Birth of Epic and Romance Literature

War was not as common a topic in lyric poetry as love, but some long vernacular poems, called **chansons de geste** ("songs of heroic deeds") and later termed epic poems, were all about warriors and their battles. They were written down

Female Musician
La comtessa de Dia was one of only a few *trobairitz*, but female musicians of various sorts were known and celebrated, as this fresco from the Cathedral of Pamplona (Navarra) proves. Here one is playing a medieval fiddle called a *vielle*.
(Gianni Dagli Orti/REX/Shutterstock.)

REVIEW QUESTION
What do the works of the troubadours and vernacular poets reveal about the nature of entertainment—its themes, its audience, its performers—in the twelfth century?

at around the same time as love poems. Like the songs of the troubadours, these epic poems implied a code of behavior for aristocrats, in this case on the battlefield. They served as heroic models for nobles and knights, whose positions were being threatened by the newly emerging merchants in the cities on the one hand and newly powerful kings on the other. The knights' ascendancy on the battlefield, where they unhorsed one another with lances and long swords and took prisoners rather than killing their opponents, was also beginning to wane in the face of mercenary infantrymen who wielded long hooks and knives that ripped easily through chain mail. A knightly ethos and sense of group solidarity emerged in the face of these social, political, and military changes. Even while heroic poems celebrated battles, they explored the moral issues that made war tragic, if inevitable.

Other long poems, later called romances, explored the relationships between men and women. Often inspired by the legend of King Arthur, romances reached their zenith of popularity during the late twelfth and early thirteenth centuries. In one romance, for example, the heroic knight Lancelot, who is in love with King Arthur's wife, Queen Guinevere, chooses humiliation over honor because of his love for the queen. When she sees him—the greatest knight in Christendom—fighting in a tournament, she tests him by asking him to do his "worst." The poor knight is obliged to lose all his battles until she changes her mind.

Lancelot was the perfect chivalric knight. The word **chivalry** derives from the French word *cheval* ("horse"); the fact that the knight was a horseman marked him as a warrior of the most prestigious sort. Perched high on his horse, his heavy lance couched in his right arm, the knight was both imposing and menacing. Chivalry made him gentle—except to his enemies on the battlefield. The chivalric hero was a knight constrained by a code of refinement, fair play, piety, and devotion to an ideal. Historians debate whether real knights lived up to the codes implicit in epics and romances, but there is no doubt that knights saw themselves mirrored there. They were the poets' audience.

Religious Fervor and Crusade

The new vernacular culture was one sign of the growing wealth, sophistication, and self-confidence of the late twelfth century. New forms of religious life were another. Unlike the reformed orders of the early half of the century, which had fled the cities, the new religious groups embraced (and were embraced by) urban populations. Rich and poor, male and female joined these movements. They criticized the existing church as too wealthy, impersonal, and spiritually superficial. Intensely interested in the life of Christ, men and women in the late twelfth century made his childhood, agony, death, and presence in the Eucharist—the bread and wine that became the body and blood of Christ in the Mass—the emotional focus of their own lives.

Religious fervor mixed with greed in new crusades that had little success in the Holy Land but were victorious on the borders of Europe and, as we have already seen, at Constantinople. These were the poisonous flowers of the Middle Ages.

New Religious Orders in the Cities

The quick rebuilding of the cathedral at Chartres reveals the religious fervor of late-twelfth-century city dwellers. This helps explain the new religious orders that appeared in the cities. The church accepted many new orders; some, however, so threatened the established doctrine and hierarchy that they were condemned as heresies.

St. Francis (1181/1182–1226) founded one of the most successful of the movements within the church, the **Franciscans**. Son of a well-to-do trader in the city of Assisi in Italy, Francis began to experience doubts, dreams, and illnesses that spurred him to religious self-examination. Eventually, he renounced his family's wealth, put on a simple robe, and went about preaching penance to anyone who would listen.

Clinging to poverty as if, in his words, "she" were his "lady" (and thus borrowing the vocabulary of chivalry), Francis accepted no money, walked without shoes, and wore only one coarse tunic. He brought religious devotion out of the monastery and into the streets. Intending to follow the model of Christ, he received, as his biographers put it, a miraculous gift of grace: the stigmata, bleeding sores corresponding to the wounds Christ suffered on the cross.

By all accounts, Francis was a spellbinding speaker, and he attracted many followers. Because they went about begging, those followers were called mendicants, from the Latin verb *mendicare* ("to beg"). Recognized as a religious order by the pope, the Brothers of St. Francis (or friars, from the Latin term for "brothers") spent their time preaching, ministering to the sick, and doing manual labor. Eventually they dispersed, setting up fraternal groups throughout Italy and then in France, Spain, Germany, England, and the Holy Land.

Francis converted not only men but women. One of these, Clare, formed the nucleus of a community of pious women that became the Order of the Sisters of St. Francis. At first, the women worked alongside the friars; but both Francis and the church hierarchy disapproved of their activities in the world, and soon Franciscan sisters were confined to cloisters under the rule of St. Benedict.

Clare was one of many women who sought outlets for religious expression. Some women joined convents; others became recluses, living alone like hermits; still others sought membership in new lay sisterhoods. In northern Europe at

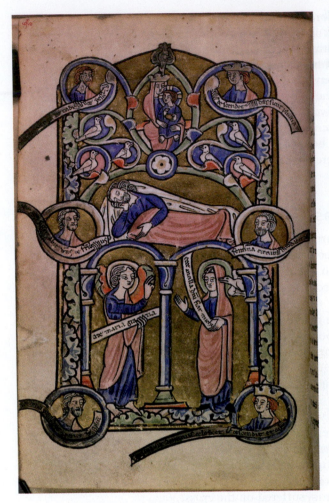

the end of the twelfth century, laywomen who lived together in informal pious communities were called Beguines. Without permanent vows or an established rule, the Beguines chose to be celibate (though they were free to leave their Beguinages to marry) and often made their living by weaving cloth or tending to the sick and old. Some of them may have prepared and illustrated their own reading materials. Although their daily occupations were ordinary, the Beguines's spiritual lives were often emotional and ecstatic, infused with the combined imagery of love and religion so pervasive in both monasteries and courts. One renowned Beguine, Mary of Oignies (1177–1213), who like St. Francis was rumored to have received stigmata, said that sometimes "she held [Christ] close to her so that He nestled between her breasts like a baby."

The church tentatively tolerated the Beguines. But other religious movements so contradicted officially accepted ideas that church authorities labeled them heresies. Heresies were not new in the twelfth century. But the eleventh-century Gregorian reform had created for the first time in the West a clear church hierarchy headed by a pope who could enforce a single doctrine and discipline. Clearly defined orthodoxy meant that people in western Europe now perceived deviant religious ideas as a serious problem.

Among those whom the church pursued most zealously were those the church called dualists. Supposedly they saw the world as being torn between two great forces—one good, the other evil. It is likely that the church was thinking of ancient dualists and pinning the accusation on dissidents who questioned the importance of the church hierarchy and its institutions. We have few of the "dualists's" own writings, but their persecutors described them in lurid terms: "They said that the Roman church was a den of thieves. . . . They ridiculed the sacraments of the church, arguing publicly that the holy water of baptism was no better than river water, that the consecrated host of the holy body of Christ was no different from common bread." And so on. In Languedoc, an area of southern France, the heretics were called Albigensians, a name derived from the town of Albi. Calling themselves "Christ's poor"—though modern historians have given them the collective name Cathars (from a Greek word meaning "pure")—they attracted both men and women, young and old, literate and unlettered. Giving women access to all but the highest positions in their church, the Cathars saw themselves as followers of Christ's original message.

Disastrous Crusades to the Holy Land

Did religious fervor also inspire the crusades of the later twelfth century? Some Europeans thought so. The pope called the Third Crusade "an opportunity for repentance and doing good." This crusade was indirectly a result of the fall of the Seljuk Empire at the hands of Nur al-Din and his successor Saladin (1138–1193). The two were Sunni Muslims eager to impose their brand of Islam in the region. They took Syria and Egypt, and, in 1187, Saladin conquered Jerusalem.

The Third Crusade was an unsuccessful bid to retake the Holy City. The greatest rulers of Europe—Emperor Frederick I (Barbarossa), Philip II of France, Leopold of Austria, and Richard I of England—led it. But they spent most of their time quarreling with one another or harassing the Byzantines. After they went home, the crusader states remained a shadow of themselves—minus Jerusalem—until they were entirely snuffed out in 1291. Islamic hegemony over the Holy Land would remain a fact of life for centuries.

The hostilities that surfaced during the Third Crusade made it a dress rehearsal for the **Fourth Crusade** (1202–1204). Antipathy toward the Byzantines had begun long before the thirteenth century. Now it combined with Venetian opportunism. As soon as the pope called the Fourth Crusade, the Venetians fitted out a fine fleet of ships and galleys for the expedition. But when the crusaders arrived in Venice, there were far fewer fighters to pay for the transport than had been anticipated. To defray the costs of the ships and other expenses, the Venetians convinced the crusaders to do them some favors before taking off against the Muslims. First, they had the crusaders attack Zara, a Christian city in Dalmatia (today's Croatia) that was Venice's competitor in the Adriatic. Then they urged the army to attack Constantinople itself, where they hoped to gain commercial advantage over their rivals (Map 11.2).

Convinced of the superiority of their brand of Christianity over that of the Byzantines, the crusaders not only took Constantinople but also killed many of its inhabitants and ransacked the city for treasure and relics. When one crusading abbot discovered a cache of relics, a chronicler recalled, he "greedily thrust in both hands, and, as he was girded for action, both he and

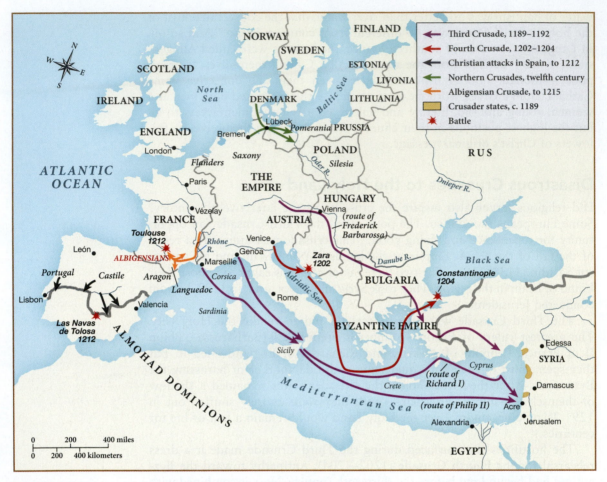

MAP 11.2 Crusades and Anti-heretic Campaigns, 1150–1215
Christian Europeans aggressively expanded their territory during the second half of the twelfth century. To the north, knights pushed into the Baltic Sea region. To the south, warriors moved against the Muslims in al-Andalus and waged war against the Cathars in southern France. To the east, new crusades were undertaken to shore up the tiny European outpost in the Holy Land. Although most of these aggressive activities had the establishment of Christianity as at least one motive, the conquest of Constantinople in 1204 had no such justification. It grew in part out of general European hostility toward Byzantium but mainly out of Venice's commercial ambitions.

the chaplain [with him] filled the folds of their habits with sacred sacrilege." The pope decried the sack of Constantinople, but he also took advantage of it, ordering the crusaders to stay there for a year to consolidate their gains. Plans to go on to the Holy Land were never carried out. The crusade leaders chose one of themselves—Baldwin of Flanders—to be emperor, and he, the other princes, and the Venetians divided the conquered Byzantine lands among themselves. Popes continued to call crusades to the Holy Land until the mid-fifteenth century, but the Fourth Crusade marked the last major mobilization of men and leaders for such an enterprise. Working against these expeditions were the new values of the late twelfth century, which placed a premium on the interior pilgrimage of the soul and valued rulers who stayed home and cared for their people.

Victorious Crusades in Europe and on Its Frontiers

Armed expeditions against those perceived as infidels were launched not only to the Holy Land but also much nearer to home. In Spain, the reconquista continued with increasing success and virulence in the second half of the twelfth century. Christian Spain took on the political configuration that would last for centuries: Aragon in the east, Castile in the middle, and Portugal in the west. The leaders of these polities competed for territory and power, but above all they sought an advantage against the Muslims to the south (Map 11.3).

Piecemeal conquests—followed by the granting of law codes to regulate relations among new Christian settlers as well as the Muslims, Mozarabs (Christians who had lived under the Muslims), and Jews who remained—gradually brought more territory under northern control. In 1212, a crusading army of Spaniards led by the kings of Aragon and Castile defeated the Muslims decisively at the battle of Las Navas de Tolosa. "On their side 100,000 armed men or more fell in the battle," the king of Castile wrote afterward, "but . . . incredible though it may be, unless it be a miracle, hardly 25 or 30 Christians of our whole army fell. O what happiness! O what thanksgiving!"

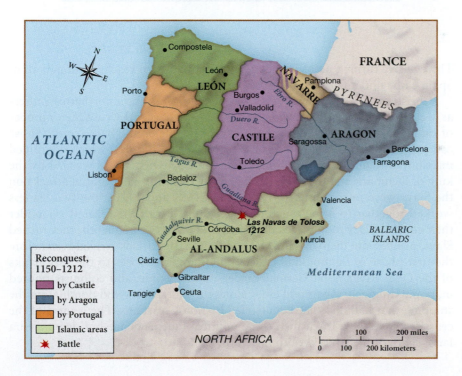

MAP 11.3 The Reconquista, 1150–1212 Slowly but surely the Christian kingdoms of the Iberian peninsula encroached on al-Andalus, taking Las Navas de Tolosa, deep in Islamic territory, in 1212. At the center of this activity was Castile. It had originally been a tributary of León, but in the twelfth century it became a power in its own right. (In 1230, León and Castile merged into one kingdom.) Meanwhile, the ruler of Portugal, who had also been dependent on León, began to claim the title of king, which was recognized officially in 1179, when he put Portugal under the protection of the papacy. Navarre was joined to Aragon until 1134, when it became, briefly, an independent kingdom. (In 1234, the count of Champagne came to the throne of Navarre, and thereafter its history was as much tied to France as to Spain.)

Almourol Castle
In the early twelfth century, the papacy recognized the reconquista as equivalent to a crusade, and the rulers of Portugal, Castile, and Aragon persuaded the Templars and other military orders to help them hold on to regions that had formerly been Muslim. When the Portuguese ruler conquered the western end of the Tagus River valley in the mid-twelfth century, he entrusted some of the Muslim strongholds there to the Templars. They rebuilt one of them as Almourol castle, using it to defend Portugal's new frontier.
(Index Fototeca/Bridgeman Images.)

The decisive turning point in the reconquista had been reached, though all of Spain came under Christian control only in 1492.

Christians flexed their military muscle along Europe's northern frontiers as well (see Map 11.2 on page 394). During the Second Crusade, a number of campaigns had been launched against the people on the Baltic coast. Those campaigns were the beginnings of the Northern Crusades, which continued intermittently until the early fifteenth century. The first phase was led by the king of Denmark and the Saxon duke Henry the Lion. Their initial attacks on the Slavs were uncoordinated, but in the 1160s and 1170s, the two leaders worked together to bring much of the region west of the Oder River under their control. They took some land outright; even more frequently, they turned Slavic princes into their vassals. Meanwhile, the Cistercians arrived even before the first phase of fighting had ended, building monasteries to the very banks of the Oder River. Soon German traders, craftspeople, and colonists poured in, populating new towns and cities along the Baltic coast and dominating the shipping that had once been controlled by non-Christians. The leaders of the crusades gave these townsmen some political independence but demanded a large share of the cities' wealth in return.

Slavic peasants suffered from the conquerors' fire and pillage, but the Slavic ruling classes ultimately benefited from the Northern Crusades. Once converted to Christianity, they found it advantageous for both their eternal salvation and their worldly profit to join new crusades to areas still farther east.

Although less well known than the crusades to the Holy Land, the Northern Crusades had far more lasting effects: they settled the Baltic region with German-speaking lords and peasants and forged a permanent relationship

REVIEW QUESTION
How did the idea of crusade change from the time of the original expedition to the Holy Land?

MAPPING THE WEST

Europe and Byzantium, c. 1215
The major transformation in the map of the West between 1150 and 1215 was the conquest of Constantinople and the establishment of a European ruler there until 1261. The Byzantine Empire was now split into two basic parts—one Latin (in purple) and the other Greek (in white). Bulgaria once again gained its independence. If Venice had hoped to control the Adriatic by conquering Constantinople, it must have been disappointed, for Hungary became its rival over the ports of the Dalmatian coast.

Analyzing the Map: What do the yellow areas on this map represent?

Making Connections: How did English territories come to include Aquitaine but not to include Normandy?

**The Albigensian Crusade,
1209–1229**

between northeastern Europe and its neighbors to the south and west. With the Baltic dotted with churches and monasteries and its peoples dipped into baptismal waters, the region gradually adopted the institutions of western medieval society—cities, guilds, universities, castles, and manors. Only the Lithuanians managed to resist western conquest, settlement, and conversion until the fourteenth century.

Crusades were also launched within Europe itself. The first of these attacked the Cathars in southern France. To be sure, the papacy initially tried conversion, and the Dominican Order had its start as preachers to the heretics. Its founder, St. Dominic (c. 1170–1221), and his followers rejected material riches and went about on foot, preaching and begging and trying to bring the Cathars back into the church. Resembling the Franciscans both organizationally and spiritually, the Dominicans, too, were called friars. But their missions did not have much success, and in 1208 the pope called upon northern princes to take up the sword, invade Languedoc, wrest the land from the heretics, and populate it with orthodox Christians.

The Albigensian Crusade (1209–1229) for the first time offered warriors fighting an enemy within Christian Europe all the spiritual and temporal benefits of a crusade to the Holy Land. Like all other crusades, the Albigensian Crusade had political as well as religious dimensions. It pitted southern French princes, who often had heretical sympathies, against northern leaders eager to demonstrate their piety and win new possessions. After sixteen years of warfare, the Capetian kings of France took over leadership of the crusade. By 1229, all resistance was broken, and Languedoc was brought under the French crown.

Conclusion

In the second half of the twelfth century, Christian Europe expanded from the Baltic Sea to the southern Iberian peninsula. European settlements in the Holy Land, by contrast, were nearly obliterated. When western Europeans sacked Constantinople in 1204, Europe and the Islamic world became the dominant political forces in the West.

Powerful territorial kings and princes established institutions of bureaucratic authority. They hired staffs to handle their accounts, record acts, collect taxes, issue writs, and preside over judicial courts. A money economy provided the finances necessary to support the new bureaucracy, and cathedral schools and universities became its training ground. A new lay vernacular culture celebrated the achievements and power of the ruling class, while Gothic architecture reflected above all the pride and power of the cities.

New religious groups blossomed—Beguines, Franciscans, Dominicans, and heretics. However dissimilar the particulars, the beliefs and lifestyles of these groups reflected the fact that people, especially city dwellers, yearned for a deeper spirituality.

Intense religiosity helped fuel the flames of crusades, which were now fought more often and against an increasing variety of foes, not only in the Holy Land but also in Spain, in southern France, and on Europe's northern frontiers. The peoples on the Baltic coast became targets for new evangelical zeal; the Byzantines became the butt of envy, hostility, and finally enmity. With heretics voicing criticisms, the church, led by the papacy, now defined orthodoxy and declared dissenters its enemies. European Christians still considered Muslims arrogant heathens, and the deflection of the Fourth Crusade did not stem the zeal of popes to call for new crusades to the Holy Land.

Confident and aggressive, the leaders of Christian Europe in the thirteenth century would attempt to impose their rule, legislate morality, and create a unified worldview impregnable to attack. But this drive for order would be countered by unexpected varieties of thought and action, by political and social tensions, and by intensely personal religious quests.

Chapter 11 Review

Key Terms and People

Be sure that you can identify the term or person and explain its historical significance.

Romanesque (p. 374)

Gothic architecture (p. 375)

Henry II (p. 377)

common law (p. 378)

Magna Carta (p. 381)

Philip II (Philip Augustus) (p. 381)

Frederick I (Barbarossa) (p. 384)

troubadours/trobairitz (p. 388)

chansons de geste (p. 389)

chivalry (p. 390)

Franciscans (p. 391)

Fourth Crusade (p. 393)

Review Questions

1. What were the innovations in education and church architecture in the twelfth and early thirteenth centuries?

2. What new sources and institutions of power became available to rulers in the second half of the twelfth century?

3. What do the works of the troubadours and vernacular poets reveal about the nature of entertainment—its themes, its audience, its performers—in the twelfth century?

4. How did the idea of crusade change from the time of the original expedition to the Holy Land?

Making Connections

1. What were the chief differences that separated the ideals of the religious life in the period 1150–1215 from those of the period 1050–1150?

2. How might you associate the gift economy with Romanesque architecture and the money economy with the Gothic style?

3. How do political developments—the growth of bureaucratic institutions, the development of strong monarchies, the growth of city governments—help explain the rise and popularity of vernacular literature and song in the twelfth and thirteenth centuries?

Important Events

1139–1153	Civil War in England
1152–1190	Reign of Frederick Barbarossa
1154–1189	Reign of King Henry II
1176	Battle of Legnano
1180–1223	Reign of Philip II Augustus
1181/1182–1226	Life of Francis of Assisi
1189–1192	The Third Crusade
1202–1204	The Fourth Crusade
1204	Fall of Constantinople to crusaders
1204	Philip takes Normandy, Anjou, Maine, Touraine, and Poitou from John
1209–1229	Albigensian Crusade
1212	Battle of Las Navas de Tolosa; triumph of the *reconquista*
1214	Battle of Bouvines
1215	Magna Carta

Consider three events

The Third Crusade (1189–1192), The Fourth Crusade (1202–1204), and the Albigensian Crusade (1209–1229). What were their various causes and results? How were they differently waged and led?

Suggested References

For the new schools, Abelard is a key primary source, while Clanchy provides perceptive background. Aurell gives insights into politics, while Christiansen covers the little-known "Northern Crusades."

*Abelard, Peter. *The Story of My Misfortunes:* http://www.fordham.edu/halsall/source/abelard-sel.html

Aurell, Martin. *The Plantagenet Empire, 1154–1224.* Trans. David Crouch. 2007.

Bouchard, Constance Brittain. *"Every Valley Shall Be Exalted": The Discourse of Opposites in Twelfth-Century Thought.* 2003.

Bruzelius, Caroline. *Preaching, Building, and Burying: Friars in the Medieval City.* 2014

Burl, Aubrey. *Courts of Love, Castles of Hate: Troubadours and Trobairitz in Southern France, 1071–1321.* 2008.

Christiansen, Eric. *The Northern Crusades.* 2nd ed. 1998.

Clanchy, Michael. *Abelard: A Medieval Life.* 1997.

Crusade of Frederick Barbarossa: The History of the Expedition of the Emperor Frederick and Related Texts. Trans. G. A. Loud. 2010.

Evergates, Theodore. *Henry the Liberal: Count of Champagne, 1127–1181.* 2016.

Freed, John B. *Frederick Barbarossa: The Prince and the Myth.* 2016.

Hudson, John. *The Formation of the English Common Law: Law and Society in England from the Norman Conquest to Magna Carta.* 1996.

Moore, R. I. *The War on Heresy.* 2012.

*Paden, William, and Frances Freeman Paden, eds. and trans. *Troubadour Poems from the South of France.* 2007.

Pegg, Mark Gregory. *A Most Holy War: The Albigensian Crusade and the Battle for Christendom.* 2008.

_____

*Primary source.

The Medieval Synthesis—and Its Cracks

1215–1340

Toward the end of the thirteenth century, a Paris workshop produced an elegantly illustrated translation of some of Aristotle's works. On the opening page of Aristotle's *Metaphysics*, in the large O of the first word, *omnes* ("all"), an artist depicted Aristotle seated on a bench and pointing to the sky. Although Aristotle was a Greek who had lived before the time of Christ, the artist showed him instructing monks while he pointed to a sky dominated by Christ himself. In this way, the artist subtly but surely incorporated the pagan Aristotle into Christian belief and practice.

In the period from 1215 to 1340, Europeans at every level, from workshop artisans to kings and popes, thought that they could harmonize all ideas with Christianity, all aspects of this world with the next, and all of nature with revelation. Sometimes, as in the case of the illumination made for Aristotle's treatise, the synthesis worked. But often it was forced, fragile, or elusive. Not everyone was willing to subordinate his or her beliefs to the tenets of Christianity; kings and popes argued, without resolution, about the limits of their power; and theologians fought over the place of reason in matters of faith. Discord continually threatened expectations of unity and harmony.

Medieval thinkers, writers, musicians, and artists attempted to reconcile faith and reason and to find the commonalities in the sacred and secular realms. At the level of philosophy, this quest led to a new method of inquiry and study known as scholasticism. Yet some scholastic thinkers pointed out cracks and disjunctions in the syntheses achieved.

« Aristotle Instructs the Monks "All men by nature desire to learn," says the opening text of this translation of Aristotle's *Metaphysics*, and that explains why the artist placed in the initial letter a depiction of Aristotle as a teacher. Notice that he wears a turban, a tribute to the fact that Aristotle's works were transmitted to Europe via Arabic scholarship. Above the sky to which Aristotle points is Christ himself. In this way, the artist revealed his certainty that the ancient teachings of Aristotle and Christian belief worked together. (Opening page of the *Metaphysics* of Artistotle, 13th century/Bibliotheque Mazarine, Paris, France/Bridgeman Images.)

CHAPTER FOCUS
In what areas of life did thirteenth-century Europeans try to find harmony and impose order, and how successful were these attempts?

To impose greater order and unity, kings and other rulers found new ways to extend their influence over their subjects. They used the tools of taxes, courts, and even representative institutions to control their realms. Popes issued new laws for Christians and established courts of inquisition to find and punish heretics (those who dissented from church teachings). Both secular and religious authorities at times persecuted Jews. Yet none of this prevented dissent, and rulers often did not gain all the power they wanted.

From 1215 to 1340, the Empire weakened, the papacy asserted itself but was eventually forced to move out of Rome, and the Mongols challenged the traditional world order. Soon, disasters—crop failures and famine—added to the tension.

The Church's Mission

The church had long sought to reform the secular world. In the eleventh century, during the Gregorian reform, it focused on the king. In the thirteenth century, it hoped to purify all of society. It tried to strengthen its institutions of law and justice to combat heresy and heretics, and it supported preachers who would bring the official views of the church to the streets. In this way, the church attempted to reorder the world in the image of heaven, with everyone following the laws of God as set forth by the church. It succeeded in this endeavor to some degree, but it also came up against the limits of control, as dissident voices and forces clashed with its vision.

Innocent III and the Fourth Lateran Council

Innocent III (r. 1198–1216) was the most powerful, respected, and prestigious of medieval popes. He allowed St. Francis's group of impoverished followers to become a new church order, and he called the Fourth Crusade, which mobilized a large force drawn from every level of European society. The first university-trained pope, Innocent studied theology at Paris and law at Bologna. From theology, he learned to tease new meaning out of canonical writings to magnify papal authority: he thought of himself as ruling in the place of

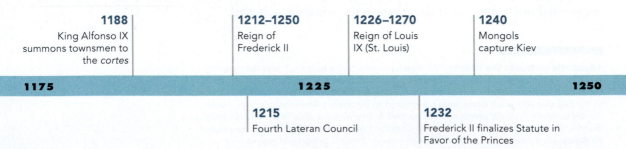

CHAPTER TIMELINE

1188 King Alfonso IX summons townsmen to the *cortes*	**1212–1250** Reign of Frederick II	**1226–1270** Reign of Louis IX (St. Louis)	**1240** Mongols capture Kiev

1175   **1225**   **1250**

1215 Fourth Lateran Council	**1232** Frederick II finalizes Statute in Favor of the Princes

Christ the King, with kings and emperors existing to help the pope. From law, Innocent gained his conceptions of the pope as lawmaker and of law as an instrument of moral reformation.

Innocent used the traditional method of declaring church law: a council. Presided over by Innocent, the **Fourth Lateran Council** (1215) attempted to regulate all aspects of Christian life. Its comprehensive legislation aimed at reforming both the clergy and the laity. Those attending the council expected Christians, clerical and lay alike, to work together harmoniously to achieve the common goal of salvation. They did not anticipate either the sheer variety of responses to their message or the persistence of those who defied it altogether.

For laypeople, perhaps the most important canons (church laws) of the Fourth Lateran Council concerned the sacraments, the rites the church believed Jesus had instituted to confer sanctifying grace. For example, Fourth Lateran required Christians to attend Mass and to confess their sins to a priest at least once a year. It also precisely defined the sacrament of the Eucharist: "[Christ's] body and blood are truly contained in the sacrament of the altar under the forms of bread and wine, the bread and wine having been changed in substance [transubstantiated], by God's power, into his body and blood." The word *transubstantiated* was meant to explain how the Eucharist could *look* like bread and wine even though it had been transformed during the Mass into Christ's body and blood.

Other canons concerned marriage. The church declared that it had the duty to discover any impediments to a union (such as a close relationship by blood), and it claimed jurisdiction over marital disputes. It insisted that children conceived within clandestine or forbidden marriages were illegitimate; they were not to receive inheritances or become priests.

The impact of the council's provisions was perhaps less dramatic than church leaders hoped. All church laws took effect only when local political powers enforced them. Well-to-do London fathers still included their bastard children in their wills. On English manors, sons conceived out of wedlock regularly took over their parents' land. Men and women continued to marry in secret, and even churchmen had to admit that the consent of both parties made any marriage valid. Nevertheless, many men and women accepted the obligation to take communion and confess once a year, and priests proceeded to call

1273	1302	1313–1321	1315–1322
Thomas Aquinas publishes the *Summa Theologiae*	First Meeting of the French Estates General	Dante writes *Divine Comedy*	Great Famine

1275   **1325**   **1350**

1265	1309–1378
English commons are summoned to Parliament	Avignon papacy

Birds' Head Haggadah

In this south German manuscript made c. 1300, the human figures have the heads of birds—or more precisely, griffins—in order to avoid representing human figures. This followed an interpretation of the Second Commandment against graven images prevalent in southern Germany since the twelfth century. The bird-men wear the conical hat that was required of Jews in Germany since the Fourth Lateran Council decreed that all Jews be marked out by a special sign. The Haggadah, the service book for Passover, tells the story of the Jews' deliverance from slavery in Egypt. Here, in this earliest surviving illustrated Haggadah, Moses parts the Red Sea to lead the Jews to the promised land. (The Israel Museum, Jerusalem, Israel/Photo © The Israel Museum, by Ardon Bar-Hama/Bridgeman Images.)

out the banns (announcements of marriages) to discover any impediments to them.

The Fourth Lateran Council wanted to control Jews as well as Christians. It required all Jews to announce their religion by some outward sign: "We decree that [Jews] of either sex in every Christian province at all times shall be distinguished from other people by the character of their dress in public." Eventually, Jews almost everywhere had to wear some sign of their second-class status. In southern France and in a few places in Spain, they wore round badges. In England, Oxford required a rectangle, while Salisbury demanded that Jews wear special clothing. In Vienna and Germany, Jews were told to put on pointed hats.

The Fourth Lateran Council's longest decree blasted heretics: "Those condemned as heretics shall be handed over to the secular authorities for punishment." If the secular authority did not carry out the punishment, the heretic was to be excommunicated. If he or she had vassals, they were to be released from their oaths of fealty and their lands taken over by orthodox Christians. Church authorities set up courts of inquisition to try cases.

Inquisition

The word *inquisition* simply means "investigation." In its zeal to end heresy, the thirteenth-century church used courts of inquisition to ferret out "heretical depravity." (See Terms of History.) Calling suspects to testify, inquisitors, aided by secular authorities, rounded up virtually entire villages, first preaching to the throngs and then questioning each man and woman who seemed to know something about heresy: "Have you ever seen any heretics? Have you heard them preach?" Those deemed guilty were handed over to secular authorities for punishment. Relatively lenient penalties were given to people who were not aware that they held heretical beliefs and to heretics who quickly recanted. But unrepentant heretics were punished severely because (according to the beliefs of the day) they threatened the salvation of all.

Inquisition

The first century of the Roman Empire witnessed the introduction of a new legal procedure called the *inquisitio*—the Latin original of the word inquisition. Before then the term had simply meant "a search." In the first century, with power now concentrated in the hands of an emperor and his officials, it became a tool of Roman magistrates, referring to their duty to investigate all aspects of legal cases before them. One technique of this investigation was torture, both of the accused and of witnesses.

Although the church had confronted heretics long before the twelfth century, it was only then that it systematically adapted aspects of the Roman *inquisitio* to ferret out those who, as churchmen put it, "no longer practice their wickedness in secret . . . but proclaim their error publicly and draw the simple and weak to join them." Heretics were seen as the worst of criminals. Murderers might kill the body, but heretics jeopardized the immortal souls of all. In 1184, the papal bull *Ad abolendam* (For the purpose of abolishing . . .) set up the procedures to be employed. Community representatives, and sometimes entire communities, were required to report any suspected heretics to their bishop—including "any who go to private meetings, or differ from the normal habits of the faithful in their demeanor or way of life." The accused were tried and, if found guilty, were turned over to the public authorities for punishment. It was regularly assumed that torture was necessary to get at the truth, so torture became routine in trials of heretics.

In the sixteenth century in Catholic Spain and elsewhere, tribunals called inquisitions were established to maintain the purity of the faith. In that same century, the Reformation created and fostered the idea that the Catholic church had set up and maintained an institution called "The Inquisition." But there was never just one inquisition; there were many, with variable powers, jurisdictions, goals, and results.

Lay Piety

The church's zeal to reform the laity was matched by the desire of many laypeople to become more involved in their religion. Men and women flocked to hear the preaching of friars, who made themselves a permanent feature of the towns. When Berthold, a Franciscan preacher who traveled the length and breadth of Germany giving sermons, came to a town, a high tower was set up for him outside the town walls. A pennant advertised his presence and let people know which way the wind would blow his voice.

Townspeople gathered to hear preachers like Berthold because they wanted to know how the Christian message applied to their daily lives. They were concerned, for example, about the ethics of moneymaking, sex in marriage, and family life. The preachers in turn met the laity on their own turf, spoke in the vernacular that all could understand, and taught them to shape their behaviors to church teachings.

Laypeople further tied their lives to the mendicants, particularly the Franciscans, by becoming tertiaries. A tertiary was one who adopted the practices of the friars—prayer and works of charity, for example—while continuing to live in the world, work at his or her usual occupation, raise a family, and tend to the normal tasks of daily life.

Although for many people religion was only one facet of life, for some—especially some women—it was a focus. Within the towns and cities, powerful families founded new nunneries for their wealthy daughters. Less well-to-do women sought the life of quiet activity and rapturous mysticism led by the Beguines. Others heeded the call of charity and service in women's mendicant orders. Still others, like Elisabeth of Hungary, raised their children while devoting their free time to fasting, prayer, and service to the poor.

The new emphasis on the holiness of the transformed wine and bread encouraged some pious women to eat nothing but the Eucharist. They believed that Christ's crucifixion was the literal sacrifice of his body, to be eaten by sinful men and women as the way to redeem themselves and others. Some bypassed their priests, receiving the Eucharist (as they explained) directly from Christ. Furthermore, renouncing all other foods became part of their pursuit of charity because many of these devout women gave the poor the food they refused to eat. Thus, pious women used their control over ordinary food to gain new kinds of social and religious prestige and power.

Jews as Outcasts

While Christian women found new roles for themselves, non-Christians were pushed further into the category of "outsiders." To be sure, the First and Second Crusades gave outlet to anti-Jewish feeling. Nevertheless, they were abnormal episodes in the generally stable if tense relationship between Christians and Jews in Europe up to the middle of the twelfth century. Then things changed dramatically as kings became more powerful, popular piety deepened, and church law singled out Jews in particular for discrimination.

Even though Jews had been ousted from manors and banned from town guilds, they were essential to their surrounding Christian communities. Although there were some Christian moneylenders (despite the Bible's prohibition against charging interest for loans), lords, especially kings, preferred to borrow from Jews because, along with their newly asserted powers, they claimed the Jews as their serfs and Jewish property as their own. In England, where Jews had arrived with the Norman conquest in 1066, a special exchequer of the Jews was created in 1194 to collect for the king any unpaid debts due after the death of a Jewish creditor. Even before that, the king of England had imposed new and arbitrary taxes on the Jewish community.

Similarly in France, persecuting Jews and confiscating their property benefited both the treasury and the authoritative image of the king. In 1198, the French king declared that Jews must be moneylenders or money changers exclusively. Their activities were to be taxed and monitored by royal officials. Limiting Jews to moneylending in an increasingly commercial economy clearly served the interests of kings. But lesser lords who needed cash also benefited: they borrowed money from Jews and then, as happened in York, England, in 1190, they orchestrated an attack to rid themselves of their debts and of the Jews to whom they owed money. Churchmen, too, borrowed from Jews but resented having to repay.

Rulers of both church and state exploited and coerced the Jews while drawing on and encouraging a wellspring of elite and popular anti-Jewish feeling.

But attacks against Jews were inspired by more than resentment against Jewish money and the desire for power and control: they also grew out of the codification of Christian religious doctrine and the anxieties of Christians about their own institutions. For example, the newly rigorous definition of the Eucharist meant to many pious Christians that the body of Christ literally lay on the altar. Even as some Christians found this thought unsettling, sensational stories (originating in clerical circles but soon widely circulated) told of Jews who secretly sacrificed Christian children in their Passover ritual—a charge that historians have termed **blood libel**. (In truth, of course, Jews had no rituals involving blood sacrifice at all.)

In 1144, in one of the earliest instances of this charge, the body of a young boy named William was found in the woods near Norwich, England. His uncle, a priest, accused local Jews of killing the child. A monk connected to the cathedral at Norwich, Thomas of Monmouth, took up the cause, writing *The Life and Martyrdom of St. William of Norwich*. According to his account, the Jews carefully prepared at Passover for the horrible ritual slaughter of the boy, whom they had chosen "to be mocked and sacrificed in scorn of the Lord's passion." Similar charges were brought against Jews elsewhere in England as well as in France, Spain, and Germany, leading to massacres of the Jewish population. Some communities expelled Jews, and in 1291, the kingdom of England cast them out entirely. Most dispersed to France and Germany, but to a sad welcome. In 1306, for example, King Philip the Fair had Jews driven from France, though they were allowed to reenter, tentatively, in 1315.

Sometimes lepers were associated with Jews. Today true leprosy is formally known as Hansen's disease, but in the Middle Ages all sorts of skin diseases were classed as leprosy. It was often considered a disease of the soul—the outward sign of inward sinfulness. Sometimes, fears of lepers and leprosy ended in violence. In 1321, mobs in southern France attacked lepers, accusing them of conspiring with Jews to poison the wells and rivers. Hauled in by local officials, lepers were tortured, made to confess, and then burned.

However, at other times, lepers were tolerated and even beloved. King Baldwin IV of Jerusalem (r. 1174–1185) had been a leper since childhood. Even so, attended by doctors, he remained on the throne until his death. As we have seen, St. Francis ministered to lepers and kissed them on their hands and mouths. Leprosaries—hospitals to isolate and care for lepers—were located near the gateways of towns so that travelers could easily offer alms. When walking about, lepers carried clappers to advertise their presence and attract the charity of the townspeople.

REVIEW QUESTION How did people respond to the teachings and laws of the church in the early thirteenth century?

Reconciling This World and the Next

Just as the church in the early thirteenth century wanted to regulate worldly life in accordance with God's plan for salvation, so thinkers, writers, musicians, and artists sought to harmonize the secular and the sacred realms. Scholars wrote treatises that reconciled faith with reason, poets and musicians sang of the links between heaven and human life on earth, and artists expressed the same ideas in stone and sculpture and on parchment. In the face of many contradictions, all of these groups were largely successful in communicating an orderly image of this world and the next.

The Achievements and Failures of Scholasticism

Scholasticism was the culmination of the method of logical inquiry and exposition pioneered by masters like Peter Abelard and Peter the Chanter (see pages 370–371). In the thirteenth century, their methods were used to summarize and reconcile all knowledge. Many of the thirteenth-century scholastics (those who practiced scholasticism) were members of the Dominican or Franciscan orders and taught in the universities. On the whole, they were confident that knowledge obtained through the senses and reason was compatible with the knowledge derived from faith and revelation.

One of the scholastics' goals was to demonstrate this harmony. The scholastic summa, or summary of knowledge, was a systematic exposition of the answer to every possible question about human morality, the physical world, society, belief, action, and theology. Another goal of the scholastics was to preach to the faithful the conclusions of these treatises.

The method of the summa borrowed much of the vocabulary and many of the rules of logic outlined by Aristotle in ancient Greece. Even though Aristotle lived before the time of Christ, scholastics considered his coherent and rational body of thought the most perfect that human reason alone could devise. They assumed that because they had the benefit of Christ's revelations, they could take Aristotle's philosophy one necessary step further and reconcile human reason with Christian faith. Confident in their method and conclusions, scholastics embraced the world and its issues.

St. Thomas Aquinas (1225–1274) was perhaps the most famous scholastic. When he was about eighteen years old, Thomas thwarted his family's wishes that he become a bishop; instead, he joined the Dominican Order. He soon became a university master. Like many other scholastics, Thomas considered Aristotle to be "the Philosopher," the authoritative voice of human reason, which he sought to reconcile with divine revelation in a universal and harmonious scheme. In 1273, he published his monumental *Summa Theologiae* (sometimes called *Summa Theologica*), intended to cover all important topics, human and divine. He divided these topics into questions, exploring each one thoroughly and concluding with a decisive position and a refutation of opposing views.

Many of Thomas's questions spoke to the keenest concerns of his day. He asked, for example, whether it was sinful to have sex outside of marriage. Arranging his discussion systematically, Thomas first quoted arguments that seemed to declare that sex was not sinful as long as the woman involved was free and willing; this was the *sic* ("yes") position. Then he cited the principle that "it is good for each person to attain his end," and that end, in the case of semen, was procreation. This was the *non* of his argument, and it represented Thomas's position. He then elaborated: procreation means the generation of offspring, and human offspring need both a mother and a father to raise them. Thomas concluded that "it is appropriate to human nature that a man remain together with a woman after the generative act." (See Primary Source Analysis on pages 412–413.)

Scholastics like Thomas were great optimists. They believed that everything had a place in God's scheme of things, that the world was orderly, and that human beings could make rational sense of it. Their logical arguments filled the classrooms, spilled into the friars' convents, found their way into the shops of artisans, and even crept under the sheets of lovers. Scholastic philosophy helped give ordinary people a sense of purpose and a guide to behavior.

Yet even among scholastics, unity was elusive. In his own day, Thomas was accused of placing too much emphasis on reason and relying too fully on Aristotle. Later scholastics argued that reason could not find truth through its own faculties and energies. In the summae of the Franciscan John Duns Scotus (d. 1308), for example, the world and God were less compatible. For Duns Scotus, human reason could know truth only through the "special illumination of the uncreated light," that is, by divine illumination. Unlike Thomas, Duns Scotus believed that this illumination came not as a matter of course, but only when God chose to intervene—in other words that God was sometimes willful rather than reasonable. Human reason could not soar to God; God's will alone determined whether or not a person could know him. In this way, Duns Scotus separated the divine and secular realms, and the medieval synthesis cracked.

New Syntheses in Writing and Music

Thirteenth-century vernacular writers, like scholastics, synthesized seemingly contradictory ideas. Dante Alighieri (1265–1321) harmonized the mysteries of faith with the poetry of love. Born in Florence in a time of political turmoil, Dante incorporated the major figures of history and his own day into his most famous poem, the *Commedia*, written between 1313 and 1321. Later known as the *Divina commedia* (*Divine Comedy*), the poem describes Dante's imaginary journey from hell to purgatory and finally to paradise. At the most literal level, it is simply a travelogue. At a deeper level, it is about the soul's search for meaning and enlightenment and its ultimate discovery of God in the radiance of divine love. Just as Thomas Aquinas employed Aristotle's logic to reach important truths, so Dante used the pagan poet Virgil as his guide through hell and purgatory. And just as Thomas believed that faith went beyond reason to even higher truths, so Dante found a new guide representing earthly love to lead him through most of paradise. That guide was Beatrice, a Florentine girl with whom Dante had fallen in love as a boy and whom he never forgot. But only faith, in the form of the divine love of the Virgin Mary, could bring Dante to the culmination of his journey—a blinding and inexpressibly awesome vision of God.

Dante's poem electrified a wide audience. By elevating one dialect of Italian—the language that ordinary Florentines used in their everyday lives— to a language of exquisite poetry, Dante was able to communicate an orderly and optimistic vision of the universe in an even more exciting and accessible way than the scholastics had done.

Thomas Aquinas Writes about Sex

Glad to broach every topic, human and divine, the scholastic Thomas Aquinas (1225–1274) took up the issue of sex in his Summa against the Gentiles. *He wrote this work around 1260 to provide arguments against the scientific views of—among others—elite Muslim scholars of ancient Greek learning, such as Averroes. The section on sex came when Thomas took up issues involved in living a moral life. As usual, he first offered arguments [here 1–3] for the position that he disagreed with: that sex outside of marriage ("fornication") was not a sin. Then he offered a long rebuttal [excerpted here as 4–6].*

The Reason Why Simple Fornication Is a Sin According to Divine Law, and That Matrimony Is Natural

[1] . . . We can see the futility of the argument of certain people who say that simple fornication is not a sin. For they say: Suppose there is a woman who is not married, or under the control of any man, either her father or another man. Now, if a man performs the sexual act with her, and she is willing, he does not injure her, because she favors the action and she has control over her own body. Nor does he injure any other person, because she is understood to be under no other person's control. So, this does not seem to be a sin.

[2] Now, to say that he injures God would not seem to be an adequate answer [against this argument]. For we do not offend God except by doing something contrary to our own good, as has been said. But this does not appear contrary to man's good. Hence, on this basis, no injury seems to be done to God.

[3] Likewise, it also would seem an inadequate answer to say that some injury is done to one's neighbor by this action, inasmuch as he may be scandalized. Indeed, it is possible for him to be scandalized by something which is not in itself a sin. In this event, the act would be accidentally sinful. But our problem is not whether simple fornication is accidentally a sin, but whether it is so essentially.

[4] Hence, we must look for a solution in our earlier considerations. We have said that God exercises care over every person on the basis of what is good for him. Now, it is good for each person to attain his end, whereas it is bad for him to swerve away from his proper end. Now, this should be considered applicable to the parts, just as it is to the whole being; for instance, each and every part of man, and every one of his acts, should attain the proper end. Now, though the male semen is superfluous in regard to the preservation of the individual, it is nevertheless necessary in regard to the propagation of the species. Other superfluous things, such as excrement, urine, sweat, and such things, are not at all necessary; hence, their emission contributes to man's good. Now, this is not what is sought in the case of semen, but, rather, to emit it for the purpose of generation, to which purpose the sexual act is directed.

Other writers of the period used different methods to express the harmony between heaven and earth. The anonymous French author of the *Quest of the Holy Grail* (c. 1225), for example, wrote about the adventures of some of the knights of King Arthur's Round Table to convey the doctrine of transubstantiation and the wonder of the vision of God. As the "good and perfect knight," Galahad himself explained, he saw "a part of the marvels of the Holy Grail which Our Lord revealed to us in His holy mercy, [and] as I beheld the mysteries which are not discovered to everyone, but only to the ministers of Jesus Christ—at that moment when I saw these things which the heart of mortal man could not conceive nor tongue describe—my heart was enthralled in such sweet bliss . . ."

Just as vernacular writers asserted the harmony of heavenly and earthly things, so musicians combined sacred and secular music—and often did so

But man's generative process would be frustrated unless it were followed by proper nutrition, because the offspring would not survive if proper nutrition were withheld. Therefore, the emission of semen ought to be so ordered that it will result in both the production of the proper offspring and in the upbringing of this offspring.

[5] It is evident from this that every emission of semen, in such a way that generation cannot follow, is contrary to the good for man. And if this be done deliberately, it must be a sin. Now, I am speaking of a way from which, in itself, generation could not result: such would be any emission of semen apart from the natural union of male and female. For which reason, sins of this type are called contrary to nature. But, if by accident generation cannot result from the emission of semen, then this is not a reason for it being against nature, or a sin; as for instance, if the woman happens to be sterile.

[6] Likewise, it must also be contrary to the good for man if the semen be emitted under conditions such that generation could result but the proper upbringing would be prevented. We should take into consideration the fact that, among some animals where the female is able to take care of the upbringing of offspring, male and female do not remain together for any time after the act of generation. This is obviously the case with dogs. But in the case of animals of which the female is not able to provide for the upbringing of offspring, the male and female do stay together after the act of generation as long as is necessary for the upbringing and instruction of the offspring. Examples are found among certain species of birds whose young are not able to seek out food for themselves immediately after hatching. In fact, since a bird does not nourish its young with milk, made available by nature as it were, as occurs in the case of quadrupeds, but the bird must look elsewhere for food for its young, and since besides this it must protect them by sitting on them, the female is not able to do this by herself. So, as a result of divine providence, there is naturally implanted in the male of these animals a tendency to remain with the female in order to bring up the young. Now, it is abundantly evident that the female in the human species is not at all able to take care of the upbringing of offspring by herself, since the needs of human life demand many things which cannot be provided by one person alone. Therefore, it is appropriate to human nature that a man remain together with a woman after the generative act, and not leave her immediately to have such relations with another woman, as is the practice with fornicators.

Source: Thomas Aquinas, *Summa contra Gentiles*, book 3, Part II. Translated by Vernon J. Bourke at http://dhspriory.org/thomas/ContraGentiles3b.htm#122

QUESTION TO CONSIDER
What were Thomas's arguments against fornication, and how convincing do you find them?

with multiple voices. The religious music of plainchant (see page 375) and the secular music of the troubadours (see page 389) had featured one sequence of notes for a given text. Sometimes a form of harmony was achieved when two voices sang exactly the same melody an interval apart. In the twelfth century, musicians experimented with new forms of polyphony, the simultaneous sounding of two or more melodies. One voice might go up the scale, for example, while the other went down, achieving even so a pleasing harmony. Or one voice might hold a pitch while the other danced around it.

In the thirteenth century, some musicians put secular and sacred tunes together. This form of music, which probably originated in Paris, was called the motet (from the French *mot*, meaning "word"). It typically had two or three melody lines, or "voices." The lowest was usually a plainchant melody

Singing a Motet
In this fourteenth-century English Psalter, the artist has illustrated the first letter of Psalm 96—which begins "O sing to the Lord a new song"—with a depiction of three clerics singing a motet. Its words and musical notation are written on a scroll draped over a lectern. (From the *Howard Psalter and Hours*, c. 1310–1320/The British Library, London, UK/Bridgeman Images.)

sung in Latin. The remaining melodies had different texts, either Latin or French (or one of each), which were sung simultaneously. Latin texts were usually sacred, whereas those in French dealt with themes made popular by the troubadours, such as love and springtime. The motet thus wove the sacred (the chant melody in the lowest voice) and the secular (the French texts in the upper voices) into a sophisticated tapestry of words and music.

Like scholastic summae, motets were written by and for a clerical elite, yet they incorporated the music of ordinary people, such as the calls of street vendors and the boisterous songs of students. In turn, they touched the lives of everyone, for polyphony influenced every form of music, from the Mass to popular songs that entertained laypeople and churchmen alike.

Complementing the motet's complexity was the development of a new notation for rhythm. Music theorists of the thirteenth century developed increasingly precise methods to indicate rhythm, with each note shape allotted a specific duration. The music of the thirteenth century reflected both the melding of the secular and the sacred and the possibilities of greater order and control.

Gothic Art

Gothic architecture—like philosophy, literature, and music—brought together this world and the next. By the end of the thirteenth century, the Gothic style had spread across most of Europe. Some of its elements began to appear as well in other forms of art, like stained glass. Because pointed arches and flying buttresses allowed the walls of a Gothic church to be pierced with large windows, stained glass became a newly important art form. To make this colored glass, workers added chemicals to sand, heated the mixture until it was liquid, and then blew and flattened it. From these colored glass sheets, artists cut shapes, holding them in place with lead strips. The size of the windows allowed the artists to depict complicated themes ranging from heaven to hell. As the sun shone through the finished windows, they glowed like jewels even when they depicted devils.

The exteriors of Gothic cathedrals were decorated with figures sculpted in the round. As if frozen in motion, the figures turned, moved, and interacted. Like stained glass, Gothic sculptures evoked complex ideas. For example, the figures flanking one of the portals of Strasbourg Cathedral depict the Wise and Foolish Virgins as if acting out the story (the parable in Matthew 25:1–13). The Wise Virgins, holding their lamps upright, follow Christ, the

REVIEW QUESTION
How did artists, musicians, and scholastics in the thirteenth and early fourteenth centuries try to link the physical world with the divine?

Foolish Virgins (see page 416) have empty lamps, and one of them flirts with the Devil.

The allure of Gothic architecture was so great that painters began to use some of its forms. Manuscript illuminations feature the pointed shapes of Gothic cathedral windows and vaults as common background themes. (See the illustration on page 418 for one example.) The colors of Gothic manuscripts echo the rich hues of stained glass. Gothic sculpture inspired painters like Giotto (1266–1337), an Italian artist. When he filled the walls of a private chapel at Padua with paintings depicting scenes of Christ's life, Giotto experimented with the illusion of depth, figures in the round, and emotional expression. By fusing naturalistic forms with religious meaning, Giotto found yet another way to fuse the earthly and divine realms.

The Politics of Control

The quest for order, control, and harmony also inspired the political agendas of princes, popes, and cities. These rulers and institutions imposed—or tried to impose—their authority ever more fully and systematically through taxes, courts, and sometimes representative institutions. Vestiges of these systems live on in modern European parliaments and in the U.S. Congress.

Last Judgment
Stained glass could illustrate complex theological truths. In this thirteenth-century depiction of the Last Judgment from the cathedral at Bourges, in France, two colorful devils force two naked sinners into the toothy mouth of hell. Licks of red flame greet them. While the devils enjoy their task (the green one is smiling), the sinners grimace and seem to cry out in pain. (Detail, 13th century stained-glass window, Saint-Étienne Cathedral, Bourges, France/Bridgeman Images.)

Louis IX of France is a good example of a ruler whose power increased during this period. In contrast, the emperor had to give up Italy and most of his power in Germany. At first powerful, the papacy was later forced to move from Rome to Avignon, a real blow to its prestige. In Italy the rise of *signori* (lords) meant that the communes, which had long governed many cities, gave way to rule by one strong man.

A new group, the Mongols, directly confronted the rulers of Europe and the Islamic world even as they opened up new trade routes to the East. But just as this was taking place, a series of calamities known as the Great Famine hit Europe.

The Weakening of the Empire

During the thirteenth century, both popes and emperors sought to dominate Italy. After Barbarossa failed in his bid for northern Italy (see pages 385–386), his son Henry VI tried a new approach to gain Italy: he married Constance, the heiress of Sicily. With Sicily as a base, Henry hoped to make good his imperial title in Italy. But he died suddenly, leaving as his heir his three-year-old son, **Frederick II** (r. 1212–1250). It was a perilous moment. The imperial office

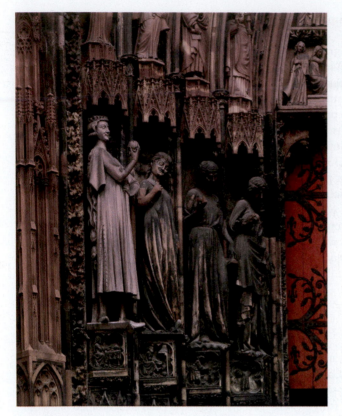

The Foolish Virgins

Figures decorating Gothic churches, such as this one at Strasbourg (in eastern France), were newly naturalistic. Carved in the round, their bodies twisted and turned, and they expressed feelings. Here the sculptor has depicted the parable of the Foolish Virgins. They should be very sad, for they have been shut out of the marriage feast with Christ—in other words, barred from Heaven. The two Virgins on the right are suitably mournful. But the one on the left is flirting with the handsome young man next to her. He is the devil (perhaps you can see the toads, snakes, and lizards climbing on his back), and her smile signals the foolish cheer of the lecherous and the damned. (akg-images/ Paul M.R. Maeyaert/Newscom.)

became the plaything of the German princes and the papacy. Pope Innocent III miscalculated, however, when, in 1212, he gave the imperial crown to Frederick, now a young man ready to take up the reins of power.

Frederick was an amazing ruler: his contemporaries called him *stupor mundi* ("wonder of the world"). Heir to two cultures, Sicilian on his mother's side and German on his father's, he cut a worldly and sophisticated figure. In Sicily, he moved easily within a diverse culture of Jews, Muslims, and Christians. Here he could play the role of all-powerful ruler. In Germany, he was less at home. There Christian princes, often churchmen with ministerial retinues, were acutely aware of their crucial role in royal elections and jealously guarded their rights and privileges.

Both emperor and pope needed to dominate Italy to maintain their power and position. The papacy under Innocent III was expansionist, gathering money and troops to make good its claim to the Papal States. The pope expected dues and taxes, military service, and the profits of justice from this region. To ensure the survival of the Papal States, the pope refused to tolerate any imperial claims to Italy.

Frederick, in turn, could not imagine ruling as an emperor unless he controlled Italy. He attempted to do this throughout his life, as did his heirs. Frederick had a three-pronged strategy. First, he revamped the government of Sicily to give himself more control and yield greater profits. His *Constitutions of Melfi* (1231), an eclectic body of laws, set up a system of salaried governors who worked according to uniform procedures. The *Constitutions* called for nearly all court cases to be heard by royal courts, regularized commercial privileges, and set up a system of taxation. Second, to ensure that he would not be hounded by opponents in Germany, Frederick granted them important concessions in his **Statute in Favor of the Princes**, finalized in 1232. These concessions allowed the German princes to turn their principalities into virtually independent states. Third, Frederick sought to enter Italy through Lombardy, as his grandfather had done.

After Innocent's death in 1216, each of the next four popes tracked Frederick's every move and excommunicated the emperor a number of times. The most

Giotto's *Birth of the Virgin*
This depiction of the Virgin Mary's birth pays attention to the homey details of a thirteenth-century Florentine aristocratic household. Those details portray a sequence: the baby is bathed and swaddled by maidservants in the bottom tier, while above she is handed to her mother, St. Anne, who reaches out eagerly for the child. (Alfredo Dagli Orti/REX/Shutterstock.)

serious of these condemnations came in 1245, when the pope and other churchmen assembled at the Council of Lyon to excommunicate and depose Frederick, absolving his vassals and subjects of their fealty to him and forbidding anyone to support him. By 1248, papal legates were preaching a crusade against Frederick and all his followers. Frederick's death, in 1250, ensured their triumph.

The fact that Frederick's vision of the Empire failed is of less long-term importance than the way it failed. His concessions to the German princes allowed them to divide Germany into discrete principalities. (In fact, Germany would not be united as a nation until the nineteenth century.) Between 1254 and 1273, the princes kept the German throne empty. Splintered into factions, they elected two different foreigners, who spent their time fighting each other.

In one of history's great ironies, it was during this low point of the German monarchy that the term *Holy* Roman Empire was coined, emphasizing its sacred character and power over Rome precisely when it was at its weakest. In 1273, the princes at last united and elected a German, Rudolf (r. 1273–1291), whose family, the Habsburgs, was new to imperial power. Rudolf used the imperial title to help him consolidate control over his own principality, Swabia, but he did not try to fulfill the meaning of the imperial title elsewhere. For the first time, the word *emperor* was freed from its association with Italy and Rome. For the Habsburgs, the title *Holy Roman Emperor* was a prestigious but otherwise meaningless honorific.

Italy at the End of the Thirteenth Century

The failure of Frederick II in Italy meant that the Italian cities would continue their independent course. To ensure that Frederick's heirs would not continue their rule in Sicily, the papacy called successively on other rulers to take over the island—first Henry III of England and then Charles of Anjou. Forces loyal to Frederick's family turned to the king of Aragon (Spain). The move left two enduring claimants to Sicily's crown—the kings of Aragon and the house of Anjou—and it spawned a long war that impoverished the region.

The popes won the war against Frederick, but at a cost. Even the king of France criticized the popes for doing "new and unheard-of things." By making its war against Frederick part of its crusade against heresy, the papacy came under attack for using religion as a political tool.

Louis IX and a New Ideal of Kingship

In hindsight, we can see that Frederick's fight for an empire that would stretch from Germany to Sicily was doomed. The successful rulers of medieval Europe were those contented with smaller, more compact, and more united polities. In France, a new ideal of a stay-at-home monarch started in the thirteenth century with the reign of **Louis IX** (r. 1226–1270). Louis's two crusades to the Holy Land made clear to his subjects just how much they needed him in France, even though his place was ably filled during his first trip by his mother, Blanche of Castile.

Louis was revered not because he was a military leader but because he was an administrator, a judge, and a "just father" of his people. On warm summer days, he would sit under a tree in the woods near his castle at Vincennes, on

Louis IX and Blanche of Castile

This miniature shows Louis IX (St. Louis), portrayed as a young boy, sitting opposite his mother, Blanche of Castile. Blanche served as regent twice in Louis's lifetime, once when he was too young to rule and a second time when he was away on crusade. The emphasis on the equality of queen and king may be evidence of Blanche's influence on and patronage of the artist. (Detail, Blanche of Castile and King Louis IX of France. Moralized Bible, France, between 1227–1234. MS M. 240, fol 8r. Purchased by J. Pierpont Morgan in 1906/The Pierpont Morgan Library, New York, NY, USA/The Morgan Library & Museum/Art Resource, NY.)

the outskirts of Paris, hearing disputes and dispensing justice personally. Through his administrators, he vigorously imposed his laws and justice over much of France. At Paris he appointed a salaried chief magistrate, who could be supervised and fired if necessary. During Louis's reign, the influence of the parlement of Paris (the royal court of justice) increased significantly. Originally a changeable and movable body, part of the king's personal entourage when he dealt with litigation, the parlement was now permanently housed in Paris and staffed by professional judges who heard cases and recorded their decisions.

Unlike his grandfather Philip Augustus, Louis did not try to expand his territory. He inherited a large kingdom that included Poitou and Languedoc (Map 12.1), and he was satisfied. Although at first Henry III, the king of England, attacked France continually to try to regain territory lost under Philip Augustus, Louis remained unprovoked. Rather than prolong the fighting, he conceded a bit and made peace. At the same time, Louis was a zealous crusader. He took seriously the need to defend the Holy Land from the Muslims when most of his contemporaries were weary of the idea.

Respectful of the church and the pope, Louis never claimed power over spiritual matters. Nevertheless, he vigorously maintained the dignity of the king and his rights. He expected royal and ecclesiastical power to work in harmony, and he refused to let the church dictate how he should use his temporal authority. For example, French bishops wanted royal officers to support the church's sentences of excommunication. But Louis declared that he would authorize his officials to do so only if he was able to judge each case himself, to see if the excommunication had been justly pronounced or not. The bishops refused, and Louis held his ground. Royal and ecclesiastical power would work side by side, neither subservient to the other.

It would be easy to fault Louis for his policies toward Jews. His hatred of them was well-known. He did not exactly advocate violence against them, but on occasion he subjected Jews to arrest, canceling the debts owed to them (but collecting part into the royal treasury) and confiscating their belongings. In 1253, he ordered Jews to live "by the labor of their hands" or leave France. He meant that they should no longer lend money, in effect taking away their one means of livelihood. Louis's contemporaries did not criticize him for his Jewish policies. If anything, his hatred of Jews enhanced his reputation.

MAP 12.1 France under Louis IX, r. 1226–1270
Louis IX did not expand his kingdom as dramatically as his grandfather Philip Augustus had done. He was greatly admired, nevertheless, for he was seen by contemporaries as a model of Christian piety and justice. After his death, he was recognized as a saint and thus posthumously enhanced the prestige of the French monarchy.

In fact, many of Louis's contemporaries considered him a saint, praising his care for the poor and sick, the pains and penances he inflicted on himself, and his regular participation in church services. In 1297, Pope Boniface VIII canonized him as St. Louis. The result was enormous prestige for the French monarchy. This prestige, joined with the renown of Paris as the center of scholarship and the repute of French courts as the hubs of chivalry, made France the cultural model of Europe.

The Birth of Representative Institutions

As thirteenth-century monarchs and princes expanded their powers, they devised a new political tool to enlist more broadly based support: all across Europe, from Spain to Poland, from England to Hungary, rulers summoned parliaments. These grew out of the ad hoc advisory sessions kings had held in the past with men from the two most powerful classes, or orders, of medieval society—the nobility and the clergy. In the thirteenth century, the advisory sessions turned into solemn, formal meetings of representatives of the orders to the kings' chief councils—the precursor of parliamentary sessions. Eventually these groups became institutions through which people not ordinarily present at court could articulate their wishes. In practice, thirteenth-century kings did not so much command representatives of the orders to come to court as they simply summoned the most powerful members of their realm—whether clerics, nobles, or important townsmen—to support their policies.

The *cortes* of Castile-León in Spain were among the earliest representative assemblies called to the king's court and the first to include townsmen. Enriched by plunder, fledgling villages soon burgeoned into major commercial centers. Like the cities of Italy, Spanish towns dominated the countryside. No wonder King Alfonso IX (r. 1188–1230) summoned townsmen to the cortes in the first year of his reign, getting their representatives to agree to his plea for military and financial support and for help in consolidating his rule. Once convened at court, the townsmen joined bishops and noblemen in formally counseling the king and assenting to royal decisions. Beginning with Alfonso X (r. 1252–1284), Castilian monarchs regularly called on the cortes to participate in major political and military decisions and to assent to new taxes to finance them.

The English Parliament also developed as a new tool of royal government.* In this case, however, the king's control was complicated by the power of the barons, manifested, for example, in Magna Carta. In the twelfth century, the king had used great councils of churchmen and barons to ratify and gain support for his policies. Although Magna Carta had nothing to do with such

---

* Although *parlement* and *Parliament* are similar words, both deriving from the French word *parler* ("to speak"), the institutions they named were very different. The parlement of France was a law court, whereas the English Parliament, although beginning as a court to redress grievances, had by 1327 become above all a representative institution. The major French representative assembly, the Estates General, first convened at the beginning of the fourteenth century (see page 422).

councils, the barons thought the document gave them an important and permanent role in royal government as the king's advisers and a solid guarantee of their customary rights and privileges. In the thirteenth century, while Henry III (r. 1216–1272) was still a child, England was governed by a council consisting of a few barons, some university-trained administrators, and a papal legate. Although not quite "government by Parliament," this council set a precedent for baronial participation in government.

A Parliament that included commoners came only in the midst of war and as a result of political weakness. Once in power, Henry III so alienated nobles and commoners alike by his wars, debts, choices of advisers, and demands for money that the barons threatened to rebel. At a meeting at Oxford in 1258, they forced Henry to dismiss his foreign advisers. Henceforth, he was to rule with the advice of a so-called Council of Fifteen, chosen jointly by the barons and the king. Chief royal officers were to serve for one year only, after which they were to account for their actions to the council. However, this new government was itself plagued by strife among the barons, and civil war erupted in 1264. At the battle of Lewes in the same year, the leader of the baronial opposition, Simon de Montfort (c. 1208–1265), routed the king's forces, captured the king, and became England's de facto ruler.

Because only a minority of the barons followed him, Simon sought new support by convening a Parliament in 1265, to which he summoned not only the earls, barons, and churchmen who backed him but also representatives from the towns, the "commons"—and he appealed for their help. Thus, for the first time, the commons were given a voice in English government. Even though Simon's brief rule ended that very year and Henry's son Edward I (r. 1272–1307) became a rallying point for royalists, the idea of representative government in England had emerged, born out of the interplay between royal initiatives and baronial revolts.

The Weakening of the Papacy

In contrast with England, representative institutions developed in France out of the conflict between Pope **Boniface VIII** (r. 1294–1303) and King Philip IV (r. 1285–1314), known as Philip the Fair. At the time, this confrontation seemed to be just one more episode in the ongoing struggle between medieval popes and secular rulers for power and authority. Throughout the thirteenth century, the papacy confidently asserted its prerogatives. In fact, however, kings were gradually gaining ground. The conflict between Boniface and Philip signaled the turning point, when royal power trumped papal power.

The conflict began over taxation. Traditionally, clerics were not taxed except in the case of religious wars. But Philip the Fair and the English king Edward I both financed their wars (mainly against one another) by taxing the clergy along with everyone else. The new principle of national sovereignty that they were claiming led them to assert jurisdiction over all people who lived within their borders, even churchmen. For the pope, however, the principle at stake was his role as head of the clergy. Thus, Pope Boniface VIII declared

Portrait of a Pope
Celebrating the power of the papacy, Pope Nicholas III (r. 1277–1280) sponsored a thorough redecoration of Rome's ancient basilica of St. Paul's Outside the Walls (the burial place of St. Paul). In the space above each of the columns running down the nave, he had his artists paint portraits of the popes, linking all to one another and ultimately to St. Peter (whose portrait was nearest the altar). In this image of Anacletus (r. c. 79– c. 91), the artist asserted the pope's gravity, solemnity, and otherworldliness. Anacletus wears a pallium, a white scarf symbolizing papal power, even though the pallium did not exist in the first century. (San Paolo fuori le Mura, Rome, Italy/Nimatallah/Art Resource, NY.)

that only the pope could authorize taxes on clerics. Threatening to excommunicate kings who taxed churchmen without papal permission, he called on clerics to disobey any such royal orders.

Edward and Philip reacted swiftly. Taking advantage of the role English courts played in protecting the peace, Edward declared that all clerics who refused to pay his taxes would be considered outlaws—that is, "outside the law." Clergymen who were robbed, for example, would have no recourse against their attackers; if accused of crimes, they would have no defense in court. Relying on a different strategy, Philip forbade the exportation of precious metals, money, or jewels—effectively sealing the French borders. Immediately, the English clergy cried out for legal protection, while the papacy itself cried out for the revenues it had long enjoyed from French pilgrims, litigants, and travelers. Boniface was forced to back down, conceding in 1297 that kings had the right to tax their clergy in emergencies.

But this concession did not end the confrontation. In 1301, Philip the Fair tested his jurisdiction in southern France by arresting Bernard Saisset, the bishop of Pamiers, on a charge of treason for slandering the king by comparing him to an owl. Saisset's imprisonment violated the principle, maintained both by the pope and by French law, that a clergyman was not subject to lay justice. Pope Boniface reacted angrily, and King Philip seized the opportunity to deride and humiliate him, orchestrating a public relations campaign against Boniface. Philip convened representatives of the clergy, nobles, and townspeople to explain, justify, and propagandize his position. This new assembly, which met in 1302, was the ancestor of the French representative institution, the Estates General. The pope's reply, the bull* *Unam Sanctam* (1302), intensified the situation to fever pitch by declaring bluntly that "it is altogether necessary to salvation for every human creature to be subject to the Roman Pontiff." At meetings of the king's inner circle, Philip's agents declared Boniface a false pope, accusing him of sexual perversion, various crimes, and heresy.

In 1303, French royal agents, acting on Philip's orders, invaded Boniface's palace at Anagni (southeast of Rome) to capture the pope, bring him to France,

---

* An official papal document is called a bull, from the *bulla*, or seal, that was used to authenticate it.

and try him. Fearing for the pope's life, the people of Anagni joined forces and drove the French agents out of town. Yet even after such public support for the pope, the king made his power felt. Boniface died very shortly thereafter, and the next two popes quickly pardoned Philip and his agents for their actions.

Just as Frederick II's failure revealed the weakness of the empire, so Boniface's humiliation demonstrated the limits of papal control. The two powers that claimed "universal" authority had very little weight in the face of new, limited, but tightly controlled national states such as France and England. After 1303, popes continued to denounce kings and emperors, but their words had less and less impact. Against newly powerful medieval states—sustained by vast revenues, judicial apparatuses, representative institutions, and even the loyalty of churchmen—the papacy could make little headway. The delicate balance between church and state, reflecting a sense of universal order and harmony and a hallmark of the reign of St. Louis, broke down at the end of the thirteenth century.

The papacy's weakness was dramatically demonstrated by its move to Avignon. In 1309, forced from Rome by civil strife, the papacy settled in this city close to France. Here it remained until 1378, and thus the period 1309–1378 marks the **Avignon papacy.** Many Europeans, ashamed that the pope lived so far from Rome, called it the Babylonian captivity. They were thinking of the Old Testament story of the Hebrews captured and brought into slavery in ancient Babylon.*

The Avignon popes, many of them French, established a sober and efficient organization that took in regular revenues and gave the papacy more say than ever before in the appointment of churchmen. Slowly, they abandoned the idea of leading all of Christendom, tacitly recognizing the growing power of the secular states to regulate their internal affairs.

The Rise of the *Signori*

During the thirteenth century, new groups, generally made up of the non-noble classes—the *popolo* ("people"), who fought on foot—attempted to take power from the nobility in many Italian communes. The popolo incorporated members of city associations such as craft and merchant guilds, parishes, and the commune itself. In fact, the popolo was a kind of alternative commune. Armed and militant, the popolo demanded a share in city government. In 1223, at Piacenza, the popolo and the nobles worked out a plan to share the election of their city's government; such power sharing was a typical result of the popolo's struggle. In some cities, however, nobles dissolved the popolo, while in others the popolo virtually excluded the nobles from government. Such factions turned northern Italian cities into centers of civil discord.

Weakened by this constant friction, the communes were tempting prey for great regional nobles who, allying with one or another urban group, often succeeded in establishing themselves as *signori* (singular *signore*, "lord") of the

*See 2 Kings 24–25.

WHAT WOULD YOU DO?

If you lived in Anagni at the moment when Pope Boniface sought refuge there from the agents of the French king, would you have joined the crowd to save the pope, remained on the sidelines, or cheered on Philip's henchmen? Why or why not?

cities, keeping the peace at the price of repression. Thirteenth-century Piacenza was typical: first dominated by nobles, the popolo gained a voice by 1225; but then by midcentury, both the nobles and the popolo were eclipsed by the power of a signore.

The Mongol Takeover

Europeans were not the only warring society in the thirteenth century: to the east, the **Mongols** (sometimes called Tatars or Tartars) created an aggressive army under the leadership of Chinghis (or Genghis) Khan (c. 1162–1227) and his sons. In part, economic necessity drove them out of Mongolia: changes in climate had reduced the grasslands that sustained their animals and their nomadic way of life. But they were also inspired by Chinghis's hope of conquering the world. By 1215, the Mongols held Beijing and most of northern China. Some years later, they moved through central Asia and skirted the Caspian Sea (Map 12.2).

In the 1230s, the Mongols began concerted attacks against Rus, Poland, and Hungary, where native princes were weak. Fighting mainly on horseback with heavy lances and powerful bows and arrows whose shots traveled far and penetrated deeply, the Mongols roared through Rus and moved onward into Hungary. Only the death of the second Great Khan, Chinghis's son Ogetei (r. 1229–1241), and disputes over his succession prevented a concentrated assault on Germany.

MAP 12.2 The Mongol Khanates after 1260 Soon after the conquests of Chinghis Khan, the Mongols split up, with the Ilkhanids taking over the traditional heartland of the Islamic world, the Golden Horde ruling Russia, and the Yuans dominating China.

In the 1250s, the Mongols took Iran and Iraq, reconfiguring the Islamic world as well as the West. By the mid-thirteenth century, they had established several fairly stable khanates under descendants of Chinghis: the Ilkhanids held Iran and Iraq, the **Golden Horde** (as they were later called) dominated Rus, the Chaghatai Khanate controlled Central Asia, and the Yuans took over China.

Kiev was the center of Mongolian power in Rus. The new rulers adopted much of the local government apparatus and left many of the old institutions in place. They allowed Rus princes to continue ruling as long as those princes paid homage and tribute to the khan, and, although their own religion was mainly shamanistic, they tolerated the Rus church, exempting it from taxes. The Mongols' chief undertaking was a series of population censuses on the basis of which they recalculated taxes and recruited troops.

The Ilkhanids, too, adopted much of Islamic culture where they conquered. They converted to Islam at the end of the thirteenth century, employed natives in their administration, and fostered the arts that their invasions had temporarily disrupted: ceramics in Iran, silk in Iraq, manuscripts at Baghdad. Mosques and madrases were built or rebuilt. Baghdad libraries flourished.

The Mongol invasion changed the political order of Europe and Asia. Because the Mongols were willing to deal with Westerners, one effect of their conquests was to open China to European travelers for the first time. Missionaries, diplomats, and merchants went to China over land routes and via the Persian Gulf. The most famous of these travelers was the Venetian Marco Polo (1254–1324), and an entire community of Venetian traders lived in the city of Yangzhou in the mid-fourteenth century. Friars, who were preachers to the cities of Europe, became missionaries in Asia as well.

The long-term effect of the Mongols on the West was to open up new land routes to the East that helped bind together the two halves of the known world. Travel stories such as Marco Polo's account of his journeys stimulated others to seek out the fabulous riches—textiles, ginger, ceramics, copper—of China and other regions of the East. In a sense, the Mongols initiated the search for exotic goods and missionary opportunities that culminated in the European "discovery" of a new world, the Americas (see Contrasting Views on pages 426–428).

Mongol Ceramics

After conquering the eastern half of the Islamic world and most of China, the Mongols settled down. The Ilkhanid dynasty, which took over Iran, Iraq, and parts of Syria, soon converted to Islam, and they revived the traditional arts of Iran, such as the ceramic dish illustrated here. Glowing with blue, black, and turquoise hues, it is decorated with leaping rams. While reviving indigenous artistic traditions, the Ilkhanids also took advantage of their links with China to draw on Chinese themes and motifs for their textiles, manuscript illuminations, and pottery. (Cincinnati Art Museum, Ohio, USA/Given in honor of Mr. and Mrs. Charles F. Williams by their children/Bridgeman Images.)

The Mongols: Instruments of God or Cruel Invaders?

When the Mongols first appeared in the West, Pope Innocent IV (r. 1243–1254) quickly wrote two letters to their "emperor"—as he thought of their Great Khan—to express his "surprise" that they would invade Christian territories. He outlined the basic beliefs of Christianity, and he called on them to do penance. Excerpt 1 is the reply of Guyuk Khan (r. 1246–1248), leader of the Mongols. A few years later (c. 1250) the king of Hungary, Béla IV (r. 1235–1270), wrote (Excerpt 2) a letter to the pope to beg him for help. His country had already been invaded by the Mongols (he called them Tartars), and he feared another assault.

1. The Mongols as God's instrument

When Guyuk Khan wrote his reply to Pope Innocent IV in 1246, he belittled the pope's standing and claimed to conquer by the favor of God.

> We, by the power of the eternal heaven,
> Khan of the great Ulus[1]
> Our command:—
>
> This is a version sent to the great Pope, that he may know and understand in the [Persian] tongue, what has been written. The petition of the assembly held in the lands of the Emperor [for our support], has been heard from your emissaries.
>
> If he reaches [you] with his own report, you who are the great Pope, together with all the Princes, come in person to serve us. At that time I shall make known all the commands of the *Yasa* [our customs and laws].
>
> You have also said that supplication and prayer have been offered by you, that I might find a good entry into baptism. This prayer of yours I have not understood. Other words which you have sent me: "I am surprised that you have seized all the lands of the Magyar and the Christians. Tell us what their fault is." These words of yours I have also not understood. The eternal God has slain and annihilated these lands and peoples because they have neither adhered to Chinghis Khan, nor to the Khagan [supreme ruler], both of whom have been sent

to make known God's command, nor to the command of God. Like your words, they also were impudent; they were proud and they slew our messenger-emissaries. How could anybody seize or kill by his own power contrary to the command of God?

> Though you also say that I should become a trembling Nestorian Christian, worship God, and be an ascetic, how do you know whom God absolves in truth, to whom He shows mercy? How do you know that such words as you speak are with God's sanction? From the rising of the sun to its setting, all the lands have been made subject to me. Who could do this contrary to the command of God?
>
> Now you should say with a sincere heart: "I will submit and serve you." You yourself, at the head of all the Princes, come at once to serve and wait upon us! At that time I shall recognize your submission.
>
> If you do not observe God's command, and if you ignore my command, I shall know you as my enemy. Likewise I shall make you understand. If you do otherwise, God knows what I know.
>
> At the end of Jumada the second in the year 644 [1246].
>
> The Seal
>
> We, by the power of the eternal Tengri [the Mongolian great god], universal Khan of the great Mongol Ulus—our command. If this reaches peoples who have made their submission, let them respect and stand in awe of it.

Source: *The Mongol Mission: Narratives and Letters of the Franciscan Missionaries in Mongolia and China in the Thirteenth and Fourteenth Centuries*, ed. Christopher Dawson (New York: Sheed and Ward, 1955), 85–86.

2. The Mongols as Cruel Invaders

Hungary considered itself to be a "frontier region," poised between greedy Germans (though Christians) to the west and pagans and heretics to the east. In his letter to Pope Innocent IV, King Béla portrayed Hungary as the fortress of Europe; if it fell, all of Europe would fall.

---

[1]Ulus is a large or small social group, here consisting of all the peoples under the supreme ruler as a community.

Already the Mongols (Tartars) had invaded Hungary in 1241–1242. Béla painted the Mongols in lurid colors. In the event, the pope did not aid Béla and the Mongols did not in fact attack again.

To the most holy father in Christ and Lord Innocent, by divine providence Supreme pontiff of the Holy Roman and Universal Church, Béla, king of Hungary by the same grace, with the respect both due and devoted. Most of the kingdom of Hungary has been reduced to a desert by the scourge of the Tartars, and it is surrounded like a sheepfold by different infidel peoples … and the Bulgarians and Bosnian heretics against whom we have been fighting until now with our armies on the southern side. On the western and northern side there are Germans, from whom, because of our common faith, our kingdom should gain the fruit of some aid. However, it is not any fruit, but rather the thorns of war that our land is forced to endure as they snatch away the wealth of the country by unexpected plundering. For this reason — and especially because of the Tartars, whom the experience of war has taught us to fear in the same way as all the other nations that they have passed through have learned — after having asked for advice from the prelates [bishops] and princes of our kingdom, we hasten to flee to the worthy vicar of Christ [the pope] and to his brethren, as to the sole and very last true protector of Christian faith in our ultimate need, so that what we all fear will not happen to us, or rather, through us, to you and to the rest of Christendom. Day after day news of the Tartars comes to us: that they have unified their forces — and not only against us, with whom they are the most enraged, because we refuse to submit to them even after all that injury, while all the other nations that they put to the test became their tributaries [states that pay tribute], especially the regions which are at the east of our kingdom. . . . It is rather against the whole of Christendom that their forces are unified, and, insofar as it is deemed certain by several trustworthy people, they have firmly decided to send their countless troops against the whole of Europe soon. Thus we are afraid that, if their people arrive, our subjects will be unable or even unwilling to withstand the cruelty of the Tartar ferocity in battle and, against our will, guided by fear, they will end up by submitting to their yoke, just as the above-mentioned neighbors have already done, unless by its careful consideration the farsighted Apostolic see securely and powerfully fortifies our kingdom in order to comfort the peoples living in it.

. . . We very much hope that it is clear to the Sanctity of your Supreme pontiff, that in these oppressive times we have received no useful aid from any prince or people of the whole Christian Europe. . . . If — God forbid! — this territory were possessed by the Tartars, the door would be open for them to [invade] the other regions of the Catholic faith. This is in part because there is no sea to hamper their passage from here to other Christians, and in part it is because they can settle their families and animals — in which they abound — marvelously well here, better than elsewhere. . . . We take God and man as our witness that our necessity and the gravity of our situation are so great that, if the various dangers of the roads did not prevent us, we would send not only messengers, as we have done so far, but would personally come as a servant and fall down at your feet to proclaim before the face of the whole Church — so that we may be justified and excused — that, if your fatherly sanctity does not send us help and the need becomes overwhelming, against our will, we may reach an arrangement with the Tartars. So we humbly beseech you that the Holy Mother Church consider, if not ours, at least the merits of our predecessors, the holy kings who, full of devotion and reverence submitted themselves and their people, preaching to them the orthodox faith, and serving you with purity of faith and in obedience. That is why the Apostolic see promised to them and to their successors all grace and favor if any necessity threatened, at a moment when they did not even ask for it, as the course of things was prosperous for them. Alas, now this heavy constraint seems to be imminent. Thus open your fatherly heart, and in this time of persecution, extend your hand with the necessary support for the defense of the faith and for the public utility. Otherwise, if our petition — which is so

(Continued)

necessary and so universally favorable for the faithful of the Roman Church—suffers a refusal (which we cannot believe) then we should be obliged by necessity, not like sons but like step-sons, excluded from the flock of the father, to beg for aid elsewhere.

Source: *Reading the Middle Ages: Sources from Europe, Byzantium, and the Islamic World,* ed. Barbara H. Rosenwein, 2d ed. (Toronto: University of Toronto Press, 2014), 381–83.

QUESTIONS TO CONSIDER

1. What were the similarities and differences between the Mongol and the papal notions of God?

2. What sort of help from the papacy could Béla expect?

The Great Famine

While the Mongols stimulated the European economy, natural disasters coupled with human actions brought on a terrible period of famine in northern Europe. The **Great Famine** (1315–1322) left many hungry, sick, and weak while it fueled social antagonisms. An anonymous chronicler looking back on the events of 1315 wrote:

> The floods of rain have rotted almost all the seed, . . . and in many places the hay lay so long under water that it could neither be mown nor gathered. Sheep generally died and other animals were killed in a sudden plague. . . . [In the next year, 1316,] the dearth of grain was much increased. Such a scarcity has not been seen in our time in England, nor heard of for a hundred years. For the measure of wheat sold in London and the neighboring places for forty pence [a very high sum], and in other less thickly populated parts of the country thirty pence was a common price.

Thus did the writer chronicle the causes and effects of the famine: uncommonly heavy rains, which washed up or drowned the crops; a disease that killed farm animals key to agricultural life not only for their meat and fleeces but also for their labor; and, finally, the effects on costs, as scarcity drove up the prices of ordinary foods. All of these led to hunger, disease, and death.

Had the rains diminished, Europeans might have recovered. But the rains continued, and the crops kept failing. In many regions, the crisis lasted for a full seven years. Hardest hit were the peasants and the poor. In rural areas, wealthy lords, churches, monasteries, and well-to-do peasants manipulated the market to profit from the newly high prices they could charge. In the cities, some merchants and ecclesiastical institutions benefited as well. But on the

A Famine in Florence

Starvation did not end with the last year of the Great Famine. This miniature from a manuscript detailing grain prices shows the effects, and the artist's interpretation, of a famine in 1329. The scene is the Orsanmichele, the Florentine grain market. The market was dominated by an image of the Virgin Mary, here depicted on the right-hand side. Extending beyond the margin on the far left, a mother with two children raises her hands and eyes to heaven in prayer. In the back, soldiers guard the market's entrance. The market itself bustles with rich buyers, who hand over their money and pack their bags with grain. Above flies an angel with broken trumpets, while a demon takes center stage and says, among other things, "I will make you ache with hunger and high prices." (Biblioteca Laurenziana, Florence, Italy/Scala/Art Resource, NY.)

whole, even the well-to-do suffered: both rural and urban areas lost fully 5 to 10 percent of their population, and loss of population meant erosion of manpower and falling productivity.

To cope with and contain these disasters, the clergy offered up prayers and urged their congregations to do penance. In the countryside, charitable monasteries gave out food, conscientious kings tried to control high interest rates on loans, and hungry peasants migrated from west to east—to Poland, for example, where land was more plentiful. In the cities, where starving refugees from rural areas flocked for food, wealthy men and women sometimes opened their storehouses or distributed coins. Other rich townspeople founded hospitals for the poor. Town councils sold municipal bonds at high rates of interest, gaining some temporary solvency. These towns became the primary charitable institutions of the era, importing grain and selling it at or slightly below cost.

Contributing to the crop failure was population growth that challenged the productive capabilities of the age. The exponential leap in population from the tenth through most of the thirteenth century slowed to zero around the year 1300, but all the land that could be cultivated had been settled by this time. No new technology had been developed to increase crop yields. The swollen population demanded a lot from the productive capacities of the land. Just a small shortfall could dislocate the whole system of distribution. This disastrous situation was mitigated somewhat in Mediterranean regions, where crops were more diversified. When wheat harvests were poor, peasants could find chestnuts or millet, or they could migrate to more flourishing regions.

The policies of rulers added to the problems of too many people and too little food. Wars between England and Scotland destroyed crops. So did the fighting between the kings of Norway, Denmark, and Sweden. These wars

MAPPING THE WEST

Europe, c. 1340

The Empire, which in the thirteenth century came to be called the Holy Roman Empire, still dominated the map of Europe in 1340, but the emperor himself had less power than ever. Each principality—often each city—was ruled separately and independently. To the east, the Ottoman Turks were just beginning to make themselves felt. In the course of the next century, they would disrupt the Mongol hegemony and become a great power.

Analyzing the Map: Where besides England was the king of England a powerful ruler?

Making Connections: When and why was the term *Holy Roman Empire* coined?

also diverted manpower and resources to arms and castles, and they disrupted normal markets and trade routes. In order to wage them, rulers imposed heavy taxes and, as the Great Famine became worse, requisitioned grain to support their troops.

As the effects of the famine became clear, people rose up in protest in many regions. In England, peasants resisted tax collectors. In a more violent reaction, poor French shepherds, artisans, and various outcasts entered Paris to storm the prisons. They then marched southward, burning royal castles and attacking officials and Jews, who had only just been readmitted to France. The king of France pursued them and succeeded in putting down the movement. But the limits of the politics of control were made clear in this confrontation, which exacerbated the misery of the famine while doing nothing to contain it.

REVIEW QUESTION
How did the search for harmony result in cooperation—and confrontation—between the secular rulers of the period 1215–1340 and other institutions, such as the church and the towns?

Conclusion

The thirteenth century sought harmony and synthesis but discovered how elusive these goals could be. Theoretically, the papacy and empire were supposed to work together; instead they clashed in bitter warfare, leaving the government of Germany to the princes and northern Italy to its communes and signori. Theoretically, faith and reason were supposed to arrive at the same truths. They sometimes did so in the hands of scholastics, but not always. Theoretically, all Christians practiced the same rites and followed the teachings of the church. In practice, local enforcement determined which church laws took effect—and to what extent. Moreover, the search for order was never able to bring together all the diverse peoples, ideas, and interests of thirteenth-century society. Heretics and Jews were set apart.

Synthesis was more achievable in the arts. Heaven, earth, and hell were melded harmoniously together in stained glass and sculpture. Musicians wove disparate melodic and poetic lines into motets. Writers melded heroic and romantic themes with theological truths and mystical visions.

Political leaders also aimed at harmony. Via representative institutions, they harnessed the various social orders to their quest for greater order and control. They asserted sovereignty over all the people who lived within their borders, asserting unity while increasing their revenues, expanding their territories, and enhancing their prestige. The kings of England and France and the governments of northern and central Italian cities largely succeeded in these goals, while the king of Germany failed miserably. Germany and Italy remained fragmented until the nineteenth century. Ironically, the Mongols, who began as invaders in the West, helped unify areas that were far apart by opening trade routes.

Events at the end of the thirteenth century thwarted the search for harmony. The mutual respect of church and state achieved under St. Louis in France disintegrated into irreconcilable claims to power under Pope Boniface VIII and Philip the Fair. The carefully constructed tapestry of St. Thomas's summae began to unravel in the teachings of John Duns Scotus. An economy stretched to the breaking point resulted in a terrible period of famine. Disorder and anxiety—but also extraordinary creativity—would mark the next era.

Chapter 12 Review

Key Terms and People

Be sure that you can identify the term or person and explain its historical significance.

Innocent III (p. 404)

Fourth Lateran Council (p. 405)

blood libel (p. 409)

scholasticism (p. 410)

Frederick II (p. 415)

Statute in Favor of the Princes (p. 416)

Louis IX (p. 418)

cortes (p. 420)

Boniface VIII (p. 421)

Avignon papacy (p. 423)

popolo (p. 423)

Mongols (p. 424)

Golden Horde (p. 425)

Great Famine (p. 428)

Review Questions

1. How did people respond to the teachings and laws of the church in the early thirteenth century?

2. How did artists, musicians, and scholastics in the thirteenth and early fourteenth centuries try to link the physical world with the divine?

3. How did the search for harmony result in cooperation—and confrontation—between the secular rulers of the period 1215–1340 and other institutions, such as the church and the towns?

Making Connections

1. Why was Innocent III more successful than Boniface VIII in carrying out his objectives?

2. How did the growth of lay piety help bolster the prestige and power of kings like Louis IX?

3. Comparing the goals and methods of Abelard's scholarship with those of Thomas Aquinas, explain the continuities and the differences between the twelfth-century schools and the scholastic movement.

Important Events

1188	King Alfonso IX summons townsmen to the *cortes*
1212–1250	Reign of Frederick II
1215	Fourth Lateran Council
1226–1270	Reign of Louis IX (St. Louis)
1232	Frederick II finalizes Statute in Favor of the Princes
1240	Mongols capture Kiev
1265	English commons are summoned to Parliament
1273	Thomas Aquinas publishes the *Summa Theologiae*

1302	First Meeting of the French Estates General
1309–1378	Avignon papacy
1313–1321	Dante writes *Divine Comedy*
1315–1322	Great Famine

Consider three events

Fourth Lateran Council (1215), Thomas Aquinas publishes the *Summa Theologiae* (1273), and Dante writes *Divine Comedy* (1313–1321). How did the papacy, scholastic philosophy, and vernacular literature represent different aspects of the medieval search for order?

Suggested References

For the church's mission, see both Bynum and Sayers. Abulafia, Jones, Maddicott, and O'Callaghan each helpfully cover the political developments of the period. Brenner has helped change our view of leprosy in the Middle Ages.

Abulafia, David. *Frederick II: A Medieval Emperor*. 1988.

Brenner, Elma. *Leprosy and Charity in Medieval Rouen*. 2015.

Bynum, Caroline Walker. *Holy Feast and Holy Fast: The Religious Significance of Food to Medieval Women*. 1987.

*Fourth Lateran Council: http://www.fordham.edu/halsall/source/lat4-select.asp

Gaposchkin, M. Cecilia. *The Making of Saint Louis: Kingship, Sanctity, and Crusade in the Later Middle Ages*. 2008.

Given, James Buchanan. *Inquisition and Medieval Society*. 2001.

Jackson, Peter. *The Mongols and the Islamic World: From Conquest to Conversion*. 2017.

*Joinville, Jean de, and Geoffroy de Villehardouin. *Chronicles of the Crusades*. Trans. M. R. B. Shaw. 1963.

Jones, Philip. *The Italian City-State: From Commune to Signoria*. 1997.

Jordan, William Chester. *The French Monarchy and the Jews: From Philip Augustus to the Last Capetians*. 1989.

Lipton, Sara. *Dark Mirror: The Medieval Origins of Anti-Jewish Iconography*. 2014.

Maddicott, J. R. *Simon de Montfort*. 1994.

Nichols, Aidan. *Discovering Aquinas: An Introduction to His Life, Work and Influence*. 2003.

O'Callaghan, Joseph F. *The Cortes of Castille-León, 1188–1350*. 1989.

Peters, Edward. *Inquisition*. 1989.

Richardson, H. G., and G. O. Sayles. *The English Parliament in the Middle Ages*. 1981.

Sayers, Jane. *Innocent III: Leader of Europe, 1198–1216*. 1994.

Strayer, Joseph R. *The Reign of Philip the Fair*. 1980.

*Thomas Aquinas. *Summa Theologiae*. http://www.newadvent.org/summa

The Quest of the Holy Grail, trans. W. W. Comfort. 2000. http://www.yorku.ca/inpar/quest_comfort.pdf

---

*Primary source.

Crisis and Renaissance

1340–1492

In 1453, the Ottoman Turks turned their cannons on Constantinople and blasted the city's walls. The fall of Constantinople, which spelled the end of the Byzantine Empire, was an enormous shock to Europeans. Some, like the pope, called for a crusade against the Ottomans; others, like the writer Lauro Quirini, sneered, calling the Ottomans "a barbaric, uncultivated race, without established customs, or laws, [who lived] a careless, vagrant, arbitrary life."

But the Turks didn't consider themselves uncultivated or arbitrary. They saw themselves as the true heirs of the Roman Empire, and they shared many of the values and tastes of the very Europeans who were so hostile to them. Sultan Mehmed II employed European architects to construct his new palace—the Topkapi Saray—in the city once known as Constantinople and now popularly called Istanbul. He commissioned the Venetian artist Gentile Bellini to paint his portrait, a genre invented in Burgundy to celebrate the status and individuality of important and wealthy patrons. He asked Costanzo da Ferrara, who had worked for various Italian patrons, to come to Istanbul to work for him, and Costanzo cast his portrait on a bronze medal nearly 5 inches in diameter (see image).

Mehmed's actions sum up the dual features of the period of crisis and Renaissance that took place from the middle of the fourteenth century to the late fifteenth century. What was a crisis from one point of view—the fall of the Byzantine Empire—was at the same time stimulus for what historians call the Renaissance. Both to confront and to mask the crises of the day, people discovered new value in ancient, classical culture:

CHAPTER PREVIEW

Crisis: Disease, War, and Schism
What crises did Europeans confront in the fourteenth and fifteenth centuries, and how did they handle them?

Renaissance: New Forms of Thought and Expression
How and why did Renaissance humanists, artists, and musicians revive classical traditions?

Consolidating Power
How did the monarchs and republics of the fifteenth century use (and abuse) their powers?

«**Medallion Portrait of Mehmed II** The Ottoman ruler Mehmed II saw himself as a Renaissance man. Like many Italian nobles of his day, he wanted to have medallions cast with his likeness on one side and with a motto of some sort on the other. This particular medallion was made by Costanzo da Ferrara. The obverse (shown here) shows the sultan in a turban, which soon became the fashion rage in Europe. The reverse presents him riding a horse. (Art Reserve/Alamy.)

they revived classical vocabulary, and they created strikingly original forms of art and music based on ancient precedents. The classical revival provided the stimulus for new styles of living, ruling, and thinking.

Along with the fall of the Byzantine Empire, other crises marked the period from 1340 to 1492. These were matched by equally significant gains. The plague, or Black Death, tore at the fabric of communities and families, but the survivors and their children reaped the benefits of higher wages and better living standards. The Hundred Years' War, fought between France and England, involved many smaller states in its slaughter and brought untold misery to the French countryside, but it also helped create the glittering court of Burgundy. By the war's end, both the French and the English kings were more powerful than ever. Following their conquest of Constantinople, the Ottoman Turks penetrated far into the Balkans, but this was a calamity only from the European point of view. Well into the sixteenth century, the Ottomans were part of the culture that nourished the artistic achievements of the Renaissance. A crisis in the church overlapped with the crises of disease and war as a schism within the papacy—pitting pope against pope—and divided Europe into separate camps. But a church council whose members included Renaissance humanists eventually resolved the papal schism by reestablishing the old system: a single pope who presided over the church from Rome.

CHAPTER FOCUS
Who suffered and who benefited from the events of the period from 1340 to 1492?

Crisis: Disease, War, and Schism

In the mid-fourteenth century, a series of crises shook the West. The Black Death swept through Europe and decimated the population, especially in the cities. Two major wars redrew the map of Europe between 1340 and 1492. The first was the Hundred Years' War, fought from 1337 to 1453 (thus actually lasting 116 years). The second was the Ottoman conquest of Constantinople in 1453. As the wars raged and attacks of the plague came and went, a crisis in the church also weighed on Europeans. Attempts to return the papacy from Avignon to Rome resulted in the Great Schism (1378–1417), when first two and then three rival popes asserted universal authority. In the wake of these crises, many ordinary folk sought solace in new forms of piety, some of them condemned by the church as heretical.

CHAPTER TIMELINE

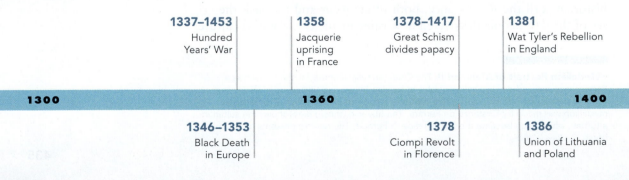

1337–1453 Hundred Years' War	**1358** Jacquerie uprising in France	**1378–1417** Great Schism divides papacy
1381 Wat Tyler's Rebellion in England		

1300   **1360**   **1400**

1346–1353 Black Death in Europe	**1378** Ciompi Revolt in Florence	**1386** Union of Lithuania and Poland

The Black Death, 1346–1353

The **Black Death**, so named by later historians, was a calamitous disease. It decimated the population wherever it struck and wreaked havoc on social and economic structures. Yet in the wake of this plague, those fortunate enough to survive benefited from an improved standard of living. Birthrates climbed, and new universities were established to educate the post-plague generations.

Already in 1346, the Byzantine scholar Nicephorus Gregoras noted a new disease and described its symptoms, including "tumorous outgrowths at the roots of thighs and arms and simultaneously bleeding ulcerations." Scientists now ascribe the Black Death to the bacterium *Yersinia pestis*, the same organism responsible for outbreaks of plague today.

Carried by fleas traveling on the backs of rats, the Black Death hitched boat rides with spices, silks, and porcelains. It hit the Genoese colony in Caffa in 1347 and soon arrived in Constantinople and southern Europe. It then crept northward to Germany, England, Scandinavia, and the state that now was starting to be called Russia.* Meanwhile, it attacked the Islamic world as well (Map 13.1). Recurring every ten to twelve years throughout the fourteenth century (though only the outbreak of 1346–1353 is called the Black Death), the disease attacked, with decreasing frequency, until the eighteenth century.

The effects of the Black Death were spread across Europe yet oddly localized. At Florence, in Italy, nearly half of the population died, yet two hundred miles to the north, Milan suffered very little. Conservative estimates put the death toll in Europe anywhere between 30 and 50 percent of the entire population, but some historians put the mortality rate as high as 60 percent. Already weakened by the Great Famine as well as by local food shortages and epidemic diseases like smallpox, Europeans were devastated by the arrival of *Yersinia*.

Many localities sought remedies. The government of the Italian city of Pistoia, for example, set up a quarantine and demanded better sanitation. Elsewhere reactions were religious. In England, the archbishop of York tried to prevent the plague from entering his diocese by ordering "devout processions." Some people took more extreme measures. Lamenting their sins—which they

---

*The Russian Orthodox church had always used the term *Russia*. In the fourteenth century, the princes who ruled the northern parts, called Muscovy, started to do so as well.

1414–1418	**1453**	**1477**	**1492**
Council of Constance ends Great Schism; Jan Hus burned at the stake	Conquest of Constantinople by Ottoman Turks; end of Hundred Years' War	Dismantling of duchy of Burgundy	Spain conquers Muslim stronghold of Granada; expels Jews

1420	**1460**		**1500**

	1454	**1478**	
	Peace of Lodi	Inquisition begins in Spain	

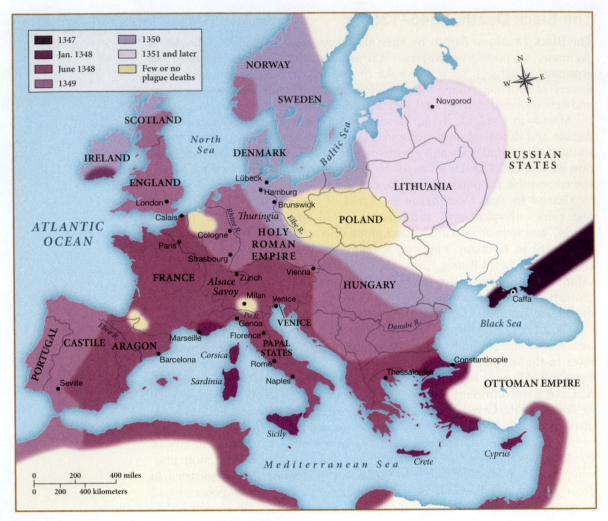

MAP 13.1 Advance of the Black Death, 1346–1353
Hitting the Mediterranean area first, the Black Death quickly worked its way northward, generally following waterways and roads. With the exception of a few regions that were spared, it killed between one-third and one-half of the population of western Europe. However, in eastern Europe its impact was far less dire. The plague recurred—at first every ten to twelve years and then at longer intervals.

believed had brought on the plague—and attempting to placate God, flagellants (men, with women praying) wandered from city to city whipping themselves. Religious enthusiasm often culminated in violence against the Jews, who were blamed for the Black Death. In Germany, thousands of Jews were slaughtered. Many Jews fled to Poland, where the epidemic affected fewer people and where the authorities welcomed Jews as productive taxpayers.

Preoccupation with death led to the popularity of a theme called the Dance of Death as a subject of art, literature, and performance. It featured a procession of people of every age, sex, and rank making their way to the grave.

Dance of Death
This fresco, painted in 1474 on a wall of a cemetery church in Croatia, depicts figures meant to represent all the "types" in medieval society. It should be read from right to left. Not pictured here, but first in line, is the pope, followed by a cardinal and a bishop. The portion shown here comes next: the king, who holds a scepter; the queen; and a landlord, carrying a small barrel. At the far left is a child. Even farther to the left (but not shown here) comes a beggar, a knight, and a shopkeeper. All the figures are flanked by gleeful, dancing skeletons. The message is clear: everyone, even the most exalted, ends up in the grave. (Church of St Mary of Rock, by Vincenzo da Castua, Beram, Istria, Croatia/De Agostini Picture Library/A. Dagli Orti/Bridgeman Images.)

In works of art, skeletal figures of Death, whirling about, laughed as they abducted their prey. Preachers, poets, and playwrights relished the theme.

At the same time that it helped inspire this bleak view of the world, the Black Death brought new opportunities for those who survived its murderous path. With a smaller population to feed, less land was needed for cultivation. Landlords allowed marginal land that had been cultivated to return to pasture, meadow, or forest, and they diversified their products. Wheat had been the favored crop before the plague, but barley—the key ingredient of beer—turned out to be more profitable afterward. Animal products continued to fetch a high price, and some landlords switched from raising crops to raising animals.

These changes in agriculture meant a better standard of living. The peasants and urban workers who survived the plague were able to negotiate better conditions or higher wages from their landlords or employers. With more money to spend, people could afford a better and more varied diet that included beer and meat. Birthrates jumped as people could afford to marry at younger ages.

The Black Death, which spared neither professors nor students, also affected patterns of education. The survivors built new local colleges and universities, partly to train a new generation for the priesthood and partly to satisfy local donors—many of them princes—who, riding on a sea of wealth left behind by the dead, wanted to be known as patrons of education. Thus, in 1348, in the midst of the Black Death, Holy Roman Emperor Charles IV chartered a university at Prague. The king of Poland founded Cracow University, and a Habsburg duke created a university at Vienna. Rather than traveling to Paris or Bologna, young men living east of the Rhine River now tended to study nearer home.

The Hundred Years' War, 1337–1453

Adding to people's miseries during the Black Death were the ravages of war. One of the most brutal was the **Hundred Years' War**, which pitted England against France. Since the Norman conquest of England in 1066, the king of England had held land in what is today France. The French kings continually chipped away at it, so that by the beginning of the fourteenth century England retained only the area around Bordeaux, called Guyenne. In 1337, after a series of challenges and skirmishes, King Philip VI of France (whose dynasty, the Valois, took over when the Capetians had no male heir) declared Guyenne to be his. In turn, King Edward III of England, son of Philip the Fair's daughter, declared himself king of France (Figure 13.1). The Hundred Years' War had begun.

The war had two major phases. In the first, the English gained ground, and a new political entity, the duchy of Burgundy, allied itself with England. This phase culminated in 1415, when the English achieved a great victory at the battle of Agincourt and took over northern France. In the second phase, however, fortunes reversed entirely after a sixteen-year-old peasant girl inspired the dauphin (the yet-uncrowned heir to the French throne) and his troops. Prompted by visions in which God told her to lead the war against the English, and calling herself "the Maid" (the virgin), **Joan of Arc** (1412–1431) arrived at the dauphin's court in 1429 wearing armor, riding a horse, and leading a small army (see Contrasting Views on pages 442–443). Radiating charisma and full of confidence at a desperate hour, Joan convinced the French that she had been sent by God when she fought courageously (and was wounded) in the successful battle of Orléans. Soon, with Joan at his side, the dauphin traveled deep into enemy territory to be anointed and crowned as King Charles VII at the cathedral in Reims, following the tradition of French monarchs. But not long afterward, Joan was captured by the Burgundians, sold to the English, and put to death by her purchasers (Map 13.2).

FIGURE 13.1 The Valois Succession
When the Capetian king Charles IV died in 1328, his daughter was next in line for the French throne, but prejudice in France against female succession was so strong that the crown went to the Valois branch of the family. Meanwhile the English king Edward III, as son of the French princess Isabella, claimed to be the rightful king of France.

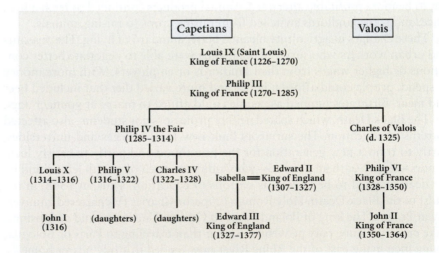

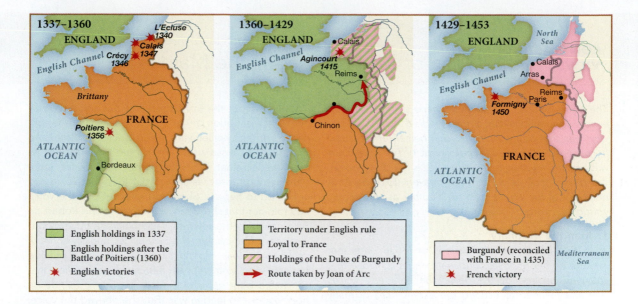

1337–1360

ENGLAND
L'Ecluse 1340
Calais 1347
Crécy 1346
English Channel
Brittany
FRANCE
Poitiers 1356
ATLANTIC OCEAN
Bordeaux

☐ English holdings in 1337
☐ English holdings after the Battle of Poitiers (1360)
✶ English victories

1360–1429

ENGLAND
Calais
English Channel
Agincourt 1415
Reims
Chinon
ATLANTIC OCEAN

☐ Territory under English rule
☐ Loyal to France
▨ Holdings of the Duke of Burgundy
➜ Route taken by Joan of Arc

1429–1453

ENGLAND
North Sea
Calais
Arras
English Channel
Reims
Formigny 1450
Paris
FRANCE
ATLANTIC OCEAN
Mediterranean Sea

☐ Burgundy (reconciled with France in 1435)
✶ French victory

As it unfolded, the Hundred Years' War drew people from much of Europe into its vortex. Both the English and the French hired mercenaries from Germany, Switzerland, and the Netherlands; the best crossbowmen came from Genoa. The duchy of Burgundy became involved in the war when the marriage of the heiress to Flanders and the duke of Burgundy in 1369 created a powerful new state. Calculating shrewdly which side—England or France—to support and cannily entering the fray when it suited them, the dukes of Burgundy created a glittering court, a center of art and culture. Had Burgundy maintained its alliance with England, the map of Europe would probably be entirely different today. But, sensing France's new strength, the duke of Burgundy broke off with England in 1435. The duchy continued to prosper until its expansionist policies led to the formation of a coalition against it. The last Burgundian duke, Charles the Bold, died fighting in 1477. His daughter, his only heir, tried to save Burgundy by marrying the Holy Roman Emperor, but the move was to little avail. The duchy broke up, with France absorbing its western bits.

Flanders, too, got drawn into the war. Its cities depended on England for the raw wool that they turned into cloth. This is why, at the beginning of the war, Flemish townsmen allied with England against their count, who supported the French king. But discord among the cities and within each town soon ended the rebellion. Although revolts continued to flare up, the count thereafter allowed a measure of self-government to the towns, maintained some distance from French influence, and managed on the whole to keep the peace.

The nature of warfare changed during the Hundred Years' War. At its start, the chronicler Jean Froissart (d. c. 1404) considered it a chivalric adventure, expecting it to display the gallantry and bravery of the medieval nobility. But even Froissart could not help but notice that most of the men who went to battle were not wealthy nobles and knights. They were not even ordinary foot soldiers,

MAP 13.2 The Hundred Years' War, 1337–1453
During the Hundred Years' War, English kings—aided by the new state of Burgundy—contested the French monarchy for the domination of France. For many decades, the English seemed to be winning, but the French monarchy prevailed in the end.

Joan of Arc: Who Was "the Maid"?

The figure of Joan of Arc gives shape to the confused events and personalities of the Hundred Years' War. But who was this young woman? Joan herself emphasized her visions and divine calling (Excerpt 1). The royal court was unsure whether to consider her a fraud (or, worse, the devil's tool) or a gift from heaven (Excerpt 2). A neighbor of the young Joan recalled her as an ordinary young country girl (Excerpt 3).

1. Joan the Visionary

Joan first referred to her visions at length after her capture by her enemies, who were eager to prove that she was inspired by the devil. The light and voices that she testified to echoed the experiences of many medieval visionaries. But we do not have Joan's exact words; her account was written up by her examiners, who composed it in Latin even though Joan spoke in French.

She confessed that when she was aged thirteen, she had a voice from God to help her to guide herself. And the first time she was greatly afraid. And this voice came around noon, in summer, in the garden of her father, and Joan had not fasted on the preceding day. She heard the voice on the right-hand side, towards the church, and she rarely heard it without a light. This light came from the same side that she heard the voice, but generally there was a great light there. And when Joan came to France [Lorraine, where Joan was raised, was not considered part of France], she often heard this voice. . . .

She said, in addition, that if she was in a wood, she clearly heard the voices coming to her. She also said that it seemed to her that it was a worthy voice and she believed that this voice had been sent from God, and that, after she had heard this voice three times, she knew that this was the voice of an angel. She said also that this voice had always protected her well and that she understood this voice clearly.

Asked about the instruction that this voice gave to her for the salvation of her soul, she said that it taught her to conduct herself well, to go to church often, and that it was necessary that she should travel to France. Joan added that her interrogator would not learn from her, on this occasion, in what form that voice had appeared to her. . . . She said moreover that the voice had told her that she, Joan, should go to find Robert de Baudricourt in the town of Vaucouleurs [a tiny holdout in eastern France that was not under English control], of which he was captain, and that he would provide her with men to travel with her. Joan then replied that she was a poor girl who did not know how to ride on horseback or to lead in war. [But she obeyed the voice, met with Robert de Baudricourt, and in the end got the escort that she needed to go to the court of the dauphin, the future Charles VII.]

Source: *Joan of Arc: La Pucelle*, trans. and annotated by Craig Taylor (Manchester: Manchester University Press, 2006), 141–42.

2. Messenger of God?

When Joan appeared at the court of the dauphin, her reputation as the messenger of God had preceded her. The French court received her with a mixture of wonder, curiosity, and skepticism. The dauphin's counselors debated about whether Joan should be taken seriously, and the dauphin referred the case to a panel of theologians to determine whether Joan's mission was of divine origin. The following account of Joan's first visit to the dauphin was given by Simon Charles, president of the royal Chamber of Accounts, at an investigation begun in 1455 to nullify Joan's sentence of 1429.

Questioned first on what he could depose and testify . . . [Simon Charles] said and declared upon oath that he only knew what follows: . . . that when Joan arrived at the town of Chinon, the council discussed whether the King should hear her or not. She was first asked why she had come and what she wanted. Although she did not wish to say anything except to the King, she was nevertheless forced on behalf of the King to reveal the purpose of her mission. She said that she had two commands from the King of Heaven, that is to say one to raise the siege [by the English army] of Orléans, and the other to conduct the King to Reims for his coronation and consecration. Having heard this, some among the King's councilors said that the King should not have any faith in this Joan, and the others said that, since she declared that she had been sent by God and that she had certain things to say to the King, the King should at least hear her. But the King decided that she should first be examined by the clerks and churchmen, which was done.

Source: *Joan of Arc: La Pucelle*, trans. and annotated by Craig Taylor (Manchester: Manchester University Press, 2006), 317–18.

3. Normal Girl?

At the same trial, various inhabitants in and near Domremy, Joan's village, recalled her as a normal young girl. The following account was given by Jean Morel, a laborer from a town near Joan's. He knew her as Jeannette.

He declared upon oath that the Jeannette in question was born at Domremy and was baptized at the parish church of Saint-Rémy in that place. Her father was named Jacques d'Arc, her mother Isabelle, both laborers living together at Domremy as long as they lived. They were good and faithful Catholics, good laborers, of good reputation, and of honest behavior. . . .

He declared upon oath that from her earliest childhood, Jeannette was well brought up in the faith as was appropriate, and instructed in good morals, as far as he knew, so that almost everyone in the village of Domremy loved her. Just like the other young girls she knew the *Credo*, the *Pater Noster*, and the *Ave Maria* [all three basic texts of Christian belief].

He declared that Jeannette was honest in her behavior, just as any similar girl is, because her parents were not very rich. In her childhood, and right up to her departure from her family home, she followed the plow and sometimes minded the animals in the fields; she did the work of a woman, spinning and making other things.

He declared upon oath that, as he saw, this Jeannette often went to church willingly to the extent that sometimes she was mocked by the other young people. . . .

He declared upon oath that on the subject of the tree called "of the Ladies," he once heard it said that women or supernatural persons—they were called fairies—came long ago to dance under that tree. But, so it is said, since a reading of the gospel of St. John, they did not come there any more. He also declared that in the present day . . . the young girls and lads of Domremy went under this tree to dance [on a particular Sunday in Lent], and sometimes also in the spring and summer on feast days; sometimes they ate at that place. On their return, they went to the spring of Thorns, strolling and singing, and they drank from the water of this spring, and all around they had fun gathering flowers. He also declared that Joan the Pucelle ["the Maid"] went there sometimes with the other girls and did as they did; he never heard it said that she went alone to the tree or to the spring, which is nearer to the village than the tree, for any other reason than to walk about and to play just like the other young girls.

Source: *Joan of Arc: La Pucelle*, trans. and annotated by Craig Taylor (Manchester: Manchester University Press, 2006), 267–68.

QUESTIONS TO CONSIDER

1. Given the norms of the time, in what ways was Joan ordinary?

2. What do you suppose was the royal court's reaction to the testimony of Simon Charles? And to the testimony of Jean Morel?

who previously had made up a large portion of all medieval armies. The soldiers of the Hundred Years' War were primarily mercenaries: men who fought for pay and plunder, heedless of the king for whom they were supposed to be fighting. During lulls in the war, these so-called Free Companies lived off the French countryside, terrorizing the peasants and exacting "protection" money.

The ideal chivalric knight fought on horseback with other armed horsemen, but in the Hundred Years' War, foot soldiers and archers were far more important than swordsmen. The French and their Genoese mercenaries used crossbows, whose heavy, deadly bolts (as their arrows were called) were released by a mechanism that even a townsman could master. The English employed longbows, which could shoot five arrows for every one launched on the crossbow. Furthermore, arrows shot by a longbow could soar more than twice as far as crossbow bolts. Meanwhile, gunpowder was slowly being introduced and cannons forged. Handguns were beginning to be used, their effect about equal to that of crossbows.

By the end of the war, chivalry was only a dream—though one that continued to inspire soldiers even up to the First World War. Heavy artillery and foot soldiers, tightly massed together in formations of many thousands of men, were the face of the new military. Moreover, the army was becoming more professional and centralized. In the 1440s, the French king created a permanent army of mounted soldiers. He paid them a wage and subjected them to regular inspection.

In addition to changing the face of warfare, the Hundred Years' War gave a new voice—however temporary—to the lower classes in France and England. When the English captured the French king John at the battle of Poitiers in 1356, Étienne Marcel, provost of the Paris merchants, and other disillusioned members of the estates of France (the representatives of the clergy, nobility, and commons) met to discuss political reform, the incompetence of the French army, and the high taxes they paid to finance the war. Under Marcel's leadership, a crowd of Parisians killed some nobles and for a short while took control of the city. But troops soon blockaded Paris and cut off its food supply. Later that year, Marcel was assassinated and the Parisian revolt came to an end.

In the same year, peasants weary of the Free Companies (who were ravaging the countryside) and disgusted by the military incompetence of the nobility rose up in protest. The French nobility called the peasant rebellion the **Jacquerie**, probably taken from a derisive name for male peasants: Jacques Bonhomme ("Jack Goodfellow"). The peasants committed atrocities against local nobles, but the nobles soon gave as good as they got, putting down the Jacquerie with exceptional brutality.

Similar revolts took place in England. The movement known as Wat Tyler's Rebellion started in much of southern and central England when royal agents tried to collect poll taxes (a tax on each household) to finance the Hundred Years' War (see Primary Source Analysis). Refusing to pay and refusing to be arrested, the commons—peasants and small householders—rose up in rebellion in 1381. They massed in various groups, vowing "to slay all lawyers, and all jurors, and all the servants of the King whom they could find." Marching

WHAT WOULD YOU DO?

If you were a French peasant in the mid-fourteenth century, confronted by the Free Companies during one of their frequent periods of unemployment, and disillusioned by the losses incurred by the French nobility during the Hundred Years' War, why would you—or why would you not—join the Jacquerie?

Wat Tyler's Rebellion (1381)

An anonymous chronicler wrote about Wat Tyler's Rebellion shortly after it took place in 1381. The author was hostile to the rebels, yet understood their motives quite well. After converging on London from various parts of southern England, the rebels, led by men like Wat Tyler, demanded that the king end the unjust taxes collected by local officials. The fourteen-year-old King Richard II (r. 1377–1399) eventually met with them and seemed to give in to their demands, but another meeting the next day led to Tyler's death and the dispersal of the demonstrators. The excerpt here chronicles the very beginning of the movement, before the march on London.

Because in the year 1380 the subsidies [taxes] were over lightly granted at the Parliament of Northampton and because it seemed to divers lords and to the commons that the said subsidies were not honestly levied, but commonly exacted from the poor and not from the rich, to the great profit and advantage of the tax-collectors, and to the deception of the king and the commons, the Council of the King ordained certain commissions to make inquiry in every township how the tax had been levied. Among these commissions, one for Essex was sent to one Thomas Bampton [one of the tax collectors]. . . . He had summoned before him the townships of a neighboring hundred, and wished to have from them new contributions. . . .

Among these townships was Fobbing, whose people made answer that they would not pay a penny more, because they already had a receipt from himself for the said subsidy. On which the said Thomas threatened them angrily. . . . And for fear of his malice the folks of Fobbing took counsel with the folks of Corringham, and the folks of these two places . . . sent messages to the men of Stanford. . . . Then the people of these three townships came together to the number of a hundred or more, and with one assent went to the said Thomas Bampton, and roundly gave him answer that they would have no traffic with him, nor give him a penny. . . .

And afterwards the said commons assembled together . . . to the number of some 50,000, and they went to the manors and townships of those who would not rise with them, and cast their houses to the ground or set fire to them. At this time they caught three clerks of Thomas Bampton, and cut off their heads, and carried the heads about with them for several days stuck on poles as an example to others. For it was their purpose to slay all lawyers, and all jurors, and all the servants of the king whom they could find.

Source: Charles Oman, *The Great Revolt of 1381* (Oxford: Clarendon Press, 1906), 186–88.

QUESTIONS TO CONSIDER

1. What did the author consider to be the main causes of the rebellion?

2. What was the issue at Fobbing?

3. Why would the people involved in the revolt single out in particular the lawyers, jurors, and servants of the king?

---

to London to see the king, they began to make a more radical demand: an end to serfdom. Although the rebellion was put down and its leaders executed, peasants returned home to bargain with their lords for better terms. The death knell of serfdom in England had been sounded.

The Ottoman Conquest of Constantinople, 1453

The end of the Hundred Years' War coincided with an event that was even more decisive for all of Europe: the conquest of Constantinople by the Ottoman Turks. The Ottomans, who were converts to Islam, were one of several tribal confederations in central Asia. Starting as a small enclave between the

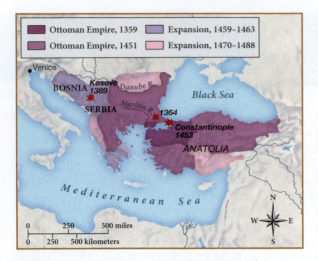

MAP 13.3 Ottoman Expansion in the Fourteenth and Fifteenth Centuries
The Balkans were the major theater of expansion for the Ottoman Empire. The Byzantine Empire was reduced to the city of Constantinople and surrounded by the Ottomans before its final fall in 1453.

Mongol Empire and Byzantium, and taking their name from a potent early leader, Othman I (d. 1324/1326), the Ottomans began to expand in the fourteenth century in a quest to wage holy war against infidels, or unbelievers.

During the next two centuries, the Ottomans took over the Balkans and Anatolia by both negotiations and arms (Map 13.3). They reduced the Byzantine Empire to the city of Constantinople and treated it as a vassal state. Under the sultan **Mehmed II** (r. 1444–1446 and 1451–1481), they besieged the city of Constantinople itself in 1453. Perhaps eighty thousand men confronted some three thousand defenders (the entire population of Constantinople was no more than fifty thousand) and a fleet from Genoa. The city held out until the end of May but was forced to capitulate when the sultan's cannons breached the city's land walls. Mehmed's troops entered the city and plundered it thoroughly, killing the emperor and displaying his head in triumph.

The conquest of Constantinople marked the end of the Byzantine Empire. But that was not the way Mehmed saw the matter. He considered himself a Renaissance prince (see the Mehmed Medallion on page 434), and he conquered Constantinople in part to be considered a successor to the Roman emperors — a Muslim successor, to be sure. He turned Hagia Sophia (the great church built by the emperor Justinian in 538) into a mosque, as he did with most of the other Byzantine churches. He retained the city's name, the City of Constantine — Qustantiniyya in Turkish — though it was popularly referred to as Istanbul, meaning, simply, "the city."

Like the French and English kings after the Hundred Years' War, the Ottoman sultans were centralizing monarchs who guaranteed law and order. The core of their army consisted of European Christian boys, who were requisitioned as tribute every five years. Trained in arms and converted to Islam, these young fighters made up the Janissaries — a highly disciplined military force also used to supervise local administrators throughout formerly Byzantine regions. Building a system of roads that crisscrossed their empire, the sultans made long-distance trade easy and profitable.

Once Constantinople was his, Mehmed embarked on an ambitious program of expansion and conquest. By 1500, the Ottoman Empire was a new and powerful state bridging Europe and the Middle East.

The Great Schism, 1378–1417

Even as war and disease threatened Europeans' material and physical well-being, a crisis in the church, precipitated by a scandal in the papacy, tore

Ottoman Conquest of Constantinople
The exterior walls of a monastery of Moldovita in Vatra, Romania, are covered with frescoes, one of which is this painting of a siege of Constantinople by Persians and Avars. The siege itself took place in 626, but the artist, Toma of Suceava, portrayed the assailants as the Ottomans and in fact depicted the conquest of Constantinople in 1453. The cannons that they used to batter down the walls are on the right, tucked into the rocky landscape. Toma, who painted the frescoes in the 1530s, was making a sly commentary on his own day, when the Ottomans were threatening the region. (Archives Charmet/ Bridgeman Images.)

at their spiritual life. The pope's relocation from Rome to Avignon in 1309 had caused an outcry, and some critics, such as Marsilius of Padua, became disillusioned with the institution of the papacy itself. In *The Defender of the Peace* (1324), Marsilius argued that the source of all power lay with the people: Christians themselves formed the church; the pope should be elected by a general council representing all Christians.

William of Ockham (d. 1347/1350), an English Franciscan, was an even more thoroughgoing critic of the papacy and clashed with it a number of times. William thought that the pope should have only spiritual power. He maintained that all knowledge came from experience, so God's existence could not be "known" or proved, though it could (and should) be taken on faith. He argued that universal concepts did not really exist; for example "humanity" existed not as an abstraction but only in the form of particular human beings. In that sense, "humanity" was just a name—which is why Ockham's philosophy came to be called nominalism. The principle that simple explanations were superior to complex ones became known as Ockham's razor (to suggest the idea of shaving away unnecessary hypotheses).

Stung by his critics, Pope Gregory XI (r. 1370–1378) left Avignon to return to Rome in 1377. The scandal of the Avignon papacy seemed to be over. Glad to have the papacy back, the Romans were determined never to lose it again. But the Italian pope chosen by the cardinals, Urban VI, immediately exalted the power of the pope and began to reduce the cardinals' wealth and privileges. The cardinals from France decided that they had made a big mistake. Many left Rome for a meeting at Anagni, where they claimed that Urban's election had been irregular and called on him to resign. When he refused, they elected a Frenchman as pope. He took the name Clement VII and soon moved his papal court to Avignon, but not before he and Urban had excommunicated each other. The **Great Schism** (1378–1417), which split the loyalties of all of Europe, had begun.

The king of France supported Clement; the king of England favored Urban. Some European states lined up on the side of France, while others supported Urban. Each pope declared that those who followed the other were to be deprived of the rights of church membership; in effect, everyone in Europe was excommunicated by one pope or the other. Church law said that only a pope could summon a general council of the church. But given the state of confusion in Christendom, many intellectuals argued that the crisis justified calling a general council to represent the body of the faithful, even against the wishes of an unwilling pope—or popes. They spearheaded the conciliar movement—a movement to have the cardinals or the emperor call a council.

In 1408, long after Urban and Clement had passed away and new popes had followed, the conciliar movement succeeded when cardinals from both sides met and declared their resolve "to pursue the union of the Church . . . by way of abdication of both papal contenders." With support from both England and France, the cardinals called for a council to be held at Pisa in 1409. Both popes refused to attend, and the council deposed them, electing a new pope, Alexander V (d. 1410).

But the "deposed" popes refused to budge, even though most of the European powers abandoned them. There were now three popes! John XXIII, the successor of Alexander, turned to the emperor to arrange for another council.

The Council of Constance (1414–1418) met to resolve the papal crisis as well as to institute church reforms. The delegates deposed John XXIII and accepted the resignation of the pope at Rome. After long negotiations with rulers still supporting the Avignon pope, all allegiance to him was withdrawn, and he was deposed. The council then elected Martin V, whom every important ruler of Europe recognized as pope. Finally, the Great Schism had come to an end.

Nevertheless, the schism had worked changes in the religious sensibilities of Europeans. Worried about the salvation of their souls now that the church was fractured by multiple popes, pious men and women eagerly sought new forms of religious solace. The church offered the plenary indulgence—full forgiveness of sins, which had been originally offered to crusaders who died while fighting for the cause—to those who made a pilgrimage to Rome and other designated holy places during declared Holy Years. People could wipe away their sins through confession and contrition, but they retained some guilt that they could remove only through good deeds or in purgatory. The idea of purgatory—the place where sins were fully purged—took precise form at this time, and with it **indulgences** became popular. These remissions of sin were offered for good works, such as pilgrimages, to reduce the time in purgatory.

Both clergy and laity became more interested than ever in the education of young people as a way to deepen their faith and spiritual life. The Brethren of the Common Life—laypeople, mainly in the Low Countries (the region comprising today's Belgium, Luxembourg, and the Netherlands), who devoted themselves to pious works—set up a model school at Deventer. In Italy, humanists (see "Renaissance Humanism" on page 450) emphasized primary school education. Priests were expected to teach the faithful the basics of the Christian religion.

Home was equally a place for devotion. Portable images of Mary, the mother of God, and of the life and passion of Christ proliferated. Ordinary Christians contemplated them at convenient moments throughout the day. People purchased or commissioned copies of Books of Hours, which contained prayers to be said at the same hours of the day that monks chanted their liturgy. Books of Hours included calendars, sometimes splendidly illustrated with depictions of the seasons and labors of the year. Other illustrations reminded their users of the life and suffering of Christ.

On the streets of towns, priests marched in dignified processions, carrying the sanctified bread of the Mass—the very body of Christ—in tall and splendid containers called monstrances that trumpeted the importance and dignity of the Eucharistic wafer. The image of a bleeding, crucified Christ was repeated over and over in depictions of the day. Viewers were supposed to think about Christ's pain and feel it themselves, mentally participating in his death on the cross.

Religious anxieties, intellectual dissent, and social unrest combined to create new heretical movements in England and Bohemia. In England were the Lollards, a term that was derogatory in the hands of their opponents and yet a proud title when used by the Lollards themselves. Inspired by the Oxford scholar John Wycliffe (c. 1330–1384), who taught that the true church was the community of believers rather than the clerical hierarchy, Lollards emphasized Bible reading in the vernacular. Although suffering widespread hostility and persecution into the sixteenth century, the Lollards were extremely active, setting up schools for children (girls as well as boys), translating the Bible from Latin into English, preaching numerous sermons, and inspiring new recruits.

On the other side of Europe were the Bohemian Hussites—named after one of their leaders, Jan Hus (1369/1371–1415), an admirer of Wycliffe. When priests celebrated Mass, they had the privilege of drinking the wine (the blood of

Book of Hours

This illustration for June in a Book of Hours made for the duke of Berry was meant for the contemplation of a nobleman. In the background is a fairy-tale depiction of the duke's palace and the tower of a Gothic church, while in the foreground graceful women rake the hay and well-muscled men swing their scythes. (Musée Condé, Chantilly, France/© RMN-Grand Palais/Art Resource, NY.)

Christ); the faithful received only the bread (the body). The Hussites, who were largely Czech laity, wanted the privilege of drinking the wine as well and with it recognition of their dignity and worth. Their demand reflected a focus on the redemptive power of Christ's blood. Furthermore, the call for communion with *both* bread and wine signified a desire for equality. Bohemia was an exceptionally divided country, with an urban German-speaking elite, including merchants, artisans, bishops, and scholars, and a Czech-speaking nobility and peasantry that was beginning to seek better opportunities. (Hus himself was a Czech of peasant stock who became a professor at the University of Prague.)

The Bohemian nobility protected Hus after the church condemned him as a heretic, but Emperor Sigismund lured him to the Council of Constance, promising him safe conduct. Hus was arrested when he arrived. When he refused to recant his views, the church leaders burned him at the stake.

Hus's death caused an uproar, and his movement became a full-scale national revolt of Czechs against Germans. Sigismund called crusades against the Hussites, but all of his expeditions were soundly defeated. Radical groups of Hussites organized several new communities in southern Bohemia, attempting to live according to the example of the first apostles. They recognized no lord, gave women some political rights, and created a simple liturgy that was carried out in the Czech language. Negotiations with Sigismund and his successor led to the Hussites' incorporation into the Bohemian political system by 1450. Though the Hussites were largely marginalized, they had won the right to receive communion in "both kinds" (wine and bread), and they had made Bohemia intensely aware of its Czech, rather than German, identity.

REVIEW QUESTION

What crises did Europeans confront in the fourteenth and fifteenth centuries, and how did they handle them?

Renaissance: New Forms of Thought and Expression

Some Europeans confronted the crises they faced by creating the culture of the Renaissance (French for "rebirth"). (See Terms of History on page 452.) The period associated with the Renaissance, about 1350 to 1600, revived elements of the classical past—the Greek philosophers before Aristotle, Hellenistic artists, and Roman rhetoricians. Disillusioned with present institutions, many people looked back to the ancient world; in Greece and Rome they found models of thought, language, power, prestige, and the arts that they could apply to their own circumstances. Humanists composed works in the Latin of Cicero rather than of the scholastics, architects embraced ancient notions of public space, artists adopted classical forms, and musicians used classical texts. In reality, Renaissance writers and artists built much of their work on medieval precedents, but they rarely acknowledged this fact. They found great satisfaction in believing that they were resuscitating the glories of the ancient world—and that everything between them and the classical past was a contemptible "Middle Age."

Renaissance Humanism

Three of the delegates at the Council of Constance—Cincius Romanus, Poggius Bracciolini, and Bartholomaeus Politianus—reveal the attitudes of the Renaissance. Although busy with church work, they decided to take time off for a "rescue mission." Cincius described the escapade to one of his Latin teachers back in Italy:

> In Germany there are many monasteries with libraries full of Latin
> books. This aroused the hope in me that some of the works of Cicero,
> Varro, Livy, and other great men of learning, which seem to have

completely vanished, might come to light, if a careful search were instituted. A few days ago, [we] went by agreement to the town of St. Gall. As soon as we went into the library [of the monastery there], we found *Jason's Argonauticon*, written by C. Valerius Flaccus in verse that is both splendid and dignified and not far removed from poetic majesty. Then we found some discussions in prose of a number of Cicero's orations.

Cicero, Varro, Livy, and Valerius Flaccus were pagan Latin writers. Even though Cincius and his friends were working for Pope John XXIII, they loved the writings of the ancients, whose Latin was, in their view, "splendid and dignified," unlike the Latin used in their own time—the Latin of the university masters—which they found debased and faulty. They saw themselves as the resuscitators of ancient language, literature, and culture, and they congratulated themselves on rescuing captive books from the "barbarian" monks of the monastery of St. Gall.

Humanism was a literary and linguistic movement—an attempt to revive classical Latin (and later Greek) as well as the values and sensibilities that came with the language. It began among men and women who, like Cincius, lived in the Italian city-states. The humanists saw parallels between their urban, independent lives and the experiences of the city-states of the ancient world. Humanism was a way to confront the crises—and praise the advances—of the fourteenth through sixteenth centuries. Humanists wrote poetry, history, moral philosophy, and grammar books, all patterned on classical models, especially the writings of Cicero.

That Cincius was employed by the pope yet considered the monks of St. Gall barbarians was no oddity. Most humanists combined sincere Christian piety with a new appreciation of the pagan past. Besides, they needed to work in order to live, and they took employment where they found it. Some humanists worked for the church, others were civil servants, and still others were notaries. A few were rich men who had a taste for literary subjects.

The first humanist, most historians agree, was **Francis Petrarch** (1304–1374). He was born in Arezzo, a town about fifty miles southeast of Florence. As a boy, he moved around a lot (his father was exiled from Florence), ending up in the region of Avignon, where he received his earliest schooling and fell in love with classical literature. He became a poet, writing in both Italian and Latin. When writing in Italian, he drew on the traditions of the troubadours, dedicating poems of longing to an unattainable and idealized woman named Laura; who she really was, we do not know. When writing in Latin, Petrarch was much influenced by classical poetry.

On the one hand, his boyhood in Avignon made Petrarch sensitive to the failings of the church: he was the writer who coined the phrase Babylonian captivity to liken the Avignon papacy to the Bible's account of the Hebrews' captivity in Babylonia. On the other hand, he took minor religious orders there, which gave him a modest living. Struggling between what he considered a life of dissipation (he fathered two children out of wedlock) and a religious vocation, he resolved the conflict at last in his book *On the Solitary Life*, in which he claimed that the solitude needed for reading the classics was akin to

TERMS OF HISTORY

Renaissance

The word *renaissance* was first used in the sixteenth century to refer to a historical moment. At that time it meant the rebirth of classical poetry, prose, and art of that period alone. Only later did historians borrow the word to refer to earlier rebirths. One of the first persons to herald the Renaissance was the Italian painter and architect Giorgio Vasari (1511–1574). In his *Lives of the Most Excellent Italian Architects, Painters, and Sculptors* (1550), Vasari argued that Greco-Roman art declined after the dissolution of the Roman Empire and was followed by a long period of barbarity. Only in recent generations had Italian artists begun to restore the perfection of the arts, according to Vasari. He called this development *la rinascita*, Italian for "the rebirth." It was the French equivalent — *la renaissance* — that stuck.

Referring initially to a rebirth in the arts and literature, the word *renaissance* came to mean a new consciousness of individuality and genius. Prizing the ancient world, Renaissance humanists were convinced that they lived in a new age that recalled that lost glory. They called the period between their age and the ancient world "the Middle Age." (That's why today we call it the Middle Ages.) They reveled in their human potential and their individuality.

The Renaissance was an important movement in Italy, France, Spain, the Low Countries, and central Europe. The word itself acquired widespread recognition with the 1860 publication of Jakob Burckhardt's *The Civilization of the Renaissance in Italy*. A historian at the University of Basel, Burckhardt considered the Renaissance a watershed in Western civilization. For him, the Renaissance ushered in a spirit of modernity, freeing the individual from the domination of society and liberating creative impulses from the repression of the church; the Renaissance represented the beginning of secular society and the preeminence of individual creative geniuses.

Although very influential, Burckhardt's ideas have also been strongly challenged by many recent scholars. Some point out the many continuities between the Middle Ages and the Renaissance, others argue that the Renaissance was not a secular but a profoundly religious age, and still others see the Renaissance as only the beginning of a long period of transition from the Middle Ages to modernity. The consensus among scholars today is that the Renaissance represents a distinct cultural period lasting from the fourteenth to the sixteenth century, centered on the revival of classical learning. Historians disagree about its significance, but they generally understand it to represent some of the complex changes that characterized the passing from medieval society to the modern age.

the solitude practiced by those who devoted themselves to God. For Petrarch, humanism was a vocation, a calling.

Less famous, but for that reason perhaps more representative of humanists in general, was Lauro Quirini (c. 1420–1474/1480), the man who (as we saw at the start of this chapter) wrote disparagingly about the Turks as barbarians. Educated at the University of Padua, Quirini eventually got a law degree there. He wrote numerous letters and essays and corresponded with other humanists. He spent the last half of his life in Crete, where he traded various commodities — alum, cloth, wine, and Greek books.

If Quirini represents the ordinary humanist, Giovanni Pico della Mirandola (1463–1494) was perhaps the most flamboyant. Born near Ferrara of a noble family, Pico received a humanistic education at home before going on to Bologna to study law and to Padua to study philosophy. Soon he was picking up Hebrew, Aramaic, and Arabic. A convinced eclectic (one who selects the best from various doctrines), he thought that Jewish mystical writings supported Christian scriptures, and in 1486, he proposed that he publicly defend at Rome nine hundred theses drawn from diverse sources. The church found some of the theses heretical, however, and banned the whole affair. But Pico's *Oration on the Dignity of Man*, which he intended to deliver before his defense, summed up the humanist view: the creative individual, armed only with his (or her) "desires and judgment," could choose to become a boor or an angel. Humanity's potential was unlimited.

Christine de Pisan (d. 1429/1430) exemplifies a humanist who chose to fashion herself into a writer and courtier. Born in Venice and educated in France, Christine was married and then soon widowed. Forced to support herself, her mother, and her three young children, she began to write poems inspired by classical models, depending on patrons to admire her work and pay her to write more. Many members of the upper nobility supported her, including Duke Philip the Bold of Burgundy, Queen Isabelle of Bavaria, and the English earl of Salisbury.

The Arts

The lure of the classical past was as strong in the visual arts as in literature—and for many of the same reasons. Architects and artists admired ancient Athens and Rome, but they also modified these classical models, melding them with medieval artistic traditions.

The Florentine architect Leon Battista Alberti (1404–1472) looked at the unplanned medieval city with dismay. He proposed that each building in a city be proportioned to fit harmoniously with all the others and that city spaces allow for all necessary public activities—there should be market squares, play areas, grounds for military exercises. In Renaissance cities, the agora and the forum (the open, public spaces of the classical world) appeared once again, but in a new guise: the piazza—a plaza or open square. Architects carved out spaces around their new buildings, and they rimmed them with porticoes—graceful covered walkways of columns and arches.

The Gothic cathedral of the Middle Ages was a cluster of graceful spikes and soaring arches. While Renaissance

The Façade of Sant'Andrea
The church of Sant'Andrea in Mantua was built in the form of an ancient Roman "temple." Its squat appearance, a silent rebuke to soaring Gothic churches, united diverse elements. The four giant pilasters that frame the windows and portal seem to support a pediment above reminiscent of the Parthenon. The archway recalls Roman triumphal arches, but the interior, with a long barrel vault, was modeled on early Christian basilicas. (De Agostini Picture Library/A. Baguzzi/Bridgeman Images.)

Lorenzo Ghiberti, *The Sacrifice of Isaac*
This bronze relief, which was entered into the competition to decorate the doors of the San Giovanni Baptistery in Florence, captures (on the right-hand side) the dramatic moment when the angel intervenes as Abraham prepares to kill Isaac, a story told in the Hebrew Scriptures. (Museo Nazionale del Bargello, Florence, Italy/Bridgeman Images.)

architects appreciated its vigor and energy, they tamed it with regular geometrical forms inspired by classical buildings. When the signore of Mantua decided to build a church to house relics of Christ's blood, for example, he called on Alberti, the man who believed in public spaces and harmonious buildings, to design it. Although Alberti died a few months before he could direct the actual construction, the finished church reflected his classicizing ideals.

The classical world inspired artists as well as architects. This explains the style Lorenzo Ghiberti (1378?–1455) chose when he competed to produce the doors of Florence's baptistery in 1400. His entry showed the sacrifice of Isaac from the Old Testament: the young, nude Isaac was modeled on the masculine ideal of ancient Greek sculpture. At the same time, Ghiberti drew on medieval models for his depiction of Abraham and for his quatrefoil frame. In this way, he gracefully melded old and new elements—and won the contest.

In addition to using the forms of classical art, Renaissance artists also mined the ancient world for new subjects. Venus, the Roman goddess of love and beauty, had numerous stories attached to her name. At first glance, *The Birth of Venus* by Sandro Botticelli (d. 1510) seems simply an illustration of the tale of Venus's rise from the sea. A closer look, however, shows that Botticelli borrowed from the poetry of Angelo Poliziano (1454–1494), who wrote of "fair Venus, mother of the cupids":

> Zephyr bathes the meadow with dew
> spreading a thousand lovely fragrances:
> wherever he flies he clothes the countryside
> in roses, lilies, violets, and other flowers.

In Botticelli's painting, Zephyr—one of the winds—blows while Venus herself is about to be clothed in a fine robe embroidered with leaves and flowers.

The Sacrifice of Isaac and *The Birth of Venus* show some of the ways in which Renaissance artists used ancient models. Other Renaissance artists perfected perspective—the illusion of three-dimensional space—to a degree that even classical antiquity had not imagined. The development of the laws of perspective accompanied the introduction of long-range weaponry, such as cannons. In one of their altarpieces, the Pollaiuolo brothers, Florentine artists, put the torment of St. Sebastian in a nearly flat space

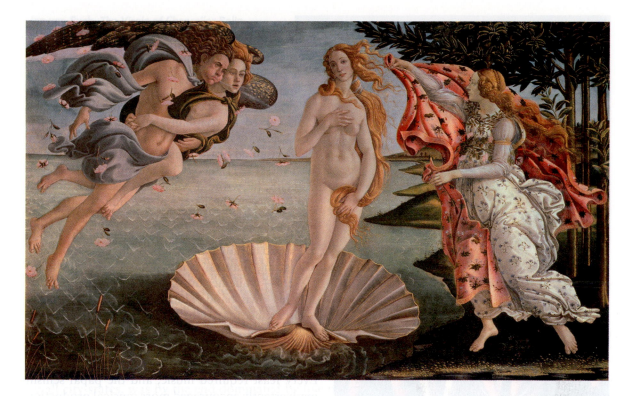

at the foreground, but behind those animated figures they created a three-dimensional space—a ruined and depleted landscape stretching far into the distance.

Ghiberti, Botticelli, and the Pollaiuolo brothers were all Italian artists. While they were creating their works, a northern Renaissance was taking place as well. At the court of Burgundy during the Hundred Years' War, the dukes commissioned portraits of themselves—sometimes unflattering ones—just as Roman leaders had once commissioned their own busts. Soon it was the fashion for those who could afford it to have a portrait made, showing them as naturalistically as possible. Around 1433, the chancellor Nicolas Rolin, for example, commissioned the Dutch artist Jan van Eyck to paint his portrait. Though opposite the Virgin and the baby Jesus, Rolin, in a pious pose, is the key figure in the picture. The grand view of a city behind the figures was meant to underscore Rolin's prominence in the community. In fact, Rolin *was* an important man: he worked for the duke of Burgundy and was also the founder of a hospital at Beaune and a religious order of nurses to serve it. Van Eyck's portrait emphasized not only Rolin's dignity and status but also his individuality. The artist took pains to show even the wrinkles of his neck and the furrows on his brow.

In music, Renaissance composers incorporated classical texts and allusions into songs that were based on the motet and other forms of polyphony. Working for patrons—whether churchmen, secular rulers, or republican

Sandro Botticelli, *The Birth of Venus*
Other artists had depicted Venus, but Botticelli was the first since antiquity to portray her in the nude. (Galleria degli Uffizi, Florence, Italy/Bridgeman Images.)

their dynasty and the security of their dominion. Philip was a lavish patron of the arts who commissioned numerous illuminated manuscripts, chronicles, tapestries, paintings, and music in his efforts to glorify himself as ruler of Burgundy.

The Burgundians' success depended on their personal relationship with their subjects. Not only did the dukes travel constantly from one part of their dominion to another, but they also staged elaborate ceremonies to enhance their power and promote their legitimacy. Their entries into cities and their presence at weddings, births, and funerals became the centerpieces of a "theater state" in which the dynasty provided the only link among diverse territories. New rituals became propaganda tools. Philip's revival of chivalry at court transformed the semi-independent nobility into courtiers closely tied to the prince. But, as mentioned earlier in this chapter (page 441), when Charles the Bold died in 1477, the duchy was parceled out between France and the Holy Roman Empire.

France's quick recovery from the Hundred Years' War allowed it to take a large bite out of Burgundy. Under Louis XI (r. 1461–1483), the French monarchy both expanded its territory and consolidated its power. Soon after Burgundy fell, Louis inherited most of southern France. When he inherited claims to the duchy of Milan and the kingdom of Naples, he was ready to exploit other opportunities in Italy. By the end of the century, France had doubled its territory, assuming boundaries close to its modern ones, and was looking to expand even further.

To strengthen royal power at home, Louis promoted industry and commerce, imposed permanent salt and land taxes, maintained western Europe's first standing army (created by his predecessor), and dispensed with the meetings of the Estates General, which included the clergy, the nobility, and representatives from the major towns of France. The French kings had already increased their power with important concessions from the papacy. The Pragmatic Sanction of Bourges (1438) asserted the superiority of a general church council over the pope, and it established what would come to be known as Gallicanism (after Gaul, the ancient Roman name for France), giving the French king effective control over ecclesiastical revenues and the appointment of French bishops.

England, too, recovered quickly from civil wars—called the Wars of the Roses—spawned by the stresses of the Hundred Years' War. The Wars of the Roses concluded with the victory of Henry Tudor, who took the title of Henry VII (r. 1485–1509). The wars did not prevent the English economy from continuing to grow during the fifteenth century. The cloth industry expanded considerably, and the English used much of the raw wool that they had been exporting to the Low Countries to manufacture fabrics at home. London merchants, taking a vigorous role in trade, also assumed greater political prominence, not only in governing London but also in serving as bankers to kings and members of Parliament. In the countryside the landed classes—the nobility, the gentry (the lesser nobility), and the yeomanry (free farmers)—benefited from rising farm and land-rent income as the population increased slowly but steadily. The Tudor monarchs took advantage of the general prosperity to bolster both their treasury and their power.

Republics

Within the fifteenth-century world of largely monarchical power were three important exceptions: Switzerland, Venice, and Florence. Republics, they prided themselves on traditions of self-rule. At the same time, however, they were in every case dominated by elites—or, in the case of Florence, even by one family.

Of the three, the Swiss Confederation was the most egalitarian. The region's cities had long had alliances with one another. In the fourteenth century, their union became more binding, and they joined with equally well-organized regional communities in rural and forested areas. The original purpose was to keep the peace, but soon the members pledged to aid one another against the Holy Roman Emperor. By the end of the fourteenth century, they had become an entity: the Swiss Confederation. While not united by a comprehensive constitution, they were nevertheless an effective political force.

Wealthy merchants and tradesmen dominated the cities of the Swiss Confederation, and in the fifteenth century they managed to supplant the landed nobility. At the same time, the power of the rural communes gave some ordinary folk political importance. No king, duke, or count ever became head of the confederation. In its fiercely independent stance against the Holy Roman Empire, it became a symbol of republican freedom. On the other hand, poor Swiss foot soldiers made their living by hiring themselves out as mercenaries, fueling the wars of kings in the rest of Europe.

Far less open to the lower classes, Venice, a city built on a lagoon, ruled an extensive empire by the fifteenth century. Its merchant ships plied the waters stretching from the Black Sea to the Mediterranean and out to the Atlantic Ocean. Now, for the first time in its career, it looked away from the sea to conquer land in northern Italy. In the early fifteenth century, Venice took over many surrounding cities, eventually coming up against the equally powerful city-state of Milan to its west. Between 1450 and 1454, two coalitions, one led by Milan, the other by Venice, fought for territorial control of the eastern half of northern Italy. Financial exhaustion and fear of an invasion by France or the Ottoman Turks led to the Peace of Lodi in 1454. Italy was no longer a collection of small cities, each with its own contado (surrounding countryside), but rather was now divided among a very few large territorial city-states.

Italy at the Peace of Lodi, 1454

It is no accident that the Peace of Lodi was signed one year after the Ottoman conquest of Constantinople: Venice wanted to direct its might against the Turks. But the Venetians also knew that peace was good for business; they traded with the Ottomans, and the two powers influenced each other's art and culture.

Venice was ruled not by a signore ("lord") but by the Great Council, which was dominated by the most important families. Far from being a hereditary monarch, the doge—the leading magistrate at Venice—was elected by the Great Council. A major question is why the lower classes at Venice did not rebel and demand their own political power, as happened in so many other Italian cities. The answer may be that Venice's foundation on water demanded

Venetian Art
When he was commissioned in the 1490s to depict the legend of Saint Ursula, Vittore Carpaccio chose Venice as the backdrop. Found in the very popular thirteenth-century *Golden Legend* by Jacobus de Voragine, the tale begins in England, where a pagan king is so inspired by hearing of the virtue of Ursula, daughter of the Christian king of Brittany, that he sends his ambassadors to ask for her hand for his son. In this detail, Carpaccio shows the English ambassadors arriving in a gondola. Note the glasslike colors and the evocation of atmosphere, both characteristic of Venetian style. (Galleria dell'Accademia, Venice, Italy/Cameraphoto Arte Venezia/Bridgeman Images.)

so much central planning, so much effort to maintain buildings and services, and such a large amount of public funding to provide the population with necessities that it fostered a greater sense of community than could be found elsewhere.

While Venice was not itself a center of humanism, its conquest of Padua in 1405 transformed its culture. After studying rhetoric at the University of Padua, young Venetian nobles returned home convinced of the values of a humanistic education for administering their far-flung territories. Lauro Quirini was one such man; his time at Padua was followed by a long period on Crete, which was under Venetian control.

Like humanism, Renaissance art also became part of the fabric of the city. Because of its trading links with Byzantium, Venice had long been influenced by Byzantine artistic styles. As it acquired a land-based empire in northern Italy, however, its artists adopted the Gothic styles prevalent elsewhere. In the fifteenth century, Renaissance art forms began to make inroads as well. Venice achieved its own unique style, characterized by strong colors, intense light, and sensuous use of paint—adapting the work of classical antiquity for its own purposes. Most Venetian artists worked on commission from churches, but lay confraternities—lay religious organizations devoted to charity—also sponsored paintings.

Florence, like Venice, was also a republic. But unlike Venice, its society and political life were turbulent, as social classes and political factions competed for power. The most important of these civil uprisings was the so-called Ciompi Revolt of 1378. Named after the wool workers (*ciompi*), laborers so lowly that they had not been allowed to form a guild, the revolt led to the creation of a guild for them, along with a new distribution of power in the city. But by 1382, the upper classes were once again monopolizing the government, and now with even less sympathy for the commoners.

By 1434, the **Medici** family had become the dominant power in this unruly city. The patriarch of the family, Cosimo de' Medici (1389–1464), founded his political power on the wealth of the Medici bank, which handled papal finances and had numerous branch offices in Italian and northern European cities. Backed by his money, Cosimo took over Florentine politics. He determined who could take public office, and he established new committees made up of men loyal to him to govern the city. He kept the old forms of the

Florentine constitution intact, governing behind the scenes not by force but through a broad consensus among the ruling elite.

Cosimo's grandson Lorenzo de' Medici (Lorenzo the Magnificent) (1449–1492), who assumed power in 1467, bolstered the regime's legitimacy with his patronage of the humanities and the arts. He himself was a poet and an avid collector of antiquities. Serving on various Florentine committees in charge of building, renovating, and adorning the churches of the city, Lorenzo employed important artists and architects to work on his own palaces. He probably encouraged the young Michelangelo Buonarroti; he certainly patronized the poet Angelo Poliziano, whose verses inspired Botticelli's *Venus*. No wonder humanists and poets sang his praises.

But the Medici family also had enemies. In 1478, Lorenzo narrowly escaped an assassination attempt, and his successor was driven out of Florence in 1494. The Medici returned to power in 1512, only to be driven out again in 1527. In 1530, the republic fell for good as the Medici once again took power, this time declaring themselves dukes of Florence.

The Tools of Power

Whether monarchies, duchies, or republics, the newly consolidated states of the fifteenth century exercised their powers more thoroughly than ever before. Sometimes they reached into the intimate lives of their subjects or citizens; at other times they persecuted undesirables with new efficiency.

A good example of the ways in which governments peeked into the lives of their citizens—and picked their pockets—is the Florentine *catasto*. This was an inventory of households within the city and its outlying territory made for the purposes of taxation in 1427. It inquired about names, types of houses, and animals, and it asked people to specify their trade. Their answers revealed the many levels of Florentine society, ranging from agricultural laborers with no land of their own to soldiers, cooks, grave diggers, scribes, great merchants, doctors, wine dealers, innkeepers, and tanners. The list went on and on. The catasto inquired about private and public investments, real estate holdings, and taxable assets. Finally, it turned to the sex of the head of the family, his or her age and marital status, and the number of mouths to feed in the household. An identification number was assigned to each household.

The catasto showed that in 1427, Florence and its outlying regions had a population of more than 260,000. Although the city itself had only 38,000 inhabitants (about 15 percent of the total population), it held 67 percent of the wealth. Some 60 percent of the Florentine households in the city belonged to the "little people" (a literal translation from the Italian term that referred to artisans and small merchants). The "fat people" (what we would call the upper middle class) made up 30 percent of the urban population and included wealthy merchants, leading artisans, notaries, doctors, and other professionals. At the very bottom of the hierarchy were slaves and servants, largely women from the surrounding countryside employed in domestic service. At the top, a tiny elite of wealthy patricians, bankers, and wool merchants controlled the

MAPPING THE WEST

Europe, c. 1492

By the end of the fifteenth century, the shape of early modern Europe was largely fixed as it would remain until the eighteenth century. The chief exception was the disappearance of an independent Hungarian kingdom after 1529.

Analyzing the Map: What had taken the place of the Byzantine Empire by 1492?

Making Connections: What do the red dots on this map represent, and why are they important?

---

state and owned more than one-quarter of its wealth. This was the group that produced the Medici family.

European kings had long fought Muslims and expelled Jews from their kingdoms, but in the fifteenth century, their powers became concentrated and centralized. Fifteenth-century kings in western Europe—England, France, Spain—commanded what we may call modern states. They used the full force of their new powers against their internal and external enemies.

Spain is a good example of this new trend. Once Ferdinand and Isabella established their rule over Castile and Aragon, they sought to impose religious uniformity and purity. They began systematically to persecute the *conversos* (converts), Jews who converted to Christianity after vicious attacks at the end of the fourteenth century. During the first half of the fifteenth century, they and their descendants (still called conversos, even though their children were born and baptized in the Christian faith) took advantage of the opportunities open to educated Christians, in many instances rising to high positions in both the church and the state and marrying into so-called Old Christian families. The conversos's success bred resentment, and their commitment to Christianity was questioned as well. Conversos were no longer Jews, so Christians justified their persecution by branding them as heretics who undermined the monarchy. In 1478, Ferdinand and Isabella set up state-sponsored courts of inquisition in Spain.

Treating the conversos as heretics, the inquisitors imposed harsh sentences, expelling or burning most of them. That was not enough (in the view of the monarchs) to purify the land. In 1492, Ferdinand and Isabella decreed that all Jews in Spain must convert or leave the country. Some did indeed convert, but the experiences of the former conversos soured most on the prospect, and a large number of Jews—perhaps 150,000—left Spain, scattering around the Mediterranean.

Meanwhile, Ferdinand and Isabella determined to rid Spain of its last Muslim stronghold, Granada. In 1492—just a few months before they expelled the Jews—the two monarchs made their triumphal entry there. In 1502, they demanded that all Muslims adopt Christianity or leave the kingdom.

> **REVIEW QUESTION**
> How did the monarchs and republics of the fifteenth century use (and abuse) their powers?

Conclusion

The years from 1340 to 1492 marked a period of crisis in Europe. The Hundred Years' War broke out in 1337, and ten years later, in 1347, the Black Death hit, taking a heavy toll. In 1378, a crisis shook the church, when first two and then three popes claimed universal authority. Revolts and riots plagued the cities and countryside. The Ottoman Turks took Constantinople in 1453, changing the very shape of Europe and the Middle East.

The revival of classical literature, art, architecture, and music helped men and women cope with these crises and gave them new tools for dealing with them. The Renaissance began mainly in the city-states of Italy, but it spread throughout much of Europe via the education and training of humanists, artists, sculptors, architects, and musicians. At the courts of great kings and dukes—even of the sultan—Renaissance music, art, and literature served as a way to celebrate the grandeur of rulers who controlled more of the apparatuses of government (armies, artillery, courts, and taxes) than ever before.

Consolidation was the principle underlying the new states of the Renaissance. Venice absorbed nearby northern Italian cities, and the Peace of Lodi confirmed its new status as a power on land as well as the sea. In eastern Europe, marriage joined together the states of Lithuania and Poland. A similar union took place in Spain with the wedding of Isabella of Castile and Ferdinand of Aragon. The Swiss Confederation became a permanent entity. The king of France came to rule over nearly the whole area that we today call France. The consolidated modern states of the fifteenth century would soon look to the Atlantic Ocean and beyond for new lands to explore and conquer.

Chapter 13 Review

Key Terms and People

Be sure that you can identify the term or person and explain its historical significance.

Black Death (p. 437)

Hundred Years' War (p. 440)

Joan of Arc (p. 440)

Jacquerie (p. 444)

Mehmed II (p. 446)

Great Schism (p. 447)

indulgences (p. 448)

humanism (p. 451)

Francis Petrarch (p. 451)

Hanseatic League (p. 457)

Medici (p. 462)

Review Questions

1. What crises did Europeans confront in the fourteenth and fifteenth centuries, and how did they handle them?

2. How and why did Renaissance humanists, artists, and musicians revive classical traditions?

3. How did the monarchs and republics of the fifteenth century use (and abuse) their powers?

Making Connections

1. How did the rulers of the fourteenth century make use of the forms and styles of the Renaissance?

2. On what values did Renaissance humanists and artists agree?

3. What tied the crises of the period (disease, war, schism) to the Renaissance (the flowering of literature, art, architecture, and music)?

Important Events

1337–1453	Hundred Years' War
1346–1353	Black Death in Europe
1358	Jacquerie uprising in France
1378–1417	Great Schism divides papacy
1378	Ciompi Revolt in Florence
1381	Wat Tyler's Rebellion in England
1386	Union of Lithuania and Poland

1414–1418	Council of Constance ends Great Schism; Jan Hus burned at the stake
1453	Conquest of Constantinople by Ottoman Turks; end of Hundred Years' War
1454	Peace of Lodi
1477	Dismantling of duchy of Burgundy
1478	Inquisition begins in Spain
1492	Spain conquers Muslim stronghold of Granada; expels Jews

Consider two events

Hundred Years' War (1337–1453) and the Black Death in Europe (1347–1353). How did these events represent both major crises and new opportunities? How was the Renaissance both a crisis itself and a response to the crises of this period?

Suggested References

Green's book is an important contribution to the study of the Black Death. Blumenfeld-Kosinski and Bynum each explore various aspects of late medieval piety. Nauert treats the many ramifications of Renaissance humanism, and Hale gives a useful overview of political developments.

Bachrach, Bernard S., and David S. Bachrach. *Warfare in Medieval Europe, c. 400–c.1453*. 2017.

The Black Death. Ed. and trans. Rosemary Horrox. 1994.

Blumenfeld-Kosinski, Renate. *Poets, Saints, and Visionaries of the Great Schism, 1378–1417*. 2006.

Bynum, Caroline. *Wonderful Blood: Theology and Practice in Late Medieval Northern Germany and Beyond*. 2006.

Cohn, Samuel K., Jr. *Lust for Liberty: The Politics of Social Revolt in Medieval Europe, 1200–1425*. 2006.

Green, Monica H., ed. *Pandemic Disease in the Medieval World: Rethinking the Black Death*. 2015.

Grendler, Paul F. *The Universities of the Italian Renaissance*. 2002.

Hale, J. R. *Renaissance Europe, 1480–1520*. 2nd ed. 2000.

Imber, Colin. *The Ottoman Empire, 1300–1650: The Structure of Power*. 2002.

Joan of Arc: La Pucelle. Trans. and ed. Craig Taylor. 2006.

Kent, F. W. *Lorenzo de' Medici and the Art of Magnificence*. 2004.

Lambert, Malcolm. *Medieval Heresy: Popular Movements from the Gregorian Reform to the Reformation*. 3rd ed. 2002.

Nauert, Charles G. *Humanism and the Culture of Renaissance Europe*. 2nd ed. 2006.

The Renaissance in Europe: An Anthology. Eds. Peter Elmer, Nick Webb, and Roberta Wood. 2000.

Rollo-Koster, Joëlle, and Thomas M. Izbicki, eds. *A Companion to the Great Western Schism (1378–1417)*. 2009.

Selections from English Wycliffite Writings. Ed. and trans. Anne Hudson. 1978.

Small, Graeme. *Late Medieval France*. 2009.

_____

*Primary source.

Global Encounters and the Shock of the Reformation

1492–1560

In 1539 in Tlaxcala, New Spain (present-day Mexico), Indians newly converted to Christianity performed a pageant organized by Catholic missionaries. It featured a combined Spanish and Indian army fighting to protect the pope, defeat the Muslims, and win control of the holy city of Jerusalem. All the parts were acted by local Tlaxcalans. In the play, after a miracle saves the Christian soldiers, the Muslims give up and convert to Christianity. Although it is hard to imagine what the locals made of this spectacle about places and people far away, the event reveals a great deal about the Europeans: the Catholic missionaries hoped that their success in converting Indians in the New World signaled God's favor for Catholicism the world over.

Led first by the Portuguese and then Spanish explorers, Europeans sailed into contact with peoples and cultures previously unknown to them. European voyagers subjugated native peoples, declared their control over vast new lands, and established a new system of slavery linking Africa and the New World. Millions of Indians died of diseases unknowingly imported by the Europeans. The discovery of new crops—corn, potatoes, tobacco, and cocoa—and of gold and silver mines brought new patterns of consumption, and new objects of conflict, to Europe. Historians now call this momentous spiral of changes in ecology, agriculture, and social patterns the Columbian exchange, after Christopher Columbus, who started the process.

«**Cortés** In this Spanish depiction of the landing of Hernán Cortés in Mexico in 1519, the ships and arms of the Spanish are a commanding presence, especially in comparison to the nakedness of the Indians and the kneeling stance of their leader. A Spanish artist painted this miniature, which measures only 6⅛ inches by 4¼ inches. It probably accompanied an account of the Spanish conquest of Mexico. On the back of the picture is a small map of the west coast of Europe and Africa and the east coast of Central America. Europeans relied on such images, and especially on maps, to help them make sense of all the new information flooding into Europe from faraway places. Many Spaniards viewed Cortés's conquests as a sign of divine favor toward Catholicism in a time of religious division. Some even believed that Cortés was born the same day, or at least the same year, as Martin Luther, the German monk who had initiated the Protestant Reformation just two years before Cortés's landing (in fact, Luther was born two years before Cortés). (The British Library, London, UK/Erich Lessing/Art Resource, NY.)

CHAPTER PREVIEW

The Discovery of New Worlds
Which European countries led the way in maritime exploration, and what were their motives?

The Protestant Reformation
How did Luther, Zwingli, Calvin, and Henry VIII each challenge the Roman Catholic church?

Reshaping Society through Religion
How did the forces for radical change unleashed by the Protestant Reformation interact with the urge for social order and stability?

Striving for Mastery
How did religious divisions complicate the efforts of rulers to maintain political stability and build stronger states?

While the Spanish were converting Indians in the New World, a different kind of challenge confronted the Catholic church in central and western Europe. Religious reformers attacked the leadership of the pope in Rome and formed competing groups of Protestants (so-called because they protested against some beliefs of the Catholic church). The movement began when the German Catholic monk Martin Luther criticized the sale of indulgences in 1517. Other reformers raised their voices, too, but did not agree with the Lutherans. Before long, religious division engulfed the German states and reached into Switzerland, France, and England. In response, Catholics undertook their own renewal, which strengthened the Catholic church. Catholic missionaries continued to dominate efforts to convert indigenous peoples for a century or more.

These two new factors—the development of overseas colonies and divisions between Catholics and Protestants within Europe—reshaped the long-standing rivalries between princes and determined the course of European history for several generations.

The Discovery of New Worlds

CHAPTER FOCUS
How did the conquest of the New World and the Protestant Reformation transform European governments and societies in this era?

Portugal's and Spain's maritime explorations brought Europe to the attention of the rest of the world. Inspired by a crusading spirit against Islam and by riches to be won through trade in spices and gold, the Portuguese and Spanish sailed across the Atlantic, Indian, and Pacific Oceans. The English, French, and Dutch followed later in the sixteenth century, creating a new global exchange of people, crops, and diseases. As a result of these European expeditions, the people of the Americas for the first time confronted forces that threatened to destroy not only their culture but even their existence.

Portuguese Explorations

The first phase of European overseas expansion began in 1434 with Portuguese exploration of the West African coast. The Portuguese hoped to find a sea route to the spice-producing lands of South and Southeast Asia in order to

CHAPTER TIMELINE

1492 Columbus reaches the Americas

1519 Cortés captures Aztec capital of Tenochtitlán

1520 Luther publishes three treatises; Zwingli breaks from Rome

1490   **1505**   **1520**

1494 Italian Wars begin; Treaty of Tordesillas divides Atlantic world between Portugal and Spain

1516 Erasmus publishes Greek edition of the New Testament

1517 Luther composes ninety-five theses to challenge Catholic church

bypass the Ottoman Turks, who controlled the traditional land routes between Europe and Asia. Prince Henry the Navigator of Portugal (1394–1460) personally financed many voyages with revenues from a noble crusading order. The first triumphs of the Portuguese attracted a host of Christian, Jewish, and even Arab sailors, astronomers, and cartographers to the service of Prince Henry and King John II (r. 1481–1495). They compiled better tide calendars and books of sailing directions for pilots that enabled sailors to venture farther into the oceans and reduced—though did not eliminate—the dangers of sea travel. Success in the voyages of exploration depended on the development in the late 1400s of the caravel, a 65-foot, easily maneuvered three-masted ship that used triangular lateen sails adapted from the Arabs. (The sails permitted a ship to tack against headwinds and therefore rely less on currents.)

Searching for gold and then slaves, the Portuguese gradually established forts down the West African coast. In 1487–1488, they reached the Cape of Good Hope at the tip of Africa; ten years later, Vasco da Gama led a Portuguese fleet around the cape and reached as far as Calicut, India, the center of the spice trade. His return to Lisbon with twelve pieces of Chinese porcelain for the Portuguese king set off two centuries of porcelain mania. Until the early eighteenth century, only the Chinese knew how to produce porcelain. Over the next two hundred years, Western merchants would import no fewer than seventy million pieces of porcelain, still known today as "china." By 1517, a chain of Portuguese forts dotted the Indian Ocean (Map 14.1). In 1519, Ferdinand Magellan, a Portuguese sailor in Spanish service, led the first expedition to circumnavigate the globe.

The Voyages of Columbus

One of many sailors inspired by the Portuguese explorations, **Christopher Columbus** (1451–1506) opened an entirely new direction for discovery. Most likely born in Genoa of Italian parents, Columbus sailed the West African coast in Portuguese service between 1476 and 1485. Fifteenth-century Europeans already knew that the world was round. Columbus wanted to sail west to reach "the lands of the Great Khan" because he hoped to find a new route

1525	1529	1536	1545–1563	1555
German Peasants' War	Colloquy of Marburg addresses disagreements between German and Swiss church reformers	Calvin publishes *Institutes of the Christian Religion*	Catholic Council of Trent condemns Protestant beliefs and confirms Catholic doctrine	Peace of Augsburg ends religious wars and recognizes Lutheran church in German states

1530		**1545**		**1560**

1527	1534	1540	1547	1559
Charles V's imperial troops sack Rome	Henry VIII breaks with Rome; Affair of the Placards in France	Jesuits established as new Catholic order	Charles V defeats Protestants at Mühlberg	Treaty of Cateau-Cambrésis ends wars between Habsburg and Valois rulers

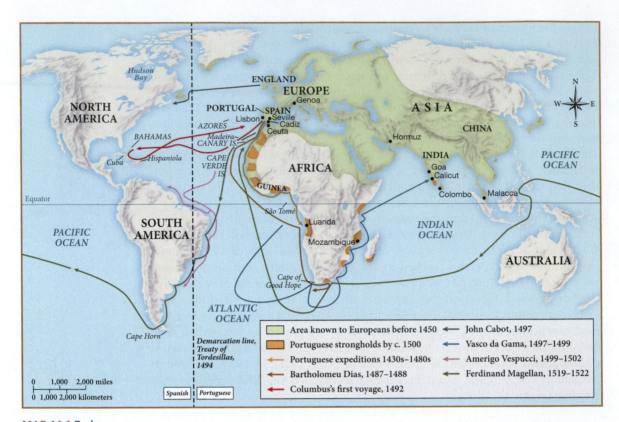

MAP 14.1 Early Voyages of World Exploration

Over the course of the fifteenth and early sixteenth centuries, European shipping dominated the Atlantic Ocean after the pioneering voyages of the Portuguese, who also first sailed around the Cape of Good Hope to the Indian Ocean and Cape Horn to the Pacific. The search for spices and the need to circumnavigate the Ottoman Empire inspired these voyages.

to the East's gold and spices. After the Portuguese refused to fund his plan, Columbus turned to the Spanish monarchs Isabella of Castile and Ferdinand of Aragon, who agreed to finance his venture.

On August 3, 1492, with ninety men on board two caravels and one larger merchant ship for carrying supplies, Columbus set sail westward. His contract stipulated that he would claim Castilian sovereignty over any new land and inhabitants and share any profits with the crown. Reaching what is today the Bahamas on October 12, Columbus mistook the islands to be part of the East Indies, not far from Japan. As the Spaniards explored the Caribbean islands, they encountered communities of peaceful Indians, the Arawaks, who were awed by the Europeans' military technology, not to mention their appearance. Although many positive entries in the ship's log testified to Columbus's personal goodwill toward the Indians, the Europeans' objectives were clear: find gold, subjugate the Indians, and propagate Christianity (see Primary Source Analysis). Excited by the prospect of easy riches, many flocked to join Columbus's second voyage. When Columbus departed the Spanish port of Cádiz in September 1493, he commanded a fleet of seventeen ships carrying some fifteen hundred men. Failing to find the imagined gold mines and spices, Columbus and his crew began capturing

PRIMARY
SOURCE
ANALYSIS
Columbus Describes His First Voyage (1493)

In this famous letter to Raphael Sanchez, treasurer to his patrons, Ferdinand and Isabella, Columbus recounts his initial journey to the Bahamas, Cuba, and Hispaniola (today Haiti and the Dominican Republic) and tells of his achievements. This passage reflects the first contact between native Americans and Europeans; already the themes of trade, subjugation, gold, and conversion emerge in Columbus's own words.

Indians would give whatever the seller required; . . . Thus they bartered, like idiots, cotton and gold for fragments of bows, glasses, bottles, and jars; which I forbad as being unjust, and myself gave them many beautiful and acceptable articles which I had brought with me, taking nothing from them in return; I did this in order that I might the more easily conciliate them, that they might be led to become Christians, and be inclined to entertain a regard for the King and Queen, our Princes and all Spaniards, and that I might induce them to take an interest in seeking out, and collecting, and delivering to us such things as they possessed in abundance, but which we greatly needed. They practise no kind of idolatry, but have a firm belief that all strength and power, and indeed all good things, are in heaven, and that I had descended from thence with these ships and

sailors, and under this impression was I received after they had thrown aside their fears. Nor are they slow or stupid, but of very clear understanding; and those men who have crossed to the neighbouring islands give an admirable description of everything they observed; but they never saw any people clothed, nor any ships like ours. On my arrival at that sea, I had taken some Indians by force from the first island that I came to, in order that they might learn our language, and communicate to us what they know respecting the country; which plan succeeded excellently, and was a great advantage to us, for in a short time, either by gestures and signs, or by words, we were enabled to understand each other. These men are still travelling with me, and although they have been with us now a long time, they continue to entertain the idea that I have descended from heaven.

Source: Christopher Columbus, *Four Voyages to the New World*, trans. R. H. Major (New York: Corinth Books, 1961), 8–9.

QUESTIONS TO CONSIDER
1. In what ways were Columbus's early impressions of native Americans both respectful and condescending?
2. Why did Columbus need the help of native Americans?

Caribs, enemies of the Arawaks, with the intention of bringing them back as slaves. The Spaniards exported enslaved Indians to Spain, and slave traders sold them in Seville. When the Spanish monarchs realized the vast potential for material gain from their new dominions, they asserted direct royal authority by sending officials and priests to the Americas, which were named after the Italian navigator Amerigo Vespucci, who led a voyage across the Atlantic from 1499 to 1502.

To head off looming conflicts between the Spanish and the Portuguese, Pope Alexander VI helped negotiate the Treaty of Tordesillas of 1494. It divided the Atlantic world between the two maritime powers, reserving for Portugal the West African coast and the route to India, and giving Spain the oceans and lands to the west (see Map 14.1 on page 472). The agreement allowed Portugal to claim Brazil in 1500, when it was accidentally "discovered" by Pedro Alvares Cabral (1467–1520) on a voyage to India.

A New Era in Slavery

The European voyages of discovery initiated a new era in slavery. Slavery had existed since antiquity and flourished in many parts of the world. Some slaves were captured in war or by piracy; others—Africans—were sold by other Africans and Bedouin traders to Christian buyers; in western Asia, parents sold their children out of poverty into servitude; and many in the Balkans became slaves when the Ottomans expanded into southeastern Europe. Slaves could be Greek, Slav, European, African, or Turkish. Many served as domestics in European cities of the Mediterranean such as Barcelona and Venice. Others sweated as galley slaves in Ottoman and Christian fleets. In the Ottoman army, slaves even formed an important elite contingent.

From the fifteenth century onward, Africans increasingly filled the ranks of slaves. Exploiting warfare between groups within West Africa, the Portuguese traded in gold and "pieces," as African slaves were called, a practice condemned at home by some conscientious clergy. Critical voices, however, could not deny the potential for profits that the slave trade brought to Portugal. Most slaves toiled in the sugar plantations that the Portuguese established on the Atlantic islands and in Brazil. African freedmen and slaves—some thirty-five thousand in the early sixteenth century—constituted almost 3 percent of the population of Portugal, a percentage that was much higher than in other European countries.

In the Americas, slavery would expand enormously in the following centuries. Even outspoken critics of colonial brutality toward indigenous peoples defended the development of African slavery. The Spanish Dominican Bartolomé de Las Casas (1474–1566), for example, argued that Africans were constitutionally more suitable for labor than native Americans and should therefore be imported to the plantations in the Americas to relieve the indigenous peoples, who were being worked to death.

Conquering the New World

The native peoples of the Americas lived in a great diversity of social and political arrangements. Some were nomads roaming large, sparsely inhabited territories; others practiced agriculture in complex organized states. Among the settled peoples, the largest groupings could be found in the Mexican and Peruvian highlands. Combining an elaborate religious culture with a strict social and political hierarchy, the Aztecs in Mexico and the Incas in Peru ruled over subjugated Indian populations in their respective empires. From their large urban capitals, the Aztecs and Incas controlled large swaths of land and could be ruthless as conquerors.

The Spanish explorers organized their expeditions to the mainland of the Americas from a base in the Caribbean. Two prominent commanders, **Hernán Cortés** (1485–1547) and Francisco Pizarro (c. 1475–1541), gathered men and arms and set off in search of gold. With them came Catholic priests intending to bring Christianity to supposedly uncivilized peoples. When Cortés first landed on the Mexican coast in 1519, the natives greeted him with gifts, thinking that he might be an ancient god returning to reclaim his kingdom. Native groups like the Tlaxcalans, who resented their subjugation by the Aztecs, joined Cortés and his soldiers. With a band of fewer than three hundred Spanish soldiers and thousands of native allies, Cortés captured the Aztec capital, Tenochtitlán (present-day Mexico City), in 1519. With 200,000 inhabitants, Tenochtitlán was bigger than any European capital. Two years later, Mexico, then named New Spain, was added to the empire of the new ruler of Spain, Charles V, grandson of Ferdinand and Isabella. To the south, Pizarro conquered the Peruvian highlands between 1532 and 1533. The Spanish Empire was now the largest in the world, stretching from Mexico to Chile.

The gold and silver mines in Mexico proved a treasure trove for the Spanish crown, but the real prize was the discovery of vast silver deposits in Potosí (today in Bolivia). When the Spaniards began importing the gold and silver they found in the New World, inflation soared in a fashion never before witnessed in Europe.

Not to be outdone by the Spaniards, other European powers joined the scramble for gold in the New World. In North America, the French went in search of a "northwest passage" to China. The French wanted to establish settlements in what became Canada, but permanent European settlements in Canada and the present-day United States would succeed only in the seventeenth century. By then the English and Dutch had also entered the contest for world mastery.

The Columbian Exchange

The movement of peoples, animals, plants, manufactured goods, precious metals, and diseases between Europe, the New World, and Africa—the Columbian exchange—was one of the most dramatic transformations of ecology,

World Map by Abraham Ortelius, 1570
European knowledge of world geography grew by leaps and bounds thanks to the voyages of exploration. Europeans had some knowledge of the West African coast before Columbus's voyages, but they knew nothing of the Americas. Ortelius was a Flemish engraver and geographer who had traveled extensively in Europe. He included this map in his Theatrum Orbis Terrarum (Theater of the World), considered to be the first modern atlas. (Photo © Tarker/Bridgeman Images.)

agriculture, and ways of life in all of human history. Columbus started the process when he brought with him firearms, unknown in the Americas, and on his second voyage, horses, which had become extinct in the Americas, as well as pigs, chickens, goats, sheep, cattle, and various plants including wheat, melons, and sugarcane. Enslaved Africans, first brought to the Caribbean in 1503 to 1505, worked on sugarcane plantations, foreshadowing the development of a massive slave economy in the seventeenth and eighteenth centuries (see Chapter 17).

The Europeans also brought with them diseases. Amerindians died in catastrophic numbers because they lacked natural immunity from previous exposure. Smallpox first appeared in the New World in 1518; it and other epidemic diseases killed as many as 90 percent of natives in some places (though the precise numbers are unknown). Syphilis, or a genetic predecessor to it, came back with the explorers to Europe.

The Spanish also brought back tobacco, cacao (chocolate), sweet potatoes, maize, and tomato seeds, changing consumption patterns in Europe. (Their native American wives, concubines, and domestics taught them to drink chocolate in the native fashion: frothy, red in color, and flavored with peppers.) At the same time, Spanish and Portuguese slave traders brought these crops and others—such as manioc, capsicum peppers, pineapples, cashew nuts, and peanuts—from the Americas to West Africa, where their cultivation altered local agriculture and diets. The slavers bought African yams, sorghum, millet, and especially rice to feed the slaves in transit, and the slaves then grew those crops in the Americas. Thus the exchange went in every conceivable direction.

REVIEW QUESTION
Which European countries led the way in maritime exploration, and what were their motives?

The Protestant Reformation

When Columbus's patrons Ferdinand and Isabella expelled all Jews from Spain in 1492 and chased the last Muslims from Granada in 1502, it appeared as if the triumph of the Catholic church had been assured. Only fifteen years later, however, Martin Luther started a movement for religious reform that would fracture the unity of Western Christianity. Instead of one Catholic church, there would be many different kinds of Christians. The invention of printing with movable type helped spread the Protestant message, which grew in part out of waves of popular piety that washed over Europe in the closing decades of the 1400s. Reformers had also been influenced by Christian humanists who focused attention on clerical abuses.

The Invention of Printing

Printing with movable type, first developed in Europe in the 1440s by Johannes Gutenberg, a German goldsmith, marked a revolutionary departure from the old practice of copying works by hand or stamping pages with individually carved woodblocks. The Chinese invented movable type in the

Printing Press

This illustration from a French manuscript of 1537 depicts typical printing equipment of the sixteenth century. An artisan is using the screw press to apply the inked type to the paper. Also shown are the composed type secured in a chase, the printed sheet (four pages of text printed on one sheet) held by the seated proofreader, and the bound volume. When two pages of text were printed on one standard-sized sheet, the bound book was called a folio. A bound book with four pages of text on one sheet was called a quarto ("in four"), and a book with eight pages of text on one sheet was called an octavo ("in eight"). The octavo was a pocket-size book, smaller than today's paperback.

eleventh century, but they preferred woodblock printing because it was more suitable to the Chinese language, with its thousands of different characters. In Europe, with only twenty-six letters to the alphabet, movable type allowed entire manuscripts to be printed more quickly than ever before. Single letters, made in metal molds, could be emptied out of a frame and new ones inserted to print each new page.

In 1467, two German printers established the first press in Rome; within five years, they had produced twelve thousand volumes, a feat that in the past would have required a thousand scribes working full-time. Printing also depended on the large-scale production of paper. Papermaking came to Europe from China via Arab intermediaries. By the fourteenth century, paper mills in Italy were producing paper that was more fragile but also much cheaper than parchment or vellum, the animal skins that Europeans had previously used for writing. Early printed books attracted an elite audience. Their expense made them inaccessible to most literate people, who comprised a minority of the population in any case. Gutenberg's famous two-volume Latin Bible was a luxury item, and only 185 copies were printed. Gutenberg Bibles remain today a treasure that only the greatest libraries possess.

The invention of mechanical printing dramatically increased the speed at which people could transmit knowledge, and it freed individuals from having to memorize everything they learned. Printed books and pamphlets, even one-page flyers, would create a wide community of scholars no longer dependent on personal patronage or church sponsorship for texts. Printing thus encouraged the free expression and exchange of ideas, and its disruptive potential did not go unnoticed by political and religious authorities. Rulers and bishops in the German states, the birthplace of the printing industry, moved quickly to issue censorship regulations, but their efforts could not prevent the outbreak of the Protestant Reformation.

Popular Piety and Christian Humanism

The Christianizing of Europe had taken many centuries to complete, but by 1500 most people in Europe believed devoutly. However, the vast majority of them had little knowledge of Catholic doctrine. More popular forms of piety—such as processions, festivals, and marvelous tales of saints' miracles—captivated ordinary believers.

Urban merchants and artisans, more likely than the general population to be literate and critical of their local priests, yearned for a faith more meaningful to their daily lives and for a clergy more responsive to their needs. They generously donated money to establish new preaching positions for university-trained clerics. The merchants resented the funneling of the Catholic church's rich endowments to the younger children of the nobility who took up religious callings to protect the wealth of their families. The young, educated clerics funded by the merchants often came from cities themselves. They formed the backbone of **Christian humanism** and sometimes became reformers, too.

Humanism had originated during the Renaissance in Italy among highly educated individuals attached to the personal households of prominent rulers. North of the Alps, however, humanists focused more on religious revival and the inculcation of Christian piety, especially through the schools of the Brethren of the Common Life. The Brethren preached religious self-discipline, specialized in the copying of manuscripts, and were among the first to print the ancient classics. Their most influential pupil was the Dutch Christian humanist Desiderius Erasmus (c. 1466–1536). The illegitimate son of a man who became a priest, Erasmus joined the Augustinian Order of monks, but the pope allowed him to leave the monastery and pursue the life of an independent scholar. An intimate friend of kings and popes, he became known across Europe. He devoted years to preparing a critical edition of the New Testament in Greek with a translation into Latin, which was finally published in 1516.

Erasmus strove for a unified, peaceful Christendom in which charity and good works, not empty ceremonies, would mark true religion and in which learning and piety would dispel the darkness of ignorance. He elaborated many of these ideas in his *Handbook of the Militant Christian* (1503), an eloquent plea for a simple religion devoid of greed and the lust for power. In *The Praise of Folly* (1509), Erasmus used satire to show that modesty, humility, and poverty represented the true Christian virtues in a world that worshipped pomposity, power, and wealth. The wise appeared foolish, he concluded, for their wisdom and values were not of this world.

Erasmus instructed the young future emperor Charles V to rule as a just Christian prince. A man of peace and moderation, Erasmus soon found himself challenged by angry younger men and radical ideas once the Reformation took hold; he eventually chose Christian unity over reform and schism. His dream of Christian pacifism crushed, he lived to see dissenters executed—by Catholics and Protestants alike—for speaking their conscience. Erasmus spent his last years in Freiburg and Basel, isolated from the Protestant community, his writings condemned by many in the Catholic church. After the Protestant

Protestant Reformation

Martin Luther started the Protestant Reformation in 1517 when he criticized the sale of indulgences and then went on to demand a whole series of reforms in Catholic church doctrine and practices. He did not call his movement the Protestant Reformation, and neither did his opponents, who condemned him as a heretic, much like the heretics of the past. In his edict of 1521, Holy Roman Emperor Charles V denounced Luther as a "reviver of the old and condemned heresies and inventor of new ones," who had propagated "numberless and endless errors." Luther's supporters only began to be called Protestants when several members of an imperial diet in 1529 published a "protest" against the decision to ban Luther and prohibit the spread of his ideas. The term Protestant then spread in usage across Europe to refer to those willing to break with the Catholic church over reform.

Luther did not anticipate either the spread of "Protestantism" or the diverse and often conflicting forms that it would take under the influence of other reformers. As divisions grew within the Protestant camp, some began to distinguish between Lutheran Protestants and Reformed Protestants, meaning the followers of Zwingli and Calvin. The term Protestant Reformation, like the term Protestantism, appeared in English in the 1600s to emphasize the similarities between the different Protestant sects and their essential difference from the "papists" or Catholics. Since "Reformation," especially when capitalized, thus became associated with anti-Catholic prejudice in the Anglophone world, some scholars began to insist that the Catholic movement for internal reform should be labeled something other than "Counter-Reformation," which implied that Catholic reform efforts originated exclusively in a reaction to "Protestantism." Given the struggles, both mental and military, that were ignited by Luther's actions, it is not surprising that the labels attached to the various sides generated such lasting controversy.

Reformation had been secured, the saying arose that "Erasmus laid the egg that Luther hatched." Some blamed the humanists for the emergence of Luther and Protestantism, despite the humanists' decision to remain in the Catholic church.

Martin Luther's Challenge

The crisis of faith of one man, **Martin Luther** (1483–1546), started the international movement known as the Protestant Reformation (see Terms of History). The son of a miner and a deeply pious mother, Luther abandoned his studies in the law and, like Erasmus, entered the Augustinian Order. There he experienced his religious crisis: despite fervent prayers, fasting, intense reading of the Bible, a personal pilgrimage to Rome (on foot), and study that led to a doctorate in theology, Luther did not feel saved.

Luther found peace inside himself when he became convinced that sinners were saved only through faith and that faith was a gift freely given by God. Shortly before his death, Luther recalled his crisis:

> Though I lived as a monk without reproach, I felt that I was a sinner before God with an extremely disturbed conscience. Secretly . . . I was angry with God. . . . At last, by the mercy of God, meditating day

and night, I gave heed to the context of the words, namely, "In [the gospel] the righteousness of God is revealed, as it is written, 'He who through faith is righteous shall live.'" There I began to understand that the righteousness of God is that by which the righteous live by a gift of God, namely by faith.

No amount of good works, Luther believed, could produce the faith on which salvation depended.

Just as Luther was working out his own personal search for salvation, a priest named Johann Tetzel arrived in Wittenberg, where Luther was a university professor, to sell indulgences. In the sacrament of penance, according to Catholic church doctrine, the sinner confessed his or her sins to a priest, who offered absolution and imposed a penance. Penance normally consisted of spiritual duties (prayers, pilgrimages), but the church also sold the monetary substitutions known as indulgences. A person could even buy indulgences for a deceased relative to reduce that person's time in purgatory and release his or her soul for heaven.

In ninety-five theses that he proposed for academic debate in 1517, Luther denounced the sale of indulgences as a corrupt practice. Printed, the theses became public and unleashed a torrent of pent-up resentment and frustration among the laypeople. What began as a theological debate in a provincial university soon engulfed the Holy Roman Empire. Luther's earliest supporters included younger Christian humanists and clerics who shared his critical attitude toward the church establishment. None of these Evangelicals, as they called themselves, came from the upper echelons of the church; many were from urban middle-class backgrounds, and most were university trained. But illiterate artisans and peasants also rallied to Luther, sometimes with an almost fanatical zeal. They and he believed they were living in the last days of the world, and that Luther and his cause might be a sign of the approaching Last Judgment. In 1520, Luther burned his bridges with the publication of three fiery treatises. In *Freedom of a Christian*, Luther argued that faith, not good works, saved sinners from damnation, and he sharply distinguished between true Gospel

Explaining the Reformation to the People
This woodcut by Lucas Cranach the Elder shows the pope himself selling indulgences to ordinary people. Luther and many other reformers believed that the sale of indulgences was corrupting the Catholic church by substituting money for true repentance. Prints such as this one from 1521 helped spread the Protestant message. (akg-images/Newscom.)

teachings and invented church doctrines. Luther advocated "the priesthood of all believers," insisting that the Bible provided all the teachings necessary for Christian living and that a professional caste of clerics should not hold sway over laypeople. These principles—"by faith alone," "by Scripture alone," and "the priesthood of all believers"—became central features of the reform movement.

In his second treatise, *To the Nobility of the German Nation*, Luther denounced the corrupt Italians in Rome and called on the German princes to defend their nation and reform the church. Luther's third treatise, *On the Babylonian Captivity of the Church*, condemned the papacy as the embodiment of the Antichrist. He had discovered a talent for polemics and made the most of it.

From Rome's perspective, the Luther Affair, as church officials called it, concerned only one unruly monk (see Contrasting Views on pages 482–483). When the pope ordered him to obey his superiors and keep quiet, Luther tore up the decree. Spread by the printing press, Luther's ideas circulated widely, letting loose forces that neither the church nor Luther could control. Social, nationalist, and religious protests fused with lower-class resentments, much as in the Czech movement that the priest and professor Jan Hus had inspired a century earlier. Like Hus, Luther appeared before an emperor: in 1521, he defended his faith at the Imperial Diet of Worms before **Charles V** (r. 1519–1556), the newly elected Holy Roman Emperor who, at the age of nineteen, ruled over the Low Countries, Spain, Spain's Italian and New World dominions, and the Austrian Habsburg lands. Luther shocked Germans by declaring his admiration for the Czech heretic. But unlike Hus, Luther enjoyed the protection of his lord, Frederick the Wise, the elector of Saxony (called an elector because he was one of seven princes charged with electing the Holy Roman Emperor). To become Holy Roman Emperor, Charles V had bribed Frederick and therefore had to treat him with respect.

Lutheran propaganda flooded German towns and villages. Sometimes only a few pages in length, these broadsheets were often illustrated with crude satirical cartoons. Magistrates began to curtail clerical privileges and subordinate the clergy to municipal authority. From Wittenberg, the reform movement quickly swelled and threatened to swamp all before it. Lutheranism spread northward to Scandinavia when reformers who studied in Germany brought back the faith and converted the kings from Catholic to Protestant beliefs.

Protestantism Spreads and Divides

Other Protestant reformers soon challenged Luther's doctrines even while applauding his break from the Catholic church. In 1520, just three years after Luther's initial rupture with Rome, the chief preacher of Zurich, Huldrych Zwingli (1484–1531), openly declared himself a reformer. Like Luther, Zwingli attacked corruption in the Catholic church hierarchy, and he also questioned fasting and clerical celibacy. Zwingli disagreed with Luther on the question of the Eucharist, the central Christian sacrament that Christians partook of in communion. The Catholic doctrine of transubstantiation held that

CONTRASTING VIEWS

Martin Luther: Holy Man or Heretic?

When Martin Luther criticized the papacy and the Catholic church, some hailed him as a godly prophet and others condemned him as a heretic. Both Protestants and Catholics used popular propaganda to argue their cause. They spread their message to a largely illiterate or semiliterate society through pamphlets, woodcuts, and broadsheets in which visual images took on increasing importance, to appeal to a wide public. These polemical works were distributed in the thousands to cities and market towns throughout the Holy Roman Empire. A few were even translated into Latin to reach an audience outside of Germany.

A positive image of Luther, published in 1521, depicts him as inspired by the Holy Spirit (Document 1). The 1523 woodcut shows Luther arguing against his Catholic opponents, who are portrayed as devils hiding in clerical robes (Document 2). An anti-Luther image from a few years later represents him as a seven-headed monster (Document 3), signifying that the reformer is the source of discord within Christianity. This image appeared in a book published in 1529 by the Dominican friar Johannes Cochlaeus, one of Luther's vociferous opponents.

Visual examples of religious propaganda worked effectively to demonize enemies and to contrast good and evil. The 1520s saw the most intense production of these cheap polemical visual prints, but the use of visual propaganda would continue for more than a century in the religious conflict.

1. Luther as Monk, Doctor, Man of the Bible, and Saint (1521)

This woodcut by an anonymous artist appeared in a volume that the Strasbourg printer Johann Schott published in 1521. In addition to being one of the major centers of printing, Strasbourg was also a stronghold of the reform movement. Note the use of traditional symbols to signify Luther's holiness: the Bible in his hands, the halo, the Holy Spirit in the form of a dove, and his friar's robes. Although the cult of saints and monasticism came under severe criticism during the Reformation, the representation of Luther in traditional symbols of sanctity stressed his conservative values instead of his radical challenge to church authorities.

2. Luther Takes On His Devilish Catholic Opponents (1523)

All three figures are wearing monk's robes, but only Luther appears as trustworthy in this woodcut printed by Melchior Ramminger. The image appears on the title page of an anonymous pamphlet called *A Pretty Dialogue between Martin Luther and Messengers Sent from Hell.* Ramminger was one of many Protestant printers in Augsburg, a free imperial city that served as a major

commercial, financial, and printing hub for the Holy Roman Empire.

3. The Seven-Headed Martin Luther by Johannes Cochlaeus (1529)

The seven heads are labeled (from left to right) doctor, Martin, Luther, ecclesiast, enthusiast, visitirer, and Barrabas. *Enthusiast* was a term of abuse, applied usually by the Catholic church to Anabaptists and religious radicals of all sorts. *Visitirer* is a pun in German on the word Tier, meaning "animal." Cochlaeus also mocks the new practice of Protestant clergy visiting parishes to check up on pastors' and parishioners' adherence to Reformed church doctrines and rituals in order to enforce Christian discipline. From left to right, Luther's many heads gradually reveal him to be a rebel: according to the Bible, the Romans had condemned the rabble-rouser Barrabas to die but instead freed him and crucified Jesus in his place. The number seven also alludes to the seven deadly sins.

QUESTIONS TO CONSIDER

1. Why did Johannes Cochlaeus condemn Martin Luther? How did he construct a negative image of Luther?

2. Evaluate the visual representations of Luther as a godly man. Which one is more effective?

when the priest consecrated them, the bread and wine of communion actually turned into the body and blood of Christ. Luther insisted that the bread and wine did not change their nature: they were simultaneously bread and wine and the body and blood of Christ. Zwingli, however, viewed the Eucharistic bread and wine as symbols of Christ's union with believers, not the real blood and body of Christ. This issue aroused such strong feelings because it concerned the role of the priest and the church in shaping the relationship between God and the believer.

In 1529, troubled by these differences and other disagreements, Protestant princes and magistrates assembled the major reformers in the Colloquy of Marburg, in central Germany. After several days of intense discussions, the reformers managed to resolve some differences over doctrine, but Luther and Zwingli failed to agree on the meaning of the Eucharist. The issue of the Eucharist would soon divide Lutherans and Calvinists as well.

Under the leadership of **John Calvin** (1509–1564), another wave of reform challenged Catholic authority. Born in Picardy, in northern France, Calvin studied in Paris and Orléans, where he took a law degree. Experiencing a crisis of faith, like Luther, Calvin sought salvation through intense theological study. Gradually, he, too, came to question fundamental Catholic teachings.

On Sunday, October 18, 1534, Parisians found church doors posted with crude broadsheets denouncing the Catholic Mass. Smuggled into France from the Protestant and French-speaking parts of Switzerland, the broadsheets provoked a wave of royal repression in the capital. In response to this so-called Affair of the Placards, the government arrested hundreds of French Protestants, executed some of them, and forced many more, including Calvin, to flee abroad.

Calvin made his way to Geneva, the French-speaking Swiss city-state where he would find his life's work. Genevans had renounced their allegiance to the Catholic bishop, and local supporters of reform begged Calvin to stay and labor there. Although it took some time for Calvin to solidify his position in the city, his supporters eventually triumphed, and he remained in Geneva until his death in 1564.

Under Calvin's leadership, Geneva became a Christian republic on the model set out in his *Institutes of the Christian Religion*, first published in 1536. No reformer prior to Calvin had expounded on the doctrines, organization, history, and practices of Christianity in such a systematic, logical, and coherent manner. Calvin followed Luther's doctrine of salvation to its ultimate logical conclusion: if God is almighty and humans cannot earn their salvation by good works, then no Christian can be certain of salvation. Developing the doctrine of **predestination**, Calvin argued that God had ordained every man, woman, and child to salvation or damnation—even before the creation of the world. Thus, in Calvin's theology, God saved only the "elect" (a small group).

Predestination could terrify, but it could also embolden. For Calvinists, a righteous life might be a sign that a person had been chosen for salvation. Thus, Calvinist doctrine demanded rigorous discipline. Fusing church and society into what followers named the Reformed church, Geneva became a theocratic city-state dominated by Calvin and the elders of the Reformed

WHAT WOULD YOU DO?

Assume that you, too, had a crisis of faith in the 1530s. Would you choose to become a follower of Luther, Zwingli, or Calvin or decide it was better in the end to remain a Roman Catholic? What reasons would you cite to members of your family for your choice? Would you go in a different direction from your mother and father?

The Progress of the Reformation

1517	Martin Luther disseminates ninety-five theses attacking sale of indulgences and other church practices
1520	Reformer Huldrych Zwingli breaks with Rome
1525	Peasants' War in German states divides reform movement
1529	Lutheran German princes protest condemnation of religious reform by Charles V
1534	The Act of Supremacy establishes King Henry VIII as head of the Church of England, severing ties to Rome
1534–1535	Anabaptists take over German city of Münster in failed experiment to create a holy community
1541	John Calvin establishes himself permanently in Geneva, making that city a model of Christian reform and discipline

church. Its people were rigorously monitored; detractors said that they were bullied. From its base in Geneva, the Calvinist movement spread to France, the Low Countries, England, Scotland, the German states, Poland, Hungary, and eventually New England.

In Geneva, Calvin tolerated no dissent. While passing through the city in 1553, the Spanish physician Michael Servetus was arrested because he had published books attacking Calvin and questioning the doctrine of the Trinity, the belief that there are three persons in one God—the Father, the Son (Jesus), and the Holy Spirit. Upon Calvin's advice, the authorities executed Servetus. Calvin was not alone in persecuting dissenters. Each religious group believed that its doctrine was absolutely true and grounded in the Bible and that therefore violence in its defense was not only justified but required. Catholic and Protestant polemicists alike castigated their critics in the harshest terms, but they often saved their cruelest words for the Jews. Calvin, for example, called the Jews "profane, unholy, sacrilegious dogs," but Luther went even further and advocated burning down their houses and their synagogues. Religious toleration was still far in the future.

The Contested Church of England

England followed yet another path, with reform led by the king rather than by men trained as Catholic clergy. Despite a tradition of religious dissent that went back to the fourteenth-century theologian John Wycliffe, Protestantism gained few English adherents in the 1520s. King **Henry VIII** (r. 1509–1547) changed that when he broke with the Roman Catholic church. The resulting Church of England retained many aspects of Catholic worship but nonetheless aligned itself in the Protestant camp.

At first, Henry opposed the Protestant Reformation, even receiving the title Defender of the Faith from Pope Leo X for a treatise he wrote against Luther. With the aid of his chancellors Cardinal Thomas Wolsey and Thomas More, Henry vigorously suppressed Protestantism and executed its leaders. More had made a reputation as a Christian humanist, publishing a controversial novel about an imaginary island called Utopia (1516), the source of the modern word for an ideal community. Unlike his friend Erasmus, More chose to serve the state directly and became personal secretary to Henry VIII, Speaker of the House of Commons, and finally Lord Chancellor.

By 1527, the king wanted to annul his marriage to Catherine of Aragon (d. 1536), the daughter of Ferdinand and Isabella of Spain and the aunt of Charles V. The eighteen-year marriage had produced a daughter, Mary (known as Mary Tudor), but Henry desperately needed a male heir to consolidate the rule of the still-new Tudor dynasty. Moreover, he had fallen in love with Anne Boleyn, a lady at court and a supporter of the Reformation. Henry claimed that his marriage to Catherine had never been valid because she was the widow of his older brother, Arthur. Arthur and Catherine's marriage, which apparently was never consummated, had been annulled by Pope Julius II to allow the marriage between Henry and Catherine to take place. Now Henry asked the reigning pope, Clement VII, to declare his marriage to Catherine invalid.

Around "the king's great matter" unfolded a struggle for political and religious control. When Cardinal Wolsey failed to secure papal approval of the annulment, Henry dismissed him and had him arrested. Wolsey died before he could be tried, and More took his place as Lord Chancellor. However, More resigned in 1532 because he opposed Henry's new direction; Henry then had him executed as a traitor in 1535. Henry now turned to two Protestants, Thomas Cromwell (1485–1540) as chancellor and Thomas Cranmer (1489–1556) as archbishop of Canterbury. Under their leadership, the English Parliament passed a number of acts that severed ties between the English church and Rome. The most important of these, the Act of Supremacy of 1534, made Henry the head of the Church of England. Other legislation invalidated the claims of Mary Tudor to the throne, recognized Henry's marriage to Anne Boleyn, and allowed the English crown to embark on the dissolution of the monasteries. In an effort to consolidate support behind his version of the Reformation, Henry sold off monastic lands to the local gentry and aristocracy. His actions prompted an uprising in 1536 in the north of the country called the Pilgrimage of Grace. Though suppressed, it revealed that many people remained deeply Catholic in their sympathies.

Henry grew tired of Anne Boleyn, who had given birth to a daughter, the future Queen Elizabeth I, but had produced no sons. He ordered Anne beheaded in 1536 on the charge of adultery. The king would go on to marry four other wives but father only one son, Edward. When Henry died in 1547, much would now depend on who held the crown. Henry himself held ambiguous views on religion: he considered himself Catholic but would not accept the supremacy of the pope; he closed the monasteries and removed shrines but kept the Mass and believed in clerical celibacy.

REVIEW QUESTION
How did Luther, Zwingli, Calvin, and Henry VIII each challenge the Roman Catholic church?

Reshaping Society through Religion

The religious reformers and their followers challenged political authority and the social order, yet in reaction to any extreme manifestation of disorder, they underlined the need for discipline in worship and social behavior. Some Protestants took the phrase "priesthood of all believers" quite literally and sided with the poor and the downtrodden. Like Catholics, Protestant authorities then became alarmed by the subversive potential of religious reforms. They viewed the Reformation as a way of instilling greater discipline in individual worship and church organization. At the same time, the Roman Catholic church undertook reforms of its own and launched an offensive against the Protestant Reformation that is sometimes called the Counter-Reformation.

Protestant Challenges to the Social Order

When Luther described the freedom of the Christian, he meant an entirely spiritual freedom. But others interpreted his call for freedom in social and political terms. In the spring of 1525, peasants in southern and central Germany rose in a rebellion known as the Peasants' War and attacked nobles' castles, convents, and monasteries (Map 14.2). Urban workers joined them, and together they looted church properties in the towns. In Thuringia (central/eastern Germany), the rebels followed an ex-priest, Thomas Müntzer (1468?–1525), who promised to chastise the wicked and thus clear the way for the Last Judgment.

The Peasants' War split the reform movement. Princes and city officials, ultimately supported by Luther, turned against the rebels. Catholic and Protestant princes joined forces to crush Müntzer and his supporters. All over the empire, princes trounced peasant armies and hunted down their leaders. By the end of the year, more than 100,000 rebels had been killed. Initially, Luther had tried to mediate the conflict, but he believed that God ordained rulers, who must therefore be obeyed even if they were tyrants. Luther considered Müntzer's mixing of religion and politics the greatest danger to the Reformation, nothing less than "the devil's work." Fundamentally conservative in its political philosophy, the Lutheran church henceforth depended on established political authority for its protection.

Some followers of Zwingli also wanted to pursue their own path to reform. They believed that true faith came only to those with reason and free will. How could a baby knowingly choose Christ? Only adults could believe and accept baptism; hence, the **Anabaptists** ("rebaptizers") rejected the validity of infant baptism and called for adult rebaptism. Many were pacifists who also refused to acknowledge the authority of law courts. The Anabaptist movement drew its leadership primarily from the artisan class and its members from the middle and lower classes—men and women attracted by a simple but radical message of peace and salvation.

Zwingli immediately attacked the Anabaptists for their refusal to bear arms and swear oaths of allegiance, sensing accurately that they were repudiating his theocratic (church-directed) order. When persuasion failed to convince the

MAP 14.2 The Peasants' War of 1525 The centers of uprisings clustered in southern and central Germany, where the density of cities encouraged the spread of discontent and allowed for alliances between urban masses and rural rebels. The proximity to the Swiss Confederation, a stronghold of the Reformation movement, also inspired antiestablishment uprisings.

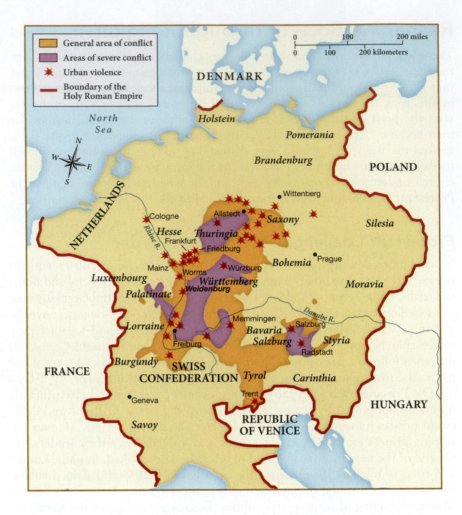

Anabaptists, Zwingli urged Zurich magistrates to impose the death sentence. Thus, the Evangelical reformers themselves created the Reformation's first martyrs of conscience.

Despite the Holy Roman Emperor's condemnation of the movement in 1529, Anabaptism spread rapidly from Zurich to many cities in southern Germany. In 1534, one Anabaptist group, believing the end of the world was imminent, seized control of the city of Münster. Proclaiming themselves a community of saints, the Münster Anabaptists abolished private property in imitation of the early Christians and dissolved traditional marriages, allowing men, like Old Testament patriarchs, to have multiple wives, to the consternation of many women. Besieged by a combined Protestant and Catholic army, the city fell in June 1535. The Anabaptist leaders died in battle or were executed, their bodies hung in cages affixed to the church tower. Their punishment was intended as a warning to all who might want to take the Reformation away from the Protestant authorities and hand it to the people. The Anabaptist movement in northwestern Europe nonetheless survived under the determined pacifist leadership of the Dutch reformer Menno Simons (1469–1561), whose followers were eventually named Mennonites.

New Forms of Discipline

Faced with the social firestorms ignited by religious reform, the middle-class urbanites who supported the Protestant Reformation urged greater religious conformity and stricter moral behavior. Protestants did not have monasteries or convents or saints' lives to set examples; they sought moral examples in their own homes, in the sermons of their preachers, and in their own reading of the Bible. Some of these attitudes had medieval roots, yet the Protestant Reformation fostered their spread, and Catholics soon began to embrace them.

Although the Bible had been translated into German before, Luther's translations (of the New Testament in 1522 and of the Old Testament in 1534) quickly became authoritative. A new Bible-centered culture began to take root, as more than 200,000 copies of Luther's New Testament were printed over twelve years, an immense number for the time. Peppered with witty phrases and colloquial expressions, Luther's Bible not only made the sacred writings more accessible to ordinary people but also helped standardize the German language. Bible reading became a common pastime undertaken in solitude or at family and church gatherings. To counter Protestant success, Catholic German Bibles soon appeared, thus sanctioning Bible reading by the Catholic laity, a sharp departure from medieval church practice.

Torture and Execution of an Anabaptist Leader
Not long after their capture in 1535, the Anabaptist leaders of Münster were tortured with hot tongs before being killed. Their bodies were placed in cages and hung from a church steeple. This print shows the cage with the body of John of Leiden. He was a tailor's apprentice from the Dutch town of Leiden. (Private Collection/Roger-Viollet, Paris, France/Bridgeman Images.)

The new emphasis on self-discipline led to growing impatience with the poor. Between 1500 and 1560, rapid economic and population growth created prosperity for some and stress—heightened by increased inflation—for many. Wanderers and urban beggars were by no means novel, but now moralists, both Catholic and Protestant, denounced vagabonds as lazy and potentially criminal.

The Reformation provided an opportunity to restructure relief for the poor. Instead of decentralized, private initiatives often overseen by religious orders, Protestant magistrates appointed officials to head urban agencies that would certify the genuine poor and distribute welfare funds to them. Catholic authorities did the same. In 1531, Henry VIII asked justices of the peace (unpaid local magistrates) to license the poor in England and to differentiate

Luther's Bible
This opening page from the Gospel of St. Matthew is taken from Luther's 1522 translation into German of the New Testament. The woodcut illustrations by Lucas Cranach, and Luther's decision to use a style of German that could be widely understood, made the book accessible to a wide audience. Bible reading became a central family activity for Protestants. (Bible Society, London, UK/Bridgeman Images.)

between those who could work and those who could not. In 1540, Charles V imposed a welfare tax in Spain to augment that country's inadequate system of private charity.

In their effort to establish order and discipline, Protestant reformers denounced sexual immorality and glorified the family. The early Protestant reformers like Luther championed the end of clerical celibacy and embraced marriage. Luther, once a celibate priest himself, married a former nun. Protestant magistrates closed brothels and established marriage courts to handle disputes over marriage promises, child support, and divorce (allowed by Protestants in some rare situations). The magistrates also levied fines or ordered imprisonment for violent behavior, fornication, and adultery.

Prior to the Reformation, despite the legislation of church councils, marriages had largely been private affairs between families; some couples never even registered with the church. The Catholic church recognized any promise made between two consenting adults (with the legal age of twelve for females, fourteen for males) in the presence of two witnesses as a valid marriage. As the Reformation took hold, Protestants asserted government control over marriage, and Catholic governments followed suit. A marriage was legitimate only if registered by both a government official and a member of the clergy.

Catholic Renewal

The Catholic church decided in the 1540s to undertake drastic action to fend off the Protestant threat. Pope Paul III convened a general council of the church in 1545 at Trent, a town on the border between the Holy Roman Empire and Italy. Meeting sporadically over eighteen years (1545–1563), the **Council of Trent** effectively set the course of Catholicism until the 1960s. Catholic leaders sought renewal of religious devotion and reform of clerical morality (some priests had had sexual relationships and fathered children) as well as clarification of church doctrine. New religious orders set out to win converts overseas or to reconvert Catholics who had turned to Protestantism. At the same time, the church did not hesitate to root out dissent by giving greater powers to the Inquisition, including the power to censor books. The papal Index, or list of prohibited books, was established in 1557 and not abolished until 1966.

Italian and Spanish clergy predominated among the 255 bishops, archbishops, and cardinals attending the Council of Trent, which condemned all the central doctrines of Protestantism. According to the council, salvation depended on faith and good works, not faith alone. On the sacrament of the Eucharist, the council reaffirmed that the bread of communion "really, truly" becomes Christ's body. It reasserted the supremacy of clerical authority over the laity; the church's interpretation of the Bible could not be challenged, and the Latin Vulgate was the only authoritative version. The council rejected divorce and reaffirmed the legitimacy of indulgences. It also called for reform from within, however, insisting that bishops henceforth reside in their dioceses and decreeing that seminaries for the training of priests be established in every diocese. Henceforth, the schism between Protestant and Catholic remained permanent, and all hopes of reconciliation faded.

The renewed energy of Catholicism expressed itself most vigorously in the founding of new religious orders such as the Society of Jesus, or **Jesuits**, founded by a Spanish nobleman, Ignatius of Loyola (1491–1556). In 1521, while recovering from an injury suffered as a soldier in the Spanish army, Ignatius read lives (biographies) of the saints; once he recovered, he abandoned his quest for military glory in favor of serving the church. In 1540, the pope recognized his small band of followers.

With Ignatius as its first general, the Jesuits became the most vigorous defenders of papal authority. The society quickly expanded; by the time of Ignatius's death in 1556, Europe had one thousand Jesuits. They established hundreds of colleges throughout the Catholic world, educating future generations of Catholic leaders. Jesuit missionaries played a key role in the Spanish and Portuguese empires and brought Roman Catholicism to Africans, Asians, and native Americans. They saw their effort as proof of the truth of Roman Catholicism and the success of their missions as a sign of divine favor, both particularly important in the face of Protestant challenge.

Catholic missionary zeal brought conflicting messages to indigenous peoples: for some, the message of a repressive and coercive alien religion; for others, a sweet sign of reason and faith. Frustrated in his efforts to convert Brazilian Indians, a Jesuit missionary wrote to his superior in Rome in 1563, "For this kind of people it is better to be preaching with the sword and rod of iron."

Catholic missionaries focused initially on winning over local elites. They learned the local languages and set up schools for the sons of conquered nobles. After an initial period of relatively little racial discrimination, the Catholic church in the Americas and Africa adopted strict rules based on color. For example, the first Mexican Ecclesiastical Provincial Council in 1555 declared that holy orders were not to be conferred on Indians, mestizos (people of mixed European-Indian parentage), or mulattoes (people of mixed European-African heritage); along with descendants of Muslims, Jews, and persons who had been sentenced by the Spanish Inquisition, these groups were deemed "inherently unworthy of the sacerdotal [priestly] office."

REVIEW QUESTION
How did the forces for radical change unleashed by the Protestant Reformation interact with the urge for social order and stability?

European missionaries in Asia greatly admired Chinese and Japanese civilization, and thus used the sermon rather than the sword to win converts. The Jesuit Francis Xavier preached in India and Japan, his work greatly assisted by a network of Portuguese trading stations. Overall the efforts of the Catholic missionaries seemed highly successful: vast multitudes of native Americans had become nominal Christians by the second half of the sixteenth century, and thirty years after Francis Xavier's 1549 landing in Japan, the Jesuits could claim more than 100,000 Japanese converts.

Striving for Mastery

Although the riches of the New World and the conflicts generated by the Reformation raised the stakes of international politics, life at court did not change all at once. Princes and popes continued to sponsor the arts and literature of the Renaissance. Henry VIII, for example, hired the German artist Hans Holbein as king's painter. While Protestantism was taking root, Catholic monarchs still fought one another and battled the powerful Ottoman Empire. Holy Roman Emperor Charles V dominated the political scene with his central position in Europe and his rising supply of gold and silver from the New World. Yet even his wealth proved insufficient to subdue all his challengers. Religious difference led to violence in every country, even Spain, where there were almost no Protestants but many Muslims who were forced to convert by Charles V in 1526. For the most part, violence failed to settle religious differences. By 1560, an exhausted Europe had achieved a provisional peace, but one sowed with the seeds of future conflict.

Courtiers and Princes

Kings, princes, and popes alike used their courts to keep an eye on their leading courtiers (cardinals in the case of popes) and impress their other subjects. Briefly defined, the court was the ruler's household. Around the prince gathered a community of household servants, noble attendants, councilors, officials, artists, and soldiers. Renaissance culture had been promoted by this political elite, and that culture now entered its "high," or most sophisticated, phase. Its acclaimed representative was Michelangelo Buonarroti (1475–1564), an immensely talented Italian artist who sculpted the gigantic nude *David* for officials in Florence and then painted the ceiling of the Sistine Chapel for the recently elected Pope Julius II.

Italian artists also flocked to the French court of Francis I (r. 1515–1547), which swelled to the largest in Europe. In addition to royal officials and guards, physicians, librarians, musicians, dwarfs, animal trainers, and a multitude of hangers-on bloated its size to more than sixteen hundred members. Although Francis built a magnificent Renaissance palace at Fontainebleau, where he hired Italian artists to produce paintings and sculpture, the French court often moved from palace to palace. It took no fewer than eighteen thousand horses to transport the people, furniture, documents, dogs, and falcons for the royal hunt. Hunting represented a form of mock combat, essential in the training of a military elite. Francis almost lost his own life when, storming a house during one mock battle, he was hit on the head by a burning log.

Two Italian writers helped define the new culture of courtesy, or proper court behavior: Ludovico Ariosto (1474–1533), in service at the Este court in Ferrara, and Baldassare Castiglione (1478–1529), a servant of the duke of Urbino and the pope. Ariosto composed an epic poem, *Orlando Furioso*, which represented court culture as the highest synthesis of Christian and classical values. The poem's captivating tales of combat, valor, love, and magic ranged across Europe, Africa, Asia, and even the moon. In *The Courtier*, Castiglione's characters debate the qualities of an ideal courtier in a series of eloquent dialogues. The true courtier, Castiglione asserts, is a gentleman who carries himself with nobility and dignity in the service of his prince and his lady.

Courtesy was recommended to courtiers, but not always to princes. The Italian politician and writer Niccolò Machiavelli (1469–1527) helped found modern political science by treating the maintenance of power as an end in itself. In his provocative essay *The Prince*, he underlined the need for pragmatic, even cold calculation. Was it better, he asked, for a prince to be feared by his people or loved? "It may be answered that one should wish to be both, but, because it is difficult to unite them in one person, [it] is much safer to be feared than loved." Machiavelli insisted that princes could benefit their subjects only by keeping a firm grip on power, if necessary through deceit and manipulation. *Machiavellian* has remained ever since a term for using cunning and duplicity to achieve one's ends.

King Francis I and His Court
In this illustration from a 1534 manuscript, the king of France is shown with his three sons listening to the reading of a translated ancient text. The translator, Antoine Macault, was the king's secretary and is shown wearing the black of officials. Renaissance kings took pride in sponsoring revivals of classical texts (in this case Diodorus of Sicily, a Greek historian from the first century B.C.E.). (Musée Condé, Chantilly, France/Bridgeman Images.)

Dynastic Wars

Even as the Renaissance developed in the princely courts and the Reformation began in the German states, the Habsburgs (the ruling family in Spain and then the Holy Roman Empire) and the Valois (the ruling family in France) fought each other for domination of Europe. French claims provoked the Italian Wars in 1494, which soon escalated into a general conflict that involved the major

Charles V and Francis I Make Peace

This fresco from the Palazzo Farnese in the town of Caprarola, north of Rome, shows French king Francis I and Holy Roman Emperor Charles V (shown pointing his finger) agreeing to the Truce of Nice in 1538, one of many peace agreements made and then broken during the wars between the Habsburgs and the Valois. Pope Paul III, who negotiated the truce, stands behind and between them. Charles is on the right pointing to Francis. The truce is the one celebrated in the Tlaxcala pageant described at the start of this chapter. (From the fresco *Sala del Consiglio Trento*, by Taddeo Zuccaro [1529–1566] and Federico Zuccaro [1542–1609]/ Palazzo Farnese, Rome, Italy/ Bridgeman Images.)

Christian monarchs and the Muslim Ottoman sultan as well. From 1494 to 1559, the Valois and Habsburg dynasties, both Catholic, remained implacable enemies. The fighting raged in Italy and the Low Countries. In 1525, the troops of Charles V crushed the French army at Pavia, Italy, counting among their captives the French king himself, Francis I. Forced to renounce all claims to Italian territory to gain his freedom, Francis furiously repudiated the treaty the moment he reached France, reigniting the conflict.

In 1527, Charles's troops captured and sacked Rome because the pope had allied with the French. Many of the imperial troops were German Protestant mercenaries, who pillaged Catholic churches and brutalized the Catholic clergy. Protestants and Catholics alike interpreted the sack of Rome by imperial forces as a punishment of God; even the Catholic church read it as a sign that reform was necessary. Finally, in 1559, the French gave up their claims in Italy and signed the Treaty of Cateau-Cambrésis, ending the conflict. To seal the peace the French king Henry II married his sister to the duke of Savoy, an ally of the Habsburgs, and his daughter to the Habsburg king of Spain, Philip II, who had succeeded his father Charles V in 1556.

The dynastic struggle (Valois versus Habsburg) had drawn in many other belligerents, who fought on one side or the other for their own benefit. Some acted purely out of power considerations, such as England, first siding with the Valois and then with the Habsburgs. Others fought for their independence, such as the papacy and the Italian states, which did not want any one power to dominate Italy. Still others chose sides for religious reasons, such as the Protestant princes in Germany, who exploited the Valois-Habsburg conflict to extract religious concessions from the emperor in 1555. The Ottoman Turks saw in this fight an opportunity to expand their territory.

The Ottoman Empire reached its height of power under Sultan Suleiman I, known as **Suleiman the Magnificent** (r. 1520–1566). In 1526, a Turkish expedition destroyed the Hungarian army at Mohács. Three years later, the Ottomans laid siege to Vienna; though unsuccessful, the attack sent shock waves throughout Christian Europe. In 1535, Charles V led a campaign to capture Tunis, the lair of North African pirates loyal to the Ottomans. Desperate to overcome Charles's superior Habsburg forces, the French king Francis I forged an alliance with the Turkish sultan. The Turkish fleet besieged the Habsburg troops holding Nice, on the southern coast of France. Francis even ordered all inhabitants of nearby Toulon to vacate the town so that he could turn it into a Muslim colony for eight months, complete with a mosque and a slave market.

The French alliance with the Turks reflected the spirit of the times: the age-old idea of the Christian crusade against Islam now had to compete with a new political strategy that considered religion only one factor among many in power politics. Religion could be sacrificed, if need be, on the altar of state building. Constantly distracted by the challenges of the Ottomans to the east and the German Protestants at home, Charles V could not crush the French with one swift blow.

The Siege of Vienna, 1529
This illustration from an Ottoman manuscript of 1588 depicts the Turkish siege of Vienna (the siege guns can be seen toward the top of the picture). Sultan Suleiman I (Suleiman the Magnificent) led an army of more than 100,000 men against Vienna, capital of the Austrian Habsburg lands. Several attacks on the city failed, and the Ottomans withdrew in October 1529. They maintained control over Hungary, but the logistics of moving so many men and horses kept them from advancing farther westward into Europe. (From the *Hunername* by Lokman/Topkapi Palace Museum, Istanbul, Turkey/Bridgeman Images.)

Financing War

The sixteenth century marked the beginning of superior Western military technology. All armies grew in size and their firepower became ever more deadly, increasing the cost of war. Heavier artillery pieces meant that the rectangular walls of medieval cities had to be transformed into fortresses with jutting ramparts and gun emplacements. Royal revenues could not keep up with war expenditures. To pay their bills, governments routinely devalued their coinage (the sixteenth-century equivalent of printing more paper money), causing prices to rise rapidly.

Charles V boasted the largest army in Europe, supported by the gold and silver coming in from the New World. Immediately after conquest, the Spanish looted gold and silver objects, melted them down, and sent the precious metals to Spain. Mining began with forced Indian labor in the 1520s, and the amount of silver extracted in Mexico and sent to Spain increased twentyfold in the 1530s and 1540s. Nevertheless, Charles could never make ends meet because of his extravagant war costs: the debt of 37 million ducats accumulated during his forty years in power exceeded by 2 million ducats all the gold and silver brought from the Americas. His opponents fared even worse. On his death in 1547, Francis I owed the bankers of Lyon almost 7 million French pounds—approximately the entire royal income for that year. Foremost among the financiers of war debts was the Fugger bank, based in the southern German imperial city of Augsburg. The enterprise began with Jakob Fugger (1459–1525), who became personal banker to Charles V's grandfather Maximilian I. By the end of his life, Maximilian was so deeply in debt to Jakob Fugger that he had to pawn the royal jewels. In 1519, Fugger assembled a consortium of German and Italian bankers to secure the election of Charles V as Holy Roman Emperor. For the next three decades, the alliance between Europe's biggest international bank and its largest empire remained very close. Charles stayed barely one step ahead of his creditors; in 1531, for example, he had to grant to the Fuggers eight years of mining rights in Spanish lands south of Peru (present-day Bolivia and Chile).

Divided Realms

European rulers viewed religious division as a dangerous challenge to the unity and stability of their rule. Subjects who considered their rulers heretics or blasphemers could only cause trouble, and religious differences encouraged the formation of competing noble factions, which easily led to violence when weak monarchs or children ruled.

In France, King Francis I tolerated Protestants until the Affair of the Placards in 1534. Even then, the government could not stop many French noble families—including some of the most powerful—from converting to Calvinism, especially in southern and western France. Francis and his successor, Henry II (r. 1547–1559), succeeded in maintaining a balance of power between Catholics and Calvinists, but after Henry's death the weakened monarchy could no longer hold together the fragile realm. The real drama of the Reformation in France took place after 1560, when the country plunged into four decades of religious wars, whose savagery was unparalleled elsewhere in Europe (see Chapter 15).

In England and Scotland religious divisions at the very top threatened the control of the rulers. Before his death in 1547, Henry VIII had succeeded in making himself head of the Church of England, but the nature of that church remained ambiguous. The advisers of the boy king Edward VI (r. 1547–1553) furthered the Protestant cause by welcoming prominent religious refugees who had been deeply influenced by Calvinism and wanted to see England move in that austere direction. But Edward died at age fifteen, opening the way to his Catholic half sister, Mary Tudor, who had been restored to the line of succession by an act of Parliament under Henry VIII in 1544.

When Mary (r. 1553–1558) came to the throne, she restored Catholicism and persecuted Protestants. Nearly three hundred Protestants perished at the stake, and more than eight hundred fled to the Protestant German states and Switzerland. Finally, when Anne Boleyn's daughter, Elizabeth, succeeded her half sister Mary, becoming Queen Elizabeth I (r. 1558–1603), the English Protestant cause gained lasting momentum. Under Elizabeth's leadership, Protestantism came to define the character of the English nation, though the influence of Calvinism within it was still a cause for dispute. Catholics were tolerated only if they kept their opinions on religion and politics to themselves. A tentative but nonetheless real peace returned to England.

Still another pattern of religious politics unfolded in Scotland, where Protestants formed a small minority until the 1550s. At the center of Scotland's conflict over religion stood Mary of Guise, a French native and Catholic married to the king of Scotland, James V. After James died in 1542, Mary surrounded herself and her daughter Mary Stuart, also a Catholic and heir to the throne, with French advisers. When, in 1558, Mary Stuart married Francis, the son of Henry II and the heir to the French throne, many Scottish noblemen, alienated by this pro-French atmosphere, joined the pro-English, anti-French Protestant cause. They gained control of the Scottish Parliament in 1560 and dethroned the regent, Mary of Guise. Eventually they forced her daughter—by then known as Mary, queen of Scots—to flee to England, and installed Mary's infant son, James, as king. Scotland would turn toward the Calvinist version of the Reformation and thus establish the potential for conflict with England.

In the German states, the Protestant princes and cities formed the Schmalkaldic League in 1531. Opposing the league were Emperor Charles V, the bishops, and the few remaining Catholic princes. Although Charles had to concentrate on fighting the French and the Turks during the 1530s, he eventually secured the western Mediterranean and then turned his attention back home to central Europe to try to resolve the growing religious differences in his lands.

After efforts to mediate between Protestants and Catholics broke down, Charles prepared to fight the Protestant Schmalkaldic League. War broke out in 1547, the year after Martin Luther's death. Using seasoned Spanish veterans and German allies, Charles occupied the German imperial cities in the south, restoring Catholic elites and suppressing the Reformation. When Protestant commanders could not agree on a joint strategy, Charles crushed the Schmalkaldic League's armies at Mühlberg in Saxony and captured the leading Lutheran princes. Jubilant, Charles restored Catholics' right to worship in Protestant lands while permitting Lutherans to keep their own rites. Protestant resistance to the declaration was deep and widespread: many pastors went into exile, and riots broke out in many cities. Charles's success did not last long. The Protestant princes regrouped, declared war in 1552, and chased a surprised, unprepared, and practically bankrupt emperor back to Italy.

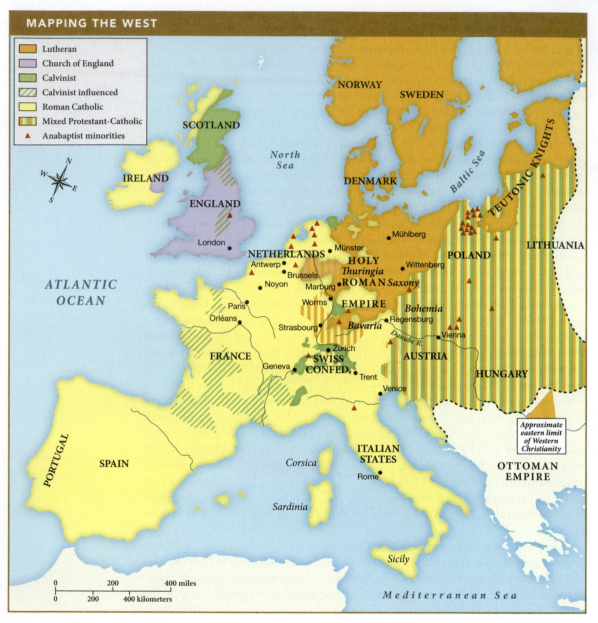

MAPPING THE WEST

Legend:
- Lutheran
- Church of England
- Calvinist
- Calvinist influenced
- Roman Catholic
- Mixed Protestant-Catholic
- ▲ Anabaptist minorities

Reformation Europe, c. 1560

The fortunes of Roman Catholicism were at their lowest point around 1560. Northern Germany and Scandinavia owed allegiance to the Lutheran church; England broke away under a national church headed by its monarchs; and the Calvinist Reformation extended across large areas of western, central, and eastern Europe. Southern Europe remained solidly Catholic.

Analyzing the Map: Where did Protestantism take hold, northern or southern Europe? Keep this in mind, as the difference will continue to have consequences for later chapters.

Making Connections: What is the relationship between the voyages of discovery and the struggles over Protestantism?

Forced to compromise, Charles V agreed to the **Peace of Augsburg** in 1555. The settlement recognized the Lutheran church in the empire; accepted the secularization of church lands but "reserved" the remaining ecclesiastical territories for Catholics; and, most important, established the principle that all princes, whether Catholic or Lutheran, enjoyed the sole right to determine the religion of their lands and subjects. Calvinist, Anabaptist, and other dissenting groups were excluded from the settlement. Ironically, the religious revolt of the common people had culminated in a princes' reformation. The Augsburg settlement preserved a fragile peace in central Europe until 1618, but the exclusion of Calvinists would prompt future conflict.

Exhausted by decades of war and dismayed by the disunity in Christian Europe, Emperor Charles V resigned his many thrones in 1555 and 1556, leaving his Netherlandish-Burgundian and Spanish dominions to his son, Philip II, and his Austrian lands to his brother, Ferdinand (who was also elected Holy Roman Emperor to succeed Charles). Retiring to a monastery in southern Spain, the most powerful of the Christian monarchs spent his last years quietly seeking salvation.

> **REVIEW QUESTION**
> How did religious divisions complicate the efforts of rulers to maintain political stability and build stronger states?

Conclusion

Charles V's decision to divide his empire reflected the tensions pulling Europe in different directions. Even as Charles's kingdom of Spain joined Portugal as a global power with new conquests overseas, Luther, Calvin, and a host of others sought converts to competing branches of Protestantism within the Holy Roman Empire. The reformers disagreed on many points of doctrine and church organization, but they all broke definitively from the Roman Catholic church. The pieces were never put together again. Portugal and Spain, the leaders in global exploration and conquest, remained resolutely Catholic, but as ruler of the Holy Roman Empire, where the Reformation began, Charles could not stifle the growing religious ferment. In the decades to come, Protestantism would spread, religious conflict would turn even more deadly, and emerging Protestant powers would begin to contest the global reach of Spain and Portugal.

Chapter 14 Review

Key Terms and People

Be sure that you can identify the term or person and explain its historical significance.

Christopher Columbus (p. 471)	John Calvin (p. 484)	Jesuits (p. 491)
Hernán Cortés (p. 474)	predestination (p. 484)	Suleiman the Magnificent (p. 495)
Christian humanism (p. 478)	Henry VIII (p. 485)	Peace of Augsburg (p. 499)
Martin Luther (p. 479)	Anabaptists (p. 487)	
Charles V (p. 481)	Council of Trent (p. 490)	

Review Questions

1. Which European countries led the way in maritime exploration, and what were their motives?

2. How did Luther, Zwingli, Calvin, and Henry VIII each challenge the Roman Catholic church?

3. How did the forces for radical change unleashed by the Protestant Reformation interact with the urge for social order and stability?

4. How did religious divisions complicate the efforts of rulers to maintain political stability and build stronger states?

Making Connections

1. In what ways did the discovery of the Americas affect Europe?

2. Why was Charles V ultimately unable to prevent religious division in his lands?

3. How did the different religious groups respond to the opportunity presented by the printing press?

4. What motives besides religious differences caused war in this period?

Important Events

1492	Columbus reaches the Americas
1494	Italian Wars begin; Treaty of Tordesillas divides Atlantic world between Portugal and Spain
1516	Erasmus publishes Greek edition of the New Testament
1517	Luther composes ninety-five theses to challenge Catholic church
1519	Cortés captures Aztec capital of Tenochtitlán
1520	Luther publishes three treatises; Zwingli breaks from Rome
1525	German Peasants' War
1527	Charles V's imperial troops sack Rome
1529	Colloquy of Marburg addresses disagreements between German and Swiss church reformers
1534	Henry VIII breaks with Rome; Affair of the Placards in France
1536	Calvin publishes *Institutes of the Christian Religion*
1540	Jesuits established as new Catholic order
1545–1563	Catholic Council of Trent condemns Protestant beliefs and confirms Catholic doctrine
1547	Charles V defeats Protestants at Mühlberg
1555	Peace of Augsburg ends religious wars and recognizes Lutheran church in German states
1559	Treaty of Cateau-Cambrésis ends wars between Habsburg and Valois rulers

Consider three events

Luther publishes three treatises (1520), German Peasants' War (1525), and Catholic Council of Trent condemns Protestant beliefs, confirms Catholic doctrine (1545–1563). How did Luther's treatises inspire the uprising of peasants and urban artisans? How did the changes wrought by the first two events prompt the Council of Trent, its goals, and its decisions?

Suggested References

A more global historical perspective is reshaping the study of both the European voyages of exploration and conquest and the Reformation, especially the Catholic renewal, which included a global missionary effort.

Banchoff, Thomas, and Casanova, José, eds. *The Jesuits and Globalization: Historical Legacies and Contemporary Challenges.* 2016.

Christopher Columbus: http://www.ibiblio.org/expo/1492.exhibit/Intro.html

Lindberg, Carter. *The European Reformations*, 2nd ed. 2010.

Manetsch, Scott M. *Calvin's Company of Pastors: Pastoral Care and the Emerging Reformed Church, 1536–1609.* 2013.

Mann, Charles C. *1493: Uncovering the New World Columbus Created.* 2013.

Norwich, John Julius. *Four Princes: Henry VIII, Francis I, Charles V, Suleiman the Magnificent and the Obsessions that Forged Modern Europe.* 2016.

O'Malley, John W. *Trent: What Happened at the Council.* 2013.

Roper, Lyndal. *Martin Luther: Renegade and Prophet.* 2016.

*Schwartz, Stuart B. *Victors and Vanquished: Spanish and Nahua Views of the Conquest of Mexico.* 2000.

*Symcox, Geoffrey, and Blair Sullivan. *Christopher Columbus and the Enterprise of the Indies: A Brief History with Documents.* 2005.

Wellman, Kathleen. *Queens and Mistresses of Renaissance France.* 2013.

Wilson, Derek. *Mrs. Luther and Her Sisters: Women in the Reformation.* 2016.

---

*Primary source.

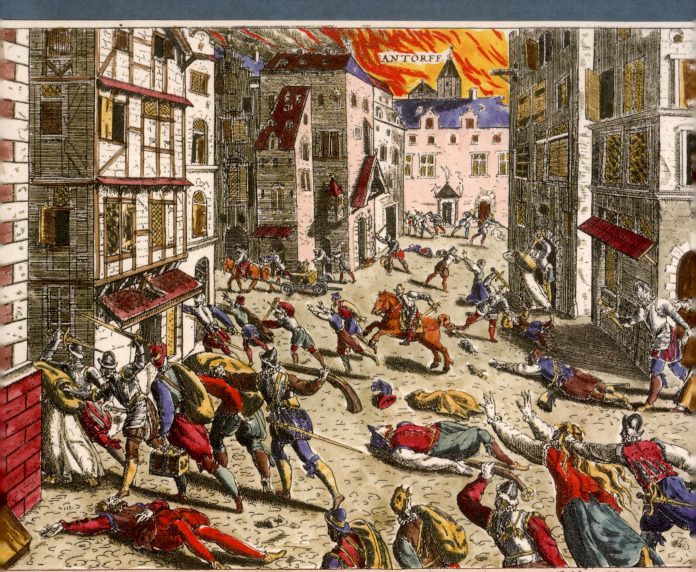

ANTORFF.

Der Spanier große tÿrannej	Der weitter welt gar wolbekant	Vil tausendt leuth vnschuldigs bloit	O Gott will dich ein mhal erbarmen
Verursachet diese wütterej	Verdorben wirt, vnd gar verbrent,	Vergossen wirt, vnd große noit	Deren so ietz seind im elend,
Da durch Antorff im niderlant	Beraubt, vnd jungfrauwen geschent	Sigtt man mitt elendigem karmen	Damitt das morden neem ein endt.

.11.

Wars of Religion and the Clash of Worldviews

1560–1648

In November 1576, Spain's soldiers sacked Antwerp, Europe's wealthiest city. In eleven days of horror known as the Spanish Fury, the troops slaughtered seven to eight thousand people and burned down a thousand buildings, including the city hall. The king of Spain had sent an army of ten thousand men in 1566 to occupy his rebellious northern domains and punish Calvinists, who had smashed stained-glass windows and statues in Catholic churches. By 1575, however, the king had run out of funds, and his men rioted after being unpaid for months. The Spanish Fury was far from an isolated incident in this time of religious upheaval. It showed, moreover, that violence often exploded from a dangerous mixture of religious, political, and economic motives.

The first two generations of battles over the Protestant Reformation had ended with the Peace of Augsburg in 1555. That agreement helped maintain a relative calm in the lands of the Holy Roman Empire, but in western Europe religious strife multiplied after 1560 as Calvinists made inroads in France, the Netherlands, and England. In 1618, fighting broke out again in the Holy Roman Empire—and before it ended in 1648, the Thirty Years' War involved most of the European powers and desolated lands and peoples across central Europe. All in all, nearly constant warfare marked the century between 1560 and 1648. Like the Spanish Fury, these struggles began as religious disputes but soon revealed other motives: political ambitions, long-standing rivalries between the leading powers, and greed—all of which raised the stakes of conflict.

Suffering only increased when a major economic downturn in the early seventeenth century led to food shortages, famine, and disease in much of Europe. These catastrophes hit especially hard in the central

«**Atrocities in Antwerp** The sixteenth-century Netherlandish artist Franz Hogenberg produced this engraving of the Spanish Fury in Antwerp not long after the events took place. It shows the kinds of atrocities—rape, murder, pillage, and burning of houses—that would be committed repeatedly on both sides of the conflict between Catholics and Protestants. (akg-images.)

European lands devastated by the fighting of the Thirty Years' War. In intellectual life a new understanding of the motion of the planets in the heavens and of mechanics on earth developed among experimenters in "natural philosophy," that is, what came to be called science. This scientific revolution ultimately reshaped Western attitudes in virtually every field of knowledge, but at its beginnings it still had to compete with traditional religious views and popular beliefs in magic and witchcraft.

Religious Conflicts Threaten State Power, 1560–1618

CHAPTER FOCUS
What were the long-term political, economic, and intellectual consequences of the conflicts over religious belief in this era?

The Peace of Augsburg made Lutheranism a legal religion in the predominantly Catholic Holy Roman Empire, but it did not extend recognition to Calvinists. The rapid expansion of Calvinism after 1560 threatened to alter the religious balance of power as Calvinists challenged Catholic dominance in France, the Spanish-ruled Netherlands, Scotland, and Poland-Lithuania. In England, they sought to influence the new Protestant monarch, Elizabeth I. Calvinists were not the only source of religious contention, however. Philip II of Spain fought the Muslim Ottoman Turks in the Mediterranean and expelled the remnants of the Muslim population in Spain. To the east, the Russian tsar Ivan IV fought to establish an empire based on Russian Orthodox Christianity.

French Wars of Religion, 1562–1598

Calvinism spread in France after 1555, when the Genevan Company of Pastors sent missionaries supplied with false passports and often disguised as merchants. By the end of the 1560s, nearly one-third of the nobles had joined the Huguenots (French Calvinists), and they raised their own armies. Conversion to Calvinism in French noble families often began with the noblewomen, who protected pastors, provided money and advice, and helped found schools and establish relief for the poor.

A series of family tragedies prevented the French kings from acting decisively to prevent the spread of Calvinism. King Henry II was accidentally killed during

CHAPTER TIMELINE

1562
French Wars of Religion begin

1569
Formation of commonwealth of Poland-Lithuania

1576
Spanish Fury erupts in Antwerp

1588
English defeat of Spanish Armada

1560   **1580**   **1600**

1566
Revolt of Calvinists against Spain begins in Netherlands

1571
Battle of Lepanto marks victory of West over Ottomans at sea

1572
St. Bartholomew's Day Massacre of French Protestants

1598
French Wars of Religion end with Edict of Nantes

a jousting tournament in 1559, and his fifteen-year-old son, Francis, died soon after. Ten-year-old Charles IX (r. 1560–1574) became king, with his mother, **Catherine de Médicis**, as regent, or acting ruler. The Huguenots followed the lead of the Bourbon family, who stood first in line to inherit the throne if the Valois kings failed to produce a male heir. The most militantly Catholic nobles took their cues from the Guise family. Catherine tried to play the Bourbon and Guise factions against each other, but civil war erupted in 1562. Both sides committed terrible atrocities. Priests and pastors were murdered, and massacres of whole congregations became frighteningly commonplace.

Although a Catholic herself, Catherine feared the rise of Guise influence, so she arranged the marriage of the king's Catholic sister, Marguerite de Valois, to Henry of Navarre, a Huguenot and Bourbon. Just four days after the wedding, in August 1572, an assassin tried but failed to kill one of the Huguenot leaders. Violence against Calvinists spiraled out of control. On St. Bartholomew's Day, August 24, a bloodbath began, fueled by years of growing animosity between Catholics and Protestants. In three days, Catholic mobs murdered some two thousand Huguenots in Paris. Three thousand Huguenots died in the provinces over the next six weeks. The pope joyfully ordered the church bells rung throughout Catholic Europe.

Huguenot pamphleteers now proclaimed their right to resist a tyrant who worshipped idols (a practice that Calvinists equated with Catholicism). This right of resistance was linked to a political notion of contract; upholding the true religion was part of the contract binding the ruler to his subjects. Both the right of resistance and the idea of a contract fed into the larger doctrine of constitutionalism—that a government's legitimacy rested on its upholding a constitution, or contract between ruler and ruled (see Contrasting Views on page 506). The religious division in France grew even more dangerous when Charles IX died and his brother Henry III (r. 1574–1589) became king. Like his brothers before him, Henry III failed to produce an heir. Convinced that Henry III lacked the will to root out Protestantism, the Guises formed the Catholic League, which requested help from Spanish king Philip II. Henry III responded in 1588 by having his men kill two Guise leaders. A few months later, a fanatical Catholic monk stabbed Henry III to death, and Henry of Navarre became Henry IV (r. 1589–1610), despite Philip II's military intervention.

1601
William Shakespeare, *Hamlet*

1625
Hugo Grotius publishes *The Laws of War and Peace*

1635
French join the Thirty Years' War by declaring war on Spain

1610   **1630**   **1650**

1618
Thirty Years' War begins

1633
Galileo Galilei forced to recant his support of heliocentrism

1648
Peace of Westphalia ends Thirty Years' War

CONTRASTING VIEWS

Political Authority and Religion: What Happened When Subjects Held Different Beliefs?

1. Defence of Liberty Against Tyrants, 1579

First published in Latin (as Vindiciae contra tyrannos) *in Edinburgh but written by a French Protestant, this tract makes a central argument that would have long-lasting influence: kings derive their power from a covenant or contract with their people, and therefore the people have a right to resist the king if the king goes against God's will in religious matters. But who was best placed to interpret God's will?*

"Now we reade of two sorts of Covenants at the Inaugurating of Kings, the first betweene God, the King, and the People, that the people might be the people of God: The second between the King and the people, that the people shall obey faithfully, and the King command justly."... The Question is, *If it be lawful to resist a Prince violating the Law of God, or ruinating the Church, or hindring the restoring of it?* If we hold ourselves to the tenure of the holy Scripture, it will resolve us. For, if in this case it have been lawful to the Jewish people (the which may be easily gathered from the books of the Old Testament) yea, if it have been injoyned them, I beleeve it will not be denyed, that the same must be allowed to the whole people of any Christian Kingdom or Country whatsoever."

Source: Hubert Languet (or Philippe de Mornay), *Vindiciae contra tyrannos, a defence of liberty against tyrants, or, Of the lawful power of the Prince over the people, and of the people over the Prince being a treatise written in Latin and French by Junius Brutus, and translated out of both into English.* London: Printed by Matthew Simmons and Robert Ibbitson, 1648, 7 and 19 (with the original spelling).

2. Jean Bodin, *The Six Books of the Commonwealth,* 1576

Even before the publication of Defence of Liberty *(no. 1), the Catholic lawyer Bodin had viewed with alarm the publication of Protestant pamphlets that justified resistance to the French king in the wake of the St. Bartholomew's Day massacre. In his* Six Books, *one of the founding texts of modern political theory, Bodin developed the idea that sovereignty must be absolute and undivided and that therefore subjects had no right to resist their king.*

"And in that the greatness and majesty of a true sovereign prince, is to be known; when the estates of all the people assembled together, in all humility present their requests and supplications to their prince, without having any power in any thing to command or determine, or to give voice, but that that which it pleaseth the king to like or dislike of, to command or forbid, is holden for law, for an edict and ordinance. Wherein they which have written of the duty of magistrates, & other such like books, have deceived themselves, in maintaining that the power of the people is greater than the prince; a thing which oft times causeth the true subjects to revolt from the obedience which they owe unto their sovereign prince, & ministreth matter of great troubles in Commonwealths. Of which their opinion, there is neither reason nor ground except the king be captive, furious [insane], or in his infancy, and so needeth to have a protector or lieutenant appointed him by the suffrages of the people. For otherwise if the king should be subject unto the assemblies and decrees of the people, he should neither be king nor sovereign; and the Commonwealth neither realm nor monarchy, but a mere Aristocracy of many lords in power equal."

Source: Jean Bodin, *Of the lawes and customes of a common-wealth. Learnedly discoursing of the power of soveraignety and majestracy [sic], and of the orders and degrees of citizens, with the priviledges of corporations and colledges: and other things pertinent to estates and societies. / Written by I. Bodin . . . Out of the French and Latin copies, done into English, by Richard Knolles, author of the Turkish history . . . ,* London: Printed by A[dam].I[slip]. and are to bee sold at the sign of the Bell in Saint Pauls Church-yard, 1606, 95.

QUESTIONS TO CONSIDER

1. What were the grounds for resistance outlined in the first document?
2. Why did Bodin reject the arguments for resisting a king on the grounds of religion?
3. How did doctrines of resistance contribute to later doctrines of constitutional protection of rights and even democracy?

With the Catholic League threatening to declare his succession invalid, Henry IV publicly embraced Catholicism, reputedly explaining, "Paris is worth a Mass." Within a few years he defeated the ultra-Catholic opposition and drove out the Spanish. In 1598, he issued the **Edict of Nantes**, in which he granted the Huguenots a large measure of religious toleration. The approximately 1.25 million Huguenots became a legally protected minority within an officially Catholic kingdom of some 20 million people. Protestants were free to worship in specified towns and were allowed their own troops, fortresses, and even courts.

Few believed in religious toleration as an ideal, but Henry IV followed the advice of those moderate Catholics and Calvinists—together called *politiques*—who urged him to give priority to the development of a durable state. The politiques believed that religious disputes could be resolved only in the peace provided by a strong government. The French Catholic writer Michel de Montaigne (1533–1592) went even further than this pragmatic position and revived the ancient doctrine of skepticism, which held that total certainty is never attainable. On the beams of his study he painted the statement "All that is certain is that nothing is certain." Like toleration of religious differences, such skepticism was repugnant to Protestants and Catholics alike, both of whom were certain that their religion was the right one.

The Edict of Nantes ended the French Wars of Religion, but Henry still needed to reestablish monarchical authority and hold the fractious nobles in check. He allowed rich merchants and lawyers to buy offices and, in exchange for an annual payment, pass their positions on to their heirs or sell them to someone else. This new social elite was known as the "nobility of the robe" (named after the robes that magistrates wore, much like the ones judges wear today). Income raised by the increased sale of offices reduced the state debt and also helped Henry strengthen the monarchy. His efforts did not, however, prevent his enemies from assassinating him in 1610 after nineteen unsuccessful attempts.

Dutch Revolt against Spain

Although he failed to prevent Henry IV from taking the French throne in 1589, **Philip II** of Spain (r. 1556–1598) was the most powerful ruler in Europe (Map 15.1). In addition to the western Habsburg lands in Spain and the Netherlands, Philip had inherited from his father, Charles V, all the Spanish colonies recently settled in the New World of the Americas. Gold and silver funneled from the colonies supported his campaigns against the Ottoman Turks and the French and the English Protestants. But all the money of the New World could not prevent Philip's eventual defeat in the Netherlands, where Calvinist rebels established the independent Dutch Republic, which soon vied with Spain, France, and England for commercial supremacy.

A deeply devout Catholic, Philip II came to the Spanish throne at age twenty-eight determined to restore Catholic unity in Europe and lead the Christian defense against the Muslims. His brief marriage to Mary Tudor

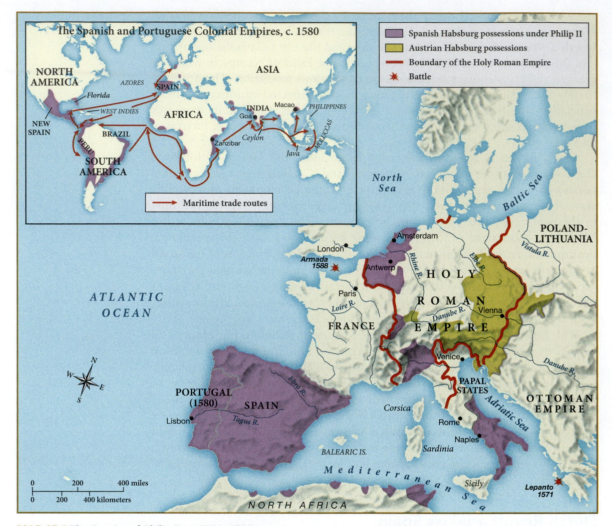

MAP 15.1 The Empire of Philip II, r. 1556–1598
Spanish king Philip II drew revenues from a truly worldwide empire. In 1580, he was the richest European ruler, but the demands of governing and defending his control of such far-flung territories eventually drained his resources.

(Mary I of England) did not produce an heir, but it and his subsequent marriage to Elisabeth de Valois, the sister of Charles IX and Henry III of France, gave him reason enough for involvement in English and French affairs. In 1578, the king of Portugal died fighting Muslims in Morocco, and two years later Philip took over this neighboring realm with its rich empire in Africa, India, and the Americas.

Philip insisted on Catholic unity in the lands under his control and worked to forge an international Catholic alliance against the Ottoman Turks. In 1571, he achieved the single greatest military victory of his reign when he joined with Venice and the papacy to defeat the Turks in a great sea battle off

The Battle of Lepanto
The Greek artist Antonio Vassilacchi painted this mural in 1600 to celebrate the Christian victory at the battle of Lepanto. Vassilacchi was working in Venice, which was one of the main Christian allies in the campaign against the Turks. The victory was considered so important that it was celebrated in writings, medals, paintings, and sculptures. The mural captures the violence and confusion of the battle. (Villa Barbarigo, Noventa Vicentina, Italy/ Bridgeman Images.)

the Greek coast at **Lepanto.** Thirty-six thousand sailors and soldiers fought on the allied side; twenty thousand for the Turks. Thousands died in artillery and gunfire and in brutal hand-to-hand fighting on board the ships. The Christian allies had the advantage of six big Venetian vessels that rode too high in the water to be boarded and carried many artillery pieces.

Spain could not pursue its advantage because of threats elsewhere. Between 1568 and 1570, the Moriscos — Muslim converts to Christianity who remained secretly faithful to Islam — had revolted in the south of Spain, killing ninety priests and fifteen hundred Christians. Philip retaliated by forcing fifty thousand Moriscos to leave their villages and resettle in other regions. In 1609, his successor, Philip III, ordered their expulsion from Spanish territory, and by 1614, some 300,000 Moriscos had been forced to relocate to North Africa.

The Calvinists of the Netherlands were less easily intimidated: they were far from Spain and accustomed to being left alone. After the Spanish Fury of 1576 outraged Calvinists and Catholics alike, Prince William of Orange (whose name came from the lands he owned in southern France) led the Netherlands' seven predominantly Protestant northern provinces into a military alliance with the ten mostly Catholic southern provinces and drove out the Spaniards. The Catholic southern provinces returned to the Spanish fold in 1579. Despite the assassination in 1584 of William of Orange, Spanish troops never regained control in the north. Spain would not formally recognize Dutch independence until 1648, but by the end of the sixteenth century, the Dutch Republic (sometimes called Holland after the most populous of its seven provinces) was a self-governing state sheltering a variety of religious groups.

Religious toleration in the Dutch Republic developed for pragmatic reasons: the central government did not have the power to enforce religious orthodoxy.

Philip II of Spain
The king of Spain is shown here (kneeling in black) with his allies at the battle of Lepanto, the doge of Venice on his left and Pope Pius V on his right. El Greco (see page 529) painted this canvas, sometimes called *The Dream of Philip II*, in 1578 or 1579. The painting is typically mannerist in the way it crowds figures into every available space, uses larger-than-life or elongated bodies, and creates new and often bizarre visual effects. What can we conclude about Philip II's character from the way he is depicted here? (Monasterio de El Escorial, Spain/Bridgeman Images.)

Each province governed itself and sent delegates to the one common institution, the States General. Although the princes of Orange resembled a ruling family, their powers paled next to those of local elites, known as regents. One-third of the Dutch population remained Catholic, and local authorities allowed them to worship as they chose in private. The Dutch Republic also had a relatively large Jewish population because many Jews had settled there after being driven out of Spain and Portugal. From 1597, Jews could worship openly in their synagogues. This openness to various religions would help make the Dutch Republic one of Europe's chief intellectual and scientific centers in the seventeenth and eighteenth centuries.

Well situated for maritime commerce, the Dutch Republic developed a thriving economy based on shipping and shipbuilding. Dutch merchants favored free trade in Europe because they could compete at an advantage. After the Dutch gained independence, Amsterdam became the main European money market for two centuries. The Dutch controlled many overseas markets thanks to their preeminence in seaborne commerce: by 1670, the Dutch commercial fleet was larger than the English, French, Spanish, Portuguese, and Austrian fleets combined.

Elizabeth I's Defense of English Protestantism

As the Dutch revolt unfolded, Philip II became increasingly infuriated with **Elizabeth I** (r. 1558–1603), who had succeeded her half sister Mary Tudor as queen of England. Philip had been married to Mary and had enthusiastically seconded Mary's efforts to return England to Catholicism. When Mary died in 1558, Elizabeth rejected Philip's proposal of marriage and promptly brought Protestantism back to England. She had to squash uprisings by Catholics in the north and at least two serious plots against her life. In the long run, however, her greatest challenges came from the Calvinist Puritans and Philip II.

The **Puritans** were strict Calvinists who opposed all vestiges of Catholic ritual in the Church of England. After Elizabeth became queen, many Puritans

Elizabeth I, Queen of England
This portrait of Elizabeth I dates from about 1575 when Elizabeth was in her 40s. The queen used cosmetics and wigs to cover up the scars of smallpox and the loss of much of her hair. The crown and scepter on the table next to her signal her sovereignty. (Print Collector/Getty Images.)

returned from exile abroad, but Elizabeth resisted their demands for drastic changes in church ritual and governance. The Church of England's Thirty-Nine Articles of Religion, issued under her authority in 1563, incorporated elements of Catholic ritual along with Calvinist doctrines. Puritans tried to undercut the crown-appointed bishops' authority by placing control of church administration in the hands of a local presbytery, that is, a group made up of the minister and the elders of the congregation. Elizabeth rejected this Calvinist presbyterianism.

The Puritans nonetheless steadily gained influence. Known for their emphasis on strict moral lives, the Puritans tried to close England's theaters and Sunday fairs. Every Puritan father—with the help of his wife—was to "make his house a little church" by teaching the children to read the Bible. Believing themselves God's elect—those whom God has chosen for mercy and salvation—and England an "elect nation," the Puritans also pushed Elizabeth to help Protestants on the continent. After Philip II annexed Portugal and began to interfere in French affairs, Elizabeth dispatched seven thousand soldiers in 1585 to help the Dutch rebels.

Philip II bided his time as long as Elizabeth remained unmarried and her Catholic cousin Mary Stuart, better known as Mary, queen of Scots, stood next in line to inherit the English throne. In 1568, Scottish Calvinists forced Mary to abdicate the throne of Scotland in favor of her one-year-old son James (eventually James I of England), who was then raised as a Protestant. After her abdication, Mary spent nearly twenty years under house arrest in England. In 1587, when a letter from Mary offering her succession rights to Philip was discovered, Elizabeth overcame her reluctance to execute a fellow monarch and ordered Mary's beheading.

Now determined to act, Philip II sent his armada (Spanish for "fleet") of 130 ships from Lisbon toward the English Channel in May 1588. The English scattered the Spanish Armada by sending blazing fire ships into its midst. A great gale then forced the Spanish to flee around Scotland. When the armada limped home in September, half the ships had been lost and thousands of sailors were dead or starving. Protestants throughout Europe rejoiced.

Retreat of the Spanish Armada, 1588

By the time Philip II died in 1598, the costs of fighting the Ottomans, Dutch, English, and French had finally bankrupted the treasury. In his novel *Don Quixote* (1605), the Spanish writer Miguel de Cervantes captured the disappointment of thwarted Spanish ambitions. Cervantes himself had been wounded at Lepanto. His novel's hero, a minor nobleman, reads so many romances and books of chivalry that he loses his sense of proportion and wanders the countryside futilely trying to mimic the heroic deeds he has come across in his reading.

Elizabeth made the most of her limited means and consolidated England's position as a Protestant power. In her early years, she held out the prospect of marriage to many political suitors; but in order to maintain her—and England's—independence, she never married. Her successor, James I (r. 1603–1625), came to the throne as king of both Scotland and England. Shakespeare's tragedies *Hamlet* (1601), *King Lear* (1605), and *Macbeth* (1606), written around the time of James's succession, might all be read as commentaries on the uncertainties faced by Elizabeth and James. But Elizabeth's story, unlike Shakespeare's tragedies, had a happy ending: she left James secure in a kingdom of growing weight in world politics.

Russia, Poland-Lithuania, and Sweden in the Late 1500s

The Clash of Faiths and Empires in Eastern Europe

In the east, the most contentious border divided Christian Europe from the Islamic realm of the Ottoman Turks. Recovering quickly from their defeat at Lepanto in 1571, the Ottomans continued their attacks, seizing Venetian-held Cyprus in 1573. In the Balkans, rather than forcibly converting their Christian subjects to Islam, the Turks allowed them to cling to the Greek Orthodox faith. They welcomed Jews expelled from Spain, and Jews soon made up 10 percent of the population of Istanbul.

The Muscovite tsars officially protected the Russian Orthodox church, which faced no competition within Russian lands. Building on the base laid by his grandfather Ivan III, Tsar Ivan IV (r. 1533–1584) stopped at nothing in his endeavor to make Muscovy (the grand duchy centered on Moscow) the heart of a mighty Russian empire. Given to unpredictable fits of rage, Ivan murdered his own son with an iron rod during a quarrel. His epithet "the Terrible" reflects not only the terror he unleashed but also the awesome impression he evoked. Cunning and cruel, Ivan came to embody barbarism in the eyes of Westerners.

Ivan initiated Russian expansion eastward into Siberia, but two formidable foes blocked his plans for expansion westward: Sweden (which then included much of present-day Finland) and Poland-Lithuania. Poland and the grand duchy of Lithuania united into a single commonwealth in 1569 and controlled an extensive territory. After Ivan IV died in 1584, a terrible period of chaos known as the Time of Troubles ensued, during which the king of Poland-Lithuania tried to put his son on the Russian throne. In 1613, an army of nobles, townspeople, and peasants finally expelled the intruders and put on

REVIEW QUESTION
How did state power depend on religious unity at the end of the sixteenth century and start of the seventeenth?

the throne a nobleman, Michael Romanov (r. 1613–1645), who established an enduring new dynasty.

The Thirty Years' War, 1618–1648

Although the eastern states managed to avoid civil wars over religion in the early seventeenth century, the rest of Europe was drawn into the final and most deadly of the wars of religion, the Thirty Years' War. It began in 1618 with conflicts between Catholics and Protestants within the Holy Roman Empire and eventually involved most European states. By its end in 1648, many central European lands lay in ruins, and the balance of power had shifted away from the Habsburg powers—Spain and Austria—toward France, England, and the Dutch Republic. Prolonged warfare created turmoil and suffering, but it also fostered the growth of armies and bureaucracies; out of the carnage would emerge centralized and powerful states that made increasing demands on ordinary people.

Origins and Course of the War

The fighting that devastated central Europe had its origins in a combination of religious disputes, ethnic competition, and political weakness. The Austrian Habsburgs officially ruled over the huge Holy Roman Empire, which comprised eight major ethnic groups. The emperor and four of the seven electors who chose him were Catholic; the other three electors were Protestants. The Peace of Augsburg of 1555 (see page 499) maintained the balance between Catholics and Lutherans, but it had no mechanism for resolving conflicts; tensions rose as Calvinism, unrecognized under the peace, made inroads into Lutheran areas. By 1613, two of the three Protestant electors had become Calvinists.

These conflicts came to a head when the Catholic Habsburg heir Archduke Ferdinand was crowned king of Bohemia (present-day Czech Republic) in 1617. The Austrian Habsburgs held not only the imperial crown of the Holy Roman Empire but also a collection of separately administered royal crowns, of which Bohemia was one. Once crowned, Ferdinand began to curtail the religious freedom previously granted to Czech Protestants. When Ferdinand was elected emperor (as Ferdinand II, r. 1619–1637), the rebellious Czechs deposed him and chose in his place the young Calvinist Frederick V of the Palatinate (r. 1616–1623). A quick series of clashes ended in 1620 when the imperial armies defeated the outmanned Czechs at the battle of White Mountain, near Prague. The Czechs would not gain their independence until 1918.

The battle of White Mountain did not end the war, which soon spread to the German lands of the empire. Private mercenary armies (armies for hire) began to form during the fighting, and the emperor had little control over them. Albrecht von Wallenstein (1583–1634), a Czech Protestant by birth, offered in 1625 to raise an army for Ferdinand II and soon had in his employ 125,000

WHAT WOULD YOU DO?

If you were a friend of Albrecht von Wallenstein, and like him a Czech Protestant by birth, how would you react to his willingness to work for the Catholic Habsburg Emperor Ferdinand II? Would you join him given the uncertainties of the time? Or would you denounce him to your friends and rejoice when he was assassinated? If you were living in the 1620s and 1630s, would religious affiliation count above all else for you? Or would the stability of the state be more important?

soldiers, who plundered much of Protestant Germany with the emperor's approval. The Lutheran king of Denmark, Christian IV (r. 1596–1648), responded by invading northern Germany. General Wallenstein's forces defeated him. Emboldened by his general's victories, Emperor Ferdinand issued the Edict of Restitution in 1629, which outlawed Calvinism in the empire and reclaimed Catholic church properties confiscated by the Lutherans.

With Protestant interests in serious jeopardy, Gustavus Adolphus (r. 1611–1632) of Sweden marched into Germany in 1630 with a highly trained army of 100,000 soldiers. Hoping to block Spanish intervention in the war, the French monarchy's chief minister, Cardinal Richelieu (1585–1642), offered to subsidize the Lutheran Gustavus. This agreement between the Swedish Lutheran and French Catholic powers to fight the Catholic Habsburgs showed that state interests could outweigh religious considerations.

Gustavus defeated the imperial army and occupied the Catholic parts of southern Germany before he was killed during a battle in 1632. Once again the tide turned, but this time it swept Wallenstein with it. Because Wallenstein was rumored to be negotiating with Protestant powers, Ferdinand had him assassinated.

France openly joined the fray in 1635 by declaring war on Spain. The two Catholic powers pummeled each other. The French king Louis XIII (r. 1610–1643) hoped to profit from the troubles of Spain in the Netherlands and from the conflicts between the Austrian emperor and his Protestant subjects. A series of internal revolts shook the perennially cash-strapped Spanish crown. In 1640, peasants in the rich northeastern province of Catalonia rebelled, overrunning Barcelona and killing the viceroy of the province. The Portuguese also revolted in 1640 and proclaimed independence like the Dutch. In 1643, the Spanish suffered their first major defeat at French hands. Although the Spanish were forced to concede independence to Portugal (annexed to Spain only since 1580), they eventually suppressed the Catalan revolt.

France, too, faced exhaustion after years of rising taxes and recurrent revolts. Richelieu died in 1642. Louis XIII followed him a few months later and was succeeded by his five-year-old son, Louis XIV. With yet another foreign queen mother—she was the daughter of the Spanish king—serving as regent and an Italian cardinal, Mazarin, providing advice, French politics once again moved into a period of instability, rumor, and crisis. All sides were ready for peace.

The Effects of Constant Fighting

When peace negotiations began in the 1640s, they did not come a moment too soon. Some towns had faced several prolonged sieges during the decades of fighting. Even worse suffering took place in the countryside. Peasants fled their villages, which were often burned down. At times, desperate peasants revolted and attacked nearby castles and monasteries. War and intermittent outbreaks of plague cost some German towns one-third or more of their population. One-third of the inhabitants of Bohemia also perished.

Soldiers did not fare all that much better. An Englishman who fought for the Dutch army in 1633 described how he slept on the wet ground, got his boots full of water, and "at peep of day looked like a drowned ratt." Governments increasingly short of funds often failed to pay the troops, and frequent mutinies, looting, and pillaging resulted. Armies attracted all sorts of displaced people desperately in need of provisions. In the last year of the Thirty Years' War, the Imperial-Bavarian Army had 40,000 men entitled to draw rations—and more than 100,000 wives, prostitutes, servants, children, and other camp followers forced to scrounge for their own food.

The Peace of Westphalia, 1648

The comprehensive settlement provided by the **Peace of Westphalia**—named after the German province where negotiations took place—would serve as a model for resolving future conflicts among warring European states. For the first time, a diplomatic congress convened to address international disputes, and those signing the treaties guaranteed the resulting settlement. A method still in use, the congress was the first to bring *all* parties together, rather than two or three at a time.

France and Sweden gained most from the Peace of Westphalia. France acquired parts of Alsace and replaced Spain as the prevailing power on the continent. Sweden took several northern territories from the Holy Roman Empire (Map 15.2). The Habsburgs lost the most. The Spanish Habsburgs

MAP 15.2 The Thirty Years' War and the Peace of Westphalia, 1648
The Thirty Years' War involved many of the major continental European powers. The arrows marking invasion routes show that most of the fighting took place in central Europe in the lands of the Holy Roman Empire. The German states and Bohemia sustained the greatest damage during the fighting. None of the combatants emerged unscathed because even ultimate winners such as Sweden and France depleted their resources of men and money.

recognized Dutch independence after eighty years of war. Each German prince in the Holy Roman Empire gained the right to establish Lutheranism, Catholicism, or Calvinism in his state, a right denied to Calvinist rulers by the Peace of Augsburg in 1555. The independence ceded to German princes sustained political divisions that prepared the way for the emergence of a new power, the Hohenzollern Elector of Brandenburg, who increased his territories and developed a small but effective standing army. After losing considerable territory in the west, the Austrian Habsburgs turned eastward to concentrate on restoring Catholicism to Bohemia and wresting Hungary from the Turks.

The Peace of Westphalia settled the distribution of the main religions in the Holy Roman Empire: Lutheranism would dominate in the north, Calvinism in the area of the Rhine River, and Catholicism in the south. Most of the territorial changes in Europe remained intact until the nineteenth century. In the future, international warfare would be undertaken for reasons of national security, commercial ambition, or dynastic pride rather than to enforce religious uniformity. As the politiques of the late sixteenth century had hoped, state interests now outweighed motivations of faith in political affairs.

The nearly constant warfare that preceded the peace had one surprising result: despite the death and destruction, warfare had increased state authority. As armies grew to bolster the war effort, governments needed more money and more supervisory officials. The rate of land tax paid by French peasants doubled in the eight years after France joined the war. In addition to raising taxes, governments deliberately depreciated the value of the currency, which often resulted in soaring prices. When all else failed, rulers declared bankruptcy. The Spanish government, for example, did so three times in the first half of the seventeenth century. From Portugal to Muscovy, ordinary people resisted new taxes by forming makeshift armies and battling royal forces. With their colorful banners, unlikely leaders, strange names (the Nu-Pieds, or "Barefooted," in France, for instance), and crude weapons, the rebels usually proved no match for state armies, but they did keep troops occupied.

To meet these new demands, monarchs relied on advisers who took on the role of modern prime ministers. Louis XIII's chief minister, Cardinal Richelieu, proclaimed the priority of ***raison d'état*** ("reason of state"), that is, the state's interest above all else. He silenced Protestants within France because they had become too independent, and he crushed noble and popular resistance to Louis's policies. He set up intendants—delegates from the king's council dispatched to the provinces—to oversee police, army, and financial affairs.

To justify the growth of state authority and the expansion of government bureaucracies, rulers carefully cultivated their royal images. James I of England argued that he ruled by divine right and was accountable only to God: "The state of monarchy is the supremest thing on earth; for kings are not only God's lieutenant on earth, but even by God himself they are called gods." He advised his son to maintain a manly appearance even as some courtiers complained of his behavior toward certain male favorites. Appearance counted for so much that most rulers regulated who could wear which kinds of cloth and decoration, reserving the richest and rarest, such as ermine and gold, for themselves.

REVIEW QUESTION
Why did a war fought over religious differences result in stronger states?

Economic Crisis and Realignment

The devastation caused by the Thirty Years' War deepened an economic crisis that was already under way. After a century of rising prices, caused partly by massive transfers of gold and silver from the New World and partly by population growth, in the early 1600s prices began to level off and even to drop, and in most places population growth slowed. International trade fell into recession. Agricultural yields also declined, and peasants and townspeople alike were less able to pay the escalating taxes needed to finance the wars. Famine and disease trailed grimly behind economic crisis and war, in some areas causing large-scale uprisings and revolts. Behind the scenes, the economic balance of power gradually shifted as northwestern Europe began to dominate international trade and broke the stranglehold of Spain and Portugal in the New World.

From Growth to Recession

Population grew and prices rose in the second half of the sixteenth century. England's population grew by 70 percent and in parts of Spain the population grew by 100 percent (that is, it doubled). The supply of precious metals from the New World reached its height in the 1590s. This flood of precious metals combined with population growth to fuel an astounding inflation in food prices in western Europe—400 percent in the sixteenth century—and a more moderate rise in the cost of manufactured goods. Wages rose much more slowly, at about half the rate of the increase in food prices.

Recession did not strike everywhere at the same time, but the warning signs were unmistakable. Foreign trade slumped as war and an uncertain money supply made business riskier. Imports of gold and silver declined, in part because so many of the native Americans who worked in Spanish colonial mines died from disease. Textile production fell in many countries, largely because of decreased demand and a shrinking labor force. The trade in African slaves grew steadily between 1580 and 1630 and then it, too, declined by a third, though its growth would resume after 1650 and skyrocket after 1700. African slaves were first transported to the new colony of Virginia in 1619, foreshadowing a major transformation of economic life in the New World colonies.

Demographic slowdown also signaled economic trouble. In the Mediterranean, growth had already stopped in the 1570s. The most sudden reversal occurred in central Europe as a result of the Thirty Years' War: one-fourth of the inhabitants of the Holy Roman Empire perished in the 1630s and 1640s. Population growth continued only in England, the Dutch Republic, the Spanish Netherlands, and Scandinavia.

Where the population stagnated or declined, agricultural prices dropped because of less demand, and farmers who produced for the market suffered. The price of grain fell most precipitously, causing many farmers to convert grain-growing land to pasture or vineyards. The only country that emerged unscathed from this downturn was the Dutch Republic, thanks to a growing population and a tradition of agricultural innovation. Inhabiting Europe's most densely populated area, the Dutch developed systems of field drainage, crop rotation, and animal husbandry that provided high yields of grain for both people and animals. Their foreign trade, textile industry, crop production, and population all grew. After the Dutch, the English fared best; unlike the Spanish, the English never depended on infusions of New World gold and silver to shore up their economy, and unlike most continental European countries, England escaped the direct impact of the Thirty Years' War.

Historians have long disagreed about the causes of the early-seventeenth-century recession. Some cite the inability of agriculture to support a growing population by the end of the sixteenth century; others blame the Thirty Years' War, the states' demands for more taxes, or the waste caused by middle-class expenditures in the desire to emulate the nobility. To this list of causes, recent researchers have added climatic changes. Cold winters and wet summers meant bad harvests, and these natural disasters ushered in a host of social catastrophes. When the harvest was bad, prices shot back up and many could not afford to feed themselves.

Consequences for Daily Life

The recession of the early 1600s had both short-term and long-term effects. In the short term, it aggravated the threat of food shortages, increased the outbreaks of famine and disease, and caused people to leave their families and homes. In the long term, it deepened the division between prosperous and poor peasants and fostered the development of a new pattern of late marriages and smaller families.

When grain harvests fell short, peasants immediately suffered because, outside of England and the Dutch Republic, grain had replaced more expensive meat as the essential staple of most Europeans' diets. By the end of the sixteenth century, the average adult European ate more than four hundred pounds of grain per year. Peasants lived on bread, soup with a little fat or oil, peas or lentils, garden vegetables in season, and only occasionally a piece of meat or fish.

When faced with famine, most people simply left their huts and hovels and took to the road in search of food and charity. Men left their families to search for better conditions elsewhere. Those left behind might be reduced to eating chestnuts, roots, bark, and grass. In eastern France in 1637, a witness reported, "The roads were paved with people. . . . Finally it came to cannibalism." Compassion sometimes gave way to fear when

The Life of the Poor
This mid-seventeenth-century painting by the Dutch artist Adriaen Pietersz van de Venne depicts the poor peasant weighed down by his wife and child. An empty food bowl signifies their hunger. In reality, many poor men abandoned their homes in search of work, leaving their wives behind to cope with hungry children and what remained of the family farm. What did the artist intend to convey about women? (*Allegory of Poverty*, 1630s, by Adriaen Pietersz van de Venne [1589–1662]/Allen Memorial Art Museum, Oberlin College, Ohio, USA/Bridgeman Images.)

hungry vagabonds became more aggressive, occasionally threatening to burn a barn if they were not given food.

Successive bad harvests led to malnutrition, which weakened people and made them more susceptible to such epidemic diseases as the plague, typhoid fever, typhus, dysentery, smallpox, and influenza. The plague was feared most: in one year it could cause the death of up to half of a town's or village's population, and it struck with no discernible pattern. Nearly 5 percent of France's entire population died just in the plague of 1628–1632.

Economic crisis widened the gap between rich and poor. Peasants paid rent to their landlords as well as fees for inheriting or selling land and tolls for using mills, wine presses, or ovens. States collected direct taxes on land and sales taxes on consumer goods such as salt, an essential preservative. Protestant and Catholic churches alike exacted a tithe (a tax equivalent to one-tenth of the parishioner's annual income); often the clergy took their tithe in the form of crops and collected it directly during the harvest. Any reversal of fortune could force peasants into the homeless world of vagrants and beggars, who numbered as much as 2 percent of the total population.

In England, the Dutch Republic, northern France, and northwestern Germany, improvements gave some peasants the means to become farmers who rented substantial holdings, produced for the market, and in good times enjoyed relative comfort and higher status. Those who could not afford to plant new crops such as maize (American corn) or to use techniques that ensured higher yields became simple laborers with little or no land of their own. One-half to four-fifths of the peasants did not have enough land to support a family. They descended deeper into debt during difficult times and often lost their land to wealthier farmers or to city officials intent on developing rural estates.

As the recession deepened, women lost some of their economic opportunities. Widows who had been able to take over their late husbands' trade now found themselves excluded by the urban guilds or limited to short tenures. Many women went into domestic service until they married, some for their entire lives. Town governments carefully regulated the work of female servants, requiring women to stay in their positions unless they could prove mistreatment by a master.

European families reacted to economic downturn by postponing marriage and having fewer children. When hard times passed, more people married and had more children. But even in the best of times, one-fifth to one-quarter of all children died in their first year, and half died before age twenty. Childbirth still carried great risks for women, about 10 percent of whom died in the process. Midwives delivered most babies; physicians were scarce, and even those who did attend births were generally less helpful than midwives. The Englishwoman Alice Thornton described in her diary how a doctor bled her to prevent a miscarriage after a fall (bloodletting, often by the application of leeches, was a common medical treatment); her son died anyway in a breech birth that almost killed her, too.

Beginning in the early seventeenth century and continuing until the end of the eighteenth, families in all ranks of society started to limit the number of children. Because methods of contraception were not widely known, they did this for the most part by marrying later; the average age at marriage during the seventeenth century rose from the early twenties to the late twenties. The average family had about four children. Poorer families seem to have had fewer children, wealthier ones more. Because Protestant and Catholic clergy alike stressed sexual fidelity and abstinence before marriage, the number of births out of wedlock was relatively small (2–5 percent of births); premarital intercourse was generally tolerated only after a couple had announced their engagement.

The Economic Balance of Power

Just as the recession of the early seventeenth century produced winners and losers among ordinary people, it also created winners and losers among the competing states of Europe. The economies of southern Europe declined during this period, whereas those of the northwest emerged stronger. Competition in the New World reflected and reinforced this shift as the English, Dutch, and French rushed to establish trading outposts and permanent settlements to compete with the Spanish and Portuguese.

The new powers of northwestern Europe, with their growing Atlantic trade, gradually displaced the Mediterranean economies, which had dominated European commerce since the time of the Greeks and Romans. England and the Dutch Republic vied with France to become the leading mercantile and slave-trading powers. Northern Italian industries were eclipsed; Spanish commerce with the New World dropped. Even the plague contributed to the new disparity in trading power. Whereas central Europe and the Mediterranean countries took generations to recover from its ravages, northwestern Europe quickly replaced its lost population, no doubt because this area's people had suffered less from the effects of the Thirty Years' War and from the malnutrition related to the economic crisis.

All but the remnants of serfdom had disappeared in western Europe, yet in eastern Europe nobles reinforced their dominance over peasants, and the burden of serfdom increased. The rise in the cost of grain in the sixteenth century prompted Polish and eastern German nobles to increase their holdings and step up their production of grain for western markets. In the economic downturn of the first half of the seventeenth century, peasants who were already dependent became serfs—completely tied to the land. Although enserfment produced short-term profits for landlords, in the long run it retarded economic development in eastern Europe and kept most of the population in a stranglehold of illiteracy and hardship.

Economic realignment also took place across the Atlantic Ocean. Because Spain and Portugal had divided between themselves the rich spoils of South America, other prospective colonizers had to carve niches in seemingly less

MAP 15.3 European Colonization of the Americas, c. 1640
Europeans coming to the Americas established themselves first in coastal areas. The English, French, and Dutch set up most of their colonies in the Caribbean and North America because the Spanish and Portuguese had already colonized the easily accessible regions in South America. Vast inland areas still remained unexplored and uncolonized in 1640.

hospitable places, especially North America and the Caribbean (Map 15.3). Eventually, the English, French, and Dutch would dominate commerce with these colonies. Many European states, including Sweden and Denmark, chartered private joint-stock companies to enrich investors by importing fish, furs, tobacco, and precious metals (if they could be found), and to develop new markets for European products. British, French, Dutch, and Danish companies also began trading slaves.

In establishing permanent colonies, the Europeans created whole new communities across the Atlantic. Careful plans could not always surmount the hazards of transatlantic shipping, however. In 1620, the *Mayflower*, which had sailed for Virginia with Pilgrim emigrants, landed off course far to the north in Massachusetts, where the settlers founded New Plymouth colony. By the 1640s, the British North American colonies had more than fifty thousand people, of whom perhaps a thousand were Africans. The Indians native to the area had been decimated in epidemics and wars.

In contrast, French Canada had only about three thousand European inhabitants by 1640. Though thin in numbers, the French rapidly moved into the Great Lakes region. Fur traders sought beaver pelts to make the hats that had taken Paris fashion by storm. Jesuit missionaries lived with native American groups, learning their languages and describing their ways of life.

Both England and France turned some attention as well to the Caribbean in the 1620s and 1630s, when they occupied the islands of the West Indies after driving off the native Caribs. These islands would prove ideal for a plantation economy of African slaves tending sugarcane and tobacco crops under the supervision of European settlers.

Even as the British and French moved into North America and the Caribbean, Spanish explorers traveled the Pacific coast up to what is now northern California and pushed into New Mexico. On the other side of the world, in the Philippines, the Spanish competed with local Muslim rulers and indigenous tribal leaders to extend their control. Spanish officials worked closely with Catholic missionaries to rule over a colony composed of indigenous peoples, Spaniards, and some Chinese merchants.

REVIEW QUESTION
What were the consequences of economic recession in the early 1600s?

The Rise of Science and a Scientific Worldview

The countries that moved ahead economically in the first half of the seventeenth century—England, the Dutch Republic, and to some extent France—turned out to be the most receptive to the rise of science and a scientific worldview. In the long-term process known as **secularization**, religion gradually became a matter of private conscience rather than public policy. Secularization did not entail a loss of religious faith, but it did prompt a search for nonreligious explanations for political authority and natural phenomena. During the late sixteenth and early seventeenth centuries, science, political theory, and even art began to break their long-standing bonds with religion. Scientists and scholars sought laws in nature to explain politics as well as movements in the heavens and on earth. The visual arts more frequently depicted secular subjects. A scientific revolution (see Terms of History on page 524) was in the making. Yet traditional attitudes did not disappear. Belief in magic and witchcraft pervaded every level of society. People of all classes believed that the laws of nature reflected a divine plan for the universe. They accepted supernatural explanations for natural phenomena, a view only gradually and partially undermined by new ideas.

The Scientific Revolution

Although the Catholic and Protestant churches encouraged the study of science and many prominent scientists were themselves clerics, the search for a secular, scientific method of determining the laws of nature undermined traditional accounts of natural phenomena. Christian doctrine had incorporated the scientific teachings of ancient philosophers, especially Ptolemy and Aristotle; now these came into question. A revolution in astronomy contested the Ptolemaic view, endorsed by the Catholic church, which held that the sun revolved around the earth. Startling breakthroughs took place in medicine, too. Supporters of these new developments argued for the **scientific method**, which combined experimental observation and mathematical deduction. The use of the scientific method culminated in the astounding breakthroughs of Isaac Newton at the end of the seventeenth century. Newton's ability to explain the motion of the planets, as well as everyday objects on earth, gave science enormous new prestige.

The traditional account of the movement of the heavens derived from the second-century Greek astronomer Ptolemy, who put the earth at the center of the cosmos. Above the earth were fixed the moon, the stars, and the planets in concentric crystalline spheres; beyond these fixed spheres dwelt God and the angels. In this view, the sun revolved around the earth, the heavens were perfect and unchanging, and the earth was "corrupted." Ptolemy insisted that the planets revolved in circular orbits (because circles were more "perfect" than other figures). To account for the actual elliptical paths that could be observed and calculated, he posited orbits within orbits, or epicycles.

TERMS OF HISTORY

Scientific Revolution

The term *scientific revolution* refers to the series of breakthroughs in the natural sciences, especially astronomy and physics, that challenged the traditional learning of ancient philosophers and Catholic teachings about the nature of the cosmos, in particular the view that the earth was the center of a fixed universe. Although it began in the sixteenth century and had origins even earlier, the most crucial developments took place in the 1600s. Among the most important were the experiments and writings of the Italian Galileo Galilei and the Englishman Isaac Newton. Galileo's experiments helped confirm that the earth was not the center of a fixed universe but one of many similar bodies revolving around the sun, and Newton established the law of universal gravitation governing the motion of bodies in the heavens and on earth. They and others like them showed that experimentation combined with human reasoning could unlock the secrets of the universe.

Neither Galileo nor Newton used the term *scientific revolution* because they considered themselves natural philosophers; the label "scientist" only began to be used in the 1800s. From the middle of the nineteenth century, writers began to refer to the "scientific revolution" as a way of signaling that a major break from the past had occurred in the 1600s: truths about nature would henceforth be determined by scientific methods (testing of hypotheses by experimentation) rather than by reference to the Bible or religious authorities.

Scholars are now divided about the validity of the term. Some argue that change did not occur all at once (it was not revolutionary), especially since the major transformations in biology and chemistry only took place later. Others draw attention to the disagreement over proper methods and procedures and the lack of any unitary notion of science as a body of knowledge. But other historians consider the seventeenth-century breakthroughs so foundational that they can only be compared to something as fundamental as the legacies of the ancient Greeks or the emergence of Christianity.

In 1543, the Polish clergyman Nicolaus Copernicus (1473–1543) began the revolution in astronomy by publishing his treatise *On the Revolution of the Celestial Spheres*. Copernicus attacked the Ptolemaic account, arguing that the earth and other planets revolved around the sun, a view known as **heliocentrism** (a sun-centered universe). He discovered that by placing the sun instead of the earth at the center of the system of spheres, he could eliminate many epicycles from the calculations and thus simplify the mathematics. Copernicus died soon after publishing his theories, but when the Italian monk Giordano Bruno (1548–1600) taught heliocentrism, the Catholic Inquisition (set up to seek out heretics) arrested him and burned him at the stake.

Copernicus's views began to attract widespread attention in the early 1600s. When the Danish astronomer Tycho Brahe (1546–1601) observed a new star in 1572 and a comet in 1577, the traditional view that the universe was unchanging came into question. Brahe still rejected heliocentrism, but the assistant he employed when he moved to Prague in 1599, Johannes Kepler (1571–1630), was won over to the Copernican view. Kepler developed three laws of planetary motion, published between 1609 and 1619, that provided mathematical backing for heliocentrism and directly challenged the claim

Galileo's Phases of the Moon
Galileo drew what he saw in his telescope. His depiction showed a moon with hills and valleys, which contradicted the dominant view supported by the Catholic church that every body in the universe except the earth was perfect. (Biblioteca Nazionale Centrale, Florence, Italy/De Agostini Picture Library/ Bridgeman Images.)

long held, even by Copernicus, that planetary motion was circular. Kepler's first law stated that the orbits of the planets are ellipses, with the sun always at one focus of the ellipse.

The Italian astronomer Galileo Galilei (1564–1642) provided more evidence to support the heliocentric view and also challenged the doctrine that the heavens were perfect and unchanging. After learning in 1609 that two Dutch astronomers had built a telescope, Galileo built a better one and observed the earth's moon, four satellites of Jupiter, the phases of Venus (a cycle of changing physical appearances), and sunspots. The moon, the planets, and the sun were no more perfect than the earth, he insisted, and the shadows he could see on the moon could only be the product of hills and valleys like those on earth. Galileo portrayed the earth as a moving part of a larger system, only one of many planets revolving around the sun, not as the fixed center of a single, closed universe.

In 1616, the Catholic church forbade Galileo to teach that the earth moves; then, in 1633, it accused him of not obeying the earlier order (see Primary Source Analysis on page 526). Forced to appear before the Inquisition, he agreed to publicly recant his assertion about the movement of the earth to save himself from torture and death. Afterward, Galileo lived under house arrest and could publish his work only in the Dutch Republic, which had become a haven for scientists and thinkers who challenged conventional ideas.

In the same year that Copernicus challenged the traditional account in astronomy (1543), the Flemish scientist Andreas Vesalius (1514–1564) did the same for anatomy. Until then, medical knowledge in Europe was based on the writings of the second-century Greek physician Galen, Ptolemy's contemporary. Drawing on public dissections (which had been condemned by the Catholic church since 1300) he performed himself, Vesalius refuted Galen's work in his illustrated anatomical text, *On the Construction of the Human Body*. The English physician William Harvey (1578–1657) used dissection to examine the circulation of blood within the body, demonstrating how the heart worked as a pump. The heart and its valves were "a piece of machinery," Harvey insisted, and they obeyed mechanical laws. Nature, he said, could be understood by experiment and rational deduction, not by following traditional authorities.

Sentence Pronounced against Galileo (1633)

In 1633, the Roman Inquisition, a committee of cardinals of the Catholic church, considered the case against Galileo and pronounced its final judgment. It found Galileo guilty of heresy against Catholic doctrine for defending heliocentrism but allowed him to recant and thus avoid the death penalty usual in cases of heresy. Nearly 350 years later, in 1980, Pope John Paul II appointed a commission to review the evidence and verdict. After four years, the commission published its findings and concluded that the judges who condemned Galileo were wrong.

We say, pronounce, sentence, and declare that you, the above-mentioned Galileo, because of the things deduced in the trial and confessed by you as above, have rendered yourself according to this Holy Office [Inquisition] vehemently suspected of heresy, namely of having held and believed a doctrine which is false and contrary to the divine and Holy Scripture: that the sun is the center of the world and does not move from east to west, and the earth moves and is not the center of the world, and that one may hold and defend as probable an opinion after it has been declared and defined contrary to Holy Scripture. Consequently you have incurred all the censures and penalties imposed and promulgated by the sacred canons and all particular and general laws against such delinquents. We are willing to absolve you from them provided that first, with a sincere heart and unfeigned faith, in front of us you abjure, curse, and detest the above-mentioned errors and heresies, and every other error and heresy contrary to the Catholic and Apostolic Church, in the manner and form we will prescribe to you.

Furthermore, so that this serious and pernicious error and transgression of yours does not remain completely unpunished, and so that you will be more cautious in the future and an example for others to abstain from similar crimes, we order that the book *Dialogue* [*Dialogue Concerning the Two Chief World Systems*, published in 1632] by Galileo Galilei be prohibited by public edict.

Source: Maurice A. Finocchiaro, ed., *The Galileo Affair: A Documentary History* (Berkeley: University of California Press, 1989), 291.

QUESTION TO CONSIDER

Why did the Catholic church go to such dramatic lengths to repress Galileo's scientific argument in support of heliocentrism?

In the 1630s, the European intellectual elite began to accept the new scientific views. Ancient learning, the churches and their theologians, and long-standing popular beliefs all seemed to be undercut by the scientific method. Two men were chiefly responsible for spreading the reputation of the scientific method in the first half of the seventeenth century: the English Protestant politician Sir Francis Bacon (1561–1626) and the French Catholic mathematician and philosopher René Descartes (1596–1650). They represented the two essential halves of the scientific method: inductive reasoning through observation and experimental research, and deductive reasoning from self-evident principles.

In *The Advancement of Learning* (1605), Bacon attacked reliance on ancient writers and optimistically predicted that the scientific method would lead to social progress. The minds of the medieval scholars, he said, had been "shut up in the cells of a few authors (chiefly Aristotle, their dictator) as their persons were shut up in the cells of monasteries and colleges," and they could therefore produce only "cobwebs of learning" that were "of no substance or profit." Knowledge, in Bacon's view, must be empirically based (that is, gained by observation and experiment).

Although Descartes agreed with Bacon's denunciation of traditional learning, he was concerned that the attack on tradition might only replace the dogmatism of the churches with the skepticism of Montaigne—that nothing at all was certain. Descartes aimed to establish the new science on more secure philosophical foundations, those of mathematics and logic. In his *Discourse on Method* (1637), he argued that mathematical and mechanical principles provided the key to understanding all of nature, including the actions of people and states. All prior assumptions must be repudiated in favor of one elementary principle: "I think, therefore I am." Everything else could—and should—be doubted, but even doubt showed the certain existence of someone thinking. Descartes insisted that human reason could not only unravel the secrets of nature but also prove the existence of God. Although he hoped to secure the authority of both church and state, his reliance on human reason rather than faith irritated authorities, and his books were banned in many places. He moved to the Dutch Republic to work in peace. Scientific research, like economic growth, became centered in the northern, Protestant countries, where it was less constrained by church control than in the Catholic south.

The power of the new scientific method was dramatically confirmed in the grand synthesis of the laws of motion developed by the English natural philosopher Isaac Newton (1642–1727). Born five years after the publication of Descartes's *Discourse on Method* and educated at Cambridge University, where he later became a professor, Newton brought his most significant mathematical and mechanical discoveries together in his masterwork, *Principia Mathematica* (1687). In it, he developed his law of universal gravitation, which explained both movement on earth and the motion of the planets. His law held that every body in the universe exerts over every other body an attractive force directly proportional to the product of their masses and inversely proportional to the square of the distance between them. This law of universal gravitation explained Kepler's elliptical planetary orbits just as it accounted for the way an apple fell to the ground.

Newtonian physics combined mass, inertia, force, velocity, and acceleration—all key concepts in modern science—and made them quantifiable. Once set in motion, in Newton's view, the universe operated like a masterpiece made possible by the ingenuity of God. Newton saw no conflict between faith and science. He believed that by demonstrating that the physical universe followed rational principles, natural philosophers could prove the existence of God and so liberate humans from doubt and the fear of chaos. Even while laying the foundation for modern physics, optics, and mechanics, Newton spent long hours trying to calculate the date of the beginning of the world and its end with the second coming of Jesus. Others, less devout than Newton, envisioned a clockwork universe that had no need for God's continuing intervention.

The Natural Laws of Politics

In reaction to the religious wars, writers not only began to defend the primacy of state interests over those of religious conformity but also insisted on secular explanations for politics. The Italian political theorist Machiavelli had pointed in this direction with his advice to Renaissance princes in the early sixteenth century, but this secular intellectual movement gathered steam in the aftermath of the religious violence unleashed by the Reformation.

The French Catholic lawyer and politique Jean Bodin (1530–1596) sought systematic secular answers to the problem of disorder in *The Six Books of the Commonwealth* (1576). Comparing the different forms of government throughout history, he concluded that there were three basic types of sovereignty: monarchy, aristocracy, and democracy. Only strong monarchical power offered hope for maintaining order, he insisted, and so he rejected any doctrine of the right to resist tyrannical authority. While Bodin's ideas helped lay the foundation for absolutism—the idea that the monarch should be the sole and uncontested source of power—his systematic discussion of types of governments implied that they might be subject to choice and undercut the notion that monarchies were ordained by God, as most rulers maintained.

During the Dutch revolt against Spain, the legal scholar Hugo Grotius (1583–1645) furthered secular thinking by attempting to systematize the notion of "natural law"—laws of nature that give legitimacy to government and stand above the actions of any particular ruler or religious group. Grotius argued that natural law stood beyond the reach of either secular or divine authority; natural law would be valid even if God did not exist (though Grotius himself believed in God). By this account, natural law—not scripture, religious authority, or tradition—should govern politics. Such ideas got Grotius into trouble with both Catholics and Protestants. His work *The Laws of War and Peace* (1625) was condemned by the Catholic church, while the Dutch Protestant government arrested him for taking part in religious controversies. Grotius's wife helped him escape prison by hiding him in a chest of books. Grotius was one of the first to argue that international conventions should govern the treatment of prisoners of war and the making of peace treaties.

Grotius's conception of natural law also challenged the widespread use of torture. Most states and the courts of the Catholic church used torture when a serious crime had been committed and the evidence seemed to point to a particular defendant but no definitive proof had been established. The judges ordered torture—hanging the accused by the hands with a rope thrown over a beam or pressing the legs in a leg screw—to extract a confession, which had to be given with a medical expert and notary present and had to be repeated without torture.

To be in accord with natural law, Grotius argued, governments had to defend natural rights, which he defined as life, body, freedom, and honor. Grotius did not encourage rebellion in the name of natural law or rights, but did hope that someday all governments would adhere to these principles and stop killing their own and one another's subjects in the name of religion.

Natural law and natural rights would play an important role in the founding of constitutional governments from the 1640s forward and in the establishment of various charters of human rights in our own time.

The Arts in an Age of Crisis

Two new forms of artistic expression — professional theater and opera — provided an outlet for secular values in an age of conflict over religious beliefs. Religion still played an important role in painting, however, even though many rulers also commissioned paintings on secular subjects.

The first professional acting companies performed before paying audiences in London, Seville, and Madrid in the 1570s. A huge outpouring of playwriting followed upon the formation of permanent professional theater companies. The Spanish playwright Lope de Vega (1562–1635) alone wrote more than fifteen hundred plays. Theaters were extremely popular despite Puritan opposition in England and Catholic objections in Spain. Shopkeepers, apprentices, lawyers, and court nobles crowded into open-air theaters to see everything from bawdy farces to profound tragedies.

The most enduring and influential playwright of the time — in fact, the man considered the greatest playwright of the English language — was William Shakespeare (1564–1616), who wrote three dozen plays (including histories, comedies, and tragedies) and was a member of a chief acting troupe. Although none of Shakespeare's plays were set in contemporary England, they reflected the concerns of his age: the nature of power and the crisis of authority. His tragedies in particular show the uncertainty and even chaos that result when power is misappropriated or misused. In *Hamlet* (1601), for example, the Danish prince Hamlet's mother marries the man who murdered his royal father and usurped the crown. In the end, Hamlet, his mother, and the usurper all die. Like many real-life people, Shakespeare's tragic characters found little peace in the turmoil of their times.

Although painting did not always touch broad popular audiences in the ways that theater could, new styles in art and especially church architecture helped shape ordinary people's experience of religion. In the late sixteenth century, the artistic style known as mannerism emerged in the Italian states and soon spread across Europe. Mannerism was an almost theatrical style that allowed painters to distort perspective to convey a message or emphasize a theme. The most famous mannerist painter, called El Greco because he was of Greek origin, trained in Venice and Rome before he moved to Spain in the 1570s. The religious intensity of El Greco's paintings found a ready audience in Catholic Spain, which had proved immune to the Protestant suspicion of ritual and religious imagery (see the illustration on page 510).

The most important new style was the **baroque**, which, like mannerism, originated in the Italian states. In place of the Renaissance emphasis on harmonious design, unity, and clarity, the baroque featured curves, exaggerated lighting, intense emotions, release from restraint, and even a kind of

The Arts and Colonial Power
Even as the Spanish Habsburg rulers were losing ground in Europe, they were consolidating their control in their colonies. This detail from the Chapel of the Rosary of the Santo Domingo Church in Puebla, Mexico, reflects the extensive use of gold and the European style baroque decoration that was favored in the effort to convert indigenous peoples. Construction of the church began in 1571 but building of the chapel only began in the 1650s. It is still considered one of the most important heritage sites in the world. (Dome of the Capilla del Rosario, Santo Domingo Church, Puebla, Mexico/Jean-Pierre Courau/Bridgeman Images.)

artistic sensationalism. Like many other historical designations, the word *baroque* ("irregularly shaped") was not used as a label by people living at the time; art critics in the eighteenth century coined the word to mean shockingly bizarre, confused, and extravagant, and art historians and collectors largely disdained the baroque until the late nineteenth century.

Closely tied to Catholic resurgence after the Reformation, the baroque melodramatically reaffirmed the emotional depths of the Catholic faith and glorified both church and monarchy. The style spread from Rome to other Italian states and then into central Europe. The Spanish built baroque churches in their American colonies as part of their massive conversion campaign.

A new secular musical form, the opera, grew up parallel to the baroque style in the visual arts. First influential in the Italian states, opera combined music, drama, dance, and scenery in a grand sensual display, often with themes chosen to please the ruler and the aristocracy. Composers could base operas on typically baroque sacred subjects or on traditional stories. Like many playwrights, including Shakespeare, opera composers often turned to familiar stories their audiences would recognize and readily follow. One of the most innovative composers of opera was Claudio Monteverdi (1567–1643), whose earliest operatic production, *Orfeo* (1607), was based on Greek mythology.

Magic and Witchcraft

Although artists, political thinkers, and scientific experimenters increasingly pursued secular goals, most remained as devout in their religious beliefs as ordinary people. Many scholars, including Newton, studied alchemy alongside their scientific pursuits. Alchemists aimed to discover techniques for turning lead and copper into gold. The astronomer Tycho Brahe defended his studies of alchemy and astrology as part of "natural magic," as opposed to demonic "black magic."

Learned and ordinary people alike also firmly believed in witchcraft, that is, the exercise of magical powers gained by a pact with the devil. The same Jean Bodin who argued against religious fanaticism insisted on death

James VI, King of Scotland, Questioning Witches
James VI personally presided over trials of Scottish witches in 1591. Some of the accused were tortured to force them to confess and then executed. As the print suggests, most of the accused were women. James became James I of England in 1603. (Private Collection/Bridgeman Images.)

for witches—and for those magistrates who would not prosecute them. Trials of witches peaked in Europe between 1560 and 1640, the very time of the celebrated breakthroughs of the new science. Montaigne was one of the few to speak out against executing accused witches: "It is taking one's conjectures rather seriously to roast someone alive for them," he wrote in 1580.

Witches had long been blamed for destroying crops and causing personal catastrophes ranging from miscarriage to madness, but never before had they been officially persecuted in such numbers. Denunciation and persecution of witches coincided with the spread of reform, both Protestant and Catholic. Witch trials concentrated especially in the German lands of the Holy Roman Empire, the boiling cauldron of the Thirty Years' War.

The victims of the persecution were overwhelmingly female: women accounted for 80 percent of the accused witches in about 100,000 trials in Europe and North America during the sixteenth and seventeenth centuries. Half of those accused were sentenced to death. Since men had been equally subject to accusation before 1400, attention had clearly shifted to women. Some official descriptions of witchcraft oozed lurid details of sexual orgies, in which women acted as the devil's sexual slaves. Social factors help explain the prominence of women among the accused. Accusers were almost always better off than those they accused. The poorest and most socially marginal people in most communities were elderly spinsters and widows. Because they were thought likely to hanker after revenge on those more fortunate, they were singled out as witches.

The tide turned against witchcraft trials when physicians, lawyers, judges, and even clergy came to suspect that accusations were based on superstition and fear. In 1682, a French royal decree treated witchcraft as fraud and imposture, meaning that the law did not recognize anyone as a witch. In 1693, the jurors who had convicted twenty people of witchcraft in Salem, Massachusetts, recanted, claiming, "We justly fear that we were sadly deluded and mistaken." The Salem jurors had not stopped believing in witches; they had simply lost

REVIEW QUESTION
How could belief in witchcraft and the rising prestige of the scientific method coexist?

MAPPING THE WEST

The Religious Divisions of Europe, c. 1648

The Peace of Westphalia recognized major religious divisions within Europe that have endured for the most part to the present day. Catholicism dominated in southern Europe, Lutheranism had its stronghold in northern Europe, and Calvinism flourished along the Rhine River. In southeastern Europe, the Islamic Ottoman Turks accommodated the Greek Orthodox Christians under their rule but bitterly fought the Catholic Austrian Habsburgs for control of Hungary.

Analyzing the Map: Which parts of Europe remained most resolutely Catholic in 1648?

Making Connections: Which were the rising powers in Europe in 1648 and which the declining ones? Why was the Atlantic Ocean becoming more important in international affairs than the Mediterranean?

confidence in their ability to identify them. When physicians and judges had believed in witches and carried out official persecutions, with torture, those accused of witchcraft had gone to their deaths in record numbers. But when the same groups distanced themselves from popular beliefs, the trials and the executions stopped.

Conclusion

The witchcraft persecutions reflected the traumas of these times of religious war, economic decline, and crises of political and intellectual authority. Deep differences over religion came to a head in the Thirty Years' War (1618–1648), which cut a path of destruction through central Europe and involved most of the European powers. Repulsed by the effects of religious violence, European rulers agreed to a peace that effectively removed disputes between Catholics and Protestants from the international arena. Almost everywhere rulers emerged from these decades of war with expanded powers that they would seek to extend further in the second half of the seventeenth century. The constant extension of state power is one of the defining themes of modern history; religious warfare gave it a jump-start.

For all their strength, however, rulers could not control economic, social, or intellectual trends. The economic downturn of the seventeenth century shifted economic power from the Mediterranean world to northwestern Europe, because England, France, and the Dutch Republic suffered less from the fighting of the Thirty Years' War and recovered more quickly from bad times. They would become even more powerful in the decades to come.

An underlying shift in cultural attitudes and intellectual expectations accompanied these changes. Secularization encompassed the establishment of the scientific method as the standard of truth, the search for nonreligious foundations of political authority, and the growing popularity of nonreligious forms of art, such as theater and opera. Proponents of these changes did not renounce their religious beliefs, and it would be foolish to claim that everyone's mental universe changed. The significance of secularization would only emerge over the long term.

Chapter 15 Review

Key Terms and People

Be sure that you can identify the term or person and explain its historical significance.

Catherine de Médicis (p. 505)

Edict of Nantes (p. 507)

politiques (p. 507)

Philip II (p. 507)

Lepanto (p. 509)

Elizabeth I (p. 510)

Puritans (p. 510)

Peace of Westphalia (p. 515)

raison d'état (p. 517)

secularization (p. 523)

scientific method (p. 523)

heliocentrism (p. 524)

baroque (p. 529)

Review Questions

1. How did state power depend on religious unity at the end of the sixteenth century and start of the seventeenth?

2. Why did a war fought over religious differences result in stronger states?

3. What were the consequences of economic recession in the early 1600s?

4. How could belief in witchcraft and the rising prestige of the scientific method coexist?

Making Connections

1. How did the balance of power shift in Europe between 1560 and 1648? What were the main reasons for the shift?

2. What were the limits to the growth of secularization?

3. What was the influence of New World colonies on Europe from 1560 to 1648?

4. How did religious conflict mix with political concerns in this period?

Important Events

1562	French Wars of Religion begin
1566	Revolt of Calvinists against Spain begins in Netherlands
1569	Formation of commonwealth of Poland-Lithuania
1571	Battle of Lepanto marks victory of West over Ottomans at sea
1572	St. Bartholomew's Day Massacre of French Protestants
1576	Spanish Fury erupts in Antwerp
1588	English defeat of Spanish Armada
1598	French Wars of Religion end with Edict of Nantes
1601	William Shakespeare, *Hamlet*
1618	Thirty Years' War begins
1625	Hugo Grotius publishes *The Laws of War and Peace*
1633	Galileo Galilei forced to recant his support of heliocentrism
1635	French join the Thirty Years' War by declaring war on Spain
1648	Peace of Westphalia ends Thirty Years' War

Consider two events

Thirty Years' War begins (1618) and Hugo Grotius publishes *The Laws of War and Peace* (1625). How does the latter event represent an effort to grapple with the climate of religious violence?

534

Suggested References

Religious conflict, the Thirty Years' War, science, witchcraft, and the travails of everyday life have all been the subject of groundbreaking research, yet the personalities of individual rulers still make for great stories, too.

Braudel, Fernand. *The Mediterranean and the Mediterranean World in the Age of Philip the Second.* Trans. Siân Reynolds. 2 vols. 1972, 1973.

Daybell, Jame, and Norrhem, Svante, eds. *Gender and Political Culture in Early Modern Europe, 1400–1800.* 2016.

*Diefendorf, Barbara B. *The Saint Bartholomew's Day Massacre: A Brief History with Documents.* 2008.

Galileo Project: http://galileo.rice.edu

Geevers, Liesbeth, and Marini, Mirella, eds. *Dynastic Identity in Early Modern Europe: Rulers, Aristocrats and the Formation of Identities.* 2016.

Ginzburg, Carlo. *The Cheese and the Worms: The Cosmos of a Sixteenth-Century Miller.* 2013.

Goodare, Julian. *The European Witch-Hunt.* 2016.

*Jacob, Margaret. *The Scientific Revolution: A Brief History with Documents.* 2010.

Kupperman, Karen Ordahl. *The Atlantic in World History.* 2012.

Lynn, John A. *Women, Armies, and Warfare in Early Modern Europe.* 2008.

Madariaga, Isabel De. *Ivan the Terrible.* 2006.

Malcolm, Noel. *Agents of Empire: Knights, Corsairs, Jesuits and Spies in the Sixteenth-Century Mediterranean World.* 2015.

*Medick, Hans, and Benjamin Marschke. *Experiencing the Thirty Years War: A Brief History with Documents.* 2013.

Pitts, Vincent J. *Henri IV of France: His Reign and Age.* 2008.

Tracy, James D. *The Founding of the Dutch Republic: War, Finance, and Politics in Holland, 1572–1588.* 2008.

_____

*Primary source.

Absolutism, Constitutionalism, and the Search for Order

1640–1700

In May 1664, King Louis XIV of France organized the first of many spectacular entertainments for his court at Versailles, where he had recently begun construction of a magnificent new palace. More than six hundred members of his court attended the weeklong series of parades, races, ballets, plays, and fireworks. In the opening spectacle, Louis was accompanied by an eighteen-foot-high float in the form of a chariot dedicated to Apollo, Greek god of the sun and Louis's personally chosen emblem. The king's favorite writers and musicians presented works specially prepared for the occasion, and each evening ended with a candlelit banquet served by masked and costumed servants.

Louis XIV designed his pageants to awe those most dangerous to him, the leading nobles of his kingdom. To make his authority and glory concrete, the king relentlessly increased the power of his bureaucracy, expanded his army, and insisted on Catholic orthodoxy. This model of state building was known as **absolutism**, a system of government in which the ruler claims sole and uncontestable power. Other mid-seventeenth-century rulers followed Louis XIV's example or explicitly rejected it, but they could not afford to ignore it.

Although absolutism exerted great influence beginning in the mid-1600s, it faced competition from **constitutionalism**, a system in which the ruler shares power with an assembly of elected representatives. Constitutionalism provided a strong foundation for state power in England, the Dutch Republic, and the British North American colonies,

«Louis Entertaining at Versailles in 1664 Louis XIV used ballets and other court entertainments to demonstrate his power. He sometimes played roles himself but in this etching by Israël Silvestre he is shown sitting in the highest seat among his chosen courtiers. The pageants of 1664 set the tone for the rest of his reign. (Heritage Images/Getty Images.)

while absolutism dominated in central and eastern Europe. Constitutionalism triumphed in England, however, only after one king had been executed as a traitor and another had been deposed. The English conflicts over the nature of authority found their most enduring expression in the writings of Thomas Hobbes and John Locke, which laid the foundations of modern political science.

The search for order took place not only in government and politics but also in intellectual, cultural, and social life. Artists sought means of glorifying power and expressing order and symmetry in new ways. As states consolidated their power, elites endeavored to distinguish themselves more clearly from the lower orders. Officials, clergy, and laypeople worked to reform the poor, now seen as a major source of disorder. Whether absolutist or constitutionalist, seventeenth-century states all aimed to extend control over their subjects' lives.

Louis XIV: Absolutism and Its Limits

French king **Louis XIV** (r. 1643–1715) personified the absolutist ruler, who in theory shared his power with no one. In 1655, he reputedly told the Paris high court of justice, *"L'état, c'est moi"* ("I am the state"), emphasizing that state authority rested in him personally. Louis cleverly manipulated the affections and ambitions of his courtiers, chose as his ministers middle-class men who owed everything to him, built up Europe's largest army, and snuffed out every hint of religious or political opposition. Yet the absoluteness of his power should not be exaggerated. Like all other rulers of his time, Louis depended on the cooperation of many people: local officials who enforced his decrees, peasants and artisans who joined his armies and paid his taxes, clergy who preached his notion of Catholicism, and nobles who joined court festivities rather than causing trouble.

CHAPTER FOCUS

What were the most important differences between absolutism and constitutionalism, and how did each system establish order?

CHAPTER TIMELINE

1642–1646
English civil war between Charles I and Parliament

1649
Charles I of England executed; new Russian legal code assigns all to hereditary class

1660
Monarchy restored in England

1635   **1645**   **1660**

1648
Peace of Westphalia ends Thirty Years' War; Fronde revolt challenges royal authority in France; Ukrainian Cossack warriors rebel against king of Poland-Lithuania; Spain formally recognizes independence of Dutch Republic

1651
Thomas Hobbes publishes *Leviathan*

The Fronde, 1648–1653

Louis XIV's absolutism (see Terms of History on page 540) built on a long French tradition of increasing centralization of state authority, but before he could establish his preeminence he had to weather a series of revolts known as the Fronde. Louis was only five when he came to the throne in 1643 upon the death of his father, Louis XIII, who with his chief minister, Cardinal Richelieu, had steered France through increasing involvement in the Thirty Years' War, rapidly climbing taxes, and innumerable tax revolts. Louis XIV's mother, Anne of Austria, and her Italian-born adviser and rumored lover, Cardinal Mazarin (1602–1661), ruled in the young monarch's name.

To meet the financial pressure of fighting the Thirty Years' War, Mazarin sold new offices, raised taxes, and forced creditors to extend loans to the government. In 1648, a coalition of his opponents presented him with a charter of demands that, if granted, would have given the parlements (high courts) a form of constitutional power with the right to approve new taxes. Mazarin responded by arresting the leaders of the parlements. He soon faced a series of revolts.

Fearing for the young king's safety, his mother took Louis and fled Paris. With civil war threatening, Mazarin and Anne agreed to compromise with the parlements. The nobles saw an opportunity to reassert their claims to power against the weakened monarchy and demanded greater local control. Leading noblewomen often played key roles in the opposition to Mazarin, carrying messages and forging alliances, especially when male family members were in prison. While the nobles sought to regain power and local influence, the middle and lower classes chafed at the repeated tax increases. Conflicts erupted throughout the kingdom as nobles, parlements, and city councils all raised their own armies to fight either the crown or one another. The urban poor, such as those in the southwestern city of Bordeaux, sometimes revolted as well.

Mazarin and Anne eventually got the upper hand because their opponents failed to maintain unity in fighting the king's forces. But Louis XIV never

1661	**1678**	**1685**	**1690**
Slave code set up in Barbados	Madame de Lafayette anonymously publishes *The Princess of Clèves*	Louis XIV revokes Edict of Nantes	John Locke publishes *Two Treatises of Government* and *Essay Concerning Human Understanding*

1665　　　　　　　　　　　　　**1680**　　　　　　　　　　　**1690**

1667	**1683**	**1688**
Louis XIV begins first of many wars that continue throughout his reign	Austrian Habsburgs break Turkish siege of Vienna	Parliament deposes James II; William, prince of Orange, and Mary take the throne

Absolutism

French king Louis XIV established the model of absolutism as a system of government without ever using the term itself. He had to constantly maneuver in order to centralize authority in his hands; he converted rebellious nobles into more docile courtiers, circumvented representative assemblies and high courts, and ruled as much as possible through hand-picked ministers who could be fired at will. Many of his counterparts in Europe also aimed to make their power absolute, that is, unlimited and unquestionable, but the term *absolutism* did not come into common usage until the 1800s. The only similar term used in the seventeenth and eighteenth centuries was *despotism*, which had entirely negative connotations because it was associated with tyranny, whereas eighteenth-century French writers such as Voltaire might refer to Louis XIV as "absolute master" in an entirely positive sense. Voltaire said of Louis XIV, "he showed that an absolute king, who wants to do good, easily accomplishes everything."[1]

By the middle of the 1800s French writers commonly referred to "the absolutism of Louis XIV" and English-language history books followed suit not long after. Having become a kind of cliché over the generations, it is perhaps not surprising that the term came into question in the 1980s and 1990s, not only in reference to France but also to central and eastern Europe. Some scholars argue that the term is anachronistic and that absolutism is a myth: the nobles did not lose their power and the state did not become truly bureaucratic. Power depended on elaborate networks of patronage that had an epicenter at the court but reached out through regional hubs to local areas, and these networks limited the ruler's ability to act unilaterally. The critics have won some points but have not carried the day. A new consensus seems to be forming that rulers faced growing fiscal demands, particularly the support of bigger armies, that prompted them to consolidate and, wherever possible, extend their powers in new ways. They may have utilized previous traditions of monarchy and faced obstacles in carrying out their designs, but the aim to centralize and expand the ruler's power reshaped politics and social life in many states.

[1] Voltaire, *Le siècle de Louis XIV*, 2 vols. (London, R. Dodsley, 1752), I: 80.

forgot the humiliation and uncertainty that marred his childhood. His own policies as ruler would be designed to prevent the recurrence of any such revolts. Yet, for all his success, peasants would revolt against the introduction of new taxes on at least five more occasions in the 1660s and 1670s, requiring tens of thousands of soldiers to reestablish order.

Court Culture as an Element of Absolutism

When Cardinal Mazarin died in 1661, Louis XIV, then twenty-two years old, decided to rule without a first minister. He described the dangers of his situation in memoirs he wrote later for his son's instruction: "Everywhere was disorder. My Court as a whole was still very far removed from the sentiments in which I trust you will find it." Louis listed many other problems in the kingdom, but none occupied him more than his attempts to control France's leading nobles, some of whom came from families that had opposed him militarily during the Fronde.

The French nobles had long exercised local authority by maintaining their own fighting forces, meting out justice on their estates, arranging jobs for underlings, and resolving their own conflicts through dueling. Louis set out to domesticate the warrior nobles by replacing violence with court ritual, such as the festivities at Versailles described at the beginning of this chapter. Using a systematic policy of bestowing pensions, offices, honors, gifts, and the threat of disfavor or punishment, Louis induced the nobles to cooperate with him. The aristocracy increasingly vied for his favor and in the process became his clients, dependent on him for advancement. Great nobles competed for the honor of holding his shirt when he dressed, foreign ambassadors squabbled for places near him, and royal mistresses basked in the glow of his personal favor (see Primary Source Analysis on page 542). Far from the court, however, nobles could still make considerable trouble for the king, and royal officials learned to compromise with them.

Those who did come to the king's court were kept on their toes. The preferred styles of behavior changed without notice, and the tiniest lapse in attention to etiquette could lead to ruin. Marie-Madeleine Pioche de La Vergne, known as Madame de Lafayette, described the court in her novel *The Princess of Clèves* (1678): "The Court gravitated around ambition. . . . Everybody was busily trying to better his or her position by pleasing, by helping, or by hindering somebody else."

Louis XIV appreciated the political uses of every form of art. Calling himself the Sun King, after Apollo, Louis stopped at nothing to burnish this radiant image. He played Apollo in ballets performed at court; posed for portraits with the emblems of Apollo (laurel, lyre, and tripod); and adorned his palaces with statues of the god. He also emulated the style and methods of ancient Roman emperors. At a celebration for the birth of his first son in 1662, Louis dressed in Roman attire, and many engravings and paintings showed him as a Roman emperor.

The king gave pensions to artists who worked for him and sometimes protected writers from clerical critics. The most famous of these writers was the playwright Molière (the pen name of Jean-Baptiste Poquelin, 1622–1673), whose comedy *Tartuffe* (1664) made fun of religious hypocrites and was loudly condemned by church leaders. Louis forced Molière to delay public performances of the play after its premiere at the festivities of May 1664 but resisted calls for his dismissal. Louis's ministers set up royal academies of dance, painting, architecture, music, and science. The government regulated the number and locations of theaters and closely censored all forms of publication.

Louis commissioned operas to celebrate royal marriages and military victories. His favorite composer, Jean-Baptiste Lully, wrote sixteen operas for court performances as well as many ballets. Playwrights often presented their new plays first to the court. Pierre Corneille and Jean Racine wrote tragedies set in Greece or Rome that celebrated the new aristocratic virtues that Louis aimed to inculcate: a reverence for order and self-control. All the characters were regal or noble, all the language lofty, all the behavior aristocratic.

PRIMARY SOURCE ANALYSIS

Marie de Sévigné, Letter Describing the French Court (1675)

Marie de Rabutin-Chantal, marquise de Sévigné (1626–1696), was the most famous letter writer of her time. A noblewoman born in Paris, she frequented court circles and wrote about her experiences to her friends and relatives, especially her daughter. Although not published in her lifetime, her letters soon gained fame and were copied and read by those in her circle. She wrote her later letters with this audience in mind and so downplayed her own personal feelings, except those of missing her daughter, to whom she was deeply attached. This letter from 1675 to her daughter recounts court intrigue surrounding Louis XIV's mistress and the shock when one of France's leading generals was killed in battle. Though Sévigné enjoyed spending time at Louis XIV's court, she could also write about it with biting wit.

They [the king and his court] were to set off today for Fontainebleau [one of the king's castles near Paris], where the entertainments were to become boring by their very multiplicity. Everything was ready when a bolt fell from the blue that shattered the joy. The populace says it is on account of *Quantova* [Sévigné's nickname for the king's mistress, Madame de Montespan, with whom Louis XIV fathered seven children], the attachment is still intense. Enough fuss is being made to upset the curé [priest] and everybody else, but perhaps not enough for her, for in her visible triumph there is an underlying sadness. You talk of the pleasures of Versailles, and at the time when they were off to Fontainebleau to plunge into joys, lo and behold M. De Turenne [commander of the French armies during the Dutch War] killed, general consternation, Monsieur le Prince [de Condé, another leading general], rushing off to Germany, France in desolation. Instead of seeing the end of the campaigns and having your brother back [Sévigné's son served in the army], we don't know where we are. There you have the world in its triumph and, since you like them, surprising events.

Source: *Madame de Sévigné: Selected Letters*, trans. Leonard Tancock (New York: Penguin, 1982), 165.

QUESTION TO CONSIDER

How did Turenne's death reflect the limits to which order could be imposed by Louis XIV?

Louis glorified his image as well through massive public works projects. Veterans' hospitals and new fortified towns on the frontiers represented his military might. Urban improvements, such as the reconstruction of the Louvre palace in Paris, proved his wealth. But his most ambitious project was the construction of a new palace at Versailles, twelve miles from the turbulent capital.

Building began in the 1660s. By 1685, the frenzied effort had engaged thirty-six thousand workers, not including the thousands of troops who diverted a local river to supply water for pools and fountains. The gardens designed by landscape architect André Le Nôtre reflected the spirit of Louis XIV's rule: their geometrical arrangements and clear lines showed that art and design could tame nature and that order and control defined the exercise of power. Versailles symbolized Louis's success at reining in the nobility and dominating Europe, and other monarchs eagerly mimicked French fashion and often conducted their business in French.

Yet for all its apparent luxury and frivolity, life at Versailles was often cramped and cold. Fifteen thousand people crowded into the palace's

Louis XIV as Apollo
King Louis XIV used every possible means to strengthen his image as an all-powerful "sun king." In the 1660s, he commissioned this gouache (a kind of watercolor painting) from Swiss artist Joseph Werner for the new Versailles palace. The painting is an allegory; no one thought that Louis was actually Apollo, but the painting makes viewers think of the king as like a Greek god, in this case driving the chariot that stands for the sun's movement in the skies. It is preceded by a female allegory for the dawn of the day. (Triumph of King Louis XIV of France driving the Chariot of the Sun preceded by Aurora, by Joseph Werner [1637–1710]/Chateau de Versailles, France/Bridgeman Images.)

apartments, including all the highest military officers, the ministers of state, and the separate households of each member of the royal family. Refuse collected in the corridors during the incessant building, and thieves and prostitutes overran the grounds. By the time Louis actually moved from the Louvre to Versailles in 1682, he had reigned as monarch for thirty-nine years. After his wife's death in 1683, he secretly married his mistress, Françoise d'Aubigné, marquise de Maintenon, and conducted most state affairs from her apartments at the palace. She inspired Louis XIV to increase his devotion to Catholicism.

Enforcing Religious Orthodoxy

Louis believed that he reigned by divine right. As Bishop Jacques-Bénigne Bossuet (1627–1704) explained: "We have seen that kings take the place of God, who is the true father of the human species. We have also seen that the first idea of power which exists among men is that of the paternal power; and that kings are modeled on fathers." The king, like a father, should instruct his subjects in the true religion, or at least make sure that others did so.

Louis's campaign for religious conformity first focused on the Jansenists, Catholics whose doctrines and practices resembled some aspects of Protestantism. Following the posthumous publication of the book *Augustinus* (1640) by the Flemish theologian Cornelius Jansen (1585–1638), the Jansenists stressed the need for God's grace in achieving salvation. They emphasized the importance of original sin and resembled the English Puritans in their austere religious practice. Prominent among the Jansenists was Blaise Pascal (1623–1662), a mathematician of genius, who wrote his *Provincial Letters* (1656–1657) to defend Jansenism against charges of heresy. Many judges in the parlements likewise endorsed Jansenist doctrine. Louis rejected any doctrine that gave priority to considerations of individual conscience over the demands of the official church hierarchy. Therefore, in 1660, he began enforcing various papal bulls (decrees) against Jansenism and closed down Jansenist theological centers.

Protestants posed an even greater obstacle to religious conformity. After many years of escalating pressure on the Calvinist Huguenots, Louis decided to eliminate all of the Calvinists' rights. Louis considered the Edict of Nantes (1598), by which his grandfather Henry IV granted the Protestants religious freedom and a degree of political independence, a temporary measure, and he fervently hoped to reconvert the Huguenots to Catholicism. In 1685, his **revocation of the Edict of Nantes** closed Calvinist churches and schools, forced all pastors to leave the country, and ordered the conversion of all Calvinists. Children of Calvinists could be taken away from their parents and raised Catholic. Tens of thousands of Huguenots responded by illegally fleeing to England, Brandenburg-Prussia, the Dutch Republic, or North America. Protestant European countries were shocked by this crackdown on religious dissent and would cite it in justification of their wars against Louis.

Extending State Authority at Home and Abroad

Louis XIV could not have enforced his religious policies without the services of a nationwide bureaucracy. **Bureaucracy**—a network of state officials carrying out orders according to a regular and routine line of authority—comes from the French word *bureau*, for "desk," which came to mean "office," both in the sense of a physical space and a position of authority. Louis personally supervised the activities of his bureaucrats and worked to ensure his supremacy in all matters. But he always had to negotiate with nobles and local officials who sometimes thwarted his will.

Louis extended the bureaucratic forms his predecessors had developed, especially the use of intendants. He handpicked an intendant for each region to represent his rule against entrenched local interests such as the parlements, provincial estates, and noble governors. The intendants supervised the collection of taxes, the financing of public works, and the provisioning of the army. In 1673, Louis decreed that the parlements could no longer vote against his proposed laws or even speak against them.

To keep tabs on all the issues before him, Louis relied on a series of talented ministers, usually of modest origins, who gained fame, fortune, and even noble status from serving the king. Most important among them was Jean-Baptiste Colbert (1619–1683), a wool merchant's son turned royal official. Colbert had managed Mazarin's personal finances and worked his way up under Louis XIV to become head of royal finances, public works, and the navy. He provided the king with pocket account books bound in red leather so that Louis could study the kingdom's finances for himself.

Colbert used the bureaucracy to establish a new economic doctrine, **mercantilism**. According to mercantilist policy, governments must intervene to increase national wealth by whatever means possible. Such government intervention inevitably increased the number of bureaucrats needed. Under Colbert, the French government established overseas trading companies and granted manufacturing monopolies. A government inspection system regulated the quality of finished goods and compelled all craftsmen to organize into guilds, in which masters could supervise the work of the journeymen and apprentices. To protect French production, Colbert rescinded many internal customs fees but enacted high foreign tariffs, which cut imports of competing goods. To compete more effectively with England and the Dutch Republic, Colbert also subsidized shipbuilding, a policy that dramatically expanded the number of seaworthy French vessels. Such mercantilist measures aimed to ensure France's prominence in world markets and to provide the resources needed to fight wars against the nation's increasingly long list of enemies. Although later economists questioned the value of mercantilism, virtually every government in Europe embraced it.

Colbert's mercantilist projects shaped life in the French colonies, too. He forbade colonial businesses from manufacturing anything already produced in mainland France. In 1663, he took control of the trading company that had founded New France (Canada). With the goal of establishing permanent settlements like those in the British North American colonies, he transplanted several thousand peasants from western France to the present-day province of Quebec, which France had claimed since 1608. He also tried to limit expansion westward, without success.

Despite the Iroquois' initial interruption of French fur-trading convoys, fur trader Louis Jolliet and Jesuit missionary Jacques Marquette reached the upper Mississippi River in 1672 and traveled downstream as far as Arkansas. In 1684, French explorer Sieur de La Salle went all the way down to the Gulf of Mexico, claiming a vast territory for Louis XIV and calling it Louisiana after him. Colbert's successors embraced the expansion he had resisted, thinking it crucial to competing successfully with the English and the Dutch in the New World.

Colonial settlement occupied only a portion of Louis XIV's attention, however, for his main foreign policy goal was to extend French power in Europe. To expand the army, Louis's minister of war centralized the organization of French troops. Barracks built in major towns received supplies—among which were uniforms to reinforce discipline—from a central distribution system. Louis's wartime army could field a force as large as that of all his enemies combined.

Absolutist governments always tried to increase their territorial holdings, and as Louis extended his reach, he gained new enemies. In

Wars of Louis XIV

1667–1668   **War of Devolution**

Enemies: Spain, Dutch Republic, England, Sweden

Ended by Treaty of Aix-la-Chapelle in 1668, with France gaining towns in Spanish Netherlands (Flanders)

1672–1678   **Dutch War**

Enemies: Dutch Republic, Spain, Holy Roman Empire

Ended by Treaty of Nijmegen, 1678–1679, which gave several towns in Spanish Netherlands and Franche-Comté to France

1688–1697   **War of the League of Augsburg**

Enemies: Holy Roman Empire, Sweden, Spain, England, Dutch Republic

Ended by Treaty of Rijswijk, 1697, with Louis returning all his conquests made since 1678 except Strasbourg

1701–1713   **War of the Spanish Succession**

Enemies: Holy Roman Empire, England, Dutch Republic, Prussia

Ended by Peace of Utrecht, 1713–1714, with Louis ceding territories in North America to the British

1667–1668, in the War of Devolution (so called because Louis claimed that lands in the Spanish Netherlands should devolve to him since the Spanish king had failed to pay the dowry of Louis's Spanish bride), Louis defeated the Spanish armies but had to make peace when England, Sweden, and the Dutch Republic joined the war. In the Treaty of Aix-la-Chapelle in 1668, he gained control of a few towns on the border of the Spanish Netherlands.

In 1672, Louis XIV opened hostilities against the Dutch because they stood in the way of his acquisition of more territory in the Spanish Netherlands. He declared war again on Spain in 1673. By now the Dutch had allied themselves with their former Spanish masters to hold off the French. Louis also marched his troops into territories of the Holy Roman Empire, provoking many of the German princes to join with the emperor, the Spanish, and the Dutch in an alliance against Louis, whom they now denounced as a "Christian Turk" for his imperialist ambitions. Faced with bloody but inconclusive results on the battlefield, the parties agreed to the Treaty of Nijmegen of 1678–1679, which ceded several Flemish towns and the Franche-Comté region to Louis, linking Alsace to the rest of France. French government deficits soared, and in 1675 increases in taxes touched off the most serious antitax revolt of Louis's reign.

Louis had no intention of standing still. Heartened by the Habsburgs' seeming weakness, he pushed eastward, seizing the city of Strasbourg in 1681 and invading the province of Lorraine in 1684. In 1688, he attacked some of the small German cities of the Holy Roman Empire. So obsessed was Louis with his military standing that he had miniature battle scenes painted on his high heels and commissioned tapestries showing his military processions into conquered cities, even those he did not take by force. It took a large coalition known as the League of Augsburg—made up of England, Spain, Sweden, the Dutch Republic, the Austrian emperor, and various German princes—to hold back the French king. When hostilities between Louis and the League of Augsburg ended in the Treaty of Rijswijk in 1697, Louis returned many of his conquests made since 1678, with the exception of Strasbourg (Map 16.1).

Four years later, Louis embarked on his last and most damaging war, the War of the Spanish Succession (1701–1713). It was caused by disagreement over who would inherit the throne of Spain. Before he died, Spanish king Charles II (r. 1665–1700) named Louis XIV's second grandson—Philip, duke of Anjou—as his heir, but the Austrian emperor Leopold I refused to agree and the British and the Dutch supported his refusal. In the ensuing war, the French lost several major battles and had to accept disadvantageous terms in the Peace of Utrecht of 1713–1714. France ceded possessions in North America (Newfoundland, the Hudson Bay area, and most of Nova Scotia) to Britain. Although Philip was recognized as king of Spain, he had to renounce any future claim to the French crown, thus barring unification of the two kingdoms. Spain surrendered its territories in Italy and the Netherlands to the Austrians, and Gibraltar to the British. Lying on his deathbed in 1715, the seventy-six-year-old Louis XIV watched helplessly as his accomplishments began to unravel.

MAP 16.1 Louis XIV's Acquisitions, 1668–1697 Every ruler in Europe hoped to extend his or her territorial control, and war was often the result. Louis XIV steadily encroached on the Spanish Netherlands to the north and the lands of the Holy Roman Empire to the east. Although coalitions of European powers reined in Louis's grander ambitions, he nonetheless incorporated many neighboring territories into the French crown.

Louis XIV's policy of absolutism fomented bitter hostility among his own subjects. Critics complained about the secrecy of Louis's government, and nobles resented his promotions of commoners to high office. Louis de Rouvroy, Duke of Saint-Simon, complained that "falseness, servility, admiring glances, combined with a dependent and cringing attitude, above all, an appearance of being nothing without him, were the only ways of pleasing him." Ordinary people suffered the most for Louis's ambitions. By the end of the Sun King's reign, one in six Frenchmen had served in the military. In addition to the higher taxes paid by everyone, those who lived on the routes leading to the battlefields had to house and feed soldiers; only nobles were exempt from this requirement.

REVIEW QUESTION
How "absolute" was the power of Louis XIV?

Constitutionalism in England

Of the two models of state building—absolutism and constitutionalism—the first seemed unquestionably more powerful because Louis XIV could raise such large armies and tax his subjects without much consultation. In the end, however, Louis could not defeat the coalition led by England's constitutional monarch. Constitutionalism had its own distinctive strengths, which came from the ruler sharing power through a representative assembly such as the English houses of Parliament. But the English rulers themselves hoped to follow Louis XIV's lead and install their own absolutist policies. Two revolutions, in 1642–1660 and 1688–1689, overturned two kings and confirmed the constitutional powers of an elected parliament, laying the foundation for the idea that government must guarantee certain rights to the people under the law.

England Turned Upside Down, 1642–1660

Disputes about the right to levy taxes and the nature of authority in the Church of England had long troubled the relationship between the English crown and Parliament. For more than a hundred years, wealthy English landowners had been accustomed to participating in government through Parliament and expected to be consulted on royal policy. Although England had no single constitutional document, it did have a variety of laws, judicial decisions, customary procedures, and charters and petitions granted by the king that all regulated relations between king and Parliament. When Charles I tried to assert his authority over Parliament, a civil war broke out. Some historians view the English civil war of 1642–1646 as the last great war of religion because it pitted Puritans against those trying to push the Church of England toward Catholicism; others see in it the first modern revolution because it gave birth to democratic political and religious movements.

When Charles I (r. 1625–1649) succeeded his father, James I, he faced an increasingly aggressive Parliament that resisted efforts to extend his personal control. In 1628, Parliament forced Charles to agree to the Petition of Right, by which he promised not to levy taxes without Parliament's consent. Charles hoped to avoid further interference with his plans by simply refusing to call Parliament into session between 1629 and 1640. Without it, the king's ministers had to find every loophole possible to raise revenues. They tried to turn "ship money," a levy on seaports in times of emergency, into an annual tax collected everywhere in the country. The crown won the ensuing court case, but many subjects still refused to pay what they considered to be an illegal tax.

Religious tensions brought conflicts over the king's authority to a head. With Charles's encouragement, the archbishop of Canterbury, William Laud (1573–1645), imposed increasingly elaborate ceremonies on the Church of England. Angered by these moves toward "popery," the Puritans responded with pamphlets and sermons filled with fiery denunciations. Laud then hauled them before the feared Court of Star Chamber, which the king personally controlled. The court ordered harsh sentences for Laud's Puritan critics; they were whipped, pilloried, branded, and even had their ears cut off and their noses split. When Laud tried to apply his policies to Scotland, however, they backfired completely: the stubborn Presbyterian Scots invaded the north of England in 1640. To raise money to fight the war, Charles called

Parliament into session and unwittingly opened the door to a constitutional and religious crisis.

The Parliament of 1640 did not intend revolution, but reformers in the House of Commons (the lower house of Parliament) wanted to undo what they saw as the royal tyranny of the 1630s. Parliament removed Laud from office, ordered the execution of an unpopular royal commander, abolished the Court of Star Chamber, repealed recently levied taxes, and provided for a parliamentary assembly at least once every three years, thus establishing a constitutional check on royal authority. Moderate reformers expected to stop there and resisted Puritan pressure to abolish bishops and eliminate the Church of England prayer book. The reformers also faced a rebellion in Ireland by native Catholics against the English and Scottish settlers who had taken over their lands. The reformers in Parliament feared that the Irish Catholics would make common cause with Charles to reestablish Catholicism as the religion of England and Scotland. Their hand was forced in January 1642, when Charles and his soldiers invaded Parliament and tried unsuccessfully to arrest those leaders who had moved to curb his power. Faced with mounting opposition within London, Charles quickly withdrew from the city and organized an army.

The ensuing civil war between king and Parliament lasted four years (1642–1646) and divided the country (see Contrasting Views on pages 550–551). The king's army of royalists, known as Cavaliers, enjoyed the most support in northern and western England. The parliamentary forces, called Roundheads because they cut their hair short, had their stronghold in the southeast, including London. Although Puritans dominated on the parliamentary side, they were divided among themselves about the proper form of church government: the Presbyterians wanted a Calvinist church with some central authority, whereas the Independents favored entirely autonomous congregations free from other church government (hence the term *congregationalism*, often associated with the Independents). The Puritans put aside their differences for the sake of military unity and united under an obscure member of the House of Commons, the country gentleman Oliver Cromwell (1599–1658), who sympathized with the Independents. After Cromwell skillfully reorganized the parliamentary troops, his New Model Army defeated the Cavaliers at the battle of Naseby in 1645. Charles surrendered in 1646.

Although the civil war between king and Parliament had ended in victory for Parliament, divisions within the Puritan ranks now came to the fore: the Presbyterians dominated Parliament, but the Independents controlled the army. The disputes between the leaders drew lower-class groups into the debate. When Parliament tried to disband the New Model Army in 1647, disgruntled soldiers protested. Called **Levellers** because of their insistence on leveling social differences, the soldiers took on their officers in a series of debates about the nature of political authority. The Levellers demanded that Parliament meet annually, that members be paid so as to allow common people to participate, and that all male heads of households be allowed to vote. Their ideal of political participation excluded servants, the propertyless, and women but offered access to artisans, shopkeepers, and modest farmers. Cromwell and

CONTRASTING VIEWS

The English Civil War

The civil war between Charles I and Parliament (1642–1646) excited furious debates about the proper forms of political authority, debates that influenced political thought for two centuries or more. The Levellers, who served in the parliamentary army, wanted Parliament to be more accountable to ordinary men like themselves (Document 1). In his statement rejecting Parliament's jurisdiction over him, Charles I reiterated the key positions of royalism (Document 2). Thomas Hobbes, in his famous political treatise Leviathan (1651), develops the consequences of the civil war for political theory (Document 3).

1. The Levellers, "The Agreement of the People, as Presented to the Council of the Army" (October 28, 1647)

Note especially two things about this document: (1) it focuses on Parliament as the chief instrument of reform, and (2) it claims that government depends on the consent of the people.

Since, therefore, our former oppressions and scarce-yet-ended troubles have been occasioned, either by want of frequent national meetings in Council [Parliament], or by rendering those meetings ineffectual, we are fully agreed and resolved to provide that hereafter our representatives be neither left to an uncertainty for the time nor made useless to the ends for which they are intended. In order whereunto we declare:—That the people of England, being at this day very unequally distributed by Counties, Cities, and Borough for the election of their deputies in Parliament, ought to be more indifferently [equally] proportioned according to the number of the inhabitants. . . . That the power of this, and all future Representatives of this Nation, is inferior only to theirs who choose them, and doth extend, without the consent or concurrence of any other person or persons [the king], to the enacting, altering, and repealing of laws,

to the erecting and abolishing of offices and courts, to the appointing, removing, and calling to account magistrates and officers of all degrees, to the making of war and peace, to the treating with foreign States [in other words, Parliament is the supreme power, not the king]. . . . These things we declare to be our native rights, and therefore are agreed and resolved to maintain them with our utmost possibilities against all opposition whatsoever.

Source: Samuel Rawson Gardiner, ed., *The Constitutional Documents of the Puritan Revolution, 1625–1660* (Oxford: Clarendon Press, 1906), 333–35.

2. Charles I's Rejection of the Jurisdiction of Parliament (1649)

In January 1649, the English Parliament voted to try Charles I for treason. Previous monarchs had been on occasion overthrown and murdered but never tried by an act of Parliament. Charles rejected the right of Parliament to try him and refused to enter a plea. He was nonetheless convicted and executed as a traitor.

Having already made my protestations, not only against the illegality of this pretended Court, but also, that no earthly power can justly call me (who am your King) in question as a delinquent, I would not any more open my mouth upon this occasion, more than to refer myself to what I have spoken, were I in this case alone concerned: but the duty I owe to God in the preservation of the true liberty of my people will not suffer me at this time to be silent: for, how can any free-born subject of England call life or anything he possesseth his own, if power without right daily make new, and abrogate the old fundamental laws of the land which I now take to be the present case! . . . There is no proceeding just against any man, but what is warranted either by God's laws or the municipal laws of the country where he lives. Now I am most

other army leaders rejected the Levellers' demands as threatening to property owners. Speaking to his advisers, Cromwell insisted, "You have no other way to deal with these men but to break them in pieces."

While political differences between Presbyterians and Independents helped spark new political movements, their conflicts over church organization

confident this day's proceeding cannot be warranted by God's laws; for, on the contrary, the authority of obedience unto Kings is clearly warranted, and strictly commanded in both the Old and New Testament, which, if denied, I am ready instantly to prove.

. . . Then for the law of this land, I am no less confident, that no learned lawyer will affirm that an impeachment can lie against the King, they all going in his name: and one of their maxims is, that the King can do no wrong. . . . And admitting, but not granting, that the people of England's commission could grant your pretended power, I see nothing you can show for that; for certainly you never asked the question of the tenth man in the kingdom, and in this way you manifestly wrong even the poorest ploughman, if you demand not his free consent. . . . Thus you see that I speak not for my own right alone, as I am your King, but also for the true liberty of all my subjects, which consists not in the power of government, but in living under such laws, such a government, as may give themselves the best assurance of their lives, and property of their goods.

Source: Samuel Rawson Gardiner, ed., *The Constitutional Documents of the Puritan Revolution, 1625–1660* (Oxford: Clarendon Press, 1906), 374–75.

3. Thomas Hobbes, *Leviathan* (1651)

In this excerpt, Hobbes depicts the anarchy of a society without a strong central authority, but he leaves open the question of whether that authority should be vested in "one Man" or "one Assembly of men," that is, a king or a parliament.

During the time men live without a common Power to keep them all in awe, they are in that condition which is called Warre [war]; and such a warre, as is of every man, against every man. . . . In such condition, there is no place for Industry; because the fruit thereof is un-

certain: and consequently no Culture of the Earth; no Navigation, nor use of the commodities that may be imported by Sea; no commodious Building; no Instrument of moving, and removing such things as require much force; no Knowledge of the face of the Earth; no account of Time; no Arts; no Letters; no Society; and which is worst of all, continuall feare, and danger of violent death; and the life of man, solitary, poore, nasty, brutish, and short. The only way to erect such a Common Power, as may be able to defend them from the invasion of Forraigners, and the injuries of one another, and thereby to secure them in such sort, as that by their owne industrie, and by the Fruites of the Earth, they may nourish themselves and live contentedly; is, to conferre all their power and strength upon one Man, or upon one Assembly of men, that may reduce all their wills, by plurality of voices, unto one Will. . . . This is more than Consent, or Concord; it is a reall Unitie of them all, in one and the same Person, made by Covenant of every man with every man. . . . This done, the Multitude so united in one Person, is called a COMMON-WEALTH, in latine CIVITAS. This is the Generation of that great LEVIATHAN, or rather (to speake more reverently) of that *Mortall God*, to which wee owe under the *Immortall God*, our peace and defence.

Source: Thomas Hobbes, *Leviathan*, eds. Richard E. Flathman and David Johnston (New York: Norton, 1997), 70, 95.

QUESTIONS TO CONSIDER

1. Why would both the king and the parliamentary leaders have found the Levellers' views disturbing?
2. What are the chief differences between the king's arguments and those of the Levellers and Hobbes?
3. Why did Hobbes's arguments about political authority upset supporters of both monarchy and Parliament?

fostered the emergence of new religious sects that emphasized the "inner light" of individual religious inspiration and a disdain for hierarchical authority. The Baptists, for example, insisted on adult baptism because they believed that Christians should choose their own church and that children should not automatically become members of the Church of England. The

Religious Society of Friends, who came to be called Quakers, demonstrated their beliefs in equality and the inner light by refusing to doff their hats to men in authority. Manifesting their religious experience by trembling, or "quaking," the Quakers believed that anyone—man or woman—inspired by a direct experience of God could preach. In keeping with their notions of equality and individual inspiration, many of the new sects provided opportunities for women to become preachers and prophets.

Parliamentary leaders feared that the new sects would overturn the whole social hierarchy. Some sects did advocate sweeping change. The Diggers promoted rural communism—collective ownership of all property. Seekers and Ranters questioned just about everything. One notorious Ranter, John Robins, even claimed to be God. A few men advocated free love. The political elite decided that tolerating the new sects would lead to skepticism, anarchism, and debauchery, and they therefore took measures to suppress the most radical ones.

The king tried to negotiate with the Presbyterians in Parliament, but Independents in the army purged the Presbyterians from Parliament in late 1648, leaving a "rump" of about seventy members. This Rump Parliament then created a high court to try Charles I. The court found him guilty of attempting to establish "an unlimited and tyrannical power" and pronounced a death sentence. On January 30, 1649, Charles was beheaded before an enormous crowd, which reportedly groaned as one when the ax fell. Although many had objected to Charles's autocratic rule, few had wanted him killed. For royalists, Charles immediately became a martyr, and reports of miracles, such as the curing of blindness by the touch of a handkerchief soaked in his blood, soon circulated.

The Rump Parliament abolished the monarchy and the House of Lords (the upper house of Parliament) and set up a Puritan republic with Oliver Cromwell as chairman of the Council of State. Cromwell did not tolerate dissent from his policies. When his agents discovered plans for mutiny within the army, they executed the perpetrators; new decrees silenced the Levellers. Although under Cromwell the various Puritan sects could worship rather freely and Jews with needed skills were permitted to return to England for the first time since the thirteenth century, Catholics could not worship publicly, nor could adherents of the Church of England use the Book of Common Prayer, thought to be too Catholic. The elites were troubled by Cromwell's religious policies but pleased to see some social order reestablished.

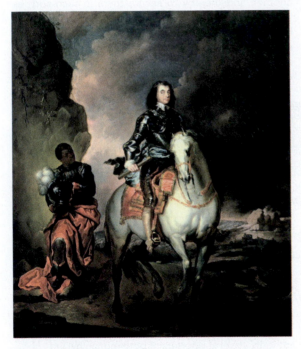

Portrait of Oliver Cromwell
In this painting by Thomas Wyck, Cromwell's pose on horseback mirrors that of King Charles I in a painting of 1633. Cromwell therefore appears quite literally as Charles's successor. The setting, however, is different. Cromwell is attended by a black servant with a backdrop that suggests North Africa. The artist may be referring to Cromwell's 1655 foray against the pirates who attacked English merchant ships from their headquarters on the Tunisian coast. Cromwell sent twenty ships to bombard the pirates' fortifications and destroy their fleet. (By Thomas Wyck [1616–1677]/Private Collection Photo © Philip Mould, Ltd., London/Bridgeman Images.)

The new regime aimed to extend state power just as Charles I had before. Cromwell laid the foundation for a Great Britain—made up of England, Ireland, and Scotland—by reconquering Scotland and brutally subduing Ireland. When his position was secured in 1649, Cromwell went to Ireland with a large force and easily defeated the rebels, massacring whole garrisons and their priests. He encouraged expropriating more lands of the Irish "barbarous wretches," and Scottish immigrants resettled the northern county of Ulster. This seventeenth-century English conquest left a legacy of bitterness that the Irish even today call "the curse of Cromwell."

In 1651, Parliament turned its attention overseas, putting mercantilist ideas into practice in the first Navigation Act, which allowed imports only if they were carried on English ships or came directly from the producers of goods. The Navigation Act was aimed at the Dutch, who dominated world trade; Cromwell tried to carry the policy further by waging naval war on the Dutch from 1652 to 1654.

At home, however, Cromwell faced growing resistance. His wars required a budget twice the size of that of Charles I, and his increases in property taxes and customs duties alienated landowners and merchants. The conflict reached a crisis in 1653: Parliament considered disbanding the army, whereupon Cromwell abolished the Rump Parliament in a military coup and made himself Lord Protector. He now silenced his critics by banning newspapers and using networks of spies to read mail and keep tabs on his enemies. Cromwell intended that his son should succeed him, but his death in 1658 only revived the prospect of civil war and political chaos. In 1660, a newly elected Parliament invited Charles II, the son of the executed king, to return from exile.

Restoration and Revolution Again

England's traditional monarchical form of government was restored in 1660 under Charles II (r. 1660–1685). More than a thousand Puritan ministers lost their positions, and attending a service other than one conforming with the Book of Common Prayer was illegal after 1664. Two natural disasters in quick succession posed new challenges. The plague struck in 1665, claiming more than thirty thousand victims in just a few months and forcing Charles and Parliament to flee from London. Then in 1666, the Great Fire swept the city. Some saw these disasters as punishment for the sins of the Cromwell era, others as an ill omen for Charles's reign.

Many in Parliament feared that Charles II wanted to emulate Louis XIV. In 1670, Charles made a secret agreement, soon leaked, with Louis in which he promised to announce his conversion to Catholicism in exchange for money for a war against the Dutch. Charles never proclaimed himself a Catholic, but in his Declaration of Indulgence (1673), he did suspend all laws against Catholics and Protestant dissenters. Parliament refused to continue funding the Dutch war unless Charles rescinded his Declaration of Indulgence. Asserting its authority further, Parliament passed the Test Act in 1673, requiring all government officials to profess allegiance to the Church of England

WHAT WOULD YOU DO?

If you were a member of the court set up to try Charles I, how would you have voted? Was he guilty of treason? Did he deserve execution? What kinds of issues would you consider in making your judgment?

Great Fire of London, 1666

This view of London shows the three-day fire at its height. The writer John Evelyn described the scene in his diary: "All the sky was of a fiery aspect, like the top of a burning oven, and the light seen above 40 miles round about for many nights. God grant mine eyes may never behold the like, who now saw above 10,000 houses all in one flame; the noise and cracking and thunder of people, the fall of towers, houses, and churches, was like an hideous storm." Everyone in London at the time felt overwhelmed by the catastrophe, and many deemed it God's punishment for the upheavals of the 1640s and 1650s. (© Museum of London, UK/Bridgeman Images.)

and in effect disavow Catholic doctrine. Then in 1678, Parliament precipitated the so-called Exclusion Crisis by explicitly denying the throne to a Roman Catholic. This action was aimed at the king's brother and heir, James, an open convert to Catholicism. Charles refused to allow it to become law.

The dynastic crisis over the succession of a Catholic gave rise to two distinct factions in Parliament: the Tories, who supported a strong, hereditary monarchy and the restored ceremony of the Church of England, and the Whigs, who advocated parliamentary supremacy and toleration of Protestant dissenters such as Presbyterians. Both labels were originally derogatory: *Tory* meant an Irish Catholic bandit; *Whig* was the Irish Catholic designation for a Presbyterian Scot. The Tories favored James's succession despite his Catholicism, whereas the Whigs opposed a Catholic monarch.

When James II (r. 1685–1688) succeeded his brother, he seemed determined to force Catholicism on his subjects. Tories and Whigs joined together when a male heir—who would take precedence over James's two adult Protestant daughters—was born to James's second wife, an Italian Catholic, in 1688. They invited the Dutch ruler **William, prince of Orange**, and his wife, James's older daughter, Mary, to invade England. Mary was brought up as a Protestant and was willing to act with her husband against her father's pro-Catholic policies. James fled to France, and Parliament offered the throne jointly to William (r. 1689–1702) and Mary (r. 1689–1694) on the condition that they accept a bill of rights guaranteeing Parliament's full partnership in a constitutional government.

In the Bill of Rights (1689), William and Mary agreed not to raise a standing army or to levy taxes without Parliament's consent. They also agreed to call meetings of Parliament at least every three years, to guarantee free elections to parliamentary seats, and to abide by Parliament's decisions. The agreement gave England's constitutional government a written, legal basis by formally recognizing Parliament as a self-contained, independent body that shared power with the rulers. Victorious supporters of the coup declared it the **Glorious Revolution** because it was achieved with so little bloodshed (at least in England).

The propertied classes who controlled Parliament prevented any resurgence of the popular turmoil of the 1640s. The Toleration Act of 1689 granted all Protestants freedom of worship, though non-Anglicans (those not in the Church of England) were still excluded from the universities; Catholics got no rights but were more often left alone to worship privately. When the Catholics in Ireland rose to defend James II, William and Mary's troops savagely suppressed them.

Social Contract Theory: Hobbes and Locke

Out of the turmoil of the English revolutions came a major rethinking of the foundations of all political authority. Although Thomas Hobbes and John Locke wrote in response to the upheavals of their times, they offered opposing arguments that were applicable to any place and any time, not just England of the seventeenth century. Hobbes justified absolute authority; Locke provided the rationale for constitutionalism. Yet both argued that all authority came not from divine right but from a **social contract** among citizens.

Thomas Hobbes (1588–1679) was a royalist who sat out the English civil war of the 1640s in France, where he tutored the future king Charles II. Returning to England in 1651, Hobbes published his masterpiece, *Leviathan*, in which he argued for unlimited authority in a ruler. Absolute authority could be vested in either a king or a parliament; it had to be absolute, Hobbes insisted, in order to overcome the defects of human nature. Believing that people are essentially self-centered and driven by the "right to self-preservation," Hobbes made his case by referring to science, not religion. To Hobbes, human life in a state of nature—that is, any situation without firm authority—was "solitary, poor, nasty, brutish, and short." Only the assurance of social order could make people secure enough to act according to law; consequently, giving up personal liberty, he maintained, was the price of collective security. Rulers derived their power, he concluded, from a contract in which absolute authority protects people's rights.

Hobbes's notion of rule by an absolute authority left no room for political dissent or nonconformity, and it infuriated both royalists and supporters of Parliament. He enraged his fellow royalists by arguing that authority came not from divine right but from the social contract. Parliamentary supporters resisted Hobbes's claim that rulers must possess absolute authority to prevent the greater evil of anarchy. Like Machiavelli before him, Hobbes became associated with a cynical, pessimistic view of human nature, and future political theorists often began their arguments by refuting Hobbes.

Rejecting both Hobbes and the more traditional royalist defenses of absolute authority, John Locke (1632–1704) used the notion of a social contract to provide a foundation for constitutionalism. Locke experienced political life firsthand as physician, secretary, and intellectual companion to the earl of Shaftesbury, a leading English Whig. In 1683, during the Exclusion Crisis, Locke fled with Shaftesbury to the Dutch Republic. There he continued work on his *Two Treatises of Government*, which, when published in 1690, served to justify the revolution of 1688. Locke's position was thoroughly anti-absolutist. He denied the divine right of kings and ridiculed the common royalist idea that political power in the state mirrored the father's authority in the family. Like Hobbes, he posited a state of nature that applied to all people. Unlike Hobbes, however, he thought people were reasonable and the state of nature peaceful.

Locke insisted that government's only purpose was to protect life, liberty, and property, a notion that linked economic and political freedom. Ultimate authority rested in the will of a majority of men who owned property, and government should be limited to its basic purpose of protection. A ruler who failed to uphold his part of the social contract between the ruler and the populace could be justifiably resisted, an idea that would become crucial for the leaders of the American Revolution a century later. For England's seventeenth-century landowners, however, Locke helped validate a revolution that consolidated their interests and ensured their privileges in the social hierarchy.

Locke defended his optimistic view of human nature in the immensely influential *Essay Concerning Human Understanding* (1690). He denied the existence of any innate ideas and asserted instead that each human is born with a mind that is a tabula rasa (blank slate). Not surprisingly, Locke devoted considerable energy to rethinking educational practices; he believed that education shaped the human personality by channeling all sensory experience. Everything humans know, he claimed, comes from sensory experience, not from anything inherent in human nature. Although Locke himself owned shares in the Royal African Company and justified slavery, his writings were later used by abolitionists in their campaign against slavery.

REVIEW QUESTION
What differences over religion and politics caused the conflict between king and Parliament in England?

Outposts of Constitutionalism

When William and Mary came to the throne in England in 1689, the Dutch and the English put aside the rivalries that had brought them to war against each other in 1652–1654, 1665–1667, and 1672–1674. The English and Dutch had much in common: oriented toward commerce, especially overseas, they both had developed representative forms of government. Also among the few outposts of constitutionalism in the seventeenth century were the British North American colonies, which developed representative government while the English were preoccupied with their revolutions at home. Constitutionalism was not the only factor shaping this Atlantic world; as constitutionalism developed in the colonies, so, too, did the enslavement of black Africans as a new labor force.

The Dutch Republic

When the Dutch Republic gained formal independence from Spain in 1648, it had already established a decentralized, constitutional state. Rich merchants called regents effectively controlled the internal affairs of each province and (through the States General) chose the *stadholder*, the executive officer responsible for defense and for representing the state at all ceremonial occasions. They almost always picked one of the princes of the house of Orange, but the stadholder resembled a president more than a king.

The Dutch Republic soon became Europe's financial capital. Praised for their industriousness, thrift, and cleanliness—and maligned as greedy, dull, and fat—the Dutch dominated overseas commerce with their shipping (Map 16.2). They imported products from all over the world: spices, tea, and silk from Asia; sugar and tobacco from the Americas; wool from England and Spain; timber and furs from Scandinavia; grain from eastern Europe. A widely reprinted history of Amsterdam that appeared in 1662 described the city as "risen through the hand of God to the peak of prosperity and greatness. . . . The whole world stands amazed at its riches and from east and west, north and south they come to behold it."

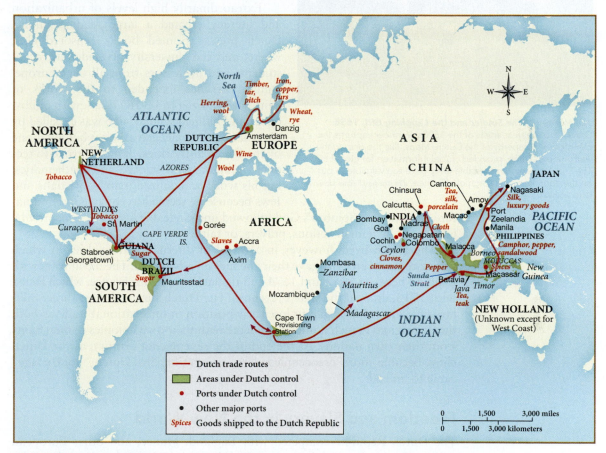

MAP 16.2 Dutch Commerce in the Seventeenth Century
Even before gaining formal independence from the Spanish in 1648, the Dutch had begun to compete with the Spanish and Portuguese all over the world. In 1602, a group of merchants established the Dutch East India Company, which soon offered investors an annual rate of return of 35 percent on the trade in spices with countries located on the Indian Ocean. Global commerce gave the Dutch the highest standard of living in Europe and soon attracted the envy of the French and the English.

Jan Vermeer, *The Soldier and the Laughing Girl*, 1658
One of the greatest artists of the 1600s, Vermeer captures the
commercial prosperity of the Dutch. Maps, like the one on the
wall in the painting, provided crucial information for global travel.
The Turkish carpet on the table (they were too valuable to put
on the floor) was a sure sign of affluence. (De Agostini Picture Library/
Getty Images.)

The Dutch rapidly became the most prosperous and best-educated people in Europe.
Whereas in other countries kings, nobles, and
churches bought art, in the Dutch Republic art
buyers were merchants, artisans, and shopkeepers. One foreigner commented that "pictures
are very common here, there being scarce an
ordinary tradesman whose house is not decorated with them." Relative prosperity decreased
the need for married women to work, so Dutch
society developed the clear contrast between
middle-class male and female roles that would
become prevalent elsewhere in Europe and in
America more than a century later.

Extraordinarily high levels of urbanization
and literacy created a large reading public.
Dutch presses printed books censored elsewhere, and the University of Leiden attracted
students and professors from all over Europe.
Dutch tolerance extended to the works of
Benedict Spinoza (1633–1677), a Jewish philosopher and biblical scholar who was expelled by
his synagogue for alleged atheism but left alone
by the Dutch authorities. Spinoza strove to reconcile religion with science and mathematics,
but his work scandalized many Christians and
Jews because he seemed to equate God and na-
ture. Like nature, Spinoza's God followed unchangeable laws and could not be
influenced by human actions, prayers, or faith.

The Dutch lived, however, in a world of international rivalries in which
strong central authority gave their enemies an advantage. The naval wars with
England between 1652 and 1674 and the land wars with France, which lasted
until 1713, drained the state's revenues. The Dutch survived these direct military challenges but began to lose their position in international trade as both
the British and French limited commerce with their own colonies to merchants
from their own nations. At the end of the seventeenth century, as the Dutch
elites became more preoccupied with ostentation, the Dutch "golden age"
came to an end.

Freedom and Slavery in the New World

The Dutch Republic competed with England, France, and other European
nations for its share of the burgeoning slave trade, but it lost its only settler
colony in North America, New Netherland (present-day New York, New
Jersey, Delaware, and Connecticut), to England in 1674. After the Spanish and
Portuguese had shown that African slaves could be transported and forced to

labor in South America and Central America, the English and French endeavored to set up similar labor systems in their new Caribbean island colonies. White planters with large tracts of land bought African slaves to work fields of sugarcane; and as they gradually built up their holdings, the planters displaced most of the original white settlers.

By the end of the seventeenth century, slavery had become codified as an inherited status that applied only to blacks. In 1661, Barbados instituted a slave code that stripped all Africans of rights under English law. Louis XIV promulgated a "black code" in 1685 to regulate the legal status of slaves in the French colonies and to prevent non-Catholics from owning slaves. The code supposedly set limits on the violence planters could exercise and required them to house, feed, and clothe their slaves. But white planters simply ignored provisions of the code that did not suit them, and in any case, because the code defined slaves as property, slaves could not themselves bring suit in court to demand better treatment.

The highest church and government authorities in Catholic and Protestant countries alike condoned the gradually expanding slave trade. In 1600, seventy-six hundred Africans were exported annually from Africa to the New World; by 1700, this number had increased more than fourfold, to thirty-three thousand. Historians advance several different ideas about which factors increased the slave trade: some claim that improvements in muskets made European slavers more effective; others cite the rising price for slaves, which made their sale more attractive for the Africans who sold them; still others focus on factors internal to Africa such as the increasing size of African armies and their use of muskets in fighting and capturing other Africans for sale as slaves. What is clear is that a combination of factors prepared the way for the development of an Atlantic economy based on slavery.

While blacks were being subjected to the most degrading forms of bondage, whites in the colonies enjoyed more freedom than ever before. Virtually left to themselves during the upheavals in England, the fledgling English colonies in North America developed representative government on their own. Almost every colony had a two-house legislature. William and Mary reluctantly allowed emerging colonial elites even more control over local affairs. The social and political elite among the settlers hoped to impose an English social hierarchy dominated by rich landowners. Ordinary immigrants to the colonies, however, took advantage of plentiful land to carve out their own farms using white servants and, later, in some colonies, African slaves.

For native Americans, the expanding European presence meant something else altogether. They faced death through disease, warfare, and the accelerating loss of their homelands. Many native Americans believed that land was a divine gift provided for their collective use and not subject to individual ownership. Europeans' claims that they owned exclusive land rights consequently resulted in frequent skirmishes. In 1675–1676, for instance, three tribes allied under Metacomet (called King Philip by the English) threatened the survival of New England settlers, who savagely repulsed the attacks and sold their captives as slaves. The benefits of constitutionalism were reserved for Europeans.

REVIEW QUESTION
Why did constitutionalism thrive in the Dutch Republic and the British North American colonies, even as their participation in the slave trade grew?

Absolutism in Central and Eastern Europe

Constitutionalism had an outpost in central and eastern Europe, too, but there it collapsed in failure. A long crisis in Poland-Lithuania virtually destroyed central state authority and pulled much of eastern Europe into its turbulent wake. Most central and eastern European rulers followed Louis XIV's model of absolutist state building, though they did not blindly emulate him, in part because they confronted conditions peculiar to their regions. Everywhere in eastern Europe, nobles lorded over their serfs but owed almost slavish obedience in turn to their rulers.

Poland-Lithuania Overwhelmed

In the version of constitutionalism adopted in Poland-Lithuania, the great nobles dominated the Sejm (parliament). To maintain an equilibrium among themselves, these nobles each wielded an absolute veto power. This "free veto" constitutional system deadlocked parliamentary government and left the monarch, elected by the nobles, with little room to maneuver.

Ukrainian Cossack warriors revolted against the king of Poland-Lithuania in 1648, inaugurating two decades of tumult known as the Deluge. *Cossack* was the name given to runaway serfs and poor nobles who formed outlaw bands in the no-man's-land of southern Russia and Ukraine. In 1654, the Cossacks offered Ukraine to Russian rule, provoking a Russo-Polish war that ended in 1667 when the tsar annexed eastern Ukraine and Kiev.

Many towns were destroyed in the fighting, and as much as a third of the Polish population perished. The once prosperous Jewish and Protestant minorities suffered greatly: some fifty-six thousand Jews were killed by the Cossacks, the Polish peasants, or the Russian troops. Surviving Jews moved from towns to shtetls (Jewish villages), where they took up petty trading, moneylending, tax gathering, and tavern leasing—activities that fanned peasant anti-Semitism. Desperate for protection amid the war, most Polish Protestants backed the violently anti-Catholic Swedes, who tried to intervene militarily, and the victorious Catholic majority branded the Protestants as traitors. In Poland-Lithuania, people came to assume that a good Pole was a Catholic. The commonwealth had ceased to be an outpost of toleration.

The commonwealth revived briefly when a man of ability and ambition, Jan Sobieski (r. 1674–1696), was elected king. Sobieski gained a reputation throughout Europe when he led twenty-five thousand Polish cavalrymen into battle in the siege of Vienna in 1683. His cavalry helped rout the Turks and turned the tide against the Ottomans. Despite his efforts to rebuild the monarchy, Sobieski could not halt Poland-Lithuania's decline into powerlessness. The Polish version of constitutionalism fatally weakened the state and made it prey to neighboring powers.

Territory lost to Russia, 1667

SWEDEN

Volga R.

RUSSIA

POLAND-LITHUANIA
BRANDENBURG-PRUSSIA
Kiev
UKRAINE

AUSTRIA
HUNGARY
Transylvania
Danube R.
Black Sea

OTTOMAN EMPIRE

Poland-Lithuania in the Seventeenth Century

Brandenburg-Prussia: Militaristic Absolutism

The contrast between Poland-Lithuania and Brandenburg-Prussia could not have been more extreme. The first was huge in territory and constitutional in government but in the end failed as a state. The second was puny, made up of disparate far-flung territories, and moving toward absolutism. In the nineteenth century Prussia would unify the different German states into modern-day Germany.

The ruler of Brandenburg was an elector, one of the seven German princes entitled to select the Holy Roman Emperor. Since the sixteenth century, the ruler of Brandenburg had also controlled the duchy of East Prussia; after 1618, the state was called Brandenburg-Prussia. Despite meager resources, **Frederick William of Hohenzollern**, who was the Great Elector of Brandenburg-Prussia (r. 1640–1688), succeeded in welding his scattered lands into an absolutist state.

Frederick William was determined to force his territories' estates (representative assemblies) to grant him a dependable income. The Great Elector struck a deal with the Junkers (nobles) of each province: in exchange for allowing him to collect taxes, he gave them complete control over their enserfed peasants and exempted them from taxation. By the end of his reign, the estates met only on ceremonial occasions. Frederick William was able to expand his army from eight thousand to thirty thousand men. Peasants filled the ranks, and Junkers became officers.

As a Calvinist ruler, Frederick William avoided the ostentation of the French court, even while following the absolutist model of centralizing state power. He boldly rebuffed Louis XIV by welcoming twenty thousand French Huguenot refugees after Louis's revocation of the Edict of Nantes. In pursuing foreign and domestic policies that promoted state power and prestige, Frederick William adroitly switched sides in Louis's wars and would stop at almost nothing to crush resistance at home. In 1701, his son Frederick I (r. 1688–1713) persuaded Holy Roman Emperor Leopold I to grant him the title "king in Prussia" in exchange for support in the War of the Spanish Succession. Prussia had arrived as an important power.

An Uneasy Balance: Austrian Habsburgs and Ottoman Turks

Holy Roman Emperor Leopold I (r. 1658–1705) ruled over a variety of territories of different ethnicities, languages, and religions, yet in ways similar to his French and Prussian counterparts, he gradually consolidated his power. Like all other Holy Roman Emperors since 1438, Leopold was an Austrian Habsburg. He was simultaneously duke of Upper and Lower Silesia, count of Tyrol, archduke of Upper and Lower Austria, king of Bohemia, king of Hungary and Croatia, and ruler of Styria and Moravia (Map 16.3). Some of these territories were provinces in the Holy Roman Empire; others were simply ruled from Vienna as Habsburg family holdings.

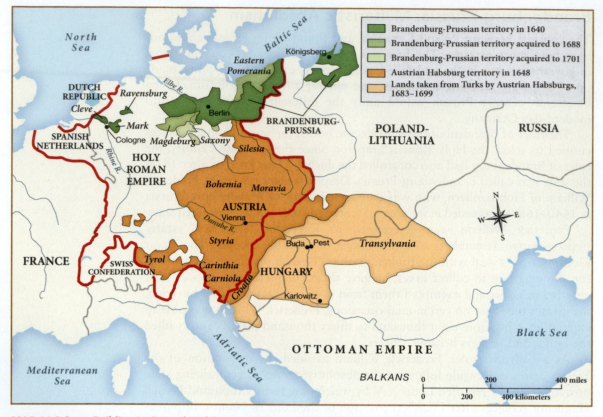

MAP 16.3 State Building in Central and Eastern Europe, 1648–1699
The Austrian Habsburgs had long contested the Ottoman Turks for dominance of eastern Europe, and by 1699 they had pushed the Turks out of Hungary. In central Europe, the Austrian Habsburgs confronted the growing power of Brandenburg-Prussia, which had emerged from relative obscurity after the Thirty Years' War to begin an aggressive program of expanding its military and its territorial base. As emperor of the Holy Roman Empire, the Austrian Habsburg ruler governed a huge expanse of territory, but the emperor's control was in fact only partial because of guarantees of local autonomy.

In response to the weakening of the Holy Roman Empire by the ravages of the Thirty Years' War, the emperor and his closest officials took control over recruiting, provisioning, and strategic planning and worked to replace the mercenaries hired during the war with a permanent standing army that promoted professional discipline. Intent on replacing Bohemian nobles who had supported the 1618 revolt against Austrian authority, the Habsburgs promoted a new nobility made up of Czechs, Germans, Italians, Spaniards, and even Irish who used German as their common tongue, professed Catholicism, and loyally served the Austrian dynasty. Bohemia became a virtual Austrian colony. In addition to holding Louis XIV in check on his western frontiers, Leopold confronted the ever-present challenge of the Ottoman Turks to the east. Austria had fought the Turks for control of Hungary for more than 150 years. In 1682, war broke out again. As they had in 1529, the Turks in 1683 pushed all the way to the gates of Vienna and laid siege to the Austrian capital.

With the help of Polish cavalry, the Austrians finally broke the siege and turned the tide in a major counteroffensive. By the Treaty of Karlowitz of 1699, the Ottoman Turks surrendered almost all of Hungary to the Austrians, marking the beginning of the decline of Ottoman power.

Once the Turks had been beaten back, Austrian rule over Hungary tightened. In 1687, the Habsburg dynasty's hereditary right to the Hungarian crown was acknowledged by the Hungarian diet, a parliament revived by Leopold in 1681 to gain the cooperation of Hungarian nobles. The diet was dominated by a core of pro-Habsburg Hungarian aristocrats, who would support the dynasty until it fell in 1918. To root out remaining Turkish influence and assert Austrian superiority, Leopold systematically destroyed Turkish buildings and rebuilt Catholic churches, monasteries, roadside shrines, and monuments in the flamboyant Austrian baroque style.

The Ottoman Turks pursued their state consolidation in a different fashion. Hundreds of thousands of Turkish families had moved with Turkish soldiers into the Balkan peninsula in the 1400s and 1500s. As locals converted to Islam, administration passed gradually into their hands. The Ottoman state, ultimately, would last longer than the French absolutist monarchy, even though the Ottoman rulers, the sultans, were often challenged by mutinous army officers. Despite frequent palace coups and assassinations of sultans, the Ottoman state continued to pose a massive military threat on Europe's southeastern borders.

Russia: Setting the Foundations of Bureaucratic Absolutism

Seventeenth-century Russia seemed a world apart from the Europe of Leopold I and Louis XIV. Straddling Europe and Asia, the Russian lands stretched across Siberia to the Pacific Ocean. Western visitors either sneered or shuddered at the "barbarism" of Russian life, and Russians reciprocated by nursing deep suspicions of everything foreign. But under the surface, Russia was evolving as an absolutist state; the tsars wanted to claim unlimited autocratic power, but like their European counterparts they had to surmount internal disorder and come to an accommodation with noble landlords.

In 1649, the Russian tsar Alexei (r. 1645–1676) convened the Assembly of the Land (consisting of noble delegates from the provinces) to consult on a sweeping law code to organize Russian society in a strict social hierarchy. The code of 1649—which held for nearly two centuries—assigned all subjects to a hereditary class according to their current occupation or state needs. Slaves and free peasants were merged into a serf class. As serfs, they could not change occupations or move; they were tightly tied to the soil and to their noble masters. To prevent tax evasion, the code also forbade townspeople to move from the community where they resided. Nobles owed absolute obedience to the tsar and were required to serve in the army, but in return no other group could own estates worked by serfs. Serfs became the chattel of their lord, who could sell them like horses or land. Their lives differed little from those of the slaves on the plantations in the Americas.

Stenka Razin in Captivity
After leading a revolt of thousands of serfs, peasants, and members of non-Russian tribes of the middle and lower Volga region, Stenka Razin was captured by Russian forces and led off to Moscow, as shown here, where he was executed in 1671. He has been the subject of songs, legends, and poems ever since. (© Imagno/ullstein bild/The Image Works.)

Some peasants resisted enserfment. In 1667, **Stenka Razin** (1630–1671), the head of a powerful band of pirates and outlaws in southern Russia, led a rebellion that promised liberation from the great noble landowners. Captured four years later by the tsar's army, Razin was taken to Moscow, where he was dismembered in front of the public and his body thrown to the dogs. Thousands of his followers also suffered grisly deaths, but Razin's memory lived on in folk songs and legends.

Like his Western rivals, Tsar Alexei wanted a bigger army, exclusive control over state policy, and a greater say in religious matters. The size of the army increased dramatically from 35,000 in the 1630s to 220,000 by the end of the century. The Assembly of the Land, once an important source of consultation for the nobles, never met again after 1653. Alexei also imposed firm control over the Russian Orthodox church. The state-dominated church took action against a religious group called the Old Believers, who rejected church efforts to bring Russian worship in line with Byzantine tradition. Whole communities of Old Believers starved or burned themselves to death rather than submit to the crown.

Nevertheless, modernizing trends prevailed. Tsar Alexei set up the first Western-style theater in the Kremlin, and his daughter Sophia translated French plays. The most adventurous nobles began to wear German-style clothing. Some even argued that service, not just birth, should determine rank. Russia's long struggle over Western influences had begun.

REVIEW QUESTION
Why did absolutism flourish everywhere in eastern Europe except Poland-Lithuania?

The Search for Order in Elite and Popular Culture

In the period of state building from 1640 to 1715, questions about obedience, order, and the limits of state power occupied poets, painters, architects, and men of science as much as they did rulers and their ministers. How much freedom of expression could be allowed? How did the individual's needs and aspirations fit with the requirements of state authority? The greatest thinkers and writers wrestled with these issues and helped frame debates for generations to come. At the same time, elites worked to distinguish themselves from the lower classes by developing new codes of correct behavior and teaching order and discipline to their social inferiors. Their repeated efforts show, however, that popular culture had its own dynamics that resisted control from above.

Freedom and Constraint in the Arts and Sciences

Most Europeans feared disorder above all else. The French mathematician Blaise Pascal vividly captured their worries in his *Pensées* (Thoughts) of 1660: "I look on all sides, and I see only darkness everywhere." Reason could not determine whether God existed or not, Pascal concluded. Poets, painters, and architects all grappled with similar issues of faith, reason, and authority, but most of them came to more positive conclusions than Pascal about human capacities.

The English Puritan poet John Milton (1608–1674) wrestled with the inevitable limitations on individual liberty. In 1643, in the midst of the civil war between king and Parliament, he published writings in favor of allowing married couples to divorce. When Parliament enacted a censorship law aimed at such literature, Milton responded in 1644 with one of the first defenses of freedom of the press, *Areopagitica*. In it, he argued that even controversial books about religion should be allowed. Forced into retirement after the restoration of the monarchy, Milton published his epic poem *Paradise Lost* in 1667. He used the biblical Adam and Eve's fall from grace to meditate on human freedom and the tragedies of rebellion. His Satan, the proud angel who challenges God and is cast out of heaven, is so compelling as to be heroic. In the end, Adam and Eve learn the limits to their freedom, yet personal liberty remains essential to their humanity.

The dominant artistic styles of the time—the baroque and the classical—both submerged the ordinary individual in a grander design. The combination of religious and political purposes in baroque art is best exemplified in the architecture and sculpture of Gian Lorenzo Bernini (1598–1680), the papacy's official artist. His architectural masterpiece was the gigantic square facing St. Peter's Basilica in Rome. Bernini's use of freestanding colonnades and a huge open space was meant to impress the individual observer with the power of the popes and the Catholic religion.

Although France was a Catholic country, French artists, like their patron Louis XIV, preferred the standards of **classicism** to those of the

Gian Lorenzo Bernini, *Ecstasy of St. Teresa of Ávila* (c. 1650)
This ultimate statement of baroque sculpture captures all the drama and even sensationalism of a mystical religious faith. Bernini based his figures on a vision reported by St. Teresa in which she saw an angel: "In his hands I saw a great golden spear, and at the iron tip there appeared to be a point of fire. This he plunged into my heart several times so that it penetrated my entrails. When he pulled it out I felt that he took them with it, and left me utterly consumed by the great love of God." (Santa Maria della Vittoria, Rome, Italy/De Agostini Picture Library/G. Nimatallah/Bridgeman Images.)

French Classicism
This painting by Nicolas Poussin, *Discovery of Achilles on Skyros* (1649–1650), shows the French interest in classical themes and ideals. In the Greek story, Thetis dresses her son Achilles as a young woman and hides him on the island of Skyros so he would not have to fight in the Trojan War. When a chest of treasures is offered to the women, Achilles reveals himself (he is the figure on the far right) because he cannot resist the sword. In telling the story, Poussin emphasizes harmony and almost a sedateness of composition, avoiding the exuberance and emotionalism of the baroque style. (Discovery of Achilles on Skyros, c. 1649–1650 (oil on canvas) by Nicolas Poussin [1594–1665]/Museum of Fine Arts, Boston, Massachusetts, USA/Juliana Cheney Edwards Collection/Bridgeman Images.)

baroque. As its name suggests, classicism reflected the ideals of the art of antiquity: geometric shapes, order, and harmony of lines took precedence over the sensuous, exuberant, and emotional forms of the baroque. Rather than being overshadowed by the sheer power of emotional display, in classicism the individual could be found at the intersection of converging, symmetrical, straight lines. These influences were apparent in the work of the leading French painters of the period, Nicolas Poussin (1594–1665) and Claude Lorrain (1600–1682), both of whom tried to re-create classical Roman values in their mythological scenes and Roman landscapes.

Art could also serve the interests of science. One of the most skilled illustrators of insects and flowers was Maria Sibylla Merian (1647–1717), a German-born painter-scholar whose engravings were widely celebrated for their brilliant realism and microscopic clarity. Merian separated from her husband and accompanied missionaries to the Dutch colony of Surinam, in South America. She painted watercolors of the exotic flowers, birds, and insects she found in the jungle around the cocoa and sugarcane plantations.

Despite the initial religious controversies associated with the scientific revolution, absolutist rulers quickly saw the potential of the new science for enhancing their prestige and glory. Various German princes supported the work of Gottfried Wilhelm Leibniz (1646–1716), who claimed that he, and not Isaac Newton, had invented modern calculus. A lawyer, mathematician, and philosopher who wrote about metaphysics, cosmology, and history, Leibniz also helped establish scientific societies in the German states. Government involvement in science was greatest in France. In 1666, Jean-Baptiste Colbert founded the Royal

Academy of Sciences, which supplied fifteen scientists with government stipends. In contrast, the Royal Society of London grew out of informal meetings of scientists at London and Oxford. It received a royal charter in 1662 but maintained complete independence.

Because of their exclusion from most universities, women only rarely participated in the new scientific discoveries. In 1667, nonetheless, the Royal Society of London invited the writer Margaret Cavendish to watch the exhibition of experiments. Labeled "mad" by her critics, she attacked the use of telescopes and microscopes because she detected in the new experimentalism a mechanistic view of the world that exalted masculine prowess and challenged the Christian belief in freedom of the will. Yet she urged the formal education of women, complaining that "we are kept like birds in cages to hop up and down in our houses."

Women and Manners

Although excluded from the universities and the professions, women played important roles not only in the home but also in more formal spheres of social interaction, such as the courts of rulers. Under the tutelage of their mothers and wives, nobles learned manners, or the fine points of social etiquette. In some ways, aristocratic men were expected to act more like women; just as women had long been expected to please men, now aristocratic men had to please their monarch or patron by displaying proper manners and conversing with elegance and wit.

European Fascination with Products of the New World
In this painting of a banana plant, Maria Sibylla Merian offers a scientific study of one of the many exotic plants and animals found by Europeans who traveled to the colonies overseas. In 1699, Merian traveled to the Dutch South American colony of Surinam with her daughter. (Inflorescence of Banana, 1705, by Maria Sibylla Graff Merian [1647–1717]/Minneapolis Institute of Arts, Minneapolis, MN, USA/The Ethel Morrison Van Derlip Fund/Bridgeman Images.)

The upper classes began to reject popular festivals and fairs in favor of private theaters, where seats were relatively expensive and behavior was formal. Clowns and buffoons now seemed vulgar; the last king of England to keep a court fool was Charles I. Some tastes spread downward from the upper classes, however. Chivalric romances that had long entranced the nobility, such as Ariosto's *Orlando Furioso*, now appeared in simplified form in cheap booklets printed for lower-class readers.

Molière, the greatest French playwright of the seventeenth century, wrote sparkling comedies of manners that revealed much about the new aristocratic behavior. His play *The Middle-Class Gentleman*, first performed for Louis XIV in 1670, revolves around the yearning of a rich middle-class Frenchman, Monsieur Jourdain, to learn to act like a *gentilhomme* (both "gentleman" and "nobleman"). Monsieur Jourdain buys fancy clothes; hires private instructors in dancing, music, fencing, and philosophy; and lends money to a debt-ridden noble in hopes that the noble will marry his daughter. Only his sensible wife and his daughter's love for a worthier commoner stand in his way. The message for the king's courtiers seemed to be a reassuring one: only born nobles can hope to act like nobles. But the play also showed how the middle classes were learning to emulate the nobility: if one could learn to act nobly through self-discipline, could not anyone with some education and money pass himself off as noble?

As Molière's play demonstrated, new attention to manners trickled down from the court to the middle class. A French treatise on manners written in 1672 explained proper behavior:

> Formerly one was permitted . . . to dip one's bread into the sauce, provided only that one had not already bitten it. Nowadays that would be a kind of rusticity. Formerly one was allowed to take from one's mouth what one could not eat and drop it on the floor, provided it was done skillfully. Now that would be very disgusting.

The key words *rusticity* and *disgusting* reveal the association of unacceptable social behavior with the peasantry, dirt, and repulsion. Similar rules governed spitting and blowing one's nose in public.

Courtly manners often permeated the upper reaches of society by means of the **salon**, an informal gathering held regularly in a private home and presided over by a socially eminent woman. The French government occasionally worried that these gatherings might challenge its authority, but the three main topics of salon conversation were love, literature, and philosophy. Before publishing a manuscript, many authors, including court favorites like Pierre Corneille and Jean Racine, would read their compositions to a salon gathering.

Some women went beyond encouraging male authors and began to write their own works, but they faced many obstacles. Madame de Lafayette wrote several short novels that were published anonymously because it was considered inappropriate for aristocratic women to appear in print. Following the publication of *The Princess of Clèves* in 1678, she denied having written it. Despite these limitations, French women began to turn out best sellers of that new type of literary form, the novel. Their success prompted the philosopher Pierre Bayle to remark in 1697 that "our best French novels for a long time have been written by women."

The new importance of women in the world of manners and letters did not sit well with everyone. Although the French writer François Poulain de la Barre, in a series of works published in the 1670s, used the new science to assert the equality of women's minds, most men resisted the idea. Clergymen, lawyers, scholars, and playwrights attacked women's growing public influence. Women, they complained, were corrupting forces and needed restraint. Molière wrote plays denouncing women's pretension to judge literary merit. English playwrights derided learned women by creating characters with names such as Lady Knowall, Lady Meanwell, and Mrs. Lovewit.

A real-life target of the English playwrights was Aphra Behn (1640–1689), one of the first professional woman authors. Her short novel *Oroonoko* (1688) told the story of an African prince mistakenly sold into slavery. The story was so successful that it was adapted by playwrights and performed repeatedly in England and France for the next hundred years.

Reforming Popular Culture

Controversies over female influence had little effect on the unschooled peasants who made up most of Europe's population. Peasant culture had three main elements: religion, which shaped every aspect of life and death; knowledge needed to work at farming or in a trade; and popular forms of entertainment such as village fairs and dances. What changed most noticeably in the seventeenth century was the social elites' attitude toward lower-class culture.

In the seventeenth century, Protestant and Catholic churches alike pushed hard to change popular religious practices. Their campaigns against popular "paganism" began during the sixteenth-century Protestant Reformation and Catholic Counter-Reformation but reached much of rural Europe only in the seventeenth century. Puritans in England tried to root out maypole dances, Sunday village fairs, gambling, taverns, and bawdy ballads. In Lutheran Norway, pastors denounced a widespread belief in the miracle-working powers of St. Olaf. The word *superstition* previously meant "false religion" (Protestantism was a superstition for Catholics, Catholicism for Protestants); in the seventeenth century it took on its modern meaning of irrational fears, beliefs, and practices that anyone educated or refined would avoid.

Catholic bishops in the French provinces trained parish priests to reform their flocks by using catechisms in local dialects and insisting that parishioners attend Mass. The church faced a formidable challenge. One bishop in France complained in 1671, "Can you believe that there are in this diocese entire villages where no one has even heard of Jesus Christ?" In some places, believers sacrificed animals to the Virgin; prayed to the new moon; and, as in pre-Christian times, worshipped at the sources of streams.

Like its Protestant counterpart, the Catholic campaign against ignorance and superstition helped extend state power. Clergy, officials, and local police worked together to limit carnival celebrations, to regulate pilgrimages to shrines, and to replace "indecent" images of saints with more restrained and decorous ones. In Catholicism, the cult of the Virgin Mary and devotions closely connected with Jesus, such as the Holy Sacrament and the Sacred Heart, took precedence over the celebration of popular saints who seemed to have pagan origins or were credited with unverified miracles.

The campaign for more disciplined religious practices helped generate a new attitude toward the poor. In the sixteenth and seventeenth centuries, the upper classes, the church, and the state increasingly regarded the poor as dangerous, deceitful, and lacking in character. The courts had previously expelled beggars from cities; now local leaders, both Catholic and Protestant, tried to reform their character. Municipal magistrates and local notables worked together to transform hospitals into houses of confinement for beggars. In Catholic France, upper-class women's religious associations, known as confraternities, set up asylums that confined prostitutes (by arrest if necessary) and rehabilitated them. Such groups advocated harsh discipline as the cure for poverty.

Even as reformers from church and state tried to regulate popular activities, villagers and townspeople pushed back with reassertions of their own values.

MAPPING THE WEST

Legend:
- Austrian territory by 1699
- Brandenburg-Prussian territory by 1701
- Spanish Habsburg lands
- Venetian possessions
- Ottoman Empire
- Boundary of the Holy Roman Empire

0   200   400 miles
0   200   400 kilometers

SCOTLAND
IRELAND
ENGLAND
London
Amsterdam
DUTCH REPUBLIC
North Sea
DENMARK-NORWAY
SWEDEN
FINLAND
Gulf of Finland
Estonia
Livonia
Moscow
RUSSIA
Baltic Sea
Danzig
POLAND-LITHUANIA
Berlin
Warsaw
Minsk
Kiev
BRANDENBURG-PRUSSIA
Leipzig
Prague
Elbe R.
Vistula R.
Dnieper R.
SPANISH NETH.
Rhine R.
English Channel
ATLANTIC OCEAN
Paris
Nantes
Loire R.
Franche-Comté
Strasbourg
Alsace
Danube R.
Vienna
Munich
AUSTRIA
Buda
Pest
HUNGARY
Bay of Biscay
FRANCE
SWITZ.
Bordeaux
Rhône R.
SAVOY
Genoa
Venice
VENETIAN REPUBLIC
Florence
Belgrade
Danube R.
SERBIA
BULGARIA
Black Sea
PORTUGAL
SPAIN
Madrid
Ebro R.
Lisbon
Tagus R.
Barcelona
Corsica
PAPAL STATES
Rome
NAPLES
Naples
MONTENEGRO
OTTOMAN EMPIRE
Constantinople
ANATOLIA
Seville
Granada
BALEARIC ISLANDS
Sardinia
Palermo
Sicily
IONIAN IS. (Venice)
Mediterranean Sea
Rhodes
Cyprus
Crete (Venice)

Europe at the End of the Seventeenth Century

Size was not necessarily an advantage in the late 1600s. Poland-Lithuania, a large country on the map, had been fatally weakened by internal conflicts. In the next century it would disappear entirely. While the Ottoman Empire still controlled an extensive territory, outside of Anatolia its rule depended on intermediaries. The Austrian Habsburgs had pushed the Turks out of Hungary and back into the Balkans. The tiny Dutch Republic, meanwhile, had become very rich through international commerce and was the envy of far larger nations.

Analyzing the Map: Look closely at the Dutch Republic. It is small compared with almost any other European country. What geographical advantages did it have that would help explain its rise to prominence in international commerce?

Making Connections: How is France as a territory different from Brandenburg-Prussia and the Holy Roman Empire? What are the consequences of those differences when it comes to fighting wars?

For hundreds of years, peasants had maintained their own forms of village justice—called variously "rough music," "charivari," or in North America, "shivaree." If a young man married a much older woman for her money, for example, villagers would serenade the couple by playing crude flutes, banging pots and pans, and firing muskets. If a man was rumored to have been physically assaulted by his wife, a reversal of the usual sex roles, he (or effigies of him and his wife) might be ridden on a donkey facing backward (to signify the role reversal) and pelted with dung before being ducked in a nearby pond or river. Others directed their mockery at tax officials, gamekeepers on big estates who tried to keep villagers from hunting, or unpopular preachers.

No matter how much care went into controlling religious festivals, such events almost invariably opened the door to popular reinterpretation and sometimes drunken celebration. When the Spanish introduced Corpus Christi processions to their colony in Peru in the seventeenth century, elite Incas dressed in royal costumes to carry the banners of their parishes. Their clothing and ornaments combined Christian symbols with their own indigenous ones. They thus signaled their conversion to Catholicism but also reasserted their own prior identities. The Corpus Christi festival, held in late May or early June, conveniently took place about the same time as Inca festivals from the pre-Spanish era. Carnival, the days preceding Lent on the Christian calendar—of which Mardi Gras ("Fat Tuesday") is the last—offered the occasion for public revelry of all sorts. Although Catholic clergy worked hard to clamp down on the more riotous aspects of Carnival, many towns and villages still held parades, like those of present-day New Orleans or Rio de Janeiro, that included companies of local men dressed in special costumes and gigantic stuffed figures, sometimes with animal skins, animal heads, or elaborate masks.

REVIEW QUESTION
How did elite and popular culture become more separate in the seventeenth century?

Conclusion

The search for order took place on various levels, from the reform of the disorderly poor to the establishment of bureaucratic routines in government. The absolutist government of Louis XIV served as a model for all those who aimed to increase the power of the central state. Even Louis's rivals—such as the Holy Roman Emperor Leopold I and Frederick William, the Great Elector of Brandenburg-Prussia—followed his lead in centralizing authority and building up their armies. Whether absolutist or constitutionalist in form, seventeenth-century states aimed to penetrate more deeply into the lives of their subjects. They wanted more men for their armed forces; higher taxes to support their projects; and more control over foreign trade, religious dissent, and society's unwanted.

Some tears had begun to appear, however, in the seamless fabric of state power. The civil war between Charles I and Parliament in England in the 1640s opened the way to new demands for political participation. When Parliament overthrew James II in 1688, it also insisted that the new king and queen, William and Mary, agree to the Bill of Rights. In the eighteenth century, new levels of economic growth and the appearance of new social groups would exert pressures on the European state system. The success of seventeenth-century rulers created the political and economic conditions in which their critics would flourish.

Chapter 16 Review

Key Terms and People

Be sure that you can identify the term or person and explain its historical significance.

absolutism (p. 537)

constitutionalism (p. 537)

Louis XIV (p. 538)

revocation of the Edict of Nantes (p. 544)

bureaucracy (p. 544)

mercantilism (p. 544)

Levellers (p. 549)

William, prince of Orange (p. 554)

Glorious Revolution (p. 555)

social contract (p. 555)

Frederick William of Hohenzollern (p. 561)

Stenka Razin (p. 564)

classicism (p. 565)

salon (p. 568)

Review Questions

1. How "absolute" was the power of Louis XIV?

2. What differences over religion and politics caused the conflict between king and Parliament in England?

3. Why did constitutionalism thrive in the Dutch Republic and the British North American colonies, even as their participation in the slave trade grew?

4. Why did absolutism flourish everywhere in eastern Europe except Poland-Lithuania?

5. How did elite and popular culture become more separate in the seventeenth century?

Making Connections

1. What accounts for the success of absolutism in some parts of Europe and its failure in others?

2. How did religious differences in the late seventeenth century still cause political conflict?

3. What were the chief differences between eastern and western Europe in this period?

4. Why was the search for order a major theme in science, politics, and the arts during this period?

Important Events

1642–1646	English civil war between Charles I and Parliament
1648	Peace of Westphalia ends Thirty Years' War; Fronde revolt challenges royal authority in France; Ukrainian Cossack warriors rebel against king of Poland-Lithuania; Spain formally recognizes independence of Dutch Republic
1649	Charles I of England executed; new Russian legal code assigns all to hereditary class
1651	Thomas Hobbes publishes *Leviathan*
1660	Monarchy restored in England

1661	Slave code set up in Barbados
1667	Louis XIV begins first of many wars that continue throughout his reign
1678	Madame de Lafayette anonymously publishes *The Princess of Clèves*
1683	Austrian Habsburgs break Turkish siege of Vienna
1685	Louis XIV revokes Edict of Nantes
1688	Parliament deposes James II; William, prince of Orange, and Mary take the throne
1690	John Locke publishes *Two Treatises of Government* and *Essay Concerning Human Understanding*

Consider three events

Thomas Hobbes publishes *Leviathan* (1651), Madame de Lafayette anonymously publishes *The Princess of Clèves* (1678), and John Locke publishes *Two Treatises of Government* (1690). How did Hobbes's new doctrine of absolute political authority, de Lafayette's novel, and Locke's emphasis on a social contract represent both an effort to create order and a challenge to the established order?

Suggested References

Recent studies have insisted that absolutism could never be entirely absolute because rulers depended on collaboration to enforce their policies. Studies of constitutional governments have emphasized the limitations of freedoms for the lower classes and especially for slaves.

*Beik, William. *Louis XIV and Absolutism: A Brief Study with Documents*. 2000.

Braddick, Michael J., ed. *The Oxford Handbook of the English Revolution*. 2015.

Brook, Timothy. *Vermeer's Hat: The Seventeenth Century and the Dawn of the Global World*. 2008.

Davies, Brian L. *Warfare, State and Society on the Black Sea Steppe, 1500–1700*. 2007.

Davis, Natalie Zemon. *Women on the Margins: Three Seventeenth-Century Lives*. 1995.

France in America (site of the Library of Congress on French colonies in North America): http://international.loc.gov/intldl/fiahtml/fiatheme.html#track1

Friedrich, Karin. *Brandenburg-Prussia, 1466–1806: The Rise of a Composite State*. 2012.

Pestana, Carla Gardina. *The English Atlantic in an Age of Revolution, 1640–1661*. 2007.

*Pincus, Steven C. A. *England's Glorious Revolution, 1688–1689: A Brief History with Documents*. 2006.

Soll, Jacob. *The Reckoning: Financial Accountability and the Rise and Fall of Nations*. 2014.

Stoye, John. *The Siege of Vienna: The Last Great Trial Between Cross and Crescent*. 2006.

Stuurman, Siep. *The Invention of Humanity: Equality and Cultural Difference in World History*. 2017.

Tezcan, Baki. *The Second Ottoman Empire: Political and Social Transformation in the Early Modern World*. 2012.

Versailles castle: http://en.chateauversailles.fr/homepage

_____

*Primary source.

The Atlantic System and Its Consequences

1700–1750

In 1699, a few coffee plants changed the history of the world. European travelers at the end of the sixteenth century noticed Middle Eastern people drinking a "black drink" called *kavah*, but the Arab monopoly on its production kept prices high. This all changed in 1699, when Dutch traders brought a few coffee plants from the east coast of India to their colony of Java (now Indonesia), which proved ideal for growing the beans. Within two decades, the trickle of beans going from Java to Europe became a flood of 200,000 pounds a year. After a shoot from a Dutch plant made its way to the Caribbean island of Martinique in 1721, coffee plants quickly spread throughout the Caribbean, where African slaves provided the plantation labor.

European consumption of coffee, tea, sugar, and other novelties increased dramatically as European nations forged worldwide economic links. At the center of this new global economy was the **Atlantic system**, the web of trade routes that bound together western Europe, Africa, and the Americas. Europeans bought slaves in western Africa, transported them to be sold in the colonies in North and South America and the Caribbean, bought raw commodities such as coffee and sugar that were produced by the new colonial plantations, and then sold those commodities in European ports for refining and reshipment. This Atlantic system, which first took clear shape in the early eighteenth century, became the hub of European expansion throughout the world.

Coffee drinking is just one example of the many new social and cultural patterns that took root between 1700 and 1750. Improvements in agricultural production at home reinforced the effects of trade overseas;

«London Coffeehouse This gouache (a variant on watercolor painting) from about 1725 depicts a scene from a London coffeehouse located in the courtyard of the Royal Exchange (merchants' bank). Middle-class men (wearing wigs) read newspapers, drink coffee, smoke pipes, and discuss the news of the day. The coffeehouse has drawn them out of their homes into a new public space. (Private Collections/Bridgeman Images.)

Europeans now had more disposable income for extras, and they spent their money not only in the new coffeehouses and cafés that sprang up all over Europe but also on newspapers, musical concerts, paintings, and novels. A new middle-class public began to make its presence felt in every domain of culture and social life.

Although the rise of the Atlantic system gave Europe new prominence in the global context, European rulers still focused most of their political, diplomatic, and military energies on their rivalries within Europe. A coalition of countries had succeeded in containing French aggression under Louis XIV, and a more balanced diplomatic system emerged. The more evenly matched competition among the great powers encouraged the development of diplomatic skills and drew attention to public health as a way of encouraging population growth.

In the aftermath of Louis XIV's revocation of the Edict of Nantes in 1685, a new intellectual movement known as the Enlightenment began to germinate. An initial impetus came from French Protestant refugees who published works critical of absolutism in politics and religion. Fed by the popularization of science and the growing interest in travel literature, the early Enlightenment encouraged greater skepticism about religious and state authority. Eventually, the movement would question almost every aspect of social and political life in Europe. The Enlightenment, which began in western Europe in those countries most affected by the new Atlantic system—Britain, France, and the Dutch Republic—can be considered a product of the age of coffee.

CHAPTER FOCUS
What were the most important consequences of the growth of the Atlantic system?

The Atlantic System and the World Economy

Although their ships had been circling the globe since the early 1500s, Europeans did not draw most of the world into their economic orbit until the 1700s. Western European nations sent ships loaded with goods to buy

CHAPTER TIMELINE

| **1700s** Beginning of rapid development of plantations in the Caribbean | | **1713–1714** Peace of Utrecht treaties end War of Spanish Succession | **1715** Death of Louis XIV | **1721** Great Northern War ends; Montesquieu publishes *Persian Letters* anonymously in the Dutch Republic |

1700   **1710**   **1720**

| | **1703** Peter the Great begins construction of St. Petersburg; founds first Russian newspaper | | **1714** Elector of Hanover becomes King George I of England | **1719** Daniel Defoe publishes *Robinson Crusoe* | **1720** Last outbreak of bubonic plague in western Europe |

slaves from local rulers on the western coast of Africa; the slaves were then transported to the colonies in North and South America and the Caribbean and sold to the owners of plantations producing coffee, sugar, cotton, and tobacco. Money from the slave trade was used to buy the raw commodities produced in the colonies and ship them back to Europe, where they were refined or processed and then sold within Europe and around the world. The Atlantic system and the growth of international trade thus helped create a new consumer society.

Slavery and the Atlantic System

In the eighteenth century, European trade in the Atlantic rapidly expanded and became more systematically interconnected (Map 17.1). By 1650, Portugal had already sent forty thousand African slaves to Brazil to work on the new plantations, which were producing some fifteen thousand tons of sugar a year. A **plantation** was a large tract of land that produced a staple crop such as sugar, coffee, or tobacco; was farmed by slave labor; and was owned by a colonial settler from western Europe.

Realizing that plantations producing staples for Europeans could bring fabulous wealth, the European powers grew less interested in the dwindling trade in precious metals and more eager to colonize. In the 1700s, large-scale planters of sugar, tobacco, and coffee began displacing small farmers who relied on one or two indentured servants (men and women who gained passage to the Americas in exchange for several years of work). Planters and their plantations won out because even cheaper slave labor allowed them to produce mass quantities of commodities at low prices.

State-chartered private companies from Portugal, France, Britain, the Dutch Republic, Prussia, and even Denmark exploited the 3,500-mile coastline of West Africa for slaves. Before 1675, most blacks taken from Africa had been sent to Brazil or Spanish America on Portuguese or Dutch ships, but by 1725, more than 60 percent of African slaves landed in the

1733
War of the Polish Succession; Voltaire's *Letters Concerning the English Nation* attacks French intolerance and narrow-mindedness

1741
George Frideric Handel composes *Messiah*

1730   **1740**   **1750**

1740–1748
War of the Austrian Succession

1748
Montesquieu publishes *The Spirit of Laws*

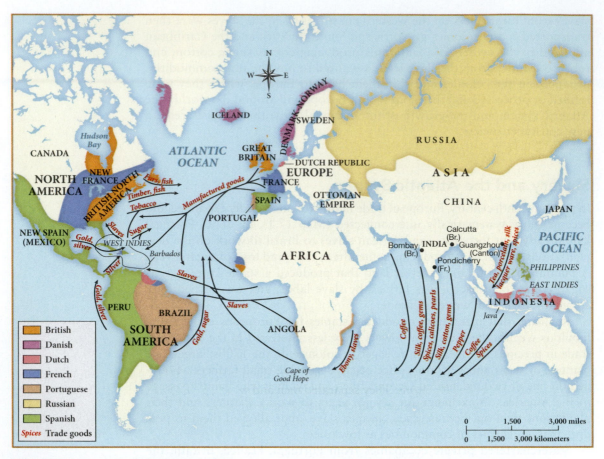

MAP 17.1 European Trade Patterns, c. 1740
By 1740, the European powers had colonized much of North and South America and incorporated their colonies there into a worldwide system of commerce centered on the slave trade and plantation production of staple crops. Europeans still sought spices and luxury goods in China and the East Indies, but few Europeans had settled permanently in these areas (with the exception of Java). How did control over colonies determine dominance in international trade in this period?

Caribbean (Figure 17.1), and more and more of them were carried on British or French ships.

After 1700, the plantation economy also began to expand on the North American mainland. The numbers stagger the imagination. In all, more than ten million Africans, not counting those who were captured but died before or during the sea voyage, were transported to the Americas before 1850, after which the slave trade finally began to wind down. Europeans traded textiles, cowries (shells from the Indian Ocean), and firearms for slaves, altering local African power structures and creating political instability. Population declined in West Africa, and because two-thirds of those enslaved were men, husbands were in short supply and men increasingly took two or more wives in a practice known as polygyny.

The enslaved women and men suffered terribly. Most had been sold to European traders by Africans from the west coast who acquired them

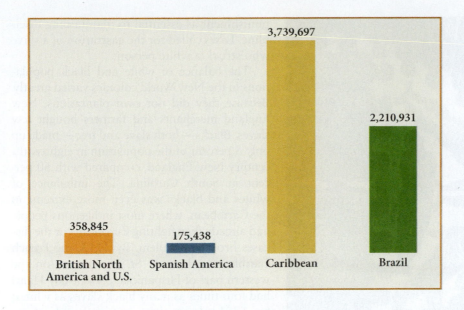

FIGURE 17.1 African Slaves Imported into American Territories, 1701–1800
During the eighteenth century, planters in the newly established Caribbean colonies imported millions of African slaves to work the new plantations that produced sugar, coffee, indigo, and cotton for the European market. The vast majority of African slaves transported to the Americas ended up in either the Caribbean or Brazil. Why were so many slaves transported to the Caribbean islands, which are relatively small compared to Spanish America or British North America? (Adapted from http://www.slavevoyages.org/.)

through warfare or kidnapping. The vast majority were between fourteen and thirty-five years old. Before cramming them onto the ships for the three-month trip, slavers shaved their heads and stripped them naked; they also branded some with red-hot irons. They separated men and women, and shackled men with leg irons. Sailors and officers raped the women at will. In the cramped and appalling conditions of the voyage, as many as one-fourth of the slaves died.

Those who survived the transit were sold and given new names, often only first names. Slaves had no social identities of their own; they were expected to learn their master's language and to do any job assigned. Slaves worked fifteen- to seventeen-hour days and were fed only enough to keep them on their feet. The death rate among slaves was high, especially on the sugar plantations, where slaves had to cut and haul sugarcane to the grinders and boilers before it spoiled. During the harvest, grinding and boiling went on around the clock. Because so many slaves died in the sugar-growing regions, more and more slaves, especially strong males, had to be imported. In North America, in contrast, where sugar was a minor crop, the slave population increased tenfold by 1863 through natural growth.

Not surprisingly, despite the threat of torture or death on recapture, slaves sometimes ran away. Outright revolt was uncommon, but slaveholders' fears about conspiracy and revolt lurked beneath the surface of every slave-based society. In 1710, the royal governor of Virginia reminded the colonial legislature of the need for unceasing vigilance: "We are not to Depend on Either Their Stupidity, or that Babel of Languages among 'em; freedom Wears a Cap which Can Without a Tongue, Call Together all Those who Long to Shake off the fetters of Slavery." Masters defended whipping and other forms of physical

Crowded Conditions on Board a Slave Ship
This wood engraving from 1789 shows a cross section of an English
slave ship built in Liverpool in 1780–1781 for the merchant Joseph
Brooks. In 1782, the ship carried 609 enslaved Africans across the
Atlantic in a space designed for 451 people; 351 of them were men,
127 women, 90 boys, and 41 girls. Abolitionists showed members of
Parliament a model of this ship to convince them of the brutality of
the slave trade. (© The Trustees of the British Museum/Art Resource, NY.)

punishment as essential to maintaining discipline. Laws called for the castration of a slave
who struck a white person.

The balance of white and black populations in the New World colonies varied greatly.
Because they did not own plantations, New
England merchants and farmers bought few
slaves. Blacks—both slave and free—made up
only 3 percent of the population in eighteenth-
century New England, compared with 60 percent in South Carolina. The imbalance of
whites and blacks was even more extreme in
the Caribbean, where most indigenous people
had already died fighting Europeans or the diseases brought by them. By 1713, the French
Caribbean colony of St. Domingue (on the
western part of Hispaniola, present-day Haiti)
had four times as many black slaves as whites;
by 1754, slaves there outnumbered whites
more than ten to one.

Plantation owners often left their colonial
possessions in the care of agents and merely
collected the revenue so that they could live
as wealthy landowners back home, where they
built opulent mansions and gained influence in
local and national politics. William Beckford,
for example, left his inherited sugar planta-
tions in Jamaica and moved the headquarters of the family business to London
in the 1730s to be close to the government and financial markets. His holdings
formed the single most powerful economic interest in Jamaica, but he preferred
to live in England, where he held political office (he was lord mayor of London
and a member of Parliament) and even loaned money to the government.

The slave trade permanently altered consumption patterns for ordinary
people. Sugar had been prescribed as a medicine before the end of the sixteenth century, but the development of plantations in Brazil and the Caribbean
made it a standard food item. By 1700, the British were sending home fifty
million pounds of sugar a year, a figure that doubled by 1730. Equally pervasive was the spread of tobacco; by the 1720s, men of every country and class
smoked pipes or took snuff.

Even though the traffic in slaves disturbed some Europeans, in the 1700s
slaveholders began to justify their actions by demeaning the mental and
spiritual qualities of the enslaved Africans. White Europeans and colonists
sometimes described black slaves as animal-like, akin to apes. A leading
New England Puritan asserted about the slaves: "Indeed their *Stupidity* is a
Discouragement. It may seem, unto as little purpose, to *Teach*, as to *wash an
Aethiopian* [Ethiopian]." One of the great paradoxes of this time was that talk

of liberty and rights, especially prevalent in Britain and its North American colonies, coexisted with the belief that some people were meant to be slaves. The churches often defended or at least did not oppose the iniquities of slavery.

World Trade and Settlement

The Atlantic system helped extend European trade relations across the globe. The textiles that Atlantic shippers exchanged for slaves on the west coast of Africa, for example, were manufactured in India and exported by the British and French East India companies. As much as one-quarter of the British exports to Africa in the eighteenth century were actually re-exports from India. To expand their trade in the rest of the world, Europeans seized territories and tried to establish permanent settlements. The eighteenth-century extension of European power prepared the way for Western global domination in the nineteenth and twentieth centuries.

In contrast to the sparsely inhabited European trading outposts in Asia and Africa, the colonies in the Americas bulged with settlers. The British North American colonies contained about 1.5 million nonnative (that is, white settler and black slave) residents by 1750. While the Spanish competed with the Portuguese for control of South America, the French competed with the British for control of North America.

Local economies shaped colonial social relations; men in French trapper communities in Canada, for example, had little in common with the men and women of the plantation societies in Barbados or Brazil. Racial attitudes also differed from place to place. Unlike the French and English, the Spanish and Portuguese tolerated intermarriage with the native populations in both America and Asia. By 1800, **mestizos**, people born to a Spanish father and an Indian mother, accounted for more than a quarter of the population in the Spanish colonies. Where intermarriage between colonizers and natives was common, conversion to Christianity proved most successful. However, greater racial diversity seems not to have improved the treatment of slaves.

In the early years of American colonization, many more men than women emigrated from Europe. Although the sex imbalance began to decline at the end of the seventeenth century, it remained substantial; for example, two and a half times more men than women were among the immigrants who left Liverpool, England, between 1697 and 1707. Women who emigrated as indentured servants ran great risks: many died of disease during the voyage, and at least one in five gave birth to an illegitimate child.

However, the uncertainties of life in the American colonies provided new opportunities for European women and men willing to live outside the law. In the 1500s and 1600s, the English and Dutch governments had routinely authorized pirates to prey on the ships of their rivals, the Spanish and Portuguese. Then, in the late 1600s, English, French, and Dutch bands made up of deserters and crews from wrecked vessels began to form their own associations of pirates, especially in the Caribbean. Called **buccaneers** from their custom of curing strips of beef, called *boucan* by the native Caribs of the

The Consumer Revolution

As imports of coffee, tea, and sugar from the colonies increased exponentially, people began to consider the effects of new patterns of consumption on their societies. In 1705, a Dutch-born English physician published a satirical poem that came to be known as "The Fable of the Bees," in which he argued that private vices, such as greed, actually contributed to the public benefit because they increased economic activity and therefore the wealth of society (Document 1). Among Mandeville's many critics was the clergyman William Law, who denounced the Fable of the Bees as immoral (Document 2). They started an argument that continues to this day about the virtues or vices of consumption.

1. Bernard de Mandeville, "The Fable of the Bees" (1705)

Mandeville used a poem to make his point that the vices of individuals could result in public benefits. In later editions, he put "private vices, public benefits" in the title itself. Although widely condemned and even threatened with government prosecution, Mandeville laid the foundation for sociology, that is, the study of the rules underpinning society.

> Vast Numbers throng'd the fruitful Hive;
> Yet those vast Numbers made 'em thrive;
> Millions endeavouring to supply
> Each other's Lust and Vanity;....
> Thus every Part was full of Vice,
> Yet the whole Mass a Paradise;
> Flatter'd in Peace, and fear'd in Wars,
> They were th'Esteem of Foreigners,
> And lavish of their Wealth and Lives,
> The Ballance of all other Hives.
> Such were the Blessings of that State;
> Their Crimes conspir'd to make them Great:
> And Virtue, who from Politicks
> Had learn'd a Thousand Cunning Tricks,
> Was, by their happy Influence,
> Made Friends with Vice: And ever since,

> The worst of all the Multitude
> Did something for the Common Good

Source: Bernard de Mandeville, *The Fable of the Bees*, 3rd ed. (London: J. Tonson, 1724), 3 and 9.

2. William Law, Denunciation of Fable of the Bees, 1724

In his long pamphlet against Mandeville, Law recalled the Christian arguments in favor of personal virtue. At issue is nothing less than a conflict over human nature and whether wanting what others have is good or bad for society.

Moral Virtue, however disregarded in Practice, has hitherto had a speculative Esteem amongst Men; her Praises have been celebrated by Authors of all kinds, as the confess'd Beauty, Ornament and Perfection of Human Nature....

You [Mandeville] consider Man, *merely* as an *Animal* having like other Animals, nothing to do but to follow his Appetites....

So that Man and Morality are here both destroy'd together; Man is declar'd to be only an *Animal*, and Morality an Imposture....

But this is not all, for you dare farther affirm in praise of Immorality, *That Evil as well moral, as natural, is the solid Basis, the Life and Support of all Trades and Employments without exception; that there we must look for the true Origin of all Arts and Sciences, and that the Moment Evil ceases, the Society must be spoil'd, if not dissolv'd.*

Source: William Law, *Remarks Upon a Late Book, Entituled [sic], The Fable of the Bees, Or Private Vices, Public Benefits: In a Letter to the Author: To Which Is Added, a Postscript, Containing an Observation Or Two Upon Mr. Bayle*, 2nd ed. (London: William and John Innys, 1725), 2–3.

QUESTIONS TO CONSIDER

1. Why would Mandeville choose bees for an analogy with human society?

2. What does Mandeville mean by "public benefits"?

3. Why is Law so disturbed by Mandeville's suggestion that humans are like other animals that follow their appetites?

islands, the pirates governed themselves and preyed on everyone's shipments without regard to national origin. After 1700, the colonial governments tried to stamp out piracy.

In comparison to those in the Americas, white settlements in Africa and Asia remained small. A handful of Portuguese trading posts in Angola and a few Dutch farms on the Cape of Good Hope provided the only toeholds in Africa for future expansion. In China, the emperors had welcomed Catholic missionaries at court in the seventeenth century, but the priests' credibility diminished as they squabbled among themselves and associated with European merchants, whom the Chinese considered pirates. In 1720, only one thousand Europeans resided in Guangzhou (Canton), the sole place where foreigners could legally trade for spices, tea, and silk (see Map 17.1 on page 578).

Europeans exercised more influence in Java (in what was then called the East Indies) and in India. Many Dutch settled in Java to oversee coffee production and Asian trade. Dutch, English, French, Portuguese, and Danish companies competed in India for spices, cotton, and silk; by the 1740s, the English and French had become the leading rivals in India, just as they were in North America. Both countries extended their power as India's Muslim rulers lost control to local Hindu princes, rebellious Sikhs, invading Persians, and their own provincial governors. A few thousand Europeans lived in India, though many thousand more soldiers were stationed there to protect them. The staple of trade with India in the early 1700s was calico—lightweight, brightly colored cotton cloth that caught on as a fashion in Europe. English and French slave traders sold calico to the Africans in exchange for slaves.

The Birth of Consumer Society

As worldwide colonization produced new supplies of goods, from coffee to calico, population growth in Europe fueled demand for them. Beginning in Britain, then in France and the Italian states, and finally in eastern Europe, population surged, growing by about 20 percent between 1700 and 1750. The gap between a fast-growing northwest and a more stagnant south and central Europe now diminished as regions that had lost population during the seventeenth-century downturn recovered. Cities, in particular, grew. Between 1600 and 1750, Paris's population more than doubled and London's more than tripled.

Although contemporaries could not have realized it then, this was the start of the modern population explosion. It appears that a decline in the death rate, rather than a rise in the birthrate, explains the turnaround. Three main factors contributed to increased longevity: better weather and hence more bountiful harvests, improved agricultural techniques, and the plague's disappearance after 1720.

By the early eighteenth century, the effects of economic expansion and population growth brought about a **consumer revolution** (see Contrasting Views). For example, at Nantes, the center of the French sugar trade, imports quadrupled between 1698 and 1733. Tea, chocolate, and coffee became

The Exotic as Consumer Item
This painting by the Venetian artist Rosalba Carriera (1675–1757) is titled *Africa*. The young black girl wearing a turban represents the African continent. Carriera was known for her use of pastels. In 1720, she journeyed to Paris, where she became an associate of Antoine Watteau and helped inaugurate the rococo style in painting. Why might the artist have chosen to paint an African girl? (bpk Bildagentur/Gemaldegalerie Alte Meister, Staaliche Kunstsammlungen Dresden, Germany/Art Resource, NY.)

virtual necessities. In 1700, England had two thousand coffeehouses; by 1740, every English country town had at least two. Paris got its first cafés at the end of the seventeenth century, and Berlin opened its first coffeehouse in 1714.

A new economic dynamic steadily took shape that has influenced all of subsequent history. More and more people escaped the confines of a subsistence economy, in which peasants produced barely enough to support themselves from year to year. As ordinary people gained more disposable income, demand for nonessential consumer goods rose. These included not only the new colonial products such as coffee and tea but also tables, chairs, sheets, chamber pots, lamps, and mirrors—and for the better-off still, coffee- and teapots, china, cutlery, chests of drawers, desks, clocks, and pictures for the walls.

Rising demand created more jobs and more income and yet more purchasing power in a mutually reinforcing cycle. In the English economic literature of the 1690s and early 1700s, writers reacted to these developments by expressing a new view of humans as consuming animals with boundless appetites. Change did not occur all at once, however. The consumer revolution spread from the cities to the countryside, from England to the continent, and from western Europe to eastern Europe only over the long run.

Europe was not the only region experiencing such changes. China's population grew even faster—it may have tripled during the 1700s—and there, too, consumption of cloth, furniture, tea, sugar, and tobacco all increased. In China, these goods could be locally produced, and China did not pursue colonization of far-flung lands. Still, foreign trade also increased, especially with lands on China's borders.

REVIEW QUESTION
How was consumerism related to slavery in the early eighteenth century?

New Social and Cultural Patterns

The rise of consumption in Europe was fueled in part by a revolution in agricultural techniques that made it possible to produce larger quantities of food with a smaller agricultural workforce. As population increased, more people moved to the cities, where they found themselves caught up in innovative urban customs such as attending musical concerts and reading novels. Along with a general increase in literacy, these activities helped create a public that responded to new writers and artists. As always, people's experiences varied depending on whether they lived in wealth or poverty, in urban or rural areas, or in eastern or western Europe.

Agricultural Revolution

Although Britain, France, and the Dutch Republic shared the enthusiasm for consumer goods, Britain's domestic market grew most quickly. In Britain, as agricultural output increased by 43 percent over the course of the 1700s, the population increased by 70 percent. The British imported grain to feed the growing population, but they also benefited from the development of techniques that together constituted an **agricultural revolution**. It was not new machinery but rather increasingly aggressive attitudes toward investment and management that propelled this revolution. The Dutch and the Flemish had pioneered many agricultural management techniques in the 1600s, but the British took them further.

Four major changes occurred in British agriculture that eventually spread to other countries. First, farmers increased the amount of land under cultivation by draining wetlands and by growing crops on previously uncultivated common lands (acreage maintained by the community for grazing). Second, those farmers who could afford it consolidated small, scattered plots into larger, more efficient units. Third, livestock raising became more closely linked to crop growing, and the yields of each increased. For centuries, most farmers had rotated their fields in and out of production to replenish the soil. Now farmers planted carefully chosen fodder crops such as clover and turnips that added nutrients to the soil, thereby eliminating the need to leave a field fallow (unplanted) every two or three years. With more fodder available, farmers could raise more livestock, which in turn produced more manure to fertilize grain fields. Fourth, selective breeding of animals combined with the increase in fodder to improve the quality and size of herds. By the 1730s and 1740s, agricultural output had increased dramatically, and prices for food had fallen because of these interconnected innovations.

Changes in agricultural practices did not benefit all landowners equally. The biggest British landowners consolidated their holdings in the enclosure movement. They put pressure on small farmers and villagers to sell their land or give up their common lands. The big landlords then fenced off (enclosed) their property. Because enclosure eliminated community grazing rights, it frequently sparked a struggle between the big landlords and villagers, and in Britain it normally required an act of Parliament. Such acts became increasingly common in the second half of the eighteenth century, and by the century's end six million acres of common lands had been enclosed and developed. In this way the English peasantry largely disappeared, replaced by a more hierarchical society of big landlords, enterprising tenant farmers, and poor agricultural laborers.

The new agricultural techniques spread slowly from Britain and the Low Countries (the Dutch Republic and the Austrian Netherlands) to the rest of western Europe. Outside a few pockets, however, subsistence agriculture (producing just enough to get by rather than surpluses for the market) continued to dominate farming in western Europe and Scandinavia. Unlike the populations of the highly urbanized Low Countries (where half the people lived in towns and cities), most Europeans, western and eastern, eked out their existence in the countryside and could barely participate in the new markets for consumer goods.

In eastern Europe, the condition of peasants worsened in the areas where landlords tried hardest to improve crop yields. To produce more for the Baltic grain market, aristocratic landholders in Prussia, Poland, and parts of Russia drained wetlands, cultivated moors, and built dikes. They also forced peasants off lands that the peasants had worked for themselves, and they increased compulsory labor services (the critical element in serfdom). Some eastern landowners grew fabulously wealthy. The Potocki family in the Polish Ukraine, for example, owned three million acres of land and had 130,000 serfs.

Social Life in the Cities

Because of emigration from the countryside, cities grew in population and consequently exercised a growing influence on culture and social life. Between 1650 and 1750, cities with at least ten thousand inhabitants increased in population by 44 percent. From the eighteenth century onward, urban growth has been continuous. Along with the general growth of cities, an important south-to-north shift occurred in the pattern of urbanization. Around 1500, half of the people in cities of at least ten thousand residents could be found in the Italian states, Spain, or Portugal; by 1700, the urbanization of northwestern and southern Europe was roughly equal. Eastern Europe, despite the huge cities of Istanbul and Moscow, was still less urban than western Europe. With 675,000 inhabitants, London was by far the most populous European city in 1750; Berlin had 90,000 people, Warsaw only 23,000.

Many landowners kept a residence in town, so the separation between rural and city life was not as extreme as might be imagined, at least not for the very rich. At the top of the ladder in the big cities were the landed nobles. Some of them filled their lives only with conspicuous consumption of fine food, extravagant clothing, carriages, books, and opera; others held key political, administrative, or judicial offices. However they spent their time, these rich families employed thousands of artisans, shopkeepers, and domestic servants. Many English peers (highest-ranking nobles) had thirty or forty servants at each of their homes.

The middle classes of officials, merchants, professionals, and landowners occupied the next rung down on the social ladder. London's population, for example, included about twenty thousand middle-class families (constituting, at most, one-sixth of the city's population). In this period the middle classes began to develop distinctive ways of life that set them apart from both the

Domestic Servant Polishing the Silver
This painting by André Bouys from 1737 depicts a scene common in prosperous households. In French towns and cities, servants made up as much as 10 percent of the population. Those at the top of the social scale employed the largest number, but even modest artisans might engage one servant to help in the home or the shop. Servants were just as important in London and Amsterdam. (Photo Josse/Leemage/Getty Images.)

rich noble landowners and the lower classes. Unlike the rich nobles, the middle classes lived primarily in the cities and towns, even if they owned small country estates.

Below the middle classes came the artisans and shopkeepers (most of whom were organized in professional guilds), then the journeymen, apprentices, servants, and laborers. At the bottom of the social scale were the unemployed poor, who survived by intermittent work and charity. Women married to artisans and shopkeepers often kept the accounts, supervised employees, and ran the household as well. Every middle-class and upper-class family employed servants; artisans and shopkeepers frequently hired them, too. Women from poorer families usually worked as domestic servants until they married. Four out of five domestic servants in the city were female. In large cities such as London, the servant population grew faster than the population of the city as a whole.

Social status in the cities was readily visible. Wide, spacious streets graced rich districts; the houses had gardens, and the air was relatively fresh. In poor districts, the streets were narrow, dirty, dark, humid, and smelly, and the houses were damp and crowded. The poorest people were homeless, sleeping under bridges or in abandoned buildings. A Neapolitan prince described his homeless neighbors as "lying like filthy animals, with no distinction of age or sex."

Like shelter, clothing was a reliable social indicator. The poorest working-women in Paris wore woolen skirts and blouses of dark colors over petticoats, a bodice, and a corset. They also donned caps of various sorts, cotton stockings, and shoes (probably their only pair). Workingmen dressed even more drably. Many occupations could be recognized by their dress: for example, no one could confuse lawyers in their dark robes with masons or butchers in their special aprons. People higher on the social ladder were more likely to sport a variety of fabrics, colors, and unusual designs in their clothing and to own many different outfits. Social status was not an abstract idea; it permeated every detail of daily life.

The ability to read and write also reflected social differences. People in the upper classes were more literate than those in the lower classes; city people were more literate than peasants. Protestant countries appear to have been more successful at promoting education and literacy than Catholic countries, perhaps because of the Protestant emphasis on Bible reading. Widespread literacy among the lower classes was first achieved in the Protestant areas of Switzerland and in Presbyterian Scotland. In France, literacy doubled in the eighteenth century thanks to the spread of parish schools, but still only one in two men and one in four women could read and write. Most peasants remained illiterate. Few schools existed, teachers received low wages, and no country had yet established a national system of education.

A new literate public nonetheless arose among the middle classes of the cities. More books and periodicals were published than ever before, another aspect of the consumer revolution. The trend began in the 1690s in England and the Dutch Republic and gradually accelerated. In 1695, new newspapers and magazines proliferated when the British government stopped demanding that each publication have a government-approved license. The first London daily newspaper came out in 1702, and in 1709, Joseph Addison and Richard Steele published the first literary magazine, *The Spectator*. They devoted their magazine to the cultural improvement of the increasingly influential middle class. By the 1720s, twenty-four provincial newspapers were published in England. In the London coffeehouses, an edition of a single newspaper might reach ten thousand male readers. Women did their reading at home. Except in the Dutch Republic, newspapers on the continent lagged behind and often consisted mainly of advertising with little critical commentary. France, for example, had no daily paper until 1777.

New Tastes in the Arts

The new literate public did not just read newspapers; its members now pursued an interest in painting, attended concerts, and besieged booksellers in search of popular novels. Because increased trade and prosperity put money into the hands of the growing middle classes, a new urban audience began to compete with the churches, rulers, and courtiers as chief patrons for new work.

Developments in painting reflected the tastes of the new public, as the **rococo** style challenged the hold of the baroque and classical schools, especially in France. *Rococo*, like *baroque*, was an invented word (from the French word *rocaille*, "shellwork") and originally a derogatory label, meaning "frivolous decoration." Many rococo paintings depicted scenes of intimate sensuality rather than the monumental, emotional grandeur favored by classical and baroque painters. Personal portraits and pastoral paintings took the place of heroic landscapes

Rococo Painting

The rococo emphasis on interiors, on decoration, and on intimacy rather than monumental grandeur are evident in François Boucher's painting *The Luncheon* (1739). The painting also draws attention to new consumer items, from the mirror and the clock to chocolate, children's toys, a small Buddha statue, and the intricately designed furniture. (Musée du Louvre, Paris, France/© DeA Picture Library/Art Resource, NY.)

and grand, ceremonial canvases. Rococo paintings adorned homes as well as palaces and served as a form of interior decoration rather than as a statement of piety. Its decorative quality made rococo art an ideal complement to newly discovered materials such as stucco and porcelain, especially the porcelain vases now imported from China.

Public music concerts were first performed in England in the 1670s and became much more regular and frequent in the 1690s. On the continent, Frankfurt organized the first regular public concerts in 1712; Hamburg and Paris began holding them within a few years. Opera continued to spread in the eighteenth century; Venice had sixteen public opera houses by 1700, and the Covent Garden opera house opened in London in 1732.

The growth of a public that appreciated and supported music had much the same effect as the extension of the reading public: like authors, composers could now begin to liberate themselves from court patronage and work for a paying audience. The composer George Frideric Handel (1685–1759) was among the first to grasp the new directions in music. A German by birth, Handel wrote operas in Italy and then moved in 1710 to Britain, where he wrote music for the court and began composing oratorios. The oratorio, a form Handel introduced in Britain, combined the drama of opera with the majesty of religious and ceremonial music and featured the chorus over the soloists. The "Hallelujah Chorus" from Handel's oratorio *Messiah* (1741) is perhaps the single best-known piece of Western classical music. It reflected the composer's personal, deeply felt piety but also his willingness to combine musical materials into a dramatic form that captured the enthusiasm of the new public.

Nothing excited the imagination of the new public more than the novel, the literary genre whose very name underscored the eighteenth-century taste for novelty. More than three hundred French novels appeared between 1700 and 1730. During this unprecedented explosion, the novel took on its modern form and became more concerned with individual psychology and social description than with the adventure tales popular earlier (such as Miguel de Cervantes's *Don Quixote*). The novel's popularity was closely tied to the expansion of the reading public, and novels were available in serial form in periodicals or from the many booksellers who served the new market.

Women figured prominently in novels as characters, and women writers abounded. The English author Eliza Haywood (1693?–1756) earned her living turning out a stream of novels with titles such as *Persecuted Virtue*, *Constancy Rewarded*, and *The History of Betsy Thoughtless*—all showing a concern for the proper place of women as models of virtue in a changing world. Haywood's male counterpart was Daniel Defoe (1660–1731), a merchant's son who had a diverse and colorful career as a manufacturer, political spy, novelist, and social commentator. Defoe is best known for his novel *Robinson Crusoe* (1719). The story of the adventures of a shipwrecked sailor, *Robinson Crusoe* portrayed the new values of the time: to survive, Crusoe had to employ fearless entrepreneurial ingenuity. He had to be ready for the unexpected and be able to improvise in every situation. He was, in short, the model for the new man in an expanding economy. Crusoe's patronizing attitude toward the black man Friday now draws much critical attention, but his discovery of Friday shows how the fate of blacks and whites had become intertwined in the new colonial environment.

Religious Revivals

Despite the novel's growing popularity, religious books and pamphlets still sold in huge numbers, and most Europeans remained devout, even as their religions were changing. In this period, a Protestant revivalist movement known as **Pietism** rocked the complacency of the established churches in northern Europe. Pietists believed in a mystical religion of the heart; they wanted a deeply emotional, even ecstatic religion. They urged intense Bible study, which in turn promoted popular education and contributed to the increase in literacy. Many Pietists attended catechism instruction every day and also went to morning and evening prayer meetings in addition to regular Sunday services. Although Pietism appealed to both Lutherans and Calvinists, it had the greatest impact in Lutheran Prussia, where it taught the virtues of hard work, obedience, and devotion to duty.

Catholicism also had its versions of religious revival, especially in France. A Frenchwoman, Jeanne Marie Guyon (1648–1717), attracted many noblewomen and a few leading clergymen to her own Catholic brand of Pietism, known as Quietism. Claiming miraculous visions and astounding prophecies, she urged a mystical union with God through prayer and simple devotion. Despite papal condemnation and intense controversy within Catholic circles in France, Guyon had followers all over Europe.

Even more influential were the Jansenists, who gained many new adherents to their austere form of Catholicism despite Louis XIV's harassment and repeated condemnation by the papacy. Under the pressure of religious and political persecution, Jansenism took a revivalist turn in the 1720s. At the funeral of a Jansenist priest in Paris in 1727, the crowd who flocked to the grave claimed to witness a series of miraculous healings. Some believers fell into frenzied convulsions, claiming to be inspired by the Holy Spirit through the intercession of the dead priest. After midcentury, Jansenism became even more politically active as its adherents joined in opposition to the crown's policies on religion.

REVIEW QUESTION
How were new social trends reflected in cultural life in the early 1700s?

Consolidation of the European State System

The spread of Pietism and Jansenism reflected the emergence of a middle-class public that now participated in every new development, including religion. The middle classes could pursue these interests because the European state system gradually stabilized despite the increasing competition for wealth in the Atlantic system. Warfare settled three main issues between 1700 and 1750: a coalition of powers held France in check on the continent, Great Britain emerged from the wars against France as the preeminent maritime power, and Russia defeated Sweden in the contest for supremacy in the Baltic. After Louis XIV's death in 1715, Europe enjoyed the fruits of a more balanced diplomatic system, in which warfare became less frequent and less widespread. States could then spend their resources establishing and expanding control over their own populations, both at home and in their colonies.

A New Power Alignment

The peace treaties that ended the War of the Spanish Succession (1701–1713) signaled a new alignment of power in western Europe (see Chapter 16). Spain began a long decline, French ambitions for dominance were thwarted, and Great Britain emerged as the new center in the balance of power. A coalition led by Britain and joined by most of the European powers had confronted Louis XIV's French forces across Europe. The conflict extended to the Caribbean and North and South America as well. The casualties mounted inexorably: in the battle of Blenheim in southern Germany in 1704, 108,000 soldiers fought and 33,000 were killed or wounded—in just one day. At Malplaquet, near the northern French border, a great battle in 1709 engaged 166,000 soldiers and cavalrymen, and 36,000 of them were killed or wounded. Those allied against Louis won at Malplaquet, but they lost twice as many men as the French did and could not pursue their advantage. Everyone rejoiced when peace came (Map 17.2).

By the terms of the peace, French king Louis XIV's grandson was confirmed as King Philip V of Spain (r. 1700–1746) but only on the condition that he renounce any claim to the French throne. None of the other powers could countenance a joint French-Spanish monarchy. Philip opened Spain further to

Territories gained after the Peace of Utrecht, 1714

- French Bourbon lands
- Spanish Bourbon lands
- Austrian Habsburg lands
- Prussian lands
- Great Britain
- To Great Britain
- To the Austrian Empire
- The Jacobite rising of 1715
- Main areas of fighting during the War of the Spanish Succession, 1701–1713
- Boundary of the Holy Roman Empire

MAP 17.2 Europe, c. 1715

Although Louis XIV succeeded in putting his grandson Philip on the Spanish throne, France emerged considerably weakened from the War of the Spanish Succession. France ceded large territories in Canada to Britain, which also gained key Mediterranean outposts from Spain as well as a monopoly on providing slaves to the Spanish colonies. Spanish losses were catastrophic. Philip had to renounce any future claim to the French crown and give up considerable territories in the Netherlands and Italy to the Austrians. How did the competing English and French claims in North America around 1715 create potential conflicts for the future?

the rest of Europe and stabilized the currency, but he could not revive Spain's military prestige or commercial position. Spain consistently imported more from Britain and France than it exported to them. As a country that had been created by a campaign against Muslims within its boundaries, Spain remained firmly in the grip of the Catholic clergy, which insisted on the censorship of dissident or heretical ideas. Although the capital city, Madrid, had 200,000 inhabitants, laws prohibited people from smoking, reading newspapers, or talking politics in the cafés and inns of the city — precisely the activities flourishing in England, France, and the Dutch Republic.

When Louis XIV died in 1715, his five-year-old great-grandson succeeded him as Louis XV (r. 1715–1774), with the duke of Orléans (1674–1723), nephew of the dead king, serving as regent for the young boy. To raise much-needed funds, in 1719, the regent encouraged the Scottish financier John Law to set up an official trading company for North America and a state bank that issued paper money and stock (without which trade depended on the available supply of gold and silver). The bank was supposed to offer lower interest rates to the state, thus cutting the cost of financing the government's debts. The value of the stock rose rapidly in a frenzy of speculation, only to crash a few months later. France finally achieved a measure of financial stability under the leadership of Cardinal Hercule de Fleury (1653–1743), the most powerful member of the government after the death of the regent. Colonial trade boomed. Peace and the acceptance of limits on territorial expansion inaugurated a century of French prosperity.

British Rise and Dutch Decline

The British and the Dutch had formed a coalition against Louis XIV under their joint ruler, William III, who was simultaneously stadholder (elected head) of the Dutch Republic and, with his English wife, Mary (d. 1694), ruler of England, Wales, and Scotland. After William's death in 1702, the British and Dutch went their separate ways. Over the next decades, England incorporated Scotland and subjugated Ireland, becoming "Great Britain" in 1707. At the same time, Dutch imperial power declined; by 1700, the British dominated the seas, and the Dutch, with their small population of less than two million, came to depend on alliances with bigger powers.

English relations with Scotland and Ireland were complicated by the problem of succession: William and Mary had no children. To ensure a Protestant succession, Parliament ruled that Mary's sister, Anne, would succeed William and Mary and that the Protestant house of Hanover in Germany would succeed Anne if she had no surviving heirs. Catholics were excluded. When Queen Anne (r. 1702–1714) died leaving no children, the elector of Hanover, a Protestant great-grandson of James I, consequently became King George I (r. 1714–1727). The house of Hanover — renamed the house of Windsor during World War I — still occupies the British throne today.

Support from the Scots and Irish for this solution did not come easily because many in Scotland and Ireland supported the claims to the throne of the deposed Catholic king, James II, and, after his death in 1701, his son James

Edward. Out of fear of this Jacobitism (from the Latin *Jacobus*, for "James"), Scottish Protestant leaders agreed to the Act of Union of 1707, which abolished the Scottish Parliament and affirmed the Scots' recognition of the Protestant Hanoverian succession. The Scots agreed to obey the Parliament of Great Britain, which would include Scottish members in the House of Commons and the House of Lords. A Jacobite rebellion in Scotland in 1715, aiming to restore the Stuart line, was suppressed (see Map 17.2 on page 592). The threat of Jacobitism nonetheless continued into the 1740s.

The Irish—90 percent of whom were Catholic—proved even more difficult to subdue. William III had to take command of the joint English and Dutch forces to defeat the Irish supporters of James II, and after that defeat, Catholics in Ireland faced yet more confiscation and legal restrictions. By 1700, Irish Catholics, who in 1640 had owned 60 percent of the land in Ireland, owned just 14 percent. The Protestant-controlled Irish Parliament passed a series of laws limiting the rights of the Catholic majority: Catholics could not marry Protestants, send children abroad for education, or establish Catholic schools at home. Moreover, Catholics could not sit in Parliament, nor could they vote for its members unless they took an oath renouncing Catholic doctrine. These and a host of other laws reduced Catholic Ireland to the status of a colony.

In Britain's constitutional system, the monarch ruled with Parliament. The crown chose ministers, directed policy, and supervised administration, while Parliament raised revenue, passed laws, and represented the interests of the people to the crown. The powers of Parliament were reaffirmed by the Triennial Act in 1694, which provided that parliaments meet at least once every three years (this was extended to seven years in 1716, after the Whigs had established their ascendancy). Only 200,000 propertied men could vote, out of a population of more than five million, and a few hundred families controlled all the important political offices.

George I and George II (r. 1727–1760) relied on one man, Sir **Robert Walpole** (1676–1745), to help them manage their relations with Parliament. From his position as First Lord of the Treasury, Walpole made himself into the first, or "prime," minister, leading the House of Commons from 1721 to 1742. Although appointed initially by the king, Walpole established an enduring pattern of parliamentary government in which a prime minister from the leading party guided legislation through the House of Commons. Walpole also built a vast patronage machine that dispensed government jobs to win support for the crown's policies.

The partisan division between the Whigs, who supported the Hanoverian succession and the rights of dissenting Protestants, and the Tories, who had backed the Stuart line and the Church of England, did not hamper Great Britain's pursuit of economic, military, and colonial power. In this period, Great Britain became a great power on the world stage by virtue of its navy and its ability to finance major military involvement in wars. The founding in 1694 of the Bank of England—which, unlike the French bank, endured—enabled the government to raise money at low interest for foreign wars. By the 1740s, the government could borrow more than four times what it could in the 1690s.

When William of Orange (William III of England) died in 1702, he left no heirs, and for forty-five years the Dutch lived without a stadholder. The merchant ruling class of some two thousand families dominated the Dutch Republic more than ever, but they presided over a country that counted for less in international power politics. The Dutch population was not growing as fast as others, and the Dutch share of the Baltic trade decreased from 50 percent in 1720 to less than 30 percent by the 1770s. The output of Leiden textiles dropped to one-third of its 1700 level by 1740. Shipbuilding, paper manufacturing, tobacco processing, salt refining, and pottery production all dwindled as well. The biggest exception to the downward trend was trade with the New World, which increased with escalating demands for sugar and tobacco. The Dutch shifted their interest away from great-power rivalries and toward those areas of international trade and finance where they could establish an enduring presence.

Russia's Emergence as a European Power

The commerce and shipbuilding of the Dutch and British so impressed Russian Tsar Peter I (r. 1689–1725) that he traveled incognito to their shipyards in 1697 to learn their methods firsthand. Known to history as **Peter the Great,** he dragged Russia kicking and screaming all the way to great-power status. Although he came to the throne while still a minor (on the eve of his tenth birthday), grew up under the threat of a palace coup, and enjoyed little formal education, his accomplishments soon matched his seven-foot-tall stature. Peter transformed public life in Russia and established an absolutist state based on the Western model. His attempts to create a society patterned after western Europe, known as **Westernization,** ignited an enduring controversy: Did Peter set Russia on a course of inevitable Westernization required to compete with the West? Or did he forever and fatally disrupt Russia's natural evolution into a distinctive Slavic society?

To pursue his goal of Westernizing Russian culture, Peter set up the first laboratories and technical schools and founded the Russian Academy of Sciences. He ordered translations of Western classics and hired a German theater company to perform the French plays of Molière. He replaced the traditional

Peter I (the Great) of Russia
This tapestry commemorates Peter I's victory over Sweden at the battle of Poltava (1709). Until then, Sweden was the dominant power in the Baltic region. Peter set Russia on a new course.
(Tapestry/Blickling Hall, Norfolk, UK/National Trust Photographic Library/John Hammond/Bridgeman Images.)

Russian calendar with the Western one,* introduced Arabic numerals, and brought out the first public newspaper. He ordered his officials and the nobles to shave their beards and dress in Western fashion.

Peter encouraged foreigners to move to Russia to offer their advice and skills, especially for building the capital city. Named St. Petersburg after the tsar, the new capital symbolized Russia's opening to the West. Construction began in 1703 in a Baltic province that had been recently conquered from Sweden. By the end of 1709, thirty thousand laborers had been enlisted in the construction. Peter ordered skilled workers to move to the new city and commanded all landowners possessing more than forty serf households to build houses there. In the 1720s, a German minister described St. Petersburg "as a wonder of the world, considering its magnificent palaces, . . . and the short time that was employed in the building of it." At Peter's death in 1725, the new city had forty thousand residents; by 1750 it had 100,000.

Peter aimed to set Russia on a new course. At his new capital he tried to improve the traditionally denigrated, secluded status of women by ordering them to dress in European styles and appear publicly at his dinners for diplomatic representatives. A foreigner headed every one of Peter's new technical and vocational schools, and for its first eight years the new Academy of Sciences included no Russians. Every ministry was assigned a foreign adviser. Upper-class Russians learned French or German, which they spoke even at home. Such changes affected only the very top of Russian society, however; the mass of the population had no contact with the new ideas and ended up paying for the innovations either in ruinous new taxation or by building St. Petersburg, a project that cost the lives of thousands of workers. Serfs remained tied to the land, completely dominated by their noble lords.

Peter also reorganized government and finance on Western models and, like other absolute rulers, strengthened his army. With ruthless recruiting methods, which included branding a cross on every recruit's left hand to prevent desertion, he forged an army of 200,000 men and equipped it with modern weapons. He not only built the first navy in Russian history but also created schools for artillery, engineering, and military medicine. Not surprisingly, taxes tripled.

The tsar allowed nothing to stand in his way. He did not hesitate to use torture, and he executed thousands. He gave a special guard regiment unprecedented power to expedite cases against those suspected of rebellion, espionage, pretensions to the throne, or just "unseemly utterances" against him. Because his only son, Alexei, had allied himself with Peter's critics, the tsar threw him into prison, where the young man mysteriously died.

To control the often restive nobility, Peter insisted that all noblemen engage in state service. The Table of Ranks (1722) classified them into military, administrative, and court categories, a codification of social and legal relationships

WHAT WOULD YOU DO?

Imagine yourself as a high-ranking Russian noble during the time of Peter the Great. Would you support his reforms or resist them? Keep in mind that you would have to build a new house in his new capital of St. Petersburg, and it might be very far away from your estates and serfs. Think about which reforms would be beneficial to you (or the country as a whole) and which might be more difficult to swallow. Would you be in favor of Westernization or opposed to it?

*Peter introduced the Julian calendar, then still used in Protestant but not Catholic countries. Later in the eighteenth century, Protestant Europe abandoned the Julian for the Gregorian calendar. Not until 1918 was the Gregorian calendar adopted in Russia, at which point Russia's calendar had fallen thirteen days behind Europe's.

in Russia that would last for nearly two centuries. Because the nobles lacked a secure independent status, Peter could command them to a degree that was un-imaginable in western Europe. State service was not only compulsory but also permanent. Moreover, the male children of those in service had to be registered by the age of ten and begin serving at fifteen. To increase his authority over the Russian Orthodox church, Peter allowed the office of patriarch (supreme head) to remain vacant, and in 1721, he replaced it with the Holy Synod, a bureaucracy of laymen under his supervision.

Peter the Great's success in building up state authority changed the balance of power in eastern Europe. First he took on Sweden, which had dominated the Baltic region since the Thirty Years' War (1618–1648). Peter joined an anti-Swedish coalition in 1700 with Denmark, Saxony, and Poland, but the en-suing Great Northern War (1700–1721) went badly for the allies at first. The Swedes defeated Denmark, quickly marched into Poland and Saxony, and then invaded Russia. Peter's rebuilt army finally defeated the Swedes at the battle of Poltava (1709), taking twenty-three thousand Swedish soldiers prisoner and marking the end of Swedish imperial ambitions in the Baltic (Map 17.3). Russia could then begin to compete with the great powers Prussia, Austria, and France.

When the tide turned in the Great Northern War, King Frederick William I of Prussia (r. 1713–1740) joined the Russian side and gained new territories. Prussia had to make the most of every military opportunity because it was much smaller in size and population than the other powers. Frederick William doubled the size of the Prussian army; though still smaller than those of his rivals, it was the best-trained and most up-to-date force in Europe. The army

MAP 17.3 Russia and Sweden after the Great Northern War, 1721
After the Great Northern War, Russia supplanted Sweden as the major power in the north. Although Russia had a much larger population from which to draw its armies, Sweden made the most of its advantages and gave way only after a great military struggle.

so dominated life in Prussia that the country earned the label "a large army with a small state attached." One of the first rulers to wear a military uniform as his everyday dress, Frederick William subordinated the entire domestic administration to the army's needs. He financed the army's growth by subjecting all the provinces to an excise tax on food, drink, and manufactured goods and by increasing rents on crown lands.

Continuing Dynastic Struggles

War broke out again in 1733 when the king of Poland-Lithuania died. France, Spain, and Sardinia joined in the War of the Polish Succession (1733–1735) against Austria and Russia, each side supporting rival claimants to the Polish throne. Prussia chose to sit on the sidelines. Although Peter the Great had been followed by a series of weak rulers, Russian forces were still strong enough to drive the French candidate out of Poland-Lithuania, prompting France to accept the Austrian candidate. In exchange, Austria gave the province of Lorraine to the French candidate, the father-in-law of Louis XV, with the promise that the province would pass to France on his death. France and Britain went back to pursuing their colonial rivalries. Prussia and Russia concentrated on shoring up their influence within Poland-Lithuania.

Because its armies still faced the Turks on its southeastern border, Austria did not want to become mired in a long struggle in Poland-Lithuania. Even though the Austrians had forced the Turks to recognize their rule over all of Hungary and Transylvania in 1699 and had occupied Belgrade in 1717, the Turks did not stop fighting. In the 1730s, the Turks retook Belgrade, and Russia now claimed a role in the struggle against the Turks. Moreover, Hungary proved less than enthusiastic about submitting to Austria. In 1703, the wealthiest Hungarian noble landlord, Ferenc Rákóczi (1676–1735), raised an army of seventy thousand men who fought for "God, Fatherland, and Liberty" until 1711. They forced the Austrians to recognize local Hungarian institutions, grant amnesty, and restore confiscated estates in exchange for confirming hereditary Austrian rule.

When Holy Roman Emperor Charles VI died without a male heir in 1740, another war of succession, the **War of the Austrian Succession** (1740–1748), began. Most European rulers recognized the emperor's chosen heiress, his daughter Maria Theresa, because Charles's Pragmatic Sanction of 1713 had given a woman the right to inherit the Habsburg crown lands. The new king of Prussia, Frederick II, who had just succeeded his father a few months earlier in 1740, saw his chance to grab territory and immediately invaded the rich Austrian province of Silesia. France joined Prussia in an attempt to further humiliate its traditional enemy Austria, and Great Britain allied with Austria to prevent the French from taking the Austrian Netherlands. The war soon expanded to the overseas colonies of Great Britain and France. French and British colonials in North America fought each other all along their boundaries, enlisting native American auxiliaries. Hostilities broke out in India, too.

Habsburg dominions, 1657
Habsburg Hungary, 1657
Expansion to 1699
Expansion to 1718
Regained by Ottoman Empire
★ Battle

POLAND-LITHUANIA

AUSTRIA   HUNGARY
Vienna   Transylvania
1683
Belgrade
1717
OTTOMAN
EMPIRE

Adriatic Sea

0   200   400 miles
0   200   400 kilometers

Austrian Conquest of Hungary, 1657–1730

Maria Theresa (r. 1740–1780) survived only by conceding Silesia to Prussia in order to split the Prussians off from France. The Peace of Aix-la-Chapelle (1748) recognized Maria Theresa as the heiress to the Austrian lands; her husband, Francis I, became Holy Roman Emperor, thus reasserting the integrity of the Austrian Empire. The peace of 1748 failed to resolve the colonial conflicts between Britain and France, however, and fighting for domination continued unofficially.

The Power of Diplomacy and the Importance of Population

No single power emerged from the wars of the first half of the eighteenth century clearly superior to the others, and the Peace of Utrecht explicitly declared that maintaining a balance of power was crucial to keeping peace in Europe. Diplomacy helped preserve that balance, and to meet the new demands placed on it, the diplomatic service, like the military and financial bureaucracies before it, had to develop regular procedures. The French set a pattern that the other European states soon imitated. By 1685, France had embassies in all the important capitals. Nobles of ancient families served as ambassadors to Rome, Madrid, Vienna, and London, whereas royal officials were chosen for Switzerland, the Dutch Republic, and Venice. The ambassador selected and paid for his own staff, which might be as large as eighty people. The diplomatic system ensured a continuation of the principles of the Peace of Westphalia (1648); in the midst of every crisis and war, the great powers would convene and hammer out a written agreement detailing the requirements for peace.

Adroit diplomacy could smooth the road toward peace, but success in war still depended on sheer numbers—of men and of muskets. Because each state's strength depended largely on the size of its army, the growth and health of the population increasingly entered into government calculations. William Petty's *Political Arithmetick* (1690) offered statistical estimates of human capital—that is, of population and wages—to determine Britain's national wealth. Government officials devoted increased effort to the statistical estimation of total population and rates of births, deaths, and marriages.

Physicians used the new population statistics to explain the environmental causes of disease, another new preoccupation in this period. Petty, trained as a physician himself, devised a quantitative scale that distinguished healthy from unhealthy places largely on the basis of air quality, an early precursor of modern environmental studies. Cities were the unhealthiest places because garbage and excrement (animal and human) accumulated where people lived densely packed together. The Irish writer Jonathan Swift described what happened in London after a big rainstorm: "Filths of all hues and colors . . . sweepings from butchers' stalls, dung, guts and blood . . . dead cats and turniptops come tumbling down the flood." Reacting to newly collected data on climate, disease, and population, local governments undertook such measures as draining low-lying areas, burying refuse, and cleaning wells.

Not all changes came from direct government intervention. Hospitals, founded originally as charities concerned foremost with the moral worthiness of the poor, gradually evolved into medical institutions that defined patients by their diseases. Physicians began to rely on postmortem dissections in the hospital to gain better knowledge, a practice most patients' families resented. Press reports of body snatching and grave robbing by surgeons and their apprentices outraged the public well into the 1800s.

Despite the change in hospitals, a medical profession with nationwide organizations and licensing had not yet emerged, and no clear line separated trained physicians from quacks. Patients in a hospital were as likely to catch a deadly disease as to be cured there. Antiseptics were virtually unknown. Because doctors believed that most insanity was caused by disorders in the system of bodily "humors," their prescribed treatments included blood transfusions; ingestion of bitter substances such as coffee, quinine, and soap; immersion in water; various forms of exercise; and burning or cauterizing the body to allow "black vapors" to escape.

Hardly any infectious diseases could be cured, though inoculation against smallpox spread from the Middle East to Europe in the early eighteenth century, thanks largely to the efforts of Lady Mary Wortley Montagu (1689–1762). Wife of the British ambassador to the Ottoman Empire, Montagu witnessed firsthand the Turkish use of inoculation. When a new smallpox epidemic threatened England in 1721, she called on her physician to inoculate her daughter. Inoculation against smallpox spread more widely only after 1796, when the English physician Edward Jenner developed a serum based on cowpox, a milder disease.

Public bathhouses had disappeared from cities in the sixteenth and seventeenth centuries because they seemed to be a source of disorderly behavior and epidemic illness. In the eighteenth century, even private bathing came into disfavor because people feared the effects of contact with water. Bathing was hazardous, physicians insisted, because it opened the body to disease. The upper classes associated cleanliness not with baths but with frequently changed linens, powdered hair, and perfume, which was thought to strengthen the body and refresh the brain by counteracting corrupt and foul air.

REVIEW QUESTION
What events and developments led to greater stability and more limited warfare within Europe?

The Birth of the Enlightenment

Economic expansion, the emergence of a new consumer society, and the stabilization of the European state system all generated optimism about the future. The intellectual corollary was the **Enlightenment**, a term used later in the eighteenth century to describe the movement begun by a loosely knit group of writers and scholars who believed that human beings could apply a critical, reasoning spirit to every problem they encountered in this world. The result of the application of reason would be progress (see Terms of History) in every aspect of life. The new secular, scientific, and critical attitude first emerged in the 1690s, scrutinizing everything from the absolutism of Louis XIV to the traditional role of women in society. After 1750, criticism took a more systematic turn as writers provided new theories for the organization of

Believing as they did in the possibilities of improvement, many Enlightenment writers preached a new doctrine about the meaning of human history. They challenged the traditional Christian belief that the original sin of Adam and Eve condemned human beings to unhappiness in this world and offered instead an optimistic vision: human nature, they claimed, was inherently good, and progress would be continuous if education developed human capacities to the utmost. Science and reason could bring happiness in this world. The idea of novelty or newness itself now seemed positive rather than threatening. Europeans began to imagine that they could surpass all those who preceded them in history, and they began to think of themselves as more "advanced" than the "backward" cultures they encountered in other parts of the world.

More than an intellectual concept, the idea of progress included a new conception of historical time and of Europeans' place within world history. Europeans stopped looking back, whether to a lost Garden of Eden or to the writings of Greek and Roman antiquity. Growing prosperity, European dominance overseas, and the scientific revolution oriented them toward the future. To distinguish it from the Middle Ages (a new

term), Europeans began to apply the word *modern* to their epoch—and they considered their modern period superior in achievement. Consequently, Europeans took it as their mission to bring their modern, enlightened ways of progress to the areas they colonized.

The economic and ecological catastrophes, destructive wars, and genocides of the twentieth century cast much doubt on this rosy vision of continuing progress. As the philosopher George Santayana (1863–1952) complained, "The cry was for vacant freedom and indeterminate progress: *Vorwarts! Avanti! Onward! Full Speed Ahead!*, without asking whether directly before you was a bottomless pit." Historians are now chastened in their claims about progress. They would no longer side with the German philosopher Georg W. F. Hegel, who proclaimed in 1832, "The history of the world is none other than the progress of the consciousness of freedom." They worry about the nationalistic claims inherent, for example, in the English historian Thomas Babington Macaulay's insistence that "the history of England is emphatically the history of progress" (1843). As with many other historical questions, the final word is not yet in: Is there a direction in human history that can correctly be called progress? Or is history, as many in ancient times thought, a set of repeating cycles?

society and politics; but as early as the 1720s, established authorities realized they faced a new set of challenges. Even while slavery expanded in the Atlantic system, Enlightenment writers began to insist on the need for new freedoms in Europe.

Popularization of Science and Challenges to Religion

The writers of the Enlightenment glorified the geniuses of the new science and championed the scientific method as the solution for all social problems. By 1700, mathematics and science had become fashionable topics in high society, and the public flocked to lectures explaining scientific discoveries.

As the prestige of science increased, some developed a skeptical attitude toward attempts to enforce religious conformity. Pierre Bayle (1647–1706), a French Huguenot refugee from Louis XIV's persecutions, launched an internationally influential campaign against religious intolerance from his safe haven in the Dutch Republic. His *News from the Republic of Letters* (first published in 1684) bitterly criticized the policies of Louis XIV and was quickly banned in Paris and condemned in Rome. After attacking Louis XIV's anti-Protestant policies, Bayle took a more general stand in favor of religious toleration. No state in Europe officially offered complete tolerance, though the Dutch Republic came closest with its tacit acceptance of Catholics, dissident Protestant groups, and open Jewish communities. In 1697, Bayle published his *Historical and Critical Dictionary*, which cited all the errors and delusions that he could find in past and present writers of all religions. Even religion must meet the test of reasonableness: "Any particular dogma, whatever it may be, whether it is advanced on the authority of the Scriptures, or whatever else may be its origins, is to be regarded as false if it clashes with the clear and definite conclusions of the natural understanding [reason]."

Bayle's insistence on rational investigation seemed to challenge the authority of faith. Other scholars challenged the authority of the Bible by subjecting it to historical criticism. Discoveries in geology in the early eighteenth century showed that marine fossils dated immensely farther back than the biblical flood story suggested. Investigations of miracles, comets, and oracles—like the growing literature against belief in witchcraft—urged the use of reason to combat superstition and prejudice. Defenders of church and state published books warning of the new skepticism's dangers. The spokesman for Louis XIV's absolutism, the bishop Jacques-Bénigne Bossuet, warned that "reason is the guide of their choice, but reason only brings them face to face with vague conjectures and baffling perplexities." Human beings, the traditionalists held, were simply incapable of subjecting everything to reason, especially in the realm of religion.

State authorities found religious skepticism equally unsettling because it threatened to undermine state power, too. The extensive literature of criticism was not limited to France, but much of it was published in French, and the French government took the lead in suppressing the more outspoken works. Forbidden books were then often published in the Dutch Republic, Britain, or Switzerland and smuggled back across the border to a public whose appetite was only whetted by censorship.

The most influential writer of the early Enlightenment was a Frenchman born into the upper middle class, François-Marie Arouet, known by his pen name, **Voltaire** (1694–1778). Voltaire took inspiration from Bayle, once giving him the following tongue-in-cheek description: "He gives facts with such odious fidelity, he exposes the arguments for and against with such dastardly impartiality, he is so intolerably intelligible, that he leads people of only ordinary common sense to judge and even to doubt." Voltaire's tangles with church and state began in the early 1730s, when he published his *Letters Concerning the English Nation* (the English version appeared in 1733), in which he devoted several chapters to scientist Isaac Newton and philosopher John Locke and used the virtues of the British as a way to attack Catholic bigotry and government rigidity in France. He spent two years in exile in Britain when the French state responded to his book with an order for his arrest.

Voltaire also popularized Newton's scientific discoveries in his *Elements of the Philosophy of Newton* (1738). The French state and many European

Voltaire and Émilie du Châtelet
In this watercolor, painted in 1750 by the French artist Louis Carmontelle (1717–1806), Voltaire is shown conversing with Gabrielle Émilie Le Tonnelier de Breteuil, marquise du Châtelet. She had died the year before, after giving birth to a daughter, an untimely end for one of the few people, man or woman, who understood Newton's mathematics. Voltaire lived in her house for a number of years (tolerated by her husband), and they set up a scientific laboratory there to pursue their mutual interests. Émilie du Châtelet prepared a French translation of Newton's *Principia Mathematica* that was published after her death; it is still the standard French translation. In his typical tongue-in-cheek fashion, Voltaire said that she was "a great man whose only fault was being a woman." (DEA/G. Dagli Orti/Getty Images.)

theologians considered Newtonianism threatening because it glorified the human mind and seemed to reduce God to an abstract, external, rationalistic force. So sensational was the success of Voltaire's book on Newton that a hostile Jesuit reported that "all Paris resounds with Newton, all Paris stammers Newton, all Paris studies and learns Newton." Voltaire's fame continued to grow, reaching truly astounding proportions in the 1750s and 1760s.

Travel Literature and the Challenge to Custom and Tradition

Just as scientific method could be used to question religious and even state authority, a more general skepticism also emerged from the expanding knowledge about the world outside of Europe. During the seventeenth and eighteenth centuries, the number of travel accounts dramatically increased as travel writers used the contrast between their home societies and other cultures to criticize the customs of European society.

Travelers to the Americas found "noble savages" (native peoples) who appeared to live in conditions of great freedom and equality; they were "naturally good" and "happy" without taxes, lawsuits, or much organized government. In China, in contrast, travelers found a people who enjoyed prosperity and an ancient civilization. Christian missionaries made little headway in China, and visitors had to admit that China's religious systems had flourished for four or five thousand years with no input from Europe or from Christianity. The basic lesson of travel literature in the 1700s, then, was that customs varied: justice, freedom, property, good government, religion, and morality all were relative to the place. One critic complained that travel encouraged the destruction of religion: "Some complete their demoralization by extensive travel, and lose whatever shreds of religion remained to them. Every day they see a new religion, new customs, new rites."

Travel literature turned explicitly political in Montesquieu's *Persian Letters* (1721) (see Primary Source Analysis on page 605). Charles-Louis de Secondat, baron of Montesquieu (1689–1755), the son of an eminent judicial

BRAMIN qui a fait vœu de porter un Colier de fer du poids de 24. livres et plus en guerre, jusqu'à ce qu'il eut amassé en aumônes une assez grande somme d'argent pour faire bâtir un Hôpital.

BRAMIN qui se balance par dévotion, pendant une demi-heure, en l'honneur du Dieu Eswara, au dessus d'un feu qu'il attise avec le bois qu'il a mis aux deux côtés.

Comparisons of Religions and the Rise of Skepticism
These two engravings come from *Religious Customs and Ceremonies of the All the Peoples of the World*, an influential encyclopedia published in French between 1723 and 1743 in Amsterdam. The artist Bernard Picart depicts a Brahmin who wears an iron collar to raise funds for a hospital and a Brahmin suspended over a fire in devotion. Picart and his fellow French Protestant refugee Jean Frédéric Bernard, the author and publisher, wanted to put Christianity and especially Catholicism in a comparative light; they emphasized the similarities in religious customs across the globe, and in this way cast doubt on claims for the absolute truth of any one religion. Their book helped inspire the early Enlightenment. (Private Collection/The Stapleton Collection/Bridgeman Images.)

family, was a high-ranking judge in a French court. He published *Persian Letters* anonymously in the Dutch Republic, and the book went into ten printings in just one year—a best seller for the times. Montesquieu tells the fictional story of two Persians, Rica and Usbek, who visit France in the last years of Louis XIV's reign and write home with their impressions. By imagining an outsider's perspective, Montesquieu could satirize French customs and politics without taking them on directly. Montesquieu chose Persians for his travelers because they came from what was widely considered the most despotic of all governments, in which rulers had life-and-death powers over their subjects. In the book, the Persians constantly compare France to Persia, suggesting that the French monarchy might verge on despotism.

Montesquieu's anonymity did not last long, and in the late 1720s, he sold his judgeship and traveled extensively in Europe, staying eighteen months in Britain. In 1748, he published a widely influential work on comparative government, *The Spirit of Laws*. Like the politique Jean Bodin before him (see page 528), Montesquieu examined the various types of government, but unlike Bodin he did not favor absolute power in a monarchy. His time in Britain made him much more favorable to constitutional forms of government. The

Montesquieu, *Persian Letters*: Letter 37 (1721)

Charles-Louis de Secondat, baron of Montesquieu (1689–1755), was one of the leading figures of the early Enlightenment. In Persian Letters, he offered a kind of reverse travel account in which fictional Persians comment on what they see in France. Politics, religion, and social customs all came under critical scrutiny. Letter 37 points to one of his and other early Enlightenment authors' main targets: the French king, Louis XIV (r. 1643–1715), and his absolutist state. Written by one of the book's two main characters, a Persian named Usbek, to a friend back home, the letter explicitly criticizes the king's vanity, ostentation, and life at court. The letter implicitly passes even more serious judgment on the aging ruler in noting his esteem for "oriental policies." Montesquieu condemns these same policies elsewhere in his letters as inhumane and unjust.

The King of France is old. We have no examples in our histories of such a long reign as his. It is said that he possesses in a very high degree the faculty of making himself obeyed: he governs with equal ability his family, his court, and his kingdom: he has often been heard to say, that, of all existing governments, that of the Turks, or that of our august Sultan, pleased him best: such is his high opinion of Oriental statecraft.[1]

I have studied his character, and I have found certain contradictions which I cannot reconcile. For example, he has a minister who is only eighteen years old,[2] and a mistress [Madame de Maintenon] who is fourscore; he loves his religion, and yet he cannot abide those [the Jansenists] who assert that it ought to be strictly observed; although he flies from the noise of cities, and is inclined to be reticent, from morning till night he is engaged in getting himself talked about; he is fond of trophies and victories, but he has as great a dread of seeing a good general at the head of his own troops, as at the head of an army of his enemies. It has never I believe happened to anyone but himself, to be burdened with more wealth than even a prince could hope for, and yet at the same time steeped in such poverty as a private person could ill brook.

He delights to reward those who serve him; but he pays as liberally the assiduous indolence of his courtiers, as the labors in the field of his captains; often the man who undresses him, or who hands him his serviette at table, is preferred before him who has taken cities and gained battles; he does not believe that the greatness of a monarch is compatible with restriction in the distribution of favors; and, without examining into the merit of a man, he will heap benefits upon him, believing that his selection makes the recipient worthy; accordingly, he has been known to bestow a small pension upon a man who had run off two leagues from the enemy, and a good government on another who had gone four.

Paris, the 7th of the moon of Maharram, 1713.

Source: Montesquieu, *Persian Letters*, trans. John Davidson (London: Privately printed, 1892), 1:85–86.

QUESTIONS TO CONSIDER

1. In the commentary of the fictional character of Usbek in this letter, in what ways is Montesquieu criticizing Louis XIV's version of absolutism?

2. Look closely at the end of the first paragraph. How does Montesquieu use "Oriental statecraft" to make a satirical comment about Louis XIV?

3. What is Montesquieu implying about Louis XIV's views on religion?

---

[1]When Louis XIV was in his sixteenth year, some courtiers discussed in his presence the absolute power of the Sultans, who dispose as they like of the goods and the lives of their subjects. "That is something like being a king," said the young monarch. Marshal d'Estrées, alarmed at the tendency revealed in that remark, rejoined, "But, sire, several of these emperors have been strangled even in my time."

[2]Barbezieux, son of Louvois, Louis's youngest minister, held office at twenty-three, not eighteen; and he was dead in 1713.

Catholic church soon listed both *Persian Letters* and *The Spirit of Laws* on its Index of forbidden books.

Raising the Woman Question

Many of the letters exchanged in *Persian Letters* focused on women because Montesquieu considered the position of women a sure indicator of the nature of government and morality. Although Montesquieu was not a feminist, his depiction of Roxana, the favorite wife in Usbek's harem, struck a chord with many women. Roxana revolts against the authority of Usbek's eunuchs and writes a final letter to her husband announcing her impending suicide: "I may have lived in servitude, but I have always been free, I have amended your laws according to the laws of nature, and my mind has always remained independent." Women writers used the same language of tyranny and freedom to argue for concrete changes in their status. Feminist ideas were not entirely new, but they were presented systematically for the first time during the Enlightenment and represented a fundamental challenge to the ways of traditional societies.

The most systematic and successful of these women writers was the English author Mary Astell (1666–1731). In 1694, she published *A Serious Proposal to the Ladies*, in which she advocated founding a private women's college to remedy women's lack of education. Addressing women, she asked, "How can you be content to be in the World like Tulips in a Garden, to make a fine *shew* [show] and be good for nothing?" In later works such as *Reflections upon Marriage* (1706), Astell criticized the relationship between the sexes within marriage: "If absolute sovereignty be not necessary in a state, how comes it to be so in a family? . . . *If all men are born free*, how is it that all women are born slaves?"

Most male writers held that women were less capable of reasoning than men and therefore did not need systematic education. Such opinions often rested on biological suppositions. The long-dominant Aristotelian view of reproduction held that only the male seed carried spirit and individuality. At the beginning of the eighteenth century, however, scientists began to undermine this belief. Physicians and surgeons began to champion the doctrine of *ovism*—that the female egg was essential in making new humans. During the decades that followed, male Enlightenment writers would continue to debate women's nature and appropriate social roles.

REVIEW QUESTION
What were the major issues in the early decades of the Enlightenment?

Conclusion

Expansion of colonies overseas and economic development at home created greater wealth, longer life spans, and higher expectations for Europeans in the first half of the eighteenth century. In these better times for many, a spirit of optimism and belief in the progress prevailed. People could now spend money on newspapers, novels, travel literature, and music as well as on coffee, tea, and cotton cloth. Not everyone shared equally in the benefits, however: slaves toiled in misery for their masters in the Americas, eastern European

MAPPING THE WEST

Austrian Habsburg territory

Prussian territory

Boundary of the Holy Roman Empire

Main areas of fighting, 1740–1748

Europe in 1750

By 1750, Europe had achieved a kind of diplomatic equilibrium in which no one power predominated despite repeated wars over dynastic succession. Spain, the Dutch Republic, Poland-Lithuania, and Sweden had all declined in power and influence while Great Britain, Russia, and Prussia gained prominence. France's ambitions to dominate had been thwarted, but its combination of a big army and rich overseas possessions made it a major player for a long time to come. In the War of the Austrian Succession, Austria lost its rich province of Silesia to Prussia.

Analyzing the Map: Consider the relative sizes of Poland-Lithuania and France. What geographic factors help explain why the smaller country—France—was more powerful?

Making Connections: Great Britain, Russia, and Prussia were all gaining power in this period. What are the different lessons that can be learned from their rising status?

serfs found themselves ever more closely bound to their noble lords, and rural folk almost everywhere tasted few fruits of consumer society.

Politics changed, too, as experts urged government intervention to improve public health, and states found it in their interest to settle many international disputes by diplomacy, which itself became more regular and routine. The consolidation of the European state system allowed a tide of criticism and new thinking about society to swell in Great Britain and France and begin to spill throughout Europe. Ultimately, the combination of the Atlantic system and the Enlightenment would give rise to a series of Atlantic revolutions.

Chapter 17 Review

Key Terms and People

Be sure that you can identify the term or person and explain its historical significance.

Atlantic system (p. 575)

plantation (p. 577)

mestizo (p. 581)

buccaneers (p. 581)

consumer revolution (p. 583)

agricultural revolution (p. 585)

rococo (p. 588)

Pietism (p. 590)

Robert Walpole (p. 594)

Peter the Great (p. 595)

Westernization (p. 595)

War of the Austrian Succession (p. 598)

Enlightenment (p. 600)

Voltaire (p. 602)

Review Questions

1. How was consumerism related to slavery in the early eighteenth century?

2. How were new social trends reflected in cultural life in the early 1700s?

3. What events and developments led to greater stability and more limited warfare within Europe?

4. What were the major issues in the early decades of the Enlightenment?

Making Connections

1. How did the rise of slavery and the plantation system change European politics and society?

2. Why was the Enlightenment born just at the moment that the Atlantic system took shape?

3. What were the major differences between the wars of the first half of the eighteenth century and those of the seventeenth century? (Refer to Chapters 15 and 16.)

4. During the first half of the eighteenth century, what were the major issues affecting peasants in France and serfs in Poland and Russia?

Important Events

1700s	Beginning of rapid development of plantations in the Caribbean
1703	Peter the Great begins construction of St. Petersburg; founds first Russian newspaper
1713–1714	Peace of Utrecht treaties end War of Spanish Succession

1714	Elector of Hanover becomes King George I of England
1715	Death of Louis XIV
1719	Daniel Defoe publishes *Robinson Crusoe*
1720	Last outbreak of bubonic plague in western Europe
1721	Great Northern War ends; Montesquieu publishes *Persian Letters* anonymously in the Dutch Republic
1733	War of the Polish Succession; Voltaire's *Letters Concerning the English Nation* attacks French intolerance and narrow-mindedness
1740–1748	War of the Austrian Succession
1741	George Frideric Handel composes *Messiah*
1748	Montesquieu publishes *The Spirit of Laws*

Consider three events

Beginning of rapid development of plantations in the Caribbean (1700s), Daniel Defoe publishes *Robinson Crusoe* (1719), and Montesquieu publishes *Persian Letters* anonymously in the Dutch Republic (1721). In what ways were these two works of literature responses to the new global economy?

Suggested References

The slave trade Web site listed here offers the most up-to-date information about the workings of the Atlantic system, and the Hypercities Web site allows the viewer to trace the growth of certain cities over time. The definitive study of the early Enlightenment is the book by Hazard, but many others have contributed biographies of individual figures or studies of women writers.

Black, Jeremy. *European Warfare in a Global Context, 1660–1815.* 2007.

Blackburn, Robin. *The American Crucible: Slavery, Emancipation and Human Rights.* 2013.

Cracraft, James. *The Revolution of Peter the Great.* 2009.

Cronk, Nicholas. *Voltaire: A Very Short Introduction.* 2017.

De Vries, Jan. *The Industrious Revolution: Consumer Behavior and the Household Economy, 1650 to the Present.* 2008.

George Frideric Handel, http://gfhandel.org/

Hazard, Paul. *The European Mind: The Critical Years, 1680–1715.* 1990.

Hunt, Lynn, Margaret C. Jacob, and W. W. Mijnhardt. *The Book That Changed Europe: Picart and Bernard's Religious Ceremonies of the World.* 2010.

Hunt, Margaret R. *Women in Eighteenth-Century Europe.* 2010.

Hypercities project (includes Berlin and Paris): http://www.hypercities.com/

Jacob, Margaret C. *The Enlightenment: A Brief History with Selected Readings*, 2nd. ed. 2017.

Norton, Marcy. *Sacred Gifts, Profane Pleasures: A History of Tobacco and Chocolate in the Atlantic World.* 2010.

Sarti, Raffaella. *Europe at Home: Family and Material Culture, 1500–1800.* Trans. Allan Cameron. 2004.

Slave trade: http://www.slavevoyages.org/

Sowall, Alice, and Penny A. Weiss, eds. *Feminist Interpretations of Mary Astell.* 2016.

Vermes, Gábor. *Hungarian Culture and Politics in the Habsburg Monarchy, 1711–1848.* 2014.

Glossary of Key Terms and People

This glossary contains definitions of terms and people that are central to your understanding of the material covered in this textbook. Each term or person in the glossary is in **boldface** in the text when it is first defined. We have also included the page number on which the full discussion of the term or person appears so that you can easily locate the complete explanation to strengthen your historical vocabulary.

For words or names not defined here, two additional resources may be useful: the index, which will direct you to many more topics discussed in the text, and a good dictionary.

Abbasids (A buh sihds) (300): The dynasty of caliphs that, in 750, took over from the Umayyads in all of the Islamic realm except for Spain (al-Andalus). From their new capital at Baghdad, they presided over a wealthy realm until the late ninth century.

absolutism (537): A system of government in which the ruler claims sole and uncontestable power.

agora (AH gore uh) (90): The central market square of a Greek city-state, a popular gathering place for conversation.

agricultural revolution (585): Increasingly aggressive attitudes toward investment in and management of land that increased production of food in the 1700s.

Alexander the Great (121): The fourth-century B.C.E. Macedonian king whose conquest of the Persian Empire led to the greatly increased cultural interactions of Greece and the Near East in the Hellenistic Age.

Alexius I (Alexius Comnenus) (353): The Byzantine emperor (r. 1081–1118) whose leadership marked a new triumph of the *dynatoi*. His request to Pope Urban II for troops to fight the Turks turned into the First Crusade.

Alfred the Great (322): King of Wessex (r. 871–899) and the first king to rule over most of England. He organized a successful defense against Viking invaders, had key Latin works translated into the vernacular, and wrote a law code for the whole of England.

Anabaptists (487): Sixteenth-century Protestants who believed that only adults could truly have faith and accept baptism.

apostolic (ah puh STAH lihk) **succession** (206): The principle by which Christian bishops traced their authority back to the apostles of Jesus.

apprentices (336): Boys (and occasionally girls) placed under the tutelage of a master craftsman in the Middle Ages. Normally unpaid, they were expected to be servants of their masters, with whom they lived, at the same time as they were learning their trade.

aretê (ah reh TAY) (53): The Greek value of competitive individual excellence.

Arianism (232): The Christian doctrine named after Arius, who argued that Jesus was "begotten" by God and did not have an identical nature with God the Father.

Aristotle (120): Greek philosopher (384–322 B.C.E.) famous for his scientific investigations, development of logical argument, and practical ethics.

asceticism (uh SEH tuh sih zuhm) (235): The practice of self-denial, especially through spiritual discipline; a doctrine for Christians emphasized by Augustine.

Atlantic system (575): The network of trade established in the 1700s that bound together western Europe, Africa, and the Americas. Europeans sold slaves from western Africa and bought commodities that were produced by the new colonial plantations in North and South America and the Caribbean.

Augustine (230): 354–430. Bishop in North Africa whose writings defining religious orthodoxy made him the most influential theologian in Western civilization.

Augustus (184): The honorary name meaning "divinely favored" that the Roman Senate bestowed on Octavian; it became shorthand for "Roman imperial ruler."

Avignon (AH vee NYAW) **papacy** (423): The period (1309–1378) during which the popes ruled from Avignon rather than from Rome.

baroque (buh ROHK) (529): An artistic style of the seventeenth century that featured curves, exaggerated lighting, intense emotions, release from restraint, and even a kind of artistic sensationalism.

Basil II (298): The Byzantine emperor (r. 976–1025) who presided over the end of the Bulgar threat (earning the name Bulgar-Slayer) and the conversion of Kievan Russia to Christianity.

battle of Hastings (360): The battle of 1066 that replaced the Anglo-Saxon king with a Norman one and thus tied England to the rest of Europe as never before.

Black Death (437): The term historians give to the disease that swept through Europe in 1347–1352.

blood libel (409): The charge that Jews used the blood of Christian children in their Passover ritual; though false, it led to massacres of Jews in cities in England, France, Spain, and Germany in the thirteenth century.

Boniface VIII (421): The pope (r. 1294–1303) whose clash with King Philip the Fair of France left the papacy considerably weakened.

buccaneers (581): Pirates of the Caribbean who governed themselves and preyed on international shipping.

bureaucracy (544): A network of state officials carrying out orders according to a regular and routine line of authority.

Calvin, John (484): French-born Christian humanist (1509–1564) and founder of Calvinism, one of the major branches of the Protestant Reformation; he led the reform movement in Geneva, Switzerland, from 1541 to 1564.

Capetian (kuh PAY shuhn) **dynasty** (323): A long-lasting dynasty of French kings, taking their name from Hugh Capet (r. 987–996).

capitalism (337): The modern economic system characterized by an entrepreneurial class of property owners who employ others and produce (or provide services) for a market in order to make a profit.

Carolingian (306): The Frankish dynasty that ruled a western European empire from 751 to the late 800s; its greatest vigor was in the time of Charlemagne (r. 768–814) and Louis the Pious (r. 814–840).

castellan (KAS tuh luhn) (319): The holder of a castle. In the tenth and eleventh centuries, castellans became important local lords. They mustered men for military service, collected taxes, and administered justice.

chansons de geste (shahn SOHN duh ZHEST) (389): Epic poems of the twelfth century about knightly and heroic deeds.

Charlemagne (SHAR luh mayn) (294): The Carolingian king (r. 768–814) whose conquests greatly expanded the Frankish kingdom. He was crowned emperor on December 25, 800.

Charles V (481): Holy Roman Emperor (r. 1519–1556) and the most powerful ruler in sixteenth-century Europe; he reigned over the Low Countries, Spain, Spain's Italian and New World dominions, and the Austrian Habsburg lands.

chivalry (390): An ideal of knightly comportment that included military prowess, bravery, fair play, piety, and courtesy.

Christ (201): Greek for "anointed one," in Hebrew *Mashiach* or in English *Messiah*; in apocalyptic thought, God's agent sent to conquer the forces of evil.

Christian humanism (478): A general intellectual trend in the sixteenth century that coupled love of classical learning, as in Renaissance humanism, with an emphasis on Christian piety.

Cicero (SIH suh roh) (166): Rome's most famous orator and author of the doctrine of *humanitas*.

city-state (9): An urban center exercising political and economic control over the surrounding countryside.

civilization (4): Ways of life especially connected with life in urban societies.

classicism (565): A seventeenth-century style of painting and architecture that reflected the ideals of the art of antiquity; in classicism, geometric shapes, order, and harmony of lines took precedence over the sensuous, exuberant, and emotional forms of the baroque.

coloni (kuh LOH ny) (225): Literally, "cultivators"; tenant farmers in the Roman Empire who became bound by law to the land they worked and whose children were legally required to continue to farm the same land.

Colosseum (193): Rome's fifty-thousand-seat amphitheater built by the Flavian dynasty for gladiatorial combats and other spectacles.

Columbus, Christopher (471): An Italian sailor (1451–1506) who opened up the New World by sailing west across the Atlantic in search of a route to Asia.

commercial revolution (332): A term for the western European development (starting around 1050) of a money economy centered in urban areas but affecting the countryside as well.

common law (378): Begun by Henry II (r. 1154–1189), the English royal law carried out by the king's justices in eyre (traveling justices). It applied to the entire kingdom and thus was "common" to all.

commune (338): In a medieval town, a sworn association of citizens who formed a legal corporate body. The commune appointed or elected officials, made laws, kept the peace, and administered justice.

Concordat of Worms (346): The agreement between pope and emperor in 1122 that ended the Investiture Conflict.

constitutionalism (537): A system of government in which rulers share power with parliaments made up of elected representatives.

consumer revolution (583): The rapid increase in consumption of new staples produced in the Atlantic system as well as of other items of daily life that were previously unavailable or beyond the reach of ordinary people.

cortes (kawr TEHZ) (420): The earliest European representative institution, called initially to consent to royal wishes; first convoked in 1188 by the king of Castile-León.

Cortés, Hernán (474): The Spanish explorer (1485–1547) who captured the Aztec capital, Tenochtitlán (present-day Mexico City), in 1519.

Council of Trent (490): A general council of the Catholic church that met at Trent between 1545 and 1563 to set Catholic doctrine, reform church practices, and defend the church against the Protestant challenge.

cult (61): In ancient Greece, a set of official, publicly funded religious activities for a deity overseen by priests and priestesses.

cuneiform (kyoo NEE uh form) (12): The earliest form of writing, invented in Mesopotamia and done with wedge-shaped characters.

curials (KYUR ee uhls) (225): The social elite in the Roman Empire's cities and towns, most of whom were obliged to serve as decurions on municipal Senates and collect taxes for the imperial government, paying any shortfalls themselves.

Cyrus (45): Founder of the Persian Empire in 557 B.C.E.

debasement of coinage (211): Putting less silver in a coin without changing its face value; a failed financial strategy during the third-century C.E. crisis in Rome.

decurions (dih KYUR ee uhns) (196): Municipal Senate members in the Roman Empire responsible for collecting local taxes.

Delian (DEE lee un) **League** (84): The naval alliance led by Athens in the Golden Age (500–400 B.C.E.) that became the basis for the Athenian Empire.

demes (DEEMZ) (72): The villages and city neighborhoods that formed the constituent political units of Athenian democracy in the late Archaic Age (750–500 B.C.E.).

Diaspora (die ASS por a) (50): The dispersal of the Jewish population from their homeland.

dominate (221): The openly authoritarian style of Roman rule from Diocletian (r. 284–305) onward; the word was derived from *dominus* ("master" or "lord") and contrasted with *principate*.

dualism (119): The philosophical idea that the human soul (or mind) and body are separate.

dynatoi (DY nuh toy) (297): The "powerful men" who dominated the countryside of the Byzantine Empire in the tenth and eleventh centuries, and to some degree challenged the authority of the emperor.

Edict of Milan (226): The proclamation of Roman co-emperors Constantine (313) and Licinius decreeing free choice of religion in the empire.

Edict of Nantes (507): The decree issued by French king Henry IV in 1598 that granted the Huguenots a large measure of religious toleration.

Elizabeth I (510): English queen (r. 1558–1603) who oversaw the return of the Protestant Church of England and, in 1588, the successful defense of the realm against the Spanish Armada.

empire (14): A political state in which one or more formerly independent territories or peoples are ruled by a single sovereign power.

Enlightenment (600): The eighteenth-century intellectual movement whose proponents believed that human beings could apply a critical, reasoning spirit to every problem.

Epicureanism (eh puh KYUR ee uh nizm) (136): The philosophy founded by Epicurus of Athens to help people achieve a life of true pleasure, by which he meant "absence of disturbance."

epigrams (134): Short poems written by women in the Hellenistic Age; many were about other women and the writer's personal feelings.

equites (EHK wih tehs) (169): Literally, "equestrians" or "knights"; wealthy Roman businessmen who chose not to pursue a government career.

Fatimids (FAT ih mihds) (301): Members of the tenth-century Shi'ite dynasty who derived their name from Fatimah, the daughter of Muhammad and wife of Ali; they dominated in parts of North Africa, Egypt, and even Syria.

feudalism (317): The whole complex of lords, vassals, and fiefs (from the Latin *feodum*) as an institution. The nature of that institution varied from place to place, and in some regions it did not exist at all.

fiefs (317): Grants of land, theoretically temporary, from lords to their noble dependents (*fideles* or, later, vassals) given in recognition of services, usually military, done or expected in the future; also called *benefices*.

First Crusade (354): The massive armed pilgrimage to Jerusalem that lasted from 1096 to 1099. It resulted in the massacre of Jews in the Rhineland (1095), the sack of Jerusalem (1099), and the setting up of the crusader states.

First Triumvirate (174): The coalition formed in 60 B.C.E. by Pompey, Crassus, and Caesar. (The word *triumvirate* means "group of three.")

Five Pillars of Islam (263): The five essential practices of Islam, namely, the *zakat* (alms); the fast of Ramadan; the *hajj* (pilgrimage to Mecca); the *salat* (formal worship); and the *shahadah* (profession of faith).

Fourth Crusade (393): The crusade that lasted from 1202 to 1204; its original goal was to recapture Jerusalem, but the crusaders ended up conquering Constantinople instead.

Fourth Lateran Council (405): The council that met in 1215 and covered the important topics of Christianity, among them the nature of the sacraments, the obligations of the laity, and policies toward heretics and Jews.

Franciscans (391): The religious order founded by St. Francis (c. 1182–1226) and dedicated to poverty and preaching, particularly in towns and cities.

Frederick I (Barbarossa) (384): King of Germany (r. 1152–1190) and emperor (crowned 1155) who tried to cement the power of the German king through conquest (for example, of northern Italy) and the bonds of vassalage.

Frederick II (415): The grandson of Barbarossa who became king of Sicily and Germany, as well as emperor (r. 1212–1250), who allowed the German princes a free hand as he battled the pope for control of Italy.

Frederick William of Hohenzollern (561): The Great Elector of Brandenburg-Prussia (r. 1640–1688) who brought his nation through the end of the Thirty Years' War and then succeeded in welding his scattered lands into an absolutist state.

Glorious Revolution (555): The events of 1688 when Tories and Whigs replaced England's monarch James II with his Protestant daughter, Mary, and her husband, Dutch ruler William of Orange; William and Mary agreed to a Bill of Rights that guaranteed rights to Parliament.

Golden Horde (425): The political institution set up by the Mongols in Russia, lasting from the thirteenth to the fifteenth century.

Gothic architecture (375): The style of architecture that started in the Île-de-France in the twelfth century and eventually became the quintessential cathedral style of the Middle Ages, characterized by pointed arches, ribbed vaults, and stained-glass windows.

Great Famine (428): The shortage of food and accompanying social ills that besieged northern Europe between 1315 and 1322.

Great Persecution (226): The violent program initiated by Diocletian in 303 to make Christians convert to traditional religion or risk confiscation of their property and even death.

Great Schism (447): The papal dispute of 1378–1417 when the church had two and even (between 1409 and 1417) three popes. The Great Schism was ended by the Council of Constance.

Gregorian reform (342): The papal movement for church reform associated with Gregory VII (r. 1073–1085); its ideals included ending three practices: the purchase of church offices, clerical marriage, and lay investiture.

Gregory of Tours (277): Bishop of Tours (in Gaul) from 573 to 594, the chief source for the history and culture of the Merovingian kingdoms.

Gregory the Great (283): The pope (r. 590–604) who sent missionaries to Anglo-Saxon England, wrote influential books, tried to reform the church, and had contact with the major ruling families of Europe and Byzantium.

guild (336): A trade organization within a city or town that controlled product quality and cost and outlined members' responsibilities. Guilds were also social and religious associations.

Hammurabi (ha muh RAH bee) (16): King of Babylonia in the eighteenth century B.C.E., famous for his law code.

Hanseatic League (457): A league of northern European cities formed in the fourteenth century to protect their mutual interests in trade and defense.

Hellenistic (126): An adjective meaning "Greek-like" that is today used as a chronological term for the period 323–30 B.C.E.

heliocentrism (524): The view articulated by Polish clergyman Nicolaus Copernicus that the earth and other planets revolve around the sun.

helot (67): A slave owned by the Spartan city-state; such slaves came from parts of Greece conquered by the Spartans.

Henry II (377): King of England (r. 1154–1189) who ended the period of civil war there and affirmed and expanded royal powers. He is associated with the creation of common law in England.

Henry IV (342): King of Germany (r. 1056–1106), crowned emperor in 1084. From 1075 until his death, he was embroiled in the Investiture Conflict with Pope Gregory VII.

Henry VIII (485): The English king (r. 1509–1547) who first opposed the Protestant Reformation and then broke with the Catholic church, naming himself head of the Church of England in the Act of Supremacy of 1534.

Heraclius (her uh KLY uhs) (268): The Byzantine emperor who reversed the fortunes of war with the Persians in the first quarter of the seventh century.

heresy (207): False doctrine; specifically, the beliefs banned for Christians by councils of bishops.

hetaira (heh TYE ruh) (95): A witty and attractive woman who charged fees to entertain at a symposium.

hierarchy (4): The system of ranking people in society according to their status and authority.

hieroglyphic (20): The ancient Egyptian pictographic writing system for official texts.

Hijra (HIJ ruh) (263): The emigration of Muhammad from Mecca to Medina. Its date, 622, marks the year 1 of the Islamic calendar.

Homer (53): Greece's first and most famous author, who composed *The Iliad* and *The Odyssey*.

hoplite (62): A heavily armed Greek infantryman. Hoplites constituted the main strike force of a city-state's militia.

hubris (HYOO bris) (105): The Greek term for violent arrogance.

humanism (451): A literary and linguistic movement cultivated in particular during the Renaissance (1350–1600) and founded on reviving classical Latin and Greek texts, styles, and values.

humanitas (166): The Roman orator Cicero's ideal of "humaneness," meaning generous and honest treatment of others based on natural law.

Hundred Years' War (440): The long war between England and France, 1337–1453 (actually 116 years); it produced numerous social upheavals yet left both states more powerful than before.

hunter-gatherers (6): Human beings who roam to hunt and gather food in the wild and do not live in permanent, settled communities.

iconoclasm (272): Literally, "icon breaking"; referring to the destruction of icons, or images of holy people.

Byzantine emperors banned icons from 726 to 787; a modified ban was revived in 815 and lasted until 843.

icons (271): Images of holy people such as Jesus, Mary, and the saints. Controversy arose in Byzantium.

indulgence (448): A step beyond confession and penance, an indulgence (normally granted by popes or bishops) lifted the temporal punishment still necessary for a sin already forgiven. Normally, that punishment was said to take place in purgatory. But it could be remitted through good works (including prayers and contributing money to worthy causes).

Innocent III (404): The pope (r. 1198–1216) who called the Fourth Lateran Council; he was the most powerful, respected, and prestigious of medieval popes.

Investiture Conflict (343): The confrontation between Pope Gregory VII and Emperor Henry IV that began in 1075 over the appointment of prelates in some Italian cities and grew into a dispute over the nature of church leadership. It ended in 1122 with the Concordat of Worms.

Jacquerie (zhah kuh REE) (444): The 1358 uprising of French peasants against the nobles amid the Hundred Years' War; it was brutally put down.

Jesuits (491): Members of the Society of Jesus, a Catholic religious order founded by Ignatius of Loyola (1491–1556) and approved by the pope in 1540. Jesuits served as missionaries and educators all over the world.

jihad (263): In the Qur'an, the word means "striving in the way of God." This can mean both striving to live righteously and striving to confront unbelievers, even as far as holy war.

Joan of Arc (440): A peasant girl (1412–1431) whose conviction that God had sent her to save France in fact helped France win the Hundred Years' War.

journeymen/journeywomen (336): Laborers in the Middle Ages whom guildmasters hired for a daily wage to help them produce their products.

Julian the Apostate (229): The Roman emperor (r. 361–363) who rejected Christianity and tried to restore traditional religion as the state religion. *Apostate* means "renegade from the faith."

Julio-Claudians (191): The ruling family of the early principate from Augustus through Nero, descended from the aristocratic families of the Julians and the Claudians.

Justinian and Theodora (246): Sixth-century emperor and empress of the eastern Roman Empire, famous for waging costly wars to reunite the empire.

Koine (koy NAY) (139): The "common" or "shared" form of the Greek language that became the international language in the Hellenistic period.

ladder of offices (159): The series of Roman elective government offices from quaestor to aedile to praetor to consul.

lay investiture (341): The installation of clerics into their offices by lay rulers.

Lepanto (509): A site off the Greek coast where, in 1571, the allied Catholic forces of Spain's king Philip II, Venice, and the papacy defeated the Ottoman Turks in a great sea battle; the victory gave the Christian powers control of the Mediterranean.

Levellers (549): Disgruntled soldiers in Oliver Cromwell's New Model Army who in 1647 wanted to "level" social differences and extend political participation to all male property owners.

Linear B (33): The Mycenaeans' pictographic script for writing Greek.

Lombards (269): The people who settled in Italy during the sixth century, following Justinian's reconquest. A king ruled the north of Italy, while dukes ruled the south. In between was the papacy, which felt threatened both by Lombard Arianism and by the Lombards' geographical proximity to Rome.

Louis IX (418): A French king (r. 1226–1270) revered as a military leader and a judge; he was declared a saint after his death.

Louis XIV (538): French king (r. 1643–1715) who in theory personified absolutism but in practice had to gain the cooperation of nobles, local officials, and even the ordinary subjects who manned his armies and paid his taxes.

Luther, Martin (479): A German monk (1483–1546) who started the Protestant Reformation in 1517 by challenging the practices and doctrines of the Catholic church and advocating salvation through faith alone.

Lyceum (120): The school for research and teaching in a wide range of subjects founded by Aristotle in Athens in 335 B.C.E.

Maat (MAH aht) (21): The Egyptian goddess embodying truth, justice, and cosmic order. (The word *maat* means "what is right.")

Magna Carta (381): Literally "Great Charter"; the charter of baronial liberties that King John was forced to agree to in 1215. It implied that royal power was subject to custom and law.

martyr (206): Greek for "witness," the term for someone who dies for his or her religious beliefs.

masters (336): Men (and occasionally women) who, having achieved expertise in a craft, ran the guilds in the Middle Ages. They had to be rich enough to have their own shop and tools and to pay an entry fee into the guild. Often their positions were hereditary.

materialism (136): A philosophical doctrine of the Hellenistic Age that denied metaphysics and claimed instead that only things consisting of matter truly exist.

Medici (MEH dih chee) (462): The ruling family of Florence during much of the fifteenth to the seventeenth centuries.

Médicis, Catherine de (505): Italian-born mother of French king Charles IX (r. 1560–1574); she served as regent and tried but failed to prevent religious warfare between Calvinists and Catholics.

Mediterranean polyculture (30): The cultivation of olives, grapes, and grains in a single, interrelated agricultural system.

Mehmed II (446): The sultan under whom the Ottoman Turks conquered Constantinople in 1453.

mercantilism (544): The economic doctrine that governments must intervene to increase national wealth by whatever means possible.

Merovingian (mehr oh VIN jian) **dynasty** (273): The royal dynasty that ruled Gaul from about 486 to 751.

mestizo (581): A person born to a Spanish father and a native American mother.

metaphysics (119): Philosophical ideas about the ultimate nature of reality beyond the reach of human senses.

metic (94): A foreigner granted permanent residence status in Athens in return for paying taxes and serving in the military.

Mongols (424): The name of a people mobilized by Chingiz Kahn (c. 1162–1227) into a formidable army that conquered China, Rus, and the eastern half of the Islamic world.

moral dualism (47): The belief that the world is the arena for an ongoing battle for control between the divine forces of good and evil.

mos maiorum (149): Literally, "the way of the elders"; the set of Roman values handed down from the ancestors.

Muhammad (260): The prophet of Islam (c. 570–632). He united a community of believers around his religious tenets, above all that there was one God whose words had been revealed to him by the angel Gabriel. Later, written down, these revelations became the Qur'an.

mystery cults (93): Religious worship that provided initiation into secret knowledge and divine protection, including hope for a better afterlife.

Neoplatonism (210): Plotinus's spiritual philosophy, based mainly on Plato's ideas, which was very influential for Christian intellectuals.

Nicene Creed (233): The doctrine agreed on by the council of bishops convened by Constantine at Nicaea in 325 to defend orthodoxy against Arianism. It declared that God the Father and Jesus were *homoousion* ("of one substance").

oblation (280): Literally "an offering," oblation was the practice by which parents confided their son or daughter at a young age to a monastery. At the time, it was considered a worthy and pious gesture, beneficial to the souls of the parents and the child.

optimates (op tee MAH tehs) (169): The Roman political faction supporting the "best," or highest, social class; established during the late republic.

orders (158): The two groups of people in the Roman republic — **patricians** (aristocratic families) and **plebeians** (all other citizens).

orthodoxy (207): True doctrine; specifically, the beliefs defined for Christians by councils of bishops.

ostracism (AHS truh sizm) (86): An annual procedure in Athenian radical democracy by which a man could be voted out of the city-state for ten years; its purpose was to prevent tyranny.

Ottonian (ah TOH nee uhn) **kings** (324): The tenth- and early-eleventh-century kings of Germany; beginning with Otto I (r. 936–973), they claimed the imperial crown and worked closely with their bishops to rule a vast territory.

palace society (29): Minoan and Mycenaean social and political organization centered on multichambered buildings housing the rulers and the administration of the state.

Parthenon (PAR thuh non) (90): The massive temple to Athena as a warrior goddess built atop the Athenian acropolis in the Golden Age of Greece.

patria potestas (PAH tree uh po TEHS tahs) (152): Literally, "father's power"; the legal power a Roman father possessed over the children and slaves in his family, including owning all their property and having the right to punish them, even with death.

patriarchy (10): Dominance by men in society and politics.

patrilineal (320): Relating to or tracing descent through the paternal line (for example, through the father and grandfather).

patron-client system (151): The interlocking network of mutual obligations between Roman patrons (social superiors) and clients (social inferiors).

Pax Romana (182): Literally "Roman Peace"; the two centuries of relative peace and prosperity in the Roman Empire under the early principate begun by Augustus.

Peace of Augsburg (499): The treaty of 1555 that settled disputes between Holy Roman Emperor Charles V and his Protestant princes. It recognized the Lutheran church and established the principle that all Catholic or Lutheran princes enjoyed the sole right to determine the religion of their lands and subjects.

Peace of God (321): A movement begun by bishops in the south of France around 990, first to limit the violence done to property and to the unarmed, and later, with the Truce of God, to limit fighting between warriors.

Peace of Westphalia (515): The settlement (1648) of the Thirty Years' War; it established enduring religious divisions in the Holy Roman Empire by which Lutheranism would dominate in the north, Calvinism in the area of the Rhine River, and Catholicism in the south.

Pericles (PEHR uh kleez) (86): Athens's political leader during the Golden Age.

Peter the Great (595): Russian tsar Peter I (r. 1689–1725), who undertook the Westernization of Russia and built a new capital city named after himself, St. Petersburg.

Petrarch, Francis (451): An Italian poet (1304–1374) who revived the styles of classical authors; he is considered the first Renaissance humanist.

Philip II (507): King of Spain (r. 1556–1598) and the most powerful ruler in Europe; he reigned over the western Habsburg lands and all the Spanish colonies recently settled in the New World.

Philip II (Philip Augustus) (381): King of France (r. 1180–1223) who bested the English king John and won most of John's continental territories, thus immeasurably strengthening the power of the Capetian dynasty.

Pietism (590): A Protestant revivalist movement of the early eighteenth century that emphasized deeply emotional individual religious experience.

plantation (577): A large tract of land that produced staple crops such as sugar, coffee, and tobacco; was farmed by slave labor; and was owned by a colonial settler.

Plato (119): A follower of Socrates who became Greece's most famous philosopher.

plebiscites (PLEH buh sites) (161): Resolutions passed by the Plebeian Assembly; such resolutions gained the force of law in 287 B.C.E.

polis (55): The Greek city-state, an independent community of citizens not ruled by a king.

politiques (poh lih TEEK) (507): Political advisers during the sixteenth-century French Wars of Religion who argued that compromise in matters of religion would strengthen the monarchy.

polytheism (11): The belief in and worship of multiple gods.

popolo (423): Literally, "people"; a communal faction, largely made up of merchants, that demanded (and often obtained) power in thirteenth-century Italian cities.

populares (poh poo LAH rehs) (169): The Roman political faction supporting the common people; established during the late republic.

praetorian guard (185): The group of soldiers stationed in Rome under the emperor's control; first formed by Augustus.

predestination (484): John Calvin's doctrine that God preordained salvation or damnation for each person before creation; those chosen for salvation were considered the "elect."

primogeniture (320): An inheritance practice that left all property to the oldest son.

principate (185): Roman political system invented by Augustus as a disguised monarchy with the *princeps* ("first man") as emperor.

proletarians (170): In the Roman republic, the mass of people so poor they owned no property.

Puritans (510): Strict Calvinists who in the sixteenth and seventeenth centuries opposed all vestiges of Catholic ritual in the Church of England.

Qur'an (kur AN/koo RAHN) (262): The holy book of Islam, considered the word of Allah ("the God") as revealed to the Prophet Muhammad.

radical democracy (86): The Athenian system of democracy established in the 460s and 450s B.C.E. that extended direct political power and participation in the court system to all adult male citizens.

raison d'état (ray ZOHN day TAH) (517): French for "reason of state," the political doctrine, first proposed by Cardinal Richelieu of France, which held that the state's interests should prevail over those of religion.

rationalism (75): The philosophic idea that people must justify their claims by logic and reason, not myth.

Razin, Stenka (564): Leader of the 1667 rebellion that promised Russian peasants liberation from noble landowners and officials; he was captured by the tsar's army in 1671 and publicly executed in Moscow.

reconquista (ray con KEE stuh) (342): The collective name for the wars waged by the Christian princes of Spain against the Muslim-ruled regions to their south. These wars were considered holy, akin to the crusades.

redistributive economy (11): A system in which state officials control the production and distribution of goods.

res publica (REHS POOB lih kuh) (150): Literally, "the people's matter" or "the public business"; the Romans' name for their republic and the source of our word *republic*.

revocation of the Edict of Nantes (544): French king Louis XIV's 1685 decision to eliminate the rights of Calvinists granted in the edict of 1598; Louis banned all Calvinist public activities and forced those who refused to embrace the state religion to flee.

rococo (588): A style of painting that emphasized irregularity and asymmetry, movement and curvature, but on a smaller, more intimate scale than the baroque.

Romanesque (374): An architectural style that flourished in Europe between about 1000 and 1150. It is characterized by solid, heavy forms and semicircular arches and vaults. Romanesque buildings were often decorated with fanciful sculpture and wall paintings.

Romanization (198): The spread of Roman law and culture in the provinces of the Roman Empire.

ruler cults (140): Cults that involved worship of a Hellenistic ruler as a savior god.

sacraments (347): In the Catholic church, the institutionalized means by which God's heavenly grace is transmitted to Christians. Examples of sacraments include baptism, the Eucharist (communion), and marriage.

salon (568): An informal gathering held regularly in a private home and presided over by a socially eminent woman; salons spread from France in the seventeenth century to other countries in the eighteenth century.

Sappho (SAF oh) (73): The most famous woman lyric poet of ancient Greece, a native of Lesbos.

scholasticism (410): The method of logical inquiry used by the scholastics, the scholars of the medieval universities; it applied Aristotelian logic to biblical and other authoritative texts in an attempt to summarize and reconcile all knowledge.

scientific method (523): The combination of experimental observation and mathematical deduction used to determine the laws of nature; first developed in the seventeenth century, it became the secular standard of truth.

Sea Peoples (34): The diverse groups of raiders who devastated the eastern Mediterranean region in the period of violence 1200–1000 B.C.E.

secularization (523): The long-term trend toward separating state power and science from religious faith, making the latter a private domain; begun in the seventeenth century, it prompted a search for nonreligious explanations for political authority and natural phenomena.

Shi'ite (265): A Muslim of the "party of Ali" and his descendants. Shi'ites are thus opposed to the Sunni Muslims, who reject the authority of Ali.

simony (SY muh nee) (341): The sin of giving gifts or paying money to get a church office.

social contract (555): The doctrine, originated by Hugo Grotius and argued by both Thomas Hobbes and John Locke, that all political authority derives not from divine right but from an implicit contract between citizens and their rulers.

Socratic method (100): The Athenian philosopher Socrates' method of teaching through conversation, in which he asked probing questions to make his listeners examine their most cherished assumptions.

Solon (70): Athenian political reformer whose changes promoted early democracy.

Sophists (SAH fists) (97): Competitive intellectuals and teachers in ancient Greece who offered expensive courses in persuasive public speaking and new ways of philosophic and religious thinking beginning around 450 B.C.E.

Statute in Favor of the Princes (416): A statute finalized by Frederick II in 1232 that gave the German princes sovereign power within their own principalities.

St. Bernard (350): The most important Cistercian abbot (early twelfth century) and the chief preacher of the Second Crusade.

Stoicism (136): The Hellenistic philosophy whose followers believed in fate but also in pursuing excellence (virtue) by cultivating good sense, justice, courage, and temperance.

Suleiman the Magnificent (495): Sultan of the Ottoman Empire (r. 1520–1566) at the time of its greatest power.

Synod of Whitby (284): The meeting of churchmen and King Oswy of Northumbria in 664 that led to the adoption of the Roman brand of Christianity in England.

tetrarchy (223): The "rule by four," consisting of two co-emperors and two assistant emperors/designated successors, initiated by Diocletian to subdivide the ruling of the Roman Empire into four regions.

theme (295): A military district in Byzantium. The earliest *themes* were created in the seventh century and served mainly defensive purposes.

Themistocles (thuh MIST uh kleez) (81): Athens's leader during the great Persian invasion of Greece.

Theodora — *See* Justinian.

Theodosius I (229): The Roman emperor (r. 379–395) who made Christianity the state religion by ending public sacrifices in the traditional cults and closing their temples. In 395, he also divided the empire into western and eastern halves to be ruled by his sons.

Torah (49): The first five books of the Hebrew Bible, also referred to as the Pentateuch. It contains early Jewish law.

Treaty of Verdun (312): The treaty that, in 843, split the Carolingian Empire into three parts; its borders roughly outline modern western European states.

triremes (TRY reems) (84): Greek wooden warships rowed by 170 oarsmen sitting on three levels and equipped with a battering ram at the bow.

troubadours/trobairitz (388): Male (troubadours) and female (trobairitz) vernacular poets in southern France in the twelfth and early thirteenth centuries who sang of love, longing, and courtesy.

Twelve Tables (159): The first written Roman law code, enacted between 451 and 449 B.C.E.

Umayyad caliphate (oo MAH yuhd KAY luhf ayt) (265): The caliphs (successors of Muhammad) who traced their ancestry to Umayyah, a member of Muhammad's tribe. The dynasty lasted from 661 to 750.

Urban II (353): The pope (r. 1088–1099) responsible for calling the First Crusade in 1095.

Visigoths (241): The name given to the barbarians whom Alaric united and led on a military campaign into the western Roman Empire to establish a new kingdom; they sacked Rome in 410.

Voltaire (602): The pen name of François-Marie Arouet (1694–1778), who was the most influential writer of the early Enlightenment.

Walpole, Robert (594): The first, or "prime," minister (1721–1742) of the House of Commons of Great Britain's Parliament. Although appointed initially by the king, through his long period of leadership he effectively established the modern pattern of parliamentary government.

War of the Austrian Succession (598): The war (1740–1748) over the succession to the Habsburg throne that pitted France and Prussia against Austria and

Britain and provoked continuing hostilities between French and British settlers in the North American colonies.

wergild (245): Under Frankish law, the payment that a murderer had to make as compensation for the crime, to prevent feuds of revenge.

Westernization (595): The effort, especially in Peter the Great's Russia, to make society and social customs resemble counterparts in western Europe, especially France, Britain, and the Dutch Republic.

William, prince of Orange (554): Dutch ruler who, with his Protestant wife, Mary (daughter of James II), ruled England after the Glorious Revolution of 1688.

wisdom literature (23): Texts giving instructions for appropriate behavior.

Acknowledgments

Chapter 1, pages 12–13: Excerpts from *Gilgamesh* by John Gardner and John Maier. Copyright © 1984 by the Estate of John Gardner and John Maier. Used by permission of Alfred A. Knopf, an imprint of the Knopf Doubleday Publishing Group, a division of Penguin Random House LLC. All rights reserved. Any third-party use of this material, outside of this publication, is prohibited. Interested parties must apply directly to Penguin Random House LLC for permission.

Chapter 6, pages 204–205: From *The Letters of the Younger Pliny*, translated with an introduction by Betty Radice (Penguin Classics, 1963; repr., 1969), Book 10, [letter] nos. 96 and 97. Copyright © Betty Radice, 1963, 1969. Reproduced by permission of Penguin Books Ltd. **Page 205:** Reproduced by permission of the publishers and the Trustees of the Loeb Classical Library from *Tertullian: Apology, De Spectaculis*, translated by T. R. Glover, Loeb Classical Library Volume 250. First published 1931. Copyright © 1931 by the President and Fellows of Harvard College. The Loeb Classical Library ® is a registered trademark of the President and Fellows of Harvard College.

Chapter 8, page 282: Excerpted from *Vita Domnae Balthildis* (The Life of Lady Balthild, Queen of the Franks) in *Late Merovingian France: History and Hagiography, 640–720* by Paul Fouracre and Richard A. Gerberding. Copyright © 1996 by Paul Fouracre and Richard A. Gerberding. Reprinted by permission of Manchester University Press.

Chapter 9, pages 304–305: James T. Monroe, "The Historical Arjūza of ibn 'Abd Rabbihi, a Tenth-Century Hispano-Arabic Epic Poem," *Journal of the American Oriental Society*, Vol. 91, No. 1 (Jan–Mar 1971), pp. 67–95. Copyright © 1971 American Oriental Society. Reprinted by permission of the author.

Chapter 9, pages 310–311: Excerpted from "12. Charlemagne and Pope Leo," translated by P. E. Dutton from *Monumenta Germaniae Historica: Poetae Latini Aevi Carolini*, vol. 1, edited by E. Dümmler (Berlin, 1881), from *Carolingian Civilization: A Reader*, 2nd edition, edited by Paul Edward Dutton. Copyright © 2004 by Paul Edward Dutton. Broadview Press/University of Toronto Press Higher Education Division. Reprinted with permission of the publisher.

Chapter 10, page 344: Excerpted from "The Life of the Emperor Henry IV" in *Imperial Lives and Letters of the Eleventh Century*, trans. Theodor E. Mommsen and Karl F. Morrison. Copyright © 2000 Columbia University Press. Reprinted by permission of the publisher and Karl Morrison. **Page 345:** Excerpted from "The Letters of Henry IV" in *Imperial Lives and Letters of the Eleventh Century*, trans. Theodor E. Mommsen and Karl F. Morrison. Copyright © 2000 Columbia University Press. Reprinted by permission of the publisher and Karl Morrison.

Chapter 11, pages 372–373: "22 (Man)" and "23 (Woman)," from *Making Love in the Twelfth Century: Letters of Two Lovers in Context* by Barbara Newman, pp. 108–9 and 111–12. Copyright © 2016 by the University of Pennsylvania Press. Reprinted with the permission of the University of Pennsylvania Press. **Pages 382–383:** From *English Historical Documents*, vol. 3, *1189–1327*, edited by Harry Rothwell. Copyright © 1975 Routledge. Reproduced by permission of Taylor & Francis Books UK. **Page 383:** From *English Historical Documents*, vol. 3, *1189–1327*, edited by Harry Rothwell. Copyright © 1975 Routledge. Reproduced by permission of Taylor & Francis Books UK.

Chapter 12, pages 412–413: Excerpt from Chapter 122, "The Reason Why Simple Fornication Is a Sin According to Divine Law, and That Matrimony Is Natural," in *Summa contra Gentiles, Book 3: Providence*, by Saint Thomas Aquinas, translated with an introduction and notes by Vernon J. Bourke. Translation copyright © 1956 by Penguin Random House LLC, copyright renewed © 1984 by Vernon J. Bourke. Used by permission of Doubleday, an imprint of the Knopf Doubleday Publishing Group, a division of Penguin Random House LLC. All rights reserved. Any third-party use of this material, outside of this publication, is prohibited. Interested parties must apply directly to Penguin Random House LLC for permission. **Page 426:** Guyuk Khan, letter to Pope Innocent IV (1246), from *The Mongol Mission [Mission to Asia]: Narratives and Letters of the Franciscan Missionaries in Mongolia and China in the Thirteenth and Fourteenth Centuries*, ed. Christopher Dawson (New York: Sheed and Ward, 1955), pp. 85–86. Copyright © 1955 Christopher Dawson. Reproduced by permission of Bloomsbury Publishing Plc. **Pages 426–428:** Excerpt from Béla IV, letter to Pope Innocent IV (c. 1250), from *Reading the Middle Ages: Sources from Europe, Byzantium, and the Islamic World*, ed. Barbara H. Rosenwein, 2nd ed. (Toronto: University of Toronto Press, 2014), 381–83. Originally from Archivio Segreto Vaticano, AA Arm. I-XVIII-605; Augustin Theiner, *Vetera monumenta historica Hungariam sacram illustrantia*, vol. 1: *1216–1352* (Rome, 1859). Translation by Piroska Nagy. Reprinted by permission of Piroska Nagy.

Chapter 13, page 442: Excerpted from *Joan of Arc: La Pucelle*, translated and annotated by Craig Taylor. Copyright © 2006 by Manchester University Press. Reprinted by permission of Manchester University Press. **Pages 442–443:** Excerpted from *Joan of Arc: La Pucelle*, translated and annotated by Craig Taylor. Copyright © 2006 by Manchester University Press. Reprinted by permission of Manchester University Press. **Page 443:** Excerpted from *Joan of Arc: La Pucelle*, translated and annotated by Craig Taylor. Copyright © 2006 by Manchester University Press. Reprinted by permission of Manchester University Press.

Index

A note about the index:
Names of individuals appear in boldface.
Letters in parenthesis following pages refer to:
(i)   illustrations, including photographs and artifacts
(f)   figures, including charts and graphs
(m)   maps

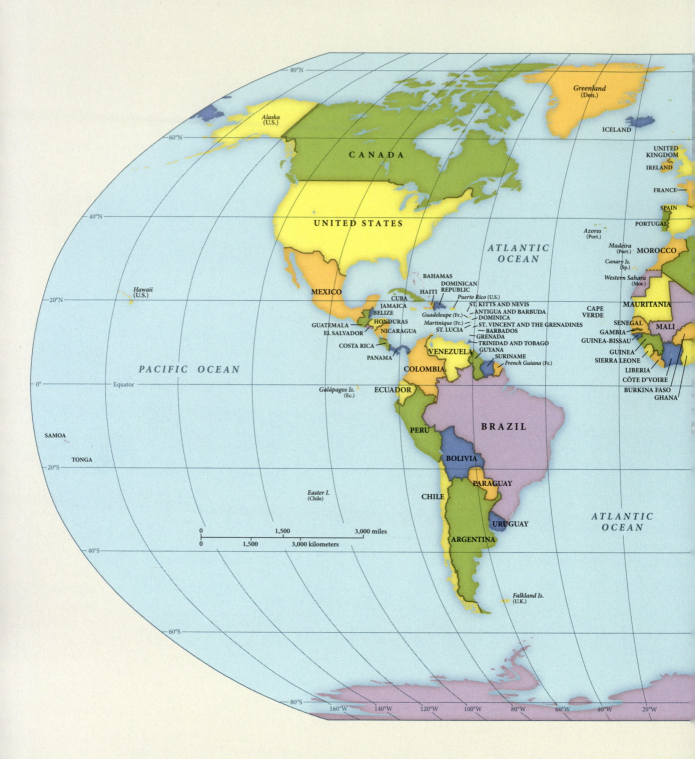

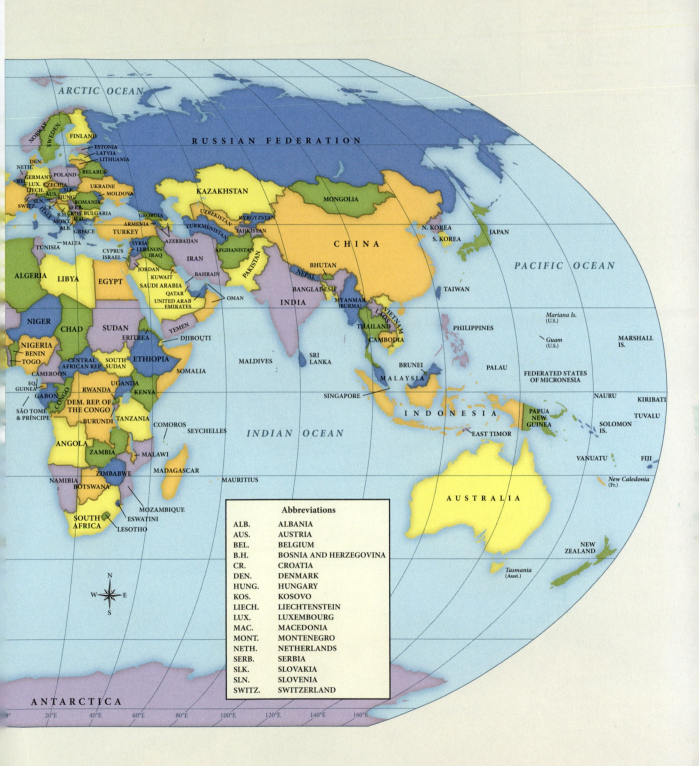

ARCTIC OCEAN

NORWAY
SWEDEN
FINLAND
ESTONIA
LATVIA
LITHUANIA
DEN.
NETH.
GERMANY
POLAND
BELARUS
BEL.
LUX.
CZECHIA
LIECH.
SLK.
UKRAINE
SWITZ.
AUS.
HUNG.
MOLDOVA
CR.
SLN.
ROMANIA
ITALY
B.H.
SERB.
MONT.
MAC.
KOS.
BULGARIA
ALB.
GEORGIA
GREECE
TURKEY
ARMENIA
AZERBAIJAN

RUSSIAN FEDERATION

KAZAKHSTAN

MONGOLIA

N. KOREA
S. KOREA
JAPAN

PACIFIC OCEAN

TUNISIA
MALTA
CYPRUS
ISRAEL
SYRIA
LEBANON
IRAQ
JORDAN
KUWAIT
ALGERIA
LIBYA
EGYPT
SAUDI ARABIA
QATAR
UNITED ARAB
EMIRATES
OMAN

UZBEKISTAN
TURKMENISTAN
KYRGYZSTAN
TAJIKISTAN
AFGHANISTAN
IRAN
PAKISTAN
BAHRAIN

CHINA

BHUTAN
NEPAL
BANGLADESH
INDIA
MYANMAR
(BURMA)

TAIWAN

Mariana Is.
(U.S.)

Guam
(U.S.)

MARSHALL
IS.

NIGER
CHAD
SUDAN
YEMEN
ERITREA
DJIBOUTI

LAOS
VIETNAM
THAILAND
CAMBODIA

PHILIPPINES

NAURU
KIRIBATI

NIGERIA
BENIN
TOGO
CAMEROON
CENTRAL
AFRICAN REP.
SOUTH
SUDAN
ETHIOPIA
SOMALIA

MALDIVES

SRI
LANKA

BRUNEI

PALAU

FEDERATED STATES
OF MICRONESIA

EQ.
GUINEA
GABON
CONGO
RWANDA
UGANDA
KENYA
SÃO TOME
& PRÍNCIPE
DEM. REP. OF
THE CONGO
BURUNDI
TANZANIA
COMOROS
SEYCHELLES

MALAYSIA

SINGAPORE

INDONESIA

PAPUA
NEW
GUINEA

SOLOMON
IS.

TUVALU

EAST TIMOR

VANUATU
FIJI

ANGOLA
ZAMBIA
MALAWI
ZIMBABWE
MADAGASCAR
NAMIBIA
BOTSWANA
MOZAMBIQUE

INDIAN OCEAN

MAURITIUS

New Caledonia
(Fr.)

AUSTRALIA

SOUTH
AFRICA
ESWATINI
LESOTHO

NEW
ZEALAND

Tasmania
(Aust.)

N
W E
S

Abbreviations	
ALB.	ALBANIA
AUS.	AUSTRIA
BEL.	BELGIUM
B.H.	BOSNIA AND HERZEGOVINA
CR.	CROATIA
DEN.	DENMARK
HUNG.	HUNGARY
KOS.	KOSOVO
LIECH.	LIECHTENSTEIN
LUX.	LUXEMBOURG
MAC.	MACEDONIA
MONT.	MONTENEGRO
NETH.	NETHERLANDS
SERB.	SERBIA
SLK.	SLOVAKIA
SLN.	SLOVENIA
SWITZ.	SWITZERLAND

ANTARCTICA

20°E   40°E   60°E   80°E   100°E   120°E   140°E   160°E